TAKING SIDES

Clashing Views on Controversial

Issues in Cultural Anthropology

Selected, Edited, and with Introductions by

Robert L. Welsch
Dartmouth College

and

Kirk M. Endicott
Dartmouth College

McGraw-Hill/Dushkin
A Division of The McGraw-Hill Companies

For Sarah and Karen

Photo Acknowledgment
Cover image: © 2003 by PhotoDisc, Inc.

Cover Art Acknowledgment
Charles Vitelli

Manufactured in the United States of America

First Edition

123456789BAHBAH6543

Library of Congress Cataloging-in-Publication Data
Main entry under title:
Taking sides: clashing views on controversial issues in cultural anthropology/selected, edited, and with introductions by Robert L. Welsch and Kirk M. Endicott.—1st ed.
Includes bibliographical references and index.
1. Anthropology, cultural. 2. Ethnology. I. Welsch, Robert L., *ed.* II. Endicott, Kirk M., *ed.* III. Series.
306
0-07-254863-0
ISSN: 1541-9207

Printed on Recycled Paper

Preface

Many courses and textbooks present cultural anthropology as a discipline that largely consists of well-established facts. In *Taking Sides: Clashing Views on Controversial Issues in Cultural Anthropology* we present the discipline in quite a different light. Here we focus on active controversies that remain unresolved. These issues represent the kind of arguments and debates that have characterized cultural anthropology for more than a century. They show the varied ways that cultural anthropologists approach the subject of their research and the kinds of anthropological evidence needed to bolster an academic argument.

Generally, we have chosen selections that express strongly worded positions on two sides of an issue. For most issues, several other reasonable positions are also possible, and we have suggested some of these in our introductions and postscripts that accompany each issue.

Taking Sides: Clashing Views on Controversial Issues in Cultural Anthropology is a tool to encourage and develop critical thinking about anthropological research questions, methods, and evidence. We have selected a range of readings and issues to illustrate the kinds of topics that cultural anthropologists study. Another goal of this volume is to provide opportunities for students to explore how cultural anthropologists frame and defend their interpretations of anthropological evidence. We have chosen issues that raise questions about research methods and the quality or reliability of different kinds of data. All of these complex matters go into shaping the positions that cultural anthropologists debate and defend in their writings. We hope that in discussing these issues students will find opportunities to explore how cultural anthropologists think about the pressing theoretical issues of the day.

Plan of the book   This book is made up of 17 issues that deal with topics that have provoked starkly different positions by different cultural anthropologists. We have divided the volume into three parts reflecting three major concerns of the discipline: Theoretical Orientations, Some Specific Issues in Cultural Anthropology, and Ethics in Cultural Anthropology. Each issue begins with an *introduction,* which sets the stage for the debate as argued in the YES and NO selections. Following these two selections is a *postscript* that makes some final observations and points the way to other questions related to the issue. In reading an issue and forming your own opinions, you should remember that there are often many alternative perspectives that are not represented in either the YES or NO selections. Most issues have reasonable positions that might appear to be intermediate between the two more extreme viewpoints represented here in the readings. There are also reasonable positions that lie totally outside the scope of the debate presented in these selections, and students should consider all of these possible positions. Each postscript also contains *suggestions for additional reading* that will help you find more resources to continue your study of any topic. Students researching any of these issues or related ones for a research paper will find these additional readings (as well as their bibliographies) a useful place to begin a more intensive analysis. At the end of the book we have also included a list of all the *contributors to this volume,* which will give you information on the anthropologists and other commentators whose views are debated here. An *On the Internet* page accompanies each part opener. This page gives you Internet site addresses (URLs) that are relevant to the issues discussed in that part of the book. Many of these sites contain links to related sites and bibliographies for further study.

A word to the instructor   An *Instructor's Manual With Test Questions* (multiple-choice and essay) is available for use with *Taking Sides.* Also available is a general guidebook, *Using Taking Sides in the Classroom,* which includes a discussion of techniques for integrating the pro-con format into an existing course. Instructors adopting this text also have access to an online version of *Using Taking Sides in the Classroom* as well as a correspondence service at http://www.dushkin.com/usingts/.

Taking Sides: Clashing Views on Controversial Issues in Cultural Anthropology is only one of many titles in the Taking Sides series. If you are interested in seeing the table of contents for any of the other titles, please visit the Taking Sides Web site at http://www.dushkin.com/takingsides/.

Acknowledgments   We received many helpful comments and suggestions from many friends and colleagues, including Hoyt Alverson, Colin Calloway, Brian Didier, Dale Eickelman, Jana Fortier, Ridie Ghezzi, Rosemary Gianno, Paul Goldstein, Alberto Gomez, Robert Gordon, Allen Hockley, Judy Hunt, Sergei Kan, Steve Kangas, Kathryn Keith, Kenneth Korey, Christine Kray, Laura Litton, Marilyn Lord, Lynn MacGillivray, Deborah Nichols, Lynn Rainville, Kevin Reinhart, Jeanne Shea, John Terrell, Robert Tonkinson, Robin Torrence, John Watanabe, Lindsay Whaley, and J. Peter White. We also want to thank John Cocklin, Lucinda Hall, Francis X. Oscadal, Cindy Shirkey, Reinhart Sonnenberg, and Amy Witzel, members of the Baker Library Reference Department, all of whom have helped track down many of the sources we have used. Special thanks go to our student research assistants Tate LeFevre, Lauren Weldon, Whitney Wilking, and Rachel Yemini. We also want to thank Ted Knight and Juliana Gribbins at McGraw-Hill/Dushkin for their constant assistance, suggestions, patience, and good humor. We also wish to thank our wives, Sarah L. Welsch and Karen L. Endicott, for their support and encouragement during the preparation of this volume.

Robert L. Welsch
Dartmouth College
Kirk M. Endicott
Dartmouth College

Contents In Brief

Contents

Cultural anthropologist Marvin Harris argues that anthropology has always
been a science and should continue to be scientific. He contends that anthropology's goal should be to discover general, verifiable laws as in the
other natural sciences. Cultural anthropologist Clifford Geertz views anthropology as a science of interpretation. He believes that anthropology's
goal should be to generate deeper interpretations of diverse cultural phenomena, using what he calls "thick description," rather than attempting to
prove or disprove scientific laws.

Cultural anthropologist Roger M. Keesing argues that what native peoples in the Pacific now accept as "traditional culture" is largely an invented
and idealized vision of their past. He contends that such fictional images
emerge because native peoples are largely unfamiliar with what life was
really like in pre-Western times and because such imagery distinguishes
native communities from dominant Western culture. Hawaiian activist and
scholar Haunani-Kay Trask asserts that Keesing's critique is fundamentally
flawed because he only uses Western documents—and native peoples
have oral traditions, genealogies, and other historical sources that are not
reflected in Western historical documents. Anthropologists like Keesing,
she maintains, are trying to hold on to their privileged position as experts
in the face of growing numbers of educated native scholars.

Postmodernist anthropologist James Clifford argues that the very act of removing objects from their ethnographic contexts distorts the meaning of objects held in museums. Exhibitions misrepresent ethnic communities by omitting important aspects of contemporary life, especially involvement with the colonial or Western world. Anthropologist Denis Dutton asserts that no exhibition can provide a complete context for ethnographic objects, but that does not mean that museum exhibitions are fundamentally flawed.

PART 2   SOME SPECIFIC ISSUES IN CULTURAL ANTHROPOLOGY   67

Social anthropologist Derek Freeman contends that Margaret Mead went to Samoa determined to prove anthropologist Franz Boas's cultural determinist agenda and states that Mead was so eager to believe in Samoan sexual freedom that she was consistently the victim of a hoax perpetrated by Samoan girls and young women who enjoyed tricking her. Cultural anthropologists Lowell D. Holmes and Ellen Rhoads Holmes contend that during a restudy of Mead's research, they came to many of the same conclusions that Mead had reached about Samoan sexuality and adolescent experiences.

Sociolinguists John J. Gumperz and Stephen C. Levinson contend that recent studies of language and culture suggest that language structures human thought in a variety of ways that most linguists and anthropologists had not believed possible. Cognitive neuropsychologist Steven Pinker draws on recent studies in cognitive science and neuropsychology to support the notion that previous studies have examined language but have said little, if anything, about thought.

Archaeologists James R. Denbow and Edwin N. Wilmsen argue that the San of the Kalahari Desert in southern Africa have been involved in pastoralism, agriculture, and regional trade networks since at least A.D. 800. They imply that the San, who were hunting and gathering in the twentieth century, were descendants of pastoralists who lost their herds due to subjugation by outsiders, drought, and livestock disease. Cultural anthropologist Richard B. Lee counters that evidence from oral history, archaeology, and ethnohistory shows that the Ju/'hoansi group of San living in the isolated Nyae Nyae-Dobe area of the Kalahari Desert were autonomous hunter-gatherers until the twentieth century. Although they carried on some trade with outsiders before then, it had minimal impact on their culture.

Cultural anthropologist Thomas N. Headland contends that tropical rain forests are poor in energy-rich wild foods that are readily accessible to humans, especially starches. Cultural anthropologists Serge Bahuchet and Igor de Garine and biologist Doyle McKey argue that rain forest foragers harvest far fewer wild foods than the forests actually contain, precisely because they now have easy access to cultivated foods.

Cultural anthropologist Maria Lepowsky argues that among the Vanatinai people of Papua New Guinea, the sexes are basically equal, although minor areas of male advantage exist. Sociologist Steven Goldberg contends that in all societies men occupy most high positions in hierarchical organizations and most high-status roles, and they dominate women in interpersonal relations. He states that this is because men's hormones cause them to compete more strongly than women for high status and dominance.

Adoptee and adoption rights advocate Betty Jean Lifton argues that there is a natural need for human beings to know where they came from. Adoption is not a natural human state, she asserts, and it is surrounded by a secrecy that leads to severe social and psychological consequences for adoptees, adoptive parents, and birth parents. Anthropologists John Terrell and Judith Modell, who are each the parent of an adopted child, contend that the "need" to know one's birth parents is an American (or Western European) cultural construct. They conclude that in other parts of the world, where there is less emphasis placed on biology, adoptees have none of the problems said to be associated with being adopted in America.

Iranian historian Parvin Paidar considers how the position of women suffered following the 1979 Iranian Revolution because of the imposition of Islamic law (shari'a), as interpreted by conservative male clerics. She contends that the Islamic Revolution marked a setback in the progressive modernist movements, which had improved women's rights during the secular regime of the Shah; new rights and opportunities have emerged since 1979 only in opposition to conservative interpretations of Islamic law. American anthropologist Erika Friedl asserts that men in Iran have consistently tried to suppress women's rights since the 1979 Iranian Revolution. Despite these efforts to repress them, women in all levels of society have access to many sources of power. In fact, argues Friedl, women have considerably more power available to them than either Western or Iranian stereotypes might suggest, even though they must work within Islamic law to obtain this power.

Anthropologist and sociobiologist Napoleon A. Chagnon argues that the high incidence of violence and warfare he observed among the Yanomami in the 1960s was directly related to man's inherent drive toward reproductive fitness (i.e., the innate biological drive to have as many offspring as possible). Anthropologist and cultural materialist R. Brian Ferguson counters that the high incidence of warfare and violence observed by Chagnon in the 1960s was a direct result of contact with Westerners at mission and government stations.

Issue 12.   Is Ethnic Conflict Inevitable?   246

Indian social researcher Sudhir Kakar analyzes the origins of ethnic conflict from a psychological perspective to argue that ethnic differences are deeply held distinctions that from time to time will inevitably erupt as ethnic conflicts. He maintains that anxiety arises from preconscious fears about cultural differences. In his view, no amount of education or politically correct behavior will eradicate these fears and anxieties about people of differing ethnic backgrounds. American sociologist Anthony Oberschall considers the ethnic conflicts that have recently emerged in Bosnia and contends that primordial ethnic attachments are insufficient to explain the sudden emergence of violence among Bosnian ethnic groups. He adopts a complex explanation for this violence, identifying circumstances in which fears and anxieties were manipulated by politicians for self-serving ends. It was only in the context of these manipulations that ethnic violence could have erupted, concludes Oberschall.

Issue 13.   Do Some Illnesses Exist Only Among Members of a Particular Culture?   268

Physician and medical anthropologist John E. Cawte asks whether or not one particular illness, called *malgri* by the Lardil Aborigines of Australia, is restricted to this one cultural group. After documenting how this condition does not fit standard psychiatric diagnoses, he concludes that *malgri* is indeed a "culture-bound syndrome" that can only occur among people who share Lardil cultural values and beliefs. Medical anthropologist Robert A. Hahn counters that the very idea of the so-called culture-bound syndrome is flawed. He contends that culture-bound syndromes are reductionist explanations for certain complex illness conditions—that is, explanations that reduce complex phenomena to a single variable. Hahn suggests that such conditions are like any illness condition; they are not so much peculiar diseases but distinctive local cultural expressions of much more common illness conditions that can be found in any culture.

PART 3   ETHICS IN CULTURAL ANTHROPOLOGY
293

Investigative journalist Patrick Tierney contends that geneticist James Neel caused a measles epidemic among the Yanomami Indians of Venezuela by inoculating them with a virulent measles vaccine. He also states that Neel's collaborator, anthropologist Napoleon Chagnon, exaggerated Yanomami aggressiveness and actually caused violence by indiscriminately giving machetes to tribesmen who helped him, sometimes even inducing them to break their own taboos. Anthropologist John Tooby counters that medical experts agree that it is impossible to produce communicable measles with the vaccine that Neel used. He also argues that Tierney systematically distorts Chagnon's views on Yanomami violence and exaggerates the amount of disruption caused by Chagnon's activities compared to that of such others as missionaries and gold miners.

Anthropologist David Stoll argues that Rigoberta Menchú misleads readers of her book by implying that she experienced events to which she could never have been a witness. Contrary to what Menchú implies, he asserts that the guerrillas used violence to force otherwise complacent Mayan peasants to join their fight. Anthropologist Carol A. Smith contends that Menchú's misrepresentations are inconsequential. She states that what is more important is that Menchú's book was instrumental in drawing national attention to the plight of the Guatemalan Maya, who, Smith maintains, were ripe for revolution and eager to fight with the guerrilla army.

Professor of the history and philosophy of science Merrilee H. Salmon argues that clitoridectomy (female genital mutilation) violates the rights of the women on whom it is performed. Professor of anthropology Elliott P. Skinner accuses feminists who want to abolish clitoridectomy of being ethnocentric. He states that African women themselves want to participate in the practice, which functions like male initiation, transforming girls into adult women.

Anthropology professor James F. Weiner asserts that anthropologists have a responsibility to defend traditional native cultures, particularly if secret cultural knowledge is involved. Applied anthropologist Ron Brunton argues that even when hired as consultants, anthropologists have a moral and professional responsibility to the truth, whether the gained knowledge is considered by the native community as secret or not.

Introduction

Studying Cultural Anthropology

Robert L. Welsch

Kirk M. Endicott

Anthropology is the study of humanity in all its biological, social, cultural, and linguistic diversity. It is the broadest social science, encompassing four major subfields—cultural anthropology, prehistoric archaeology, biological anthropology, and anthropological linguistics—and several smaller ones. Cultural anthropology, the topic of this book, is the comparative study of human ways of life. Cultural anthropologists try to explain why these ways of life—cultures —take the form they do and what they mean to the people who follow them. Historically, cultural anthropologists have focused on small-scale non-Western societies, especially tribes and peasant communities, but nowadays they apply their methods and concepts to the study of groups in complex societies as well, such as occupational groups in the United States.

Several features of cultural anthropology distinguish it from other social sciences, like sociology and political science. One feature is the basic method of data collection—*ethnographic fieldwork* or *participant observation*. Typically, cultural anthropologists live with the people they are studying for a year or more, learn their language, and participate in the daily life of the community as much as possible, thus enabling them to gain a personal understanding of the people and their world. Another feature is the cultural anthropologists' use of the concept of culture—which may be thought of as socially learned ways of acting, thinking, and feeling—both for describing specific ways of life and for analyzing and explaining particular practices and beliefs. Cultural anthropologists attempt to understand a wide variety of practices, ranging from child-rearing techniques to religious rituals, largely in terms of culture and cultural conditioning. Cultural anthropologists also try to understand a culture as a whole rather than focusing on only one or a few subsystems, such as a people's economy or religion. They are interested in how these subsystems fit together to form coherent—or sometimes discordant—wholes. Finally, cultural anthropologists use comparisons between different cultures to try to answer broad questions about similarities and differences in human behavior. They use cross-cultural comparison to look for patterns of association; for example, between certain religions and certain forms of government. Because cultural anthropologists study so many aspects of so many different cultures from so many different points of view, it may seem that no two anthropologists actually study the same things, yet they all are working toward a greater understanding of the cultural capabilities and productions of the human species.

Cultural anthropology as we know it today (called *social anthropology* in Great Britain) developed in the late nineteenth century out of European scholars' attempts to understand the radically different ways of life of the peoples outside Europe who were encountered by explorers, traders, missionaries, travelers, and colonial administrators. The standard explanatory concept at that time was *social evolution,* the idea that civilization as known in Europe was the culmination of a series of incremental changes from simpler beginnings. Scholars proposed hypothetical evolutionary sequences leading up to all the major components of European civilization. One of the more general schemes, that of the American anthropologist Lewis Henry Morgan, divided human history into the stages of "Savagery," "Barbarism," and "Civilization," the first two having three subdivisions, based mainly on advances in technology, such as the invention of pottery. All societies were thought to have followed the same evolutionary path, but those outside Europe and North America suffered from arrested development, getting stuck at some lower stage of development. The Australian Aborigines, for instance, were commonly seen as living examples of the lowest stage of social evolution ("Lower Savagery" for Morgan), one that Europeans had passed through thousands of years before. The slow progress of non-Europeans was attributed to their inferior intellectual endowment, a racist interpretation used by scholars and laypeople alike. Yet the notion that such peoples could overcome their inherent limitations with help from more talented Europeans was one of the justifications given for colonialism, the so-called *white man's burden* to civilize and Christianize the "backward" peoples outside Europe and North America. Most cultural anthropologists today vehemently reject the idea that any society is superior to any other, but notions of cultural evolution are still used in some theories of culture change.

The defining features of cultural anthropology—the idea of culture and the modern fieldwork method—developed along separate paths, only becoming firmly joined in the twentieth century. The first influential definition of culture in the anthropological sense was that of the British scholar E. B. Tylor. As he writes in *Primitive Culture* (J. Murray, 1871), "Culture or Civilization, taken in its wide ethnographic sense, is that complex whole which includes knowledge, belief, art, morals, law, custom, and any other capabilities and habits acquired by man as a member of society." Since then anthropologists, especially in North America, have repeatedly defined and redefined what they mean by culture. In a 1952 survey of the literature, Alfred Kroeber and Clyde Kluckhohn found over 157 different definitions of culture in print, reflecting numerous different emphases and points of view (*Culture: A Critical Review of Concepts and Definitions,* Papers of the Peabody Museum of American Archaeology and Ethnology, vol. 47, no. 1 [Harvard University]). However, a few common threads run through the theorizing and debate about culture that went on during the first half of the twentieth century. Cultural anthropologists were trying to establish that culture was a thing in itself, a so-called *emergent phenomenon,* not something that could be reduced to the sum of the actions and ideas of the individuals making up a society and therefore not explainable in terms of individual psychology or biological instincts. Culture was thought of as having an existence of its own, apart from the individuals who happened to carry it at any given time; it needed to be explained in its own terms, with distinctively cultural theories. The founder of American academic anthropology, Franz Boas, considered each culture to be a unique tradition or way of life, the result of a particular history of innovations and borrowings from other cultures. However, subsequent generations of cultural anthropologists were not content to view cultures as merely the outcome of the accidents of history. They attempted to explain the forms cultures took in terms of environmental adaptation or other forces. Cultural anthropologists like Margaret Mead (see Issue 4, "Was Margaret Mead's Fieldwork on Samoan Adolescents Fundamentally Flawed?") debated whether biologically inherited instincts ("nature") or cultural conditioning ("nurture") was the predominant influence on human behavior, with most cultural anthropologists coming down strongly on the side of nurture. The debate about the importance of instinct versus culture in shaping behavior continues today. (See Issue 8, "Do Sexually Egalitarian Societies Exist?"; Issue 10, "Has the Islamic Revolution in Iran Subjugated Women?"; and Issue 14, "Did Napoleon Chagnon and Other Researchers Harm the Yanomami Indians of Venezuela?")

Today anthropologists still argue about how best to conceptualize culture and even about whether or not such a concept is needed and useful. Nevertheless, in practice most cultural anthropologists treat all enduring social groups, from clubs to whole nations, as having a set of typical practices, ideas, and feelings that can be discovered and described in the form of a cultural description. Those practices, ideas, and feelings are shared because they are part of an interconnected—though not entirely coherent—tradition, which is learned, internalized, valued, and followed by each new generation. Cultures can change due to the innovations of creative individuals, but they also have great inertia, giving them a recognizable identity over time. For example, American culture can be defined as the set of practices, ideas, and feelings shared by all Americans, regardless of their ancestry, due to their learning and participating in a common tradition. Such a view does not deny that there are many layers of subcultures within the common American culture (e.g., working-class Mexican American culture) or that cultures continuously change.

The anthropological fieldwork method arose through a series of innovations by American and British researchers. The social evolutionists had generally been content to use the reports of European travelers, missionaries, officials, and so on rather than gathering their own data. Needless to say, the quality and accuracy of those reports were highly variable. The first systematic research into the customs of non-European peoples in North America were the studies made by officials of the U.S. government's Bureau of Indian Affairs on Indian reservations in the late nineteenth century. Typically an official would stay at the administrator's house and interview elderly members of the tribe about how they lived before they were defeated and placed on reservations, a process jokingly called "kitchen-table anthropology." Boas carried out his own research among Eskimos and the Kwakiutl Indians of British Columbia. He made numerous trips to the Kwakiutl and employed an educated Kwakiutl man as a research assistant and correspondent. Boas emphasized the importance of face-to-face research to his graduate students.

The modern method of fieldwork, however, derives from the pioneering research of the Polish-born British anthropologist Bronislaw Malinowski in the Trobriand Islands, off the east coast of New Guinea, beginning in 1914. Malinowski began his studies in New Guinea in the typical fashion of the day—living with a white administrator, visiting villages during the day or interviewing informants "on the veranda" through interpreters. However, with the outbreak of World War I, the Australian governor of Papua limited the movements of Malinowski, technically an enemy alien since he was Polish, to the Trobriand Islands. Making a virtue of necessity, Malinowski moved into a village, learned the Trobriand language, and stayed for more than two years. His findings formed the basis for a series of important monographs on Trobriand culture. Because of the unprecedented depth and richness of information Malinowski was able to obtain, his procedure became the standard fieldwork method for British anthropologists. However, that method spread only slowly to the United States, finally becoming fully established in the 1960s. In part the question of whether or not Mead's 1924 research in Samoa was flawed (Issue 4) is a question of whether or not her Boasian method of research was inferior to the Malinowskian approach followed by her critic, Derek Freeman. Today, most data used by cultural anthropologists are ultimately derived from observations, informal conversations, and interviews carried out by a researcher living within a study community. The fieldwork methodology distinguishes most anthropological research from that of sociologists, psychologists, economists, and other social scientists.

The information fieldworkers collect does not speak for itself; cultural data must be interpreted. Interpretation begins with the creation of the research questions themselves, for this reflects what investigators consider important to find out and directs their observations and questions in the field. At each step of data collection and analysis, the investigators' theories and interests shape their understandings of other cultures. In their reports (called *ethnographic monographs*), anthropologists draw on theories to create and test hypotheses or to shape their interpretations. It is easy to see why cultural anthropologists can arrive at different conclusions, even when studying the same society.

Much explanation in cultural anthropology is based on comparison of cultural features in different societies. Some anthropologists explicitly make cross-cultural comparisons, using statistics to measure the significance of apparent correlations between such variables as child-rearing practices and typical adult personalities. Even anthropologists who concentrate on explaining or interpreting features of particular cultures use their knowledge of similar or different features in other societies as a basis for insights. By viewing cultures in a comparative framework, anthropologists become aware of what is "missing" in a particular culture—in other words, what is found in other similar cultures —as well as what is there. Comparison is fundamental to the anthropological perspective.

Recently, cultural anthropologists have begun asking questions about anthropologists and the culture of anthropology, specifically about possible biases in the ways anthropologists depict and represent other cultures through writing, films, and other media. This movement has been called *post-modern anthropology* or *critical anthropology*. Post-modernists ask, among other things: Do our theories and methods of representation inadvertently portray the people we study as exotic "Others," in exaggerated contrast with Western peoples? This is the question that lies behind Issue 3, "Do Museums Misrepresent Ethnic Communities Around the World?"

Theoretical orientations In Part 1 of this volume we look at controversies concerning general theoretical orientations in cultural anthropology. The first issue considers whether cultural anthropology should model itself on the natural sciences or view itself as an interpretive branch of the humanities. Although most cultural anthropologists consider themselves social scientists, much anthropological analysis comes from interpretations of cultural data rather than from the material basis of human societies. In this issue, Marvin Harris argues that anthropology is a science and should model itself directly on the natural sciences, especially biology and environmental studies. Clifford Geertz counters that anthropology is nothing without cultural interpretations of symbols, meaning, and behavior. But for him such interpretations come from the fact that in anthropology, unlike the natural sciences, the anthropologist is the instrument through which all understanding must emerge. Issue 2 asks whether or not native peoples continually invent and reinvent their traditions. This debate between the late anthropologist Roger M. Keesing and Hawaiian activist Haunani-Kay Trask concerns who is best able to speak about native culture. Do anthropologists have a privileged view that allows them to see native custom and beliefs more accurately or do native peoples themselves have a better understanding of their culture? Clearly native peoples understand the nuances of their culture better than most foreign anthropologists, but do anthropologists bring an objectivity that allows them to see things that native peoples miss? Finally, Issue 3 questions the nature of anthropological interpretations. For more than a century, museums have been closely linked to anthropology, and until the 1950s most anthropologists made collections and studied various aspects of material culture in the course of their ethnographic studies. During the 1950s, 1960s, and 1970s the role of the museum in anthropology was in decline, and few anthropologists were trained to work with museum collections. But since the mid-1980s there has been a growing interest among cultural anthropologists about how the peoples anthropologists study are represented in museum collections.

Some specific issues in cultural anthropology Part 2 considers a variety of controversies that are being debated in cultural anthropology today. Because of the great breadth of subject matter in cultural anthropology, most cultural anthropologists become specialists in one or a few topics or subfields of cultural anthropology. Major subfields include kinship and social organization, economic anthropology, political anthropology, anthropology of religion, ethnicity, gender and culture, language and culture, psychological anthropology, and medical anthropology. We have tried to include at least one issue from each of these subfields.

Issue 4, which asks about the adequacy of Mead's fieldwork in Samoa, questions Mead's belief that the amount of sexual freedom offered to adolescents makes a difference in their transition to adulthood. Issue 5, "Does Language Determine How We Think?" concerns the question of whether a people's language shapes their culture. Issue 6, "Are San Hunter-Gatherers Basically Pastoralists Who Have Lost Their Herds?" and Issue 7, "Do Hunter-Gatherers Need Supplemental Food Sources to Live in Tropical Rain Forests?" deal with so-called hunter-gatherer societies, focusing specifically on their social organization and economic systems. Issue 8, concerning sexually egalitarian societies, and Issue 10, concerning the Islamic Revolution in Iran, deal with the question of gender and society. Issue 9, "Is It Natural for Adopted Children to Want to Find Out About Their Birth Parents?" concerns one of the most pressing contemporary issues in kinship studies. In the United States many adoptees feel driven to find their birth parents. However, the question is not whether American adoptees believe this urge is a natural one or not, but whether it is a universal—and thus a biological—urge or a culturally inspired one. Similarly, Issue 11, "Are Yanomami Violence and Warfare Natural Human Efforts to Maximize Reproductive Fitness?" raises the question of whether or not the violence observed by anthropologist Napoleon Chagnon among the Yanomami Indians of Venezuela is a natural drive inherent in men to maximize the number of sexual partners and thus maximize their biological offspring. Issue 12, "Is Ethnic Conflict Inevitable?" deals with Muslim-Hindu tension in India and ethnic violence in Bosnia specifically but raises questions about whether or not ethnic tension is universal. Finally, Issue 13, "Do Some Illnesses Exist Only Among Members of a Particular Culture?" raises a question from medical anthropology.

This set of issues is by no means exhaustive, either in representing the kinds of questions currently debated by anthropologists or the range of subfields in cultural anthropology. Nevertheless, these issues illustrate how cultural anthropology can and has weighed in on several pressing social issues of the day.

Ethics in cultural anthropology   Part 3 looks at controversies concerning the ethics of research, a topic that has become increasingly important in contemporary anthropology. The American Anthropological Association has developed a Code of Ethics covering both research and teaching (see the American Anthropological Association Web site at http://www.aaanet.org). It recognizes that researchers sometimes have conflicting obligations to the people and animals studied, host countries, the profession, and the public. One basic principle is that researchers should do nothing that could harm or distress the people or animals they study.

Here we consider four specific examples of ethical questions that affect cultural anthropologists. Issue 14 asks whether Chagnon and his colleagues actually harmed the Yanomami people (also spelled Yanomamö) with whom they worked. This issue rose suddenly in September 2000, when most American anthropologists received e-mails about charges leveled against the researchers by investigative journalist Patrick Tierney. This issue is thus timely, and it is also very important to the discipline because so many undergraduates have read one of Chagnon's books about the Yanomami or seen one of the ethnographic films he produced with Timothy Asch. Issue 15 asks whether it matters if Nobel Peace Prize winner Rigoberta Menchú's memoir contains inaccuracies. In 1999 anthropologist David Stoll published a challenge to the literal veracity of Menchú's book *I, Rigoberta Menchú* (Verso, 1984). But the ethical issues involved also concern whether or not Stoll is himself guilty of an ethnical breach by undermining one of Guatemala's national heroes and the interests of Guatemalan peasants by challenging Menchú's account. Issue 16, "Should Anthropologists Work to Eliminate the Practice of Female Circumcision?" concerns whether or not anthropologists have an obligation to try to stop a traditional cultural practice that some see as at odds with international human rights. This is the practice of female circumcision, which some call female genital mutilation. Can anthropologists sit still while women in African and Middle Eastern countries are mutilated? Or do anthropologists have an obligation to help preserve traditional customs? Finally, Issue 17 asks whether anthropologists have a moral responsibility to defend the interests of "less advantaged" communities. At issue is whether "traditional customs" of aboriginal women were being violated by the building of a certain bridge in South Australia or whether anthropologists have actually encouraged their informants to create new versions of their traditional secrets for political reasons. Just how far should an anthropologist go to help protect the interests of disadvantaged native peoples?

Some Basic Questions

On the surface, the issues presented in this book are very diverse. What has attracted us to the issues presented here is that each raises much broader questions that affect the entire discipline. In this section we briefly describe some of the basic questions lying behind specific issues.

Is Anthropology a Science or a Humanity?

Science is a set of ideas and methods intended to describe and explain phenomena in a naturalistic way, seeing individual things and events as the outcome of discoverable causes and as conforming to general laws. Anthropologists taking a scientific approach are concerned with developing broad theories about the processes that lead to observed patterns of variation in human biology, language, and culture. The humanities, on the other hand, are concerned with understanding people's cultural creations in terms of their meanings to their creators and the motivations behind their creation.

Cultural anthropologists are sharply divided over whether cultural anthropology should model itself on the natural sciences or on the humanities. Issue 11 explores how sociobiologists and their critics approach explanations for certain patterns in human behavior. Here Chagnon argues that anthropologists can use biologically based models from sociobiology to understand why native peoples behave the way they do. Anthropologist Brian Ferguson counters that Chagnon has misinterpreted his data, suggesting that Chagnon's own behavior during fieldwork created the native behaviors that he is trying to explain.

Is Biology or Culture More Important in Shaping Human Behavior?

Most anthropologists accept that both genetically transmitted behavioral tendencies (instincts) and cultural ideas and norms influence human behavior, thought, and emotion. However, anthropologists diverge widely over the amount of weight they assign to these two influences. *Biological determinists* believe that all human behavior is ultimately determined by the genes, and culture merely lends distinctive coloration to our genetically driven behaviors. At the other extreme, *cultural determinists* believe that any instincts humans may have are so weak and malleable that cultural learning easily overcomes them. The conflict between supporters of the two extreme views, called the *nature-nurture debate,* has been going on for many years and shows no sign of being resolved soon.

Several of the issues in this volume deal directly with the nature-nurture question, including Issue 8 concerning sexually egalitarian societies, Issue 11 concerning Yanomami violence and warfare, and Issue 13 concerning illnesses that may or may not exist only among members of a particular culture. In addition, Issue 4, about the Mead-Freeman controversy, concerns two diametrically opposed positions on whether adolescence is shaped more by biology or by culture.

Is the Local Development of Culture or Outside Influence More Important in Shaping Cultures?

In trying to explain the form a particular culture takes, different anthropologists place different amounts of emphasis on the local development of culture and on outside influence. Those who favor local development emphasize unique innovations and adaptations to the natural environment, while those favoring outside influences emphasize the borrowing of ideas from neighbors (*diffusion*) and changes forced upon a people by more powerful groups (*acculturation*). Most anthropologists recognize some influence from both sources, but some attribute overriding importance to one or the other.

Three issues in this volume are about the relative importance of local cultural development and external influences: Issue 6 concerning San hunter-gatherers, Issue 7 concerning hunter-gatherers and supplemental food sources, and Issue 12 concerning ethnic conflict.

Is a Feminist Perspective Needed in Anthropology?

Although female anthropologists—like Mead and Ruth Benedict—have been very influential in the development of anthropology, there was a bias in early anthropological studies toward emphasizing the social and political lives of men.

Over the past 30 years feminist anthropologists have argued that these male-biased accounts have overlooked much of what goes on in traditional societies because male anthropologists have been preoccupied with men's activities and the male point of view. Feminist anthropologists want ethnographers and theorists to give full weight to the activities and perspectives of women and to recognize that gender identities and values pervade all cultures.

Issue 8 concerning sexually egalitarian societies considers whether or not a feminist perspective is needed to recognize sexual equality. In a somewhat different way Issue 10 reassesses what a feminist anthropology might actually look like by presenting two opposed perspectives on what has happened to women's rights following the Iranian Revolution of 1979. Feminist anthropologists have also asserted that male bias affects anthropological methodologies as well. Issue 4 concerning Mead's fieldwork on Samoan adolescents hinges in part on different methods available to male and female researchers.

Some Theoretical Approaches

Cultural anthropologists draw on many theories of widely varying scope and type. We present brief summaries of a number of theoretical approaches used by authors in this book so that you will recognize and understand them when you see them. We have arranged these theories in a rough continuum from most scientific in approach to most humanistic.

Sociobiology   Sociobiology is a theory that attempts to use evolutionary principles to explain all behavior of animals, including humans. The best-known practitioner is biologist E. O. Wilson, whose book *Sociobiology: The New Synthesis* (Harvard University Press, 1975) sets out the basic concepts. Sociobiologists believe that human behavior is determined by inherited behavioral tendencies. The genes promoting behaviors that lead to survival and successful reproduction are favored by natural selection and thus tend to become more common in a population over the generations. For sociobiologists such behaviors as selfishness, altruism to close kin, violence, and certain patterns of marriage are evolutionarily and biologically determined. They see individual and cultural ideas as mere rationalizations of innate patterns of behavior. In their view, no culture will persist that goes against the "wisdom of the genes."

Cultural ecology   The theory of cultural ecology was developed by cultural anthropologist Julian Steward in the 1930s as a corrective to the overly simple schemes of cultural evolution. Emphasizing the process of adaptation to the physical environment, he postulated that societies in different environments would develop different practices, though the general trend was toward higher levels of complexity, a process he called *multilinear evolution*. His idea of adaptation, like natural selection, explained why some societies and practices succeeded and were perpetuated, while other less well-adapted ones died out.

Many archaeologists and cultural anthropologists use versions of cultural ecology to explain why certain practices exist in certain environments. Harris's widely-used theory of *cultural materialism* is a further development of cultural ecology. The basic idea behind all versions of cultural ecology is that societies must fulfill their material needs if they are to survive. Therefore those institutions involved with making a living must be well adapted to the environment, while others, like religions, are less constrained by the environment.

Culture history   Boas rejected the cultural evolution schemes of the nineteenth century, with their fixed stages of cultural development. He pointed out that all societies had unique histories, depending on local innovations and diffusion of ideas from neighboring societies. Also, change is not always toward greater complexity; civilizations crumble as well as rise. Boas advocated recording the particular events and influences that contributed to the makeup of each culture.

World system theory   The world system theory, which has gained great prominence in the social sciences in recent years, asserts that all societies, large and small, are—and long have been—integrated in a single worldwide political-economic system. This approach emphasizes the connections among societies, especially the influence of politically powerful societies over weak ones, as in colonialism, rather than local development of culture.

Cultural interpretation   Humanist anthropologists emphasize their role as interpreters, not explainers, of culture. They focus on the task of describing other cultures in ways that are intelligible to Western readers, making sense of customs that at first glance seem incomprehensible. The most prominent practitioner of cultural interpretation is Geertz, who coined the term *thick description* for this process. This approach is used especially for dealing with aspects of culture that are products of human imagination, like art and mythology, but even the institutions involved in physical survival, like families and economic processes, have dimensions of meaning that warrant interpretation.

Feminist anthropology   Feminist anthropology began in the 1970s as an approach meant to correct the lack of coverage of women and women's views in earlier anthropology. It has now developed into a thoroughgoing alternative approach to the study of culture and society. Its basic idea is that gender is a cultural construction affecting the roles and meanings of the sexes in particular societies. The aim of feminist anthropology is both to explain the position of women and to convey the meanings surrounding gender. Feminist anthropologists emphasize that all social relations have a gender dimension.

How Anthropologists Reach Conclusions

None of the issues considered in this volume have been resolved, and several are still the subject of heated, and at times, acrimonious debate. The most heated controversies typically arise from the most extreme points of view. When reading these selections students should bear in mind that only two positions are presented formally, although in the introductions and postscripts we raise questions that should guide you to consider other positions as well. We encourage you to question all of the positions offered before coming to any conclusions of your own. Remember, for more than a century anthropology has prided itself on revealing how our own views of the world are culturally biased. Try to be aware of how your own background, upbringing, ethnicity, religion, likes, and dislikes affect your assessments of the arguments presented here.

In our own teaching we have often used controversial issues as a way to help students understand how anthropologists think about research questions. We have found that five questions often help students focus on the most important points in these selections:

1. Who is the author?
2. What are the author's assumptions?
3. What methods and data does an author use?
4. What are the author's conclusions?
5. How does the author reach his or her conclusions from the data?

For each issue we suggest that you consider what school of thought, what sort of training, and what sort of research experience each author has. We often find it useful to ask why this particular author finds the topic worth writing about. Does one or the other author seem to have any sort of bias? What assumptions does each author hold? Do both authors hold the same assumptions?

For any anthropological debate, we also find it useful to ask what methods or analytical strategies each author has used to reach the conclusions he or she presents. For some of the issues presented in this book, authors share many of the same assumptions and are generally working with the same evidence, but disagree as to how this evidence should be analyzed. Some authors disagree most profoundly on what kinds of data are most suitable for answering a particular research question. Some even disagree about what kinds of questions anthropologists should be asking.

Finally, we suggest that you consider how the author has come to his or her conclusions from the available data. Would different data make any difference? Would a different kind of evidence be more appropriate? Would different data likely lead to different conclusions? Would different ways of analyzing the data suggest other conclusions?

If you can answer most of these questions about any pair of selections, you will be thinking about these problems anthropologically and will understand how anthropologists approach controversial research questions. After weighing the various possible positions on an issue you will be able to form sound opinions of your own.

Cultural Materialism

The Cultural Materialism Web site, created by Dr. M. D. Murphy of the University of Alabama, features an explanation of cultural materialism, a summary of the history of cultural materialism, and a list of pertinent scholars. This site also gives links to other relevant Web sites.

`http://www.as.ua.edu/ant/Faculty/murphy/cultmat.htm`

Exhibitions at the Smithsonian: National Museum of the American Indian

This Web site of the National Museum of the American Indian was created by the Smithsonian Institution and provides images of current and recent exhibits about Native American art and society. The links provided on this site allow students to evaluate how this museum represents the Native American community.

`http://www.nmai.si.edu/exhibits/index.html`

Exhibitions at the Smithsonian: National Museum of African Art

Students can compare this Web site of the National Museum of African Art, also created by the Smithsonian Institution, with that of the previous Web site. How is this ethnic community represented differently?

`http://www.nmafa.si.edu/exhibits/currexhb.htm`

PART 1

Theoretical Orientations

*C*ultural anthropologists study the cultures and societies of living communities. Like other social scientists they try to find patterns in social behavior and often develop and test models about the human condition and the range of human possibilities. However, many cultural anthropologists disagree on the extent to which cultural anthropology is a science or one of the humanities. Should anthropology model itself on the natural sciences or should the anthropologist's role be seen as interpretive? If anthropologists are interpreters of other cultures, what are the guidelines and limits that should be set for interpretations? Here we address the first question in a general way before turning to two specific cases to address the second question. The first case asks whether or not native peoples invent their traditions. The second asks whether or not museums exhibitions misrepresent native peoples as exotic "others." All of these issues suggest tensions and unresolved directions within cultural anthropology that will likely be with us for some time to come.

- Should Cultural Anthropology Model Itself on the Natural Sciences?

- Do Native Peoples Today Invent Their Traditions?

- Do Museums Misrepresent Ethnic Communities Around the World?

ISSUE 1

Should Cultural Anthropology Model Itself on the Natural Sciences?

YES: Marvin Harris, from "Cultural Materialism Is Alive and Well and Won't Go Away Until Something Better Comes Along," in Robert Borofsky, ed., *Assessing Cultural Anthropology* (McGraw-Hill, 1994)

NO: Clifford Geertz, from *The Interpretation of Cultures: Selected Essays by Clifford Geertz* (Basic Books, 1973)

ISSUE SUMMARY

YES: Cultural anthropologist Marvin Harris argues that anthropology has always been a science and should continue to be scientific. He contends that the most scientific approach to culture is cultural materialism, which he has developed specifically to be a "science of culture." Anthropology's goal should be to discover general, verifiable laws as in the other natural sciences, concludes Harris.

NO: Cultural anthropologist Clifford Geertz views anthropology as a science of interpretation, and as such he argues that anthropology should never model itself on the natural sciences. He believes that anthropology's goal should be to generate deeper interpretations of diverse cultural phenomena, using what he calls "thick description," rather than attempting to prove or disprove scientific laws.

For more than a century, anthropologists have viewed their discipline as a science of humankind or as a science of culture. But not all anthropologists agree about what being a science should mean. At issue has been the question: Just what kind of science is anthropology?

Nineteenth- and early-twentieth-century anthropologists generally viewed anthropology as one of the natural sciences, and most early theorists, such as Edward Tylor, James Fraser, and Lewis Henry Morgan, saw anthropology as an extension of biology. Like biology, anthropology is a comparative discipline, and ethnographic descriptions of particular societies resemble the systematic descriptions that biologists provide about different species. Most early anthropologists were also attracted to the theories of the naturalist Charles Darwin, whose theory of natural selection attempted to explain how natural species evolved. For anthropologists evolution meant explaining how one social form evolved into another, how one kind of society developed into another.

With the rise of functionalism in the 1920s, evolutionary models became much less important as sociocultural anthropologists made detailed studies of individual societies, conducting ethnographic fieldwork lasting a year or two. Research became a total immersion into the culture, and anthropologists were expected to learn the local language, conduct participant observation, and try to understand the indigenous culture from the "native's point of view."

Although many anthropologists abandoned evolutionary questions in the 1920s, several new kinds of evolutionary models emerged after the Second World War. Leslie White proposed a unilineal model, arguing that cultural evolution could be explained in terms of how much energy a people could capture with their technology. Julian Steward proposed a rather different multilinear model to explain how societies in widely scattered parts of the world respond similarly to environmental and ecological constraints.

Building on these kinds of evolutionary models, Marvin Harris developed an approach he has called "cultural materialism." For Harris cultural materialism makes anthropology a science that parallels the evolutionary and biological sciences. But whereas biologists try to explain the physical evolution of species through natural selection, Harris argues that anthropologists should explain cultural evolution by understanding "cultural selection." Some cultural practices, whether actual behaviors or ideas, directly influence the community's successful adaptation to its material environment. Harris contends that anthropology's research agenda should be to establish regular, predictable, and verifiable laws just as scientists in other scientific fields do.

In his selection, Clifford Geertz argues that anthropologists should not attempt any kind of positivist science at all and that it is futile to seek scientific laws to explain human behavior. He contends that such laws would be either so general as to be meaningless, so obvious as to be trivial, or so specific to particular cultural settings as to have no relevance to other communities. The interpretation of cultures requires "thick description," in which the anthropologist is sensitive to cultural meanings and can provide a nuanced understanding of what he or she has observed, heard, and experienced in the field. Thus, for Geertz, anthropology should develop as a science of interpretation, and by definition such a science of interpretation cannot consist of verifiable laws; instead, it depends on the personal interpretive abilities of each individual anthropologist.

These selections pose several questions that lie at the heart of all sociocultural anthropology. Should anthropologists focus their attention on developing evolutionary theories, such as the kinds of cultural materialist explanations Harris seeks? Or, should anthropology primarily seek a more modest role in the multicultural world of today, attempting to translate and make sense of other people's cultural practices? And finally, is anthropology big enough to hold both of these perspectives and others as well?

Cultural Materialism Is Alive and Well and Won't Go Away Until Something Better Comes Along

Cultural materialism is a paradigm whose principles are relevant to the conduct of research and the development of theory in virtually all of the fields and subfields of anthropology. Indeed, it has been guesstimated (Thomas 1989:115) that half of the archaeologists in the United States consider themselves to be cultural materialist to some degree. For cultural materialists, whether they be cultural anthropologists, archaeologists, biological anthropologists, or linguists, the central intellectual experience of anthropology is not enthnography but the exchange of data and theories among different fields and subfields concerned with the global, comparative, diachronic, and synchronic study of humankind: the origin of the hominids, the emergence of language and culture, the evolution of cultural differences and similarities, and the ways in which biocultural, mental, behavioral, demographic, environmental and other nomothetic processes have shaped and continue to shape the human world.

Culture

... The culture in cultural materialism refers to the socially conditioned repertories of activities and thoughts that are associated with particular social groups or populations. This definition of culture stands opposed to the fixed, "essentialist" notions that inspire those who define culture as a realm of pure and uniform ideas hovering over the hub-bub of the daily life of specific individuals. For cultural materialists, culture elements are constructed (more specifically, abstracted) from the bedrock of the immensely variable thoughts and behavior of specific individuals (Harris 1964a).... [C]ultural materialists have long argued that culture is at bottom an unfolding material process (viz. the concept of "behavior stream") rather than an emanation of a platonic archetype.... Yet, it would be completely self-defeating to limit the definition of culture and the scope of the social sciences ... to the bedrock of individual thought and activity. Although we cannot see or touch entities such as a mode of production or a transnational corporation or a sociocultural system, to the extent that these are logical and empirical abstractions built up out of the observation of individual-level events, they possess a reality that is not inferior to any other reality. Indeed, it is imperative for human survival and well-being that we learn to rise above individual thoughts and actions to the level at which we can begin to examine the aggregate effects of social life and the behavior of such higher-order entities as institutions and whole sociocultural systems. Political economies are as real as the individuals who fall under their sway, and a lot more powerful.

Paradigms

Paradigms stipulate the principles which govern the conduct of research. Principles fall into two classes: rules for acquiring, testing, and validating knowledge (i.e., epistemological principles) and rules for generating and evaluating theories (i.e., theoretical principles). A widely misunderstood aspect of scientific paradigms is that neither the epistemological or theoretical principles nor the paradigm as a whole has the status of a scientific theory. Principles such as creationism, natural selection, or the priority of infrastructure are not falsifiable. This does not mean however that paradigms are "ships that pass in the night." Paradigms can be compared with each other and evaluated from two standpoints: (1) their logical structure and internal coherence and (2) their respective abilities to produce scientific theories in conformity with the criteria discussed below. From this vantage point, the alternatives to cultural materialism presented in this [selection] offer slight hope of safe passage. I see a lot of sunken ships in the muddy waters of post-postmodernism—ships built out of flawed accounts of the history of anthropological theory, parochial agendas, inchoate conceptions of the nature of human society and human cultures, and a lack of well-formed epistemological and theoretical principles or useful substantive achievements that might justify a future—any future—for anthropology.

Epistemological Principles: Science

Cultural materialism is based on certain epistemological principles which are held in common by all disciplines which claim to have scientific knowledge. Scientific knowledge is obtained by public, replicable operations (observations and logical transformations). The aim of scientific research is to formulate explanatory theories which are (1) predictive (or retrodictive), (2) testable (or falsifiable), (3) parsimonious, (4) of broad scope, and (5) integratable or cumulative within a coherent and expanding corpus of theories.

The same criteria distinguish scientific theories which are more acceptable from those which are less acceptable. Scientific theories find acceptance in accordance with their relative powers of predictability, testability, parsimony, scope, and integratability as compared with rival theories about the same phenomena. Since one can only approach, but never completely reach, perfection in this regard, scientific theories are held as tentative approximations, never as "facts."

This view of science derives from the logical positivist and empiricist philosophical traditions.... Note that it makes no claim to being "value free." Rather it proposes to overcome the inevitable biases of all forms of knowledge by methodological rules that insist upon opening to public scrutiny the operations by which particular facts and theories come to be constructed. The oft-repeated charge by postmodernist science-bashers that there is no community of observers who can or do scrutinize anthropological, especially ethnographic operations... is belied by the intense criticisms to which crucial facts and theories are regularly subjected in the pages of anthropology's principal journals. Challenges by other observers to the ethnographic accuracy of the work of Boas, Mead, Benedict, Redfield, Evans-Pritchard, Malinowski, Lee, Vayda, and Chagnon just for starters, whether based on fresh fieldwork or written sources, clearly do fulfill the scientific model for independent testing by other observers.... It may take awhile, but ethnographers working in the same region if not the same village do help to keep each other in touch with basic ethnographic facts. However, I certainly agree... that the future of ethnography lies in greatly expanding the use of field teams and the number of restudies rather than, as Marcus proposes... increasing the number of experimental, personalistic, and idiosyncratic field studies carried out by untrained would-be novelists and ego-tripping narcissists afflicted with congenital logo-diarrhea.

... The reason that cultural materialists favor knowledge produced in conformity with the epistemological principles of science is not because science guarantees absolute truth free of subjective bias, error, untruths, lies, and frauds. It is because science is the best system yet devised for reducing subjective bias, error, untruths, lies, and frauds....

Following the lead of Clifford Geertz and under the direct influence of postmodern philosophers and literary critics such as Paul De Man, Jacques Derrida, and Michel Foucault, interpretationist anthropologists have adopted an increasingly arrogant and intolerant rhetoric aimed at ridding anthropology of all vestiges of scientific "totalizing" paradigms. According to Stephen Tyler, for example, sociocultural anthropologists should abandon

> the inappropriate mode of scientific rhetoric that entails "objects," "facts," "descriptions," "inductions," "generalizations," "verification," "experiment," "truth," and like concepts that, except as empty invocations, have no parallels either in the experience of ethnographic fieldwork or in the writing of ethnographies. The urge to conform to the canons of scientific rhetoric has made the easy realism of natural history the dominant mode of ethnographic prose, but it has been an illusory realism, promoting, on the one hand, the absurdity of "describing" nonentities such as "culture" or "society" as if they were fully observable, though somewhat ungainly, bugs, and, on the other, the equally ridiculous behaviorist pretense of "describing" repetitive patterns in isolation from the discourse that actors use in constituting and situating their action, and all in simpleminded surety that the observers' grounding discourse is itself an objective form sufficient to the task of describing acts. (1986:130)

Tyler's totalizing renunciation of the search for objects, facts, descriptions, inductions, generalizations, verification, experiment, truth, and "like concepts"(!) in human affairs mocks itself so effectively that any attempt at rebuttal would be anticlimactic. I do think it may be useful, however, to point out that the "simpleminded surety" with which positivists and behaviorists are alleged to view human social life flagrantly distorts the entire history of science in general, during which all sureties, simpleminded or not, have been subject to relentless skepticism, and the history of logical positivism in particular, during which the struggle to create objective data languages has constituted the central focus of a vast and continuing philosophical effort.

Anthropology's dedicated science-bashers are not mollified by the assurance that cultural materialists seek probabilities rather than certainties, generalizations rather than laws. . . .

Questions and Answers

The fallacies that embolden these queries are so transparent that one must wonder if the interlocutors really intend to be taken seriously. . . .

Question: Just how often does something have to recur in order for it to serve as the basis for a generalization?

Answer: The more times the better.

Question: If generalizations cannot be expected to be applicable to any specific case, what good are they?

Answer: The better the generalization, the more *probable* its applicability to the particular case, the more useful it is. (It is definitely useful to know that a particular person who smokes four packs of cigarettes a day is ten times more likely to get lung cancer than one who doesn't smoke, even though not all heavy smokers get lung cancer.)

Question: Why must science be equated with generalizing?

Answer: Because science is by definition a generalizing form of knowledge.

Question: Is the mandate to generalize nothing but a "procedural rule"?

Answer: Of course. And anyone is free to ignore the rule but to do so is to cease doing science. (It is also likely to get you killed the next time you step off the curb against the light, or the next time you strike a match to look inside your gas tank.)

Last question: Instead of generalizing, why not consider "all the particularity of the individual case"?

Answer: Because there are no limits to particularity. Any project that proposes to deliver *all* the particularities of any macrophysical event, human or not human, therefore makes a preposterous claim on our time and resources. For this reason, in science endless particularity is the exact equivalent of endless ignorance.

Epistemological Principles: Emics and Etics

In addition to the general epistemological principles shared with other scientific disciplines, cultural materialism is also based on epistemological principles which are specific to the study of human sociocultural systems. These involve: (1) the separation of mental events (thoughts) from behavior (actions of body parts and their environmental effects) and (2) the separation of emic from etic views of thoughts and behavior... The reason for the epistemological distinction between mental and behavioral events is that the operations (observational procedures) used to obtain knowledge of mental events are categorically distinct from those needed to obtain knowledge of behavioral events. In the former, observers depend directly or indirectly on participants to communicate what is going on inside their heads; in the latter observers are not dependent on actors to identify the actor's body motions and the environmental effects of those motions. The reason for the further distinction between emic and etic events is that the separation of mental from behavioral events does not exhaustively specify the epistemological status of the categories (data language) employed in the identification of mental or behavioral events. Observers have the option of describing both kinds of events in terms of categories that are defined, identified, and validated by the community of participants (emics) or by the community of observers (etics). Four types of knowledge stem from these distinctions: (1) emics of thought; (2) emics of behavior; (3) etics of behavior; (4) etics of thought.

To illustrate, consider the practice of indirect infanticide in northeast Brazil: (1) A sample of economically and socially deprived mothers condemns and abhors infanticide. (2) These mothers insist that their own behavior has been devoted to sustaining the life of their infants. (3) Observers note, however, that some of these mothers actually withhold food and drink from certain infants, especially from infants that are first and last born. (4) On the basis of the observed occurrence of maternal neglect and high infant mortality, it can be inferred that these disadvantaged women have thoughts that are contrary to or that modify their elicited emics of thought and behavior.... Emic and etic versions of social life are often but not necessarily contradictory.... But failure to distinguish between emic and etic and between mental and behavior data renders much of the sociocultural literature of cultural anthropology useless by literally preventing researchers from understanding the referential significance of their descriptive discourse (Harris 1968; Marano 1982; Headland, Pike, and Harris 1990).

Despite a persistent barrage of uninformed or malicious assertions to the contrary, cultural materialists insist that the proper study of humankind is both emics and etics and both thought and behavior....

While no cultural materialist has ever advocated making the subject matter of cultural anthropology exclusively etic or behavioral, the postmodernists and their idealist predecessors have relentlessly advocated essentialist exclusions with regard to what cultural anthropologists ought to study....

Theoretical Principles

These rest on the assumption that certain categories of behavioral and mental responses are more directly important to the survival and well-being of human individuals than others and that it is possible to measure the efficiency with which such responses contribute to the achievement of an individual's survival and well-being. This assumption lies at the basis of the "costing" of alternative patterns of behavior which in turn is essential for identifying optimizing behavior and thought... and the development of materialist theories of the causes of sociocultural differences and similarities.

The categories of responses whose costs and benefits underwrite cultural selection and cultural evolution are empirically derived from the biological and psychological sciences that deal with the genetically given needs, drives, aversions, and behavioral tendencies of *Homo sapiens*: sex, hunger, thirst, sleep, language acquisition, need for affective nurturance, nutritional and metabolic processes, vulnerability to mental and physical disease and to stress by darkness, cold, heat, altitude, moisture, lack of air, and other environmental hazards. This list is obviously not intended to encapsulate the whole of human nature. It remains open-ended and responsive to new discoveries about the human biogram and population-specific genetic differences....

Infrastructure, Structure, and Superstructure

The components of social life which most directly mediate and facilitate the satisfaction of biogram needs, drives, aversions, and behavioral tendencies constitute the causal center of sociocultural systems. The burden of this mediation is borne by the conjunction of demographic, technological, economic, and ecological processes—the modes of production and reproduction—found in every socio-cultural system. More precisely, it is the etic behavioral aspect of the demo-techno-econo-environmental conjunction that is salient.... Infrastructure constitutes the interface between nature in the form of unalterable physical, chemical, biological, and psychological constraints on the one hand, and culture which is *Homo sapiens*'s primary means of optimizing health and well-being, on the other.... Cultural optimizations and adaptations must in the first and last instance conform to the restraints and opportunities of the environment and of human nature.

In addition to infrastructure, every human sociocultural system consists of two other major subsystems: structure and superstructure, each with its mental/behavioral and emic/etic aspects. Structure denotes the domestic and political subsystems, while superstructure denotes the realm of values, aesthetics, rules, beliefs, symbols, rituals, religions, philosophies, and other forms of knowledge including science itself.

The basic theoretical principles of cultural materialism can now be stated: (1) optimizations of the cost/benefits of satisfying biogram needs probabilistically (i.e. with more than chance significance) determine (or select for) changes in the etic behavioral infrastructure; (2) changes in the etic behavioral infrastructure probabilistically select for changes in the rest of the sociocultural system. The combination of 1 and 2 is the principle of the primacy of infrastructure.

As a guide to theory-making, the primacy of infrastructure enjoins anthropological researchers concerned with the explanation of sociocultural differences and similarities to concentrate on and to give priority to the formulation of hypotheses and theories in which components of the etic behavioral infrastructure are treated as independent variables while components of structure and superstructure are treated as dependent variables. The practical consequence of such a commitment of research effort is that the search for causal infrastructural variables will be conducted with decisively greater persistence and in greater detail than is likely under the auspices of alternative paradigms. The history of anthropological theory demonstrates that those who lack a paradigmatic commitment inevitably "quit early" when confronted with difficult, puzzling phenomena. . . .

Another aspect of the principle of the primacy of infrastructure that is surrounded by misinformation is the feedback between infrastructure and structure or superstructure. It would be convenient for materialist-bashers if the principle of the primacy of infrastructure meant that cultural materialists regard the mental, emic, and symbolic-ideational aspects of sociocultural systems as mere mechanical reflexes or epiphenomena of infrastructure. ("Harris thinks ideas, symbols, values, art, and religion are unimportant aspects of human life. Ugh!") Again I quote from Murphy's paper: "As for the materialists, they fail to recognize that cultural forms have lives of their own and are not mere epiphenomena of underlying 'infrastructures'" (page 57). The attempt by Murphy and others to portray cultural materialism as a paradigm in which "the ideas by which men [sic] live have no importance for their action" (Bloch 1985b:134) is totally at variance with the prominence of the phrase "sociocultural system" in the specification of cultural materialist principles. Why does one bother to talk about the systemic role of structure and superstructure if infrastructure alone has importance for action? Do cultural materialists propose that people go about producing and reproducing at random and without an idea in their heads? Could sociocultural life as we know it exist if there was nothing but infrastructure? Certainly not. No more than one can imagine people living without an infrastructure, i.e., living on ideas alone. . . . The issue is not whether thought is important for action, but whether thoughts and actions are equally important in the explanation of the evolution of sociocultural systems. Cultural materialism—indeed any genuinely materialist paradigm in the social sciences—says no. The system is asymmetrical. Infrastructural variables are more determinative of the evolution of the system. But this does not mean that the infrastructure can do without its superstructure . . . .

To illustrate, consider the changes in U.S. family life since World War II with reference to the disappearance of the male breadwinner role, the demise of the multiparous stay-at-home housewife, and the rise of feminist ideologies emphasizing the value of sexual, economic, and intellectual independence for women. As I have proposed elsewhere (Harris 1981a), these structural and superstructural transformations are the determined outcome of a shift from goods-producing industrialism to service-and-information-producing industrialism, mediated by the call-up of a reserve army of housewives into low-paying service-and-information nonunion jobs. The infrastructural transformations themselves were related to the use of electronic technologies and to declining productivity in the unionized smokestack industries which had created and sustained the male-breadwinner-stay-at-home-housewife families. The rise of a feminist ideology which glamorized the wage labor market and the intellectual, sexual, and emotional independence of women was the determined outcome of the same infrastructural force. However, it is clear that both the structural and superstructural changes have exerted and continue to exert an amplifying, positive-feedback effect on the infrastructural transformations. As the consequences of the call-up of the female labor force manifest themselves in higher divorce rates, lower first marriage rates, and historically low fertility rates, service-and-information industrialism is in turn amplified into an ever-more dominant mode of production and reproduction. Similarly, as feminist ideologies continue to raise consciousness against the vestiges of male breadwinner sexism, men and women find themselves locked into the labor force as competitors, wages for both are driven down, unions are driven out, and the profitability of the service-and-information industries rises, encouraging more diversion of capital from goods-producing enterprises into service-and-information production....

Power and Cultural Materialist Theories

For proposing that changes in sociocultural systems are selected for in conformity with optimizing principles, cultural materialism has been caricatured as a form of functionalism in which all is for the best in the best of all possible worlds (Diener, Nonini, and Robkin 1978). This accusation cannot be reconciled with cultural materialism's long-standing focus on problems of class, caste, racial, and sexual inequality and exploitation....

The fact that modes of production and reproduction are selected for in conformity with optimizing principles does not mean that every member of a society benefits equally from this selection process. Where marked differences of power have evolved as between sexes and stratified groups, the benefits may be distributed in a completely lopsided and exploitative fashion. Under such circumstances, the costs and benefits must be reckoned not only with respect to individuals in their infrastructural context but with respect to the political-economic decisions of power holders. This does not mean that all changes which benefit ruling-class interests necessarily have adverse effects on everyone else, as Marxists have wanted us to believe. For example, as indicated above, the rise of the service and information sectors in hyperindustrial mixed economies reflects the higher rates of profit to be obtained from unorganized labor. Thus, an increasing portion of the industrial labor force consists of women who have to some extent risen above their previous condition as unpaid housewife-mothers dominated by blue-collar male chauvinist husbands. There is no contradiction involved in holding that the greater advantages accruing to U.S. capitalist interests are facilitated by a lesser but still favorable balance of benefits over costs accruing to women. The behavior of both strata exhibits the predicted optimizations even though one might hold that the gain for most women, especially for minority women, is slight by comparison.

Cultural materialism is thus no less emphatic about the importance of political-economic inequality as a modifier of optimization process than are various Marxist theoreticians who claim to have a monopoly on the defense of the oppressed (Harris 1991).... One can never escape the question of benefits for whom or of costs for whom. Far from neglecting or "covering up" the effects of political factors on optimizations, cultural materialists recognize regular systemic feedbacks from the structural to the infrastructural level which give rise to political economy, political demography, political technology, and political ecology. One cannot for example explain the adoption and spread of technological devices such as shotguns, of new varieties of wheat and rice, tractors, or solar cell generators apart from the interests of trading companies, agribusiness, and petrochemical transnational corporations, local landowners, banks, etc....

Where Is Cultural Anthropology Going?

A popular myth among interpretationist science-bashers is that positive anthropology deservedly collapsed because of its failure to produce a coherent body of scientific theories about society and culture. Marcus and Fischer for example assert that there is a crisis in anthropology and related fields because of the "disarray" in the "attempt to build general and comprehensive theories that would subsume all piecemeal research" (1986:118). This implies that the postmodernists have made a systematic study of the positivist corpus of theories that deal with the parallel and convergent evolution of sociocultural systems. But they have not done this. It was only after World War II that nonbiological, positivist cultural and archaeological paradigms gained acceptance among anthropologists. In the ensuing years unprecedented strides have been made in solving the puzzles of sociocultural evolution through a genuinely cumulative and broadening corpus of sophisticated and powerful theories based on vastly improved and expanded research methods. The cumulative expansion of knowledge has been especially marked within archaeology and at the interface between archaeology and cultural anthropology (see e.g. Johnson and Earle 1987). It is ironic, then, that at the very moment when anthropology is achieving its greatest scientific successes, anthropologists who have never tested the positivist theoretical corpus which they condemn hail the death of positivist anthropology and the birth of a "new" humanistic paradigm. Only those who know little about the history of anthropological theories could hail such a paradigm as "new," much less as "a refiguration of social thought" (Darnell 1984:271).

This raises the question of why antipositivistic humanism has become so attractive to a new generation of anthropologists (and other practitioners of social "science"). One reason may be that the generation of students reared during the 1960s and early 1970s believes that positivist social science is responsible for such twentieth-century scourges as fascism, Stalinism, U.S. imperialism, corpocracies, and the educational-industrial-military complex. No doubt hyperindustrialism, high tech, and the "technological fix" lead to feelings of dehumanization and alienation. But the association between all of this and positivist social science is spurious. The problem is not that we have had too much of positivist social science but that we have had too little (Harris 1974:264ff). The atrocities of the twentieth century have been carried out precisely by people who were ignorant of or vehemently opposed to positivist social science (e.g., Lenin, Stalin, Hitler, Mussolini). Too many anthropologists seem to have forgotten that there is a flip side to relativism, phenomenology, and antipositivism—the side on which relativists who denounce reason and scientific knowledge construct the world in their own image.

Clifford Geertz  **NO**

Thick Description: Toward an Interpretive Theory of Culture

I

[Here I argue] for a narrowed, specialized, and, so I imagine, theoretically more powerful concept of culture to replace E. B. Tylor's famous "most complex whole," which, its originative power not denied, seems to me to have reached the point where it obscures a good deal more than it reveals.

The conceptual morass into which the Tylorean kind of *pot-au-feu* theorizing about culture can lead, is evident in what is still one of the better general introductions to anthropology, Clyde Kluckhohn's *Mirror for Man*. In some twenty-seven pages of his chapter on the concept, Kluckhohn managed to define culture in turn as: (1) "the total way of life of a people"; (2) "the social legacy the individual acquires from his group"; (3) "a way of thinking, feeling, and believing"; (4) "an abstraction from behavior"; (5) a theory on the part of the anthropologist about the way in which a group of people in fact behave; (6) a "storehouse of pooled learning"; (7) "a set of standardized orientations to recurrent problems"; (8) "learned behavior"; (9) a mechanism for the normative regulation of behavior; (10) "a set of techniques for adjusting both to the external environment and to other men"; (11) "a precipitate of history"; and turning, perhaps in desperation, to similes, as a map, as a sieve, and as a matrix. In the face of this sort of theoretical diffusion, even a somewhat constricted and not entirely standard concept of culture, which is at least internally coherent and, more important, which has a definable argument to make is (as, to be fair, Kluckhohn himself keenly realized) an improvement. Eclecticism is self-defeating not because there is only one direction in which it is useful to move, but because there are so many: it is necessary to choose.

The concept of culture I espouse... is essentially a semiotic one. Believing, with [German sociologist and political economist] Max Weber, that man is an animal suspended in webs of significance he himself has spun, I take culture to be those webs, and the analysis of it to be therefore not an experimental science in search of law but an interpretive one in search of meaning. It is explication I am after, construing social expressions on their surface enigmatical. But this pronouncement, a doctrine in a clause, demands itself some explication.

II

... [I]f you want to understand what a science is, you should look in the first instance not at its theories or its findings, and certainly not at what its apologists say about it; you should look at what the practitioners of it do.

In anthropology, or anyway social anthropology, what the practitioners do is ethnography [the study of human cultures]. And it is in understanding what ethnography is, or more exactly *what doing ethnography is,* that a start can be made toward grasping what anthropological analysis amounts to as a form of knowledge. This, it must immediately be said, is not a matter of methods. From one point of view, that of the textbook, doing ethnography is establishing rapport, selecting informants, transcribing texts, taking genealogies, mapping fields, keeping a diary, and so on. But it is not these things, techniques and received procedures, that define the enterprise. What defines it is the kind of intellectual effort it is: an elaborate venture in, to borrow a notion from [British philosopher] Gilbert Ryle, "thick description."

Ryle's discussion of "thick description" appears in two recent essays of his (now reprinted in the second volume of his *Collected Papers*) addressed to the general question of what, as he puts it, *"Le Penseur"* is doing: "Thinking and Reflecting" and "The Thinking of Thoughts." Consider, he says, two boys rapidly contracting the eyelids of their right eyes. In one, this is an involuntary twitch; in the other, a conspiratorial signal to a friend. The two movements are, as movements, identical; from an I-am-a-camera, "phenomentalistic" observation of them alone, one could not tell which was twitch and which was wink, or indeed whether both or either was twitch or wink. Yet the difference, however unphotographable, between a twitch or wink is vast; as anyone unfortunate enough to have had the first taken for the second knows. The winker is communicating, and indeed communicating in a quite precise and special way: (1) deliberately, (2) to someone in particular, (3) to impart a particular message, (4) according to a socially established code, and (5) without cognizance of the rest of the company. As Ryle points out, the winker has now done two things, contracted his eyelids and winked, while the twitcher has done only one, contracted his eyelids. Contracting your eyelids on purpose when there exists a public code in which so doing counts as a conspiratorial signal *is* winking. That's all there is to it: a speck of behavior, a fleck of culture, and—*voilà!*—a gesture.

That, however, is just the beginning. Suppose, he continues, there is a third boy, who, "to give malicious amusement to his cronies," parodies the first boy's wink, as amateurish, clumsy, obvious, and so on. He, of course, does this in the same way the second boy winked and the first twitched: by contracting his right eyelids. Only this boy is neither winking nor twitching, he is parodying someone else's, as he takes it, laughable, attempt at winking. Here, too, a socially established code exists (he will "wink" laboriously, overobviously, perhaps adding a grimace—the usual artifices of the clown); and so also does a message. Only now it is not conspiracy but ridicule that is in the air. If the others think he is actually winking, his whole project misfires as completely, though with somewhat different results, as if they think he is twitching. One can go further: uncertain of his mimicking abilities, the would-be satirist may practice at home before the mirror, in which case he is not twitching, winking, or parodying, but rehearsing; though so far as what a camera, a radical behaviorist, or a believer in protocol sentences would record he is just rapidly contracting his right eyelids like all the others. Complexities are possible, if not practically without end, at least logically so. The original winker might, for example, actually have been fake-winking, say, to mislead outsiders into imagining there was a conspiracy afoot when there in fact was not, in which case our descriptions of what the parodist is parodying and the rehearser rehearsing of course shift accordingly. But the point is that between what Ryle calls the "thin description" of what the rehearser (parodist, winker, twitcher . . .) is doing ("rapidly contracting his right eyelids") and the "thick description" of what he is doing ("practicing a burlesque of a friend faking a wink to deceive an innocent into thinking a conspiracy is in motion") lies the object of ethnography: a stratified hierarchy of meaningful structures in terms of which twitches, winks, fake-winks, parodies, rehearsals of parodies are produced, perceived, and interpreted, and without which they would not (not even the zero-form twitches, which, *as a cultural category,* are as much nonwinks as winks are nontwitches) in fact exist, no matter what anyone did or didn't do with his eyelids.

Like so many of the little stories Oxford philosophers like to make up for themselves, all this winking, fake-winking, burlesque-fake-winking, rehearsed-burlesque-fake-winking, may seem a bit artificial.

. . . In finished anthropological writings, . . . this fact—that what we call our data are really our own constructions of other people's constructions of what they and their compatriots are up to—is obscured because most of what we need to comprehend a particular event, ritual, custom, idea, or whatever is insinuated as background information before the thing itself is directly examined. . . . There is nothing particularly wrong with this, and it is in any case inevitable. But it does lead to a view of anthropological research as rather more of an observational and rather less of an interpretive activity than it really is. Right down at the factual base, the hard rock, insofar as there is any, of the whole enterprise, we are already explicating: and worse, explicating explications. Winks upon winks upon winks.

. . . The point for now is only that ethnography is thick description. What the ethnographer is in fact faced with—except when (as, of course, he must do) he is pursuing the more automatized routines of data collection—is a multiplicity of complex conceptual structures, many of them superimposed upon or knotted into one another, which are at once strange, irregular, and inexplicit, and which he must contrive somehow first to grasp and then to render. And this is true at the most down-to-earth, jungle field work levels of his activity: interviewing informants, observing rituals, eliciting kin terms, tracing property lines, censusing households . . . writing his journal. Doing ethnography is like trying to read (in the sense of "construct a reading of") a manuscript—

foreign, faded, full of ellipses, incoherencies, suspicious emendations, and ten-dentious commentaries, but written not in conventionalized graphs of sound but in transient examples of shaped behavior.

III

Culture, this acted document, thus is public, like a burlesqued wink or a mock sheep raid. Though ideational, it does not exist in someone's head; though unphysical, it is not an occult entity. The interminable, because unterminable, debate within anthropology as to whether culture is "subjective" or "objective," together with the mutual exchange of intellectual insults ("idealist!" —"materialist!"; "mentalist!"—"behaviorist!"; "impressionist!"—"positivist!") which accompanies it, is wholly misconceived. Once human behavior is seen as (most of the time; there *are* true twitches) symbolic action—action which, like phonation in speech, pigment in painting, line in writing, or sonance in music, signifies—the question as to whether culture is patterned conduct or a frame of mind, or even the two somehow mixed together, loses sense. The thing to ask about a burlesqued wink or a mock sheep raid is not what their ontological status is. It is the same as that of rocks on the one hand and dreams on the other—they are things of this world. The thing to ask is what their import is: what it is, ridicule or challenge, irony or anger, snobbery or pride, that, in their occurrence and through their agency, is getting said.

This may seem like an obvious truth, but there are a number of ways to obscure it. One is to imagine that culture is a self-contained "super-organic" reality with forces and purposes of its own; that is, to reify it. Another is to claim that it consists in the brute pattern of behavioral events we observe in fact to occur in some identifiable community or other; that is, to reduce it. But though both these confusions still exist, and doubtless will be always with us, the main source of theoretical muddlement in contemporary anthropology is a view which developed in reaction to them and is right now very widely held—namely, that, to quote [anthropologist] Ward Goodenough, perhaps its leading proponent, "culture [is located] in the minds and hearts of men."

Variously called ethnoscience, componential analysis, or cognitive an-thropology (a terminological wavering which reflects a deeper uncertainty), this school of thought holds that culture is composed of psychological struc-tures by means of which individuals or groups of individuals guide their behav-ior. "A society's culture," to quote Goodenough again, this time in a passage which has become the *locus classicus* of the whole movement, "consists of whatever it is one has to know or believe in order to operate in a manner ac-ceptable to its members." And from this view of what culture is follows a view, equally assured, of what describing it is—the writing out of systematic rules, an ethnographic algorithm, which, if followed, would make it possible so to op-erate, to pass (physical appearance aside) for a native. In such a way, extreme subjectivism is married to extreme formalism, with the expected result: an ex-plosion of debate as to whether particular analyses (which come in the form of taxonomics, paradigms, tables, trees, and other ingenuities) reflect what the natives "really" think or are merely clever simulations, logically equivalent but substantively different, of what they think.

As, on first glance, this approach may look close enough to the one being developed here to be mistaken for it, it is useful to be explicit as to what divides them. If, leaving our winks and sheep behind for the moment, we take, say, a Beethoven quartet as an, admittedly rather special but, for these purposes, nicely illustrative, sample of culture, no one would, I think, identify it with its score, with the skills and knowledge needed to play it, with the understanding of it possessed by its performers or auditors, nor, to take care, *en passant,* of the reductionists and reifiers, with a particular performance of it or with some mysterious entity transcending material existence. The "no one" is perhaps too strong here, for there are always incorrigibles. But that a Beethoven quartet is a temporarily developed tonal structure, a coherent sequence of modeled sound—in a word, music—and not anybody's knowledge of or belief about anything, including how to play it, is a proposition to which most people are, upon reflection, likely to assent.

To play the violin it is necessary to possess certain habits, skills, knowledge, and talents, to be in the mood to play, and (as the old joke goes) to have a violin. But violin playing is neither the habits, skills, knowledge, and so on, nor the mood, nor (the notion believers in "material culture" apparently embrace) the violin. To make a trade pact in Morocco, you have to do certain things in certain ways (among others, cut, while chanting Quranic Arabic, the throat of a lamb before the assembled, undeformed, adult male members of your tribe) and to be possessed of certain psychological characteristics (among others, a desire for distant things). But a trade pact is neither the throat cutting nor the desire. . . .

Culture is public because meaning is. You can't wink (or burlesque one) without knowing what counts as winking or how, physically, to contract your eyelids, and you can't conduct a sheep raid (or mimic one) without knowing what it is to steal a sheep and how practically to go about it. But to draw from such truths the conclusion that knowing how to wink is winking and knowing how to steal a sheep is sheep raiding is to betray as deep a confusion as, taking thin descriptions for thick, to identify winking with eyelid contractions or sheep raiding with chasing woolly animals out of pastures. The cognitivist fallacy—that culture consists (to quote another spokesman for the movement, [anthropologist] Stephen Tyler) of "mental phenomena which can [he means "should"]—be analyzed by formal methods similar to those of mathematics and logic"—is as destructive of an effective use of the concept as are the behaviorist and idealist fallacies to which it is a misdrawn correction. Perhaps, as its errors are more sophisticated and its distortions subtler, it is even more so.

The generalized attack on privacy theories of meaning is, since early [Edmund] Husserl and late [Ludwig] Wittgenstein, so much a part of modern thought that it need not be developed once more here. What is necessary is to see to it that the news of it reaches anthropology; and in particular that it is made clear that to say that culture consists of socially established structures of meaning in terms of which people do such things as signal conspiracies and join them or perceive insults and answer them, is no more to say that it is a psychological phenomenon, a characteristic of someone's mind, personality, cognitive structure, or whatever, than to say that Tantrism, genetics, the progressive form of the verb, the classification of wines, the Common Law, or the notion of "a conditional curse" ... is. What, in a place like Morocco, most prevents those of us who grew up winking other winks or attending other sheep from grasping what people are up to is not ignorance as to how cognition works ... as a lack of familiarity with the imaginative universe within which their acts are signs....

IV

... [T]he aim of anthropology is the enlargement of the universe of human discourse. That is not, of course, its only aim—instruction, amusement, practical counsel, moral advance, and the discovery of natural order in human behavior are others; nor is anthropology the only discipline which pursues it. But it is an aim to which a semiotic concept of culture is peculiarly well adapted. As interworked systems of construable signs (what, ignoring provincial usages, I would call symbols), culture is not a power, something to which social events, behaviors, institutions, or processes can be causally attributed; it is a context, something within which they can be intelligibly—that is, thickly—described....

In short, anthropological writings are themselves interpretations, and second and third order ones to boot. (By definition, only a "native" makes first order ones: it's *his* culture.) They are, thus, fictions; fictions, in the sense that they are "something made," "something fashioned"—the original meaning of *fictiō* —not that they are false, unfactual, or merely "as if" thought experiments....

V

Now, this proposition, that it is not in our interest to bleach human behavior of the very properties that interest us before we begin to examine it, has sometimes been escalated into a larger claim: namely, that as it is only those properties that interest us, we need not attend, save cursorily, to behavior at all. Culture is most effectively treated, the argument goes, purely as a symbolic system (the catch phrase is, "in its own terms"), by isolating its elements, specifying the internal relationships among those elements, and then characterizing the whole system in some general way—according to the core symbols around which it is organized, the underlying structures of which it is a surface expression, or the ideological principles upon which it is based. Though a distinct improvement over "learned behavior" and "mental phenomena" notions of what culture is, and the source of some of the most powerful theoretical ideas in contemporary anthropology, this hermetical approach to things seems to me to run the danger (and increasingly to have been overtaken by it) of locking cultural analysis away from its proper object, the informed logic of actual life. There is little profit in extricating a concept from the defects of psychologism only to plunge it immediately into those of schematicism.

Behavior must be attended to, and with some exactness, because it is through the flow of behavior—or, more precisely, social action—that cultural

forms find articulation. They find it as well, of course, in various sorts of artifacts, and various states of consciousness; but these draw their meaning from
the role they play (Wittgenstein would say their "use") in an ongoing pattern
of life, not from any intrinsic relationships they bear to one another....

A further implication of this is that coherence cannot be the major test of
validity for a cultural description. Cultural systems must have a minimal degree of coherence, else we would not call them systems; and, by observation,
they normally have a great deal more. But there is nothing so coherent as a
paranoid's delusion or a swindler's story. The force of our interpretations cannot rest, as they are now so often made to do, on the tightness with which they
hold together, or the assurance with which they are argued. Nothing has done
more, I think, to discredit cultural analysis than the construction of impeccable
depictions of formal order in whose actual existence nobody can quite believe.

If anthropological interpretation is constructing a reading of what happens, then to divorce it from what happens—from what, in this time or that
place, specific people say, what they do, what is done to them, from the whole
vast business of the world—is to divorce it from its applications and render it
vacant. A good interpretation of anything—a poem, a person, a history, a ritual,
an institution, a society—takes us into the heart of that of which it is the interpretation. When it does not do that, but leads us instead somewhere else—into
an admiration of its own elegance, of its author's cleverness, or of the beau-
ties of Euclidean order—it may have its intrinsic charms; but it is something
else than what the task at hand—figuring out what all that rigamarole with the
sheep is about—calls for....

The ethnographer "inscribes" social discourse; *he writes it down.* In so doing, he turns it from a passing event, which exists only in its own moment
of occurrence, into an account, which exists in its inscriptions and can be
reconsulted....

The situation is even more delicate, because, as already noted, what we
inscribe (or try to) is not raw social discourse, to which, because, save very
marginally or very specially, we are not actors, we do not have direct access,
but only that small part of it which our informants can lead us into understanding....

VI

So, there are three characteristics of ethnographic description: it is interpretive;
what it is interpretive of is the flow of social discourse; and the interpreting
involved consists in trying to rescue the "said" of such discourse from its per-
ishing occasions and fix it in perusable terms. The *kula* is gone or altered; but,
for better or worse, *The Argonauts of the Western Pacific* remains. But there is, in
addition, a fourth characteristic of such description, at least as I practice it: it is
microscopic.

This is not to say that there are no large-scale anthropological interpretations of whole societies, civilizations, world events, and so on. Indeed, it is

such extension of our analyses to wider contexts that, along with their theoretical implications, recommends them to general attention and justifies our
constructing them. . . .

It is merely to say that the anthropologist characteristically approaches
such broader interpretations and more abstract analyses from the direction
of exceedingly extended acquaintances with extremely small matters. He confronts the same grand realities that others—historians, economists, political
scientists, sociologists—confront in more fateful settings: Power, Change, Faith,
Oppression, Work, Passion, Authority, Beauty, Violence, Love, Prestige; but
he confronts them in contexts obscure enough . . . to take the capital letters
off them. These all-too-human constancies, "those big words that make us all
afraid," take a homely form in such homely contexts. But that is exactly the
advantage. There are enough profundities in the world already.

Yet, the problem of how to get from a collection of ethnographic minia-
tures—. . . an assortment of remarks and anecdotes—to wall-sized culturescapes
of the nation, the epoch, the continent, or the civilization is not so easily passed
over with vague allusions to the virtues of concreteness and the down-to-earth
mind. For a science born in Indian tribes, Pacific islands, and African lineages
and subsequently seized with grander ambitions, this has come to be a major
methodological problem, and for the most part a badly handled one. The models that anthropologists have themselves worked out to justify their moving
from local truths to general visions have been, in fact, as responsible for undermining the effort as anything their critics—sociologists obsessed with sample
sizes, psychologists with measures, or economists with aggregates—have been
able to devise against them.

Of these, the two main ones have been: the Jonesville-is-the-USA "mi-
crocosmic" model; and the Easter-Island-is-a-testing-case "natural experiment"
model. Either heaven in a grain of sand, or the farther shores of possibility.

The Jonesville-is-America writ small (or America-is-Jonesville writ large)
fallacy is so obviously one that the only thing that needs explanation is how
people have managed to believe it and expected others to believe it. The notion
that one can find the essence of national societies, civilizations, great religions,
or whatever summed up and simplified in so-called "typical" small towns and
villages is palpable nonsense. What one finds in small towns and villages is
(alas) small-town or village life. If localized, microscopic studies were really
dependent for their greater relevance upon such a premise—that they captured
the great world in the little—they wouldn't have any relevance.

But, of course, they are not. The locus of study is not the object of study.
Anthropologists don't study villages (tribes, towns, neighborhoods . . .); they
study *in* villages. You can study different things in different places, and some
things—for example, what colonial domination does to established frames of
moral expectation—you can best study in confined localities. But that doesn't
make the place what it is you are studying. . . .

The "natural laboratory" notion has been equally pernicious, not only
because the analogy is false—what kind of a laboratory is it where *none* of the
parameters are manipulable?—but because it leads to a notion that the data
derived from ethnographic studies are purer, or more fundamental, or more

solid, or less conditioned (the most favored word is "elementary") than those derived from other sorts of social inquiry. The great natural variation of cultural forms is, of course, not only anthropology's great (and wasting) resource, but the ground of its deepest theoretical dilemma: how is such variation to be squared with the biological unity of the human species? But it is not, even metaphorically, experimental variation, because the context in which it occurs varies along with it, and it is not possible (though there are those who try) to isolate the y's from x's to write a proper function. . . .

The methodological problem which the microscopic nature of ethnography presents is both real and critical. But it is not to be resolved by regarding a remote locality as the world in a teacup or as the sociological equivalent of a cloud chamber. It is to be resolved—or, anyway, decently kept at bay—by realizing that social actions are comments on more than themselves; that where an interpretation comes from does not determine where it can be impelled to go. Small facts speak to large issues, winks to epistemology, or sheep raids to revolution, because they are made to.

VII

There is an Indian story—at least I heard it as an Indian story—about an Englishman who, having been told that the world rested on a platform which rested on the back of an elephant which rested in turn on the back of a turtle, asked (perhaps he was an ethnographer; it is the way they behave), what did the turtle rest on? Another turtle. And that turtle? "Ah, Sahib, after that it is turtles all the way down."

. . . Cultural analysis is intrinsically incomplete. And, worse than that, the more deeply it goes the less complete it is. It is a strange science whose most telling assertions are its most tremulously based, in which to get somewhere with the matter at hand is to intensify the suspicion, both your own and that of others, that you are not quite getting it right. But that, along with plaguing subtle people with obtuse questions, is what being an ethnographer is like.

There are a number of ways to escape this—turning culture into folklore and collecting it, turning it into traits and counting it, turning it into institutions and classifying it, turning it into structures and toying with it. But they *are* escapes. The fact is that to commit oneself to a semiotic concept of culture and an interpretive approach to the study of it is to commit oneself to a view of ethnographic assertion as, to borrow W. B. Gallie's by now famous phrase, "essentially contestable." Anthropology, or at least interpretive anthropology, is a science whose progress is marked less by a perfection of consensus than by a refinement of debate. What gets better is the precision with which we vex each other. . . .

My own position in the midst of all this has been to try to resist subjectivism on the one hand and cabbalism on the other, to try to keep the analysis of symbolic forms as closely tied as I could to concrete social events and occasions, the public world of common life, and to organize it in such a way that the connections between theoretical formulations and descriptive interpretations were unobscured by appeals to dark sciences. I have never been impressed by the argument that, as complete objectivity is impossible in these matters (as, of course, it is), one might as well let one's sentiments run loose. As [economist] Robert Solow has remarked, that is like saying that as a perfectly aseptic environment is impossible, one might as well conduct surgery in a sewer. Nor, on the other hand, have I been impressed with claims that structural linguistics, computer engineering, or some other advanced form of thought is going to enable us to understand men without knowing them. Nothing will discredit a semiotic approach to culture more quickly than allowing it to drift into a combination of intuitionism and alchemy, no matter how elegantly the intuitions are expressed or how modern the alchemy is made to look.

The danger that cultural analysis, in search of all-too-deep-lying turtles, will lose touch with the hard surfaces of life—with the political, economic, stratificatory realities within which men are everywhere contained—and with the biological and physical necessities on which those surfaces rest, is an ever-present one. The only defense against it, and against, thus, turning cultural analysis into a kind of sociological aestheticism, is to train such analysis on such realities and such necessities in the first place. It is thus that I have written about nationalism, about violence, about identity, about human nature, about legitimacy, about revolution, about ethnicity, about urbanization, about status, about death, about time, and most of all about particular attempts by particular peoples to place these things in some sort of comprehensible, meaningful frame.

To look at the symbolic dimensions of social action—art, religion, ideology, science, law, morality, common sense—is not to turn away from the existential dilemmas of life for some empyrean realm of de-emotionalized forms; it is to plunge into the midst of them. The essential vocation of interpretive anthropology is not to answer our deepest questions, but to make available to us answers that others ... have given, and thus to include them in the consultable record of what man has said.

POSTSCRIPT

Should Cultural Anthropology Model Itself on the Natural Sciences?

Cultural anthropology is often viewed as a big tent capable of embracing many diverse points of view, as the selections by Harris and Geertz suggest. One can see a number of parallels between anthropology and biology in this respect as well. Biology has always included those who provide systematic descriptions of natural species as well as theoretical biologists who develop and test evolutionary models. Some view anthropology in a similar way, arguing that Geertz's interpretive anthropology is merely the descriptive side of anthropology, while Harris's cultural materialism together with other evolutionary and ecological approaches provide the theoretical grounding. As Harris notes, most biological anthropologists and archaeologists either explicitly or implicitly draw on some form of cultural materialist theory, and it is this shared evolutionary theory that unifies the three main subfields of anthropology.

Geertz strongly disagrees with this view of anthropology, arguing that any positivist, nomothetic anthropology misses the nuance and subtlety that makes human cultures worth studying in the first place. But while Geertz is the most prominent champion of this viewpoint, he is not the harshest critic of efforts to turn anthropology into a law-based science. A number of younger scholars, such as James Clifford, George Marcus, and Stephen Tylor, have been much more vocal in their attacks on positivism in anthropology. Many of their arguments have origins in the interpretive approach developed by Geertz in the 1960s, but they have urged anthropology to become a self-reflective social science, which is often referred to as "critical theory." For these scholars, anthropologists should illuminate the implicit, underlying assumptions that have motivated anthropologists. Sometimes called "postmodernism," this perspective encourages anthropologists to deconstruct the assumptions of Western cultures. Some have suggested that critical theorists are more concerned with studying the culture of anthropology than with understanding anthropology's traditional subjects. In this sense, positivism in anthropology has become one of their most visible targets.

Cultural materialism is one direction for an evolutionary science of culture to develop, but it is not the only kind of "scientific" anthropology that has been proposed. Another evolutionary anthropology is "sociobiology," which takes a somewhat different approach from Harris. Sociobiologists argue that humans, like all animals, are genetically programmed to respond in certain ways, and cultural practices are just an external manifestation of inner biological drives. For example, sociobiologists argue that, like other species, humans are internally driven to pass on their genes to the next generation. Thus, they expect individuals to be altruistic toward their offspring as well as others who are closely related to them and therefore share some of the same genetic material. Increasingly, sociobiologists have developed theories that they maintain are both testable and verifiable.

Must all anthropologists have the same perspective, or is the discipline strengthened by having diverse theoretical points of view? Is there some middle ground between cultural materialism and an interpretive (or even a critical) anthropology?

For an extended treatment of Harris's views, see his *Cultural Materialism: The Struggle for a Science of Culture* (Random House, 1979). Two of Harris's other books put his theories into practice: *Cows, Pigs, Wars, and Witches* (Random House, 1974) and *Cannibals and Kings: The Origins of Cultures* (Random House, 1977).

Geertz's *The Interpretation of Cultures* (Basic Books, 1973), for which his selection was written, is the most coherent statement outlining the breadth and scope of an interpretive anthropology. It contains what is probably his best-known interpretive essay, "Deep Play: Notes on the Balinese Cockfight." Students should also consult his *Local Knowledge: Further Essays in Interpretive Anthropology* (Basic Books, 1983) and *Works and Lives: The Anthropologist as Author* (Stanford University Press, 1988). Michael Fisher's review essay "Interpretive Anthropology," *Reviews in Anthropology* (vol. 4, no. 4, 1977) offers a useful overview.

For background on sociobiology, see Edmund O. Wilson's *Sociobiology: The New Synthesis* (Belknap Press, 1975), Daniel G. Freedman's *Human Sociobiology: a Holistic Approach* (Free Press, 1979), and Georg Breuer's *Sociobiology and the Human Dimension* (Cambridge University Press, 1992). For an alternative view, see Marshall Sahlins's critique *The Use and Abuse of Biology: An Anthropological Critique of Sociobiology* (University of Michigan Press, 1976).

Important essays from a critical perspective are contained in two edited volumes: George E. Marcus and Michael M. J. Fisher's *Anthropology as Cultural Critique: An Experimental Moment in the Human Sciences* (University of Chicago Press, 1986) and James Clifford and George E. Marcus's *Writing Culture: The Poetics and the Politics of Anthropology* (University of California Press, 1986).

ISSUE 2

Do Native Peoples Today Invent Their Traditions?

YES: Roger M. Keesing, from "Creating the Past: Custom and Identity in the Contemporary Pacific," *The Contemporary Pacific* (Spring/Fall 1989)

NO: Haunani-Kay Trask, from "Natives and Anthropologists: The Colonial Struggle," *The Contemporary Pacific* (Spring 1991)

ISSUE SUMMARY

YES: Cultural anthropologist Roger M. Keesing argues that what native peoples in the Pacific now accept as "traditional culture" is largely an invented and idealized vision of their past. He contends that such fictional images emerge because native peoples are largely unfamiliar with what life was really like in pre-Western times and because such imagery distinguishes native communities from dominant Western culture.

NO: Hawaiian activist and scholar Haunani-Kay Trask asserts that Keesing's critique is fundamentally flawed because he only uses Western documents—and native peoples have oral traditions, genealogies, and other historical sources that are not reflected in Western historical documents. Anthropologists like Keesing, she maintains, are trying to hold on to their privileged position as experts in the face of growing numbers of educated native scholars.

I n 1983 Eric Hobsbawm and Terence Ranger published a collection of essays entitled *The Invention of Tradition* (Cambridge University Press). For many anthropologists trained in a structural-functionalist style of research, this volume was striking because it suggested two points that seemed to fly in the face of many cherished anthropological ideas. First, they argued that traditions in all societies change as a response to the political, economic, and social needs of the community. Second, they contended that the "historical" traditions societies celebrated were often invented in the recent past as a way of distinguishing one indigenous group from a dominant one. By 1983 most anthropologists had

26

accepted the axiom that all societies change over time. Culture and social institutions may work to inhibit changes and keep society functioning as it had in the previous generation, but innovations inevitably occurred. What made Hobsbawm and Ranger's book so important was that it used several Western examples to demonstrate that even in Western countries with rich historical documentation, institutions such as Scottish tartans could become routinized and accepted as a traditional and essential marker of Scottish ethnicity, even though the custom had existed for barely a century. They argued that the idea that tartans had ancient origins was particularly appealing to the Scots because it distinguished them from the dominant English culture that had long oppressed them.

In the following selection, Roger M. Keesing builds on Hobsbawm and Ranger's argument by turning his attention to the "invention of tradition" in Pacific countries. Throughout the Pacific, people now accept as historical traditions and customs practices that could only have emerged following the invasion and conquest of their islands by Western people. Keesing contends that because colonial intrusion has been so comprehensive, Pacific islanders know almost nothing about what their precolonial societies were really like. As a result, islanders have grasped onto certain idealized images of their past as themes and motifs to celebrate the distinctiveness of their cultures from dominant Western society. These idealized and largely fictional images have great political power for oppressed people, and they have often become a rallying point for various social movements. Nevertheless, concludes Keesing, these images of Pacific traditions find little support in historical documents and should largely be understood as modern mythmaking for the political ends of modern Pacific elites.

Hawaiian activist Haunani-Kay Trask attempts to turn Keesing's argument on its head by suggesting that Keesing's assertions about the "inventions" of Hawaiian traditions are yet another example of colonialism, racism, and white presumptions of superiority. She contends that Keesing only accepts Western historical sources, completely ignoring oral tradition, local mythologies, genealogies, and even rituals. Historical documents were biased by Western culture, argues Trask, and often represented an inaccurate understanding of native culture and social institutions. She questions whether or not white anthropologists have a privileged view of native customs, suggesting that most of Keesing's claims are racist attempts to further belittle native understanding and appreciation of the past.

Do native peoples or Western anthropologists have a better understanding of the native past? Have native traditions changed as much as Keesing would have us believe? Have these changes been the direct result of Western colonialism or have native peoples been active agents in such changes? Are Western historical sources biased and inaccurate when describing native practices? Are native oral traditions today accurate and authentic visions of traditional ways of life? Is there an authentic cultural tradition in any society, or, as Keesing suggests, are there different traditions for chiefs and for commoners, for men and for women? And, finally, are these " traditions" powerful as tools to fight oppression?

Roger M. Keesing

 **YES**

Creating the Past: Custom and Identity in the Contemporary Pacific

Across the Pacific, from Hawai'i to New Zealand, in New Caledonia, Aboriginal Australia, Vanuatu, the Solomon Islands, and Papua New Guinea, Pacific peoples are creating pasts, myths of ancestral ways of life that serve as powerful political symbols. In the rhetoric of postcolonial nationalism (and sometimes separatism) and the struggles of indigenous Fourth World peoples, now minorities in their own homelands, visions of the past are being created and evoked.

Scholars of Pacific cultures and history who are sympathetic to these political struggles and quests for identity are in a curious and contradiction-ridden position in relation to these emerging ideologies of the past. The ancestral ways of life being evoked rhetorically may bear little relation to those documented historically, recorded ethnographically, and reconstructed archaeologically—yet their symbolic power and political force are undeniable.

Perhaps it does not matter whether the pasts being recreated and invoked are mythical or "real," in the sense of representing closely what actual people did in actual times and places. Political symbols radically condense and simplify "reality," and are to some extent devoid of content: that is how and why they work. Perhaps it matters only whether such political ideologies are used for just causes, whether they are instruments of liberation or of oppression. In the contemporary Pacific they are being used both to recapture just rights and to deny them. The question is less simple than that.

The process of recapturing the past, of reconstructing, of questioning Western scholarship—historical and anthropological—is important and essential. My intention is neither to defend established versions of the past from a standpoint of vested scholarly interest, nor to debunk emerging political myths by comparing them to actual pasts to which I claim privileged access. Rather, in showing contradictions in this process of political mythmaking and in showing how in many ways the contemporary discourses of cultural identity derive from Western discourses, I seek to promote a more genuinely radical stance in relation to both the more distant and the more recent past—and to Western domination, of minds as well as societies.

From Roger M. Keesing, "Creating the Past: Custom and Identity in the Contemporary Pacific," *The Contemporary Pacific*, vol. 1, nos. 1 & 2 (Spring/Fall 1989). Copyright © 1989 by University of Hawaii Press. Reprinted by permission. Notes and references omitted.

The discourse of identity, legitimacy, and historical origins—the political mythmaking of our time—is not as different from the political mythmaking of the pre-European Pacific as it might seem.

The "invention of tradition" has been extensively explored in recent years..., in relation to theoretical issues of ideology and representation, questions of political economy (such as the invention and evocation of a symbolically constructed Scottish Highlands culture, replete with woollen kilts from British mills as well as bagpipes..., and the dynamics of national-identity construction in postcolonial nation states. These phenomena have not been extensively explored for the Pacific. Nonetheless, they have occurred in other times and places and are going on at present in other settings. Contemporary Malaysia, where a mythic "Malay culture," a conflation of indigenous (but heavily Indianized) court traditions and Islam, is being used to persecute and disenfranchise Chinese and Indian minorities and indigenous ethnic groups, is a case in point.

Modern Mythmaking in the Pacific

Before I turn to some of the important theoretical issues raised by contemporary movements and ideologies of cultural identity, let me sketch briefly the range of phenomena I am concerned with.

Beginning with ideologies of *kastom* in contemporary Melanesia, I will illustrate four variants, or levels, mainly with reference to the Solomon Islands. These phenomena have counterparts in Vanuatu and Papua New Guinea.

First, at a national and regional level, are rhetorical appeals to "The Melanesian Way," and idealizations of custom (most often emanating from a Westernized elite). In Vanuatu in particular, the ideologies and charters of the postcolonial state enshrine customary law and institutions.

Second, are ritualized celebrations of custom in the form of the arts —music, dance, "traditional" dress—as dramatically enacted in art festivals, tourist events, and rituals of state.

Third, the rhetoric of custom is invoked with reference to a particular region or island or province within a postcolonial state. This may take the form of competition for state resources and political power, regional separatism, or even secessionist demands.... In the emergence of Papua New Guinea, secessionist claims by North Solomons and East New Britain were cast partly in terms of customary unity....

Fourth, if the field of view is narrowed to particular language groups, particularly on islands like Malaita (or Tanna) where the commitment to "traditional" culture remains strong, we find ideologies of *kastom* used to resolve the contradictions between ancestral ways and Christianity. As Burt has documented, the Kwara'ae of central Malaita have produced origin myths that trace their ancestors back to wandering tribes of Israelites and codify ancestral rules in the style of Biblical commandments. The creation of mythical customs has been encouraged and even demanded by institutions of the postcolonial state that empower and legitimize "paramount chiefs" or other "traditional" leaders:

contemporary Melanesia is now filled with "paramount chiefs" in areas that in precolonial times had no systems of chiefly authority or hereditary rank. . . .

In Australia, idealized representations of the pre-European past are used to proclaim Aboriginal identity and the attachment of indigenous peoples to the land, and are being deployed in environmentalist as well as Aboriginal political struggles. In New Zealand, increasingly powerful and successful Maori political movements incorporate idealized and mythicized versions of a precolonial Golden Age, the mystical wisdom of Aotearoa.

Hawai'i and New Caledonia exhibit further variants on the themes of Fourth World political struggle, with idealized representations of precolonial society deployed to assert common identity and to advance and legitimate political demands. In the Hawaiian case, a cultural tradition largely destroyed many decades ago must be reconstituted, reclaimed, revived, reinvented. A denial that so much has been destroyed and lost is achieved by political mythology and the sanctification of what survives, however, altered its forms. In New Caledonia, the issues are not simply the desperate struggle for political power and freedom from colonial oppression, but also the creation of both common bonds and common cultural identity among peoples whose ancestors were deeply divided, culturally and linguistically, into warring tribes speaking mutually unintelligible languages.

Some Theoretical Themes

These discourses of cultural identity in the contemporary Pacific, although they depict the precolonial past and claim to produce countercolonial images, are in many ways derived from Western ideologies.

. . .[C]ontemporary Third World (and Fourth World) representations of their own cultures have been shaped by colonial domination and the perception of Western culture through a less direct reactive process, a dialectic in which elements of indigenous culture are selected and valorized (at the levels of both ideology and practice) as *counters to* or *commentaries on* the intrusive and dominant colonial culture. That is, colonized peoples have distanced themselves from (as well as modeling their conceptual structures on) the culture of domination, selecting and shaping and celebrating the elements of their own traditions that most strikingly differentiate them from Europeans.

. . .Pacific Island elites, and Aboriginal Australians, Maori, and Hawaiians in a position to gain leadership roles and become ideologues, have been heavily exposed, through the educational process, to Western ideologies that idealize primitivity and the wisdom and ecological reverence of those who live close to Nature. Idealizations of the precolonial past in the contemporary Pacific have often been derivatives of Western critiques of modern technology and progress; ironically, those in the Pacific who in their rhetorical moments espouse these idealized views of the past are mainly (in their political actions and life-styles) hell-bent on technology, progress, materialism, and "development."

In the process of objectification, a culture is (at the level of ideology) imagined to consist of "traditional" music, dances, costumes, or artifacts. Periodically performing or exhibiting these fetishized representations of their cultures, the elites of the new Pacific ritually affirm (to themselves, the tourists, the village voters) that the ancestral cultural heritage lives on.

...[A]ssertions of identity based on idealizations of the ancestral past draw heavily on anthropological concepts—particularly ideas about "culture" —as they have entered Western popular thought. It is ironic that cultural nationalist rhetoric often depicts anthropologists as villains who appropriate and exploit, although that anti-anthropological rhetoric is itself squarely shaped by anthropology's concepts and categories. . . .

European scholars are implicated in a more direct way in some of the misrepresentations of ancestral cultures. Some of the classic accounts and generalizations about the cultures of Polynesia and Melanesia by expatriate scholars —to which Islanders have been exposed through books and other media—are misleading. Western scholars' own misrenderings and stereotypes have fed back into contemporary (mis)representations of the Pacific past.

In questioning the political myths of our time, I am not defending the authority of anthropological representations of the Pacific past, or the hegemonic position of scholarly discourse in relation to the aspirations of indigenous peoples to recapture their own pasts. The past . . . is contested ground. I am urging that in contesting it, Pacific Islanders be more relentlessly radical and skeptical —not that they relinquish it to the "experts." (We who claim expertise, too, can well reflect on the politics and epistemology of our privileged authority.)

Finally (and critically), if I seem to imply a gulf between the authenticity of actual precolonial societies and cultures and the inauthenticity of the mythic pasts now being invented in the Pacific, such a characterization in fact perpetuates some of anthropology's own myths. The present political contexts in which talk of custom and ancestral ways goes on are of course very different from precolonial contexts. Nonetheless, such mystification is inherent in political processes, in all times and places. Spurious pasts and false histories were being promulgated in the Pacific long before Europeans arrived, as warrior leaders draped veils of legitimacy over acts of conquest, as leaders sought to validate, reinforce, [and] institutionalize, . . . and as factions battled for dominance. Ironically, then, the "true" and "authentic" cultures of the Pacific past, overlain and distorted by today's political myths, represent, in part at least, cumulations of the political myths of the ancestors.

In Pacific communities on the eve of European invasion, there were multiple "realities"—for commoners and for chiefs, for men and for women, for young and for old, for free persons and for captives or slaves, for victors and for vanquished. Genealogies, cosmologies, rituals were themselves contested spheres. The "authentic" past was never a simple, unambiguous reality. The social worlds of the Pacific prior to European invasion were, like the worlds of the present, multifaceted and complex.

Moreover, however the past may be constructed as a symbol, and however critical it may be for historically dominated peoples to recapture this ground, a people's cultural heritage poses a challenge to radical questioning. We are all to some degree prisoners of "real" pasts as they survive into the present—in the form of patriarchal values and institutions, of patterns of thought, of structures of power. A deeply radical discourse (one that questions basic assumptions) would aspire to liberate us from pasts, both those of our ancestors and those of (colonial or other) domination, as well as to use them as political symbols.

Let me develop these arguments. . . .

The Fetishization of "Culture"

Not only in the Pacific are dramatizations and ritual enactments of cultural traditions being celebrated—in the form of dress, music, dance, handicrafts —while actual cultural traditions are vanishing. The two processes—the celebration of fossilized or fetishized cultures and the destruction of cultures as ways of life and thought—are going on in the Soviet Union, eastern Europe, and China and also in the Andean states, Brazil, Malaysia, and Indonesia. Perhaps it is an essential element in the process of nation building, where populations are ethnically diverse. Most often, a dominant national population imposes its language and cultural tradition on minority groups while appearing to value and preserve minority cultures: they are preserved like specimens in jars. . . . What greater alienation than watching those who dominate and rule you perform symbolically central elements of your cultural heritage: selling *your* culture?

What makes the Pacific distinctive here is the way, particularly in the Melanesian countries, the specimens in the jars are the cultures those with political power have themselves left behind. Members of the Westernized elites are likely to be separated by gulfs of life experience and education from village communities where they have never lived: their ancestral cultures are symbols rather than experienced realities. Bringing the specimens out of the jars on special occasions—cultural festivals, rituals of state—is a denial of alienation at a personal level, and a denial that cultural traditions are being eroded and destroyed in the village hinterlands. . . .

By the same logic, the "cultures" so commoditized and packaged can be sold to tourists. I have commented elsewhere on the way this commoditization shapes Pacific cultures to fit Western fantasies:

> Mass tourism and the media have created a new Pacific in which what is left or reconstructed from the ruins of cultural destruction of earlier decades is commoditized and packaged as exoticism for the tourists. The Pacific [is] Fantasy Land for Europe and the United States (and now for Japan) . . . to be symbolically constructed—and consumed by a consumerist society, to serve its pleasures and needs.
>
> The commoditization of their cultures has left tens of thousands of Pacific Islanders as aliens in their own lands, reduced to tawdry commercialized representations of their ancestors, histories and cultures. Beneath the veneer of fantasy, the Islanders are pauperized in village hinterlands or themselves commoditized as menial employees. Serving the comforts as well as the fantasies of rich tourists, they are constrained to smile and "be happy," because that is part of their symbolic image.

We need only think of tourism in Fiji. There, at least, the elements of culture enacted for tourists represent a version, if an edited and Christianized one (no strangling of widows in the hotel dining rooms), of a past that actually existed. The representations of "Hawaiian culture" for tourists, with hula dances,

ukuleles, and pineapples, illustrate that where there is a gulf between historical realities and the expectations of tourists, the fantasies will be packaged and
sold.

Invented Pasts and Anthropology

The objectification of a way of life, the reification of the customs of ancestors
into a symbol to which a political stance is taken—whether of rejection or idealization—is not new in the Pacific, and is not confined to Islanders who have
learned the Western concept of "culture." The so-called Vailala Madness of the
Gulf Division of Papua in 1919, where villagers destroyed cult objects in a wave
of iconoclasm, and proclaimed their rejection of the ways of ancestors who had
withheld material riches from them, is but one example. Other classic "cargo
cults" echoed the same theme.

The political stances being taken toward the ways of the ancestors in the
contemporary Pacific reflect some of the same mechanisms. When massively
confronted with an engulfing or technologically dominating force—whether
early colonial invaders or more recently the world capitalist system and late-
twentieth-century technology and wealth—one is led to take an objectified,
externalized view of one's way of life that would hardly be possible if one
were simply *living* it. Land, and spiritual connection to it, *could not* have, other
than in a context of invasion and displacement and alienation, the ideological
significance it acquires in such a context.

The ideologies of our time, unlike cargo cult ideologies, are phrased in
terms of "culture" and other anthropological concepts, as they have passed into
Western popular thought and intellectual discourse. This is hardly surprising,
given the educational experiences of Pacific Island leaders, but it is problematic nonetheless, because the concepts that have been borrowed oversimplify in
ways that have bedeviled anthropology for decades. First, "culture" represents a
reification. A complex system of ideas and customs, attributed a false concreteness, is turned into a causal agent. Cultures are viewed as doing things, causing
things to happen (or not happen).

In the framework of functionalist anthropology, societies and cultures
have been attributed a spurious coherence and integration and portrayed in
a timeless equilibrium. The timelessness and integration of the ideologically
constructed Pacific pasts represent in part a projection of anthropology's own
conceptual simplifications into contemporary political myths.

...Pacific Island peoples asserting their identity and their continuity with
the past are led to seek, characterize, and proclaim an "essence" that has endured despite a century or more of change and Westernization.

In a different and older anthropological tradition—one that lives on in
anthropology museums, hence is represented in the contemporary Pacific—
a culture is metonymically represented by its material artifacts. This museological tradition, which has old roots in the nineteenth-century folklorism of
Europe, has fed as well into the discourse on cultural identity, as I have noted.
From it derives the view that in preserving the material forms and performance
genres of a people, one preserves their culture.

In borrowing from anthropological discourse, ideologies of cultural identity in the contemporary Pacific have not only acquired conceptual oversimplifications but have incorporated some empirical distortions and misinterpretations for which anthropologists (and other European scholars) are ultimately responsible.

It is not that Aboriginal or Maori activists, or contemporary Samoans or Trobriand Islanders, are uncritical in their acceptance of what anthropologists have written about them. In Aboriginal struggles for land rights, for example, one of the battles has been waged against orthodox views, deriving ultimately from Radcliffe-Brown, of the patrilineality of local territorial groups—views incorporated into federal land rights legislation. The ironies and contradictions of Aboriginal peoples being denied rights they believe are culturally legitimate on grounds that they do not fit an anthropological model have chilling implications for those of us who would claim privileged authority for our "expertise" or *our* constructions of the past.

There is a further twist of irony when scholarly interpretations that may be faulty, or at least misleadingly oversimplified or overgeneralized, have been incorporated by Pacific Islanders into their conceptions of their own pasts. Let me illustrate with the concept of *mana* in Oceanic religion.... When I was at the University of South Pacific in 1984 and spoke on *mana*, I discovered that Polynesian students and faculty had been articulating an ideology of a common Polynesian cultural heritage and identity in which *mana* was central. Yet, as I pointed out, in many languages in Western Polynesia *mana* is used as a noun only to describe thunder, lightning, or other meteorological phenomena. Where *mana is* used as a noun to refer to spiritual power, in a number of Polynesian languages, it seems to be a secondary usage, less common than its usage as a stative verb ('be effective', 'be potent', 'be sacred').

Mana in the sense it has acquired in anthropology seems centrally important only in a few languages of eastern Polynesia, notably Maori and Hawaiian....

The imputation of mystical wisdom to Polynesians (who in the process were distinguished from their dark-skinned, savage, cannibal neighbors to the west) has roots in European theories of race. The construction of the Polynesians in European thought, a process going back to the early explorers, has been brilliantly examined by Bernard Smith. Most striking has been the construction of Maori culture in European imagination.... The cosmic philosophy of the Maori, the mystical worldview, is as much a European as a Polynesian creation. Even though contemporary Maori ideologues attempt to discredit some aspects of the representation of Maori culture by Western scholars, the counterrepresentation advanced as authentic seems deeply infused by early Western romanticizations of the Maori....

Political Mythology and Cultural "Authenticity": A Wider View

So far, I have implied that there is a wide gulf between the authentic past—the real ways of life that prevailed in the Pacific on the eve of European invasion

—and the representations of the past in contemporary ideologies of cultural identity. This gulf requires a closer look.

...My point is ... that the real past was itself highly political. Pacific societies, in pre-European times, were far from stable and static...: they were, as the archaeological record makes very clear, marked by political expansions and contractions, regional systems, warfare, trade—and change. Anthropological models have by and large failed to capture the dynamics of cultural production and change. Cultures are often imagined to be like coral reefs, the gradual accumulation of countless "polyps." ...To the contrary, ... cultural production is a highly political process. The symbolic material of cultures—rules imputed to ancestors, rituals, myths—serves ideological ends, reinforcing the power of some, the subordination of others.

From such a viewpoint, the authentic ancestral cultures of the past begin to appear in a different light. The rituals, the myths, the ideologies of hierarchy and the sanctity of chiefs, served political purposes. Conquering chiefs—or their priestly retinues—invented genealogies connecting them to the gods, and discrediting fallen rivals. Those individuals or classes acquiring sufficient political power to control symbolic production could bend cultural rules and roles to their own ends, reinforcing and legitimating their power. (The old Polynesian process whereby ascendant chiefly factions produce and impose versions of the past that legitimate their ascendancy in cosmic and genealogical terms has clearly continued into the latter twentieth century, notably in Tonga.) "Ancestral cultures" themselves represented legitimations of political power and aspirations; cultures were contested spheres. In this sense, the political myths of the contemporary Pacific that refashion the past to advance the interests of the present are not so different from the political myths of the past, dutifully recorded by the early ethnographers.

There are political contexts where it is important for an idealized vision of the past to be used as counter to the present: to the world capitalist system as it incorporates poor Third World countries on its margins as primary producers and consumers; to mindless materialism, disintegration of bonds of kinship and community, narcissistic individualism, destruction of environments for short-term profit. There is a place for pastoral visions, in the West and in the Pacific.

And there is certainly a place for discourses of resistance cast in terms of cultural identity. For Fourth World indigenous minorities in the Pacific—Maori, Aboriginal Australians, Kanaks, Hawaiians—a reverence for what survives of the cultural past (however altered its forms), and for a lost heritage, is a necessary counterpoint to deep anger over the generations of destruction.

But such ideologies become self-delusory if they are not interspersed with visions of "real" pasts that cast into relief not simply their idealized virtues, but their cracks of contradictions.... European scholars of the Pacific have been complicit in legitimating and producing male-oriented and elitist representations of societies that were themselves male- and (in many cases) elite-dominated. A critical skepticism with regard to pasts and power, and a critical deconstruction of conceptualizations of "a culture" that hide and neutralize subaltern voices and perspectives, should, I think, dialectically confront idealizations of the past. I am encouraged by the emergence, in the last several years, of critical writings in this vein by Pacific Islanders, including Epeli Hau'ofa and a number of feminist critics.

This is not the time to leave the past to the "experts," whether of the present generation or their predecessors....

A more radical Pacific discourse would also be more deeply self-reflexive about the hegemonic force of Western education, of Christianity (an integral part of the colonial-imperialist project), of Western pastoral myths as appropriations of Otherness....

A similar self-reflexivity is a continuing challenge for scholars working in the Pacific. Both the political implications and epistemology of our projects and representations are deeply problematic. The frame of certainty that surrounds scholarly expertise—like mythical history—is less solid than it seems: it dissolves in the right mixture of astute skepticism and self-reflexivity. But specialists on the Pacific do not best serve the interests of a less hegemonic scholarship or best support the political struggles of decolonizing and internally colonized Pacific peoples by suspending their critical judgment or maintaining silence—whether out of liberal guilt or political commitment—regarding mythic pasts evoked in cultural nationalist rhetoric. Our constructions of real pasts are not sacrosanct, but they are important elements in a continuing dialogue and dialectic.

NO

Haunani-Kay Trask

Natives and Anthropologists: The Colonial Struggle

As a Hawaiian, a long-time outspoken defender of my people's claim to nationhood, a scholar, and a Native who knows her history and people, I found Roger Keesing's article... a gem of academic colonialism. Knowing old-fashioned racism too crude to defend but bitterly clinging to his sense of white superiority, Keesing plows the complaining path of the unappreciated missionary who, when confronted by ungrateful, decolonizing Natives, thinly veils his hurt and anger by the high road of lamentation: Alas, poor, bedeviled Natives "invent" their culture in reaction to colonialism, and all in the service of grimy politics!

Keesing's peevishness has a predictably familiar target: Native nationalists —from Australia and New Zealand through the Solomons and New Caledonia to Hawai'i. The problem? These disillusioned souls idealize their pasts for the purpose of political mythmaking in the present. Worse, they are so unoriginal (and, by implication, unfamiliar with what Keesing calls their "real" pasts) as to concoct their myths out of Western categories and values despite their virulent opposition to same. Thus the romanticization of pre-European Native pasts (the "Golden Age" allegedly claimed by the Maori); the assertion of a common Native identity (eg, Fijian "culture"); the "ideology" of land as spiritually significant (supposedly argued by Hawaiians, Solomon Islanders, Kanaks, and Aborigines). The gospel, according to Keesing, is that these claims are "invented." To be specific, there never was a "Golden Age," a common identity, or a spiritual attachment to the land.

Proof? Keesing supplies none, either on the charge that Native nationalists have made such claims or that their claims are false. He merely asserts fabrication then proceeds to belabor, through the mumbo jumbo of academic "discourse," the crying need for Natives (and academics) to face "our" pasts with "skepticism," while pursuing a "critical deconstruction of conceptualizations" to achieve "dialectical confrontation." The final intention should be to "liberate us" from our pasts.

Well, my answer to Keesing has been said by modern-day Natives to would-be White Fathers many times: What do you mean "us," white man?

From Haunani-Kay Trask, "Natives and Anthropologists: The Colonial Struggle," *The Contemporary Pacific* (Spring 1991). Copyright © 1991 by University of Hawaii Press. Reprinted by permission. References and some notes omitted.

Among Hawaiians, people like Keesing are described as *maha'oi haole*, that is, rude, intrusive white people who go where they do not belong. In Keesing's case, his factual errors, cultural and political ignorance, and dismissive attitude qualify him perfectly as *maha'oi*. Unlike Keesing; I cannot speak for other Natives. But regarding Hawaiian nationalists, Keesing neither knows whereof he speaks, nor given his *maha'oi* attitude, does he care.

Example   Keesing only cites works by *haole* academics on the current situation in Hawai'i. Obviously, he hasn't bothered to read our Native nationalists and scholars, including those, like myself, who have been very critical of these same *haole* academics. Indeed, most of his comments on Hawaiian nationalists come from one problematic and contested article (contested by Natives, that is) by anthropologist Jocelyn Linnekin, hardly a sound evidentiary base for sweeping claims that we invent our past.

Beyond his poverty of sources, there is Keesing's willful ignorance of solid evidence from Native forms of history—genealogy—which reveal that in pre-*haole* Hawai'i our people looked on land as a mother, enjoyed a familial relationship with her and other living things, and practiced an economically wise, spiritually based ethic of caring for the land, called *mālama 'āina*.

Contrary to Linnekin's claims, and Keesing's uncritical acceptance of them, the value of *mālama 'āina* has been "documented historically," and "recorded ethnographically," (as Keesing might learn if he read Native sources), two of the criteria Keesing cites as central to any judgment of the accuracy of "ancestral ways of life being evoked rhetorically" by Native nationalists today.[1] If Natives must be held to Keesing's criteria, why should he be allowed to escape them?

The answer is that Keesing, with many Western academics, shares a common assumption: Natives don't know very much, even about their own life-ways, thus there is no need to read them. (The only "real" sources are *haole* sources, hegemony recognizing and reinforcing hegemony).

Keesing's racism is exposed here. Not only has he refused to read what we Native nationalists write and say, he has refused to look at our sources of knowledge. But then, Keesing believes, Natives are so colonized, why bother?

Example   Keesing has also failed to distinguish between what Hawaiian nationalists say about our ways of life and what the mammoth tourist industry advertises "Hawaiian culture" to be, including "hula dances, ukuleles, and pineapples." Because he is totally ignorant of modern Hawaiian resistance, he is also totally ignorant of the Native criticism of the tourist industry, including the myth of happy Natives waiting to share their "culture" with tourists. In fact, after years of Native resistance to tourism, the churches in Hawai'i (with the push of Native nationalists and international ecumenical groups) sponsored a conference on the impact of tourism on Hawaiian people and culture in 1989. At that conference, Hawaiians from each of our major islands spoke eloquently of tourism's damage to Hawaiian sites, dance, language, economics, land, and way of life. The declaration issued from that conference listed ways to halt this damage, including a ban on all resorts in Hawaiian communities. Keesing should be reading this kind of primary evidence if he wants to learn what Hawaiian nationalists think about tourism and our culture.

Example   Keesing claims that Native nationalists hark back to an "authentic," "simple, unambiguous reality," when, in fact, "there were multiple 'realities' —for commoners and chiefs, for men and for women..." in cultures where "genealogies, cosmologies, rituals were themselves contested spheres."

As usual, the critical reader finds not a single reference here to a single Native nationalist statement. More *haole* sources follow, especially Keesing on Keesing. But where are the Natives?

In the dark, naturally.

The truth is that Keesing has made a false charge. Those of us in the current Hawaiian nationalist movement know that genealogies are claimed and contested all the time. Some of the chiefly lineages have legal claims on lands taken by the United States government at the American annexation of Hawai'i in 1898, which means that genealogies have an impact beyond the Hawaiian community. Cosmologies are also contested, with nationalists citing and arguing over accuracy and preferability.[2]

Finally, at the Center for Hawaiian Studies—which generates nationalist positions, sponsors nationalist conferences, and teaches the historical background and political substance of nationalist arguments—students are required to take a course on genealogies.

Given Roger Keesing's shameless claims about us Hawaiian nationalists, I invite him to take this course, or any other offered at our center. We Natives might teach him something.

Example   Keesing asserts that "cultural nationalist rhetoric often depicts anthropologists as villains who appropriate and exploit." In a note, he adds that anthropologists are "imagined to be appropriating and profiting from other people's cultures...."

In Hawai'i, contract work is a major source of funding for archaeologists and anthropologists. These people are hired by investors and state or private institutions to survey areas and deem them ready for use. In highly controversial cases regarding removal of Hawaiian bones and destruction of Hawaiian temple and house sites, many archaeologists and anthropologists have argued *for* development and *against* preservation while receiving substantial sums of money. At its worst, these controversies have exposed the racist paternalism of anthropologists who pit (in their own words) *emotional* Hawaiians who try to stop disinterment and development against *scientific* anthropologists who try to increase the store of (Western) knowledge.

Of course, these *haole* anthropologists would be outraged were we Hawaiians to dig up *their* relatives for osteological analysis, search for evidence of tuberculosis and other diseases, and, not coincidentally, get paid handsomely for our troubles. To my knowledge, no anthropologist has ever dug up missionary bones, despite their plentiful presence. Nor has any haole "expert" ever argued that missionary skeletons should be subjected to osteological analysis, despite historical evidence that missionaries did bring certain diseases to

Hawai'i. White colonialism in Hawai'i ensures that it is the colonizers who determine disinterment. Since we are the colonized, we have no power to disinter the bones of the colonizer. Thus, Native remains are dug up and studied. Missionary and explorer remains are sacrosanct.

Apart from contract work, anthropologists make academic careers and employment off Native cultures. Keesing may not think this is "profiting," but anthropologists who secure tenure by studying, publishing, and lecturing about Native peoples are clearly "profiting" through a guaranteed lifetime income. Of course, Keesing is disingenuous, at best. He knows as well as Native nationalists that anthropologists without Natives are like entomologists without insects.

For Hawaiians, anthropologists in general (and Keesing in particular) are part of the colonizing horde because they seek to take away from us the power to define who and what we are, and how we should behave politically and culturally.[3] This theft testifies to the stranglehold of colonialism and explains why self-identity by Natives elicits such strenuous and sometimes vicious denials by members of the dominant culture.

These denials are made in order to undermine the legitimacy of Native nationalists by attacking their motives in asserting their values and institutions. But motivation is laid bare through the struggle for cultural expression. Nationalists offer explanations at every turn: in writing, in public forums, in acts of resistance. To Natives, the burst of creative outpouring that accompanies cultural nationalism is self-explanatory: a choice has been made for things Native over things non-Native. Politically, the choice is one of decolonization.

The direct links between mental and political decolonization are clearly observable to representatives of the dominant culture, like Keesing, who find their status as "experts" on Natives suddenly repudiated by Natives themselves. This is why thinking and acting like a native is a highly politicized reality, one filled with intimate oppositions and psychological tensions. But it is not Natives who create politicization. *That* was begun at the moment of colonization.

In the Hawaiian case, the "invention" criticism has been thrown into the public arena precisely at a time when Hawaiian cultural and political assertion has been both vigorous and strong willed. Since 1970, Hawaiians have been organizing for land rights, including claims to restitution for the American overthrow of our government in 1893 and for forced annexation in 1898. Two decades of struggle have resulted in the contemporary push for Hawaiian sovereignty, with arguments ranging from complete secession to legally incorporated land-based units managed by Hawaiians, to a "nation-within-a-nation" government akin to Native American Indian nations. The US government has issued two reports on the status of Hawaiian trust lands, which encompass nearly half the State of Hawai'i. And finally, a quasi-governmental agency—the Office of Hawaiian Affairs—was created in 1978, partly in response to Hawaiian demands.

This kind of political activity has been accompanied by a flourishing of Hawaiian dance, a move for Hawaiian language immersion schools, and a larger public sensitivity to the destructive Western relationship to the land compared to the indigenous Hawaiian way of caring for the land.

Non-Native response to this Hawaiian resistance has varied from humor, through mild denial that any wrong has been committed against the Hawaiian people and government, to organized counteraction, especially from threatened agencies and actors who hold power over Hawaiian resources. Indeed, representatives of the dominant culture—from historians and anthropologists to bureaucrats and politicians—are quick to feel and perceive danger because, in the colonial context, all Native cultural resistance is political: it challenges hegemony, including that of people like Keesing who claim to encourage a more "radical stance" toward our past by liberating us from it.

But Keesing obviously knows nothing about Hawaiians. He has failed to distinguish land claims from cultural resurgence, although both have nationalist origins. And he has little or no background regarding the theft of Hawaiian domain and dominion by the American government in the nineteenth century. Given this kind of ignorance of both our recent and distant past, Keesing would do better to take a "radical" look at the racism and arrogance of *his* culture which originated anthropology and its "search for the primitive."

As for nationalist Hawaiians, we know our future lies in the ways of our ancestors, not in the colonial world of *haole* experts. Our efforts at "liberation" are directed against the colonizers, whether they be political agencies, like the American government, or academics, like Keesing himself. We do not need, nor do we want to be "liberated" from our past because it is the source of our understanding of the cosmos and of our *mana*.

In our language, the past (*ka wā mamua*) is the time in front or before; the future (*ka wā mahope*) is the time that comes after. In the words of one of our best living Native historians, Lilikalā Kameʻeleihiwa (whom Keesing did not read), "The Hawaiian stands firmly in the present, with his back to the future, and his eyes fixed upon the past, seeking historical answers for present-day dilemmas. Such an orientation is to the Hawaiian an eminently practical one, for the future is always unknown whereas the past is rich in glory and knowledge."

Notes

1. In her article, Linnekin writes, "For Hawaiʻi, 'traditional' properly refers to the precontact era, before Cook's arrival in 1778." But later on the same page, she admits that "tradition is fluid..." Despite this confusion she criticizes Hawaiians for a "reconstruction of traditional Hawaiian society" in the present.

   But what constitutes "tradition" to a people is ever-changing. Culture is not static, nor is it frozen in objectified moments in time. Without doubt, Hawaiians were transformed drastically and irreparably after contact, but remnants of earlier lifeways, including values and symbols, have persisted. One of these values is the Hawaiian responsibility to care for the land, to make it flourish, called *mālama 'āina* or *aloha 'āina*. To Linnekin, this value has been invented by modern Hawaiians to protest degradation of the land by developers, the military, and others. What Linnekin has missed here—partly because she has an incomplete grasp of "traditional" values but also because she doesn't understand and thus misapprehends Hawaiian cultural nationalism—is simply this: the Hawaiian relationship to land has persisted into the present. What has changed is ownership and use of the land (from collective use by Hawaiians for subsistence to private use by whites and other non-Natives for profit). Asserting the Hawaiian relationship in this changed context results in politicization. Thus, Hawaiians assert a "traditional" relationship to the land *not* for political ends, as Linnekin (and Keesing) argue, but because they continue to believe in the cultural value of caring for the land. That land use is now contested makes such a belief political. This distinction is crucial because the Hawaiian cultural motivation reveals the persistence of traditional values, the very thing Linnekin (and Keesing) allege modern Hawaiians to have "invented."

2. In Hawai'i the Kawananakoa line contests the loss of governance, since they were heirs to the throne at the time of the American military-backed overthrow of Hawaiian Queen Lili'uokalani. The Salazar family lays claim to part of the Crown lands for similar reasons. Regarding land issues, the Ka'awa family occupied Makapu'u Point in 1988 in protest over its current use. Their argument revolved around their claim to ownership because of their genealogical connection to the Kamehameha line. Among nationalist organizations, 'Ohana o Hawai'i, led by Peggy Ha'o Ross, argues claims to leadership based on genealogy. These examples illustrate the continuity of genealogy as profoundly significant to Hawaiians in establishing mana and, thus, the power to command recognition and leadership. Keesing obviously knows nothing about any of these families or their claims.

3. The United States government defines Native Hawaiians as those with 50 percent or more Hawaiian blood quantum. Those with less than 50 percent Hawaiian blood are not considered to be "Native" and are thus not entitled to lands and monies set aside for 50 percent bloods. Hawaiians are the only human beings in the State of Hawai'i who are categorized by blood quantum, rather like Blacks in South Africa.

   While bureaucrats are happily dividing up who is and is not Native, the substance of *what* constitutes things Hawaiian is constantly asserted by anthropologists against Native nationalists. Of course, the claim to knowledge by anthropologists is their academic training applied to the field. Native nationalists' claim to knowledge is their life experience as Natives.

   The problem is more serious than epistemology, however. In a colonial world, the work of anthropologists and other Western-trained "experts" is used to disparage and exploit Natives. What Linnekin or Keesing or any other anthropologist writes about Hawaiians has more potential power than what Hawaiians write about themselves. Proof of this rests in the use of Linnekin's argument by the US Navy that Hawaiian nationalists have invented the sacred meaning of Kaho'olawe Island (which the US Navy has controlled and bombed since the Second World War) because nationalists need a "political and cultural symbol of protest" in the modern period. Here, the connection between anthropology and the colonial enterprise is explicit. When Natives accuse Western scholars of exploiting them, they have in mind the exact kind of situation I am describing. In fact, the Navy's study was done by an anthropologist who, of course, cited fellow anthropologists, including Linnekin, to argue that the Hawaiian assertion of love and sacredness regarding Kaho'olawe was "fakery." Far from overstating their case, Native nationalists acutely comprehend the structure of their oppression, including that perpetuated by anthropologists.

POSTSCRIPT

Do Native Peoples Today Invent Their Traditions?

Building on Hobsbawm and Ranger's notion of the "invention of traditon," Keesing makes the case that in most—if not all—Pacific societies, the history and cultural traditions that are regarded as authentic are substantially different from the events and practices that actually occurred. In his mind, there can also be little doubt that controlling what is accepted as tradition has become politically important. How does Trask's concern over professional bias impact Keesing's other arguments? What criteria would Trask suggest as a substitute as a way of judging which practices are authentic traditions and which are modern innovations?

Many other anthropologists have addressed the question of the invention of tradition. In Hawaii, the best-known work is by Jocelyn Linnekin, especially her 1983 essay "Defining Tradition: Variations on the Hawaiian Identity," *American Ethnologist* (vol. 10) and her book *Children of the Land* (Rutgers University Press, 1985). See also Trask's review of the latter in the *Hawaiian Journal of History* (vol. 20, 1986).

Questions about the invention of traditions have become important in North America as well. In 1997 Brian D. Haley and Larry R. Wilcoxon published an essay in *Current Anthropology* (vol. 38) entitled "Anthropology and the Making of Chumash Tradition." They argued that anthropologists and environmentalists had encouraged Chumash Indians to exaggerate claims that a site proposed for industrial development was traditionally sacred. The following year, archaeologist John McVey Erlandson published a reply to Haley and Wilcoxon in *Current Anthropology* (vol. 39). Like Keesing, Erlandson drew on historical (white American) sources to defend his position that the site was held to be sacred.

Another anthropologist, Alan Hanson, wrote a similar but more focused argument about the invention of tradition among the Maori of New Zealand in "The Making of the Maori: Culture Invention and Its Logic," *American Anthropologist* (vol. 91, no. 4, 1989). This essay prompted a vigorous and at times hostile debate within New Zealand, and at one point some Maori threatened to censure the American Anthropological Association because of this article, which some considered racist and anti-Maori. Stephen Webster discusses this topic in light of the so-called Maori renaissance, a revival of Maori cultural values within the modern bicultural state of New Zealand in his book, *Patrons of Maori Culture: Power, Theory and Ideology in the Maori Renaissance* (University of Otago Press, 1998).

ISSUE 3

Do Museums Misrepresent Ethnic Communities Around the World?

YES: James Clifford, from *The Predicament of Culture: Twentieth-Century Ethnography, Literature, and Art* (Harvard University Press, 1988)

NO: Denis Dutton, from "Mythologies of Tribal Art," *African Arts* (Summer 1995)

ISSUE SUMMARY

YES: Postmodernist anthropologist James Clifford argues that the very act of removing objects from their ethnographic contexts distorts the meaning of objects held in museums. He contends that whether these objects are displayed in art museums or anthropological museums, exhibitions misrepresent ethnic communities by omitting important aspects of contemporary life, especially involvement with the colonial or Western world.

NO: Anthropologist Denis Dutton asserts that no exhibition can provide a complete context for ethnographic objects, but that does not mean that museum exhibitions are fundamentally flawed. Dutton suggests that postmodernists misunderstand traditional approaches to interpreting museum collections, and what they offer as a replacement actually minimizes what we can understand of ethnic communities from museum collections.

In the late nineteenth and early twentieth centuries, museums were a major focus of anthropological research. In the United States, for example, until after the First World War more anthropologists were employed in museums than in universities. By 1940 cultural anthropologists had largely moved out of museums as they focused on intensive fieldwork. This change was directly related to a shift in paradigms from cultural evolution to functionalism, which happened in the 1920s and 1930s.

As anthropologists later began to focus on functional questions about how societies and their institutions worked, museum collections became increasingly unimportant. Many anthropologists believed that differences in the bindings of stone axes have little to say about how marriages were contracted or how clans were linked together; objects cannot explain how leadership worked or what role religious ideas might have had in maintaining social order.

The following selections deal with the question of how museums should exhibit and interpret ethnographic collections that were obtained during the "museum period" of anthropology. Both authors are critical of certain exhibitions, particularly art historian William Rubin's "Primitivism" show from 1984, and both feel that a good exhibition should contextualize museum objects historically. But the authors differ profoundly in their approach to the study of museum objects.

James Clifford surveys several different kinds of museum exhibits in New York and asks, Do any of them do justice to the peoples who made and used these objects? For Clifford, objects and the cultures from which they come have histories. He questions how much of these histories are present in the several exhibitions he visited. By definition, each and every non-Western object in a Western museum has been removed from its original ethnographic context, a process often referred to as "decontextualization."

Clifford explains in his selection how museums offer a "representation" of tribal peoples as if these societies were timeless and without history. By focusing on particular features of tribal culture, each exhibition makes statements about the relationship between modern Americans and "primitive" peoples. For him, these are fundamentally misleading representations.

Denis Dutton accepts that exhibitions such as those discussed by Clifford are inevitably incomplete, but the lack of a full context does not completely invalidate the exercise of exhibiting objects from tribal societies. He argues that Clifford and the other postmodernist critics of museum exhibitions go too far in their criticisms and that they, too, have an agenda that is itself misleading. Referring to this postmodernist agenda as a "new mythology" about tribal art, Dutton contends that the new mythologists have exaggerated their interpretations of museum exhibitions.

Dutton argues that museums can never offer complete representations of ethnic communities; but this does not mean that exhibitions cannot be both informative and enlightening even if they are incomplete. He asserts that Clifford's analysis leads us away from any understanding of museum objects; instead Clifford prefers to present his understandings of the culture through museum curators in our own modern culture. For Dutton, the goal should be to discover the meanings and significance of objects from the point of view of their original communities, and such meanings will never emerge from critiques of museum exhibitions like Clifford's.

How serious are the inevitable distortions of a museum exhibit? Does the omission of the current historical and global economic context misinform the public? How much context can a museum exhibition realistically provide? If such misrepresentations do occur, would it be better not to exhibit "primitive" art at all? What solutions to the problem of distortion do Clifford and Dutton propose?

Histories of the Tribal and the Modern

During the winter of 1984–85 one could encounter tribal objects in an unusual number of locations around New York City. This [selection] surveys a half-dozen, focusing on the most controversial: the major exhibition held at the Museum of Modern Art (MOMA), " 'Primitivism' in 20th Century Art: Affinity of the Tribal and the Modern." The... "ethnographic present" is late December 1984.

The "tribal" objects gathered on West Fifty-third Street have been around. They are travelers—some arriving from folklore and ethnographic museums in Europe, others from art galleries and private collections. They have traveled first class to the Museum of Modern Art, elaborately crated and insured for important sums. Previous accommodations have been less luxurious: some were stolen, others "purchased" for a song by colonial administrators, travelers, anthropologists, missionaries, sailors in African ports. These non-Western objects have been by turns curiosities, ethnographic specimens, major art creations. After 1900 they began to turn up in European flea markets, thereafter moving between avant-garde studios and collectors' apartments. Some came to rest in the unheated basements or "laboratories" of anthropology museums, surrounded by objects made in the same region of the world. Others encountered odd fellow travelers, lighted and labeled in strange display cases. Now on West Fifty-third Street they intermingle with works by European masters— Picasso, Giacometti, Brancusi, and others. A three-dimensional Eskimo mask with twelve arms and a number of holes hangs beside a canvas on which Joan Miró has painted colored shapes. The people in New York look at the two objects and see that they are alike.

Travelers tell different stories in different places, and on West Fifty-third Street an origin story of modernism is featured. Around 1910 Picasso and his cohort suddenly, intuitively recognize that "primitive" objects are in fact powerful "art." They collect, imitate, and are affected by these objects. Their own work, even when not directly influenced, seems oddly reminiscent of non-Western forms. The modern and the primitive converse across the centuries and continents. At the Museum of Modern Art an exact history is told featuring individual artists and objects, their encounters in specific studios at precise moments. Photographs document the crucial influences of non-Western artifacts

From James Clifford, *The Predicament of Culture: Twentieth-Century Ethnography, Literature, and Art* (Harvard University Press, 1988). Originally published as "Histories of the Tribal and the Modern" in *Art in America* (April 1985). Copyright © 1985 by Brant Publications, Inc. Reprinted by permission of *Art in America*. Notes and references omitted.

on the pioneer modernists. This focused story is surrounded and infused with another—a loose allegory of relationship centering on the word *affinity.* The word is a kinship term, suggesting a deeper or more natural relationship than mere resemblance or juxtaposition. It connotes a common quality or essence joining the tribal to the modern. A Family of Art is brought together, global, diverse, richly inventive, and miraculously unified, for every object displayed on West Fifty-third Street looks modern.

The exhibition at MOMA is historical and didactic. It is complemented by a comprehensive, scholarly catalogue, which includes divergent views of its topic and in which the show's organizers, William Rubin and Kirk Varnedoe, argue at length its underlying premises. One of the virtues of an exhibition that blatantly makes a case or tells a story is that it encourages debate and makes possible the suggestion of other stories. Thus in what follows different histories of the tribal and the modern will be proposed in response to the sharply focused history on display at the Museum of Modern Art. But before that history can be seen for what it is, however—a specific story that excludes other stories—the universalizing allegory of affinity must be cleared away.

This allegory, the story of the Modernist Family of Art, is not rigorously argued at MOMA. (That would require some explicit form of either an archetypal or structural analysis.) The allegory is, rather, built into the exhibition's form, featured suggestively in its publicity, left uncontradicted, repetitiously asserted —"Affinity of the Tribal and the Modern." The allegory has a hero, whose virtuoso work, an exhibit caption tells us, contains more affinities with the tribal than that of any other pioneer modernist. These affinities "measure the depth of Picasso's grasp of the informing principles of tribal sculpture, and reflect his profound identity of spirit with the tribal peoples." Modernism is thus presented as a search for "informing principles" that transcend culture, politics, and history. Beneath this generous umbrella the tribal is modern and the modern more richly, more diversely human.

⋅❦⋅

The power of the affinity idea is such (it becomes almost self-evident in the MOMA juxtapositions) that it is worth reviewing the major objections to it. Anthropologists, long familiar with the issue of cultural diffusion versus independent invention, are not likely to find anything special in the similarities between selected tribal and modern objects. An established principle of anthropological comparative method asserts that the greater the range of cultures, the more likely one is to find similar traits. MOMA's sample is very large, embracing African, Oceanian, North American, and Arctic "tribal" groups. A second principle, that of the "limitation of possibilities," recognizes that invention, while highly diverse, is not infinite. The human body, for example, with its two eyes, four limbs, bilateral arrangement of features, front and back, and so on, will be represented and stylized in a limited number of ways. There is thus a priori no reason to claim evidence for affinity (rather than mere resemblance or coincidence) because an exhibition of tribal works that seem impressively "modern" in style can be gathered. An equally striking collection could be made demonstrating sharp dissimilarities between tribal and modern objects.

The qualities most often said to link these objects are their "conceptualism" and "abstraction" (but a very long and ultimately incoherent list of shared traits, including "magic," "ritualism," "environmentalism," use of "natural" materials, and so on, can be derived from the show and especially from its catalogue). Actually the tribal and modern artifacts are similar only in that they do *not* feature the pictorial illusionism or sculptural naturalism that came to dominate Western European art after the Renaissance. Abstraction and conceptualism are, of course, pervasive in the arts of the non-Western World. To say that they share with modernism a rejection of certain naturalist projects is not to show anything like an affinity. Indeed the "tribalism" selected in the exhibition to resemble modernism is itself a construction designed to accomplish the task of resemblance. Ife and Benin sculptures, highly naturalistic in style, are excluded from the "tribal" and placed in a somewhat arbitrary category of "court" society (which does not, however, include large chieftainships). Moreover, pre-Columbian works, though they have a place in the catalogue, are largely omitted from the exhibition. One can question other selections and exclusions that result in a collection of only "modern"-looking tribal objects. Why, for example, are there relatively few "impure" objects constructed from the debris of colonial culture contacts? And is there not an overall bias toward clean, abstract forms as against rough or crude work?

The "Affinities" room of the exhibition is an intriguing but entirely problematic exercise in formal mix-and-match. The short introductory text begins well: "AFFINITIES presents a group of tribal objects notable for their appeal to modern taste." Indeed this is all that can rigorously be said of the objects in this room. The text continues, however, "Selected pairings of modern and tribal objects demonstrate common denominators of these arts that are independent of direct influence." The phrase *common denominators* implies something more systematic than intriguing resemblance. What can it possibly mean?... The affinity idea itself is wide-ranging and promiscuous, as are allusions to universal human capacities retrieved in the encounter between modern and tribal or invocations of the expansive human mind—the healthy capacity of modernist consciousness to question its limits and engage otherness.

... The affinities shown at MOMA are all on modernist terms. The great modernist "pioneers" (and their museum) are shown promoting formerly despised tribal "fetishes" or mere ethnographic "specimens" to the status of high art and in the process discovering new dimensions of their ("our") creative potential. The capacity of art to transcend its cultural and historical context is asserted repeatedly....

At West Fifth-third Street modernist primitivism is a going Western concern....

Indeed an unintended effect of the exhibition's comprehensive catalogue is to show once and for all the incoherence of the modern Rorschach of "the primitive."... [T]he catalogue succeeds in demonstrating not any essential affinity between tribal and modern or even a coherent modernist attitude toward the primitive but rather the restless desire and power of the modern West to collect the world.

❧

... If we ignore the "Affinities" room at MOMA, however, and focus on the "serious" historical part of the exhibition, new critical questions emerge. What is excluded by the specific focus of the history? Isn't this factual narration still infused with the affinity allegory, since it is cast as a story of creative genius recognizing the greatness of tribal works, discovering common artistic "informing principles"? Could the story of this intercultural encounter be told differently? It is worth making the effort to extract another story from the materials in the exhibition—a history not of redemption or of discovery but of reclassification. This other history assumes that "art" is not universal but is a changing Western cultural category. The fact that rather abruptly, in the space of a few decades, a large class of non-Western artifacts came to be redefined as art is a taxonomic shift that requires critical historical discussion, not celebration. That this construction of a generous category of art pitched at a global scale occurred just as the planet's tribal peoples came massively under European political, economic, and evangelical dominion cannot be irrelevant. But there is no room for such complexities at the MOMA show. Obviously the modernist appropriation of tribal productions as art is not simply imperialist. The project involves too many strong critiques of colonialist, evolutionist assumptions. As we shall see, though, the scope and underlying logic of the "discovery" of tribal art reproduces hegemonic Western assumptions rooted in the colonial and neocolonial epoch.

Picasso, Léger, Apollinaire, and many others came to recognize the elemental, "magical" power of African sculptures in a period of growing *négrophilie,* a context that would see the irruption onto the European scene of other evocative black figures: the jazzman, the boxer (Al Brown), the *sauvage* Josephine Baker. To tell the history of modernism's recognition of African "art" in this broader context would raise ambiguous and disturbing questions about aesthetic appropriation of non-Western others, issues of race, gender, and power. This other story is largely invisible at MOMA.... Overall one would be hard pressed to deduce from the exhibition that all the enthusiasm for things *nègre,* for the "magic" of African art, had anything to do with race. Art in this focused history has no essential link with coded perceptions of black bodies— their vitalism, rhythm, magic, erotic power, etc.—as seen by whites. The modernism represented here is concerned only with artistic invention, a positive category separable from a negative primitivism of the irrational, the savage, the base, the flight from civilization.

A different historical focus might bring a photograph of Josephine Baker into the vicinity of the African statues that were exciting the Parisian avant-garde in the 1910s and 1920s; but such a juxtaposition would be unthinkable in the MOMA history, for it evokes different affinities from those contributing to the category of great art. The black body in Paris of the twenties was an ideological artifact. Archaic Africa (which came to Paris by way of the future—that is,

America) was sexed, gendered, and invested with "magic" in specific ways. Standard poses adopted by "La Bakaire," like Léger's designs and costumes, evoked a recognizable "Africanity"—the naked form emphasizing pelvis and buttocks, a segmented stylization suggesting a strangely mechanical vitality. The inclusion of so ideologically loaded a form as the body of Josephine Baker among the figures classified as art on West Fifty-third Street would suggest a different account of modernist primitivism, a different analysis of the category *nègre* in *l'art nègre* and an exploration of the "taste" that was something more than just a backdrop for the discovery of tribal art in the opening decades of this century.

Such a focus would treat art as a category defined and redefined in specific historical contexts and relations of power....

Since 1900 non-Western objects have generally been classified as either primitive art *or* ethnographic specimens. Before the modernist revolution associated with Picasso and the simultaneous rise of cultural anthropology associated with Boas and Malinowski, these objects were differently sorted—as antiquities, exotic curiosities, orientalia, the remains of early man, and so on. With the emergence of twentieth-century modernism and anthropology figures formerly called "fetishes" (to take just one class of object) became works either of "sculpture" or of "material culture." The distinction between the aesthetic and the anthropological was soon institutionally reinforced. In art galleries non-Western objects were displayed for their formal and aesthetic qualities; in ethnographic museums they were represented in a "cultural" context. In the latter an African statue was a ritual object belonging to a distinct group; it was displayed in ways that elucidated its use, symbolism, and function. The institutionalized distinction between aesthetic and anthropological discourses took form during the years documented at MOMA, years that saw the complementary discovery of primitive "art" and of an anthropological concept of culture."...

Cultural background is not essential to correct aesthetic appreciation and analysis: good art, the masterpiece, is universally recognizable. The pioneer modernists themselves knew little or nothing of these objects' ethnographic meaning. What was good enough for Picasso is good enough for MOMA. Indeed an ignorance of cultural context seems almost a precondition for artistic appreciation. In this object system a tribal piece is detached from one milieu in order to circulate freely in another, a world of art—of museums, markets, and connoisseurship.

Since the early years of modernism and cultural anthropology non-Western objects have found a "home" either within the discourses and institutions of art or within those of anthropology.... Both discourses assume a primitive world in need of preservation, redemption, and representation. The concrete, inventive existence of tribal cultures and artists is suppressed in the process of either constituting authentic, "traditional" worlds or appreciating their products in the timeless category of "art."

⟨❖⟩

Nothing on West Fifty-third Street suggests that good tribal art is being produced in the 1980s. The non-Western artifacts on display are located either in a vague past (reminiscent of the label "nineteenth-twentieth century" that accompanies African and Oceanian pieces in the Metropolitan Museum's Rockefeller Wing) or in a purely conceptual space defined by "primitive" qualities: magic, ritualism, closeness to nature, mythic or cosmological aims. In this relegation of the tribal or primitive to either a vanishing past or an ahistorical, conceptual present, modernist appreciation reproduces common ethnographic categories.

The same structure can be seen in the Hall of Pacific Peoples, dedicated to Margaret Mead, at the American Museum of Natural History. This new permanent hall is a superbly refurbished anthropological stopping place for non-Western objects. In *Rotunda* (December 1984), the museum's publication, an article announcing the installation contains the following paragraph:

> Margaret Mead once referred to the cultures of Pacific peoples as "a world that once was and now is no more." Prior to her death in 1978 she approved the basic plans for the new *Hall of Pacific Peoples*. (p. 1)

We are offered treasures saved from a destructive history, relics of a vanishing world. Visitors to the installation (and especially members of *present* Pacific cultures) may find a "world that is no more" more appropriately evoked in two charming display cases just outside the hall. It is the world of a dated anthropology. Here one finds a neatly typed page of notes from Mead's much-disputed Samoan research, a picture of the fieldworker interacting "closely" with Melanesians (she is carrying a child on her back), a box of brightly colored discs and triangles once used for psychological testing, a copy of Mead's column in *Redbook*. In the Hall of Pacific Peoples artifacts suggesting change and syncretism are set apart in a small display entitled "Culture Contact." It is noted that Western influence and indigenous response have been active in the Pacific since the eighteenth century. Yet few signs of this involvement appear anywhere else in the large hall, despite the fact that many of the objects were made in the past 150 years in situations of contact, and despite the fact that the museum's ethnographic explanations reflect quite recent research on the cultures of the Pacific. The historical contacts and impurities that are part of ethnographic work—and that may signal the life, not the death, of societies—are systematically excluded.

The tenses of the hall's explanatory captions are revealing. A recent color photograph of a Samoan *kava* ceremony is accompanied by the words: "STATUS and RANK were [sic] important features of Samoan society," a statement that will seem strange to anyone who knows how important they remain in Samoa today. Elsewhere in the hall a black-and-white photograph of an Australian Arunta woman and child, taken around 1900 by the pioneer ethnographers Spencer and Gillen, is captioned in the *present* tense. Aboriginals apparently must always inhabit a mythic time. Many other examples of temporal incoherence could be cited—old Sepik objects described in the present, recent Trobriand photos labeled in the past, and so forth.

The point is not simply that the image of Samoan *kava* drinking and status society presented here is a distortion or that in most of the Hall of Pacific Peoples history has been airbrushed out. (No Samoan men at the *kava* ceremony are wearing wristwatches; Trobriand face painting is shown without noting that it is worn at cricket matches.) Beyond such questions of accuracy is an issue of systematic ideological coding. To locate "tribal" peoples in a nonhistorical time and ourselves in a different, historical time is clearly tendentious and no longer credible (Fabian 1983). This recognition throws doubt on the perception of a vanishing tribal world, rescued, made valuable and meaningful, either as ethnographic "culture" or as primitive/modern "art." ...

At the Hall of Pacific Peoples or the Rockefeller Wing the actual ongoing life and "impure" inventions of tribal peoples are erased in the name of cultural or artistic "authenticity." Similarly at MOMA the production of tribal "art" is entirely in the past. Turning up in the flea markets and museums of late nineteenth-century Europe, these objects are destined to be aesthetically redeemed, given new value in the object system of a generous modernism.

The story retold at MOMA, the struggle to gain recognition for tribal art, for its capacity "like all great art ... to show images of man that transcend the particular lives and times of their creators," is taken for granted at another stopping place for tribal travelers in Manhattan, the Center for African Art on East Sixty-eighth Street. Susan Vogel, the executive director, proclaims in her introduction to the catalogue of its inaugural exhibition, "African Masterpieces from the Musee de l'Homme, " that the "aesthetic-anthropological debate" has been resolved. It is now widely accepted that "ethnographic specimens" can be distinguished from "works of art" and that within the latter category a limited number of "masterpieces" are to be found. Vogel correctly notes that the aesthetic recognition of tribal objects depends on changes in Western taste. For example it took the work of Francis Bacon, Lucas Samaras, and others to make it possible to exhibit as art "rough and horrifying [African] works as well as refined and lyrical ones." Once recognized, though, art is apparently art. Thus the selection at the Center is made on aesthetic criteria alone. A prominent placard affirms that the ability of these objects "to transcend the limitations of time and place, to speak to us across time and culture ... places them among the highest points of human achievement. It is as works of art that we regard them here and as a testament to the greatness of their creators."

There could be no clearer statement of one side of the aesthetic anthropological "debate" (or better, *system*). On the other (anthropological) side, across town, the Hall of Pacific Peoples presents collective rather than individual productions—the work of "cultures." At the American Museum of Natural History ethnographic exhibits have come increasingly to resemble art shows. Indeed the Hall of Pacific Peoples represents the latest in aestheticized scientism. Objects are displayed in ways that highlight their formal properties.... While these artistically displayed artifacts are scientifically explained, an older, functionalist attempt to present an integrated picture of specific societies or culture areas is no longer seriously pursued. There is an almost dadaist quality to the labels on eight cases devoted to Australian aboriginal society (I cite the complete series in order): "CEREMONY, SPIRIT FIGURE, MAGICIANS AND SORCERERS, SACRED ART, SPEAR THROWERS, STONE AXES AND KNIVES, WOMEN, BOOMERANGS." Elsewhere the hall's pieces of culture have been recontextualized within a new cybernetic, anthropological discourse. For instance flutes and stringed instruments are captioned: "MUSIC is a system of organized sound in man's [sic] aural environment" or nearby: "COMMUNICATION is an important function of organized sound."

In the anthropological Hall of Pacific Peoples non-Western objects still have primarily scientific value. They are in addition beautiful. Conversely, at the Center for African Art artifacts are essentially defined as "masterpieces," their makers as great artists. The discourse of connoisseurship reigns. Yet once the story of art told at MOMA becomes dogma, it is possible to reintroduce and co-opt the discourse of ethnography. At the Center tribal contexts and functions are described along with individual histories of the objects on display. Now firmly classified as masterpieces, African objects escape the vague, ahistorical location of the "tribal" or the "primitive." The catalogue, a sort of *catalogue raisonné*, discusses each work intensively. The category of the masterpiece individuates: the pieces on display are not typical; some are one of a kind. The famous Fon god of war or the Abomey shark-man lend themselves to precise histories of individual creation and appropriation in visible colonial situations. Captions specify *which* Griaule expedition to West Africa in the 1930s acquired each Dogon statue.... We learn in the catalogue that a superb Bamileke mother and child was carved by an artist named Kwayep, that the statue was bought by the colonial administrator and anthropologist Henri Labouret from King N'Jike. While tribal names predominate at MOMA, the Rockefeller Wing, and the American Museum of Natural History, here personal names make their appearance.

In the "African Masterpieces" catalogue we learn of an ethnographer's excitement on finding a Dogon hermaphrodite figure that would later become famous. The letter recording this excitement, written by Denise Paulme in 1935, serves as evidence of the aesthetic concerns of many early ethnographic collectors. These individuals, we are told, could intuitively distinguish masterpieces from mere art or ethnographic specimens. (Actually many of the individual ethnographers behind the Musée de l'Homme collection, such as Paulme, Michel Leiris, Marcel Griaule, and André Schaeffner, were friends and collaborators of the same "pioneer modernist" artists who, in the story told at MOMA, constructed the category of primitive art. Thus the intuitive aesthetic sense in question is the product of a historically specific milieu.) The "African Masterpieces" catalogue insists that the founders of the Musée de l'Homme were art connoisseurs, that this great anthropological museum never treated all its contents as "ethnographic specimens." The Musee de l'Homme was and is secretly an art museum. The taxonomic split between art and artifact is thus healed, at least for self-evident "masterpieces," entirely in terms of the aesthetic code. Art is art in any museum. . . .

The non-Western objects that excited Picasso, Derain, and Léger broke into the realm of official Western art from outside. They were quickly integrated, recognized as masterpieces, given homes within an anthropological-aesthetic object system. By now this process has been sufficiently celebrated. We need exhibitions that question the boundaries of art and of the art world, an influx of truly indigestible "outside" artifacts. The relations of power whereby one portion of humanity can select, value, and collect the pure products of others need to be criticized and transformed. This is no small task. In the meantime one can at least imagine shows that feature the impure, "inauthentic" productions of past and present tribal life; exhibitions radically heterogeneous in their global mix of styles; exhibitions that locate themselves in specific multicultural junctures; exhibitions in which nature remains "unnatural"; exhibitions whose principles of incorporation are openly questionable. The following would be my contribution to a different show on "affinities of the tribal and the postmodern." I offer just the first paragraph from Barbara Tedlock's superb description of the Zuni Shalako ceremony, a festival that is only part of a complex, living tradition.

> Imagine a small western New Mexican village, its snow-lit streets lined with white Mercedes, quarter-ton pickups and Dodge vans. Villagers wrapped in black blankets and flowered shawls are standing next to visitors in blue velveteen blouses with rows of dime buttons and voluminous satin skirts. Their men are in black Stetson silver-banded hats, pressed jeans, Tony Lama boots and multicolored Pendleton blankets. Strangers dressed in dayglo orange, pink and green ski jackets, stocking caps, hiking boots and mittens. All crowded together they are looking into newly constructed houses illuminated by bare light bulbs dangling from raw rafters edged with Woolworth's red fabric and flowered blue print calico. Cinderblock and plasterboard white walls are layered with striped serapes, Chimayó blankets, Navajo rugs, flowered fringed embroidered shawls, black silk from Mexico and purple, red and blue rayon from Czechoslovakia. Rows of Hopi cotton dance kilts and rain sashes; Isleta woven red and green belts; Navajo and Zuni silver concha belts and black mantas covered with silver brooches set with carved lapidary, rainbow mosaic, channel inlay, turquoise needlepoint, pink agate, alabaster, black cannel coal and bakelite from old '78s, coral, abalone shell, mother-of-pearl and horned oyster hang from poles suspended from the ceiling. Mule and white-tailed deer trophy-heads wearing squash-blossom, coral and chunk-turquoise necklaces are hammered up around the room over rearing buckskins above Arabian tapestries of Martin Luther King and the Kennedy brothers, The Last Supper, a herd of sheep with a haloed herder, horses, peacocks.

Denis Dutton

Mythologies of Tribal Art

Forty years ago Roland Barthes defined a mythology as those "falsely obvious" ideas which an age so takes for granted that it is unaware of its own belief. An example of what he means can be seen in his 1957 critique of Edward Steichen's celebrated photographic assemblage "The Family of Man." Barthes declares that the myth this exhibition promotes first seems to stress exoticism, projecting a Babel of human diversity over the globe. From this picture of diversity, however, a pluralistic humanism "is magically produced: man is born, works, laughs and dies everywhere in the same way...." The implicit mythological background of the show postulates "a human essence."

Barthes is exactly on target about the philosophic intentions of "The Family of Man." In his introduction to the published version of the exhibition, Steichen had written that the show was "conceived as a mirror of the universal elements and emotions in the everydayness of life—as a mirror of the essential oneness of mankind throughout the world." Such juxtapositions as that which places Nina Leen's *Life* magazine image of an American farm family next to a family in Bechuanaland (now Botswana), photographed by another *Life* photographer, Nat Farbman, are therefore meant to convey the idea that despite all differences of exterior form, of cultural surface, the underlying nature of all families and peoples is essentially the same. This position is what Barthes views as the sentimentalized mythology of "classic humanism," and he contrasts it with his own "progressive humanism," which must try "constantly to scour nature, its 'laws' and its 'limits' in order to discover History there, and at last to establish Nature itself as historical." While classic humanism regards the American and African families as embodying, beneath culture and skin color, abiding natural relationships of kin and affection, progressive humanism would insist that these bourgeois conceptions of the natural are themselves historically determined. Barthes claims that such imperialistic juxtapositions ignore the political and economic roots of diversity.

Although "The Family of Man" had a potently relevant message for the generation that had witnessed the genocidal horrors of the Second World War, it was also worth paying attention to Barthes's claim that Steichen's collection, for all its antiracism and humanist charms, conveyed an implicit illusion

Excerpted from Denis Dutton, "Mythologies of Tribal Art," *African Arts*, vol. 28, no. 3 (Summer 1995). Copyright © 1995 by The Regents of the University of California. Reprinted by permission of *African Arts* and the author. Notes and references omitted.

of equality of power among the cultures it portrayed. It is now two genera-tions later, however, and critics who accept the importance of exposing cultural mythologies and covert ideologies have new work to do. One area of criticism that especially stands in need of fresh examination is the shell-pocked field where battles have raged over the status and understanding of ethnographic arts. Barthes's reaction to MOMA's "The Family of Man" is particularly per-tinent in this regard, because much of what he says adumbrates reactions to another exhibition, " 'Primitivism' in 20th Century Art," which took place over a quarter of a century later in that same museum. That show displayed side-by-side images of Africa and Europe, not photographs of people, but works of art. And it too was denounced as complacently positing, without regard to cultural difference, a specious universalism—aesthetic instead of moral.

But a sea change in academic thinking separates Barthes's critique of "The Family of Man" from the more strident critics of the "Primitivism" show. In the middle 1950s, Barthes was nearly alone in his dissent against a much loved and widely praised exhibition. The generation of critics who questioned (or de-nounced) "Primitivism" represented a manner of thinking that had become a virtual academic fashion. Some of these later critics were arguing from a set of ideas that had themselves come to embody a virtual mythology in precisely the Barthesian sense. Their views presuppose and constitute, in point of fact, a New Mythology of tribal arts—a prevailing set of presuppositions, prejudices, and articles of political and philosophical faith which govern many discussions of these arts and their relations to European criticism, art, and aesthetics. A con-temporary Africanist art historian [Sidney Kasfir] for example, writes in a recent *African Arts* article on the authenticity of African masks and carvings: "That from an African perspective, these objects are *not* art in the current Western sense is too well known to discuss here." The phrase "too well known to discuss here" is symptomatic of a mythology. Barthes claimed his intention to unmask "the mystification which transforms petit-bourgeois culture into universal na-ture." Today we should be just as willing to deal with those mystifications that transform prevailing conventions of academic culture into validated truth.

This vigorous New Mythology of tribal arts takes on its life against the backdrop of what it posits as the Old Mythology. As with other ideologies, the New Mythology would no more describe its precepts as "mythology" than would the Old: both operate according to the familiar adage "Your views are so much mythology; mine speak the truth." Nevertheless, much contemporary theorizing and criticism about tribal arts are founded on a complacent accep-tance of a substrate of givens and unsupported hypotheses which constitute the central tenets of the New Mythology. To be sure, not all of the theses are false. On the other hand, not all of the beliefs the New Mythologists stigmatize as Old Mythology are false either. Independent, critical thinkers should want to choose the component ideas of these mythologies that are worth rejecting, preserving, or reviving.

Providing a disinterested assessment of these ideas is not easy in the present ideologically charged and factious atmosphere. This indeed is part of the problem: so many contemporary theorists of tribal arts posit enemies who have it all wrong, in contrast to themselves, who have it right. This lack of any generosity whatsoever toward one's perceived (or invented) opposition increasingly stultifies writing in this area. The New Mythology finds itself expressed by a wide range of writers, including, for example, the more vociferous critics of the "Primitivism" show such as Thomas McEvilley and Hal Foster; James Clifford in his treatment of museums and ethnographic art; Arnold Krupat in *Ethnocriticism;* Sidney Kasfir in her article "African Art and Authenticity," published in this journal; Sally Price in *Primitive Art in Civilized Places;* Marianna Torgovnick in *Gone Primitive;* and Christopher B. Steiner in *African Art in Transit.*

Mythologies, Old and New

There are actually two phases of the Old Mythology to which these writers tend to react. What I will call *premodernist* or *colonialist* Old Mythology includes the elements of nineteenth-century imperialism—racism, contempt for "childish" artifacts, and regard for "primitive" art as representing a lower evolutionary stage of human development, with missionaries burning "fetishes" and the wholesale looting of indigenous art, as in Benin. The later, more enlightened, *modernist* Old Mythology, exemplified by such figures as Picasso, Roger Fry, and the "Primitivism" exhibition itself, is, from a New Mythological perspective, perhaps even more insidious, because while it pretends to valorize these arts, it perpetuates acts of imperialism, appropriation, and ethnocentric insensitivity toward Third World peoples—all in the name of enlightened, magnanimous liberalism. The grounds for my three-fold distinction—between premodernist/colonialist Old Mythology, modernist Old Mythology, and the New Mythology —can be usefully developed in terms of the following key ideas. Again, some of these notions included within these mythologies are entirely valid, some constitute half-truths, and some are plainly false; no one of these sets of ideas has a monopoly on truth.

> *(1) According to the premodernist Old Mythology, at least as the New Mythology likes to imagine it, tribal artifacts weren't works of art at all, but merely "fetishes," "idols," "fertility symbols," "ancestor figures," and the like, which colonialists collected as they might botanical specimens. The later, post-Picasso modernist version of the Old Mythology insists, on the contrary, that they are works of art, embodying universal aesthetic values.*

Curiously, the New Mythology frequently sides with the colonialist Old Mythology by aggressively questioning the status of tribal artifacts as works of art: in the New Mythological view, the Old Mythology at least acknowledged difference. This convergence of opinion, however, is complicated. Philistine colonialists often regarded artifacts as demonstrating little skill and no sense of form: the colonialists were applying nineteenth-century European aesthetic criteria to genres of work they did not begin to comprehend, and so were reluctant to call them "art." The New Mythologists' reluctance to identify tribal artifact genres as "art" is based on the notion that this would be hegemonic or imperialistic. Such reluctance is frequently supported by unthinking repetition of the folk legend that pretechnological peoples have no art because they have no word that refers to what Europeans call "art." Patrick R. McNaughton recognizes another aspect of this New Mythologists' doctrine and has stressed the importance of challenging it, "because so many scholars still recite what has become a kind of maxim asserted by outsiders about Africans, that they unlike us treat what we call art as a functional part of life" rather than something for aesthetic contemplation.

(2) The Old Mythology essentialized the primitive, subsuming the endless variety of tribal cultures under a few crude stereotypes.

The New Mythology, on the other hand, while eager to recognize the diverse and frequently unique characteristics that distinguish tribal societies, essentializes "the West," creating, in an inversion of Edward Said's familiar formulation, a kind of Occidentalism. Thus, in the example cited earlier, Kasfir qualifies her discussion of authenticity with the remark that the artifacts in question should not be considered art "in the current Western sense." The quaintness of this last phrase should not go unnoticed: among Praxiteles, Donatello, Rembrandt, Judy Chicago, Duchamp, and Koons—not to mention the myriad genres of European folk craft and popular art—there is no "current Western sense" of art, but various, radically different, and rival senses of the concept, each partially implicated in competing social practices and theories of art. In fact, in its crudity, the very phrase "the West" is the New Mythologists' answer to "the Primitive" as that term might have been used a century ago. The latter was a lazy and misleading way of lumping together such cultures as Hopi, Sepik, Benin, and !Kung—even Aztec, in some understandings of "primitive." In the New Mythology, "the West" refers to twelfth-century French villages, horror movies, the Industrial Revolution, the theology of St. Augustine, New Zealand public education, the international banking system, modern toy retailing, medieval concepts of disease, Thanksgiving dinner, electronic mail, Gregorian chants, Linnaean botany, napalm, the Chopin études, and bar codes —as though the values and ideologies found therein can be the subject of useful generalization. The New Mythology replaces one set of stereotypes with another set, equally banal.

(3) In the Old Mythology, precontact tribal societies were seen as largely isolated, unchanging, coherent, and unbroken in their cultural tradition. Colonialism was supposed to have destroyed their structure and belief base. Their Golden Age of aesthetic and cultural achievement, and hence authenticity, predates European contact. Postcolonial culture and artifacts are culturally "inauthentic."

The New Mythology asserts to the contrary that these societies never were isolated, were not necessarily "unified" or "coherent," and underwent profound breaks in their traditions before European contact. The Old Mythology's "people without a history" view was a convenient colonialist construction. The New Mythology responds to claims of "inauthenticity" by variously claiming

(a) indigenous belief systems were not destroyed but only occulted during the colonial period, and are now coming again into flower; (b) what is truly authentic is now found in the process of mutual appropriation by indigenous and colonial cultures; and in any event, (c) authentic cultural values must always be defined by the people who hold them: therefore, whatever indigenous people claim as authentic is, *ipso facto*, authentic, whether traditional, postcolonial, or merely imported.

Old and New Mythologists for the most part agree that small-scale indigenous societies have been permanently altered or obliterated by the encounter with the West's political systems, media, missionaries, technology, commerce, wage labor, and so forth. New Mythologists, however, are especially keen to emphasize that this has involved imperialist domination and exploitation. What is awkward for them is the fact that less desirable elements of culture change have been enthusiastically (and voluntarily) embraced by many indigenous peoples: cigarettes, soft drinks, movies, pop music, and Jack Daniels. By stressing that tribal cultures were always borrowing and in a state of flux, the New Mythology places in benign perspective the obliteration (or active abandonment) of traditional indigenous values: all cultures, it seems, are in the process of being altered by history.

(4) The Old Mythology, especially in its colonial form, held it unproblematic that traders or travelers might buy or barter for artifacts. Alternatively, artifacts might be accepted as gifts. None of this disturbs their meanings in the Old Mythology, and if anything the native should be thankful for receiving payment for the work before the termites got to it.

The New Mythology sees buying, selling, and trading as essentially Western concepts. Even to accept these objects as gifts is to become, as Kasfir puts it, implicated in "the web of conflicting interests that surround them." There is hence no "noninterventionist" way of obtaining these artifacts, since somewhere in the scheme power relations will obtrude, leading to the exploitation of the indigenous maker or owner of the object. In other words, the native always gets cheated. The New Mythology seems to impute to precontact tribal societies a premercantile edenic state, as though trade and barter (not to mention theft or conquest) of ritual or other valuable artifacts did not occur among these peoples until Europeans came along.

(5) The only reason to collect primitive artifacts, according to premodernist Old Mythology, was as curiosities, examples perhaps of an early stage of Social Darwinist development: they were to be placed in a cabinet alongside fossils and tropical insects. After Picasso & Co., the Old Mythology proclaimed that primitive art embodied the aesthetic sensibilities found in all art, and therefore was as much worth collecting as Constables or Utamaros, and for precisely the same reasons.

The New Mythology displays an oddly ambivalent attitude toward collecting. On the one hand, collecting is persistently disparaged, for instance as a "hegemonic activity, an act of appropriation... a largely colonial enterprise... the logical outcome of a social-evolutionary view of the Other." McEvilley speaks of "captured" tribal objects, a trope suggesting they exist in Western collections as prisoners or slaves. Given the reprehensible nature of collecting, one would expect New Mythologists to demand that the trade in ethnographic art cease, but I have not encountered any such suggestions (except, of course, for the criminal trade in looted antiquities). Even those writers who take moral satisfaction from criticizing collecting appear themselves to have "captured" the occasional artifact.

(6) On puritanical grounds the Old Mythology often forbade taking pleasure in works of tribal art: the sexual element in carvings offended missionary and nineteenth-century colonial sensibilities. In New Zealand, as elsewhere, genitals were hacked off Maori figures, and some overtly sexual carvings were simply burned, lest prurient pleasure be aroused.

The New Mythology replaces this attitude with a new and asexual form of puritanism. Enjoyment of any sort derived from the experience of ethnographic art is considered a cultural mistake at best, a form of visual imperialism at worst: "the colonialist gaze." Angst-ridden New Mythologists are reluctant to record appreciation or enthusiastic emotional reactions to artifacts. Thus Torgovnick heaps contempt on Roger Fry, among many others, for his "insensitive" and "racist" readings in praise of African art, but she never provides, in her own voice, nonracist, sensitive readings to instruct us on how to do it right. Nicholas Thomas is simply bemused: of the museums crammed with indigenous artifacts —"carved bowls, clubs, spears, baskets, pots," etc.—he honestly admits that "I have never understood why people want to look at such things (although I often look at them myself)." Christopher B. Steiner makes the bizarre claim that the objects are valued by Westerners as a way to "celebrate" the loss of the utility they had in their original cultural contexts. Other New Mythologists, such as James Clifford and James Boon (whose article title "Why Museums Make Me Sad" is clear enough), write about ethnographic arts with such a brooding sense of guilt about the historical treatment of conquered cultures that no sense of joy or love for the art is ever allowed to emerge.

(7) Colonialist Old Mythology held that though primitive cultures were to some degree capable of adopting Western technologies and manufactured articles, they could not possibly understand Western culture. In fact, having no adequate comparative perspective, the primitives could not even fully understand their own cultures. Their simple little societies were, however, transparent to the educated, sophisticated Westerner.

The New Mythology, on the contrary, contends that it is the "educated" West which fails to grasp the vast subtleties offered by these cultures, ranging from ethnobotany and folk medicines to spiritual wisdom. Instead, the West ethnocentrically imposes on them its own categories, such as "individual," "religion," or "work of art," when in actuality these concepts have no place in the cultural landscape of the Other. In the matter of borrowing, the New Mythology holds that indigenous artists are, in its preferred parlance, free to appropriate from European culture, infusing their new work with "transformed meanings," fresh associations given to foreign elements introduced into a new cultural context. The reverse—Europeans borrowing from indigenous arts—is to be discouraged. This inversion of the Old Mythology means that an innovative Sepik dancer who incorporates cigarette wrappers in an elaborate headdress is participating in an exciting fusion of cultures, while a Swedish office-worker who wears a New Guinea dog-tooth necklace is implicated in hegemonic, colonialist appropriation.

As a frontispiece for *Gone Primitive,* Torgovnick presents a heavily ironic, not to say sneering, painting (by Ed Rihacek) of a stylish European woman wearing sunglasses and sitting before a zebra skin, surrounded by a collection of "primitive art." In his derisory essay on the "Primitivism" exhibition, Clifford reproduces a 1929 photograph of Mrs. Pierre Loeb, seated in her Paris apartment filled with Melanesian and African carvings. Clifford labels this as an "appropriation" which was "not included in the 'Primitivism' Show" (a curious observation inasmuch as this very photograph appears in the show's catalogue). Both of these images suggest a kind of disapproval of European cultural appropriation that it would be unthinkable to direct toward their cultural inversion —for example, the 1970s posed village photograph Susan Vogel has published showing a Côte d'Ivoire man seated before a wrinkled, painted backdrop of an airplane, a cassette radio proudly displayed on his lap.

(8) The Old Mythology at its colonialist worst posited an ethnocentric aesthetic absolutism: advanced, naturalistic European art forms were seen, especially because of their naturalism, as demonstrating a higher stage in the evolution of art. Modernist Old Mythology retained the idea of universal aesthetic standards, but argued that tribal arts fully met these criteria for excellence, which were formalist rather than naturalistic.

In rejecting both these positions, some New Mythologists urge the abandonment of any idea of transcultural aesthetic criteria (which would be implicitly imperialistic) in favor of complete aesthetic relativism. McEvilley imputes to Kant an epistemology which "tacitly supported the violent progress of 19th- and 20th-century imperialisms" and which justified a view of the Western aesthetic sense as superior to that of non-Western cultures. The New Mythology owes its aesthetic relativism entirely to the climate of poststructural thought rather than to any empirical study of ethnographic and other world arts.

(9) More generally, both colonialist and modernist Old Mythologies imply or presuppose an epistemic realism: they both presume to describe the actual, existent characteristics of tribal societies and their arts.

Under the influence of poststructuralism, the New Mythology often presupposes various forms of constructivism, the idea that categories of human existence are constituted entirely by our own mental activity: we "invent" or "construct" the "primitive," tribal "art," "religion," and so on. The knots into which theorists become tied in trying to introduce such poststructural rhetoric into the study of indigenous arts is illustrated by Barbara Kirshenblatt-Gimblett who writes: "Ethnographic artifacts are objects of ethnography. They are artifacts created by ethnographers. Objects become ethnographic by virtue of being defined, segmented, detached, and carried away by ethnographers." From her first sentence, a dictionary definition, Kirshenblatt-Gimblett deduces a constructivist howler: the trivial fact that ethnographers define the ethnographic status of artifacts does not entail that *they create the artifacts.* Nor do they create the artifacts' meanings; it is the people being studied who determine that, and this awkward reality gets obviously in the way of attempts by New Mythologists to relativize cultural knowledge and meaning. Constructivism is a strong force among New Mythologists most influenced by literary theory, and is less persistent among those who come from a background of academic anthropology. Despite their tendency to toy with the jargon of literary theory, anthropologists generally acquire a robust respect for the independent existence and integrity of the peoples they study.

> *(10) Finally, premodernist Old Mythology, especially in its Victorian colonialist guises, preached the superiority of Western culture. It proposed to bring moral enlightenment to people it viewed as savages, mainly through Christianity, but also with science and modern medicine. In this, it stands starkly apart from modernist Old Mythology, and even from some eighteenth-century explorers of the South Pacific, who claimed that the moral sense and intellectual capacities of "primitive man" were at least equal to those of Europeans.*

The air of smug moral superiority has returned with a vengeance with the arrival of the New Mythology, whose champions patronize, censure, and jeer at any Old Mythology text they find wanting. The New Mythology of tribal arts displays a sense of righteous certitude that would fit the most zealous Victorian missionary.

At Play in the Fields of the Text

In some respects, the New Mythology's frequent borrowing from poststructuralism and the general intellectual climate of postmodernism is healthy and appropriate. For example, the approach to tribal arts must necessarily involve "blurred genres" and fused disciplines, bringing together ethnography, art history, philosophical aesthetics, and general cultural, including literary, criticism. This is fully in the poststructural/postmodern spirit, as is calling into question the peculiarly European distinction between the so-called fine arts and the popular and folk arts and crafts, which normally has no clear application in understanding tribal arts. But there are other aspects of poststructuralism which sit uneasily with the study of tribal arts.

One such notion is the pervasive poststructuralist attack on the authority of the artist or author in aesthetic interpretation. Barthes, whose thinking was again seminal in this regard, proclaimed the death of the god-author, along with the end of the ideologies of objectivity and truth, insisting that the meaning of a literary text is a critical construction instead of a discovered fact. In the theory of literature and the practice of criticism, such constructivist ideas have had their uses, liberating criticism from traditional demands to invoke authorial intention as a validating principle for critical interpretation.

However, the poststructural abandonment of the notion that texts contain meanings placed there by their authors (which it is criticism's job to determine) is only possible in a cultural landscape in which there is enough prior agreement on meanings to allow criticism to become thus freely creative. The poststructural death of the author could only take hold in literary theory because there was already in place an extensive tradition of interpretation of, say, *Madame Bovary* or *Moby Dick*. These novels enjoy a canonical status as works of literary art: they observe the conventions of established genres and were written in European languages by recognized literary artists. The cultural conditions that form the context of their creation and reception are solid enough to enable a generation of critics—notably Barthes, Foucault, and Derrida, but also the New Critics of the Anglo-American world—to declare the hypothetical death of the author and advocate a liberated, creative criticism of *jouissance.*

But do these doctrines and strategies of contemporary theory provide useful models for the critical ethnography of indigenous arts? Hardly. Poststructuralism's image of the free-spirited critic at play in textual fields goes counter to one of the most strongly held (indeed, in my opinion, indispensable) principles of the New Mythology: respect for the autonomous existence of tribal artists, including respect for their intentions and cultural values. Declaring the death of the (European) author may be jolly sport for jaded literary theorists, but an analogous ideological death of the tribal artist is not nearly so welcome in the New Mythology, nor should it be in any anthropology department. The study of tribal arts—indeed, all non-Western arts—cannot presuppose a sufficiently stable, shared background understanding against which one might declare artists' intentions irrelevant or passé. Moreover, the New Mythology gains its sense of identity by pitting itself against what it takes to be the Old Mythology's ethnocentric disregard not only for the intentions of tribal artists but for their very names as well. (Price calls this "the anonymization of Primitive Art," and it was a major complaint lodged against the " 'Primitivism' in 20th Century Art" exhibition. If such ethnocentrism is not to be actively encouraged, the tribal artist's interpretations *must* enjoy special status, defining in the first instance the object of study. In order to respect the cultures and people from which tribal works of art are drawn, the New Mythology must treat indigenous intentions—ascertained or, where unavailable, at least postulated—as constituting the beginning of all interpretation, if not its exhaustive or validating end.

This deep conflict between doctrines of the New Mythology and the poststructuralism it seems so eager to appropriate keeps breaking out despite efforts to paper it over. McEvilley and Clifford enthusiastically adopt the discourse of constructivism, so long as they are talking about how "we," or "the West," or the "omniscient" curatorial mind, construct the generalized primitive, but New Mythologists are not nearly so keen to revert to constructivist parlance when it comes to discussing the actual meanings of works of tribal art. Thus Kasfir asks, "Who creates meaning for African art?," where "for" indicates "on behalf of," implying that Western collectors and exhibitors make a meaning for African art to satisfy the Western eye and mind.

This, however, avoids the more obvious wording of the question "Who creates the meaning *of* African art?" If there is any answer at all to this question, it must begin with the artists and cultures that produce the art. The West can "construct" in the poststructuralist manner to its heart's content, but its understandings will always be about the indigenous constructions of the cultures from which African works derive. It is indigenous intentions, values, descriptions, and constructions which must be awarded theoretical primacy. If an African carving is intended by its maker to embody a spirit, and that is an ascertainable fact about it, then any ethnography that constructs its meaning in contradiction to that fact is false. Of course, ethnography need not culminate with indigenous meanings and intentions, any more than literary criticism comes to an end when an author's intended meaning for a work of fiction has been determined. But ethnography has no choice except to begin with indigenous meanings, which it does not construct, but discovers.

POSTSCRIPT

Do Museums Misrepresent Ethnic Communities Around the World?

Clifford, like many critical theorists, is deeply suspicious of all representations of others. Dutton, in contrast, seems to question both the motives and the logic of this suspicion. He is especially critical of Clifford's lack of historical accuracy when describing the goals and motivations of museums and their curators. Are Clifford's postmodernist conclusions guilty of misrepresenting the museum world in ways that parallel his critique of particular exhibits? Does Dutton's critique of the postmodernists solve the historical problems that are present in both museums and the writings of their critics? Is there a middle ground that would allow for exhibitions with more sensitive context?

Clifford has also dealt with museum exhibits in his book *Routes: Travel and Translation in the Late Twentieth Century* (Harvard University Press, 1997). Related approaches to the problem of representation in museums include Sally Price's *Primitive Art in Civilized Places* (University of Chicago Press, 1989) and Shelly Errington's *The Death of Authentic Primitive Art and Other Tales of Progress* (University of California Press, 1998).

Nicholas Thomas's *Entangled Objects: Exchange, Material Culture and Colonialism in the Pacific* (Harvard University Press, 1991) considers the problem of representation among ethnographic objects in the Pacific. Enid Schildkraut and Curtis A. Keim's *The Scramble for Art in Central Africa* (Cambridge University Press, 1998), Ruth B. Phillips and Christopher B. Steiner's *Unpacking Culture: Art and Commodity in Colonial and Post Colonial Worlds* (University of California Press, 1999), and Michael O'Hanlon and Robert L. Welsch's *Hunting the Gatherers: Ethnographic Collectors, Agents, and Agency in Melanesia* (Berghahn, 2000) provide examples of the rich historical context of museum collections of the sort Dutton seeks.

Both Clifford and Dutton build their arguments on the premise that objects have complex histories, an idea that was originally developed in slightly different ways by anthropological historian George W. Stocking, Jr.'s *Objects and Others: Essays on Museums and Material Culture* (University of Wisconsin Press, 1985) and by anthropologist Arjun Appadurai's *The Social Life of Things: Commodities in Cultural Perspective* (Cambridge University Press, 1986). Both books make two crucial points: objects have histories, and the meanings of objects change when the objects themselves move from one context to another. Also, both argue that objects can take on many different meanings depending on context and viewpoint. Together these books have redefined museological studies and transformed what had been an anthropological backwater into a thriving specialization within the discipline.

On the Internet . . .

Margaret Mead

This Web site on Margaret Mead was prepared for the centennial of her birth and offers information on research currently being carried out in Samoa.

http://www.mead2001.org

The !Kung of the Kalahari Desert

The !Kung of the Kalahari Desert Web site contains general information about this group of people who are now called the Ju/'hoansi by most scholars.

http://www.ucc.uconn.edu/~epsadm03/Kung.html

Images of Foraging in Africa

This Web site, entitled Images of Foraging in Africa, focuses on foragers and contains information on the Kalahari debate as well as links to more sites about the Ju/'hoansi.

http://www.c-sap.bham.ac.uk/anthropology%20_pilot/conflicting.htm

Islam for Today

Islam for Today provides basic information about Islam for non-Muslims. Explore the links to basic Islamic beliefs, Muslim history and civilizations, and articles on Islam.

http://www.islamfortoday.com

Collisions of Religions and Violence: Redux

Collisions of Religions and Violence: Redux is a Web site that contains a special issue of the journal *Cross Currents* and deals specifically with the question of whether or not conflict and violence emerge from immutable religious and ethnic differences.

http://www.crosscurrents.org/violencespecial.htm

Culture-Bound Syndromes

The Culture-Bound Syndromes Web site has links to information on culture-bound psychopathology and a glossary of culture-bound syndromes.

http://web.utk.edu/~wmorgan/psy573/culture.htm

PART 2

Some Specific Issues in Cultural Anthropology

*A*lthough cultural anthropologists often examine the interconnections among many aspects of a culture, most have customarily specialized in several subfields. This part deals with research methods and asks questions about different aspects of social and cultural life, including gender roles, kinship, and ethnicity, and it also addresses issues in cognitive anthropology, economic anthropology, political anthropology, sociobiology, the anthropology of religion, and medical anthropology.

- Was Margaret Mead's Fieldwork on Samoan Adolescents Fundamentally Flawed?

- Does Language Determine How We Think?

- Are San Hunter-Gatherers Basically Pastoralists Who Have Lost Their Herds?

- Do Hunter-Gatherers Need Supplemental Food Sources to Live in Tropical Rain Forests?

- Do Sexually Egalitarian Societies Exist?

- Is It Natural for Adopted Children to Want to Find Out About Their Birth Parents?

- Has the Islamic Revolution in Iran Subjugated Women?

- Are Yanomami Violence and Warfare Natural Human Efforts to Maximize Reproductive Fitness?

- Is Ethnic Conflict Inevitable?

- Do Some Illnesses Exist Only Among Members of a Particular Culture?

ISSUE 4

Was Margaret Mead's Fieldwork on Samoan Adolescents Fundamentally Flawed?

YES: Derek Freeman, from *Margaret Mead and Samoa: The Making and Unmaking of an Anthropological Myth* (Harvard University Press, 1983)

NO: Lowell D. Holmes and Ellen Rhoads Holmes, from *Samoan Village: Then and Now,* 2d ed. (Harcourt Brace Jovanovich College Publishers, 1992)

ISSUE SUMMARY

YES: Social anthropologist Derek Freeman argues that Margaret Mead was wrong when she stated that Samoan adolescents had sexual freedom. He contends that Mead went to Samoa determined to prove anthropologist Franz Boas's cultural determinist agenda and states that Mead was so eager to believe in Samoan sexual freedom that she was consistently the victim of a hoax perpetrated by Samoan girls and young women who enjoyed tricking her.

NO: Cultural anthropologists Lowell D. Holmes and Ellen Rhoads Holmes contend that Margaret Mead had a very solid understanding of Samoan culture in general. During a restudy of Mead's research, they came to many of the same conclusions that Mead had reached about Samoan sexuality and adolescent experiences. Mead's description of Samoan culture exaggerates the amount of sexual freedom and the degree to which adolescence in Samoa is carefree but these differences, they argue, can be explained in terms of changes in Samoan culture since 1925 and in terms of Mead's relatively unsophisticated research methods as compared with field methods used today.

In 1925 a student of anthropologist Franz Boas named Margaret Mead set off for a nine-month study of adolescent women in Samoa. At only 23 years old, Mead was just barely beyond adolescence herself. Concerned about Mead's safety in a remote and distant place, Boas arranged for her to stay with an

American family. Here she could live in a European-style house and her physical safety would be ensured. For the next several months she studied the culture and lives of young Samoan women by visiting their village.

On her return to New York in 1925, she wrote up her dissertation for Boas, revising this volume for publication in 1928. She titled the book *Coming of Age in Samoa: A Psychological Study of Primitive Youth for Western Civilization.* Mead concluded that because Samoan culture was so much more relaxed about sexuality than Western culture, Samoan adolescents had a much more tranquil transition from childhood to adulthood than was observed in America and other Western countries. *Coming of Age in Samoa* was an immediate best-seller and it earned Mead renown as a scientist.

In 1983 Derek Freeman published his book entitled *Margaret Mead and Samoa: The Making and Unmaking of an Anthropological Myth* (Harvard University Press), an excerpt of which is provided as the Yes-side selection. Freeman argues that Mead was so eager to find support for her model that she blatantly biased her Samoan fieldwork findings and in effect falsified her data.

Freeman had worked in Western Samoa from 1940 to 1943, returning for further fieldwork from 1965 to 1967. During his research he found evidence that challenges some of Mead's published field data as well as a number of her conclusions regarding Samoan adolescence. He contends that his findings call into question Mead's entire project. He also contends that Mead's young Samoan informants perpetrated a hoax on her by making up stories about their promiscuity.

Freeman's selection is countered by a selection written by Lowell D. Holmes and Ellen Rhoads Holmes, who, in the 1950s, had conducted a restudy of the same community that Mead had visited. Holmes and Holmes had expressly intended to test the reliability and validity of Mead's findings. They conclude that while Mead's characterizations of Samoans are in some ways exaggerated, the characterizations are by no means fundamentally wrong.

These selections allow us to ask a number of questions about Mead's research: Did Mead unintentionally exaggerate her findings about sexual freedom? Or did she intentionally falsify her field data, specifically so that she could support Boas's model of cultural determinism? Could Mead's excesses be explained as the consequence of her being a youthful and inexperienced field researcher? Or can differences between Mead's findings and those of the selection authors be explained in other ways?

These selections raise a number of questions about the replicability of anthropological fieldwork, as well. Is it possible to conduct a systematic restudy of another anthropologist's field subjects? Can an anthropologist working in another village or on another island reliably challenge the findings of another anthropologist?

Derek Freeman  **YES**

Margaret Mead and Samoa

Preface

By far the most widely known of Margaret Mead's numerous books is *Coming of Age in Samoa,* based on fieldwork on which she embarked in 1925 at the instigation of Franz Boas, her professor at Columbia University. Boas had sent the 23-year-old Mead to Samoa to study adolescence, and she returned with a startling conclusion. Adolescence was known in America and Europe as a time of emotional stresses and conflicts. If, Mead argued, these problems were caused by the biological processes of maturation, then they would necessarily be found in all human societies. But in Samoa, she reported, life was easy and casual, and adolescence was the easiest and most pleasant time of life. Thus in anthropological terms, according to Mead, Samoa was a "negative instance"—and the existence of this one counterexample demonstrated that the disturbances associated with adolescence in the United States and elsewhere had cultural and not biological causes. In the controversy between the adherents of biological determinism and those of cultural determinism, a controversy that was at its height in the 1920s, Mead's negative instance appeared to be a triumphant outcome for believers in the sovereignty of culture.

When *Coming of Age in Samoa* was published in 1928 it attracted immense attention, and its apparently conclusive finding swiftly entered anthropological lore as a jewel of a case. Since that time Mead's finding has been recounted in scores of textbooks, and through the vast popularity of *Coming of Age in Samoa,* the best-selling of all anthropological books, it has influenced the thinking of millions of people throughout the world. It is with the critical examination of this very widely accepted conclusion that I am concerned [here].

Scientific knowledge, as Karl Popper has shown, is principally advanced through the conscious adoption of "the critical method of error elimination." In other words, within science, propositions and theories are systematically tested by attempts to refute them, and they remain acceptable only as long as they withstand these attempts at refutation. In Popper's view, "in so far as a scientific statement speaks about reality it must be falsifiable," and rational criticism entails the testing of any particular statement in terms of its correspondence with the facts. Mead's classing of Samoa as a negative instance obviously depends on the adequacy of the account of Samoan culture on which it is based. It is thus very much a scientific proposition, for it is fully open to testing against the relevant empirical evidence.

While the systematic testing of the conclusions of a science is always desirable, this testing is plainly imperative when serious doubts have been expressed about some particular finding. Students of Samoan culture have long voiced such doubts about Mead's findings of 1928.... I adduce detailed empirical evidence to demonstrate that Mead's account of Samoan culture and character is fundamentally in error. I would emphasize that I am not intent on constructing an alternative ethnography of Samoa. Rather, the evidence I shall present has the specific purpose of scientifically refuting the proposition that Samoa is a negative instance by demonstrating that the depictions on which Mead based this assertion are, in varying degree, mistaken.

In undertaking this refutation I shall limit my scrutiny to those sections of Mead's writings which have stemmed from, or refer to, her researches on Samoa. My concern, moreover, is with the scientific import of these actual researches and *not* with Margaret Mead personally, or with any aspect of her ideas or activities that lies beyond the ambit of her writings on Samoa. I would emphasize also that I hold in high regard many of the personal achievements of Margaret Mead, Franz Boas, and the other individuals certain of whose assertions and ideas I necessarily must question in the pages that follow.

... When I reached Western Samoa in April 1940, I was very much a cultural determinist. *Coming of Age in Samoa* had been unreservedly commended to me by [Ernest] Beaglehole, and my credence in Mead's findings was complete.

After two years of study, during which I came to know all the islands of Western Samoa, I could speak Samoan well enough to converse in the company of chiefs with the punctilio that Samoan etiquette demands, and the time had come to select a local polity for intensive investigation. My choice was Sa'anapu, a settlement of 400 inhabitants on the south coast of Upolu. On my first visit to Sa'anapu I had become friendly with Lauvi Vainu'u, a senior talking chief.... I was to become his adopted son. From that time onward I lived as one of the Lauvi family whenever I was in Sa'anapu.

In my early work I had, in my unquestioning acceptance of Mead's writings, tended to dismiss all evidence that ran counter to her findings. By the end of 1942, however, it had become apparent to me that much of what she had written about the inhabitants of Manu'a in eastern Samoa did not apply to the people of western Samoa. After I had been assured by Samoans who had lived in Manu'a that life there was essentially the same as in the western islands, I realized that I would have to make one of the objectives of my research the systematic testing of Mead's depiction of Samoan culture.

Soon after I returned to Sa'anapu its chiefs forgathered one morning at Lauvi's house to confer on me one of the chiefly titles of their polity. I was thus able to attend all *fono,* or chiefly assemblies, as of right, and I soon came to be accepted by the community at large. From this time onward I was in an exceptionally favorable position to pursue my researches into the realities of Samoan life.

By the time I left Samoa in November 1943 I knew that I would one day face the responsibility of writing a refutation of Mead's Samoan findings. This would involve much research into the history of early Samoa. This task I began in 1945 in the manuscript holdings of the Mitchell Library in Sydney and later continued in England, where I thoroughly studied the Samoan archives of the London Missionary Society.

During 1946–1948, while studying anthropology at the University of London, I wrote a dissertation on Samoan social organization. . . . There then came, however, the opportunity to spend some years among the Iban of Borneo. With this diversion, . . . the continuation of my Samoan researches was long delayed.

I finally returned to Western Samoa, accompanied by my wife and daughters, at the end of 1965. Sa'anapu, now linked Apia by road, was once again my center of research. The chiefs of Sa'anapu immediately recognized the title they had conferred on me in 1943, and I became once again an active member of the Sa'anapu *fono*. My family and I remained in Samoa for just over two years, making frequent visits elsewhere in the district to which Sa'anapu belongs, as also to numerous other parts of the archipelago, from Saua in the east to Falealupo in the west.

Many educated Samoans, especially those who had attended college in New Zealand, had become familiar with Mead's writings about their culture. A number of them entreated me, as an anthropologist, to correct her mistaken depiction of the Samoan ethos. Accordingly, early in 1966 I set about the systematic examination of the entire range of Mead's writings on Samoa, seeking to test her assertions by detailed investigation of the particulars of the behavior or custom to which they referred. . . .

[I]n 1967 organized a formal traveling party to [the island of] Ta'ū. We visitors were received as long-lost kinsmen, and in the company of chiefs from both Ta'ū and Sa'anapu I was able to review all those facets of Mead's depiction of Samoa which were then still at issue. In Ta'ū I also recorded the testimony of men and women who remembered the period to which Mead's writings refer. In many instances these recollections were vivid and specific; as one of my informants remarked, the happenings of the mid 1920s were still fresh in their memories.

As my inquiries progressed it became evident that my critical scrutiny of Mead's conclusions would have to extend to the anthropological paradigm of which *Coming of Age in Samoa* was a part. . . .

My researches were not completed until 1981, when I finally gained access to the archives of the High Court of American Samoa for the 1920s. Thus my refutation of Mead's depiction of Samoa appears some years after her death. In November 1964, however, when Dr. Mead visited the Australian National University, I informed her very fully, during a long private conversation, of the empirical basis of my disagreement with her depiction of Samoa. From that time onward we were in correspondence, and in August 1978, upon its first completion, I offered to send her an early draft of my refutation of the conclusions she had reached in *Coming of Age in Samoa.* I received no reply to this offer before Dr. Mead's death in November of that year.

In September 1981 I returned to Western Samoa with the specific purpose of submitting a draft of [my] book to the critical scrutiny of Samoan scholars.... In the course of the refutation of Mead's misleading account of their culture, which many Samoans encouraged me to undertake, I have had to deal realistically with the darker side of Samoan life. During my visit of 1981 I found among contemporary Samoans both a mature appreciation of the need to face these realities and a clear-headed pride in the virtues and strengths of the Samoan way of life....

Mead's Misconstruing of Samoa

... [The] notion that cultural determinism was absolute was "so obvious" to Mead that... she also avowed it in *Coming of Age in Samoa,* in respect of adolescent behavior.

That this doctrine of the absoluteness of cultural determinism should have seemed "so obvious" to Mead is understandable. Anthropology, when she began its study in 1922, was dominated by Boas' "compelling idea," as Leslie Spier has called it, of "the complete moulding of every human expression—inner thought and external behavior—by social conditioning," and by the time she left for Samoa in 1925 she had become a fervent devotee of the notion that human behavior could be explained in purely cultural terms. Further, although by the time of Mead's recruitment to its ranks cultural anthropology had achieved its independence, it had done so at the cost of becoming an ideology that, in an actively unscientific way, sought totally to exclude biology from the explanation of human behavior. Thus as, [Alfred] Kroeber declared, "the important thing about anthropology is not the science but an attitude of mind"—an attitude of mind, that is, committed to the doctrine of culture as a superorganic entity which incessantly shapes human behavior, "conditioning all responses." It was of this attitude of mind that Mead became a leading proponent, with (as Marvin Harris has observed) her anthropological mission, set for her by Boas, being to defeat the notion of a "panhuman hereditary human nature." She pursued this objective by tirelessly stressing, in publication after publication, "the absence of maturational regularities."

In her own account of this mission, Mead describes it as a battle which she and other Boasians had had to fight with the whole battery at their command, using the most fantastic and startling examples they could muster. It is thus evident that her writings during this period, about Samoa as about other South Seas cultures, had the explicit aim of confuting biological explanations of human behavior and vindicating the doctrines of the Boasian school. By 1939 this battle, according to Mead, had been won....

For Mead's readers in North America and elsewhere in the Western world, there could be no more plausible location for the idyllic society of which she wrote than in the South Seas, a region that since the days of Bougainville has figured in the fantasies of Europeans and Americans as a place of preternatural contentment and sensual delight. So, as Mead reports, her announcement in 1925 that she was going to Samoa caused the same breathless stir as if she had been "setting off for heaven." Indeed, there were many in the 1920s, according to Mead, who longed to go to the South Sea islands "to escape to a kind of divine nothingness in which life would be reduced to the simplest physical terms, to sunshine and the moving shadows of palm trees, to bronze-bodied girls and bronze-bodied boys, food for the asking, no work to do, no obligations to meet."

... How did the young Margaret Mead come so to miscronstrue ethos and ethnography of Samoa? The fervency of her belief in cultural determinism and her tendency to view the South Seas as an earthly paradise go some way in accounting for what happened, but manifestly more was involved.

The Ph.D. topic that Boas assigned to Mead was the comparative study of canoe-building, house-building, and tattooing in the Polynesian culture area. During 1924 she gathered information on these activities from the available literature on the Hawaiians, the Marquesans, the Maori, the Tahitians, and the Samoans. These doctoral studies did not have any direct relevance to the quite separate problem of adolescence in Samoa that Boas set her in 1925, and, indeed, the fact that her reading was mainly on Eastern rather than Western Polynesia concealed from her the marked extent to which the traditional culture and values of Samoa differ from those of Tahiti. Again, during the spring of 1925 she had little time for systematic preparation for her Samoan researches. Indeed, the counsel she received from Boas about these researches prior to her departure for Pago Pago lasted, she tells us, for only half an hour. During this brief meeting Boas' principal instruction was that she should concentrate on the problem he had set her and not waste time doing ethnography. Accordingly, when in the second week of November 1925 Mead reached Manu'a, she at once launched into the study of adolescence without first acquiring, either by observation or from inquiry with adult informants, a thorough understanding of the traditional values and customs of the Manu'ans. This, without doubt, was an ill-advised way to proceed, for it meant that Mead was in no position to check the statements of the girls she was studying against a well-informed knowledge of the fa'aSamoa [Samoan way of life]

It is also evident that Mead greatly underestimated the complexity of the culture, society, history, and psychology of the people among whom she was to study adolescence. Samoan society, so Mead would have it, is "very simple," and Samoan culture "uncomplex." ...

As any one who cares to consult Augustin Krämer's *Die Samoa-Inseln*, Robert Louis Stevenson's *A Footnote to History*, or J. W. Davidson's *Samoa mo Samoa* will quickly discover, Samoan society and culture are by no means simple and uncomplex; they are marked by particularities, intricacies, and subtleties quite as daunting as those which face students of Europe and Asia. Indeed, the fa'aSamoa is so sinuously complex that, as Stevenson's step-daughter, Isobel Strong, once remarked, "one may live long in Samoa without understanding the whys and wherefores." Mead, however, spent not even a few months on the systematic study of Manu'a before launching upon the study of adolescence immediately upon her arrival in Ta'ū in accordance with Boas' instructions. Thus, she has noted that while on her later field trips she had "the more satisfactory task of learning the culture first and only afterwards working on a special problem" in Samoa this was "not necessary."

... Another problem was that of being able to communicate adequately with the people she was to study. Mead had arrived in Pago Pago without any knowledge of the Samoan language.... In this situation Mead was plainly at some hazard pursuing her inquiries in Manu'a, for Samoans, when diverted by the stumbling efforts of outsiders to speak their demanding language, are inclined not to take them seriously.

Mead, then, began her inquiries with her girl informants with a far from perfect command of the vernacular, and without systematic prior investigation of Manu'an society and values. Added to this, she elected to live not in a Samoan household but with the handful of expatriate Americans who were the local representatives of the naval government of American Samoa, from which in 1925 many Manu'ans were radically disaffected.... Of the immense advantage that an ethnographer gains by living among the people whose values and behavior he is intent on understanding there can be not the slightest doubt. Mead, however, within six weeks of her arrival in Pago Pago, and before she had spent any time actually staying in a traditional household, had come to feel that the food she would have to eat would be too starchy, and the conditions of living she would have to endure too nerve-racking to make residence with a Samoan family bearable. In Ta'ū, she told Boas, she would be able to live "in a white household" and yet be in the midst of one of the villages from which she would be drawing her adolescent subjects. This arrangement to live not in a Samoan household but with the Holt family in their European-style house, which was also the location of the government radio station and medical dispensary, decisively determined the form her researches were to take.

According to Mead her residence in these government quarters furnished her with an absolutely essential neutral base from which she could study all of the individuals in the surrounding village while at the same time remaining "aloof from native feuds and lines of demarcation." Against this exiguous advantage she was, however, depriving herself of the close contacts that speedily develop in Samoa between an ethnographer and the members of the extended family in which he or she lives. Such contacts are essential for the gaining of a thorough understanding of the Samoan language and, most important of all, for the independent verification, by the continuous observation of actual behavior, of the statements being derived from informants. Thus, by living with the Holts, Mead was trapping herself in a situation in which she was forced to rely not on observations of the behavior of Samoans as they lived their lives beyond the precincts of the government station on Ta'ū, but on such hearsay information as she was able to extract from her adolescent subjects....

It is evident then that although, as Mead records, she could "wander freely about the village or go on fishing trips or stop at a house where a woman was weaving" when she was away from the dispensary, her account of adolescence in Samoa was, in the main, derived from the young informants who came to talk with her away from their homes in the villages of Lumā, Si'ufaga, and Faleasao. So, as Mead states, for these three villages, from which all her adolescent informants were drawn, she saw the life that went on "through the eyes" of the group of girls on the details of whose lives she was concentrating. This situation is of crucial significance for the assessment of Mead's researches in Manu'a, for we are clearly faced with the question of the extent to which the lens she fashioned from what she was being told by her adolescent informants and through which she saw Samoan life was a true and accurate lens.

... [M]any of the assertions appearing in Mead's depiction of Samoa are fundamentally in error, and some of them preposterously false. How are we to account for the presence of errors of this magnitude? Some Samoans who have read *Coming of Age in Samoa* react, as Shore reports, with anger and the insistence "that Mead lied." This, however, is an interpretation that I have no hesitation in dismissing. The succession of prefaces to *Coming of Age* in Samoa published by Mead in 1949, 1953, 1961, and 1973 indicate clearly, in my judgment, that she did give genuine credence to the view of Samoan life with which she returned to New York in 1926. Moreover, in the 1969 edition of *Social Organization of Manu'a* she freely conceded that there was a serious problem in reconciling the "contradictions" between her own depiction of Samoa and that contained in "other records of historical and contemporary behavior." ...

Mead's depiction of Samoan culture, as I have shown, is marked by major errors, and her account of the sexual behavior of Samoans by a mind-boggling contradiction, for she asserts that the Samoans have a culture in which female virginity is very highly valued, with a virginity-testing ceremony being "theoretically observed at weddings of all ranks," while at the same time adolescence among females is regarded as a period "appropriate for love-making," with promiscuity before marriage being both permitted and "expected." And, indeed, she actually describes the Samoans as making the "demand" that a female should be "both receptive to the advances of many lovers and yet capable of showing the tokens of virginity at marriage." Something, it becomes plain at this juncture, is emphatically amiss, for surely no human population could be so cognitively disoriented as to conduct their lives in such a schizophrenic way. Nor are the Samoans remotely like this, for ... they are, in fact, a people who traditionally value virginity highly and so disapprove of premarital promiscuity as to exercise a strict surveillance over the comings and goings of adolescent girls. That these values and this regime were in force in Manu'a in the mid 1920s is, furthermore, clearly established by the testimony of the Manu'ans themselves who, when I discussed this period with those who well remembered it, confirmed that the fa'aSamoa in these matters was operative then as it was both before and after Mead's brief sojourn in Ta'ū. What then can have been the source of Mead's erroneous statement that in Samoa there is great premarital freedom, with promiscuity before marriage among adolescent girls, being both permitted and expected?

The explanation most consistently advanced by the Samoans themselves for the magnitude of the errors in her depiction of their culture and in particular of their sexual morality is, as [Eleanor Ruth] Gerber has reported, "that Mead's informants must have been telling lies in order to tease her." Those Samoans who offer this explanation, which I have heard in Manu'a as well as in other parts of Samoa, are referring to the behavior called *tau fa'ase'e*, to which Samoans are much prone. *Fa'ase'e* (literally "to cause to slip") means "to dupe," as in the example given by Milner, *"e fa'ase'e gofie le teine,* the girl is easily duped"; and the phrase *tau fa'ase'e* refers to the action of deliberately duping someone, a pastime that greatly appeals to the Samoans as a respite from the severities of their authoritarian society.

Because of their strict morality, Samoans show a decided reluctance to discuss sexual matters with outsiders or those in authority, a reticence that is especially marked among female adolescents. Thus, Holmes reports that when he and his wife lived in Manu'a and Tutuila in 1954 "it was never possible to obtain details of sexual experience from unmarried informants, though several of these people were constant companions and part of the household." Further, as Lauifi Ili, Holmes's principal assistant, observes, when it comes to imparting information about sexual activities, Samoan girls are "very close-mouthed and ashamed." Yet it was precisely information of this kind that Mead, a liberated young American newly arrived from New York and resident in the government station at Ta'ū, sought to extract from the adolescent girls she had been sent to study. And when she persisted in this unprecedented probing of a highly embarrassing topic, it is likely that these girls resorted, as Gerber's Samoan informants have averred, to *tau fa'ase'e*, regaling their inquisitor with counterfeit tales of casual love under the palm trees.

This, then, is the explanation that Samoans give for the highly inaccurate portrayal of their sexual morality in Mead's writings. It is an explanation that accounts for how it was that this erroneous portrayal came to be made, as well as for Mead's sincere credence in the account she has given in *Coming of Age* in Samoa, for she was indeed reporting what she had been told by her adolescent informants. The Manu'ans emphasize, however, that the girls who, they claim, plied Mead with these counterfeit tales were only amusing themselves, and had no inkling that their tales would ever find their way into a book.

While we cannot, in the absence of detailed corroborative evidence [but see addendum following], be sure about the truth of this Samoan claim that Mead was mischievously duped by her adolescent informants, we can be certain that she did return to New York in 1926 with tales running directly counter to all other ethnographic accounts of Samoa, from which she constructed her picture of Manu'a as a paradise of free love, and of Samoa as a negative instance, which, so she claimed, validated Boasian doctrine. It was this negative instance that she duly presented to Boas as the ideologically gratifying result of her inquiries in Manu'a....

We are thus confronted in the case of Margaret Mead's Samoan researches with an instructive example of how, as evidence is sought to substantiate a cherished doctrine, the deeply held beliefs of those involved may lead them unwittingly into error. The danger of such an outcome is inherent, it would seem, in the very process of belief formation....

In the case of Mead's Samoan researches, certainly, there is the clearest evidence that it was her deeply convinced belief in the doctrine of extreme cultural determinism, for which she was prepared to fight with the whole battery at her command, that led her to construct an account of Samoa that appeared to substantiate this very doctrine. There is, however, conclusive empirical evidence to demonstrate that Samoa, in numerous respects, is not at all as Mead depicted it to be.

A crucial issue that arises from this historic case for the discipline of anthropology, which has tended to accept the reports of ethnographers as entirely empirical statements, is the extent to which other ethnographic accounts may have been distorted by doctrinal convictions, as well as the methodological question of how such distortion can best be avoided. These are no small problems. I would merely comment that as we look back on Mead's Samoan researches we are able to appreciate anew the wisdom of Karl Popper's admonition that in both science and scholarship it is, above all else, indefatigable rational criticism of our suppositions that is of decisive importance, for such criticism by "bringing out our mistakes . . . makes us understand the difficulties of the problem we are trying to solve," and so saves us from the allure of the "obvious truth" of received doctrine.

Addendum: New Evidence of the Hoaxing of Margaret Mead

In my book *The Fateful Hoaxing of Margaret Mead* (1998) there is an account, based on the sworn testimony of Fa'apua'a, of how Margaret Mead in March of 1926 on the island of Ofu in American Samoa was hoaxed about the sexual mores of the Samoans by her two Samoan traveling companions, Fa'apua'a and Fofoa.

I [have recently discovered] direct evidence, from Mead's own papers, that Margaret Mead was indeed taken in by the "whispered confidences" (as she called them) of Fa'apua'a and Fofoa. This incontrovertible historical evidence finally brings to closure the long-running controversy over Margaret Mead's Samoan fieldwork. . . .

The crucially important direct evidence in question is contained in a little known book entitled *All True! The Record of Actual Adventures That Have Happened To Ten Women of Today* that was published in New York in 1931 by Brewer, Warren and Putnam. The "adventure" by Dr. Margaret Mead is entitled "Life as a Samoan Girl". It begins with a wistful reference to "the group of reverend scientists" who in 1925 sent her to study (Mead, 1925) "the problem of which phenomena of adolescence are culturally and which physiologically determined" among the adolescent girls of Samoa, with "no very clear idea" of how she was "to do this." It ends with an account of her journey to the islands of Ofu and Olosega in March of 1926 with the "two Samoan girls," as she calls them, Fa'apua'a and Fofoa. In fact, Fa'apua'a and Fofoa were both twenty-four years of age and slightly older than Dr. Mead herself. Dr. Mead continues her account of her visit to the islands of Ofu and Olosega with Fa'apua'a and Fofoa by stating: "In all things I had behaved as a Samoan, for only so, only by losing my identity, as far as possible, had I been able to become acquainted with the Samoan girls receive their whispered confidences and learn at the same time the answer to the scientists' questions."

This account, by Mead herself, is fully confirmed by the sworn testimony of Fa'apua'a (cf. Freeman, 1998, Chapter 11). It can be found on p. 141 of the second and paperback edition (1999) of my book *The Fateful Hoaxing of Margaret Mead: A historical analysis of her Samoan research*. It is definitive historical evidence that establishes that Martin Orans is in outright error in asserting (1996:92) that it is "demonstrably false that Mead was taken in by Fa'apua'a and Fofoa". It is also evidence that establishes that *Coming of Age in Samoa,* far from being a "scientific classic" (as Mead herself supposed) is, in certain vitally significant respects (as in its dream-like second chapter), a work of anthropological fiction.

References

Freeman, Derek, 1999, *The Fateful Hoaxing of Margaret Mead,* Boulder: Westview, 2nd. edition.

Mead, Margaret, 1925, Plan of Research Submitted to the National Research Council of the U.S.A. (Archives of the National Academy of Sciences).

Mead, Margaret, 1928, *Coming of Age in Samoa.* New York: Morrow.

Mead, Margaret, 1931, "Life as a Samoan Girl," in *All True! The Record of Actual Adventures That Happened to Ten Women of Today.* New York: Brewer, Warren and Putnam.

Orans, Martin, 1996, *Not Even Wrong: Margaret Mead, Derek Freeman and the Samoans,* Novato: Chandler and Sharp.

Samoan Character and
the Academic World

On January 31, 1983, the *New York Times* carried a front-page article, the headline of which read, "New Samoa Book Challenges Margaret Mead's Conclusions." The book that precipitated this somewhat unexpected turn of events was *Margaret Mead and Samoa: The Making and Unmaking of an Anthropological Myth* by Derek Freeman, an emeritus professor of anthropology at Australian National University in Canberra. This work, which some claim set off the most heated controversy in sociocultural anthropology in one hundred years, is described by its author as a "refutation of Mead's misleading account" of Samoan culture and personality as presented in her 1928 ethnography, *Coming of Age in Samoa.*

The *New York Times* article was of special interest to me because, in 1954, I had conducted a year-long methodological restudy of the Mead data under attack. I had lived in Ta'ū village, where Mead had worked twenty-nine years earlier, and had used many of her informants in a systematic and detailed evaluation of every observation and interpretation she had made about the lifestyle of the people in that Samoan village. A methodological restudy, incidentally, involves a second anthropologist going into the field with the *express purpose* of testing the reliability and validity of the findings of a former investigator. This restudy is made in order to establish what kinds of errors of data collection or interpretation might have been made by certain kinds of people, in certain kinds of field research situations, researching certain kinds of problems. For example, Margaret Mead was a twenty-three-year-old woman investigating a male-dominated society that venerates age. She was a student of Franz Boas and, therefore, went equipped with a particular theoretical frame of reference. She was also on her first field trip—at a time when research methods were crude. My task in this methodological restudy was not only to analyze how my findings might be different from hers (if that would be the case), but I would also attempt to speculate on how differences in the status of the investigators (for example, sex, age, family situation, education) and other personal factors might affect the collection and interpretation of data.

My critique of Margaret Mead's study was presented in my doctoral dissertation, *The Restudy of Manu'an Culture. A Problem in Methodology,* which by

From Lowell D. Holmes and Ellen Rhoads Holmes, *Samoan Village: Then and Now,* 2d ed. (Harcourt Brace Jovanovich College, 1992). Copyright © 1992, 1974 by Holt, Rinehart and Winston, Inc.

1983 had been collecting dust on a Northwestern University library shelf for some twenty-seven years. I was therefore eager to obtain a copy of Freeman's new evaluation of Mead's work from its publisher, Harvard University Press. In reading the book this is what I found.

In *Margaret Mead and Samoa: The Making and Unmaking of an Anthropological Myth* (1983), Derek Freeman argues that Mead perpetuated a hoax comparable in consequence to that of Piltdown Man when, in 1928, she described Samoa as a paradise where competition, sexual inhibition, and guilt were virtually absent. Refusing to believe that adolescents in all societies inevitably experience emotional crises—storm and stress—because of biological changes associated with puberty (as hypothesized in *Adolescence* in 1904 by psychologist G. Stanley Hall), Mead set out to discover a society where the passage to adulthood was smooth and without trauma. She described such a society in *Coming of Age in Samoa*. In delineating this "negative instance" (which challenged Hall's theory of universal adolescent rebellion and strife), Margaret Mead had in effect established that nurture (culture) is more critical than nature (biology) in accounting for adolescent maturation behavior in the human species. Derek Freeman, on the other hand, rejects the idea that human behavior is largely shaped by culture and believes that Mead and her mentor, Franz Boas (commonly called the "Father of American Anthropology"), were guilty of *totally* ignoring the influence of biological heredity. He believes that Mead's "negative instance" results entirely from faulty data collection and that Mead's Samoan findings have led anthropology, psychology, and education down the primrose path of pseudoscience. Freeman's book, therefore, is an attempt to set the record straight through his own, more accurate, observations of Samoa and Samoans—although his observations of Samoan behavior were in another village, on another island, in another country, and fourteen years later.

Freeman's main theoretical approach in this evaluation of Mead's work derives from the German philosopher of science, Karl Popper, who maintains that science should be deductive, not inductive, and that progress in scientific research should consist essentially of attempts to refute established theories. Thus, Derek Freeman is out to destroy the credibility of what he interprets as the "absolute cultural determinism" to be found in the work of Margaret Mead as well as in much of the work of Boas and his other students. This claim is, of course, spurious, as any student of American anthropological theory knows. For example, in Melville J. Herskovits' biography of Franz Boas, we find the statement that, because of his "rounded view of the problem Boas could perceive so clearly the fallacy of the eugenicist theory, which held the destiny of men to be determined by biological endowment, with little regard for the learned, cultural determinants of behavior." By the same token, he "refused to accept the counter-dogma that man is born with a completely blank slate, on which can be written whatever is willed. He saw both innate endowment and learning—or, as it was called popularly, heredity and environment—as significant factors in the making of the mature individual" (1953:28). Herskovits also points out that "numerous examples can be found, in reports on the various studies he conducted, of how skillfully Boas was able to weave cultural and biological factors into a single fabric" (*Ibid.*).

Marvin Harris concurs: "American anthropology has always been concerned with the relationships between nature (in the guise of habitat and genic programming) and culture (in the guise of traditions encoded in the brain, not in the genes). Neither Boas nor his students ever denied that *Homo sapiens* has a species-specific nature" (1983:26). In his book, *The Rise of Anthropological Theory,* Harris writes, "Boas systematically rejected almost every conceivable form of cultural determinism" (1968:283).

Evaluation of the Mead Data

My restudy experience in Ta'ū village in 1954 led me to conclude that Margaret Mead often overgeneralized; that, in many cases, we interpreted data differently; and that, because of her age and sex, some avenues of investigation apparently were closed to her—particularly those having to do with the more formal aspects of village political organization and ceremonial life. However, her overall characterization of the nature and dynamics of the culture were, in my judgment, quite valid and her contention that it was easier to come of age in Samoa than in America in 1925–1926 was undoubtedly correct. In spite of the greater possibilities for error in a pioneer study, Mead's age (only 23), her sex (in a male-dominated society), and her inexperience, I believe the reliability and validity of the Ta'ū village research is remarkably high.

I look upon an ethnographic account as a kind of map to be used in finding one's way about in a culture—in comprehending and anticipating behavior. Mead's account never left me lost or bewildered in my interactions with Samoan islanders, but I also felt that if one were to come to a decision about the comparative difficulties of coming of age in Samoa and the United States, it would be necessary to know something about what life was like for adolescents in America in 1925–1926. Joseph Folsom's book, *The Family,* published in 1934, but researched about the time Mead was writing *Coming of Age in Samoa,* provided that information. Folsom describes the social environment in which children came of age at that time as follows:

> Children are disciplined and trained with the ideal of absolute obedience to parents. Corporal punishment is used, ideally in cold blood.... All sexual behavior on the part of children is prevented by all means at the parents' disposal.... For the sake of prevention it has been usual to cultivate in the child, especially the girl, an attitude of horror or disgust toward all aspects of sex.... Premarital intercourse is immoral though not abhorrent.... Violations are supposedly prevented by the supervision of the girl's parents.... Illegitimate children are socially stigmatized.... The chief stigma falls upon the unmarried mother, because she has broken an important sex taboo (1934: 10–25)....

While Freeman contends that Mead was absolutely wrong about nearly everything (partly, he maintains, because the teenage girls she used as informants consistently lied to her), I found discrepancies mainly in such areas as the degree of sexual freedom Samoan young people enjoy, the competitive nature of the society, the aggressiveness of Samoan behavior, and the degree of genuine affection and commitment between lovers and spouses.

I saw Samoan culture as considerably more competitive than Mead, although I never considered it as inflexible or aggressive as Freeman does. I observed a great preoccupation with status, power, and prestige among men of rank and, on more than one occasion, was present at fierce verbal duels between Talking Chiefs trying to enhance their own prestige and, incidentally, that of their village....

I also found that Samoan culture was not as simple as Margaret Mead claimed, nor was Ta'ū village the paradise she would have us believe. She often romanticized, overgeneralized, and, on some occasions, took literary license in her descriptions of Samoan lifeways. For example, her very dramatic chapter, "A Day in Samoa," crowds typical activities (some of which occur only at particular times of the year) into a typical day and thereby presents a village scene that was much more vibrant, bustling, and picturesque than I ever encountered in any twenty-four hour period. Mead's chapter is good prose, but is it good anthropology?...

I also did not agree with Mead on the degree of sexual freedom supposedly enjoyed by her informants, but I believe her characterization comes closer to the truth than that of Freeman. Samoans have a very natural and healthy attitude toward sex. Judging by the number of illegitimate children in Ta'ū village when I was there and by the fact that divorce frequently involved claims of adultery, I would conclude that, while Samoans are far from promiscuous, they are not the puritanical prudes Freeman paints them to be. However, I must admit that it was difficult to investigate anything of a sexual nature, primarily because of pressure from the London Missionary Society church. Even today, older Samoans seem more distressed over Mead's claims that they are sexually active than Freeman's claims that they are aggressive with strong passions, even psychopathological tendencies. I would assume, however, that Mead was better able to identify with, and therefore establish rapport with, adolescents and young adults on issues of sexuality than either I (at age 29—married with a wife and child) or Freeman, ten years my senior.

Freeman maintains that Mead imposed her own liberated ideas of sexuality onto the Samoans and that her teenage informants consistently lied to her about these matters solely out of mischief. He has recently made contact with one of Mead's informants, Fa'apua'a Fa'amu, who lived in Fitiuta while Mead was working in Ta'ū village. Freeman believes this informant when she says that she consistently lied to Mead (while also identifying her as a good friend), but Freeman does not seem to consider the possibility that she may be lying to him. The possibility of Mead's informants being successful at such long-term deception is simply not credible considering the fact that Mead was an extremely intelligent, well-trained Ph.D. who constantly cross-checked her data with many informants. Anyone who has studied her field notes in the Library of Congress, as I have, must be impressed with her savvy and sophistication.

I must also disagree with Mead's statements that all love affairs are casual and fleeting, and no one plays for very heavy emotional stakes. Custom dictates that displays of affection between spouses and between lovers not take place in public. However, expressions of love and affection were often observed in the families of my informants....

Although I differed with Margaret Mead on many interpretations, the most important fact that emerged from my methodological restudy of her Samoan research is that, without doubt, Samoan adolescents have a less difficult time negotiating the transition from childhood to adulthood than American adolescents....

Critique of the Freeman Refutation

My objections to Derek Freeman's picture of Samoa are much more substantial than to the picture presented by Margaret Mead. Basically, I question Freeman's objectivity and believe he is guilty of an age-old temptation in science, which was recognized as early as 1787 by Thomas Jefferson—no slouch of a scientist himself. In a letter to his friend Charles Thomson, Jefferson wrote, "The moment a person forms a theory, his imagination sees, in every object, only the traits which favor that theory" (Martin 1952:33).

Not only does Freeman ignore counterevidence, he also ignores time and space and assumes that it is legitimate to assess data obtained by Mead in Manu'a in 1925–1926 in terms of the data he collected in Western Samoa in the 1940s, 1960s, and 1980s.

Time differences.   Freeman plays down the fact that Mead did her study of Ta'ū village in the Manu'a Island group of American Samoa fourteen years before he arrived as a teacher (not as an anthropologist) in Western Samoa and that he did not return to Samoa with the express purpose of refuting Mead's study until forty-three years after her visit. Minimizing this time gap, he arbitrarily states that "there is no ... reason to suppose that Samoan society and behavior changed in any fundamental way during the fourteen years between 1926, the year of the completion of Mead's inquiries, and 1940, when I began my own observation of Samoan behavior" (1983:120).

However, Freeman did not visit Ta'ū village, the site of Mead's research, until 1968. Having established to his satisfaction that there had been few changes in Samoan culture during this long period of time, Freeman went on to state that he would "draw on evidence of my own research in the 1940s, the years 1965 to 1968, and 1981" (1983:120). I might add that he would draw upon historical sources, some of which go back as far as the early eighteenth century, to prove his points. My own analysis of Samoan cultural change, as published in *Ta'ū, Stability and Change in a Samoan Village* (1958), indicates, however, that while there was relative stability in the culture from 1850 to 1925 and from 1925 to 1954, change definitely did take place, particularly in the twentieth century. There is absolutely no basis for Freeman's dealing with Samoa as though it existed in a totally static condition despite its long history of contact with explorers, whalers, missionaries, colonial officials and bureaucrats, entrepreneurs, anthropologists, and, more recently, educators with Western-style curricula and television networks.

Place differences.   It also must be kept in mind that Sa'anapu (where Freeman observed Samoan culture) is not Ta'ū village (where Mead did her study). They are different villages, on different islands, in different countries, and there are great historical and political differences between the island of Upolu in Western Samoa and Ta'ū island in the isolated Manu'a Group of American Samoa. Western Samoa has experienced a long and often oppressive history of colonialism under Germany and New Zealand, while the Manu'a Group and American Samoa in general have been spared this. The U.S. Navy administration (1900–1951) exerted little influence outside the Pago Pago Bay area on the island of Tutuila, and the Department of the Interior, which took over from the Navy, has been an ethnocentric—but still benevolent—force in the political history of the territory. While Sa'anapu is on the opposite side of Upolu from Apia, it has daily bus communication with that port town, with all of its banks, supermarkets, department stores, theaters, bookstores, and nightclubs. Cash cropping has always been more important in Western Samoa than in American Samoa, and today, the economies of the two Samoas are vastly different.... On five separate research trips to Manu'a, I have never witnessed a single physical assault or serious argument that threatened to get out of hand. However, urban centers such as Apia in Western Samoa and Pago Pago in American Samoa have a very different character. As early as 1962, there were delinquency problems in the Pago Pago Bay area involving drunkenness, burglary, assaults, and rapes. Young people who migrate to urban areas such as Pago Pago and Apia are no longer under the close supervision and control of their *matai* [chief of the family] and often behave in very nontraditional ways. It is difficult, indeed, to make a blanket statement that all villages in Samoa are the same and that all behavior within the two Samoas is comparable. I have studied several villages during my thirty-seven-year contact with Samoa, and I find each unique in numerous, social, ceremonial, economic, and political respects.

Freeman's subjective use of literature.   A serious scientist considers all the literature relating to his or her research problem. One does not select data that supportive and ignore that which is not. Freeman violates that principle repeatedly.... When [Ronald Rose's book, *South Seas Magic* (1959)] can be used to corroborate or advance Freeman's position, he is quoted; however, where Rose's statements concerning Samoan sexual behavior run contrary to Freeman's claims, and fall in line with Mead's observations, his work is ignored. For example, while Freeman insists that Samoans are puritanical and sexually inhibited, Rose writes that "sexual adventures begin at an early age. Although virginity is prized, it is insisted on only with the taupo.... If a girl hasn't had a succession of lovers by the time she is seventeen or eighteen, she feels she is 'on the shelf' and becomes the laughing stock among her companions" (1959:61).

   With regard to the matter that Freeman believes was Mead's spurious example of a "negative instance"—a culture where coming of age is relatively less stressful—Rose writes (but understandably is not quoted by Freeman) as follows:

> Mental disturbances, stresses and conflicts occur at puberty but, as might
> be expected. these are not quite as common as in our society where taboos
> associated with sex abound (*Ibid.*: 164).

One can question the objectivity of a scientist who describes Samoans as "an unusually bellicose people" (1983:157) and attempts to substantiate the claim with citations from the eighteenth century, but fails to quote the favorable impressions of the very first European to come in contact with Samoan islanders from the village of Ta'ū, the very village Mead studied. In 1722, Commodore Jacob Roggeveen anchored his vessel off the village of Ta'ū and allowed a number of the islanders to come aboard. After a two-hour visit, the Commodore wrote in his log:

> They appeared to be a good people, lively in their manner of conversing, gentle in their deportment towards each other, and in their manners nothing was perceived of the savage.... It must be acknowledged that this was the nation the most civilized and honest of any that we had seen among the Islands of the South Sea. They were charmed with our arrival amongst them, and received us as divinities. And when they saw us preparing to depart, they testified much regret (Bumey 1816:576).

Rather than quote Roggeveen, Freeman chooses to discuss, as an example of Samoan bellicosity, the La Perouse expedition's visitation at Tutuila in 1787 that ended in tragedy. It is true that Samoans in the village of A'asu attacked a shore party, killing several crew members, but what Freeman fails to mention is that the attack occurred only after crew members punished a Samoan for pilfering by hanging him by his thumbs from the top of the longboat mast....

It also should be noted that the eminent writer, Robert Louis Stevenson, who lived among Samoans the last four years of his life, recorded in his chronicle of Samoan events, *A Footnote to History,* that Samoans were "easy, merry, and pleasure loving; the gayest, though by no means the most capable or the most beautiful of Polynesians" (1892:148) and that their religious sentiment toward conflict was "peace at any price" (*Ibid.*: 147).

Observers contemporary with Mead in Samoa also record descriptions of Samoan chararacter that do not square with Freeman's allegations or his citations from early literature. For example, William Green, the principal of the government school in American Samoa in the 1920s writes:

> Personal combats and fist fights are rather rare today. I believe there has been no murder case in American Samoa since our flag was raised in 1900. Natives will suffer indignities for a long time before resorting to a fight but they remain good fighters. Boxing contests are held occasionally.... Respect for elders and magistrates has, I suppose, tended to discourage frequent combats. Life is easy, and one's habitual tendencies and desires are seldom blocked (1924:134).

Professional Reactions

... It is questionable whether any anthropology book to date has created such a media circus or produced such a media hero as *Margaret Mead and Samoa, The Making and Unmaking of an Anthropological Myth.* It is also doubtful whether any academic press ever mounted such a campaign of Madison Avenue hype to market a book as did Harvard University Press. The early reviews of the book and feature articles about the controversy were primarily penned by journalists and tended to be highly supportive of Freeman's critique, but once the anthropologists began evaluating the Freeman book, the tide took a definite turn. George Marcus of Rice University called the book a "work of great mischief," the mischief being that Freeman was attempting to reestablish "the importance of biological factors in explanations of human behavior" (1983:2).... Marvin Harris observed in his review that Freeman "seems obsessed with the notion that to discredit Mead's Samoan material is to discredit any social scientist who holds that 'nurture' is a more important determinant of the differences and similarities in human social life than nature" (1983:26).

It is only fair to point out that Derek Freeman had, and continues to have, a cadre of anthropological supporters, mostly in Europe and Australia, and the Samoans are mixed in their support of Mead or Freeman....

Like most American anthropologists, and a few scholarly Samoans, we believe the Freeman book has done a disservice to Samoans and to the memory of Margaret Mead. *Margaret Mead and Samoa* is not an objective analysis of Mead's work in Manu'a, but an admitted refutation aimed at discrediting not only Margaret Mead, but Franz Boas and American cultural anthropology in general. Anthropology has often been referred to as a "soft science" throughout much of this rhubarb over Samoa and nature/nurture. It is little wonder, since Freeman's diatribe, published by a supposedly scholarly press, has been accepted by the media, by a select group of anthropologists, and by a number of distinguished ethologists and sociobiologists as legitimate anthropology. Margaret Mead would have loved to have debated the issues with Derek Freeman, but unfortunately, the book was not published while she was alive. It would have been great sport and good for the science of anthropology. As a friend wrote immediately after the publication of Freeman's book, "Whatever else she was, Margaret was a feisty old gal and would have put up a spirited defense which would quickly have turned into a snotty offense." We would have put our money on the plump little lady with the no-nonsense attitude and the compulsion to "get on with it."

References

Burney, James. 1816. *A chronological history of the voyages and discoveries in the South Seas or Pacific Ocean.* London: Luke Hansard and Sons.

Folsom, Joseph K. 1934. *The family: Its sociology and psychiatry.* New York: J. Wiley and Sons.

Freeman, Derek. 1983. *Margaret Mead and Samoa: The making and unmaking of an anthropological myth.* Cambridge, MA: Harvard University Press.

Green, William M. 1924. "Social traits of Samoans." *Journal of Applied Sociology* 9:129 135.

Hall, G. Stanley. 1904. *Adolescence: Its psychology and its relations to physiology, anthropology, sociology, sex, crime, religion and education.* New York: D. Appleton and Company.

Harris, Marvin. 1968. *The rise of anthropological theory.* New York: Thomas Y. Crowell Company.

———. 1983. "The sleep-crawling question." *Psychology Today* May:24–27.

Herskovits, Melville J. 1953. *Franz Boas.* New York: Charles Scribner's Sons.

Holmes, Lowell D. 1958. *Taʻū: Stability and change in a Samoan village.* Reprint No. 7, Wellington, New Zealand: Polynesian Society.

Marcus, George, 1983. "One man's Mead." *New York Times Book Review* March 27, 1983:2–3, 22–23.

Martin, Edwin T. 1952. *Thomas Jefferson: Scientist.* New York: Henry Schuman.

Rose, Ronald. 1959. *South Seas magic.* London: Hale.

Stevenson, Robert Louis. 1892. *Vailima papers and A footnote to history.* New York: Charles Scribner's Sons.

POSTSCRIPT

Was Margaret Mead's Fieldwork on Samoan Adolescents Fundamentally Flawed?

The response to Freeman's *Margaret Mead and Samoa* was quite extraordinary and included books, journal articles, editorials, and conference papers. Special sessions at the annual meetings of the American Anthropological Association were devoted exclusively to the Mead-Freeman debate. The first reaction was largely defensive. But as the initial shock of Freeman's assertions wore off, scholars began to address some of the specific points of criticism. A representative sample of these would include Lowell D. Holmes's *Quest for the Real Samoa: The Mead/Freeman Controversy and Beyond* (Bergin and Garvey, 1987) and Hiram Caton's edited volume, *The Samoa Reader: Anthropologists Take Stock* (University Press of America, 1990).

A number of scholars have pointed out that Samoan life has changed significantly since Mead's fieldwork. The Christian Church now exerts a much stronger pressure over the very same women that Mead had interviewed. Another point is that Mead's informants themselves have become much more puritanical as old women than they were as girls. These women now have reputations of social propriety to uphold that would not have concerned them in their youth. Can we believe that they had the same views so many years ago?

In the 1980s Freeman returned to Ta'u with an Australian documentary film crew, specifically to interview some of Mead's now elderly informants. When asked what they had told Mead 60 years earlier, the women stated that they fibbed continuously and explained that it is a cherished Samoan custom to trick people in these ways. Freeman and the film crew take such statements as incontrovertible evidence that Mead was hoaxed. But if it is Samoan custom to trick others, how can Freeman and his film crew be certain that they are not victims of a similar hoax?

Another Samoa specialist, Martin Orans, approaches the controversy in his book *Not Even Wrong: Margaret Mead, Derek Freeman, and the Samoans* (Chandler & Sharp, 1996). Orans contends that neither Mead nor Freeman framed their research questions about cultural determinism in ways that can be tested. Arguing that anthropologists must frame their conclusions as testable hypotheses, Orans asserts that Mead and Freeman are so vague that neither makes their case, and both are so ambiguous that they are "not even wrong." But if Orans is correct, how can anthropologists frame the nature-versus-nurture debate in more specific and testable ways in specific field settings?

ISSUE 5

Does Language Determine How We Think?

YES: John J. Gumperz and Stephen C. Levinson, from "Introduction: Linguistic Relativity Re-examined" and "Introduction to Part 1," in John J. Gumperz and Stephen C. Levinson, eds., *Rethinking Linguistic Relativity* (Cambridge University Press, 1996)

NO: Steven Pinker, from *The Language Instinct: How the Mind Creates Language* (Perennial Classics, 2000)

ISSUE SUMMARY

YES: Sociolinguists John J. Gumperz and Stephen C. Levinson contend that recent studies of language and culture suggest that language structures human thought in a variety of ways that most linguists and anthropologists had not believed possible.

NO: Cognitive neuropsychologist Steven Pinker draws on recent studies in cognitive science and neuropsychology to support the notion that previous studies have examined language but have said little, if anything, about thought.

For more than a century, anthropologists and linguists have observed that the world's languages differ in a number of significant ways. While some languages, such as French or Spanish, require speakers to mark the gender of most nouns, English does not. Some languages in Africa, New Guinea, and Latin America have only two, three, or four basic color terms, while English has eleven. Some languages are rich in cover terms such as tree, bird, or animal, while others have many terms for the different species but may lack any single term that would include all kinds of trees, birds, or animals. Do such differences among the world's languages have any effect on how different people think about the world in which they live?

The idea that human thought changes with different languages has come to be known as the question of linguistic relativity. It is most widely associated with the linguistic anthropologist Edward Sapir and his sometime student Benjamin Lee Whorf. Early in the twentieth century Sapir had drawn on his studies of Native American languages to suggest that different lexical (vocabulary) items and different grammatical features did lead various Indian groups to view the world differently from white English-speaking Americans. By the 1950s the idea that the language people spoke shaped the way they were inclined to think about the world had become known as the Sapir-Whorf hypothesis.

Although the Sapir-Whorf hypothesis had been generally accepted by most American anthropologists, few accepted the hypothesis in its strongest and most deterministic form. Derived from Whorf's writings, the strong version implied that humans were prisoners of their native language and could only think in terms of that language's grammatical and lexical categories. Since most anthropologists learned these exotic languages and with training were themselves able to understand both the words and the exotic worldviews, most anthropologists recognized that language could not be so deterministic. On the other hand, most anthropologists recognized that their informants approached the world quite differently from themselves.

The first formal test of linguistic relativity came in 1969 when cognitive anthropologist Brent Berlin and Paul Kay published *Basic Color Terms* (Berkeley, University of California Press). Examining the color terminologies of more than 100 languages from around the world, they concluded that the number of key or basic color terms a language might have is highly variable, from as few as two to as many as twelve. But the particular hues that would be coded was highly predictable and not at all random. Berlin and Kay suggested that all people perceive colors the same, but how they assign particular color chips to different color terms is anything but arbitrary.

In the 1970s these and other studies of how different people classified their natural, biological, and social worlds suggested to most anthropologists that language's role in culture was primarily limited to prescribing how people classified the world they inhabited rather than on people's thought processes. Thus, for about two decades the Sapir-Whorf hypothesis was relegated to the dustbin of bad anthropological theories. But in the 1990s a growing number of linguists and linguistic anthropologists began to reevaluate the hypothesis, and a growing number has come to see the relationship between language and thought in a variety of new ways.

The first selection, by John J. Gumperz and Stephen C. Levinson, examines some new studies, suggesting that new findings on the issue of linguistic relativity are emerging from many quarters in linguistics and anthropology. Accepting a nondeterministic reading of Sapir and Whorf, they explore some of the directions this new research is taking.

As anthropologists and linguists began to reexamine Sapir-Whorf, new criticisms have arisen from the new field of cognitive neuroscience. Here, Steven Pinker evaluates the linguistic relativity question, drawing on recent studies by cognitive neuroscience. He tends to view the relativity problem in more determinist terms than do Gumperz and Levinson, as well as most of the anthropologists who are currently working on this problem.

John J. Gumperz and
Stephen C. Levinson

 **YES**

Rethinking Linguistic Relativity

Introduction: Linguistic Relativity Re-Examined

Language, Thinking, and Reality

Every student of language or society should be familiar with the essential idea of linguistic relativity, the idea that culture, *through* language, affects the way we think, especially perhaps our classification of the experienced world. Much of our experience seems to support some such idea, for example the phenomenology of struggling with a second language, where we find that the summit of competence is forever over the next horizon, the obvious absence of definitive or even accurate translation (let alone the ludicrous failure of phrasebooks), even the wreck of diplomatic efforts on linguistic and rhetorical rocks.

On the other hand, there is a strand of robust common sense that insists that a stone is a stone whatever you call it, that the world is a recalcitrant reality that imposes its structure on our thinking and our speaking and that the veil of linguistic difference can be ripped aside with relative ease. Plenty of subjective experiences and objective facts can be marshalled to support this view: the delight of foreign friendships, our ability to "read" the military or economic strategies of alien rivals, the very existence of comparative sciences of language, psychology, and society.

These two opposing strands of "common sense" have surfaced in academic controversies and intellectual positions over many centuries of Western thought. If St. Augustine (354–430) took the view that language is a mere nomenclature for antecedently existing concepts, Roger Bacon (1220–92) insisted, despite strong views on the universal basis of grammar, that the mismatch between semantic fields in different languages made accurate translation impossible. The Port Royal grammarians of the seventeenth century found universal logic thinly disguised behind linguistic difference, while the German romantics in a tradition leading through to Humboldt in the nineteenth century found a unique *Weltanschauung*, "world view," in each language. The first half of our own century was characterized by the presumption of radical linguistic and cultural difference reflecting profound cognitive differences, a presumption to be found in anthropology, linguistics and behaviourist psychologies, not to mention philosophical emphasis on meaning as use. The second half of the century has been dominated by the rise of the cognitive sciences, with their treatment of mind as inbuilt capacities for information processing, and their associated universalist and rationalist presuppositions. St. Augustine would probably recognize the faint echoes of his views in much modern theorizing about how children acquire language through prior knowledge of the structure of the world.

There is surely some spiral ascent in the swing of this pendulum. Nevertheless it is important to appreciate how little real scientific progress there has been in the study of lexical or morphosyntactic meaning—most progress in linguistics has been in the study of syntax and sound systems, together with rather general ideas about how the meaning of phrases might be composed out of the meaning of their constituents. Thus there is still much more opinion (often ill-informed) than solid fact in modern attitudes to "linguistic relativity."

There are three terms in the relation: language, thought, and culture. Each of these are global cover terms, not notions of any precision. When one tries to make anything definite out of the idea of linguistic relativity, one inevitably has to focus on particular aspects of each of these terms in the relation. This [selection] will show how each can be differently construed and, as a consequence, the relation reconsidered. In addition the connecting links can be variously conceived. Thus by the end of the [selection] the reader will find that the aspects of language and thinking that are focused on are selective, but also that the very relation between culture and community has become complex. Readers will find the original idea of linguistic relativity still live, but functioning in a way that differs from how it was originally conceived.

Linguistic Relativity Re-Examined

The original idea, variously attributable to [Wilhelm von] Humboldt, [Franz] Boas, [Edward] Sapir, [and Benjamin Lee] Whorf, was that the semantic structures of different languages might be fundamentally incommensurable, with consequences for the way in which speakers of specific languages might think and act. On this view, language, thought, and culture are deeply interlocked, so that each language might be claimed to have associated with it a distinctive worldview.

These ideas captured the imagination of a generation of anthropologists, psychologists, and linguists, as well as members of the general public. They had deep implications for the way anthropologists should conduct their business, suggesting that translational difficulties might lie at the heart of their discipline. However, the ideas seemed entirely and abruptly discredited by the rise of the cognitive sciences in the 1960s, which favoured a strong emphasis on the commonality of human cognition and its basis in human genetic endowment. This emphasis was strengthened by developments within linguistic anthropology, with the discovery of significant semantic universals in color terms, the structure of ethnobotanical nomenclature, and (arguably) kinship terms.

However, there has been a recent change of intellectual climate in psychology, linguistics, and other disciplines surrounding anthropology, as well as within linguistic anthropology, towards an intermediate position, in which more attention is paid to linguistic and cultural difference, such diversity being viewed within the context of what we have learned about universals (features shared by all languages and cultures). New work in developmental psychology, while acknowledging underlying universal bases, emphasizes the importance of the socio-cultural context of human development. Within sociolinguistics and linguistic anthropology there has also been increasing attention to meaning and discourse, and concomitantly a growing appreciation of how interpretive differences can be rooted as much in the systematic uses of language as in its structure.

...[T]he ideas we associate today so especially with Whorf and Sapir have a long and distinguished lineage on the one hand, while perhaps being no more than one of two opposing perennial strands of thought, universalism vs. relativism, on the other. Nevertheless, they crystallized in a particular fashion in American intellectual life of the 1940s. The idea of a close link between linguistic and conceptual categories took on a new meaning in the context of three further background assumptions characteristic of the first half of the century. One was the presumption of a (sometimes tempered) empiricist epistemology, that is, the view that all knowledge is acquired primarily through experience. The other was the structuralist assumption that language forms a system of oppositions, such that formal distinctions directly reflect meaning distinctions. The third was the idea of an unconscious mental life, and thus the possibility of linguistic effects beyond conscious awareness. It was the conjunction of these background ideas together with the specific formulation of the "linguistic relativity" hypothesis that gave the hypothesis its particular character in the history of ideas.

Sapir may have originated the phrase, but the *locus classicus* (though by no means the most careful statement) of the concept of linguistic relativity is the popular articles by Whorf, where the following oft-quoted passages may be found which illustrate all the central themes.

Epistemology

We dissect nature along lines laid down by our native languages. The categories and types that we isolate from the world of phenomena we do not find there because they stare every observer in the face; on the contrary, the world is presented in a kaleidoscopic flux of impressions which has to be organized by our minds—and this means largely by the linguistic systems of our minds.

— (1956:213) ...

Unconscious Thought

[T]he phenomena of language are to its own speakers largely of a background character and so are outside the critical consciousness and control of the speaker.

— (1956:211)

Linguistic Relativity

> The phenomena of language are background phenomena, of which the talkers are unaware or, at most, dimly aware... These automatic, involuntary patterns of language are not the same for all men but are specific for each language and constitute the formalized side of the language, or its "grammar" ...
>
> From this fact proceeds what I have called the "linguistic relativity principle," which means, in informal terms, that users of markedly different grammars are pointed by their grammars toward different types of observations and different evaluations of externally similar acts of observation, and hence are not equivalent as observers, but must arrive at somewhat different views of the world.
>
> — (1956:221)...

The boldness of Whorf's formulation prompted a succession of empirical studies in America in the 1950s and early 1960s aimed at elucidating and testing what now became known as the Sapir–Whorf hypothesis. Anthropological and linguistic studies by Trager, Hoijer, Lee, Casagrande, and others have been well reviewed elsewhere. These studies hardly touched on cognition, but in the same period a few psychologists (notably Lenneberg, Brown, Stefflre) did try to investigate the relation between lexical coding and memory, especially in the domain of color, and found some significant correlations. This line of work culminated, however, in the celebrated demonstration by Berlin & Kay of the language-independent saliency of "basic colors," which was taken as a decisive anti-relativist finding, and effectively terminated this tradition of investigations into the Sapir-Whorf hypothesis. There followed a period in which Whorf's own views in particular became the butt of extensive criticism.

It is clear from this background that the "Sapir-Whorf" hypothesis in its classical form arose from deep historical roots but in a particular intellectual climate. Even though (it has been closely argued by Lucy the original hypothesis has never been thoroughly tested, the intellectual milieu had by the 1960s entirely changed. Instead of empiricism, we now have rationalistic assumptions. Instead of the basic tenets of structuralism, in which each linguistic or social system must be understood first in internal terms before comparison is possible, modern comparative work (especially in linguistics) tends to presume that one can isolate particular aspects or traits of a system (e.g. aspect or subjecthood) for comparison. The justification, such as it is, is that we now have the outlines of a universal structure for language and perhaps cognition, which provides the terms for comparison. It is true that the assumption of unconscious processes continues, but now the emphasis is on the unconscious nature of nearly all systematic information processing, so that the distinctive character of Whorf's habitual thought has been submerged.

In this changed intellectual climate, and in the light of the much greater knowledge that we now have about both language and mental processing, it would be pointless to attempt to revive ideas about linguistic relativity in their original form. Nevertheless, there have been a whole range of recent intellectual shifts that make the ground more fertile for some of the original seeds to grow into new saplings. It is the purpose of this [selection] to explore the implications of some of these shifts in a number of different disciplines for our overall view of the relations between language, thinking, and society.

The Idea Behind the Present [Selection]

This [selection] explores one chain of reasoning that is prompted by these recent changes in ideas. The line of argument runs in the following way.

Linguistic relativity is a theory primarily about the nature of meaning, the classic view focusing on the lexical and grammatical coding of language-specific distinctions. In this theory, two languages may "code" the same state of affairs utilizing semantic concepts or distinctions peculiar to each language; as a result the two linguistic descriptions reflect different construals of the same bit of reality. These semantic distinctions are held to reflect cultural distinctions and at the same time to influence cognitive categorizations, an issue re-examined... below.

Assuming that there is such a link between linguistic structure and conceptual categories, the possibility of conceptual relativity would seem at first sight to depend on whether linguistic codings are significantly different across languages. Very little, however, is actually known about substantive semantic or conceptual universals. It is true that there are demonstrations of universal semantic principles in a few domains like color terminology, ethnobiological taxonomies, perhaps also in systems of kinship terminology. However, these demonstrations carry no necessary general implications, and the same holds for studies of grammatical meaning....

Yet, on further reflection, distinctive linguistic (grammatical or lexical) codings are not the only ways in which "meanings" or interpretations can vary systematically across cultures. This is brought out by recent developments in the theory of meaning. These developments show that "meaning" is not fully encapsulated in lexicon and grammar, which provide only schematic constraints on what the speaker will be taken to have meant in a particular utterance....

A large part of the burden of interpretation is thus shifted from theories of context-free lexical and grammatical meaning to theories of use in context. Some important principles of the use of language may plausibly be argued to be universal.... Yet others seem much more clearly culture-specific. For example, the ethnography of speaking has shown how diverse can be the principles governing the production and interpretation of utterances in specific speech events—court proceedings, formal greetings, religious rituals, councils, and the like....

This [selection] therefore spans a large terrain, from the classic Whorfian issues of the relation of grammar to thought on the one hand to consideration of language use in sociolinguistic perspective on the other. One key idea that supports this span is the notion of indexicality, conceived not just in terms of the contextual dependence of deictic items, but also in the broader Peircean sense, as a broad relationship between interpreters, signals, and the context of interpretation. Indexicality necessarily anchors meaning and interpretation to the context of language use and thus to wider social organization. Issues of linguistic relativity are in this way directly related to the variable cultural structuring of contexts....

Introduction to Part I...

The Very Idea: Causal Links Between Language and Thinking

Might the language we speak affect the way we think? Generations of thinkers have been intrigued by this idea. Aarsleff summarized Humboldt's influential views thus: "Humboldt's entire view of the nature of language is founded on the conviction that thinking and speaking, thought and language form so close a union that we must think of them as being identical, in spite of the fact that we can separate them artificially. Owing to this identity, access to one of the two will open nearly equal access to the other."

Whorf, as we saw [earlier], brought to the idea a new and heady mix of an empiricist epistemology, an insistence on the underlying systematicity of language as a structured semantical system, and an emphasis on the unconscious influence of language on habitual thought....

The phrase "linguistic determinism" has come to stand for these views that there is a causal influence from linguistic patterning to cognition. Despite phrases like "linguistic conditioning," "linguistic legislation," "inexorable control," etc., Whorf's own considered position seems to have been that language influences unconscious habitual thought, rather than limiting thought potential. Thus the phrase "linguistic determinism" should be understood to imply that there is *at least some* causal influence from language categories to non-verbal cognition; it was not intended to denote an exclusive causal vector in one direction—probably no proponent has held the view that what cannot be said cannot be thought.

The idea that language could determine (however weakly) the nature of our thinking nowadays carries more than a faint whiff of anachronism; rather it seems to belong to an altogether different age, prior to the serious study of mind as an information processing device. That device, in the predominant metaphor of our time, is instantiated in "wetware," whose properties are in turn dictated by the genetic code of the species. Although those properties are only dimly understood, still it is generally presumed, as Fodor has influentially put it, that the mind is "modular," composed of subsystems specialized to the automatic unconscious processing of particular kinds of information, visual, auditory, haptic, and so on. Since we can, for example, talk about what we see, the output of these specialized systems must, it seems, be available to some central information processing system, where "thinking," in the sense of ratiocination and deliberation, occurs. This picture (a close analogy of course to the computers of the day) of a single generalized central processor with specialized input/output devices is beginning to give way to a more complex version: each specialized input/output device is itself a system of modules, while "central processes" may themselves be differentiated into different "languages of thought" (propositional, imagistic, and so on)…. Nevertheless the essentials of the Fodorean view are very generally held.

Thus, on this widespread view, we can expect thinking in all essentials to have universal properties, to be couched in an inner language structurally the same for all members of the species, and to be quite unrelated to the facts of linguistic diversity. The tenor of the anti-Whorfian assumptions can be gauged from the following quotations: "For the vocabulary of the language, in and of its self, to be a moulder of thought, lexical dissections and categorizations of nature would have to be almost accidentally formed, rather as though some Johnny Appleseed had scattered named categories capriciously over the earth"; "Whorf's hypothesis [of linguistic determinism] has engendered much confusion, and many circular arguments. Its converse often seems more plausible" and "there is no evidence for the strong version of the hypothesis—that language imposes upon its speakers a particular way of thinking about the world"; "The discussions that assume that language determines thought carry on only by a collective suspension of disbelief."

In short, many authors find the thesis of linguistic determinism wildly adventurous or even ridiculous. On the other hand, others have recently claimed to find it sober and plausible. It is therefore useful to attempt to clarify the issues by dissecting the relativity hypothesis into its component parts, and in particular by isolating the "determinism" hypothesis from other linked ideas. Clearly, the hypothesis of linguistic relativity relies on the presumption of linguistic difference. Thus the discovery of universals may have a bearing on that hypothesis. But the hypothesis that linguistic categories might determine aspects of non-linguistic thinking is quite independent of facts about linguistic difference. Let us therefore spell out the nexus of interlinked hypotheses (where the numbers *[1]* and *[2]* refer to the premises and the number *[3]* to an implied conclusion).

[1] Linguistic Difference

Languages differ substantially in their semantic structure: both the intensions (the senses) and extensions (the denotations) of lexical and morpho-syntactic categories may differ across languages (and may do so independently).

[2] Linguistic Determinism

Linguistic categorizations, implicit or explicit, may determine or codetermine or influence aspects of non-linguistic categorization, memory, perception or thinking in general.

This is often said to have a "strong" and a "weak" form: under the strong claim, linguistically uncoded concepts would be unattainable; under the weak form, concepts which happen to be linguistically coded would be facilitated or favored (e.g. would be more accessible, easier to remember, or the default coding for non-linguistic cognition).

❧◈❧

The mechanisms whereby semantic distinctions may have an influence on cognition can be left open; a prior task is to show that there is indeed some correlation. Whorf himself of course held the view that the unconscious "compulsive patterning" of grammatical oppositions would play a special role in habitual unreflective patterns of thought.

Linguistic Relativity

Given that:

(1) differences exist in linguistic categories across languages;
(2) linguistic categories determine aspects of individuals' thinking;
    then:
(3) aspects of individuals' thinking differ across linguistic communities according to the language they speak.

Note that the conclusion here will hold even under the weakest versions of (1) and (2). Thus if there is *at least some* aspect of semantic structure that is not universal, *and at least some* cognitive effect of such distinctive semantic properties, then there must be *at least some* systematic cognitive variation in line with linguistic difference. That would seem... to be as trivially true as the strongest version of linguistic relativity (that one's semantic inventory of concepts provides one's total vocabulary of thoughts) is trivially false. Thus the central problem is to illuminate the degrees of language difference, and the ways in which semantics and cognitive categories and processes interact.

Now notice that modern views complicate this picture by apparently subscribing to various aspects of these propositions while robustly denying the conclusion in the syllogism above. For example, a common modern stance is:

(1') languages differ in semantic structure, but only at a molecular level—at an atomic level, the conceptual "atoms" (e.g. "male," "adult," etc.) are identical, and are merely assembled into some culture-specific notion like "uncle";
(2') "determinism" between semantic categories and conceptual categories is in a sense trivially complete, since they are one and the same—the meanings of words are expressed in a "language" that is identical to the "language of thought." ...

Thus although the identity of linguistic and conceptual categories in (2') alone might be thought to entail linguistic relativity, it is in fact usually associated with some claim (often implicit) like that in (1'), allowing subscribers to presume that the "language of thought" (alias: system of semantic representations) is universal. Then the conclusion in (3) no longer follows. In schematic form we may now oppose the two views thus:

The Whorfian Syllogism

(1) Different languages utilize different semantic representation systems which are informationally non-equivalent (at least in the sense that they employ different lexical concepts);

(2) semantic representations determine aspects of conceptual representations;

> *therefore*

(3) users of different languages utilize different conceptual representations.

The Anti-Whorfian Syllogism

(1′) Different languages utilize the same semantic representation system (if not at the molecular then at least at the atomic level of semantic primes);

(2′) universal conceptual representations determine semantic systems, indeed THE semantic representation system just is identical to THE propositional conceptual system (the innate "language of thought");

> *therefore*

(3′) users of different languages utilize the identical conceptual representation system.

Despite the fact that the doctrines appear diametrically opposed, they are nevertheless, on suitable interpretations, *entirely compatible*, as long as one subscribes to the distinction between atomic and molecular levels of semantic representation. Then, on an atomic level, semantic representations, and their corresponding conceptual representations, are drawn from a universal language of thought, while on the molecular level there are language-specific combinations of universal atomic primitives, which make up lexical meanings (and meanings associated with morpho-syntactic distinctions) and which may have specific conceptual effects.

Most semantic analysts in practice work with an assumption of such "semantic decomposition" of linguistic expressions. But it is worth pointing out that there are in fact fundamental problems with that assumption which have long been recognized, and some of those who subscribe enthusiastically to (2′) might lose some of their enthusiasm if they realized that without (1′), (2′) implies the strongest version of linguistic relativity.

Let us take stock. Proposition (1) is evidently true, in the sense that languages clearly employ distinct lexical meanings. (1′) may or may not be tenable, but is in fact compatible with (1). Likewise (2) and (2′) are compatible if we make a distinction between atomic and molecular concepts: the inventory of concepts in the language of thought could determine the range of possible lexical concepts, but such lexical concepts once selected could in turn determine the concepts we employ when solving non-linguistic problems. (3) would be the conclusion from (1) and (2). All thus hinges on (2). Is it even remotely plausible?

Although the thesis of linguistic determinism seems at first sight to have an anachronistic flavor, it can easily be brought to bear on modern theorizing in a way that makes it look anything but silly. First, note that there is considerable psychological evidence that our working memory is restricted to about half a dozen chunks of information, but is indifferent to the underlying complexity of those chunks. Thus mental operations are facilitated by grouping elementary concepts into larger chunks. And this is just what lexical items do for us. Thus there is every reason to think that such chunks might play an important role in our thinking....

Within such a framework, it is quite easy to show that in certain respects and for certain phenomena linguistic determinism *beyond* thinking-for-speaking is not only plausible, but must be correct. The reasoning can be exemplified as follows. Consider a language that has no words for *'in front,'* *'behind,'* *'left,'* *'right,'* and so on, preferring instead to designate all such relations, however microscopic in scale, in terms of notions like 'North,' 'South,' 'East,' 'West,' etc. Now a speaker of such a language cannot remember arrays of objects in the same way as you or I, in terms of their relative location from a particular viewing angle. If I think of the visual array currently in front of me, I think of it as, say, "boy in front of tree, dog to left of tree." Later I can so describe it. But that will not do for the speaker of the language with 'North'/ 'South'/'East'/'West' notions: remembering the array in terms of notions like 'front' and 'left' will not allow him to reconstruct the cardinal directions. So if he remembers it that way, he will not be able to describe it later; while if he remembers the array in a way congruent with the linguistic coding (in terms of 'North' and 'East', etc.), then he will be able to code it linguistically. So it seems *prima facie* quite clear that the speaker of such a language and I simply MUST code our experiences differently for memory in order to speak our different languages. In short, thinking in a special way for speaking will not be enough: we must mentally encode experiences in such a way that we can describe them later, in the terms required by our language.

There are in fact just such languages that require the use of cardinal directions. Furthermore, this *prima facie* argument about the cognitive consequences of speaking such different languages can be backed up by empirical investigation: it turns out that in non-linguistic tasks speakers of languages that use 'North'/'South'/'East'/'West' systems instead of 'front'/'back'/'left'/'right' systems do indeed remember spatial arrays differently, in ways that can be demonstrated experimentally and observationally.

Is this a peculiar case? One needs to think afresh to assess the possibilities. From the perspective of speech production, there are three different kinds of ways in which a particular language might determine how we think. First, the grammatical or lexical categories may force a specific way of thinking at the time of speaking (the "regimentation" of thoughts described above). Second, such thinking-for-speaking may itself require the coding of situations in specific forms at the time that they are experienced. This is clearly so in the North/South/East/West case above. It is also clearly so in many other cases: for example, obligatory coding of number in languages with plural marking will require noticing for all possible referents whether or not they are singletons—some languages without plural marking will let one say in effect "I saw bird on the lawn," but in English I must say either a *bird* or *birds* and must therefore have remembered how many relevant birds there were; or in systems of honorifics based on relative age, I must have ascertained before speaking whether the referent is senior or junior to me; or in systems of aspect requiring distinctions between perfective and imperfective, I must attend to the exact nature of event-overlap. These are language-specific distinctions that seem to require noticing special properties of the world so that one is ready to encode them linguistically should the need arise. Such examples suggest that those theorists who reluctantly subscribe to a relativity in thinking-for-speaking, will have also to subscribe to a consequent relativity in thinking at the time at which events are experienced. Thirdly, one may also go on to consider the consequences, or after-effects, of thinking-for-speaking in a particular way. There may for example be memory effects: it may be easier to remember aspects of events that have been coded for speaking during prior verbalization (hence we may indulge in speaking-for-thinking). Since some languages will enforce particular codings (e.g. in systems of aspect, honorifics, number-marking, etc.), they may ensure that their speakers recall certain features of situations better than others.

NO

Steven Pinker

Mentalese

Is thought dependent on words? Do people literally think in English, Chero-kee, [or] Kivunjo...? Or are our thoughts couched in some silent medium of the brain—a language of thought, or "mentalese"—and merely clothed in words whenever we need to communicate them to a listener? No question could be more central to understanding the language instinct.

In much of our social and political discourse, people simply assume that words determine thoughts. Inspired by [George] Orwell's essay "Politics and the English Language," pundits accuse governments of manipulating our minds with euphemisms like *pacification* (bombing), *revenue enhancement* (taxes), and *nonretention* (firing). Philosophers argue that since animals lack language, they must also lack consciousness—[Ludwig] Wittgenstein wrote, "A dog could not have the thought 'perhaps it will rain tomorrow'"—and therefore they do not possess the rights of conscious beings. Some feminists blame sexist thinking on sexist language, like the use of *he* to refer to a generic person. Inevitably, reform movements have sprung up. Many replacements for *he* have been suggested over the years, including *E, hesh, po, tey, co, jhe, ve, xe, he'er, thon,* and *na.* The most extreme of these movements is General Semantics, begun in 1933 by the engineer Count Alfred Korzybski and popularized in long-time best-sellers by his disciples Stuart Chase and S. I. Hayakawa. (This is the same Hayakawa who later achieved notoriety as the protest-defying college president and snoozing U.S. senator.) General Semantics lays the blame for human folly on insidious "semantic damage" to thought perpetrated by the structure of language. Keep-ing a forty-year-old in prison for a theft he committed as a teenager assumes that the forty-year-old John and the eighteen-year-old John are "the same per-son," a cruel logical error that would be avoided if we referred to them not as *John* but as $John_{1972}$ and $John_{1994}$, respectively. The verb *to be* is a particu-lar source of illogic, because it identifies individuals with abstractions, as in *Mary is a woman,* and licenses evasions of responsibility, like Ronald Reagan's famous nonconfession *Mistakes were made.* One faction seeks to eradicate the verb altogether.

And supposedly there is a scientific basis for these assumptions: the fa-mous Sapir-Whorf hypothesis of linguistic determinism, stating that people's thoughts are determined by the categories made available by their language,

From Steven Pinker, *The Language Instinct: How the Mind Creates Language* (Perennial Classics, 2000). Copyright © 1994 by Steven Pinker. Reprinted by permission of HarperCollins Publishers, Inc.

and its weaker version, linguistic relativity, stating that differences among languages cause differences in the thoughts of their speakers. People who remember little else from their college education can rattle off the factoids: the languages that carve the spectrum into color words at different places, the fundamentally different Hopi concept of time, the dozens of Eskimo words for snow. The implication is heavy: the foundational categories of reality are not "in" the world but are imposed by one's culture (and hence can be challenged, perhaps accounting for the perennial appeal of the hypothesis to undergraduate sensibilities).

But it is wrong, all wrong. The idea that thought is the same thing as language is an example of what can be called a conventional absurdity: a statement that goes against all common sense but that everyone believes because they dimly recall having heard it somewhere and because it is so pregnant with implications. (The "fact" that we use only five percent of our brains, that lemmings commit mass suicide, that the *Boy Scout Manual* annually outsells all other books, and that we can be coerced into buying by subliminal messages are other examples.) Think about it. We have all had the experience of uttering or writing a sentence, then stopping and realizing that it wasn't exactly what we meant to say. To have that feeling, there has to be a "what we meant to say" that is different from what we said. Sometimes it is not easy to find *any* words that properly convey a thought. When we hear or read, we usually remember the gist, not the exact words, so there has to be such a thing as a gist that is not the same as a bunch of words. And if thoughts depended on words, how could a new word ever be coined? How could a child learn a word to begin with? How could translation from one language to another be possible?

The discussions that assume that language determines thought carry on only by a collective suspension of disbelief....

As we shall see in this [selection], there is no scientific evidence that languages dramatically shape their speakers' ways of thinking. But I want to do more than review the unintentionally comical history of attempts to prove that they do. The idea that language shapes thinking seemed plausible when scientists were in the dark about how thinking works or even how to study it. Now that cognitive scientists know how to think about thinking, there is less of a temptation to equate it with language just because words are more palpable than thoughts. By understanding *why* linguistic determinism is wrong, we will be in a better position to understand how language itself works....

The linguistic determinism hypothesis is closely linked to the names Edward Sapir and Benjamin Lee Whorf. Sapir, a brilliant linguist, was a student of the anthropologist Franz Boas. Boas and his students (who also include Ruth Benedict and Margaret Mead) were important intellectual figures in this century, because they argued that nonindustrial peoples were not primitive savages but had systems of language, knowledge, and culture as complex and valid in their world view as our own. In his study of Native American languages Sapir noted that speakers of different languages have to pay attention to different aspects of reality simply to put words together into grammatical sentences. For example, when English speakers decide whether or not to put -*ed* onto the end of a verb, they must pay attention to tense, the relative time of occurrence of the event they are referring to and the moment of speaking. Wintu speakers need not bother with tense, but when they decide which suffix to put on their verbs, they must pay attention to whether the knowledge they are conveying was learned through direct observation or by hearsay.

Sapir's interesting observation was soon taken much farther. Whorf was an inspector for the Hartford Fire Insurance Company and an amateur scholar of Native American languages, which led him to take courses from Sapir at Yale. In a much-quoted passage, he wrote:

> We dissect nature along lines laid down by our native languages. The categories and types that we isolate from the world of phenomena we do not find there because they stare every observer in the face; on the contrary, the world is presented in a kaleidoscopic flux of impressions which has to be organized by our minds—and this means largely by the linguistic systems in our minds. We cut nature up, organize it into concepts, and ascribe significances as we do, largely because we are parties to an agreement to organize it in this way—an agreement that holds throughout our speech community and is codified in the patterns of our language. The agreement is, of course, an implicit and unstated one, *but its terms are absolutely obligatory*; we cannot talk at all except by subscribing to the organization and classification of data which the agreement decrees.

What led Whorf to this radical position? He wrote that the idea first occurred to him in his work as a fire prevention engineer when he was struck by how language led workers to misconstrue dangerous situations. For example, one worker caused a serious explosion by tossing a cigarette into an "empty" drum that in fact was full of gasoline vapor. Another lit a blowtorch near a "pool of water" that was really a basin of decomposing tannery waste, which, far from being "watery," was releasing inflammable gases. Whorf's studies of American languages strengthened his conviction. For example, in Apache, *It is a dripping spring* must be expressed "As water, or springs, whiteness moves downward." "How utterly unlike our way of thinking!" he wrote.

But the more you examine Whorf's arguments, the less sense they make. Take the story about the worker and the "empty" drum. The seeds of disaster supposedly lay in the semantics of *empty*, which, Whorf claimed, means both "without its usual contents" and "null and void, empty, inert." The hapless worker, his conception of reality molded by his linguistic categories, did not distinguish between the "drained" and "inert" senses, hence, flick... boom! But wait. Gasoline vapor is invisible. A drum with nothing but vapor in it looks just like a drum with nothing in it at all. Surely this walking catastrophe was fooled by his eyes, not by the English language.

The example of whiteness moving downward is supposed to show that the Apache mind does not cut up events into distinct objects and actions. Whorf presented many such examples from Native American languages. The Apache equivalent of *The boat is grounded on the beach* is "It is on the beach pointwise as an event of canoe motion." *He invites people to a feast* becomes "He, or somebody, goes for eaters of cooked food." *He cleans a gun with a ramrod* is translated as "He directs a hollow moving dry spot by movement of tool." All this, to be sure, is utterly unlike our way of talking. But do we know that it is utterly unlike our way of thinking?

As soon as Whorf's articles appeared, the psycholinguists Eric Lenneberg and Roger Brown pointed out two non sequiturs in his argument. First, Whorf did not actually study any Apaches; it is not clear that he ever met one. His assertions about Apache psychology are based entirely on Apache grammar—making his argument circular. Apaches speak differently, so they must think differently. How do we know that they think differently? Just listen to the way they speak.

Second, Whorf rendered the sentences as clumsy, word-for-word translations, designed to make the literal meanings seem as odd as possible. But looking at the actual glosses that Whorf provided, I could, with equal grammatical justification, render the first sentence as the mundane "Clear stuff—water— is falling." Turning the tables, I could take the English sentence "He walks" and render it "As solitary masculinity, leggedness proceeds." Brown illustrates how strange the German mind must be, according to Whorf's logic, by reproducing Mark Twain's own translation of a speech he delivered in flawless German to the Vienna Press Club:

> I am indeed the truest friend of the German language—and not only now, but from long since—yes, before twenty years already.... I would only some changes effect. I would only the language method—the luxurious, elaborate construction compress, the eternal parenthesis suppress, do away with, annihilate; the introduction of more than thirteen subjects in one sentence forbid; the verb so far to the front pull that one it without a telescope discover can. With one word, my gentlemen, I would your beloved language simplify so that, my gentlemen, when you her for prayer need, One her yonder-up understands.
>
> ... I might gladly the separable verb also a little bit reform. I might none do let what Schiller did: he has the whole history of the Thirty Years' War between the two members of a separate verb inpushed. That has even Germany itself aroused, and one has Schiller the permission refused the History of the Hundred Years' War to compose—God be it thanked! After all these reforms established be will, will the German language the noblest and the prettiest on the world be.

Among Whorf's "kaleidoscopic flux of impressions," color is surely the most eye-catching. He noted that we see objects in different hues, depending on the wavelengths of the light they reflect, but that physicists tell us that wavelength is a continuous dimension with nothing delineating red, yellow, green, blue, and so on. Languages differ in their inventory of color words: Latin lacks generic "gray" and "brown"; Navajo collapses blue and green into one word; Russian has distinct words for dark blue and sky blue; Shona speakers use one word for the yellower greens and the greener yellows, and a different one for the bluer greens and the nonpurplish blues. You can fill in the rest of the argument. It is language that puts the frets in the spectrum; Julius Caesar would not know shale from Shinola.

But although physicists see no basis for color boundaries, physiologists do. Eyes do not register wavelength the way a thermometer registers temperature. They contain three kinds of cones, each with a different pigment, and the cones are wired to neurons in a way that makes the neurons respond best to red patches against a green background or vice versa, blue against yellow, black against white. No matter how influential language might be, it would seem preposterous to a physiologist that it could reach down into the retina and rewire the ganglion cells.

Indeed, humans the world over (and babies and monkeys, for that matter) color their perceptual worlds using the same palette, and this constrains the vocabularies they develop. Although languages may disagree about the wrappers in the sixty-four crayon box—the burnt umbers, the turquoises, the fuchsias— they agree much more on the wrappers in the eight-crayon box—the fire-engine reds, grass greens, lemon yellows. Speakers of different languages unanimously pick these shades as the best examples of their color words, as long as the language has a color word in that general part of the spectrum. And where languages do differ in their color words, they differ predictably, not according to the idiosyncratic taste of some word-coiner. Languages are organized a bit like the Crayola product line, the fancier ones adding colors to the more basic ones. If a language has only two color words, they are for black and white (usually encompassing dark and light, respectively). If it has three, they are for black, white, and red; if four, black, white, red, and either yellow or green. Five adds in both yellow and green; six, blue; seven, brown; more than seven, purple, pink, orange, or gray. But the clinching experiment was carried out in the New Guinea highlands with the Grand Valley Dani, a people speaking one of the black-and-white languages. The psychologist Eleanor Rosch found that the Dani were quicker at learning a new color category that was based on fire-engine red than a category based on an off-red. The way we see colors determines how we learn words for them, not vice versa.

The fundamentally different Hopi concept of time is one of the more startling claims about how minds can vary. Whorf wrote that the Hopi language contains "no words, grammatical forms, constructions, or expressions that refer directly to what we call 'time,' or to past, or future, or to enduring or lasting." He suggested, too, that the Hopi had "no general notion or intuition of TIME as a smooth flowing continuum in which everything in the universe proceeds at an equal rate, out of a future, through a present, into a past." According to Whorf, they did not conceptualize events as being like points, or lengths of time like days as countable things. Rather, they seemed to focus on change and process itself, and on psychological distinctions between presently known, mythical, and conjecturally distant. The Hopi also had little interest in "exact sequences, dating, calendars, chronology."

What, then, are we to make of the following sentence translated from Hopi?

Then indeed, the following day, quite early in the morning at the hour when people pray to the sun, around that time then he woke up the girl again.

Perhaps the Hopi are not as oblivious to time as Whorf made them out to be. In his extensive study of the Hopi, the anthropologist Ekkehart Malotki, who reported this sentence, also showed that Hopi speech contains tense, metaphors for time, units of time (including days, numbers of days, parts of the day, yesterday and tomorrow, days of the week, weeks, months, lunar phases, seasons, and the year), ways to quantify units of time, and words like "ancient," "quick," "long time," and "finished." Their culture keeps records with sophisticated methods of dating, including a horizon-based sun calendar, exact ceremonial day sequences, knotted calendar strings, notched calendar sticks, and several devices for timekeeping using the principle of the sundial. No one is really sure how Whorf came up with his outlandish claims, but his limited, badly analyzed sample of Hopi speech and his long-time leanings toward mysticism must have contributed.

Speaking of anthropological canards, no discussion of language and thought would be complete without the Great Eskimo Vocabulary Hoax. Contrary to popular belief, the Eskimos do not have more words for snow than do speakers of English. They do not have four hundred words for snow, as it has been claimed in print, or two hundred, or one hundred, or forty-eight, or even nine. One dictionary puts the figure at two. Counting generously, experts can come up with about a dozen, but by such standards English would not be far behind, with *snow, sleet, slush, blizzard, avalanche, hail, hardpack, powder, flurry, dusting,* and a coinage of Boston's WBZ-TV meteorologist Bruce Schwoegler, *snizzling.*

Where did the myth come from? Not from anyone who has actually studied the Yupik and Inuit-Inupiaq families of polysynthetic languages spoken from Siberia to Greenland. The anthropologist Laura Martin has documented how the story grew like an urban legend, exaggerated with each retelling. In 1911 Boas casually mentioned that Eskimos used four unrelated word roots for snow. Whorf embellished the count to seven and implied that there were more. His article was widely reprinted, then cited in textbooks and popular books on language, which led to successively inflated estimates in other textbooks, articles, and newspaper columns of Amazing Facts.

The linguist Geoffrey Pullum, who popularized Martin's article in his essay "The Great Eskimo Vocabulary Hoax," speculates about why the story got so out of control: "The alleged lexical extravagance of the Eskimos comports so well with the many other facets of their polysynthetic perversity: rubbing noses; lending their wives to strangers; eating raw seal blubber; throwing Grandma out to be eaten by polar bears." It is an ironic twist. Linguistic relativity came out of the Boas school, as part of a campaign to show that nonliterate cultures were as complex and sophisticated as European ones. But the supposedly mind-broadening anecdotes owe their appeal to a patronizing willingness to treat other cultures' psychologies as weird and exotic compared to our own. As Pullum notes,

> Among the many depressing things about this credulous transmission and elaboration of a false claim is that even if there *were* a large number of roots for different snow types in some Arctic language, this would *not*, objectively, be intellectually interesting; it would be a most mundane and

unremarkable fact. Horsebreeders have various names for breeds, sizes, and ages of horses; botanists have names for leaf shapes; interior decorators have names for shades of mauve; printers have many different names for fonts (Carlson, Garamond, Helvetica, Times Roman, and so on), naturally enough.... Would anyone think of writing about printers the same kind of slop we find written about Eskimos in bad linguistics textbooks? Take [the following] random textbook..., with its earnest assertion "It is quite obvious that in the culture of the Eskimos... snow is of great enough importance to split up the conceptual sphere that corresponds to one word and one thought in English into several distinct classes..." Imagine reading: "It is quite obvious that in the culture of printers... fonts are of great enough importance to split up the conceptual sphere that corresponds to one word and one thought among non-printers into several distinct classes..." Utterly boring, even if true. Only the link to those legendary, promiscuous, blubber-gnawing hunters of the ice-packs could permit something this trite to be presented to us for contemplation.

If the anthropological anecdotes are bunk, what about controlled studies? The thirty-five years of research from the psychology laboratory is distinguished by how little it has shown. Most of the experiments have tested banal "weak" versions of the Whorfian hypothesis, namely that words can have some effect on memory or categorization. Some of these experiments have actually worked, but that is hardly surprising. In a typical experiment, subjects have to commit paint chips to memory and are tested with a multiple-choice procedure. In some of these studies, the subjects show slightly better memory for colors that have readily available names in their language. But even colors without names are remembered fairly well, so the experiment does not show that the colors are remembered by verbal labels alone. All it shows is that subjects remembered the chips in two forms, a nonverbal visual image and a verbal label, presumably because two kinds of memory, each one fallible, are better than one. In another type of experiment subjects have to say which two out of three color chips go together; they often put the ones together that have the same name in their language. Again, no surprise. I can imagine the subjects thinking to themselves, "Now how on earth does this guy expect me to pick two chips to put together? He didn't give me any hints, and they're all pretty similar. Well, I'd probably call those two 'green' and that one 'blue,' and that seems as good a reason to put them together as any." In these experiments, language is, technically speaking, influencing a form of thought in some way, but so what? It is hardly an example of incommensurable world views, or of concepts that are nameless and therefore unimaginable, or of dissecting nature along lines laid down by our native languages according to terms that are absolutely obligatory...

✿

People can be forgiven for overrating language. Words make noise, or sit on a page, for all to hear and see. Thoughts are trapped inside the head of the thinker. To know what someone else is thinking, or to talk to each other about the nature of thinking, we have to use—what else, words! It is no wonder that many commentators have trouble even conceiving of thought without words— or is it that they just don't have the language to talk about it?

As a cognitive scientist I can afford to be smug about common sense being true (thought is different from language) and linguistic determinism being a conventional absurdity. For two sets of tools now make it easier to think clearly about the whole problem. One is a body of experimental studies that break the word barrier and assess many kinds of nonverbal thought. The other is a theory of how thinking might work that formulates the questions in a satisfyingly precise way....

Now we are in a position to pose the Whorfian question in a precise way. Remember that a representation does not have to look like English or any other language; it just has to use symbols to represent concepts, and arrangements of symbols to represent the logical relations among them, according to some consistent scheme. But though internal representations in an English speaker's mind don't *have* to look like English, they *could*, in principle, look like English— or like whatever language the person happens to speak. So here is the question: Do they in fact? For example, if we know that Socrates is a man, is it because we have neural patterns that correspond one-to-one to the English words *Socrates, is, a,* and *man,* and groups of neurons in the brain that correspond to the subject of an English sentence, the verb, and the object, laid out in that order? Or do we use some other code for representing concepts and their relations in our heads, a language of thought or mentalese that is not the same as any of the world's languages? We can answer this question by seeing whether English sentences embody the information that a processor would need to perform valid sequences of reasoning—without requiring any fully intelligent homunculus inside doing the "understanding."

The answer is a clear no. English (or any other language people speak) is hopelessly unsuited to serve as our internal medium of computation. Consider some of the problems.

The first is ambiguity. These headlines actually appeared in newspapers:

- Child's Stool Great for Use in Garden
- Stud Tires Out
- Stiff Opposition Expected to Casketless Funeral Plan
- Drunk Gets Nine Months in Violin Case
- Iraqi Head Seeks Arms...

Each headline contains a word that is ambiguous. But surely the thought underlying the word is *not* ambiguous; the writers of the headlines surely knew which of the two senses of the words *stool, stud,* and *stiff* they themselves had in mind. And if there can be two thoughts corresponding to one word, thoughts can't be words.

The second problem with English is its lack of logical explicitness. Consider the following example, devised by the computer scientist Drew McDermott:

> Ralph is an elephant.
> Elephants live in Africa.
> Elephants have tusks.

Our inference-making device, with some minor modifications to handle the English grammar of the sentences, would deduce "Ralph lives in Africa" and "Ralph has tusks." This sounds fine but isn't. Intelligent you, the reader, knows that the Africa that Ralph lives in is the same Africa that all the other elephants live in, but that Ralph's tusks are his own. . . .

A third problem is called "co-reference." Say you start talking about an individual by referring to him as *the tall blond man with one black shoe*. The second time you refer to him in the conversation you are likely to call him *the man*; the third time, just *him*. But the three expressions do not refer to three people or even to three ways of thinking about a single person; the second and third are just ways of saving breath. Something in the brain must treat them as the same thing, English isn't doing it.

A fourth, related problem comes from those aspects of language that can only be interpreted in the context of a conversation or text—what linguists call "deixis." Consider articles like *a* and *the*. What is the difference between *killed a policeman* and *killed the policeman*? Only that in the second sentence, it is assumed that some specific policeman was mentioned earlier or is salient in the context. Thus in isolation the two phrases are synonymous, but in the following contexts (the first from an actual newspaper article) their meanings are completely different:

- A policeman's 14-year-old son, apparently enraged after being disciplined for a bad grade, opened fire from his house, *killing a policeman* and wounding three people before he was shot dead.
- A policeman's 14-year-old son, apparently enraged after being disciplined for a bad grade, opened fire from his house, *killing the policeman* and wounding three people before he was shot dead.

Outside of a particular conversation or text, then, the words *a* and *the* are quite meaningless. They have no place in one's permanent mental database. Other conversation-specific words like *here, there, this, that, now, then, I, me, my, here, we,* and *you* pose the same problems, as the following old joke illustrates:

First guy: I didn't sleep with my wife before we were married, did you?

Second guy: I don't know. What was her maiden name? . . .

These examples (and there are many more) illustrate a single important point. The representations underlying thinking, on the one hand, and the sentences in a language, on the other, are in many ways at cross-purposes. Any particular thought in our head embraces a vast amount of information. But when it comes to communicating a thought to someone else, attention spans are short and mouths are slow. To get information into a listener's head in a reasonable amount of time, a speaker can encode only a fraction of the message into words and must count on the listener to fill in the rest. But *inside a single head*, the demands are different. Air time is not a limited resource: different parts of the brain are connected to one another directly with thick cables that can transfer huge amounts of information quickly. Nothing can be left to the imagination, though, because the internal representations *are* the imagination.

We end up with the following picture. People do not think in English or Chinese or Apache; they think in a language of thought. This language of thought probably looks a bit like all these languages; presumably it has symbols for concepts, and arrangements of symbols that correspond to who did what to whom.... But compared with any given language, mentalese must be richer in some ways and simpler in others. It must be richer, for example, in that several concept symbols must correspond to a given English word like *stool* or *stud*. There must be extra paraphernalia that differentiate logically distinct kinds of concepts, like Ralph's tusks versus tusks in general, and that link different symbols that refer to the same thing, like *the tall blond man with one black shoe* and *the man*. On the other hand, mentalese must be simpler than spoken languages; conversation-specific words and constructions (like *a* and *the*) are absent, and information about pronouncing words, or even ordering them, is unnecessary. Now, it could be that English speakers think in some kind of simplified and annotated quasi-English, with the design I have just described, and that Apache speakers think in a simplified and annotated quasi-Apache. But to get these languages of thought to subserve reasoning properly, they would have to look much more like each other than either one does to its spoken counterpart, and it is likely that they are the same: a universal mentalese.

Knowing a language, then, is knowing how to translate mentalese into strings of words and vice versa. People without a language would still have mentalese, and babies and many nonhuman animals presumably have simpler dialects. Indeed, if babies did not have a mentalese to translate to and from English, it is not clear how learning English could take place, or even what learning English would mean.

POSTSCRIPT

Does Language Determine
How We Think?

In many respects the two positions on linguistic relativity differ largely on whether they accept the "strong" version of Sapir-Whorf or the more widely held "weaker" version in which language provides people with the concepts with which they can view the world. It is not clear that anyone, including Whorf, ever accepted the most deterministic position that has often been attributed to him. Sapir's writings on the subject are ambiguous but have generally been interpreted as a weaker formulation. Pinker and other critics from neuropsychology typically frame the question in its strongest and most deterministic reading. See Paul Kay and Willett Kempton's 1984 article "What Is the Sapir-Whorf Hypothesis?" *American Anthropologist* (vol. 86) for a similar view by anthropologists. Cognitive psychologist Jerry A. Fodor takes a similar point of view in *The Language of Thought* (Harvard University Press, 1975). Such differences in approach raise the question of whether or not these two groups of scholars are actually talking past one another. Since the strong version of the hypothesis is rarely accepted, would it not be more productive to explore the limits of the weaker version?

In mainstream anthropology the relativity question has often been framed in terms of language's effect on a people's worldview, which is another version of the weak hypothesis. See, for example, Jane Hill and Bruce Mannheim's "Language and World View," *Reviews in Anthropology* (vol. 21, 1992). Two books by linguists suggest ways in which the weak version of linguistic relativity can help us understand the relationship between language and culture even in our own language: George Lakoff's *Women, Fire and Dangerous Things* (University of Chicago Press, 1987) and George Lakoff and Mark Johnson's *The Metaphors We Live By* (University of Chicago Press, 1980).

The most important early statements by Whorf are to be found in a volume of his papers from the 1930s, collected in 1956 by John B. Carroll in *Language, Thought, and Reality: Selected Writings* (Technology Press). For a more recent and detailed survey of anthropological approaches to the Sapir-Whorf hypothesis, see John A. Lucy's review article, "Linguistic Relativity," *Reviews in Anthropology* (vol. 26, 1997).

ISSUE 6

Are San Hunter-Gatherers Basically Pastoralists Who Have Lost Their Herds?

YES: James R. Denbow and Edwin N. Wilmsen, from "Advent and Course of Pastoralism in the Kalahari," *Science* (December 19, 1986)

NO: Richard B. Lee, from *The Dobe Ju/'hoansi*, 3rd ed. (Wadsworth, 2003)

ISSUE SUMMARY

YES: Archaeologists James R. Denbow and Edwin N. Wilmsen argue that the San of the Kalahari Desert in southern Africa have been involved in pastoralism, agriculture, and regional trade networks since at least A.D. 800. They imply that the San, who were hunting and gathering in the twentieth century, were descendants of pastoralists who lost their herds due to subjugation by outsiders, drought, and livestock disease.

NO: Cultural anthropologist Richard B. Lee counters that evidence from oral history, archaeology, and ethnohistory shows that the Ju/'hoansi group of San living in the isolated Nyae Nyae-Dobe area of the Kalahari Desert were autonomous hunter-gatherers until the twentieth century. Although they carried on some trade with outsiders before then, it had minimal impact on their culture.

Can hunter-gatherers (also called "foragers") be economically self-sufficient and politically autonomous even when in contact with more powerful food-producing peoples? This is the basic question behind the "Great Kalahari Debate," which is illustrated by the following selections.

Even in the late nineteenth century, hunting-and-gathering peoples living outside the disruptive influence of complex societies and colonialism were scarce. By then most Native American hunter-gatherers were on reservations or incorporated into the fur trade, and others, like the Veddas of Sri Lanka, had been absorbed and transformed by the dominant societies that surrounded them. The most striking exception was the Australian Aborigines, who were still nomadic hunter-gatherers using stone tools at the time of European contact.

Aborigines became the model of the earliest stage of cultural evolution as discussed by Emile Durkheim in *The Elementary Forms of the Religious Life* (George Allen and Unwin Ltd., 1915) and Sigmund Freud in *Totem and Taboo* (Moffat, Yard, 1918). By the 1950s, however, most Aborigines, too, had been settled on ranches, missions, or government settlements, and their cultures had been radically disrupted. Anthropologists' waning hopes of studying other "pristine" foragers were suddenly raised when an American family, the Marshalls, found and studied a group of Ju/'hoansi (!Kung) San living by independent foraging in the Kalahari Desert of Southwest Africa (now Namibia). Lorna Marshall's scholarly articles (later collected in her book *The !Kung of Nyae Nyae* [Harvard University Press, 1976]), her daughter Elizabeth Marshall Thomas's popular book *The Harmless People* (Knopf, 1959) and her son John's films (e.g., *The Hunters*) attracted great attention to the San.

In 1963 then–graduate student Richard B. Lee went to northwestern Bechuanaland (now Botswana) in search of an independent foraging San group. He found such a group in the Ju/'hoansi at Dobe waterhole. Although he recognized that they interacted with Bantu-speaking herding people in the region, his research focused on their adaptation to the natural environment. His findings led to a radically new image of the San and, eventually, of foragers in general. Once thought to live in a precarious struggle for survival, he found that the Ju/'hoansi actually needed to work less than 22 hours a week to get an adequate amount of food. The key to their success was their dependence on plant foods, mostly gathered by women, rather than meat, and the emphasis placed on food sharing.

By the early 1970s, however, some anthropologists had begun to question the popular image of San as isolated people with a continuous history of independent foraging since preagricultural times. In their selection, James R. Denbow and Edwin N. Wilmsen make the case that the Kalahari San have long participated in the regional economy and political system. They argue that the Ju/'hoansi and other inhabitants of the Kalahari Desert were agropastoralists (farmer-herders) and commodity traders until the late nineteenth century, when dominating outsiders, drying climate, and livestock diseases caused some of them to lose their herds and revert (temporarily) to full-time foraging.

Richard B. Lee responds that some San groups—such as the Ju/'hoansi of the Nyae Nyae-Dobe area—were quite isolated from outsiders until the late nineteenth century, when Europeans and Bantu-speaking Africans began to make occasional journeys into their homeland. Thus, his research suggests that foraging societies can live in contact with food-producers without being economically or politically subjugated by them.

This debate raises a number of important questions. Can small-scale, politically weak societies have economic and political ties with powerful outsiders without being dominated and fundamentally changed? Can one generalize from one case like the Dobe Ju/'hoansi to other foraging peoples? If foragers were herders or farmers in the past, can they still tell us something about the hunting-and-gathering way of life before the advent of agriculture?

James R. Denbow and
Edwin N. Wilmsen

 **YES**

Advent and Course of Pastoralism in the Kalahari

It has long been thought that farming and herding were compara-tively recent introductions into the Kalahari and that it has been a preserve of foraging "Bushmen" for thousands of years. Agropastoral Bantu-speakers were thought to have entered this region only within the last two centuries. However, fully developed pastoralism and met-allurgy are now shown to have been established in the Kalahari from A.D. 500, with extensive grain agriculture and intracontinental trade added by A.D. 800. Archeological, linguistic, and historical evidence delineates the continuation of mixed economies in the region into the present. Consequences of this revised view for anthropological theory and for policy planning concerning contemporary Kalahari peoples are indicated.

When the principal ethnographic studies of southern African peoples, then called "Bushmen" (1), were undertaken in the 1950's and 1960's, very little was known of their prehistory or of the history of their association with herd-ing and farming peoples; a similar lack of historic depth characterized earlier southern Bantu studies (2). At the time, it was universally assumed that Bantu-speaking farming-herding peoples had intruded into the Kalahari no more than two or three centuries ago. The region was presumed to have been peopled pre-viously only by San-speaking foragers who had, until then, remained isolated from external influences.

Before the mid-1970's, only two systematic archeological investigations had been carried out in Botswana, an area approximately the size of Texas (575,000 square kilometers); only one attempt had been made to integrate the history of relations among hunting and herding Kalahari peoples. In addi-tion, the climatic history of the Kalahari and its potential influence on local economies was entirely unknown. Likewise, linguistic studies, with their im-plications for revealing the history of social interaction and diversification in the region, were in their infancy. The assumption that pastoralism and social heterogeneity in the Kalahari were very recently introduced appeared to be correct.

From James R. Denbow and Edwin N. Wilmsen, "Advent and Course of Pastoralism in the Kala-hari," *Science*, vol. 234 (December 19, 1986). Copyright © 1986 by American Association for the Advancement of Science. Reprinted by permission. Some notes omitted.

Current work in archeology, geology, linguistics, and anthropology renders that assumption untenable. Since 1975, excavations have been carried out at 34 archeological sites in Botswana as well as at other sites in Zimbabwe and Namibia. Seventy-nine radiocarbon dates now delineate the chronology of domesticated food production in Botswana during the past 2000 years. These investigations indicate that cattle (*Bos taurus*) and ovicaprids were introduced along with ceramics into the northern Kalahari in the final centuries B.C. and first centuries A.D. Slightly later, grain cultivation and metallurgy were part of the economic repertoire of Early Iron Age (EIA) pastoralists in the region. By the ninth century, these peoples were engaged in trade networks that brought exotic goods such as glass beads and marine shells from the Indian Ocean into the Kalahari.

Geologic evidence suggests that significantly higher rainfall may have created an environment that encouraged the initial establishment of pastoral economies in the region. Linguistic evidence points to the diversification of Khoisan and southern Bantu languages coincident with this agropastoral expansion. Archival sources from the 18th and 19th centuries as well as oral histories document varying conjunctions of pastoralism and foraging in the economies of both Khoisan and Bantu-speakers that existed in precolonial time and characterize the region to this day. These sources also confirm the continued involvement of these peoples in ancient intracontinental trade networks that were not dominated by European colonial merchants until the second half of the 19th century. As a result of these studies, relations among hunters and herders in the Kalahari are shown to be both of longer duration and more integrated than has been thought.

The Context of Initial Pastoralism

Excavations of Late Stone Age (LSA) sites in the Kalahari reveal forager subsistence patterns differing from those recorded ethnographically among San in the region. Brooks and Helgren report that, in at least some LSA sites in the Makgadikgadi Pans area, fish and other aquatic resources complemented land animals in the subsistence of foragers between 4000 and 2000 years ago. At Lotshitshi, on the southeastern edge of the Okavango Delta, a LSA stratum dating within this period was found to contain fish, bullfrogs, and turtles along with large land mammals. Reconnaissance in the Makgadikgadi complex located over 50 additional LSA sites; two of these include small quantities of Bambata ceramics in their assemblages; eight others contain somewhat later EIA Gokomere or Kumadzulo pottery types. At Bambata Cave, in Zimbabwe, ceramics with remains of domesticated sheep are dated tentatively as early as the second century B.C. Maunatlala, in eastern Botswana, has ceramics and pole-and-clay hut remains at the end of the fourth century A.D.

The middle LSA level of Lotshitshi dates in the third century A.D. Faunal remains from this component indicate a broadly based economy including cattle (*B. taurus*) along with zebra, wildebeest, duiker, warthog, smaller game, and fish. Ceramics from this site are too fragmented for accurate identification, but their thin, charcoal-tempered fabric and finely incised decoration are compatible with Bambata types. Farther westward, in Namibia, ceramics (not Bambata ware) were present before A.D. 400 at Mirabib (with domestic sheep) and Falls Rock. Of the sites mentioned thus far, only Maunatlala has yielded evidence of metal use.

Radiocarbon dates placing sheep, and possibly cattle, but not metal, as far south as the Cape of Good Hope in the first century A.D. have been available for some years, consequently, a gap in data existed between these very early pastoralist manifestations in the far south and older centers north of the Okavango and Zambezi Rivers. The early pastoralist sites in the Kalahari and its margins begin to fill that gap. Consistent association of ceramics and domestic animals with LSA assemblages and their early dates indicate that pastoralist elements were introduced from the north into indigenous foraging economies here before the currently documented beginning of the Iron Age in southern Africa.

Recently acquired geomorphological evidence for fluctuating climates in the region has implications for these changes in LSA economies. At the Cwihaba caverns in western Ngamiland, periodically more humid climatic conditions are indicated by episodes of rapid sinter formation. In order to account for these episodes, Cooke suggests that rainfall in western Ngamiland reached 300 percent of the present annual mean between 2500 and 2000 years ago and again around 750 years ago. In general, these dates parallel those obtained for the sequence of beach levels found around the Makgadikgadi, Ngami, and Mababe basins where a number of higher lake levels with intervening regressions are indicated between 3000 and 1500 years ago.

Although it cannot be assumed that these high lake levels were caused solely by increased rainfall, Shaw argues for generally wetter conditions over the delta at dates congruent with those of Cwihaba. He estimates that rainfall over the Okavango increased between 160 and 225 percent. Under such a regime, many currently ephemeral pans and springs would also have contained more constant supplies of available water. Brain and Brain found evidence, in the form of microfaunal proportions, for episodes of climatic amelioration between about 4000 and 500 years ago at Mirabib in Namibia. Thus, several independent studies indicate higher rainfall during the millennium embracing the initial spread of agropastoral economies through the region 2500 to 1500 years ago.

In recent years, studies of Khoe (Central Khoisan) languages have proliferated in the Kalahari; all lead to an estimate that Khoe diversification in this region began about 2000 years ago. Vossen finds words for cattle and milking with apparent Proto-Khoe roots in the Khoe languages of north central Botswana. Köhler finds such words, along with a Khoe crop vocabulary, among the Kxoe (Khoe-speakers of northern Namibia). Both conclude that pastoralism must have been familiar to these peoples for a long time.

Ehret also argues that the basic separation of Khoi and Central Khoisan languages took place in the Botswana-Angola border region shortly after 500 B.C. He proposed further, from lexical evidence, that the basic pastoralist vocabulary of southern Bantu is derived through a Khoisan intermediary in this area, implying that these Bantu-speakers, but not others farther north, acquired cattle and sheep from Khoisan-speaking peoples. Pfouts suggests diversification of the Bantu languages of Namibia and southern Angola beginning about 1500 to 2000 years ago, whereas Ehret and Kinsman specifically place diversification of Proto-southeast Bantu in the EIA of this time frame. These authors suggest that economic factors contributed to this process of linguistic differentiation; their conclusions are compatible with the archeological evidence regarding initiation of pastoralism and socioeconomic heterogeneity in southern Africa. Elphick reconstructs historical data to reach a similar conclusion.

The Early Iron Age

The western sandveld.   The presence of Iron Age agropastoral communities in the Kalahari by the middle of the first millennium is now attested for Ngamiland as well as for eastern Botswana. At Tsodilo Hills, in the sandveld, 70 kilometers west of the Okavango, extensive excavations have uncovered settlements that span the period from the 6th to the 11th centuries A.D. Ceramics from the earliest (A.D. 550–730) of these sites, Divuyu, indicate that it belongs to an EIA variant, the distribution of which appears to extend northward into Angola. There are no close parallels in known EIA assemblages to the south, either in Zimbabwe or South Africa. Common decoration motifs consist of multiple parallel bands of combstamping separated by spaces that are either blank or filled-in with incised motifs. Divuyu ceramics are charcoal tempered but have substantial inclusions of calcrete.

A wide variety of iron and copper implements and ornaments were recovered from Divuyu but only a single stone tool. The presence of slag and bloomery waste indicates that metal working took place on the site. An amorphous scatter of friable burned clay fragments with stick impressions marks the probable location of a pole-and-clay hut. Fragments of perforated ceramic strainers indicate that salt was extracted from local sources. Unidentified marine shells provide firm evidence for coastal links, possibly through Angolan sites. Local trade with peoples of the Okavango system is indicated by the presence of fish bones and river mollusk shells (*Unio* sp. or *Aspartharin* sp.). Domesticated ovicaprids made up a large portion of the diet at Divuyu; domesticated *Bos* was rare. Large quantities of carbonized mongongo nut shells (*Ricinodendron rautanenii*) attest to the importance of foraging in the economy.

In the second Iron Age site at Tsodilo, Nqoma, a lower stratum contains Divuyu ceramics contemporary with the final dates at Divuyu itself. The major components at Nqoma stratigraphically overlie this material and are dated in the ninth and tenth centuries. Ceramics from these later components are uniformly charcoal tempered with few inclusions of other materials; decoration is most often applied as bands of interlocking triangles or in pendent triangles filled with hatching, combstamping, or linear punctuating. False-relief chevron designs occur frequently. Only a few dated sites are presently available for comparison. We see affinities with Sioma, in southwestern Zambia, and Dundo, in northeastern Angola, dated to the sixth through eighth centuries in the range of Divuyu and the beginning of Nqoma occupations at Tsodilo, but systematic ceramic comparisons of these sites have yet to be undertaken. Nqoma ceramics are similar to those from the ninth century site at Kapako on the Okavango River in Namibia; charcoal-tempered ceramics have been dated to the same period far out in the sandveld at NxaiNxai and are found in adjacent parts of Botswana and Namibia.

Evidence for metal working is attested at Nqoma by the presence of tuyeres as well as slag and bloom. Iron and copper ornaments are common and include finely made chains and necklaces with alternating links of copper and iron as well as bracelets with designs sometimes preserved by rust and oxidation. Moderate numbers of stone tools of LSA types are present. Dense areas of burned clay with pole and stick impressions mark the locations of substantial house structures.

Cattle (*Bos taurus*) were paramount in the pastoral economy of Nqoma; preliminary analysis suggests they outnumber ovicaprids by a factor of 2. Bifid thoracic vertebrae indicate that at least some of these cattle were of a humpbacked variety. Carbonized seeds of sorghum (*Sorghum bicolor* caffra), pearl millet (*Pennisetum americannum* thyphoides), and perhaps melons (*Cucurbita* sp.) provide direct evidence for cultivation. Remains of wild game along with carbonized mongongo nuts and *Grewia* seeds indicate that foraging continued to form an important part of the diet of this Iron Age population. Fish bones and river mollusk shells document continuing trade connections with the Okavango to the north and east.

Many glass beads and marine shells, primarily cowrie, along with worked ivory, one piece in the shape of a conus shell, provide evidence that Nqoma was an important local center in an intracontinental trade network extending to the Indian Ocean in the ninth century.

The river systems. Although the origins of the EIA communities at Tsodilo point consistently northward to Angola, contemporary agropastoralist sites on the eastern margins of the Okavango Delta as well as on the Chobe River belong firmly within the Kumadzulo-Dambwa complex documented by Vogel for the Victoria Falls area. This complex forms a regional facies of the widespread Gokomere tradition of western Zimbabwe and northeastern Botswana. Kumadzulo-Dambwa complex ceramics and small clay figurines of hump-backed cattle were found at the eighth century site of Serondela, on the Chobe River, and cattle bones along with LSA lithics and similar ceramics were recovered at Hippo Tooth on the Botletle River dating to the early ninth century. At the island site of Qugana, in the eastern delta, the same ceramic complex with burned, reed-impressed clay hut remains dates to the eighth century; as yet, no domestic fauna have been recovered from this site.

Matlhapaneng, on the southeastern Okavango, is an extensive site dated between the late seventh and tenth centuries, contemporary with the Nqoma sequence at Tsodilo. Ceramics are charcoal tempered with Kumadzulo-Dambwa decoration motifs. Pole-and-clay structures, iron, copper, and ivory ornaments, slag, and bloomery waste mark this as a fully formed EIA community. LSA stone tools are also present. Although this site is not as rich as Nqoma, long-distance trade connections are attested by the presence of cowrie shells and glass beads. Carbonized remains of sorghum (*S. bicolor* caffra), millet (*P. americanum* typhoides), and cow peas (*Vigna unguiculata*) provide evidence for agriculture; cattle and ovicaprids dominate faunal remains. Foraging was important here as it was at Tsodilo; carbonized marula (*Sclerocarya caffra*) and *Grewin* seeds are present and wild animal remains are common.

The eastern hardveld.   Similar developments took place simultaneously in the eastern hardveld where thick kraal dung deposits vitrified by burning have been found at more than 200 sites, indicating that large herds were kept in the region. The same EIA suite of materials already described is present, although ceramics are of Gokomere-Zhizo types with affinities eastward to Zimbabwe and northern Transvaal. East coast trade, documented by glass beads and marine shells, is dated in the late first millennium at a number of these sites as well as at contemporary sites in Zimbabwe and the Transvaal.

Major chiefdoms developed along this eastern margin of the Kalahari at the end of the first millennium, marking a transition to later centralized state development. A tripartite hierarchy of settlement size and complexity is discernible at this time. Large towns of approximately 100,000 square meters, Toutswe, K2, and Mapungubwe, dominated extensive hinterlands containing smaller villages and many small hamlets. Rulers of these chiefdoms succeeded in controlling the Indian Ocean trade into the Kalahari; it is possible that a system supplying valued goods in tribute to these chiefdoms from the western sandveld was instituted at this time, displacing previous exchange relations in which foreign imports as well as local exports had circulated widely.

Supporting evidence for changes in social relations of economic production is found in a comparison of age distributions of cattle and ovicaprid remains at the middle-order sites, Nqoma, Matlhapaneng and Taukome, with those at the capital towns, Mapungubwe and K2. At the first set of sites, a bimodal culling pattern is found similar to that of present-day cattle posts in Botswana, where slaughter is highest in nonreproductive age classes. Such a strategy conserves breeding stock and emphasizes rates of herd growth rather than meat production. Producers and consumers of herd products at these sites probably belonged to the same local social units.

In contrast, at Mapungubwe and K2, both primary centers, the majority of cattle slaughtered were in prime age classes; offtake appears not to have followed the conservative strategy found at the secondary sites. In other studies, this form of distribution has been associated with differential social stratification among occupants of a site. This appears to be the most plausible explanation for the contrasting culling patterns observed in our study. Elites at primary centers appear to have been selective consumers of prime rather than very old animals, many of which would have been produced elsewhere.

The Kalahari in the Second Millennium

These eastern Kalahari chiefdoms collapsed around the beginning of the 13th century. Great Zimbabwe emerged at this time, supplanting the political role played earlier at Toutswe, K2, and Mapungubwe. The extent of this new hegemony is indicated by stone-walled Zimbabwe-Khami outposts found far out in the Kalahari on the margins of the Makgadikgadi Pans. Control of trade became the prerogative of this kingdom. The final component at Toutswe (A.D. 1500) is devoid of exotic goods and no long-distance trade items have been recovered from two rock shelters, Qomqoisi and Depression, excavated at Tsodilo and dated to the 16th and 17th centuries, nor in an upper stratum at Lotshitshi, which, though undated, probably falls in this period.

Glass beads reappear at Xaro in Ngamiland at the beginning of the 17th century. These and cowrie shells are abundant at the 18th century site, Kgwebe, as well as in a probably contemporary (though not yet dated) upper stratum at Nqoma. Portuguese, through their Atlantic trade into the Kongo and Angola, were the probable source of these beads, which reached the interior along trade routes that had functioned since the Early Iron Age. Many of the first Europeans to enter the region from the Cape record that this trade in Portuguese goods was active south of the Orange River and to the east at least as far as the Zambezi by the 18th century. Native peoples including San-speakers, not Portuguese themselves, are specified in these records as the interior agents of this trade.

Archival records as well as oral histories testify to the importance of pastoralism throughout the Kalahari long before Europeans arrived. Every European who first observed the region from the 18th century on reports the presence of peoples of different languages, appearance, and group designation —Bantu and Khoissan—everywhere they went. Virtually every one of these Europeans remarks on the importance of pastoralism in all parts of the region and on the involvement of San-speakers in herding; several specifically mention San owners of livestock. Indeed, the herds of subsequently subjugated peoples were one inducement for Tswana expansion into Ngamiland in 1795. So rich in cattle was the northwestern Kalahari that 12,000 head were exported annually from it alone to the Cape during the 1860's through the 1880's, while unknown but apparently large numbers of interior cattle had been supplied to the Atlantic trade since the late 18th century.

In addition to cattle, 100,000 pounds of ivory along with many bales of ostrich feathers and hides are recorded to have been exported annually from the region as a whole during those decades in exchange for guns, tobacco, sugar, coffee, tea, cloth, beads, and other European goods. These were newly developed markets, but the trade networks they followed were continuations of Iron Age systems. Both Khoisan- and Bantu-speakers are reliably recorded by many observers to have been thoroughly involved in production for precolonial regional exchange networks. When first seen by Europeans in the 19th century, the copper mines and salt pans of northern Namibia were exclusively under San control; 50 to 60 tons of ore were estimated to be taken annually from those mines and traded to Bantu smiths. Trade routes were linked to wider subcontinental networks. Salt, manufactured into loaves, was traded far into the interior and is reported to have been at least as important an exchange commodity as copper.

In extension of this economic activity, San are credited with producing the bulk of ivory and ostrich feathers exported through Bantu and Nama middlemen during the 19th century. Relations of production and exchange were thus not strictly bounded by ethnic or linguistic divisions but cut across them. More than anything else, it is this negotiable lattice of relations among peoples and production that characterizes the last two millennia in the Kalahari.

Discussion

We have summarized a large body of data pertaining to prehistoric and historic economies of Kalahari peoples, and those surrounding them, which has been accumulated by a number of investigators.... We have concentrated on the early introduction and subsequent local transformations of agropastoralism in the region because these have been the least known aspects of those economies. Pastoralism has been treated in the ethnographies cited at the beginning of this article as if its history in and adjacent to the Kalahari has been recent and separate from that of indigenous foraging. A guiding assumption of these anthropological studies was that 20th-century foraging there is a way of life that has remained unchanged for millennia. Practitioners of these segregated economies have been rather strictly supposed to have had distinct ethnic and racial origins, in contact only for the last two centuries or less. This position can no longer be supported.

Many problems remain to be investigated. Much of the central Kalahari is unexplored archeologically, and the extent to which Iron Age pastoralism penetrated this area is unknown. A hiatus exists in our knowledge of the entire region between the 12th and 16th centuries. While large centralized states with many satellite communities flourished in the east, few if any sites are presently known for this period in the entire western half of southern Africa, with some possible exceptions at the Cape. Drier conditions may have led to shifts in settlement size and location, making detection of sites in the Kalahari difficult under present conditions. A reasonable hypothesis posits a concentration of population along the river systems and permanent springs leaving less densely peopled the drier hinterland, where foraging may have waxed and waned in accordance with changing environmental and regional economic conditions, particularly after European influence penetrated the region. It is unlikely that herders withdrew entirely from the sandveld; more likely, they at least continued to exploit seasonal surface water and grazing. At present, there is no evidence either to support or refute these propositions.

All of the peoples of the Kalahari during the past two millennia have been linked by extensive social and economic networks; thus, during this period of time, the Kalahari was never the isolated refuge of foragers it has been thought to be. It was the vastly intensified extraction of commoditized animal products in the colonial period, abetted by a drying climatic trend and stock diseases, especially rinderpest, which killed 75 percent of all cattle and antelope in southern Africa at the end of the 19th century, that combined to pauperize the region. These forces became factors leading to increased labor migration to the newly opened South African mines. In the process, the dues and privileges of earlier native states became increasingly translated into private family fortunes of a colonially favored aristocracy, while previously flexible relations among Khoisan and Bantu-speakers were transformed into ethnic categories defined by criteria of race, language, and economic class. The resultant divisions gave, to anthropological observers in the 20th century, the false impression of a Kalahari eternally empty, its peoples long segregated and isolated from each other.

An unresolved problem concerns the presence of Bantu-speakers in the western half of the subcontinent, a presence that now appears to have been more pervasive and much earlier than previously assumed. There is no doubt that the introduction of EIA economies from central Africa brought with it a complex interdigitation of people south of the Zambezi-Okavango-Cunene Rivers. In the eastern half of the subcontinent, it is well established that Iron Age Bantu agropastoralists gained a dominant position over indigenous foragers and pastoralists, ultimately subjugating, absorbing, or eliminating them. This did not happen in the west where, in fact, Khoi-speaking (Nama) herders dominated a large part of the area when first encountered by Europeans. It has been thought that a major reason for this difference lay in the short history of association of these peoples in the west. The perceived isolating severity of the Kalahari environment has been seen as a primary factor protecting San foragers from Bantu pastoralist domination. Neither supposition finds support in the research reported here.

This research has profound implications for understanding relations among contemporary southern African peoples. In particular, those relegated to the ethnographic categories "Bushman" and "hunter-gatherers" are seen to have a history radically different from that hitherto assumed. It is clear that, rather than being static, uniform relics of an ancient way of life, San societies and cultures have undergone transformations in the past 2000 years that have varied in place and time in association with local economic and political alterations involving a variety of peoples.

Two important consequences flow from this new understanding. The first forces reevaluation of models of social evolution based on assumptions brought to the anthropological study of these peoples. At the very least, ethnographic analogies formulated on modern San "foragers" and applied to studies of evolving social forms must be modified to take into account the millennia-long association of these peoples with both pastoralism and Bantu-speakers. Following on this, and more immediately important, is the need to bring the results of this research into the arena of policy planning. In this arena, San are routinely dismissed as rootless "nomads," without legitimate claim to full participation in modern national politics because they are conceived to be unprepared by history to cope with complex decisions involving economic and political alternatives. That this is no more true of them than of any other peoples should be clear in even this brief account of their recent past.

Notes

1. Etymologies of the terms "Bushmen" and "San" are debated; a long-standing derogatory connotation is acknowledged for the first of these, but San, as also "Bantu," has acquired segregating racial and ethnic overtones. To avoid such implications, we use Khoisan and Bantu as adjectives to designate speakers of two different language families, retaining San only where necessary to specify peoples so labeled in ethnographies. We use Setswana spelling, in which c and x represent the front clicks and q the back clicks of Khoisan words.

2. L. Marshall, *The !Kung of NyaeNyae* (Harvard Univ. Press, Cambridge, MA, 1976); R. Lee, *The !Kung San* (Harvard Univ. Press, Cambridge, MA, 1979); J. Tanaka, *The San* (Univ of Tokyo Press, Tokyo, 1980); G. Silberbauer, *Hunter and Habitat in the Central Kalahari Desert* (Cambridge Univ. Press, Cambridge, 1981); I. Schapera, *The Bantu-Speaking Tribes of Southern Africa* (Routledge, London, 1937); W. Hammond-Tooke, Ed., *The Bantu-Speaking Peoples of Southern Africa* (Routledge, London, 1974).

Richard B. Lee

 **NO**

The Kalahari Debate: Ju/'hoan Images of the Colonial Encounter

The Kalahari Debate, also known as Kalahari revisionism, sprung up in the late 1980s and early 1990s, and has been a topic of discussion among anthropologists ever since. What is at stake in the Kalahari Debate is the question of who the San peoples are historically—autonomous foragers or dependent serfs. The position taken [here] is that the Ju/'hoansi of the Dobe area, despite recent changes, show an unbroken history as independent hunters and gatherers that can be traced back far into the past. The "revisionists" argue that the Nyae Nyae and Dobe area Ju/'hoansi have been bound into regional trade networks and dominated by distant power holders for centuries. In this view they were not even hunters in the past but cattle-keepers, or servants of cattle people, raising the possibility that the Ju/'hoansi's unique cultural features of sharing and egalitarianism come not from their hunting and gathering traditions, but rather from being outcasts, at the bottom of a social hierarchy.

Curiously, until recently, neither the revisionists or their opponents had bothered to systematically ask the Ju people themselves for their views of their own history. How do the Ju/'hoansi interpret their past and how does that picture square with the evidence from archaeology and history? . . .

Beginning in 1986–1987 when the revisionist debate began to heat up, I started to ask Botswana Ju elders focused questions about the time they refer to as *n//a k'aishe* or "first time." The goal was to elicit collective memories of their pre-colonial past, a time we could date historically to the pre-1870s. Subsequently I returned for two more periods of interviewing, in 1995 and 1997, with informants from the Nyae Nyae and Cho/ana areas of Namibia. Now there are five major areas of Ju settlement represented in the oral history accounts. In this discussion, I will draw on three bodies of evidence on the Nyae Nyae-Dobe area Ju/'hoansi: their own oral histories, archaeology, and ethnohistory. . . .

Oral Histories

During my fieldwork in the Dobe area starting in the 1960s, the Ju/'hoansi were acutely aware that they were living under the gaze and control of the Tawana chiefdom and, beyond it, the British colonial authority. However in speaking of the area's past, Ju/'hoansi informants spoke of their own autonomy in the nineteenth century as a given: they were foragers who lived entirely on their own without agriculture or domesticated animals.

The existence of many Later Stone Age archeological sites in the Dobe area with thousands of stone artifacts and debris supports this view. But left unexplained is the presence on these same sites of small quantities of pottery and iron, indicating Iron Age presence or contact with Iron Age cultures. The Ju/'hoansi themselves explain the presence of these goods in terms of their long-standing trade relations with riverine peoples. On the other hand, Kalahari revisionists have argued that these archeological traces are proof positive of domination of the Dobe area by Iron Age peoples and the incorporation of the Ju/'hoansi into a regional polity. Wilmsen has further argued that people labeled Bushmen had raised cattle in centuries past:

> [I]n this century... an overwhelming majority of peoples so labeled have pursued a substantially pastoral way of life in symbiosis with, employed by, or enserfed to Bantu-speaking cattle owners... this is equally true of earlier centuries.

Remarkably, in all the voluminous writings on the Kalahari Debate..., neither side had systematically investigated how the Ju/'hoansi themselves articulate their own history.

An Interview With Kumsa N ≠whin

Kumsa n≠whin, a 70-year-old Dobe man, was a former tribal policeman and famous healer I interviewed in 1987. I began by asking him if long ago his ancestors had lived with cattle.

"No," he replied. "My father's father saw them for the first time. My father's father's father did not know them. The first non-San to come to the region were Europeans, not Blacks. We worked for them, got money and obtained our first cattle from the Tswana with that money. The Whites first came to !Kubi [south of Dobe], killed elephants and pulled their teeth [i.e., ivory]. In the old days the Ju/'hoansi also killed elephants with spears for the meat. At least 15 men were required for a hunt. They dumped the tusks [they didn't have a use for them].

"The Whites came by ≠dwa-/twe [lit. "giraffe-horse" [i.e., camels]. The Whites had no cattle, they had horses and camels. 'Janny' came from the south. Another one made a well at Qangwa [also called Lewisfontein]. My father said 'Oh, can water come out of there?' They used metal tools but not engines. This well is not used today. They spoke Burusi [Afrikaans]."

I asked, "Before the Whites came did you know 'Ju sa jo' [Black people] here?" His response was unequivocal: "No. We only knew ourselves. Ju/'hoansi exclusively."

"But when the Blacks did come, who was first?"

"The first Black was Mutibele, a Tswana, and his older brother, Mokgomphata. They came from the east following the paths made by the Whites going in the opposite direction. They were shown the waterholes by Ju/'hoansi including my father/Twi. They were shown the killing sites of the elephants, where the bones lay, the sites where Whites killed. And they said 'Oh, the Whites have already got the n!ore [territory] from us.' Then [Mutibele's] father claimed the land and all the Ju/'hoansi on it, but he deceived us."

"How did he deceive you? When the Tswana claims he is master of you all, do you agree?"

"If he was the master, he didn't give us anything, neither clothes nor pots, or even one calf. The Europeans had given the Ju/'hoansi guns. When the Tswana saw this they decided to give guns to other Ju/'hoansi, so that they could hunt eland and giraffe."

Later in the conversation I explored the nature of San-Black interactions in the precolonial period. What had they received from the Blacks?

"When I was young," Kumsa replied, "we had no iron pots. We used the clay pots of the Goba. We couldn't make them ourselves."

"Then how do you account for the fact that there are many potsherds on old Ju/'hoansi sites around here?"

"Our fathers' fathers and their fathers' fathers got them from the Gobas. They would trade for them with skins. The Gobas didn't come up here. They stayed where they were [on the rivers] and we went to them. This went on for a very long time [so that is why there are so many potsherds]."

"We [always] got two things from them: iron and pots. If you go to Danega today you will find the right earth. But the Gobas didn't come here. We always went to them."

⊷◉⊶

Kumsa's statements are congruent with a model of autonomy. Others had also made the point that a long-standing trade existed with riverine peoples *in which the Ju did the travelling.* It would be hard to argue that the Blacks could dominate the Dobe area without any physical presence, but I suppose it is not impossible. The trading trips made by the Ju to the east and elsewhere would certainly account for the presence of Iron Age materials on the Dobe area sites. In fact Polly Wiessner has argued that the levels of iron and pottery found on Dobe area Later Stone Age (LSA) sites can be accounted for by *hxaro* trade, a traditional form of delayed exchange still practiced by the Ju/'hoansi that historically has been a vehicle for long-distance trade.

One suggestive point was Kumsa's intriguing statement that the precolonial Ju hunted elephant but discarded the tusks; remarkable because it indicates that the Dobe Ju/'hoansi were hunting elephant for subsistence and were not part of a mercantile *or* a tributary network, since in either case elephant ivory would have been a prime valuable item.

Also interesting is Kumsa's rather dismissive view of the Tswana as overlords. For Kumsa the criterion for being a chief [lit. in San, "wealth-person"] is giving away in this context, not exercising power *per se.* The Europeans were chiefs because they gave guns, the Tswana were "deceivers" because in Kumsa's terms they claimed chiefly status but gave nothing.

A !Goshe Commentary on the Early Days of Contact

/Ti!kai-n!a, aged 80 at the time of the interview (1987), and /Ti!kai-tsau ("tooth") age 63, were two of the leading men of !Goshe, 16 kilometers east of Qangwa, and the easternmost and most economically "progressive" of the Dobe area villages. !Goshe is the jumping-off point for travel to the east, and the village has kept Tswana cattle since the 1910s. With their strong ties to the east where most Blacks reside, !Goshe people, by reason of history and geography, are the most attuned to links to "Iron Age" peoples.

"Certain Europeans in Gaborone," I began, "argue that long ago you Ju/'hoansi, [that is] your fathers' fathers' fathers' fathers had cattle. Do you agree?"

"No! Not a bit!" was the younger /Ti!kai's emphatic answer. "Long ago our fathers' fathers' fathers' fathers, the only meat *they* had was what they could shoot with arrows. We only got cows from the Tswana."

I persisted. "But when you dig holes deep down beneath where you live, you find pieces of pottery. Where did they come from?"

"Oh those pots were our own work!" replied the elder /Ti!kai. "Our ancestors made them. They would put them on the fire and cook with them. But since we got iron pots from you Europeans we lost the knowledge of pottery making."

Shifting the topic, I asked, "What about iron?"

"We got that from the Mbukushu," said /Ti!kai. "But we learned how to work it ourselves.... You stick it in the fire, heat it up, and hammer it.... We did it ourselves. We saw how the Gobas did it and we learned from them."

"Where did you get the iron itself from?"

Their answer surprised me. "The Europeans," said /Ti!kai. "The Tswana and Gobas didn't have it. They also got it from the Europeans."

I had to disagree. "But," I said, "in the oldest abandoned villages of the Gobas, iron is there. Long before the Europeans came."

At this point the older /Ti!kai intervened. "Yes! /Tontah is right. Long ago the Mbukushu had the pieces of iron that they worked."

The younger /Ti!kai turned to the older and asked, incredulously, "Well, where did they get the iron from?"

Matter-of-factly, the older man replied, "From the earth."

Much discussion followed on this point. The younger man was unconvinced that the Gobas had iron before the Europeans, but old /Ti!kai stuck to his story.

Shifting topic again, I asked, "Long long ago, did your fathers' fathers' fathers' fathers practice //*hara* [farming]?"

There was no disagreement on this point. "No, we didn't. We just ate the food that we collected from the bush."

The older /Ti!kai added, "When I was a boy we had learned about //*hara* from the Tswanas. They showed us how [to do it]."

The !Goshe interviews corroborate the account of Kumsa on the absence of cattle and agriculture before the twentieth-century arrival of the Tswana. They add detail on Ju/'hoan understandings of the history of pottery and iron use. In the first case they spoke of Ju manufacture of pottery, whereas other informants spoke of it as only imported. In the second case there was an intriguing difference of opinion. There was agreement that iron was imported from the Gobas but only in the recent past, but some believed that iron was so recent that the Gobas only obtained iron *after* the arrival of the Europeans, a view that we were to encounter elsewhere.

N!ae and /Kunta at Cho/ana

Another round of oral history interviews took place in 1995 at Cho/ana, a former Ju/'hoan waterhole, 65 kilometers northwest of Dobe, now located in Namibia's Kaudom Game Reserve. The informants were N!ae and her husband /Kunta (/Tontah) one of my namesakes. Cho/ana has long been known to historians as a meeting point for Ju/'hoansi from several regions. It was a convenient water hole for Ju/'hoan parties engaged in *hxaro* trade to meet.

In tracing the earliest history of the place, /Kunta saw the original owners as Ju/'hoansi, not Blacks or any other ethnic group. In the beginning, asserted /Kunta, only Ju/'hoansi lived here; there were no Gobas. Ju people would come from Nyae Nyae and from the north, to do *hxaro* here. It was a waterhole that always held water. People from the South (Nyae Nyae) would bring /*do* (ostrich eggshell beads). People from the North brought /*an* (glass beads). In /Kunta's words, "*Hxaro* brought them together."

A point of emphasis in our interviews was the question of whether the Gobas made trips to the interior to trade or to make their presence felt. /Kunta was emphatic: "No, [they didn't come to us] we went to them. We saw pots on their fires and wanted them, so they gave us some."

"And what did you give them in return?"

"We gave Gobas /*do* in exchange for pots."

The interior Ju/'hoansis' proximity to Iron Age peoples on their periphery and the use of iron as a marker of Iron Age overlordship has been a particular point of emphasis for the revisionists. I was anxious to hear /Kunta and N!ae's views of the pre-colonial use of iron and its source.

"Did your ancestors have *!ga* (iron)?"

"Are you joking? We didn't know *!ga*. If we needed arrows we used ≠*dwa* (giraffe) or *n!n* (eland) bones."

"Who gave Ju/'hoansi the iron?"

"We visited north and east and saw this wonderful stuff for arrows and knives; we asked Gobas for it and got some. It was very valuable; when others saw it their hearts were sad because they didn't have it; they wanted it so badly they would even fight other Ju for it. Parties went north to seek it; Gobas gave it to them in exchange for steenbok and duiker skins and other things."

"Where did Goba get iron from?"

Without hesitation /Kunta replied, "From the European."

"Are you saying that before Europeans came Gobas had no iron?"

"Yes, they had no iron."

✺

It is interesting that informants see iron coming ultimately from Europeans; they saw the appearance of iron and Europeans in their areas as so close in time that iron was associated with Europeans. While it is true that the amount of iron on Nyae Nyae-Dobe LSA sites is miniscule, it is striking that the long history of Iron Age occupation on their periphery, for example at the Tsodilo Hills with radiocarbon dates as early as 500 A.D., doesn't have much resonance with the Ju/'hoansi informants. When they did obtain iron from the Gobas, it was clearly an item of trade and not a marker of overlordship. In any event the very (post-European) regency of the trade in iron challenges the revisionist view of a deep antiquity of Ju/'hoan subservience.

Discussion

In all interviews there was repeated insistence that no Gobas or any other Blacks occupied their area or even visited prior to the late nineteenth century; several spoke of the Gobas' preference for staying on the river and avoiding the dry interior. All these accounts illuminate the pragmatic and matter-of-fact approach of Dobe and Nyae Nyae area people to questions of history. These, after all, are questions of the most general nature and the accounts agree closely, not only about the autonomy of the area from outside domination but also about the absence of cattle and agriculture in pre-colonial times (though not of pottery and iron). There are interesting divergences of opinion on whether pottery was imported or locally made, and on whether the Gobas had iron before the Europeans. Taken together these accounts along with others... constitute a fair representation of mid and late twentieth-century Ju/'hoan views of their forebearers' nineteenth-century history of autonomy.

One other indication of the Ju sense of their history is the largely positive self-image of their past. They see themselves as actors, not victims, and this contrasts with the negative self-imagery expressed by other San people, (such as Hai//om or Nharo views of their present and past.

Archaeological Tie-ins

The oral history interviews in both 1995 and 1997 accompanied archaeological excavation, designed to link archaeology with the knowledge that was part of the living tradition of the Ju/'hoansi. Professor Andrew Smith of the University of Cape Town started excavating a rich Later Stone Age archaeological site at Cho/ana, which provided a continual stimulus for oral history as new and interesting materials came to light in the excavations. The Ju informants' comments provided a valuable adjunct to the archaeological work (and vice versa). They identified plant remains, made tentative suggestions regarding fragmentary bone materials, and provided a social context in which the material could be interpreted. For example, the elders described a kind of white glass bead as one of the earliest of the European trade goods obtained through intermediaries to the north. A few days after the interview, precisely such a bead was found in a sealed level in association with an LSA industry.

But the most stunning confirmation of the direct late nineteenth-century encounter between people with advanced stone-working skills and colonialists was a piece of bottle glass (mouth and neck) showing signs of delicate micro-retouching that the South African Later Stone Age is famous for. This gave a further indication of the persistence of LSA stone-working techniques into the colonial contact period.

The oral history's insistence on the absence of cattle and Blacks in the interior was confirmed by the complete lack in the archaeological record of the presence of domesticated animals or of non-Ju/'hoan people in the area prior to the latter part of the nineteenth century....

Colonial Constructions of the Ju/'hoansi

Turning to the third body of evidence, what light do ethnohistoric documents shed on these Ju accounts of their own past? Do they support or contradict Ju accounts of relative autonomy? In general, the few historical accounts we do have support the Ju/'hoansi view of autonomy....

One of the earliest detailed accounts of the Nyae Nyae-Dobe Ju/'hoansi comes relatively late when Hauptman Müller, a German colonial officer, traveled through the Nyae Nyae area in 1911. Müller offers some unusually detailed observations on the situation of the Nyae Nyae-Dobe area Ju/'hoansi some 30 years after colonial trade had been established. In Müller's account (1912) the area remained remote and inaccessible. His visit was the first to the interior from the west in five years.

Most telling is Müller's ethnographic description of the bushman inhabitants of this stretch of land he calls "virginal" [jungfräulich]. He depicts their state as "noch uberuhrt von aller Zivilisation, in alter Ursprunglichkeit" [still untouched by all civilization in their old pristine state]. He reports with amusement how European objects such as matches and mirrors were unknown to them, as well as the camels of his troopers, which startled them and caused the women to grab their children and scatter into the bush. However, he did find them using such things as wooden bowls, glass and iron beads, cooper rings, and "Ovambo knives," all obtained through trade with Black neighbors.

Of particular interest is Müller's descriptions of the Bushman themselves. In his account they were well nourished and relatively tall, thanks to an ample diet of meat (hunted with bone-tipped arrows) and a variety of wild plants. There is no mention in Müller's account of any resident cattle or Bantu-speaking overlords, though BaTswana were visiting the area during his stay. For Müller the association of the Nyae Nyae Bushmen with the BaTswana was not ancient; it was of recent date and was based on trade and assistance rendered at the latters' hunting expeditions. The Bushmen were rewarded with gifts for their services and the relationship with the hunter/herders is described as equitable and friendly:

> The Bushmen seem, however, to be good friends with the BaTswanas. When
> I asked a Bushman if it didn't bother him that the BaTswanas were killing
> off so much game every year he said "Yes, but we are getting presents!" ...

Müller's is one of the earliest accounts to be based on actual reports of what he observed, as distinguished from second-hand accounts at a distance. And the preceding short quotation is among the very first to cite the actual words of a Ju/'hoan person.

∙◦❀◦∙

To sum up this section, both German and Ju/'hoan testimony are consistent and mutually supportive. The detail presented by Müller and the others (such as Hans Schinz and James Chapman) attests to five propositions that accord closely with statements made by the Ju/'hoansi themselves:

1. The relative isolation of the Nyae Nyae-Dobe area from the West and the low volume of European traffic, 1880–1911
2. The absence of cattle in pre-colonial Ju subsistence
3. The absence of Bantu overlords or tributary relations
4. The relatively favorable terms of trade between Blacks and San
5. The relatively good foraging subsistence base and nutritional status of the San

These lines of evidence argue the case that the views of the Ju/'hoansi about their historical autonomy are not sharply at odds with the ethnohistoric sources.

Hunter-Gatherer Discourse and Agrarian Discourse

Both the Ju oral histories and the German and other historical texts are cultural constructions, and yet, how are we to account for the correspondences between these two bodies of evidence? Why do they corroborate one another? To argue that both are careful fabrications still leaves open the question of why they agree so closely. One would have to invoke conspiracy or coincidence, in either case a tough sell. Surely it would be more reasonable to assume that they agree because they are describing the same reality. If Kumsa's, the two /Ti!kai's, N!ae and /Kunta's and others' collective accounts of the Ju/'hoansi autonomous past gibe so closely with those of European eyewitnesses such as Müller, then on what grounds rests the view of the historic Ju/'hoansi as enserfed pastoralists? And why has this view gained such currency in anthropological circles?

A more fruitful approach to understanding the recent debates is to attempt to place them in the context of the intellectual currents of the late twentieth century. How does the current conjuncture shape our perceptions of the situation of indigenous "others"?

Obviously, by the 1990s, the processes affecting the Dobe Ju/'hoansi had brought them to becoming clients, laborers, and rural proletarians, subject to and dependent on regional and world economies. Their current predicament is well understood by recourse to theories arising from political economy, dependency theory, or colonial discourse. Current theorizing is much weaker, however, in understanding the antecedent conditions. Part of the inability of contemporary theory to encompass hunters and gatherers as historical subjects is the lack of attention to the *differences* between discourses about hunters and gatherers and the discourses concerning agrarian societies and the emerging world system.

In agrarian discourse the presence of structures of domination are taken as given; it is the *forms* of domination and the modes of exploitation and surplus extraction that are problematic. In the literature on the agrarian societies of the Third World, stratification, class and class struggle, patriarchy, accumulation, and immiseration constitute the basic descriptive and analytical vocabulary.

In hunter-gatherer discourse it is not the forms and modes of domination that are at issue; rather the prior question to be asked is whether domination is *present*. I have been struck by the eagerness of otherwise competent analysts to gloss over, sidestep, or ignore this question.

There is no great mystery about what separates hunter-gatherer from agrarian societies. The former usually live lightly on the land at low densities; they can move and still survive, an escape route not available to sedentary farmers. The latter, with high densities and fixed assets, can no longer reproduce themselves outside the system, and are rendered far more vulnerable to domination.

In the recent debate some analysts seem to have taken the world systems/ political economy position so literally that every culture is seen as nothing more than the sum total of its external relations. But surely there is more to a culture than its links of trade, tribute, domination, and subordination. There is the internal dynamic of the means by which a social group reproduces itself ecologically, socially, and in terms of its collective consciousness. . . .

An historically informed ethnography can offer an alternative to the totalizing discourses of world systems theory. The unself-conscious sense of their own nineteenth- and early twentieth-century autonomy expressed by Ju/'hoan hunter-gatherers and its corroboration by contemporaneous colonial observers is one example of how these powerful assumptions can be challenged. They bear testimony that in the not very distant past other ways of being were possible.

That said, autonomy should not be taken as an article of faith, nor is it an all-or-nothing proposition. It is, or should be, an empirical question, and each society may exhibit a complex array of more or less autonomy at stages in its history. Even in agrarian societies spaces are opened up, however small, for the expression of autonomous thought and behavior. Thus it need not be the exclusive preserve of non-hierarchical or noncolonized societies. . . .

With reference to the latter though, a final point: What is desperately needed is to theorize the communal mode of production and its accompanying world view. Without it there is a theoretical vacuum filled far too facilely by imputing capitalist relations of production, bourgeois subjectivity, or "culture of poverty" frameworks to hunter-gatherer peoples.

POSTSCRIPT

Are San Hunter-Gatherers Basically Pastoralists Who Have Lost Their Herds?

These selections express two radically different worldviews. Denbow and Wilmsen's view—which has been called the "revisionist" view—emphasizes the interconnectedness of societies and the tendency for powerful polities to exert control over their less powerful neighbors. On the other hand, Lee's view —called the "traditionalist" view—emphasizes the people's adaptation to their natural environment and sees their relations with outsiders as variable, depending on local circumstances. Most anthropologists recognize that all cultures are influenced by local conditions and by the larger social environment, including, to some extent, the entire "world system." The question is, How much weight should one give to these two types of influence?

The disagreement between these scholars and their supporters is not merely a matter of theoretical emphasis. They also disagree about the facts and their proper interpretation. In subsequent publications Wilmsen and Lee, in particular, have argued over such matters as the precise locations of groups and trade routes mentioned in travelers' journals and whether or not the presence of cattle bones, for example, in an archaeological site indicates trade or outside domination. For elaboration of Wilmsen and Denbow's views see "Paradigmatic History of San-Speaking Peoples and Current Attempts at Revision," *Current Anthropology* (vol. 31, no. 5, 1990) and Wilmsen's book *Land Filled With Flies: A Political Economy of the Kalahari* (University of Chicago Press, 1989). For Lee's critique of these sources see his and Mathias Guenther's "Problems in Kalahari Historical Ethnography and the Tolerance of Error," *History in Africa* (vol. 20, 1993) and "Oxen or Onions? The Search for Trade (and Truth) in the Kalahari," *Current Anthropology* (vol. 32, 1991).

The literature on the San is voluminous. Alan Barnard's book *Hunters and Herders of Southern Africa: A Comparative Ethnography of the Khoisan Peoples* (Cambridge University Press, 1992) is an excellent overview of the various San and Khoi (formerly called "Hottentot") peoples. Important expressions of the revisionist view include Carmel Schrire's article "An Inquiry Into the Evolutionary Status and Apparent Identity of San Hunter-Gatherers," *Human Ecology* (vol. 8, no. 1, 1980) and her chapter entitled "Wild Surmises on Savage Thoughts," in her edited volume *Past and Present in Hunter Gatherer Studies* (Academic Press, 1984). A crucial source on the history of the San is Robert Gordon's *The Bushman Myth: The Making of a Namibian Underclass* (Westview Press, 1992). Works supporting the traditionalist view include Susan Kent's "The Current Forager Controversy: Real vs. Ideal Views of Hunter-Gatherers," *Man* [n.s.] (vol. 27, 1992).

ISSUE 7

Do Hunter-Gatherers Need Supplemental Food Sources to Live in Tropical Rain Forests?

YES: Thomas N. Headland, from "The Wild Yam Question: How Well Could Independent Hunter-Gatherers Live in a Tropical Rain Forest Ecosystem?" *Human Ecology* (1987)

NO: Serge Bahuchet, Doyle McKey, and Igor de Garine, from "Wild Yams Revisited: Is Independence From Agriculture Possible for Rain Forest Hunter-Gatherers?" *Human Ecology* (1991)

ISSUE SUMMARY

YES: Cultural anthropologist Thomas N. Headland hypothesizes that hunter-gatherers could never have lived in tropical rain forests without some access to cultivated foods. He contends that such forests are poor in energy-rich wild foods that are readily accessible to humans, especially starches.

NO: Cultural anthropologists Serge Bahuchet and Igor de Garine and biologist Doyle McKey argue that rain forest foragers harvest far fewer wild foods than the forests actually contain, precisely because they now have easy access to cultivated foods. They present evidence that Aka Pygmies in the central African rain forest can live entirely off of wild foods and have done so in the past.

Some of the best-documented hunting and gathering peoples live in tropical rain forests. They are generally pictured as small groups living in temporary camps and supporting themselves by gathering wild tubers, fruits, and honey and by killing game with spears, bows and arrows, and blowpipes with poisoned darts. Yet all, or almost all, of these peoples obtain some agricultural produce through trading with nearby farmers, working for farmers in return for food, or growing a few crops themselves. The classic example is the Mbuti Pygmies of the Ituri Forest in the Congo (formerly Zaire). As described by Colin Turnbull in his book *Wayward Servants: The Two Worlds of the African Pygmies* (The Natural History Press, 1965), the Mbuti spend part of each year as nomadic foragers in the forest living off of wild foods and part of each year living in camps near the villages of farmers, with whom they trade meat for cultivated foods, like bananas and manioc (tapioca root). The villagers think of their Mbuti trade partners as their servants or even slaves, but the Mbuti see the villagers as mere resources that they can exploit or ignore according to their own wishes.

During the 1980s a number of hunter-gatherer specialists began questioning just how independent tropical forest foragers like the Mbuti were from their agricultural trading partners. Some scholars began to argue that the foragers' trading for food was not voluntary but was probably a necessity, at least some of the time. This argument was based on the contention that in tropical forests, contrary to appearances, wild foods accessible to humans are scarce, seasonally absent, and time-consuming to obtain and process; in terms of foraging potential such forests are in fact "green deserts."

Thomas N. Headland, a specialist on the Agta of northeastern Luzon in the Philippines, carried this reasoning to its logical conclusion. In his selection, he questions whether or not full-time independent foraging is possible in any tropical rain forest. Drawing on his knowledge of the Agta and their environment and on the literature on other tropical forest foragers, he argues that rain forests contain so few readily accessible carbohydrates that foragers cannot survive there without obtaining supplementary agricultural produce by trade, working for farmers, or growing some crops themselves. Therefore, foragers could not have moved into tropical forests before pioneering farmers with whom they could maintain a symbiotic relationship based on the exchange of forest products or labor for cultivated food.

Serge Bahuchet, Doyle McKey, and Igor de Garine respond to Headland's challenge. They maintain that the fact that tropical forest foragers today obtain carbohydrates from farmers does not mean that they are incapable of living without those food sources or that they have not lived by independent foraging in the past. Using data collected by Annette Hladik and Marcel Hladik on the density of wild yams in the territory of the Aka Pygmies, the authors conclude that there is an ample amount of starch available to support the current Aka population if they choose to live exclusively off of wild foods. They also give linguistic evidence to suggest that the Pygmies had a well-established foraging tradition well before farmers settled in the forest. The authors contend that the Pygmies trade for agricultural produce today because trading for food is more efficient than gathering it from wild sources.

This issue raises a number of important questions for anthropologists. What difference does it make to our understanding of human prehistory and history if people could not have lived in any tropical rain forests before the advent of agriculture? If tropical forest foragers are truly dependent upon farmers for some of their food, can we legitimately consider them hunter-gatherers? What sort of evidence is needed to test Headland's hypothesis decisively? In general, how can we know what a people are capable of doing if they do not actually do it?

Thomas N. Headland

 **YES**

The Wild Yam Question

Introduction

Anthropologists and others have generally represented hunter-gatherer societies found today in tropical forest environments as having always lived in such biomes, until recently isolated and separated from other peoples, and surviving solely on wild foods.... Though a number of anthropologists have recently criticized this view, one still finds what Barnard (1983) calls a "Rousseauian notion of natural purity and cultural pollution [that] permeates the field of hunter-gatherer studies" (p. 194).

This [selection] presents an alternative hypothesis. Increasing evidence suggests that for foraging humans, tropical rain forests are food-poor, not food-rich. Wild starch foods, and especially wild yams, may be too scarce in such biomes to sustain independent hunter-gatherers without recourse to cultivated foods. Prehistoric hunter-gatherers either did not live in tropical rain forests, or else they lived there following an economy of symbiotic trade with food producers, exchanging forest products for cultivated plant foods. They may even have practiced cultivation themselves.... Pure foraging, with no iron tools, no cultivation, and no trade would at best have been a difficult and meager existence in closed tropical forests.

Tropical Forest Typology

There are two general classes of tropical forest. These are "rain forests" and "monsoon forests." ... Both classes occur in areas with a mean annual temperature of at least 24°C and which are essentially frost-free. "Rain forests," however, receive more, and more evenly distributed rainfall, at least 4000 mm per year, and not less than 100 mm in any month for 2 out of 3 years. "Monsoon forests" usually have less rainfall, but their defining characteristic is in their having a marked dry season....

In contrast to rain forests, the plant growth in monsoon forests slackens and may turn brown for want of water during several months of the year. Many trees lose their leaves, and much more sunlight penetrates to the forest floor during the dry season. Biomass in monsoon forests is only one-fifth that of rain forests. The implications of this for the ecology of wild tubers will become apparent.

The Case of the Agta Negritos

The Philippine archipelago was once completely covered with unbroken forest of one type or another. The western parts of the Philippines fall generally into the category of monsoon forest, while the eastern sections are classed as rain forest.

... In the past, primary lowland dipterocarp forest covered from 80–90% of eastern Luzon, but today much has been cut back. In the 700 km² Casiguran area of Aurora Province, approximately 58% of the area was still dipterocarp forest in 1983. Originally, most of this was "full-closure" primary forest. Today, about 75% of this lowland forest remains primary (about 300 km²), but most of this (about 260 km²) is now "partial closure." The remaining area of lowland forest (about 100 km²) is "secondary forest."...

Scattered throughout this rain forest live several nomadic groups of Negrito hunter-gatherers, all of whom refer to themselves as Agta. All of these Agta carry on symbiotic trade relationships with neighboring non-Agta farming populations. The salient characteristic of this symbiosis is the exchange by the Agta of forest products, especially wild meat, for starch foods from the farmers. One aspect of my model hypothesizes that the Agta may never have lived for long periods isolated and independent from agricultural neighbors, following a paleolithic lifestyle. If they ever did, either they must have practiced some type of minor horticulture, or, in past millennia, they lived in a different ecosystem than rain forest....

While wild meat and fish are plentiful at times in areas of eastern Luzon very distant from human residence sites, wild plant foods are not readily available there to humans. Though the Agta sometimes harvest wild tubers, and the starch from the pith of a wild palm (*Caryota cumingii*), the labor they expend to obtain these is quite high for the small amount of starch they get, and the plants are not abundant in any of the five forest microhabitats of eastern Luzon.... Caryota resembles the sago palm, but the amount of starch secured per tree is far less than from the true sago. The Agta also eat several types of wild fruits and plants, usually as snack food, and the hearts or buds of some small palms, usually as a cooked vegetable, especially a few species of *Calamus*. These do not, of course, sustain a person for long because of their low caloric content, though they are used as a famine food among indigenous peoples in the Philippines. Honey is an extremely undependable resource, as it is plentiful during only 1 out of every 4–6 years when the dipterocarps blossom.

In late 1985, Clark (in preparation) completed a six-month ethnographic field study among an Agta Negrito group on the eastern coast of Cagayan Province. The expressed purpose of her research was to live among Agta residing in a remote river area who have less access to trading opportunities than most Agta bands. Clark presumed that these Agta would be subsisting on wild roots during periods when trading was not possible. Though she lived with one of the most isolated Negrito groups in the Philippines, she found that roughly

99% of their starch food was cultivated crops, gained by trade with outsiders for forest, riverine, and marine resources. These Agta did dig up wild yams on three occasions, but twice these were at Clark's request. . . .

Of the many ethnographers who have described the Agta . . . , there are no references to anyone ever observing an Agta band living off wild plant food, even for short periods. These include published and unpublished descriptions written by Europeans who lived in or traveled through Agta areas in the eighteenth and nineteenth centuries. In fact, the earliest Spanish reports of the eastern coast of Luzon describe eighteenth century Agta as trading heavily then with farming populations, and as having swiddens of their own. . . .

This concords with statements by the Griffins who, after several years of field work with the Cagayan Agta, suggest that the Agta environment is plant food-poor (Estioko-Griffin, 1984, p. 211; Griffin, 1984, pp. 96, 100, 117). They also state, "Wild roots and vegetables . . . are probably not available in quantities adequate to support the present density of Agta" (Estioko-Griffin and Griffin, 1981, p. 143).

In 1984, the Casiguran Agta ate some type of cultivated starch food, usually rice, at 98% of their meals. Almost all of this starch was secured through trade. Wild carbohydrate food was eaten at only 2% of their meals during the same period (in those nine cases, the food was wild yam . . .).

These data suggest that the energy Agta expend to secure rice is less than it would take to dig up the nutritional equivalent in wild roots. While mere food preference may play a role here, the Agta are far from being affluent foragers. My time allocation study shows that healthy Casiguran Agta men work 6 days a week, 7 hours a day, on the average, much of this as farm laborers for outsiders. Healthy women without suckling children work only slightly less at the same type of labor. The same study presents evidence showing that these Agta suffer chronic undernutrition, with a life expectancy at birth of only 21.5 years, and an alarming death rate which is higher than the birth rate. Securing sufficient rice to sustain themselves is a serious daily problem for the Agta; if wild starch foods are available, why don't they dig them up when they are short of rice or root crops?

I suggest that such wild plant foods are not only not readily available today in Southeast Asian rain forests, but in the distant past they were so scarce and so difficult to secure and process, especially when Negritos did not have iron tools, that early Holocene foragers could have lived only a very marginal existence in such biomes. . . .

The Question of Wild Yam Abundance

. . . Except for two short preliminary investigations, one by James Eder and one by Douglas Yen, and some data from Karen Endicott from the Malay Peninsula, no empirical data have yet been collected from Southeast Asia which could satisfactorily answer "the wild yam question." The question concerns whether there were, in prehistoric times, enough wild plant foods, specifically wild tubers, to sustain a Southeast Asian (or African or Amazonian) hunter-gatherer population living independently in a tropical rain forest. The argument is that the wild foods necessary to meet human nutritional carbohydrate requirements were so scarce or seasonal in rain forest environments that they could not support human foraging populations year round unless they supplemented their diet by part-time cultivation and/or trade with neighboring farmers. Even a very low population density would not satisfy the conditions, if wild starch foods were not available all year round. As we know from Liebig's "law of the minimum," it doesn't matter how abundant food is for 11 months of the year if there is none during the twelfth....

Rambo (1982, p. 261) has proposed that the Malaysian rain forest is a "virtual desert" for human forager groups, because of the scarcity of edible wild plants and animals. He refers here specifically to the scarcity of wild yams, and to tubers too difficult to harvest because they are buried deep beneath the soil (Rambo, 1982, p. 263). Hutterer (1983) believes that tropical rain forests are "deficient in carbohydrate plant foods for human occupants" (p. 179) because potential plant foods are either out of reach in the forest canopy or are poisonous to humans, and because most rain forest plants store relatively little energy as starch or fat in their fruits, nuts, or seed, or in their underground roots.

Richards (1973, p. 62) makes the more general statement that there is a shortage of edible plants in tropical rain forests, and "this is why jungle hunter-gatherers have very low population densities." ... Most recently, in a review of Amazonian human ecology, Sponsel (1986) also states, "*Homo sapiens*... would have a difficult time obtaining adequate food solely by foraging [in the Amazonian rain forest]" (p. 74). Besides the problem of wild foods being inaccessible or poisonous to humans, Sponsel also points out that "most [neotropical] wild plants are not cost effective in terms of time and energy input/output ratios" (Sponsel, 1986, p. 74)....

Evidence Supporting the Wild Yam Hypothesis

In this section, we will review the archeological data, some botanical information concerning the evolution and ecology of yams, the linguistic evidence for Luzon (and for the African rain forests), and the archival evidence for Luzon. These bodies of evidence support the present argument.

The archeological evidence.   Unfortunately, there is little archeological evidence relating directly to the present yam hypothesis, either for or against, although there are three reports on excavations in northeastern Luzon which suggest that Agta Negritos were trading with farmers there during the second millennium B.C. There are no empirical data concerning the use of wild yams by pre-agricultural man anywhere in the tropics, although it is a logical enough deduction that yams were an important food, if not a major staple, at the end of the Pleistocene....

Bellwood (1985), a leading specialist on Southeast Asian prehistory, takes the view that human occupation in equatorial rain forests during the Pleistocene and early Holocene was minimal (p. 161). He suggests that late Pleistocene hunting societies were probably concentrated more in regions of seasonal climates. He bases this idea on the dearth of archeological evidence from rain forest areas, and because most of the flaked stone assemblages come from seasonally dry regions of Java, Sulawesi, the Lesser Sundas, and the Philippines. He notes, however, the "the inland forests of Malaya were widely settled by Hoabinhians from the beginning of the Holocene" (Bellwood, 1985). Dunn (1975) hypothesizes that these Hoabinhian hunter-fisher-gatherers were practicing some cultivation of root crops and other plants by 8000 B.C. (p. 135), and that by 3000 B.C., "root crops probably had assumed an important place in [the] subsistence economy [of Malayan Neolithic people]" (p. 136). In fact, Dunn suggests that Upper Pleistocene peoples 20,000 years ago in the same area "possibly supplement[ed] their diet through some form of incipient root crop cultivation" (Dunn, 1975, p. 132)....

Archeology in northeastern Luzon.   The earliest solid evidence for humans living in today's Agta area is that of Thiel (1980). Thiel's study neither supports nor contradicts the present hypothesis. She does establish that pre-agricultural man was living in northeastern Luzon at the end of the Pleistocene. However, it must be remembered that this area was then probably still a tree savanna ecosystem, not a rain forest....

The earliest established date we have for rice farming in northeastern Luzon, in the same area as Thiel's excavation, is 1400 B.C. (Snow, Shutler, Nelson, Vogel, and Southon, 1986). Cultivation of taro and yam in the same area almost surely predates that by 1000–2000 years. Ceramic manufacturing cultures in northeastern Luzon date back to approximately 3000 B.C. (Snow and Shutler, 1985). Peterson (1974a, b) excavated what he calls an "incipient agricultural site" (Peterson, 1974b, p. 227) in the center of the Palanan Agta area which was probably occupied between 2500–1500 B.C.... I am suggesting that by the second millennium B.C. the ancestors of today's Agta were practicing intense exchange relationships with these non-Negrito populations in Palanan, and certainly with the farmers just 80 km to the northwest who were growing rice in 1400 B.C.

Botanical evidence.   The following botanical information lends some inferential support to the present hypothesis.... Botanists and geographers agree that *Dioscorea* spp. [yams] evolved in the tropical lowlands, but this probably did not occur in rain forest biomes. Coursey (1967) states, "Yams appear to have evolved... in a climate with well marked wet and dry seasons" (p. 32), and "the tuberous development of the edible yams is essentially an evolutionary adaption to a prolonged dry season" (p. 71).... Yams are generally specialized for starch storage, adapted to survive dry seasons, and with roots which grow quickly to maturity each year when the rains return. Botanists point out that varieties of *Dioscorea* in seasonal biomes grow large esculent tubers annually, which gradually wither away as the plants draw energy from them during the dry season. But rain forest varieties in general, and there may be some expectations, have perennial tubers, and these are very small, having no need to store up reserves for survival until the next rains.

Burkill (1951) mentions that many wild yams have evolved in a way which protects their tubers by deep burial in the soil, and others which are not buried deeply protect themselves with much tannin in their tubers or with thorny roots. This hardly speaks in favor of their easy use by stone-age foragers. Referring specifically to the poisonous quality of wild yams, Burkill (1951) states,

> Many wild yams from the forests are eaten [only] after prolonged boiling and others after an all-night boiling along with wood-ashes to mitigate their acridity. Many hold tannin enough to make them unsavoury, yet not prevent the needy from eating them (p. 302).

... The botanical information, then, mostly supports the hypothesis that yams probably did not evolve in rain forests, and most species are not adapted to grow there. Those found in such biomes today tend to be inadequate as a dependable food staple for humans because the plants are widely dispersed, have small roots, are hard to dig up even with iron tools, and are often poisonous. Furthermore, as Hutterer (1982) points out, "Nobody has ever counted the number, or measured the productivity of wild edible roots occurring per hectare in a seasonal rain forest" (p. 135). Endicott (1984, p. 51) makes a similar statement. Two exceptions to this, for the rain forests in Central Africa, have recently been published by Hladik, Bahuchet, Ducatillion, and Hladik (1984) and Hart and Hart (1986). A discussion of this will follow.

The linguistic evidence. A strong body of support for the argument presented comes from the science of historical-comparative linguistics. These data have been presented elsewhere (Headland, 1986, pp. 17–19, 174–178; Headland and Reid, to appear; Reid, 1987). Philippine Negritos long ago, somewhere around the middle of the second millennium B.C., lost their original languages and adopted those languages of their Austronesian-speaking neighbors, a non-Negrito people who first began migrating into Luzon around 3000 B.C. (Bellwood, 1985, pp. 120, 232). This could only have happened if these two populations were living in intense inter-ethnic symbiosis. The subsequent differentiation today between the languages of the Negritos and those of their non-Negrito neighbors shows that the prehistoric interaction was ancient.

The linguistic evidence defines approximately when the linguistic switch took place, but it cannot tell us why. It is suggested here that the logical reason Negritos established such relationships with these ancient farmers was because of their desire for trade goods, especially carbohydrate foods. The Negritos received food from these farmers in exchange not only for forest products, but for their own labor, just as they still do today. ...

The archival evidence. There are a few archival references which tell us that Agta Negritos were practicing some minor cultivation of their own, actually making tiny swiddens during Spanish times.... These mostly eighteenth-century references to Agta agriculture are too many to cite here (see Headland, 1986).... If sufficient wild starch foods were available in the Agta areas, then we may ask why the Agta were going to the trouble to plant gardens in the 1700s.

We may also ask, at this point, how dependent Agta were on food bartered from non-Negrito farmers in eastern Luzon during early Spanish times. There are a good number of references to Agta/farmer interaction in the Spanish archives, most of them indicating that there was intense mutualistic symbiosis between the Agta and local farming populations. These documents show that throughout the Spanish period the Agta were continually exchanging forest products and labor for rice, as well as tobacco, knives, clothing, beads, and pots (see Headland, 1986)....

Examples from Southeast Asia.   Ethnographers who studied Negritos early in this century mentioned the importance of wild tubers, that many of the types contained poison, and that a good deal of labor was expended in leaching out the poison (see Garvan, 1964, pp. 55–56 on Negritos in western Luzon; Radcliffe-Brown, 1964 on the Andamanese; Schebesta, 1927, pp. 84, 115–117; Evans, 1937, pp. 58–60 on Negritos in West Malaysia). With the exception of Radcliffe-Brown, all mention that cultivated food was also a major resource among these Negritos.

... Dentan (1968, p. 46) in his "conjectural history" of the Semai (who live in the same general area as the West Malaysian Batek), proposes that in the distant past they probably lived completely off of wild vegetables, roots, and fruits. Yet, he states in the same paragraph,

> Present-day Semai rarely dig up wild roots except in emergencies. Should the crops fail, however, they know where to find patches of yams, especially the giant *takuub* yam (*Dioscorea orbiculata, D. pyrifolia*) whose tuber is often over 6 feet long. It may take all day for a group of men using machetes and dibbles to dig up a single *takuub* tuber and carry it home (p. 47).

... Labang and Medway (1979, p. 56) report that the Penan they observed in Sarawak rain forests secured starch from three species of (wild?) palm, but found and cooked a wild yam only once, when they were requested to do so by one of the investigators....

These reports from Southeast Asia, while not conclusive, do lend support to the wild yam hypothesis. The evidence that yams ever served as more than an emergency "famine food," much less a staple, is absent. I suspect that, in at least some of the ethnographic reports describing wild yam use, what the ethnographers may have observed was the digging up of feral, rather than wild yams, say in long-abandoned swiddens, or the digging of wild yams in secondary forest rather than primary forest. Only a very few Western researchers highly specialized in tropical botany, such as Yen, would be able to recognize the difference between wild vs. ferel vs. cultivated root plants.

Examples from Africa.   ... [A] very recent body of empirical ethnographic data has been presented concerning the wild yam question for central Africa. Hart and Hart have challenged the view held by several anthropologists (Hart and Hart, 1986, p. 30) that the Mbuti pygmies lived independently in the equatorial forest prior to its recent penetration by farming immigrants....

The Harts ... argue that there is simply not enough wild food in the central African forests to support a pure hunting and gathering economy year round. Using a large body of data on wild food resources of the area, they demonstrate that none of the calorically important forest fruits and seeds are available in the Ituri forest for 5 months out of the year. Honey is also scarce during this season. Game is available year round, but the main animals caught have low fat content.

Concerning wild yams specifically, Hart and Hart (1986) found that they are widely dispersed, not abundant, small in size, not available year round, hard to harvest and process, poor in taste, and especially, that they do not grow in primary tropical forest, but in secondary forest areas previously cleared by swiddeners. "Most of the important [wild plant] food species gathered by the Mbuti do not regenerate in closed forest environments, but are associated instead with more open habitats" (p. 50). It is their hypothesis that the Ituri evergreen forest was "essentially uninhabited until recently" (p. 51).

The Harts' thesis is supported by a new paper by Bailey and Peacock (in press), which is based on their field work among the Efe pygmies of Zaire. Bailey also challenges the idea that pygmies ever lived in the Congo Basin rain forest independently of agriculture. Though Bailey and Peacock report that there is a 3-month dry season in the Efe forest area, they hypothesize that the Efe do not, could not, and never had lived for more than a few weeks in the forest solely on wild foods. They say this even though they note that wild yams are found in this biome, and that Efe women sometimes forage for them.

The Harts' thesis is also supported by a recent report by Hladik *et al.* (1984) on the interior forests of Lobaya, Central African Republic. Tubers there are very scarce, as compared to the forest margins and areas of secondary forest growth (97 tuber plants/ha in the former, in contrast to 9400 plants/ha in the latter; Vincent, 1985). ...

Examples from South America.   Ethnographies have been written describing Amazonian foraging groups which, at first reading, seem to provide examples contradicting the wild yam hypothesis, since these groups appear to have been isolated hunter-gatherers living independently of cultivated foods or outside trade. A careful reading of such reports, and more recent data, however, provide support for the hypothesis.

For example, Kloos (1977) describes the Akuriyo of Surinam as such an isolate group up to 1968. This was a group he studied for "several months" in 1973, 5 years after they were "(re)discovered," and 3 years after they had moved into villages with other Amerindian farmers. The Akuriyo were a group of only 60 individuals in 1973, former swidden cultivators (pp. 14, 19), who Kloos thinks changed to "a completely nomadic way of life" (p. 7) about 80 years previously. Kloos admits that his reconstruction of their pre-1968 life is only an hypothesis (p. 19), and no empirical data are presented. ... Kloos suggests they ate only wild foods, but states that "getting enough food ... requires all their energy for most of their time" (p. 10). He also notes that they suffered from diseases "possibly contracted from visitors" (p. 20), and that they were "acquainted with

manioc but not in great quantities" (p. 21). If they had visitors and ate manioc, this case supports, rather than contradicts the wild yam hypothesis. Most
significant, Kloos (1977) states,

> The Akuriyo distinguish six edible tubers.... Most of them are small (many
> of them not exceeding the size of a finger) and often a day of hard work is
> rewarded by not more than a pound of tiny tubers (p. 10).

... The Ache (or Guayaki) of eastern Paraguay appear to be a hunter-
gatherer group who lived independently of trade and cultivated foods. Clastres
(1972), the first ethnographer to describe them, said they knew nothing of agriculture (pp. 140, 142), though the group he studied in 1962 was then living on
a plantation under the protection of a Paraguayan farmer (p. 144). Hawkes and
Hill believe that the Ache they studied in the early 1980s were formerly "full
time hunter-gatherers until the mid-1970s" (Hill, Kaplan, Hawkes, and Hurtado,
1985, p. 30). At the time of their study, the Ache were living on a mission station, hunting, cultivating several crops, and raising livestock (Hawkes, Hill,
and O'Connel, 1982, p. 381). The Ache were, indeed, very successful hunters.
If their particular ecosystem really allowed them to live independently of cultivation (an hypothesis based on a reconstructed model of their "ethnographic
present"), it may be because the area is not a rain forest. Hill and Hawkes
(1983) describe many microhabitats (pp. 140–141). The western area is nontrop-
ical, with several days of frost every year. Valleys are filled with grasses. Wild
foods may be abundant, but Hawkes *et al.* (1982, p. 384) report that the Ache
always took manioc or corn with them on their foraging trips from the mission
station....

The nomadic Siriono of the Bolivian tropical forest, often used as an illustration of extremely primitive Amazonian nomads, grew several kinds of crops
in tiny plots (Holmberg, 1969, pp. 67–68, 101–102). Their "digging of [wild]
roots and plants ... are almost negligible occupations" (p. 65). This is true in
spite of Holmberg's depiction of them as suffering chronic hunger frustration.
The Kaingang Indians in Brazil, a deculturated group studied by Henry in the
1930s, were supposedly forest nomads before 1914 who lived mainly by hunting meat, and did little plant gathering. They are reported as eating pine nuts
in season, but wild fruits were of slight dietary importance, and Henry says he
"never heard of the Kaingang using any [wild] roots for food" (Henry, 1964, p. 161,
emphasis added)....

Conclusion

... This [selection] has presented the hypothesis that wild carbohydrate foods,
and specifically wild yams, are scarce in climax tropical rain forests, and that
prehistoric foragers attempting to follow a "pure" hunter-gatherer economy
could not have survived in such ecosystems without some type of direct or
indirect access to cultivated foods. The symbiotic relationships found today

throughout the world between tropical forest hunter-gatherers and food producers are therefore not a recent phenomenon. This argument has been illustrated with a case study of the Agta Negritos in the Philippines, as well as data from other areas.

I fully agree with Hart and Hart (1986) that further investigation of the distribution and abundance of yams in tropical forest ecosystems is clearly needed (p. 52). If what they found for central Africa, and what I have observed in eastern Luzon, is general for other areas of the tropical forest world, then we may need to revise our views of human prehistory in the tropics.

References

Bailey, R., and Peacock, N. Efe pygmies of northeast Zaire: Subsistence strategies in the Ituri Forest. In de Garine, I., and Harrison, G. (eds.), *Coping with Uncertainty in the Food Supply.* Oxford University Press, Oxford. In press.

Barnard, A. (1983). Contemporary hunter-gatherers: Current theoretical issues in ecology and social organization. *Annual Review of Anthropology* 12: 193–214.

Bellwood, P. (1985). *Prehistory of the Indo-Malaysian Archipelago.* Academic Press, New York.

Burkill, I. (1951). Dioscoreaceae. *Flora Malesiana* 4: 293–335.

Clark, C. *Trading Networks of the Northeastern Cagayan Agta.* Unpublished Master's thesis in anthropology, University of Hawaii. In preparation.

Clastres, P. (1972). The Guayaki. In Bicchieri, M. (ed.), *Hunters and Gatherers Today.* Holt, Rinehart and Winston, New York, pp. 138–174.

Coursey, D. (1967). *Yams: An Account of the Nature, Origins, Cultivation and Utilisation of the Useful Members of the Dioscoreaceae.* Longmans, London.

Dentan, R. (1968). *The Semai: A Nonviolent People of Malaya.* New York: Holt, Rinehart and Winston.

Dunn, F. (1975). *Rain-Forest Collectors and Traders: A Study of Resource Utilization in Modern and Ancient Malaya.* Monograph 5, Malaysian Branch, Royal Asiatic Society, Kuala Lumpur.

Endicott, K. (1984). The economy of the Batek of Malaysia: Annual and historical perspectives. *Research in Economic Anthropology* 6: 29–52.

Estioko-Griffin, A. (1984). *The Ethnography of Southeastern Cagayan Agta Hunting.* Unpublished Master's thesis in anthropology, University of the Philippines.

Estioko-Griffin, A., and Griffin, P. B. (1981). Woman the hunter: The Agta. In Dahlberg, F. (ed.), *Woman the Gatherer.* Yale University Press, New Haven, pp. 121–149.

Evans, I. (1937). *The Negritos of Malaya.* Frank Cass, London.

Garvan, J. (1964). In Hochegger, H. (ed.), *The Negritos of the Philippines.* Verlag Ferdinand Berger Horn, Vienna.

Griffin, P. (1984). Forager resource and land use in the humid tropics: The Agta of northeastern Luzon, the Philippines. In Schrire, C. (ed.), *Past and Present in Hunter Gatherer Studies.* Academic Press, Orlando, pp. 95–121.

Hart, T., and Hart, J. (1986). The ecological basis of hunter-gatherer subsistence in African rain forests: The Mbuti of Eastern Zaire. *Human Ecology* 14: 29–55.

Hawkes, K., Hill, K., and O'Connell, J. (1982). Why hunters gather: Optimal foraging and the Ache of eastern Paraguay. *American Ethnologist* 9: 379–398.

Headland, T. (1986). Why foragers do not become farmers: A historical study of a changing ecosystem and its effect on a Negrito hunter-gatherer group in the Philippines. University Microfilms International, Ann Arbor.

Headland, T., and Reid, L. Hunter-gatherers and their relationships to agriculturalists from prehistory to the present. To appear.

Henry, J. (1964). *Jungle People: A Kaingang Tribe of the Highlands of Brazil.* Random House (Vintage), New York.

Hill, K., and Hawkes K. (1983). Neotropical hunting among the Ache of eastern Paraguay. In Hames, R., and Vickers, W. (eds.), *Adaptive Responses of Native Amazonians.* Academic Press, New York, pp. 139–188.

Hill, K., Kaplan, H., Hawkes, K., and Hurtado, A. (1985). Men's time allocation to subsistence work among the Ache of eastern Paraguay. *Human Ecology* 13: 29–47.

Hladik, A., Bahuchet, S., Ducatillion, C., and Hladik, C. (1984). Les plantes a tubercule de la foret dense d'Afrique centrale. *Le Terre et la Vie* 39: 249–290.

Holmberg, A. (1969). *Nomads of the Long Bow: The Siriono of Eastern Bolivia.* Natural History Press, Garden City, New York.

Hutterer, K. (1982). Interaction between tropical ecosystems and human foragers: Some general considerations. Working paper, Environment and Policy Institute, East-West Center, Honolulu.

Hutterer, K. (1983). The natural and cultural history of Southeast Asian agriculture: Ecological and evolutionary considerations. *Anthropos* 78: 169–212.

Kloos, P. (1977). The Akuriyo of Surinam: A case of emergence from isolation. IWGIA Document No. 27, International Work Group for Indigenous Affairs, Copenhagen.

Labang, D., and Medway, L. (1979). Preliminary assessments of the diversity and density of wild mammals, man and birds in alluvial forest in the Gunong Mulu National Park, Sarawak. In Marshall, A. (ed.), *The Abundance of Animals in Malaysian Rain Forests.* Department of Geography, University of Hull, and Institute of Southeast Asian Biology, University of Aberdeen, Aberdeen, pp. 53–66.

Peterson, W. (1974a). Summary report of two archaeological sites from northeastern Luzon. *Archaeology and Physical Anthropology in Oceania* 9: 26–35.

Peterson, W. (1974b). Anomalous archaeology sites of northern Luzon and models of Southeast Asian prehistory. Unpublished Ph.D. dissertation in anthropology. University of Hawaii, Honolulu.

Radcliffe-Brown, A. (1964). *The Andaman Islanders.* Free Press of Glencoe, New York.

Rambo, A. (1982). Orang Asli adaptive strategies: Implications for Malaysian natural resource development planning. In MacAndrews, C., and Chia, L-S. (eds.), *Too Rapid Rural Development: Perceptions and Perspectives from Southeast Asia.* Ohio University Press, Athens, pp. 251–299.

Reid, L. (1987). The early switch hypothesis: Linguistic evidence for contact between Negritos and Austronesians. *Man and Culture in Oceania* 3: 41–59.

Richards, P. (1973). The tropical rainforest. *Scientific American* 229(6): 58–67.

Schebesta, P. (1927). *Among the Forest Dwarfs of Malaya.* Hutchinson, London.

Snow, B., and Shutler, R., Jr. (1985). *The Archaeology of Fuga Moro Island: New Approaches for the Isolation and Explanation of Diagnostic Ceramic Assemblages in Northern Luzon, Philippines.* San Carlos Publication, Cebu City, Philippines.

Snow, B., Shutler, R., Jr., Nelson, D., Vogel, J., and Southon, J. (1986). Evidence of early rice cultivation in the Philippines. *Philippine Quarterly of Culture and Society* 14: 3–11.

Sponsel, L. (1986). Amazon ecology and adaptation. *Annual Reviews of Anthropology* 15: 67–97.

Thiel, B. (1980). Excavations in the Pinacanauan valley, northern Luzon. *Bulletin of the Indo-Pacific Prehistory Association* 2: 40–48.

Vincent, A. (1985). Plant foods in savanna environments: A preliminary report of tubers eaten by the Hadza of northern Tanzania. *World Archaeology* 17: 131–148.

NO

Serge Bahuchet, Doyle McKey,
and Igor de Garine

Wild Yams Revisited

Introduction

The Cultivated Calories Hypothesis

At the conceptual core of this new view of subsistence in rain forest foragers is a set of ideas that, for convenience, we will refer to collectively as "the cultivated calories hypothesis." Headland (1987) and Bailey et al. (1989) argue that subsistence based purely on foraging is difficult in tropical rain forest because of the scarcity of energy-rich wild foods, such as fat-rich animals, oilseeds, and carbohydrate-rich tubers and tuberous roots such as those of wild yams. Energy-rich storage organs are scarce in wild plants of tropical rain forest, and those that exist are often chemically defended. Those that can be used as food by humans are too scarce or too uncertain in supply, or the energy too difficult to extract (because tubers are deeply buried, or laborious processing is necessary for detoxification), to supply energy requirements. Animal fat is calorie-rich, but meat is leanest at the same time that plant foods are least plentiful (Hart and Hart, 1986). Thus, tropical rain forests offer only a scarce and uncertain supply of energy-rich wild foods. Access of foraging peoples to starchy staples cultivated by their farming neighbors frees them from a major constraint limiting human use of these environments. Many of the farmer–forager symbioses existing today have a long history, and may have evolved thousands of years ago as an adaptive strategy for exploiting tropical forest.

But Headland (1987) and Bailey et al. (1989) also examine a much bolder hypothesis: Not only are there no peoples currently living independently of agriculture in tropical rain forest, they argue, but subsistence based purely on foraging is impossible in these environments, and humans have never lived in tropical rain forest independently of domesticated plants and animals. This hypothesis appears to be a logically compelling corollary of their ideas, an extension back in time of the ecological constraints they invoke to explain current patterns. We find this extension of their ideas to the past, however, to be much more problematical than their conclusions about contemporary patterns. Lest it be accepted uncritically, the notion that foraging without recourse to cultivated plant foods is impossible in rain forest, and has thus never occurred, must be

From Serge Bahuchet, Doyle McKey, and Igor de Garine, "Wild Yams Revisited: Is Independence From Agriculture Possible for Rain Forest Hunter-Gatherers?" *Human Ecology*, vol. 19, no. 2 (1991). Copyright © 1991 by Plenum Publishing Corporation. Reprinted by permission of Kluwer Academic/Plenum Publishers. Some references omitted.

teased apart from the finding (which we accept) that this mode of subsistence seems not to occur in such environments today. We offer a critique on several grounds. We hope that our constructive criticism will lead to clearer definition and more rigorous tests of a hypothesis that is guiding research on an important question in the history of human adaptation to environment.

Our objectives, however, transcend criticism. Starting from the same observations about ecological constraints on foraging in rain forest as the cultivated calories hypothesis, we propose an alternative hypothesis about the history of subsistence patterns in rain forest foraging peoples, and attempt to test it using ecological and ethnographic data concerning pygmy foraging peoples of the western Congo basin. These data indicate that subsistence based purely on foraging, with wild yams (one conspicuous group of energy-rich wild plant foods) supplying a large proportion of calories, might indeed be possible in this environment....

Critique of the Cultivated Calories Hypothesis

The Argument Is Not Logically Compelling

The argument for the impossibility of subsistence based purely on foraging in rain forest is not logically compelling. The absence of a postulated mode of subsistence among contemporary peoples is not evidence that this mode of subsistence never occurred in the past nor that it is impossible. Were we to conclude that subsistence based on foraging without recourse to agriculture is only possible in environments where this way of life occurs today, then the set of environments that could have been exploited by pre-agricultural people would be vanishingly small indeed! Nowhere in the contemporary world do foragers live independently of other people. But agriculture had definite origins, and before agriculture people lived as foragers. Where did they live? We suspect that in the absence of archeological evidence favoring one position or the other (as in tropical rain forest...), hypotheses could be proposed *post hoc* to explain the impossibility of independent foraging in many of the other environments in which this way of life does not occur contemporarily....

Some Versions of the Hypothesis Are Unfalsifiable

Overly restrictive definitions of "rain forest" render some versions of the cultivated calories hypothesis virtually unfalsifiable. "True rain forest" may be so narrowly defined, along various dimensions, that any one of several escape routes becomes available to avoid refutation of the hypothesis by contradictory data. For example, Headland (1987) proposes a definition of tropical rain forest so restrictive in terms of amount of rainfall ("at least 4000 mm per year, and not less than 100 mm in any month for 2 out of 3 years," p. 464) that his version of the cultivated calories hypothesis effectively removes all of Africa, most of Amazonia, and much of tropical Asia from the discussion. His [selection] includes several examples in which possible exceptions to the cultivated calories hypothesis (e.g., the Batak Negritos of Palawan, Philippines, p. 470, and aborigines in tropical forest of northern Australia, p. 472) are discounted because they seem not to occur in "true rain forest." . . .

In a similar vein, proponents of the hypothesis sometimes seem to employ a rather too typological distinction between "mature climax forest" and "secondary forest," discounting some examples (of plant species, assemblages of species, or entire ethnic groups) that tend to contradict the cultivated calories hypothesis because they occur in "secondary forest" rather than in "climax forest" (Hart and Hart, 1986, p. 32; Headland, 1987, p. 485). A certain imprecision also creeps into the use of these terms; "secondary forest" is associated with semideciduous forest, "climax forest" with evergreen forest (Hart and Hart, 1986, pp. 30–31). Discussions of the hypothesis have tended not to reflect in full measure the realization that even "mature" tropical forest is a dynamic mosaic of vegetation in various phases of succession, and that it was that way long before human intervention. . . .

Bailey et al. (1989) largely avoid these pitfalls, admitting by their definition of "tropical rain forest" virtually all evergreen and semideciduous forests of the tropics and subtropics. This broad version of the hypothesis, which admits into the discussion an important diversity of environments, is also the most useful, we feel, because it is bold and can be falsified; the escape routes for avoiding refutation are fewer. We suggest that in many cases it will be refuted. . . .

Archeology Is Neutral on the Question

Archeological data could settle this debate, and indeed the absence of archeological evidence for pre-agricultural sites in rain forest has been perceived as supporting the cultivated calories hypothesis. Bailey et al. (1989) state that "it is impossible at present to support the hypothesis that people lived in the tropical moist forest of Africa without the aid of cultivated foods." It must be emphasized that there is no support from archeology for the converse hypothesis, either, because the data are simply too scant. Archeology is neutral on the question.

There is little reason to be sanguine that pre-agricultural sites, even if they existed, might be found in greater numbers. As Bailey et al. (1989) note, tropical forest is not a favorable environment for preserving cultural remains. Furthermore, hunter-gatherers are unlikely to leave distinctive remains, since they leave no agricultural implements, pottery, and the like. . . . In tropical moist forest, there are many possible campsites, so that concentration of accumulated material at a few particular sites is less likely. . . .

Nevertheless, numerous sites are known from central Africa—although our knowledge of each remains quite fragmentary—and many of these certainly predate the origin of agriculture. . . . The uncertainty lies in whether the rain forest vegetation that now covers the areas in which these preagricultural sites are found also characterized them during the period of habitation. This uncertainty derives from difficulties of dating of many artifacts, other than typologically, and from uncertainty surrounding the history of climate and vegetation in equatorial Africa.

... The extent to which moist forest vegetation was reduced during the Pleistocene, and the timing of its disappearance and reappearance in different parts of central Africa, are still controversial; but current consensus holds that at 18,000 B.P. the forest was broken into refugia, from which forest re-expanded beginning about 12,000 to 8000 B.P. Even considering the checkered history of the African forest zone, there still existed—as Bailey et al. (1989) duly point out (but not, we feel, with sufficient emphasis)—a span of at least several thousand years during which foraging peoples could have occupied rain forest prior to the advent of agriculture. Again, archeology is neutral as to whether such pre-agricultural occupation of rain forest environments actually occurred.

The Cultivated Calories Hypothesis Lacks Ecological Supporting Data

We have seen that contemporary absence of pure foragers in tropical rain forests does not allow us to conclude that foraging independently of farmers is impossible here, and that archeology is largely silent on whether the world's rain forests were ever inhabited by pre-agricultural peoples. Resolution, however tentative, of the question thus hinges for the present on ecological data. From what we know about the density, distribution, and biological characteristics of wild plant foods in tropical forests, and the subsistence activities and food requirements of foraging peoples, is independent foraging possible in this environment?

This is the empirical core of the cultivated calories hypothesis, and it is much less firm than is generally realized. In only one study (Hladik et al., 1984) has the abundance in rain forest environments of a major group of wild plant foods—in this case, wild yams—actually been measured, and this case . . . does not appear to offer support for the cultivated calories hypothesis. Although the argument centers on the availability of wild plant foods, data on this point are notably lacking. In those studies that do provide quantitative information of some sort (e.g., Headland, 1987), it usually concerns extent of use, rather than availability. The tacit assumption seems to be that use reflects availability. The current reliance of the cultivated calories hypothesis on inferences about wild plant food availability, rather than actual measures of it, is in fact its principal weakness. As long as availability of wild plant foods is inferred from extent of use, rather than actually measured, a plausible alternative hypothesis cannot be excluded. In the following section, we present this alternative and argue that it provides a better explanation of data concerning pygmy foraging peoples of the western Congo basin than does the cultivated calories hypothesis.

An Alternative Hypothesis

According to the cultivated calories hypothesis, energy-rich wild plant foods make low contributions to the diets of rain forest-dwelling foraging peoples because their availability is low, so low that subsistence based on them would be impossible. However, availability has not been measured; rather, the tacit assumption seems to have been made that low use reflects low availability. For a very simple reason, though, "extent of use" may consistently and grossly underestimate "availability" of wild plant foods, particularly starch-rich roots and tubers such as wild yams. One of the most confident predictions of foraging theory is that a food item will not be used, or will be used sparingly, if qualitatively similar items that give greater net returns are available. Based on everything we know about wild and cultivated starchy plant foods, optimal foraging theory leads us to predict that cultivated plants would be preferred if both are available. Use of wild plant foods may thus consistently underestimate their abundance. Edible wild roots and tubers, sparsely distributed and requiring more effort to remove and process, are likely to be neglected if starch-rich cultivated plant foods are available. Because such cultivated plant foods have long been readily available to foragers through contact with farmers, wild plant foods formerly used more heavily are now neglected. Starting from the same observations about ecological constraints as the cultivated calories hypothesis, it is thus possible, in the absence of direct measurements of resource abundance, to construct an equally plausible but very different hypothesis.

This alternative hypothesis generates two testable predictions: (1) Wild plant foods that are currently used are not used to the limit of their availability. In the absence of cultivated plant foods, they could supply a larger proportion of the diet than they currently do. (2) With long-term access to cultivated plant foods, some low-preference wild plant foods may have been abandoned, some of them so thoroughly that even knowledge about them was lost. Tropical forest habitats may contain potential foodstuffs, used in the past but no longer classified as food....

Ecological Evidence

Biology of Forest Yams

In viewing rain forests as poor in energy-rich wild-plant foods, proponents of the cultivated calories hypothesis argue that yams are principally adapted to environments outside rain forest, and, when present in the forest zone, are found mostly in secondary-forest habitats (Hart and Hart, 1986; Headland, 1987; Bailey et al., 1989). These authors draw upon a literature that has long emphasized species of savanna, savanna-forest ecotone, or anthropogenic clearings in forest, and that has treated the storage tubers of yams as adaptations to strongly seasonal environments (e.g., Coursey, 1976). In such environments, the reserves stored in tubers enable the plants, dormant during the dry season, to produce quickly a new aerial stem at the beginning of each rainy season. If the advantage of underground storage organs is understood solely in terms of seasonability, then it is easy to see why yams and other tuber-bearing plants might be thought not to characterize the relatively less seasonal environments of tropical moist forests.

Contrary to the impression one might gain from this literature, however, distinct forest-adapted species of *Dioscorea* do exist, though only one study has examined them (Hladik et al., 1984). Furthermore, forest *Dioscorea*, as well as a number of other plants (principally vines) of rain forests of the western Congo basin, regularly possess starchy tubers, sometimes quite large (Hladik et al.,

1984). What role do starch-rich tubers play in the biology of yams found in these less seasonal environments?

We believe that the significance of the underground storage organs of forest yams and other vines of western Congo basin rain forest is linked to the successional dynamics of tropical forest (Hladik et al., 1984). In Africa, as elsewhere, tropical forest consists of a mosaic of vegetation in various successional stages following natural disturbances, such as treefalls. In the context of the dynamic mosaic of vegetation, which may for convenience be classified as gap, building, and mature phases, notions like "climax forest" have little meaning. Though human activities have resulted in an increased proportion of forest in relatively young successional stages, in Africa as elsewhere, "secondary forest" and species considered typical of it have been components of tropical forest vegetation since long before human occupation of this habitat.

What we know thus far about rain forest yams suggests that the energy they store in tubers enables them to persist as suppressed juveniles in light-poor environments, and to respond with rapid growth when conditions become favorable. . . .

Is Tuber Density High Enough to Support Subsistence?

Using data on yam abundance, Aka food consumption, size of their camps, and their ranging behavior, we attempted to determine the feasibility of a mode of subsistence in which the cultivated food plants that the Aka currently use as starchy staples—manioc and plantains—would be completely replaced by wild tubers.

We used 2 kg/ha as our estimate of standing crop density of edible tubers in rain forest occupied by the Aka. This was based on a conservative rounding-off of the average density (2.39 kg/ha) found in four C.A.R. plots. An average Aka camp is comprised of seven households and about 26 people, including ten children less than 12 years old (Bahuchet, 1985). Studies of food intake have shown that each Aka consumes 0.5–1.0 kg of starchy plant foods (manioc and plantains) per day. Because food consumption varies in a complex fashion and is difficult to measure, we used two different estimates of the amount of wild tubers that would be required to replace the cultivated starchy staples of the current Aka diet. The minimum estimate is 2 kg/day/household, or 14 kg/day for the entire camp. The maximum estimate is 1 kg/day/person, or 26 kg/day for the camp.

Several factors might determine whether the wild yams in their territory would constitute a resource sufficient for Aka subsistence. First, are there enough tubers there? The territory of an Aka camp covers about 250 km^2, or 25,000 ha (Bahuchet, 1985). At 2 kg/ha, it contains 50,000 kg of edible wild tubers. The camp requires from 5100 kg (based on consumption of 14 kg/day) to 9490 kg (based on 26 kg/day) each year, or ca. 10–19% of the standing crop of yams in its territory each year.

The problem can also be examined on a finer spatial and temporal scale. Aka women gather food within a circle of ca. 2 km radius around a campsite (Bahuchet, 1985). Using our estimate of 2 kg of edible wild tubers/ha, the area within this foraging radius (1250 ha) would contain 2500 kg of edible tubers.

With the minimum estimate of carbohydrate consumption by the camp of 14 kg/day, the area within the foraging radius of a campsite contains enough yams for about 6 months' subsistence (178 days), and even with the maximum estimate of carbohydrate consumption by the camp of 26 kg/day, the quantity of yams around a campsite might support subsistence for up to 96 days. Actual residence times of the Aka in forest campsites between moves averaged ca. 60 days (Bahuchet, 1985). Thus, assuming the Aka can locate them, enough yams are present around each campsite to support the Aka for substantially longer periods than they actually stay.

Second, would tuber density remain high enough to support subsistence in the face of increased levels of exploitation? In the absence of long-term studies of yam population dynamics, it is impossible to know whether the standing crops of edible tubers measured by Hladik et al. (1984) could be maintained under more intense human exploitation. There is reason, however, to suspect that they might. . . . [T]he Aka move their camps with a frequency that might be high enough to prevent depletion of tubers within the foraging radius of each campsite. Furthermore, the total territory of the camp, 25,000 ha (Bahuchet, 1985), is about 20 times the gathering area around each campsite. Since camps are moved only every 60 days or so, this means that a given area might be exploited for yams less than once every 3 years, and even then may not be greatly depleted of yams.

Third, are the Aka good enough at locating and excavating the tubers that are there? Can an Aka woman locate, excavate, and process wild tubers at the rate necessary to supply her household with 2 kg (minimum consumption) to 3.7 kg (maximum consumption) of edible tubers per day? On this point our data are least satisfactory. We lack estimates of search times. Once yams are located, their excavation is not very time consuming. Data on excavation of a total of 16 tubers of at least four species show that tubers ranging in weight from 0.25–6.70 kg can be dug up by one woman in 10–20 min with a wooden digging stick. Estimating from these excavations, one Aka woman could dig up an average-sized tuber (1.945 kg) in 15 min. Though these data lack precision and only concern excavation time, there are several reasons to suspect that Aka women could supply wild tubers at the rate required. First, Aka population density is such that less than 20% of the yams actually present in their territory must be harvested each year. The Aka may thus be able to concentrate their foraging in areas where tuber density and/or renewal rates are high. They may thus be foraging in areas where yam density is often substantially higher than the average of 2 kg/ha that we are assuming and the returns from their foraging activities might be correspondingly higher. Second, as already noted, yams in rain forests of the western Congo basin generally can be eaten after simple cooking (boiling or roasting). . . .

Fourth, would edible wild tubers support subsistence throughout the year? . . . Again, we are hampered by the absence of any long-term studies of yam dynamics. Our view of the biology of rain forest yams suggests that their tubers may show less seasonality in density, size, and composition than those of savanna yam species. Data on the Aka show relatively constant usage of wild yams over the year, but as we have argued, the relationship between use and availability is not simple.

Availability of Other Wild Plant Foods

In our analysis of the feasibility of Aka subsistence based purely on foraging, we have concentrated on one class of wild-plant foods, wild yams, in order to develop a bold alternative to the cultivated calories hypothesis. This has necessarily resulted in some oversimplification. In practice, there are additional ecological considerations that make it even more likely that a purely foraging mode of subsistence is possible in rain forest. [R]ain forest offers other tubers as well as a variety of other energy-rich wild plant foods, including nuts and other seeds. Like wild yams, these could have contributed to the calories now supplied by cultivated plants. . . .

Linguistic Evidence

. . . Data from historical linguistics, in turn, demonstrate that hunting and gathering have long been central components in the economy of these people, and suggest that prior to contact with farmers, they were already living as foragers in rain forest environments similar to ones in which they now live.

. . . The Aka and Baka are geographically separated (found east and west of the Sangha River, in C.A.R. and Cameroon, respectively). Though they share many cultural traits, they speak two different languages, belonging to two different families (Bantu and Oubanguian for the Aka and Baka, respectively). These languages were borrowed by Pygmies from villagers at some earlier stage of their history, and since then have undergone divergence from respective related languages spoken by farmers.

Though they speak very different languages, comparison of their vocabularies shows that 20% of words (identical and/or cognate terms) are common to the two languages. These words shared between Aka and Baka are not present in the languages of any farming group. This fact, and the cultural coherence of this shared vocabulary that will be described [later] allow us to conclude that the Aka and Baka are descended from a common ancestral group of Pygmies termed "*Baakaa*" (Bahuchet, 1989a).

The majority (75%) of the vocabulary shared by Aka and Baka is concerned with forest ethnobiology, tools, and technical skills. This common vocabulary is not just isolated names of many rain forest species of trees (Bahuchet, 1989b), mammals, and other organisms, but—even more informatively—the shared terms form very specific and detailed ensembles. The cultural complexes characterized by common Aka-Baka vocabulary correspond to particular activities that are not only important in the material and symbolic worlds of these two pygmy groups, but also characterize pygmies in the eyes of farmers.

The major cultural complexes for which Aka and Baka share a largely common vocabulary are the following:

1. Honey gathering. Twenty-four words are shared, including names of several bee species and terms describing their biology, terms for different sounds made by bees, terms for combs, and terms for techniques and implements used in honey gathering (e.g., terms for the axe used for cutting toeholds to climb honey trees and to open the hive, and the bark box used for collecting honey).

2. Hunting. Forty words are shared, including ethnobiology of prey animals and techniques and tools employed in hunting. Shared terms relating to elephants and their hunting are especially well developed (e.g., shared words for six different "castes" (age-sex groups) of elephants.

3. Yams. Nine words are shared, including names of three species and terms for growth phases, fruit, and even yam-feeding beetles. There is also a shared term for a specific tool, the special and extremely long wooden digging stick used in extracting the deeply buried tubers of *Dioscorea semperflorens.* . . .

Based on this shared terminology, we conclude that the way of life of the ancestral **Baakaa* was already based upon hunting and gathering in rain forest ecosystems. When the **Baakaa* met the ancestral villagers, they had a characteristic culture, different from that of the non-pygmy villagers. At this time, they were already specialists in rain forest ethnobiology. . . .

Historical Development of Relationships Between Pygmies and Farmers in the Western Congo Basin

The cultivated calories hypothesis and the alternative we present offer two very different perspectives on the historical development of contemporary relationships between pygmies and horticulturists. Bailey et al. (1989) suggest that foraging peoples may only have been able to enter the rain forest together with farmers, who brought along the starch-rich cultivated plants that provided the energy source necessary for specialized hunting and gathering, and whose activities increased the extent of secondary forests, thereby increasing the returns from hunting and gathering.

We suggest that pygmy foraging peoples already occupied the equatorial forests when Bantu farmers began to spread into this environment. Furthermore, instead of the pygmies requiring symbiosis with farmers to exploit the rain forest environment, we argue that dependence may well have been the other way around. The knowledge of rain forest hunter/gatherers about starch-rich wild plants in this environment—plants that could be successfully cultivated in rain forest farms—may have been a key component in the spread of agriculture into African rain forests. . . .

Conclusion

Ecological Evidence for the Possibility of Hunting and Gathering Independently of Agriculture in Tropical Forest Environments

Summarizing the ecological evidence, we find the following: (1) Densities of wild yams and other edible tubers in the rain forest habitat of the Aka are high enough that the wild tubers could be exploited much more heavily than they are by the Aka today. (2) There is evidence that several kinds of wild plant foods, including wild tubers, were formerly more heavily used than they are today, some apparently having been abandoned altogether. These findings support our hypothesis that the limited use of wild-plant foods cannot be attributed to scarcity that prevents any greater use of them, but instead is due to their replacement by cultivated plant foods that became available upon contact (often ancient) of the Aka with farming villagers, a replacement that has continued until the present. Wild plant foods may well have been so extensively replaced by cultivated foods precisely because the latter are more easily available, less seasonal, or otherwise free foragers from ecological constraints. But, we believe, these wild plant foods did allow subsistence in these environments purely by foraging, before the cultivated plants arrived.

References

Bahuchet, S. (1985). *Les Pygmées Aka et la Forêt Centrafricaine, Ethnologie Écologique.* SELAF, Paris, "Ethnosciences 1."

Bahuchet, S. (1989a). *Les Pygmées Aka et Baka: Contribution de l'Ethnolonguistique à l'Histoire des Populations Forestières d' Afrique Centrale.* Thèse de doctorat d'etat es lettres et sciences humaines, Université René Descartes Paris V.

Bahuchet, S. (1989b). Les noms d'arbres des Pygmées de l'Ouest du bassin congolais. *Adansonia, Bulletin du Museum National d'Histoire Naturelle, Série Botanique* (Paris), 11 (4e série): 355–365.

Bailey, R. C., Head, G., Tenike, M., Owen, B., Rechtman, R., and Zechenter, E. (1989). Hunting and gathering in tropical rainforest: Is it possible? *American Anthropologist* 91: 59–82.

Coursey, D. G. (1976). The origins and domestication of yams in Africa. In Harlan, J. R., De Wet, J. M. J., and Stemler, A. B. L. (eds.), *Origins of African Plant Domestication.* Mouton, Paris/The Hague, pp. 383–408.

Hart, T., and Hart, J. (1986). The ecological basis of hunter-gatherer subsistence in African rain forests: The Mbuti of eastern Zaire. *Human Ecology* 14: 29–55.

Headland, T. (1987). The wild yam question: How well could independent hunter-gatherers live in a tropical rainforest ecosystem? *Human Ecology* 15: 463–491.

Hladik, A., Bahuchet, S., Ducatillion,C., and Hladik, C. (1984). Les plantes à tubercule de la forêt dense d'Afrique Centrale. *La Terre et la Vie* 39: 249–290.

POSTSCRIPT

Do Hunter-Gatherers Need Supplemental Food Sources to Live in Tropical Rain Forests?

The hypothesis put forward by Headland and R. C. Bailey, G. Head, M. Tenike, B. Owen, R. Rechtman, and E. Zechenter in "Hunting and Gathering in Tropical Rain Forests: Is It Possible?" *American Anthropologist* (vol. 91, 1989), that foragers cannot live independently in tropical rain forests, has stimulated much new research and careful reanalysis of data already collected. Some research shows that there is great variation from one rain forest to another in the types and amounts of plants and animals suitable for human consumption. One resource not fully recognized in the original formulations of the hypothesis is the starch found in the pith of sago palms, which are abundant in the rain forests of Indonesia and Melanesia. Sago starch is the staple food of the Penan foragers of Borneo, for example. Some scholars have complained that the proponents have defined tropical forest foraging so narrowly that it does not fit the reality of how such foragers live. For example, Peter Brosius criticizes Headland and Bailey for ignoring the fact that foragers both unintentionally and intentionally increase the density of valued plant resources (a point also made by Bahuchet, McKey, and de Garine in the unabridged version of their selection) and that foragers utilize many different microenvironments in the rain forest, including streams and naturally occurring clearings, not just the tree-dominated climax forest. See "Foraging in Tropical Rain Forests: The Case of the Penan of Sarawak, East Malaysia (Borneo)," *Human Ecology* (vol. 19, no. 2, 1991). The debate continues as new research findings appear.

For concise overviews of this controversy see McKey's article, "Wild Yam Question," in the *Encyclopedia of Cultural Anthropology, vol. 14*, (Henry Holt, 1996) and Headland's "Could 'Pure' Hunter-Gatherers Live in a Rain Forest?" at http://www.sil.org/sil/roster/headland-t/wildyam.htm. The latter contains an extensive and current bibliography, including works both supporting and opposing the hypothesis. Considered the best single source of articles is the special issue of *Human Ecology* (vol. 19, no. 2, 1991) from which the selection by Bahuchet, McKey, and de Garine was taken. It includes an introduction and conclusion by Headland and Bailey and five articles examining the applicability of the hypothesis in various places, including Borneo, the Malay Peninsula, New Guinea, the western Congo basin, and Bolivian Amazonia.

ISSUE 8

Do Sexually Egalitarian Societies Exist?

YES: Maria Lepowsky, from *Fruit of the Motherland: Gender in an Egalitarian Society* (Columbia University Press, 1993)

NO: Steven Goldberg, from "Is Patriarchy Inevitable?" *National Review* (November 11, 1996)

ISSUE SUMMARY

YES: Cultural anthropologist Maria Lepowsky argues that among the Vanatinai people of Papua New Guinea, the sexes are basically equal, although minor areas of male advantage exist. Men and women both have personal autonomy; they both have similar access to material possessions, influence, and prestige; and the activities and qualities of males and females are valued equally.

NO: Sociologist Steven Goldberg contends that in all societies men occupy most high positions in hierarchical organizations and most high-status roles, and they dominate women in interpersonal relations. He states that this is because men's hormones cause them to compete more strongly than women for high status and dominance.

In most of the world's societies, men hold the majority of leadership positions in public organizations, from government bodies, to corporations, to religious institutions. In families, husbands usually serve as heads of households and as primary breadwinners, while wives take responsibility for children and homes. Is the predominance of men universal and inevitable, a product of human nature, or is it a cultural fact that might vary or be absent under different circumstances? Are sexually egalitarian societies—in which men and women are equally valued and have equal access to possessions, power, and prestige— even possible?

Some nineteenth-century cultural evolutionists, including J. J. Bachofen and J. F. MacLellan, postulated that a matriarchal stage of evolution, in which women ruled, had preceded the patriarchal stage known to history. Today most anthropologists doubt that matriarchal societies ever existed, but it is well established that some societies trace descent matrilineally, through women, and that in these societies women generally play a more prominent public role than in patrilineal ones, where descent is traced from father to children.

Whether or not matriarchal societies ever existed, by the twentieth century European and American societies were firmly patriarchal. Most people considered this state of affairs not only natural but God-given. Both Christian and Jewish religions gave scriptural justification for the predominance of men and the subordination of women.

The anthropology of women (later termed "feminist anthropology"), which arose in the early 1970s, challenged the claim that the subordination of women was either natural or inevitable. The rallying cry of feminists was "Biology is not destiny." Women, it was said, could do anything society permits them to do, and patriarchal society, like any other social institution, could be changed.

Some feminist anthropologists considered male dominance to be universal but attributed it to universal cultural, not biological, causes. The groundbreaking volume *Woman, Culture, and Society,* Michelle Rosaldo and Louise Lamphere, eds. (Stanford University Press, 1974) presents some possible cultural reasons for universal male dominance. Rosaldo and Lamphere proposed that all societies distinguish between "domestic" and "public" domains and that women are always associated with the domestic domain, with the home and the raising of children, while men are active in the public domain, where they have opportunities to obtain wealth, power, and ties with other men.

Some anthropologists contend that sexually egalitarian societies once existed (e.g., Eleanor Leacock's "Women's Status in Egalitarian Society: Implications for Social Evolution," *Current Anthropology* [vol. 19, 1978]). They attribute the scarcity of such societies today to historical circumstances, particularly the spread of European patriarchal culture to the rest of the world through colonialism and Christian missionization.

In her selection, Maria Lepowsky argues that in the Vanatinai culture of Sudest Island in Papua New Guinea, the sexes are basically equal. She describes the numerous features of Vanatinai culture, including social practices and beliefs, that make this possible. She contends that matrilineal descent is one contributing factor, but that it alone does not guarantee sexually egalitarian social relations.

Steven Goldberg counters that males have more of the hormones that cause individuals to strive for dominance than women do. Therefore, regardless of cultural variations, men occupy most positions in hierarchical organizations and most high-status roles, and they are dominant in interpersonal relations with women. Goldberg would argue that even in a matrilineal society like the Vanatinai, more men than women would occupy positions of power and prestige.

While reading these selections, ask yourself whether or not the Vanatinai case actually contradicts Goldberg's assertion that all societies are male dominated. Do you know of any other societies in which men and women are apparently equal? Would a single sexually egalitarian society disprove Goldberg's thesis? If you accept Goldberg's contention that males have an innate tendency toward domination, do you think that any cultural arrangements could neutralize this or keep it in check?

Gender and Power

Vanatinai customs are generally egalitarian in both philosophy and practice. Women and men have equivalent rights to and control of the means of production, the products of their own labor, and the products of others. Both sexes have access to the symbolic capital of prestige, most visibly through participation in ceremonial exchange and mortuary ritual. Ideologies of male superiority or right of authority over women are notably absent, and ideologies of gender equivalence are clearly articulated. Multiple levels of gender ideologies are largely, but not entirely, congruent. Ideologies in turn are largely congruent with practice and individual actions in expressing gender equivalence, complementarity, and overlap.

There are nevertheless significant differences in social influence and prestige among persons. These are mutable, and they fluctuate over the lifetime of the individual. But Vanatinai social relations are egalitarian overall, and sexually egalitarian in particular, in that at each stage in the life cycle all persons, female and male, have equivalent autonomy and control over their own actions, opportunity to achieve both publicly and privately acknowledged influence and power over the actions of others, and access to valued goods, wealth, and prestige. The quality of generosity, highly valued in both sexes, is explicitly modeled after parental nurture. Women are not viewed as polluting or dangerous to themselves or others in their persons, bodily fluids, or sexuality.

Vanatinai sociality is organized around the principle of personal autonomy. There are no chiefs, and nobody has the right to tell another adult what to do. This philosophy also results in some extremely permissive childrearing and a strong degree of tolerance for the idiosyncrasies of other people's behavior. While working together, sharing, and generosity are admirable, they are strictly voluntary. The selfish and antisocial person might be ostracized, and others will not give to him or her. If kinfolk, in-laws, or neighbors disagree, even with a powerful and influential big man or big woman, they have the option, frequently taken, of moving to another hamlet where they have ties and can expect access to land for gardening and foraging. Land is communally held by matrilineages, but each person has multiple rights to request and be given space to make a garden on land held by others, such as the mother's father's matrilineage. Respect and tolerance for the will and idiosyncrasies of individuals is reinforced by fear of their potential knowledge of witchcraft or sorcery.

Anthropological discussions of women, men, and society over the last one hundred years have been framed largely in terms of "the status of women," presumably unvarying and shared by all women in all social situations. Male dominance and female subordination have thus until recently been perceived as easily identified and often as human universals. If women are indeed universally subordinate, this implies a universal primary cause: hence the search for a single underlying reason for male dominance and female subordination, either material or ideological.

More recent writings in feminist anthropology have stressed multiple and contested gender statuses and ideologies and the impacts of historical forces, variable and changing social contexts, and conflicting gender ideologies. Ambiguity and contradiction, both within and between levels of ideology and social practice, give both women and men room to assert their value and exercise power. Unlike in many cultures where men stress women's innate inferiority, gender relations on Vanatinai are not contested, or antagonistic: there are no male versus female ideologies which vary markedly or directly contradict each other. Vanatinai mythological motifs, beliefs about supernatural power, cultural ideals of the sexual division of labor and of the qualities inherent to men and women, and the customary freedoms and restrictions upon each sex at different points in the life course all provide ideological underpinnings of sexual equality.

Since the 1970s writings on the anthropology of women, in evaluating degrees of female power and influence, have frequently focused on the disparity between the "ideal" sex role pattern of a culture, often based on an ideology of male dominance, publicly proclaimed or enacted by men, and often by women as well, and the "real" one, manifested by the actual behavior of individuals. This approach seeks to uncover female social participation, overt or covert, official or unofficial, in key events and decisions and to learn how women negotiate their social positions. The focus on social and individual "action" or "practice" is prominent more generally in cultural anthropological theory of recent years. Feminist analyses of contradictions between gender ideologies of female inferiority and the realities of women's and men's daily lives—the actual balance of power in household and community—have helped to make this focus on the actual behavior of individuals a wider theoretical concern.

In the Vanatinai case gender ideologies in their multiple levels and contexts emphasize the value of women and provide a mythological charter for the degree of personal autonomy and freedom of choice manifested in real women's lives. Gender ideologies are remarkably similar (though not completely, as I discuss [later]) as they are manifested situationally, in philosophical statements by women and men, in the ideal pattern of the sexual division of labor, in taboos and proscriptions. myth, cosmology, magic, ritual, the supernatural balance of power, and in the codifications of custom. Women are not characterized as weak or inferior. Women and men are valorized for the same qualities of strength, wisdom, and generosity. If possessed of these qualities an individual woman or man will act in ways which bring prestige not only to the actor but to the kin and residence groups to which she or he belongs.

Nevertheless, there is no single relationship between the sexes on Vanatinai. Power relations and relative influence vary with the individuals, sets of roles, situations, and historical moments involved. Gender ideologies embodied in myths, beliefs, prescriptions for role-appropriate behavior, and personal statements sometimes contradict each other or are contradicted by the behavior of individuals.

As Ortner points out, a great deal of recent social science theory emphasizes "the centrality of domination" and the analysis of "asymmetrical social relations" in which one group has more power than the other, as the key to understanding a social system. A focus upon asymmetry and domination also tends to presuppose its universality as a totalizing system of belief and practice and thus to distort analyses of gender roles and ideologies in places with egalitarian relations.

Gender Ideologies

... More men than women are widely known for their wealth of ceremonial valuables and their involvement in exchange and mortuary ritual. Still, Vanatinai is an equal opportunity society where this avenue to prestige and renown is open to both sexes. A few women are well known throughout the archipelago for their exceptional wealth, generosity, and participation in ritualized exchanges. All adult women as well as men are expected to participate in exchange to a certain minimum, particularly when a father, spouse, or close affine dies. Besides the opportunity to be the owner or the eater of a feast, women have an essential ritual role as life-givers, the role of principal female mourner who represents her matrilineage in the ritual work of compensating death to ensure the continuity of life.

Women have a complementary power base as life-givers in other spheres that counterbalances the asymmetry of men's tendency to be more heavily involved in exchange, an advantage that results in part from male powers to bring death. The most exclusive is of course the fact that women give birth to children. These children enrich and enlarge the kin group of the mother and her mothers, sisters, and brothers, ensuring the continuity and the life of the matrilineage itself. Her role of nurturer is highly valued, and the idiom of nurturing or feeding is applied as well to fathers, maternal uncles, and those who give ceremonial valuables to others. In ideological pronouncements she is called, by men and women alike, the owner of the garden, even though garden land is communally held by the matrilineage, and individual plots are usually worked with husbands or unmarried brothers. She is, in verbalized ideology of custom, the giver of yams, the ghanika moli, or true food, with which all human beings are nurtured, whether she grew them or her husband or brother. She is likely to raise pigs, which she exchanges or sacrifices at feasts. She is prominent in the life-giving work of healing, a form of countersorcery. And life-giving, Vanatinai people say, is more highly valued than the life-taking associated with male warfare and sorcery....

An overview of the life courses of males and females on Vanatinai and the ideologies of gender associated with them reveals two more potential sources of contradiction to prevailing ideologies of gender equivalence. One seems clear to an outside observer: men may have more than one wife, if they are strong enough to fulfill multiple affinal obligations and if the co-wives consent to enter into or remain in the marriage. Women may not have two husbands. Even though polygyny is rare, and women need not, and do not necessarily, agree to it, it is a customary and continuing form of marriage and an indication of gender asymmetries. A big man may distribute his procreative power and the strength of his affinal labor and personal wealth to two or more spouses and matrilineages, enlarging his influence and his reputation as a gia. Women may not....

Vanatinai menstrual taboos, such as those prohibiting the menstruating woman from visiting or working in a garden and, especially, from participating in the communal planting of yams, are multivalent cultural markers of female power. The symbolic complexity and multiple meanings of such taboos have been emphasized in recent writings on the anthropology of menstruation. Earlier anthropological constructions have emphasized the relation of menstrual taboos to ideologies of female pollution and thus, directly, of female inferiority or gender asymmetry. In the Vanatinai case there is no ideology of contamination through physical contact with the menstruating woman, who continues to forage, prepare food, and have sexual intercourse. Both men and women who have had intercourse in the last few days are barred from the new yam planting, and the genital fluids of both sexes are inimical, at this earliest and most crucial stage, to the growth of yams. (Later on, marital intercourse in the garden will help the yams to flourish.) Vanatinai menstrual taboos, which bar women from what islanders see as the most tedious form of subsistence labor, weeding gardens, are not regarded by women as a burden or curse but as a welcome interlude of relative leisure. Their predominant cultural meaning may be the ritual separation of the sacred power of female, and human, fertility and regeneration of life from that of plants, especially yams, whose parallels to humans are indicated by anthropomorphizing them in ritual spells. Menstrual taboos further mark woman as the giver of life to human beings.

The Sexual Division of Labor

Vanatinai custom is characterized by a marked degree of overlap in the sexual division of labor between what men normally do and what women do. This kind of overlap has been suggested as a primary material basis of gender equality, with the mingling of the sexes in the tasks of daily life working against the rise of male dominance.

Still, sorcerers are almost all male. Witches have less social power on Vanatinai and are blamed for only a small fraction of deaths and misfortunes. Only men build houses or canoes or chop down large trees for construction or clearing garden lands. Women are forbidden by custom to hunt, fish, or make war with spears, although they may hunt for possum and monitor lizard by climbing trees or setting traps and catching them and use a variety of other fishing methods. Despite the suppression of warfare men retain greater control of the powers that come with violence or the coercive threat of violent death.

Some Vanatinai women perceive an inequity in the performance of domestic chores. Almost all adult women are "working wives," who come home tired in the evening, often carrying both a young child in their arms and a heavy basket of yams or other produce on their heads for distances of up to three miles. They sometimes complain to their husbands or to each other that, "We come home after working in the garden all day, and we still have to fetch water, look for firewood, do the cooking and cleaning up and look after the children while all men do is sit on the verandah and chew betel nut!" The men usually retort that these are the work of women. Here is an example of contested gender roles.

Men are tender and loving to their children and often carry them around or take them along on their activities, but they do this only when they feel like it, and childcare is the primary responsibility of a mother, who must delegate it to an older sibling or a kinswoman if she cannot take care of the child herself. Women are also supposed to sweep the house and the hamlet ground every morning and to pick up pig excrement with a sago-bark "shovel" and a coconut-rib broom. . . .

Vanatinai is not a perfectly egalitarian society, either in terms of a lack of difference in the status and power of individuals or in the relations between men and women. Women in young and middle adulthood are likely to spend more time on childcare and supervision of gardens and less on building reputations as prominent transactors of ceremonial valuables. The average woman spends more of her time sweeping up the pig excrement that dots the hamlet from the unfenced domestic pigs wandering through it. The average man spends more time hunting wild boar in the rain forest with his spear (although some men do not like to hunt). His hunting is more highly valued and accorded more prestige by both sexes than her daily maintenance of hamlet cleanliness and household order. The sexual division of labor on Vanatinai is slightly asymmetrical, despite the tremendous overlap in the roles of men and women and the freedom that an individual of either sex has to spend more time on particular activities—gardening, foraging, fishing, caring for children, traveling in quest of ceremonial valuables—and to minimize others.

Yet the average Vanatinai woman owns many of the pigs she cleans up after, and she presents them publicly during mortuary rituals and exchanges them with other men and women for shell-disc necklaces, long axe blades of polished greenstone, and other valuables. She then gains status, prestige, and influence over the affairs of others, just as men do and as any adult does who chooses to make the effort to raise pigs, grow large yam gardens, and acquire and distribute ceremonial valuables. Women who achieve prominence and distribute wealth, and thus gain an enhanced ability to mobilize the labor of others, are highly respected by both sexes. An overview of the life course and the sexual division of labor on Vanatinai reveals a striking lack of cultural restrictions upon the autonomy of women as well as men and the openness of island society to a wide variety of lifestyles....

Material and Ideological Bases of Equality

Does equality or inequality, including between men and women, result from material or ideological causes? We cannot say whether an idea preceded or followed specific economic and social circumstances. Does the idea give rise to the act, or does the act generate an ideology that justifies it or mystifies it?...

On Vanatinai, where there is no ideology of male dominance, the material conditions for gender equality are present. Women—and their brothers— control the means of production. Women own land, and they inherit land, pigs, and valuables from their mothers, their mothers' brothers, and sometimes from their fathers equally with men. They have the ultimate decison-making power over the distribution of staple foods that belong jointly to their kinsmen and that their kinsmen or husbands have helped labor to grow. They are integrated into the prestige economy, the ritualized exchanges of ceremonial valuables. Ideological expressions, such as the common saying that the woman is the owner of the garden, or the well-known myth of the first exchange between two female beings, validate material conditions.

I do not believe it would be possible to have a gender egalitarian society, where prevailing expressions of gender ideology were egalitarian or valorized both sexes to the same degree, without material control by women of land, means of subsistence, or wealth equivalent to that of men. This control would encompass anything from foraging rights, skills, tools, and practical and sacred knowledge to access to high-paying, prestigious jobs and the knowledge and connections it takes to get them. Equal control of the means of production, then, is one necessary precondition of gender equality. Vanatinai women's major disadvantage is their lack of access to a key tool instrumental in gaining power and prestige, the spear. Control of the means of production is potentially greater in a matrilineal society.

Matriliny and Gender

... Matrilineal descent provides the preconditions favorable to the development of female political and economic power, but it does not ensure it. In the cases of Vanatinai, the Nagovisi, the Minangkabau, and the Hopi, matriliny, woman-centered postmarital residence (or the absence of a virilocal residence rule), female autonomy, extradomestic positions of authority, and ideologies of gender that highly value women seem closely connected. Nevertheless matriliny by itself does not necessarily indicate, or generate, gender equality. As earlier comparative studies of matrilineal societies have emphasized, in many cases brothers or husbands control the land, valuables, and persons of sisters and wives....

Gender Ideologies and Practice in Daily Life

... The small scale, fluidity, and mobility of social life on Vanatinai, especially in combination with matriliny, are conducive of egalitarian social relations between men and women and old and young. They promote an ethic of respect for the individual, which must be integrated with the ethic of cooperation essential for survival in a subsistence economy. People must work out conflict through face to face negotiation, or existing social ties will be broken by migration, divorce, or death through sorcery or witchcraft.

Women on Vanatinai are physically mobile, traveling with their families to live with their own kin and then the kin of their spouse, making journeys in quest of valuables, and attending mortuary feasts. They are said to have traveled for these reasons even in precolonial times when the threat of attack was a constant danger. The generally greater physical mobility of men in human societies is a significant factor in sexual asymmetries of power, as it is men who generally negotiate and regulate relationships with outside groups.

Vanatinai women's mobility is not restricted by ideology or by taboo, and women build their own far-ranging personal networks of social relationships. Links in these networks may be activated as needed by the woman to the benefit of her kin or hamlet group. Women are confined little by taboos or community pressures. They travel, choose their own marriage partners or lovers, divorce at will, or develop reputations as wealthy and generous individuals active in exchange.

Big Men, Big Women, and Chiefs

Vanatinai giagia, male and female, match Sahlin's classic description of the Melanesian big man, except that the role of gia is gender-blind. There has been renewed interest among anthropologists in recent years in the big man form of political authority. The Vanatinai case of the female and male giagia offers an intriguing perspective.

In the Massim, except for the Trobriand Islands, the most influential individuals are those who are most successful in exchange and who gain a reputation for public generosity by hosting or contributing significantly to mortuary feasts. Any individual on Vanatinai, male or female, may try to become known as a gia by choosing to exert the extra effort to go beyond the minimum contributions to the mortuary feasts expected of every adult. He or she accumulates ceremonial valuables and other goods both in order to give them away in acts of public generosity and to honor obligations to exchange partners from the local area as well as distant islands. There may be more than one gia in a particular hamlet, or even household, or there may be none. A woman may have considerably more prestige and influence than her husband because of her reputation for acquiring and redistributing valuables. While there are more men than women who are extremely active in exchange, there are some women who are far more active than the majority of men.

Giagia of either sex are only leaders in temporary circumstances and if others wish to follow, as when they host a feast, lead an exchange expedition, or organize the planting of a communal yam garden. Decisions are made by consensus, and the giagia of both sexes influence others through their powers of persuasion, their reputations for ability, and their knowledge, both of beneficial magic and ritual and of sorcery or witchcraft....

Images of Gender and Power

... On Vanatinai power and influence over the actions of others are gained by achievement and demonstrated superior knowledge and skill, whether in the realm of gardening, exchange, healing, or sorcery. Those who accumulate a surplus of resources are expected to be generous and share with their neighbors or face the threat of the sorcery or witchcraft of the envious. Both women and men are free to build their careers through exchange. On the other hand both women and men are free not to strive toward renown as giagia but to work for their own families or simply to mind their own business. They can also achieve the respect of their peers, if they seek it at all, as loving parents, responsible and hard-working lineage mates and affines, good gardeners, hunters, or fishers, or skilled healers, carvers, or weavers....

What can people in other parts of the world learn from the principles of sexual equality in Vanatinai custom and philosophy? Small scale facilitates Vanatinai people's emphasis on face-to-face negotiations of interpersonal conflicts without the delegation of political authority to a small group of middle-aged male elites. It also leaves room for an ethic of respect for the will of the individual regardless of age or sex. A culture that is egalitarian and nonhierarchical overall is more likely to have egalitarian relations between men and women.

Males and females on Vanatinai have equivalent autonomy at each life cycle stage. As adults they have similar opportunities to influence the actions of others. There is a large amount of overlap between the roles and activities of women and men, with women occupying public, prestige-generating roles. Women share control of the production and the distribution of valued goods, and they inherit property. Women as well as men participate in the exchange of valuables, they organize feasts, they officiate at important rituals such as those for yam planting or healing, they counsel their kinfolk, they speak out and are listened to in public meetings, they possess valuable magical knowledge, and they work side by side in most subsistence activities. Women's role as nurturing parent is highly valued and is the dominant metaphor for the generous men and women who gain renown and influence over others by accumulating and then giving away valuable goods.

But these same characteristics of respect for individual autonomy, role overlap, and public participation of women in key subsistence and prestige domains of social life are also possible in large-scale industrial and agricultural societies. The Vanatinai example suggests that sexual equality is facilitated by an overall ethic of respect for and equal treatment of all categories of individuals, the decentralization of political power, and inclusion of all categories of persons (for example, women and ethnic minorities) in public positions of authority and influence. It requires greater role overlap through increased integration of the workforce, increased control by women and minorities of valued goods —property, income, and educational credentials—and increased recognition of the social value of parental care. The example of Vanatinai shows that the subjugation of women by men is not a human universal, and it is not inevitable. Sex role patterns and gender ideologies are closely related to overall social systems of power and prestige. Where these systems stress personal autonomy and egalitarian social relations among all adults, minimizing the formal authority of one person over another, gender equality is possible.

NO

Steven Goldberg

Is Patriarchy Inevitable?

In five hundred years the world, in all likelihood, will have become homogenized. The thousands of varied societies and their dramatically differing methods of socialization, cohesion, family, religion, economy, and politics will have given way to a universal culture. Fortunately, cultural anthropologists have preserved much of our present diversity, which may keep our descendants from too hastily allowing their natural human ego- and ethno-centricity to conclude that theirs is the only way to manage a society.

However, the anthropological sword is two-edged. While diversity is certainly apparent from anthropological investigations, it is also clear that there are realities which manifest themselves no matter what the varied forms of the aforementioned institutions. Because these universal realities cut across cultural lines, they are crucial to our understanding of what society *by its nature* is and, perhaps, of what human beings are. It is important, then, that we ask why, when societies differ as much as do those of the Ituri Pygmy, the Jivaro, the American, the Japanese, and a thousand others, some institutions are universal.

It is always the case that the universal institution serves some need rooted in the deepest nature of human beings. In some cases the explanation of universality is obvious (e.g., why every society has methods of food gathering). But there are other universalities which are apparent, though without any obvious explanation. Of the thousands of societies on which we have any evidence stronger than myth (a form of evidence that would have us believe in cyclopes), there is no evidence that there has ever been a society failing to exhibit three institutions:

1. Primary hierarchies always filled primarily by men. A Queen Victoria or a Golda Meir is always an exception and is always surrounded by a government of men. Indeed, the constraints of royal lineage may produce more female societal leaders than does democracy—there were more female heads of state in the first two-thirds of the sixteenth century than there were in the first two-thirds of the twentieth.

2. The highest status roles are male. There are societies in which the women do most of the important economic work and rear the children, while the men seem mostly to hang loose. But, in such societies, hanging loose is given higher status than any non-maternal role primarily served by women. No doubt this is partly due to the fact that the males hold the positions of power. However, it is also likely that high-status roles are male not primarily because they are male (ditch-digging is male and low status), but because they are high status. The high status roles are male because they possess—for whatever socially determined reason in whichever specific society—high status. This high status exerts a more powerful influence on males than it does on females. As a result, males are more willing to sacrifice life's other rewards for status dominance than are females.

In their *Not in Our Genes,* Richard Lewontin, Leon Kamin, and Stephen Rose—who, along with Stephen Jay Gould are the best-known defenders of the view that emphasizes the role of environment and de-emphasizes that of heredity—attempt to find fault with my work by pointing out that most family doctors in the Soviet Union are women. However, they acknowledge that in the Soviet Union "family doctoring [had] lower status than in the United States."

Which is precisely the point. No one doubts that women can be doctors. The question is why doctors (or weavers, or load bearers, etc.) are primarily women only when being a doctor is given lower status than are certain roles played mostly by men—and furthermore, why, even when this is the case (as in Russia) the upper hierarchical positions relevant to that specific area are held by men.

3. Dominance in male-female relationships is always associated with males. "Male dominance" refers to the feeling, of both men and women, that the male is dominant and that the woman must "get around" the male to attain power. Social attitudes may be concordant or discordant with the reality of male dominance. In our own society there was a time when the man's "taking the lead" was positively valued by most women (as 30s' movies attest); today such a view is purportedly detested by many. But attitudes toward male-dominance behavior are causally unimportant to the reality they judge—and are not much more likely to eliminate the reality than would a social dislike of men's being taller be able to eliminate men's being taller.

Over the past twenty years, I have consulted every original ethnographic work invoked to demonstrate an exception to these societal universalities. Twenty years ago many textbooks spoke cavalierly of "matriarchies" and "Amazons" and pretended that Margaret Mead had claimed to find a society in which sex roles were reversed. Today no serious anthropologist is willing to claim that any specific society has ever been an exception.

It is often claimed that "modern technology renders the physiological differentiation irrelevant." However, there is not a scintilla of evidence that modernization alters the basic "motivational" factors sufficiently to cast doubt on the continued existence of the universals I discuss. The economic needs of modern society probably do set a lower limit on the status of women; no modern society could give women the low status they receive in some non-modern societies. But modernization probably also sets an upper limit; no modern society is likely to give women the status given to the maternal roles in some other matrilineal societies.

Scandinavian nations, which have long had government agencies devoted to equalizing women's position, are often cited by social scientists as demonstrating modernization's ability to override patriarchy. In fact, however, Norway has 454 municipal councils; 443 are chaired by men. On the Supreme Court, city courts, appellate courts, and in Parliament, there are between five and nine times as many men as there are women. In Sweden, according to government documents, men dominate "senior positions in employer and employee organizations as well as in political and other associations" and only 5 of 82 directors of government agencies, 9 of 83 chairpersons of agency boards, and 9 per cent of judges are women.

One may, of course, hope that all this changes, but one cannot invoke any evidence implying that it will.

Of course, there are those who simply try to assert away the evidence. Lewontin *et al.* write, "Cross cultural universals appear to lie more in the eye of the beholder than in the social reality that is being observed." In fact, with reference to the universalities mentioned above, they do not. If these universals were merely "in the eye of the beholder," the authors would merely have to specify a society in which there was a hierarchy in which males did not predominate and the case would be closed.

The answer to the question of why an institution is universal clearly must be parsimonious. It will not do to ascribe causation of a universal institution to capitalism or Christianity or modernization, because many hundreds of societies lacked these, but not the universal institutions. If the causal explanation is to be at all persuasive, it must invoke some factor present in every society from the most primitive to the most modern. (Invoking the male's physical strength advantage does meet the requirement of parsimony, but does not counter the evidence of the central importance of neuro-endocrinological psycho-physiological factors.)

When sociologists are forced to acknowledge the universals, they nearly always invoke "socialization" as explanation. But this explanation faces two serious problems. First, it does not explain anything, but merely forces us to ask another question: *Why* does socialization of men and women always work in the same direction? Second, the explanation implicitly assumes that the social environment of expectations and norms acts as an *independent* variable capable of acting as counterpoise to the physiological constituents that make us male and female.

In individual cases, of course, anything can happen.

Even when a causation is nearly entirely hereditary, there are many exceptions (as tall women demonstrate). Priests choose to be celibate, but this does not cast doubt on the physiological basis of the "sex drive." To be sure, there is also feedback from the environmental to the physiological, so that association of physical strength with males results in more males lifting weights.

However, in principle, a society could find itself with women who were physically stronger than men if women lifted weights throughout their lives and men remained sedentary.

But, in real life, this can't happen because the social environment is a *dependent* variable whose limits are set by our physiological construction. In real life we all observe a male's dominance tendency that is rooted in physiological differences between males and females and, because values and attitudes are not of primary causal importance here, we develop expectations concordant with the male–female behavioral differences.

Most of the discussion of sex differences has emphasized the neuro-endocrinological differentiation of males and females and the cognitive and behavioral differentiation this engenders. This is because there is an enormous amount of evidence demonstrating the role of hormones in fetally differentiating the male and female central nervous systems, CNS response to the potentiating properties of certain hormones, and the thoughts and actions of males and females.

There is not room here for detailed discussion of the neuro-endocrinological mechanism underlying dominance behavior. But a useful analogy is iron and magnet. Iron does not have a "drive" or a "need" to find a magnet, but when there is a magnet in the area, iron, as a result of the very way it is built, tends to react in a certain way. Likewise, the physiological natures of males and females predispose them to have different hierarchies of response to various environmental cues. There is no response that only one sex has; the difference between men and women is the relative strengths of different responses. Males react more readily to hierarchical competitiveness than do females; females react more readily to the needs of an infant-in-distress. Norms and socialization do not cause this difference, but reflect it and make concrete a specific society's specific methods for manifesting the response. (Cleaning a rifle and preparing Spaghetti-Os are not instinctive abilities).

The iron–magnet analogy makes clear the role of social environment. Were there to be a society without hierarchy, status, values, or interdependence of the sexes, there would be no environmental cue to elicit the differentiated, physiologically rooted responses we discuss. But it is difficult to imagine such a society and, indeed, there has never been such a society.

Even if we had no neuro-endocrinological evidence at all, the anthropological evidence alone would be sufficient to force us to posit a mechanism of sexual psycho-physiological differentiation and to predict its discovery. We do, however, possess the neuro-endocrinological evidence and the anthropological evidence permits us to specify the institutional effects—the limits of societal variation that the neuro-endocrinological engenders.

For thousands of years, everyone, save perhaps some social scientists and others ideologically opposed to the idea, have known perfectly well that men and women differ in the physiological factors that underlie masculine and feminine thought and behavior. They may not have known the words to describe the linkage of physiology with thought and behavior, but they knew the linkage was there. (I recently read a comment of a woman in Pennsylvania: "They keep telling us that men and women are the way they are because of what they've been taught, but you can go a hundred miles in any direction and not find a single person who really believes that.") And even the most feminist parent, once she has children, can't help but notice that it is nearly impossible to get small boys to play with dolls not named "Killer Joe, the Marauding Exterminator," or at least with trucks—*big* trucks.

None of this is to deny tremendous variation on the level of roles. Even in our own society, in just a century the role of secretary changed from virtually solely male to virtually solely female. With the exception of roles associated with child nurturance, political leadership, warfare, security, and crime, virtually every specific role is male in some societies and female in others. No one doubts that the women who exhibit the dominance behavior usually exhibited by men encounter discrimination. But the question remains: why is dominance behavior usually exhibited by *men*?

The implication of all this depends on context. Clearly the correctness or incorrectness of the theory I present is important to an understanding of human behavior and society. But to the individual man or woman, on the other hand, the universals are largely irrelevant. The woman who wishes to become President has a sufficient number of real-life equivalents to know that there is not a constraint rendering impossible a female head of state. But there is no more reason for such a woman to deny that the motivation to rule is more often associated with male physiology than there is for the six-foot woman to pretend that women are as tall as men.

POSTSCRIPT

Do Sexually Egalitarian Societies Exist?

In these two selections, Lepowsky and Goldberg disagree both on the interpretation of the facts and on the types of forces, cultural or biological, that determine relations between the sexes. Lepowsky argues that Vanatinai culture is basically sexually egalitarian and that this is due to a particular constellation of social and ideological features of their culture. Goldberg contends that men are dominant in every culture—the Vanatinai people would be no exception—and that men's innate drive to dominate would lead them to occupy most of the positions of authority and high status and to dominate women in interpersonal relations.

During the last 30 years, anthropologists have conducted many studies focusing specifically on gender ideas and roles in particular societies, especially in non-Western and tribal societies. Their general finding is that gender relations are much more complicated and variable than scholars thought in the early days of feminist anthropology. For example, studies have shown that not all societies make a simple distinction between domestic and public domains, associate women exclusively with a domestic domain, or evaluate activities outside the home as superior to those inside it. Scholars have also realized that analytical concepts like "male dominance" and the "status of women" are too crude. They have attempted to break them up into components that can be sought and measured in ethnographic field studies.

The question of whether or not males are dominant in a particular society is not as clear-cut as it once seemed. One important distinction now made, and reflected in Lepowsky's excerpt, is that between the actual practice of male-female roles and interactions and the ideologies that contain bases for evaluating the sexes and their activities. Studies show that in some societies women and men have similar amounts of influence over daily life, but the cultural ideology (or at least the men's ideology) portrays women as inferior to men. In some cases men's and women's spheres of activity and control are separate and independent. Some societies have competing ideologies, in which both men and women portray their own gender as superior. And some societies, such as the Hua of Papua New Guinea, have multiple ideologies, which simultaneously present women as inferior, superior, and equal to men (see Anna Meigs's book *Food, Sex, and Pollution: A New Guinea Religion* [Rutgers University Press, 1984]). Despite these complications, it may still be useful to term a culture in which both practice and ideology consistently point to equality or balance between the sexes as "sexually egalitarian," as Lepowsky does in the case of the Vanatinai. Of course Goldberg would say that such societies do not exist.

For more information on the Vanatinai people, see Lepowsky's book *Fruit of the Motherland: Gender in an Egalitarian Society* (Columbia University

Press, 1993). A very readable introduction to feminist anthropology is Henrietta Moore's book *Feminism and Anthropology* (University of Minnesota Press, 1988). An interesting collection of articles showing variations in male-female relations is Peggy Sanday and Ruth Goodenough's edited volume *Beyond the Second Sex: New Directions in the Anthropology of Gender* (University of Pennsylvania Press, 1990). For a discussion of gender equality and inequality among hunter-gatherers, see Karen L. Endicott's article "Gender Relations in Hunter-Gatherer Societies," in *The Cambridge Encyclopedia of Hunters and Gatherers,* Richard B. Lee and Richard Daly, eds. (Cambridge University Press, 1999).

For a full explication of Goldberg's theory of innate male dominance, see his book *Why Men Rule: A Theory of Male Dominance* (Open Court, 1993). Other works that argue for a biological basis for male dominance include Lionel Tiger's book *Men in Groups* (Holt, Rinehart & Winston, 1969); Lionel Tiger and Robin Fox's book *The Imperial Animal* (Holt, Rinehart & Winston, 1971); Robert Wright's article "Feminists Meet Mr. Darwin," *The New Republic* (November 28, 1994); and Barbara Smuts's article "The Origins of Patriarchy: An Evolutionary Perspective," in A. Zagarell's edited volume *Origins of Gender Inequality* (New Issues Press, in press).

Is It Natural for Adopted Children to Want to Find Out About Their Birth Parents?

YES: Betty Jean Lifton, from *Journey of the Adopted Self: A Quest for Wholeness* (Basic Books, 1994)

NO: John Terrell and Judith Modell, from "Anthropology and Adoption," *American Anthropologist* (March 1994)

ISSUE SUMMARY

YES: Adoptee and adoption rights advocate Betty Jean Lifton argues that there is a natural need for human beings to know where they came from. Adoption is not a natural human state, she asserts, and it is surrounded by a secrecy that leads to severe social and psychological consequences for adoptees, adoptive parents, and birth parents.

NO: Anthropologists John Terrell and Judith Modell, who are each the parent of an adopted child, contend that the "need" to know one's birth parents is an American (or Western European) cultural construct. They conclude that in other parts of the world, where there is less emphasis placed on biology, adoptees have none of the problems said to be associated with being adopted in America.

The 1976 television miniseries *Roots*, based on the book by Alex Haley, led many Americans to try to search out their own family stories, to find their own "roots." For most the effort merely meant asking grandparents about their ancestors. But for adopted children in America, information about their forebears was sealed by court order, and there was rarely any knowledge about their birth parents available to them from their adopted parents. Information about birth parents was usually kept secret to protect the birth parents from public scandal, since most adopted children were conceived out of wedlock and quietly put up for adoption with the understanding that the child and the public would never be able to link the birth parents with the adoptee. As social mores have changed in the United States, relatively little stigma now surrounds being an unwed mother or a single parent. But court records for most adoptions remain sealed, leading to a growing movement advocating open adoption records.

For several decades, adoptees' attempts to find their birth parents have become a growing social movement, with advocacy organizations, support groups, and self-help groups all attempting to help adoptees find their birth parents and which often help birth parents find the children they put up for adoption in their youth. Many of these groups insist that there is an inherent human right for adoptees to know their biological parents and for parents to know their natural children. These groups contend that there is a natural bond between parents and children that has been severed by adoption.

In the following selection, Betty Jean Lifton considers the psychological factors at play when children are put up for adoption, where knowledge of their birth parents is denied them. Drawing on her personal experiences as an adoptee as well as on interviews with dozens of other adoptees, Lifton considers how psychologically damaging this veil of secrecy is on adoptees, both as children and as adults. For her, people have a natural need to know where they came from. It is unnatural to grow up separated from and without knowledge of one's natural clan, she argues. The lack of such knowledge of one's roots has a negative impact on the child's psyche and leads them to seek out their roots, concludes Lifton.

Anthropologists John Terrell and Judith Modell counter that the "natural" need to know one's parents, as so often discussed by the adoption rights movement, is an American cultural construct. American and Western European culture emphasizes the difference between biological and adoptive families, viewing adoptive relationships as less real than biological ones. In most non-Western societies, people have very different views of adoption, typically viewing adoptive relationships as equal to biological ones. Citing examples from Hawaii and other parts of Oceania, they challenge the primacy of blood relationships over all other kinds of kinship ties. They argue that in America open adoptions would probably be healthier for all concerned parties but that it would be better still if Americans had a better understanding of the diverse ways other peoples have for understanding and dealing with adoption.

Are kin relations based on biology stronger than relationships based on other ties? Is there something in our genes that makes us have a more important relationship with our biological or birth parents than with others? Are adoptees likely to have stronger bonds with their adopted parents than with their birth parents? What do the experiences of Hawaiians and other Pacific Islanders say about how natural it is to want to know one's birth parents? Is the adoption rights movement in America a social phenomenon that could only emerge in America or does it touch on universal values and psychological needs?

Betty Jean Lifton

 **YES**

Betwixt and Between

"Then I shan't be exactly human?" Peter asked.
"No."
"What shall I be?"
"You will be Betwixt-and-Between," Solomon said, and
certainly he was a wise old fellow, for that is exactly how
it turned out.

— James Barrie, *Peter Pan in Kensington Gardens*

Many people identify with the familiar condition of being Betwixt and Between, just as they identify with Peter Pan, the boy who did not want to grow
up and face the responsibilities of the real world.

Peter, James Barrie tells us, is "ever so old," but really always the same age:
one week. Though he was born "so long ago," he never had a birthday, nor is
there the slightest chance of his having one. He escaped from his home when
he was seven days old by flying out the window to Kensington Gardens.

Barrie doesn't tell us what was going on in Peter's family that after only
seven days he knew he had to take off. But adoptees recognize Peter Pan as a
brother. They, too, became lost children when they separated as babies from
their natural families and disappeared into a place very much like never-never
land. Like Peter, they are fantasy people. Denied the right to see their real birth
certificates and the names of those who brought them into the world, they can't
be sure they ever had a real *birth* day. They can never grow up because they are
always referred to as an "adopted child."

I didn't realize that, like Peter, I wasn't "exactly human" until I was seven
years old. It was the moment my mother told me I was adopted. Like most adoptive parents faced with breaking such bleak news, she tried to make adoption
sound special, but I could feel the penetrating chill of its message. I was not
really her child. I had come from somewhere else, a place shrouded in mystery,
a place that, like myself, was Betwixt and Between.

As I listened, I could feel a part of myself being pulled into the darkness of
that mystery—a place already carved out by Peter and the lost children. I would
never be the same again.

This was to be our secret, my mother said. Hers and mine. I was not to share it with anyone—not even my father. It would break his heart if he suspected I knew. In this way I learned that secrecy and adoption were inextricably mixed, as in a witch's brew. By becoming a keeper of the secret, I was to collaborate in the family conspiracy of silence.

I didn't know then that our little family secret was connected to the *big* secret in the closed adoption system, just as our little conspiracy was connected to the larger social conspiracy around adoption. My mother and father had been assured that my birth records would be sealed forever, that I would never be able to learn the identity of my original family. Secrecy was the magic ingredient that would give our adoptive family the aura of a blood-related one. Secrecy was the magic broom that would sweep away all feelings of grief and loss on the part of any of the parties involved.

As I played my role of the good daughter—repressing a natural need to know where I came from—I was unaware that the secrecy inherent in the adoption system was shaping and constricting the self through which I organized my perception of reality. By denying my natural curiosity about where I came from, and my grief for my lost birth parents and for the child I might have been, I was shrinking my emotional space to the size permitted by that system. So, too, were my adoptive parents forced by the secrecy to shrink their emotional space as they denied their need to grieve for the natural child they might have had.

We were trapped in a closed family system where secrecy cut off real communication. We were not unlike those families who keep secrets around alcoholism, divorce, incest, and all the other things that family members are prone to hide from their neighbors and from one another.

I had no idea of this as a child. Having repressed my real feelings, I was not consciously aware of my pain. And as a consequence, I was not consciously aware of myself, except as someone unreal pretending to be real. I did things that my human friends did, even looked real in my high school and college graduation pictures, and in the photographs taken at my wedding, before I flew off with my husband to the Far East.

Perhaps I might have never been in touch with my feelings if, shortly after my return from Japan, a relative, recently married into my adoptive family, had not remarked about something she heard—that my natural parents had been killed in a car accident. Her statement was like a Zen slap, knocking me into another state of consciousness. I had been told my parents were dead, but I had not been told this story. When I tried to clear up the mystery of how they died, I was shocked to learn that they had been very much alive at the time of my adoption—and might still be.

Much that had lain repressed in me now began stirring. I started to wonder how my mind had been able to cut off the primal subject of who my parents were. Even if it were true that they were dead, why had I not asked any questions about them? After all, dead people have names; they have relatives they have left behind; they have graves. Why had I behaved as if death had wiped out all traces of their existence? It was my first conscious brush with the psychological mystery that forms the core of this [selection]: How does a child's mind close down when it senses danger, and stay closed until some life event or crisis inadvertently jars it open? And what traumatic effects does this have on the child's growing sense of self?

◈

As a writer, I set out to explore the psychological complexities of being adopted in my book *Twice Born: Memoirs of an Adopted Daughter.* I was amazed, even alarmed, at what surfaced. The compliant adopted child within, as elusive as ever, was in many ways a stranger to the adult I had become. The anger, barely contained under what passed as irony and wit, could no longer be disguised as I dredged up memories of that child's helplessness in the face of mysteries too dark to comprehend. Even as I wrote about my search and reunion, I felt burdened with guilt, as if it were a disloyalty to my deceased adoptive parents. Nor had I fully absorbed the depths of what I had been through. I found a birth mother who had tried to hold on to me but, as an unmarried seventeen-year-old with no emotional or financial support, finally had to let go. Once she was defeated, she put on the scarlet letter—S for secrecy and shame—and did not tell either of her two husbands or her son about me. We met secretly twice before I had to leave for a summer in Japan. The psychic chaos I felt during those two months in Tokyo—as if I had fallen into a black hole—was so great that when I returned to the States I did not call her for fear of falling back into that dark place: a place, as we will see, that is not unfamiliar to many adoptees who have internalized the taboos of the closed adoption system. At the time of my reunion, there were no books to sanction my search for my mother or to prepare me for what I might experience.

My next book, *Lost and Found, the Adoption Experience,* was an attempt to write such a book and, in so doing, to illuminate the existential condition of being adopted. I explored the psychological pitfalls that await adoptees all through the life cycle when they are forced to close off their real feelings and live *as if* their families of origin were not an inherent part of their identity. I laid out the difficult stages of awakening that adoptees experience before they dare to set out in search of the missing pieces in their lives.

As the search phenomenon was still relatively new at that time, the last part of the book gave an overview of the varieties of reunion experience and the psychological growth and accommodation that everyone—adoptee, adoptive parents, and birth parents—has to make....

◈

[Looking at my own life,] I found an adopted woman waiting there, one who was more sensitive than ever to the lack of respect for the rights of adopted children to know who they are, and who was still absorbed with the psychological mysteries inherent in adoption. Once again I was faced with the same questions I had been grappling with earlier: Why do adopted people feel so alienated? Why do they feel unreal, invisible to themselves and others? Why do they feel unborn? Now, however, I had a new question that I felt would shed light on the others: How do adopted people form a sense of self in the closed adoption system?

The psychoanalyst Karen Horney defined the real self as the alive, unique, personal center of ourselves that wants to grow. When the real self is prevented from free, healthy growth because of abandoning its needs to others, one can become alienated from it. She quotes Kierkegaard on the alienation and loss of self as "sickness unto death." Adoptees, who often say they feel they have no self, can be seen as expressing this despair. Having abandoned their need to know their origins for the sake of their adoptive parents, they are left with a hole in the center of their being. They feel they don't exist.

Of course, everyone has some kind of self. The adoptee born psychologically into the closed adoption system and shaped by its myths, secrets, and taboos from first conscious memory, and even before, has a unique self, an adopted self. But this fragile self has a basic inner division brought about by the need for denial that is built into the closed adoption system.

When I began research for this [selection], I was primarily interested in how secrecy affects the formation of the adopted self. I saw it as emotional abuse (of which adoptive parents are unaware) because it distorts the child's psychic reality. In the course of interviewing adoptees, however, I realized that it is not just secrecy that affects their sense of self but rather a series of traumas. This "cumulative adoption trauma" begins when they are separated from the mother at birth; builds when they learn that they were not born to the people they call mother and father; and is further compounded when they are denied knowledge of the mother and father to whom they were born.

I was not unfamiliar with the literature on trauma. My husband, Robert Jay Lifton, has been preoccupied with trauma on a massive scale. As a journalist, I have reported on the war-wounded, orphaned, and traumatized children of Hiroshima, Korea, Vietnam, and the Holocaust. Still, as an adopted person, loyal to my adoptive parents, I didn't allow myself to see that closed adoption is also a form of trauma—an invisible and subtle one—until years later when I began noticing parallels between adopted children and children of alcoholics, children of survivors (even survivors themselves), and children who have been abused.

There has already been some misunderstanding about the linking of adoption to trauma. Far from being regarded as traumatic, adoption is still widely viewed as fortunate for the child who is rescued from homelessness, and for the adoptive parents who are rescued from childlessness. And in most cases it is. Yet the word *trauma* has been slipping into the psychological literature on adoption with increasing frequency in the last decade as clinicians come to realize the high psychic cost that both parent and child pay when they repress their grief and loss.

I have come to believe in the course of my research that it is unnatural for members of the human species to grow up separated from and without knowledge of their natural clan, that such a lack has a negative influence on a child's psychic reality and relationship with the adoptive parents. By enveloping their origins with secrecy, the closed adoption system asks children to disavow reality, to live *as if* they were born to the parents who raise them. They grow up feeling like anonymous people cut off from the genetic and social heritage that gives everyone else roots.

⊷⊙⊶

As I write this, we are Betwixt and Between change and stasis in the adoption field. We are between two systems: the traditional closed one that for almost half a century has cut adopted children off from their heritage, and an open one in which birth mothers choose the adoptive parents of their baby and maintain some contact with the family. It is a time when the best interests of the child, for which the adoption system was originally created, have become subordinate to the best interests of the adults, as fierce custody battles are waged over the few available healthy white infants.

Meanwhile, adoption records remain sealed in all but two states due to the influence of a conservative lobby group, the National Council for Adoption, that has managed to polarize the field by labeling those who seek reform as "anti-adoption." Reformers who are working to open the system, as well as the records, however, are not anti-adoption but rather anti–closed adoption and pro–adopted children.

While no amount of openness can take away the child's trauma of being separated from his mother, or save the child from the trauma of learning she was not born into the adoptive family, we can remove the secrecy that compounds those two traumas. We can begin to demystify the adoptive family and to see it with much of the strengths and weaknesses of other families. The conservatives argue for the myth of the happy adoptive family that has no problems because love conquers all. But we will see that something more is expected of the adopted family: an excess of happiness that is meant to make up for the excess of loss that everyone in the triad experiences, and an excess of denial to cover that loss. Exposing the myths of the adoptive family while still holding on to the very real need and love that parents and child have for each other has been the challenge facing me. . . .

The adoptees [I studied] are mostly successful people in that they are productive in their work and their private lives. But, . . . much of their psychic energy has been taken up with adjusting to the mystery of their origins by disavowing their need to have some knowledge of and contact with their blood kin. . . .

The adoptive family has managed to "pass" until now; it remains, for the most part, an unexplored constellation that has escaped psychological detection. Many professionals regard its psychodynamics as being the same as that of other families, overlooking the trauma that the parents as well as the child experience due to the conspiracy of silence built into the closed system.

Because it is a social rather than a natural construct, we can see the strengths and malfunctions of the adoptive family as a laboratory to illuminate some of the most fundamental issues around mothering and mother loss, attachment and bonding, separation and loss, denial and dissociation, and the human need for origins. We can see the deep need that parents and child fill for each other, but we can also see the problems that occur between parents and child when secrets prevent open communication between them.

In *Lost and Found* I spoke of what I called the Adoption Game, a family system that operates by unspoken rules that require everyone in it to live a double life. While seeming to exist in the real world with their adoptive family, the children are at the same time inhabiting an underground world of fantasies and fears which they can share with no one. The adoptive parents also live a double life. Believing themselves to be doing everything for their children, they withhold from them the very knowledge they need to develop into healthy adults. This double role of savior/withholder eventually works against the adoptive parents, estranging them from their children. So, too, the birth mother is forced to live a double life from the moment she surrenders her baby. Advised to go on as if nothing has happened, she keeps secret what is probably the most important and traumatic event of her life.

In [*Journey of the Adopted Self: A Quest for Wholeness*], I speak not of adoption games but of adoption ghosts. In many ways [the] book is a ghost story, for it tells of the ghosts that haunt the dark crevices of the unconscious and trail each member of the adoption triangle (parents and child alike) wherever they go. Unless one is aware of these ghosts, one will never be able to understand or to help the child who is adopted, the parents who adopt, or the parents who give up a child to adoption.

Who are these ghosts?

The adopted child is always accompanied by the ghost of the child he might have been had he stayed with his birth mother and by the ghost of the fantasy child his adoptive parents might have had. He is also accompanied by the ghost of the birth mother, from whom he has never completely disconnected, and the ghost of the birth father, hidden behind her.

The adoptive mother and father are accompanied by the ghost of the perfect biological child they might have had, who walks beside the adopted child who is taking its place.

The birth mother (and father, to a lesser extent) is accompanied by a retinue of ghosts. The ghost of the baby she gave up. The ghost of her lost lover, whom she connects with the baby. The ghost of the mother she might have been. And the ghosts of the baby's adoptive parents.

All of these ghosts are members of the extended adoptive family, which includes the birth family. . . .

[The] book, then, is about the search for the adopted self. It is not about the literal search in the material world, where one sifts through records and archives for real people with real names and addresses; but rather about the internal search in which one sifts through the pieces of the psyche in an attempt to understand who one was so that one can have some sense ot who one is and who one can become. It is the quest for all the missing pieces of the self so that one can become whole.

It is the search for the answer to that universal question—Who am I?—behind which, for the adoptee, lurks: Who is the mother who brought me into this mysterious world?

 **NO**

Anthropology and Adoption

Anthropologists, we believe, are likely to forget that "what every anthropologist knows" is not necessarily what everyone else knows. In the quest for tenure, professional visibility, and academic achievement, anthropologists may also overlook the possibility that what they know could be important to people who are not anthropologists, too, if only they know. Here is one example.

Adoption in America

In North America, most children grow up living with at least one of the parents they were born to; most children grow up assuming they will live with children born to them. Consequently, perhaps, many people in our society think of adoption as a second-best way of becoming a family (Schaffer and Lindstrom 1989:15). The psychological and social ties binding an adoptive family together are looked on as weaker than "natural" ties of blood. And adoption is seen as difficult and risky. The risk is held to be especially great when a child does not "match"—look like or share the background of—its adoptive parents (Bates 1993). This is preeminently true of transracial and international adoptions, in which a child, who has no say in the matter, is severed not only from its "real" family but also from ethnic roots and cultural heritage: in a word, from its true identity.

Recently, advocates of adoption have been emphasizing the difference between adoptive and biological families (e.g., Melina 1986; Register 1991; Schaffer and Lindstrom 1989), often as a way of helping parents through such "alternative parenthood" (Kirk 1984). Adoptive families are different, for one thing, because adoption is not typical in American society. They are more profoundly different because, it is said, all parties in the "adoption triad" (birth parents, adoptees, and adoptive parents) must cope with psychological pain and feelings of loss. Adoptive parents "lose" the chance to have a biological child and the perpetuation of their blood line. An adopted child loses its natural heritage. And birth parents lose their children.

Moreover, it is presumed that adoptive parents must deal with feelings of inadequacy, and birth parents with feelings of incompetence or frustration. Adoptees, in this argument, suffer throughout their lives because "adoption cuts off people from a part of themselves" (Brodzinsky et al. 1992:3). Even children who were adopted in the first days or weeks of life "grieve not only for the parents they never knew, but for the other aspects of themselves that have been lost through adoption: the loss of origins, of a completed sense of self, of genealogical continuity" (Brodzinsky et al. 1992:11–12). Because they have not been raised by those who gave them life, even the most well-adjusted adoptees, we are told, go through predictable ups and downs of psychological adaptation that distinguish them as a recognizable class of persons who may need special counseling and professional help (Brodzinsky et al. 1992; Samuels 1990:87–113).

Adoption in Oceania

Anthropologists know that what is problematic or self-evident in one society may not be so in another. Oceanic societies—Hawaii among them—are well known in anthropological literature for the frequency and apparent casualness of adoption. What most Americans know about our 50th state, however, does not usually include the information that the last reigning monarch was an adopted, or *hanai,* child. Moreover, this was a crucial fact in her story and remains significant in the interpretations Hawaiians make of their culture and history. In her autobiography, Queen Liliuokalani wrote:

> Immediately after my birth I was wrapped in the finest soft tapa cloth, and taken to the house of another chief, by whom I was adopted. Konia, my foster-mother, was a granddaughter of Kamehameha I., and was married to Paki, also a high chief; their only daughter, Bernice Pauahi, afterwards Mrs. Charles R. Bishop, was therefore my foster-sister. In speaking of our relationship, I have adopted the term customarily used in the English language, but there was no such modification recognized in my native land. I knew no other father or mother than my foster-parents, no other sister than Bernice.
> [Liliuokalani 1990:4]

She goes on to say that Paki treated her exactly as any other father would treat his child, and that when she would meet her biological parents, she would respond with perhaps more interest, but always with the same demeanor that was due all strangers who noticed her.

Liliuokalani adds that her biological mother and father had other children, ten in all. Most of them were adopted into other chiefs' families. She says it is difficult to explain to outsiders why these adoptions seem perfectly natural to Hawaiians. "As intelligible a reason as can be given is that this alliance by adoption cemented the ties of friendship between chiefs. It spread to the common people, and it has doubtless fostered a community of interest and harmony" (Liliuokalani 1990:4).

Given what anthropologists know about adoption throughout Oceania, (for example, Brady 1976; Carrol 1970; Howard 1990; Levy 1973; Mandeville 1981; Webster 1975), what this royal informant says about the place and popularity of adoption in her native land is not peculiar. For her—and not uniquely—adoption was a loving and generous transaction, not a response to need or crisis. Furthermore, such a loving and generous gesture benefited the whole society as well as the particular individuals involved.

The point of view represented by Queen Liliuokalani—and by other people in Pacific Island societies who share her experiences (Modell 1994a)—ought to be a lesson for Americans, with our quite different story of adoption. As Bartholet (1993) argues, birth parents, adoptive parents, and adoptees should know that people elsewhere in the world may look on adoption in a variety of ways that do not resemble our assumptions and biases about this form of kinship. They need to know that what adoption means, and what it signifies for participants, is malleable, contingent, pragmatic: a "social construction," not a natural fact or a universal cultural given.

Anthropology and Adoption

Anthropologists are likely to find this observation self-evident; adoption is made —*fictio*—by those who practice this mode of child having and child rearing. But, with some exceptions (e.g., Modell 1994b), anthropologists have not been drawn to study the politics and practice of adoption in Western societies: apparently what anthropologists find interesting elsewhere may be less interesting, or deeply private, at home. A glance over the abundant published literature on kinship, in fact, suggests that studying adoption generally plays a peripheral role in anthropology: as a way of illuminating a kinship system, as a mechanism of social mobility, or as a way of transmitting property. Little disciplinary attention has been paid to the diverse ways people think about, react to, and represent the meaning of adoption.

This is not to say that nothing exists on the subject. In the early 20th century, Lowie remarked on the frequency of adoption in Pacific Island societies, forgetting his cultural relativism to claim that child exchange in such societies went "well beyond the rational" (Lowie 1933). His surprise prompted others to inquire into the consequences of the unfamiliar behavior of moving large numbers of children from household to household. Three decades later, in the early 1960s, Levy discovered in a small village in Tahiti that more than 25 percent of children were adopted; this was not untypical for Polynesian societies. Levy went on to analyze the impact of this generous "transaction in parenthood" in his path-breaking account of Tahitian culture and personality (Levy 1973).

Anthropologists such as Marshall picked up other threads in the (slowly) growing tapestry on adoption in the Pacific. In an article examining created kin in Trukese society, Marshall concludes that what is common to kinship is a notion of sharing, differently enacted and represented in different contexts (1977:656–657). To analyze kinship cross-culturally and without bias, he argues, one must explore the nature of nurture and of sharing. His article demonstrates the significance of creating kin through constructed sibling and parent-child bonds for revealing the meanings of kinship. To act like kin is to be kin; to care for reciprocally is to have a relationship. Conduct and performance make (and unmake) kin, with a fluidity that differs from "biogenetic" notions of kinship characteristic of American society (Marshall 1977).

Marshall's article confirms the extent to which kinship is not "natural" but "cultural," representing an intense experience of love and of obligation between individuals. Moreover, these experiences may change over the course of a person's life, depending on circumstances and on perceptions of the "useful-ness" and rewards of being related.

Two volumes on adoption in Oceania underscored the importance of created kinship in Pacific Island societies: [Vern] Carroll's *Adoption in Ocea-nia* (1970) and [Ivan] Brady's *Transactions in Kinship* (1976). In both volumes the contributing anthropologists explore the structure and the functions of adoption, with varying degrees of attention to Carroll's initial warning about applying the single term *adoption* to diverse arrangements across cultures. The goal of challenging the universality of a definition of *adoption* is, as Ward Good-enough concludes in the epilogue to the 1970 volume, only imperfectly met. Treating adoption largely as a social institution, the articles in these volumes tended not to explore the meanings of the experience for the individuals in-volved or to establish a framework for interpretive analysis of the cultural and personal significance of "child exchange" wherever, and however, it occurs.

Silk offers an alternative to the conventional treatment of adoption in an-thropological literature. In a 1980 article, she notes the frequency of adoption in Pacific Island societies compared with almost all others in the world, and asks why. Her answer draws on sociobiological theory. Silk argues that as a way of modifying extreme family size, adoption is adaptive for the group, though it may be a risk for the individual child. Following her theoretical premise, the risk lies in the tendency of parents to treat their biological—more *closely related* —children differently from the way they treat an adopted child (Silk 1980:803). She further suggests that, consequently (and necessarily), biological parents re-tain an interest in the child they have given away; thus, bonds are maintained, not severed, by adoption. In offering a sociobiological explanation, Silk does not mean to exclude the social and cultural factors that affect the transaction; her primary aim is to distinguish societies in which adoption occurs frequently from those in which it occurs rarely (Silk 1980:816). She does not question the concept of adoption itself.

Frequency has continued to be a feature that brings adoption to the atten-tion of anthropologists, most of whom come from a society in which adoption affects "only" about 2 or 3 percent of children in any one year (Adamec and Peirce 1991). Anthropologists of Eskimo (Inuit) societies, sounding rather like anthropologists of the Pacific, remark on the astonishing ease with which chil-dren are moved from parent to parent, for shorter or longer stays (Guemple 1979). Several of these studies inquire into the impact of this movement on the affective as well as the structural and functional domains of social life.

The frequency of adoption in large-scale, complex societies has also piqued anthropological interest, though without major impact on the disci-pline. In 1980, for instance, [Arthur] Wolf and [Chieh-shan] Huang published an exhaustive study of adoption in China whose importance has mainly been acknowledged by other Sinologists. *Marriage and Adoption in China 1845–1945* traces trends in the transactions of women and of children as these reflect social and political changes. With a century's worth of historical records, Wolf and Huang had data other anthropologists might envy. Yet their analysis remains conventional, assuming that the meaning of adoption can be transferred from "us" to "them" and describing the social to the exclusion of the psychological ramifications of the phenomenon.

The silence accorded to full-scale studies of adoption continues. To take a final example: Esther Goody's pioneering analysis of "child exchange" in West African societies and among West Africans in London recognizes the range of meanings and functions moving a child may have (Goody 1982). Discussing numerous particular cases in which parenthood is delegated, Goody reminds her readers that words like *adoption* and *fosterage* are culturally and historically relative as well as individually negotiated. Her book speaks a quiet warning against assuming that the meaning of adoption holds from group to group, time to time, or even person to person.

One cannot, of course, leave the subject of adoption and kinship without referring to the work of Jack Goody—especially his under-appreciated article, "Adoption in Cross Cultural Perspective." The point he made in this 1969 piece remains all too appropriate: "For I know of no attempt to do a systematic survey of the distribution of this phenomenon, which is not for example included in the data recorded in the Ethnographic Atlas (1967) nor mentioned in Goody's study of changing family patterns (1963)" (Goody 1969:56). As far as we know, his agenda for the comparative study of adoption has not been followed. Nor have the issues raised in the ethnographic writings cited above been taken as far as they might.

If anthropologists embrace the goal of examining rather than imposing meanings of core concepts on others—or, for that matter, our own society—then adoption would seem to be a crucial area of study. For it is here that the multivocal meanings of personhood and identity, of kinship and social bonds, can be thoroughly explored—and from the point of view of those who "make" these kinds of relationships. Existing writings on adoption suggest there is more to be said about the self-conscious gesture involved in creating kin and its diverse manifestations. Virtually everywhere it occurs, adoption inscribes and perpetuates understandings of birth, blood, and belonging, of essence and accident or choice. In the late 19th century, the British jurist Sir Henry Maine articulated the premise of his own culture's understanding of adoption: fictive kinship, he wrote, replicates "real" kinship; the bond of law "imitates" the bond of birth and the child is "as if begotten" (Maine 1861). The ramifications of this premise in Western society, and the import of transferring it to other societies, have too rarely been seen as problematic.

The treatment of adoption in anthropological literature perpetuates a sense that the concept is nonproblematic. The transaction of a child, evidently, is not considered either a major social event or a key cultural text; rather, child exchange is analyzed as "only" an aspect of kinship, form of social solidarity, or response to demographic conditions. The neglect also speaks to a conservatism about our methods and categories of analysis, despite (or perhaps because of) the popularity of postmodernist writings in the discipline. Further confirming this is the modest reception given to several recently published radical reexaminations of kinship, of kinship and gender, and of theories of identity and ethnicity (e.g., Collier and Yanagisako 1987; Linnekin and Poyer 1990a; Schneider 1984; Weston 1991). These studies do show, however, that at least some anthropologists are drastically rethinking the context and meaning of fundamental aspects of social life.

Kinship and Adoption

Adoption as a category of meaning, like adoption as social practice, is problematic. Western common sense says the distinction between kin and non-kin is self-evident, a distinction that allows for the concept of "*as if* begotten." Adoption is thus a phenomenological category betwixt categories, a category that straddles the fence, a category in our society that dooms those who fall within it to be both kin and non-kin—real and "fictive." As Schneider has demonstrated through his brilliant analysis of the cultural unit on Yap called *tabinau,* there is much to be gained by recognizing how considerably varied and flexible the meanings of words can be (Schneider 1984:21).

Although Western ideas about kinship and adoption assume the primacy of blood ties and biological inheritance and see people as discrete and bounded individuals (Linnekin and Poyer 1990b:2, 7), anthropologists know that these presuppositions are not universal. Pomponio, for example, notes that while children on Mandok Island, Papua New Guinea, are thought to share the substance of their parents and other kin, "substance" means more than it does in Western thought: not just shared biogenetic endowment but the combination of blood, food, and work. "The transubstantial nature of Mandok personhood is evidenced by their belief that firstborns can be 'created' through adoption, and adoption is not limited to married couples." Many children (13 of 81, or 16 percent of her sample), in fact, are adopted specifically for this purpose. She concludes, "The important substance here is not contained in blood or semen, but food and work (i.e., caretaking). By feeding and caring for a child, the substance of the adult is transferred to that child" (Pomponio 1990:54).

Lieber argues that what Pomponio observes about the nature of kinship and adoption on Mandok may be true of Oceanic societies generally. What it means to be a person in many Pacific Island societies is structured, he says, by local theories of ontogeny (Lieber 1990:71) in which what a person becomes is not "in their blood," but is credited instead to the nurturing social and physical environment within which they mature. In other words, as Howard has summarized the argument, kinship in Oceania is considered to be contingent rather than absolute.

> Thus, on the one hand, kinship has to be validated by social action to be recognized; on the other, kinship status can be achieved through social action (i.e., by consistently acting as kinsmen even though genealogical linkages may be questionable or unknown). [Howard 1990:266]

A similar argument made by Sahlins chastens anthropologists for separating adoption—and kinship—from all aspects of culture and social structure. In Hawaii, where belonging comes from action and relationships are contingent, Sahlins claims: "From family to state, the arrangements of society were in constant flux, a set of relationships constructed on the shifting sands of love" (Sahlins 1985:20). The civil state, he might have added, rests upon chosen attachments much like the relationship between parents and child.

Anthropology and the Public

The process of rethinking theories of the person, of kinship, and of social and cultural life that is essential to our discipline also bears on current debates about multiculturalism occurring throughout the American university environment. Anthropologists have expressed amazement that scholars from across the disciplinary spectrum have discovered "the other," "multivocality," and "multiculturalism" without discovering anthropology (Perry 1992). But it is equally fair to argue that anthropologists have not actively guided the debate or introduced an anthropological vocabulary to a public that will feel the effects of such debate.

Anthropologists—or at least anthropologists who read the *Anthropology Newsletter*—do not need to be told that it is important to be "public or perish" (Givens 1992). Nevertheless—all too often, it seems—anthropologists focus on what their colleagues will say about their work and overlook opportunities to be heard and appreciated by others. Even when they cannot grab newspaper headlines with startling news about lost tribes, missing links, or the oldest potsherds in the world, they need to ask themselves: who might be interested to know what I know?

Thanks to anthropologists such as Schneider, it may no longer be intellectually strategic to study adoption simply to refute the conventional wisdom that the bonds of kinship are genealogical—given by "birth" (Schneider 1984:169–177). Studying adoption can also be a way of discovering the meanings and implications of aspects of culture and social order that remain problematic for both anthropologists and the public. Adoption not only belies what Schneider has called "biologistic" ways of marking and defining human character, human nature, and human behavior (Schneider 1984:175), it also reveals interpretations of concepts like identity, family, and ethnicity.

Thus, for instance, a study of adoption can shed light on definitions of and criteria for "citizenship": What does it mean to belong to a group or nation, and is this linked with ideas about what it means to belong to a family? Nor is adoption irrelevant to larger concerns about assimilation, "true" cultural identity, and ethnic purity, raising as it does the problem of being "*as if* begotten" when contract has been the mode of entry. At core, adoption is about who belongs and how—a subject of immense political as well as disciplinary significance. It is also, and increasingly, about power, privilege, and poverty. Concerns are properly raised about babies moving from the poor to the rich, or, a new version of the old "baby-selling" cry, about residents of impoverished nations and regions putting their babies on the international market. But anthropologists have not addressed those concerns. Moreover, these are issues that touch the lives of a general public, well beyond those who may experience, or know about, an adoptive relationship.

Conclusion

In societies such as ours where caring for children who are not one's own by birth is seen as risky, painful, and unnatural, learning through anthropology's eyes that what adoption does to people is not written in stone would undoubtedly be beneficial to birth parents, adoptive parents, and adoptees. It seems equally apparent that studying adoption in different societies can be a window through which anthropologists may learn about other facets of life.

Our own interest in adoption (beyond the powerful consideration that we are both adoptive parents) lies in both these directions. We are interested in adoption as an empirical question. What are the meanings, values, and contexts of caring for children "other than your own" in different societies? What determines the place and popularity (or lack thereof) of adoption in different societies? The agenda Jack Goody set over twenty years ago can benefit from recent literature on reflexivity and multivocalism, so that adoption is considered not only a social transaction but also a cultural text. The comparative task, then, will involve analyzing the forms of attachment and the representations of experience constituted by adoption—or, broadly, "child exchange"—as practiced by diverse cultural groups.

A study of adoption becomes an inquiry into fundamental beliefs about the person and personal connections as these intertwine with political, economic, and historical developments. Taking the perspective of constructed kinship and making the most of the "construction" it entails, so that adoption is not assumed to be univocal or universal in meaning, can advance theories of culture creativity, human agency, and identity formation. Ideally, studying adoption will preserve the centrality of individual experiences in the composition of social worlds and cultural texts.

We also want to strengthen public awareness of the diverse ways that people in different parts of the world—and in different ethnic communities here in North America—build and value human relationships and family ties and obligations. In the process we should demonstrate that anthropology importantly is, as it historically has been, a "way of seeing" for those other than its practitioners.

References

Adamec, Christine, and William Peirce, 1991, The Encyclopedia of Adoption. New York: Facts on File.

Bartholet, Elizabeth, 1993, Family Bonds. Adoption and the Politics of Parenting. Boston: Houghton Mifflin.

Bates, J. Douglas, 1993, Gift Children. A Story of Race, Family, and Adoption in a Divided America. New York: Ticknor and Fields.

Brady, Ivan, ed., 1976, Transactions in Kinship: Adoption and Fosterage in Oceania. Honolulu: University of Hawaii Press.

Brodzinsky, David M., Marshall D. Schechter, and Robin Marantz Henig, 1992, Being Adopted. The Lifelong Search for Self. New York: Doubleday.

Carrol, Vern, ed., 1970, Adoption in Eastern Oceania. Honolulu: University of Hawaii Press.

Collier, Jane Fishburne, and Sylvia Junko Yanagisako, eds., 1987, Gender and Kinship. Essays toward a Unified Analysis. Stanford: Stanford University Press.

Givens, David B., 1992, Public or Perish. Anthropology Newsletter 33(5):1, 58.

Goody, Esther, 1982, Parenthood and Social Reproduction. New York: Cambridge University Press.

Goody, Jack, 1969, Adoption in Cross-Cultural Perspective. Comparative Studies in Society and History 2:55–78.

Guemple, D. L., 1979, Inuit Adoption. Ottawa: National Museums of Canada.

Howard, Alan, 1990, Cultural Paradigms, History, and the Search for Identity in Oceania, *In* Cultural Identity and Ethnicity in the Pacific. Jocelyn Linnekin and Lin Poyer, eds. Pp. 259–279. Honolulu: University of Hawaii Press.

Kirk, H. David, 1984, Shared Fate. A Theory and Method of Adoptive Relationships. Port Angeles, WA: Ben-Simon Publications.

Levy, Robert, 1973, The Tahitians: Mind and Experience in the Society Islands. Chicago: University of Chicago Press.

Lieber, Michael D., 1990, Lamarckian Definitions of Identity on Kapingamarangi and Pohnpei. *In* Cultural Identity and Ethnicity in the Pacific. Jocelyn Linnekin and Lin Poyer, eds. Pp. 71–101. Honolulu: University of Hawaii Press.

Liliuokalani, 1990, Hawaii's Story by Hawaii's Queen. Honolulu: Mutual Publishing.

Linnekin, Jocelyn, and Lin Poyer, 1990a, [eds.] Cultural Identity and Ethnicity in the Pacific. Honolulu: University of Hawaii Press.

_____, 1990b, Introduction. *In* Cultural Identity and Ethnicity in the Pacific. Jocelyn Linnekin and Lin Poyer, eds. Pp. 1–16. Honolulu: University of Hawaii Press.

Lowie, Robert, 1933, Adoption. *In* Encyclopedia of the Social Sciences. E. A. Seligman and A. Johnson, eds. Pp. 459–460. New York: Macmillan and Company.

Maine, Sir Henry, 1861, Ancient Law. London: Macmillan.

Mandeville, Elizabeth, 1981, Kamano Adoption. Ethnology 20:229–244.

Marshall, Mac, 1977, The Nature of Nurture. American Ethnologist 4(4):643–662.

Melina, Lois Ruskai, 1986, Raising Adopted Children. A Manual for Adoptive Parents. New York: Harper and Row.

Modell, Judith, 1994a, Nowadays Everyone Is *Hanai:* Child Exchange and the Construction of Hawaiian Urban Culture. *In* Urban Cultures in the Pacific. C. Jourdan and J. M. Philibert, eds. Forthcoming.

_____, 1994b, Kenship with Strangers: Adoption and Interpretations of Kinship in American Culture. Berkeley: University of California Press.

Perry, Richard J., 1992, Why Do Multiculturalists Ignore Anthropologists? Chronicle of Higher Education 38(26):A52.

Pomponio, Alice, 1990, Seagulls Don't Fly into the Bush: Cultural Identity and the Negotiations of Development on Mandok Island, Papua New Guinea. *In* Cultural Identity and Ethnicity in the Pacific. Jocelyn Linnekin and Lin Poyer, eds. Pp. 43–70. Honolulu: University of Hawaii Press.

Register, Cheri, 1991, "Are Those Kids Yours?" American Families with Children Adopted from Other Countries. New York: Free Press.

Sahlins, Marshall, 1985, Islands of History. Chicago: University of Chicago Press.

Samuels, Shirley C., 1990, Ideal Adoption: A Comprehensive Guide to Forming an Adoptive Family. New York: Plenum.

Schaffer, Judith, and Christina Lindstrom, 1989, How to Raise an Adopted Child. A Guide to Help Your Child Flourish from Infancy through Adolescence. New York: Penguin Books.

Schneider, David M., 1984, A Critique of the Study of Kinship. Ann Arbor: University of Michigan Press.

Silk, Joan, 1980, Adoption and Kinship in Oceania. American Anthropologist 82(4):799–820.

Webster, Steven, 1975, Cognatic Descent Groups and the Contemporary Maori: A Preliminary Reassessment. Journal of the Polynesian Society 84:121–152.

Weston, Kath, 1991, Families We Choose: Lesbians, Gays, Kinship. New York: Columbia University Press.

Wolf, Arthur, and Chieh-shan Huang, 1980, Marriage and Adoption in China, 1845–1945. Stanford: Stanford University Press.

POSTSCRIPT

Is It Natural for Adopted Children to Want to Find Out About Their Birth Parents?

Lifton's argument is clearly situated within the adoption rights movement and draws upon her personal experiences as much as on the experiences of those she has interviewed. She and her American informants clearly have a burning need to know who their birth parents are, and she concludes that it is unnatural for anyone to be deprived of this information. She and her informants feel a certain amount of psychic pain and emptiness, as well as lack of wholeness.

Terrell and Modell, on the other hand, argue that however real such feelings may be, they are cultural constructs rather than natural, biological ones. They cite examples from Pacific Island societies to show that such feelings are not human universals but culturally specific responses to a particular normative kinship structure.

This issue raises questions about just how "natural" are kinship systems in different societies. American society has long placed emphasis on biological families, just as Americans have long accepted biologically or physiologically based illnesses as more real than psychological ones. As Terrell and Modell note, some anthropologists have not found it easy to ignore their own culture's views on adoption. Nevertheless, they argue that anthropologist David Schneider was essentially correct in his description of American kinship. In *American Kinship: A Cultural Account* (Prentice-Hall, 1968), he argues that while Americans contend that kinship is about biological relatedness, in practice it is those who "act" like close kin who are accepted as one's closest kinsmen. Thus, it is the social behavior rather than the genetic relationship that is most important in shaping our social worlds.

To what extent do significantly higher rates of adoption in Oceania or other parts of the world challenge American views that biologically based parent-child relationships are inherently more "real" than socially constructed relationship created by adoption? How are we to explain the strongly held views of Lifton and other adoption rights advocates, who clearly feel something lacking in their own lives if they do not and cannot know who their birth parents are?

Some of Lifton's other books include *Twice Born: Memoirs of an Adopted Daughter* (Penguin, 1977) and *Lost and Found: The Adoption Experience* (HarperCollins, 1988). Somewhat earlier versions of the same argument are provided by John Triseliotis's *In Search of Origins: The Experiences of Adopted People* (Routledge & Kegan Paul, 1973) and H. David Kirk's *Adoptive Kinship: A Modern Institution in Need of Reform* (Butterworths, 1981), as well as his *Shared*

Fate: A Theory and Method of Adoptive Relationships (Ben-Simon Publications, 1984). See also David M. Brodzinsky, Marshall D. Schechter, and Robin M. Henig's *Being Adopted: The Lifelong Search for Self* (Doubleday, 1992).

Modell has written a more extended view of the cultural construction of American adoption in *Kinship With Strangers: Adoption and Interpretations of Kinship in American Culture* (University of California Press, 1994). For similar perspectives, see Karen March's *The Stranger Who Bore Me: Adoptee-Birth Mother Relationships* (University of Toronto Press, 1995) and Katarina Wegar's *Adoption, Identity and Kinship: The Debate Over Sealed Birth Records* (Yale University Press, 1997). For a survey of current views of the problems of modern adoption, readers should consult a special issue of *Family Relations* (vol. 49, no. 4, October 2000), edited by Karen March and Charlene Miall.

For discussions of adoption in Pacific Island cultures, see *Adoption in Eastern Oceania* (University of Hawaii Press, 1970), edited by Vern Carroll. See also Jocelyn Linnekin and Lin Poyer's collection, *Cultural Identity and Ethnicity in the Pacific* (University of Hawaii Press, 1990), and Mac Marshall's essay "The Nature of Nurture," *American Ethnologist* (vol. 4, 1977).

ISSUE 10

Has the Islamic Revolution in Iran Subjugated Women?

YES: Parvin Paidar, from "Feminism and Islam in Iran," in Deniz Kandiyoti, ed., *Gendering the Middle East: Emerging Perspectives* (Syracuse University Press, 1996)

NO: Erika Friedl, from "Sources of Female Power in Iran," in Mahnaz Afkhami and Erika Friedl, eds., *In the Eye of the Storm: Women in Post-Revolutionary Iran* (Syracuse University Press, 1994)

ISSUE SUMMARY

YES: Iranian historian Parvin Paidar considers how the position of women suffered following the 1979 Iranian Revolution because of the imposition of Islamic law (shari'a), as interpreted by conservative male clerics. She contends that the Islamic Revolution marked a setback in the progressive modernist movements, which had improved women's rights during the secular regime of the Shah; new rights and opportunities have emerged since 1979 only in opposition to conservative interpretations of Islamic law.

NO: American anthropologist Erika Friedl asserts that men in Iran have consistently tried to suppress women's rights since the 1979 Iranian Revolution. Despite these efforts to repress them, women in all levels of society have access to many sources of power. In fact, argues Friedl, women have considerably more power available to them than either Western or Iranian stereotypes might suggest, even though they must work within Islamic law to obtain this power.

Perhaps nowhere has Islam's role in shaping the position of women been more obvious than in Afghanistan where the theocratic Taliban regime prevented women from working outside the home, from attending school, and from participating in the political process in any meaningful way. In Iran one of the effects of the 1979 revolution was that women suddenly lost most of the rights they had gradually obtained over the previous century. In both countries religious leaders have defended their actions and policies in terms of Islamic law, or *shari'a*, leading many Western observers to argue that this legal code inherently subjugates women. However, Muslim clerics have long argued that Islamic law does not subjugate women but merely defines men's and women's roles in society in complementary ways as prescribed by God.

At issue is whether or not Islamic customs, such as wearing head scarves, necessarily subordinate and subjugate women, as many feminist observers have argued. Or does Islamic law as interpreted by conservative male clerics merely delineate complementary social roles for men and women, as many Muslim scholars and religious leaders insist? Most importantly, if *shari'a* does not inherently subjugate women, why is it that the reimposition of *shari'a* law in the late twentieth century has so often included the loss of rights for Muslim women rather than enhancing their legal protections? In these countries, the more anti-Western and fundamentalist the religious and political leaders have become, the lower the apparent position of women.

Islam has traditionally depicted women as the weaker sex, in need of protection from the men in their lives. Such a view has shaped the social roles available to Islamic women in both conservative and progressive Muslim countries. Women in most Muslim countries have a much less obvious political voice in the affairs of the state than in Western countries, since politics is defined in Islamic law as the domain of men. But many observers have argued that within the household, women have considerably more power than Western observers have generally acknowledged.

The following selections consider the role and position of women in Iran. Parvin Paidar, herself an Iranian, documents the changing position of women since the nineteenth century. Here, she shows how women were able to draw on Western feminist ideas during the reign of the Shah to gain individual rights and improve the status of women. But when the Ayatollah Khomeini took control following the 1979 revolution, women's rights were sharply and suddenly curtailed. All of these changes were justified by the need to return to the "true" faith, as outlined in *shari'a* law. For Paidar, improvements in women's position in society have only been possible following Khomeini's death, when less conservative and more secular voices have emerged.

Erika Friedl acknowledges that Iranian women do not have the rights enjoyed by most Western women. But she argues that, working within conservative readings of Islamic law, Iranian women have many sources of power available to them. Such power can emerge in part through resistance to male authority. Or Iranian women can achieve control over their own lives and over the lives of their sons and husbands through work, religion, and the government itself. In a male-dominated society such as Iran, women have many "weapons of the weak" at their disposal, believes Friedl, with which they can achieve power within their households.

Parvin Paidar  **YES**

Feminism and Islam in Iran

$\mathbf{F}$eminism(s) in the Middle East and their articulations with Islam have attracted substantial interest in recent years. This [selection] will focus on the interaction between feminism and Islam in Iran. It will trace, in general terms, the development of feminism in that country and the ways in which it has interacted with Islam at various historical moments since the turn of the century. While in recent decades feminisms in the Arab Middle East by and large make reference to utopian Islam(s) to defend women's rights, in Iran the interaction between feminism and Islam has taken place in the context of a militant Shi'i state which claims to have implemented 'true Islam'. The contrast between these contexts may provide a useful contribution to an understanding of the interaction between feminism and Islam in various Middle Eastern contexts.

The approach adopted in this [selection] emanates from the view that far from being an optional extra, gender is situated at the heart of political discourses in Iran. Indeed, any political discourse aiming at the social reorganization of Iranian society has necessarily entailed a redefinition of gender relations and of women's position in society. Therefore, this [selection] will place the interaction between Islam and feminism in the broader context of political process in twentieth-century Iran.

Early Twentieth-Century Nationalist Feminism

In tracing the historical development of feminism in relation to Islam, a natural starting point would be the constitutional movement of the early twentieth century, since this was the context within which the 'woman question' was first explicitly raised in Iran.

The Constitutional Revolution of 1906–11 took place against the background of Western intrusion and the rise of nationalism. It revolved around the demand for constitutional monarchy to curb the power of the monarch in favour of the power of parliament and the rule of law on the one hand, and to protect Iran's national interests in the face of Western economic and political intervention on the other. It rested upon a diverse urban alliance which included merchants, traders, land owners, secular intellectuals and the Shi'i clergy. The importance of the constitutional movement for women was in the creation of a particular vision of modern Iran. The concept of modernity encapsulated justice, democracy, independence and women's emancipation. The movement created a conceptual link between national independence and progress and women's emancipation. It constructed women as social actors for the first time and facilitated the formation of a network of women's rights activists which gradually developed into a loosely formed women's movement.

Since the very idea of women's emancipation was grounded in the need for national progress, women activists prioritized the general developmental gains implicit in the improvement of women's position. The main demands of the women's movement included education and the abolition of practices such as seclusion and early marriage, which were regarded as serious impediments to women's contribution to national development. The way in which women's emancipation became associated with national progress during the constitutional period, created a generic link between feminism and nationalism which has shaped the course of Iranian feminism ever since. This has had at least two consequences. First, it has made it impossible to talk about the interaction between feminism and Islam without taking into account the links between Islam and nationalism. Second, this has been one of the main reasons why individualistic types of feminism based on women's personal experience and individual choice, a stance commonly associated with feminism in the West, have not developed in Iran.

The type of nationalism that developed in Iran in the first half of the century was on the whole secular. It was constructed as an alternative discourse, as Islam was associated with traditionalism and backwardness. During the constitutional period, secular intellectuals played an important role in constructing concepts such as constitutionalism, nationalism, modernity and women's emancipation.... Babism was ... one of the main indigenous sources of inspiration for women's emancipation at the turn of the century since one of its female protagonists Tahereh Qorrat ol-Eyn took off her veil in public and challenged the *ulama* (Muslim clergy) to debate women's position with her.

From the beginning of this century, then, the concept of women's emancipation became grounded in concepts associated with nationalism and modernity.... However, the debate on women was conducted in a way which avoided outright confrontation with religion. Feminists of this period complained against social conservatism rather than Islam as such. For example, Bibi Khanum Astarabadi argued that 'The obstacle to women's emancipation is not Islam but the male interest to preserve his privileges....'

Although the secular debate on women avoided outright opposition to Islam, nevertheless the expression of ideas inspired by non-Islamic sources was considered to be a serious threat by many Shi'i clerics. The Shi'i establishment focused on opposing the practical steps taken to emancipate women. For example, the opening of each new school for women was accompanied by a campaign by local mollahs to close it down. This is not to say that the clergy were united on the question of women's education—on the contrary....

[W]hile women's protests against subordination were conducted within an acceptable cultural framework which avoided overt criticism of Islam, the main point of reference for these women was secular nationalism. The secular nature of early twentieth-century feminism was strengthened further in the post-Constitutional period as a result of two particular developments; the rise of socialism and establishment of the Bolshevik state across the border in Russia and the emergence of the state as an agent of social reform.....

The emergence of the state as an agent of social reform was an even more important development affecting Iranian feminism in the early part of the century. The state established by Reza Shah Pahlavi in 1925 had a national-ist outlook and valorized pre-Islamic Iran. It set out to transform Iran from a dependent, backward society to a modern, independent nation-state and as a result the state became the initiator and implementor of social reform and as-sumed responsibility for the health, welfare and education of the population, at least in rhetoric.

Statist Feminism and the Rise of Cultural Nationalism in Mid Twentieth-Century Iran

However, in imposing reform on women's position, Reza Shah's state adopted a forceful and centralist approach and ended an era of women's independent activities by creating a state-sponsored women's organization to lead the way on women's emancipation. The measures proclaimed included compulsory un-veiling, free education and, potentially, the creation of new employment oppor-tunities. These measures had been demanded by many constitutionalists and feminists since the turn of the century, and by implementing them the state took the initiative on women's issues away from independent socialists, liberal nationalists and feminists. With a silent Shi'i establishment, co-opted national-ism, a suppressed socialist movement, and a partly co-opted, partly suppressed women's movement, the only voice allowed on behalf of women was that of the state.

The second Pahlavi state, established in 1941 after the abdication of Reza Shah in favour of his son, Mohammad Reza Shah, continued the same pattern of modernization, co-option and political suppression. The initial period of constitutional rule under the Shah resulted in the formation of a short-lived liberal nationalist government by Mohammad Mosaddeq who led a coalition of nationalist forces. The nationalist government, however, did not have a spe-cific gender agenda and its half-hearted attempt to introduce a new electoral bill which included enfranchisement for women failed. A CIA-sponsored coup in 1953 against Mosaddeq restored the Shah's autocratic rule. The post-coup pe-riod of 1960s and 1970s witnessed heightened suppression of most autonomous political groupings. But it also resulted in further state initiatives on women's rights. The campaign for political rights conducted by prominent feminists, such as Fatemeh Sayyah, had some success despite substantial opposition by the clergy.

The 1960s and 1970s also saw the growth of cultural nationalism and Islamic modernism. This occasioned a shift in the interaction between femi-nism, nationalism and Islam. The rise of cultural nationalism as a new political force closely associated with Islam resulted in the Shi'i establishment reclaiming lost moral ground on women and family issues as a result of several new developments.

First, on the religious front, after the death in 1961 of Ayatollah Borujerdi, the highest Shi'i authority of his time, a group of high-ranking clerics shared similar high status and gained their own followers. These Ayatollahs, including Khomeini, published and circulated widely their religious opinions on a broad range of issues, including women and the family. These religious views about women's position found political expression in a campaign by an Iranian version of the Muslim Brotherhood in the 1960s which presented a new fundamentalist defence of the Shi'i *shari'a* on women.

Second, on the political front, reformist clerics such as Ayatollah Motahhari and lay religious radicals such as Ali Shari'ati articulated new models of Muslim womanhood for Iranian women. The ideas of Shari'ati were adopted by the Mojahedin-e Khalq, who represented the Islamic tendency within the Marxist-Leninist guerrilla movement of the 1960s and 1970s which led a crusade against the Pahlavi state.

The success of these new Islamic trends in regaining the initiative on women and the family was due to both ideological and political factors. The Pahlavi state's unwillingness to introduce fundamental changes on women's position within the family enabled the Shi'i establishment to regain the initiative fairly easily. Both Reza Shah and Mohammad Reza Shah focused their reforms on the civic aspects of women's roles as opposed to the familial ones. Despite tremendous opposition by the Shi'i establishment, both Pahlavi regimes pushed forward with women's education, unveiling and de-segregation, while the reforms that they carried out on the family remained relatively limited. Pahlavi reforms did not go beyond a codification of traditional Shi'i law on women and family as part of the Civil Code of 1936, and an attempt to limit arbitrary male power in the family through the introduction of Family Protection Laws in 1967 and 1975. These limitations were due not so much to clerical opposition as to deeper concerns about the wider implications of granting women real power and independence within the family. The Pahlavi regimes opposed women's independence in the family and their independent presence in the public sphere, and this influenced the logic behind state-sponsored women's organizations which made sure that women's lives inside and outside the home remained under the control of male guardians. This strengthened the clergy's ideological hold over matters concerning women and the family, which was translated so effectively into a successful political campaign by the Shi'i movement during the 1970s.

However, the existence of new Shi'i ideas on women would not by itself have affected feminism in Iran if the political developments of the 1970s had not pushed them to the forefront. The rise of Shi'ism as a serious modern political movement in the context of anti-Shah politics became a major factor in the adoption of Shi'i ideas on women. The revolutionary context provided fertile ground for the first serious confrontation of secular feminisms (such as statist and socialist feminism) by political Islam. For the first time, Islamic activism became a serious political option for Iranian women, and many women from the younger generation who were totally alienated from state feminism took it up. The Pahlavi state's claim to be liberating women was politically untenable; the nationalist opposition was not able to present an alternative gender policy to that of the state and the socialist alternative only attracted a small minority of women. As a result, the campaign on women's issues became the preserve of the Islamic opposition.

The Islamic campaign on women included appeals to reject 'Westerniza-tion' and the exploitation of women as 'sex objects' which was seen as the consequence of Iran's economic and cultural dependence on the West. Instead, women were urged to embrace the new Shi'i model of womanhood which rep-resented 'authenticity' and 'independence' and emphasized women's dual role as mothers and revolutionaries. This found credence with large groups among both religious and secular women because it promised political freedom, eco-nomic equality, social justice, cultural integrity and personal fulfilment. It facilitated women's massive participation in the Revolution of 1979.

The contrast between women's participation in the 1979 Revolution and the earlier Constitutional Revolution could not be sharper, and was rooted in the different interactions between Islam and feminism in each revolutionary period. The 1979 Revolution was the second attempt in this century, apart from the brief Mosaddeq period, to redefine and change existing relations between the state and Western powers with the aim of establishing independence and democracy in Iran. But while the former revolutionary movement aimed to achieve this through emulation of the Western liberal model of society, the lat-ter aimed to achieve it by constructing an 'indigenous' and 'authentic' Islamic model of society in Iran. Moreover, while the flavour of the first revolution-ary discourse was that of a liberal nationalism associated with secularism, the second revolved around a cultural nationalism associated with Islam.

In summary, Iranian feminism was essentially secular until the rise of Shi'i modernism in the 1970s. It was only then that the new trend of Islamist fem-inism (gender activism within an Islamic framework) joined other feminisms in Iran.

Islamist Feminism and State Policy in the Islamic Republic

Let us now consider the development of Islamist feminism under the Islamic Republic. After the establishment of the Islamic Republic, the new constitution gave a prominent place to women, defining them as mothers and citizens. It stressed that the establishment of an Islamic nation was dependent on the Is-lamization of women and constructed the ideal Islamic woman in opposition to Western values on womanhood. The constitution attempted to create harmony between the Islamic family and nation by advocating a set of patriarchal rela-tions to strengthen male control over women in the family on the one hand, and granting women the right to be active citizens on the other.

The link between nationalism and Islam was crucial in determining the gender policies of the Islamic Republic. After the Islamic Republic settled into a theocracy, nationalism as a mobilizing force was transformed and re-defined.

The state attempted this by constructing nationalism as synonymous with anti-imperialism on the one hand, and replacing nationalism with Islam as the main mass mobilization force on the other. The new alliance between Islam and anti-imperialism, for which historical precedents existed in Iran, constituted the cornerstone of the Islamization policy of the state. The context of revolutionary populism, anti-imperialism, the effects of a war economy and struggle for state power between Islamic factions determined which concepts and ideas on women were defined as 'Islamic' and which ones as 'un-Islamic'. The result was a significant reversal of the history of clerical opposition to women's participation in politics. For example, the same clerics who had in the 1960s objected to women's enfranchisement on religious grounds were in the 1980s prepared to grant women the right to vote in the name of Islam.

With regard to women's social role, the Islamic Republic formulated policies on women's education, employment and political participation to ensure the continuation of women's mass support. Women's political participation was approved because it legitimized the state's Islamization policies and created an image of popular support and stability internally and internationally. These policies, however, were based on the premise that women's presence outside the home had to be accompanied with a process of de-sexualization of male-female interaction to protect the Islamic family and nation from its harmful moral consequences. A number of policies were developed to ensure this.

First, the protection of the family required the strengthening of male privilege through the Islamization of the Iranian household. The Family Protection Law was abolished and the Civil Code of 1936 was reinstated. This meant that the modest safeguards created for women in matters of divorce, marriage, child custody and abortion were all revoked overnight. Second, an extensive policy of gender segregation and compulsory *hejab* (head cover and loose clothes) for women was implemented. Third, measures were introduced in order to police the integrity of the family. These measures became known as the 'anti-corruption crusade', with a broad definition of corruption covering any social mixing between men and women as well as adultery, homosexuality, consumption of drugs and alcohol, gambling and a whole range of leisure activities.

Having thus structured the social role of women, the post-revolutionary Islamic state encouraged the development of an Islamic women's movement to counter the threat posed by secular feminism. The spontaneous movement of secular women to defend their rights against the Islamic state was crushed and secular feminism was driven into exile. Like preceding secular regimes, the Islamic state has ensured that the women's movement remained under tight state control. Different factions of the state and the state-sponsored revolutionary organizations attempted to harness women's tremendous mobilization potential by creating platforms for Islamic women activists.

The hard-line factions of the state took control of women's mass mobilization by organizing mass rallies in support of state Islamization and against the secular and Islamic opposition. Women's mass support was also manipulated in relation to two other areas of importance to the survival of the state—elections and the war against Iraq.

While women from the lower classes provided the mass support that the Islamic regime needed, Islamic women leaders became involved in philanthropic, religious, and feminist activities. Many of the state-funded welfare agencies, health and education centres, charities and foundations were run by women. Women who managed such organizations often came from clerical families and were well-connected within the circle of Islamic leadership.

A third category of Islamist women took up feminist activities under the patronage of the moderate factions of the state. The Women's Society of the Islamic Revolution (WSIR) was founded soon after the Revolution by a group of women to preserve and build upon the revolutionary demand for a culturally authentic gender identity. The popular, formerly pro-Pahlavi, women's magazine, *Zan-e Ruz* (Woman of Today), was taken over by an editorial board of Islamic feminists and transformed into a popular Islamic women's magazine. These women tended to be highly educated, often with doctorates from Western universities, and professionals in various fields. Their activities included not only publishing women's magazines, but also running women's organizations and formulating Islamic policies on women.

During the post-revolutionary transitional period of 1979–81, Islamist feminists drew their support from the religious faction of the Provisional Government and later, in some cases, the office of President Banisadr. The same period witnessed the forceful imposition of a hasty Islamization programme by Ayatollah Khomeini. This went against the views of Islamist feminists who wanted instead a long-term, gradualist Islamization programme based on educating women about the values of Islam.

Islamist feminists set out to create a vision of the 'ideal Islamic society' and the role of women in it. The idealization of the future Islamic society entailed a critique of the past and the present. The Islamist feminist theory of women's oppression and liberation was constructed in opposition to 'traditional Islam'. 'True Islam', according to Islamic feminists, transcended the 'traditional, deviatory and colonized Islam' in relation to women. The failures of traditional Islam were seen as rooted in male-dominated culture and distorted interpretations of Islamic laws.

Ayatollah Khomeini's Islamization measures received coded criticisms from the Islamist feminists. Azam Taleghani and Zahra Rahnavard, two well-known activists, warned the authorities about the negative effects of forcing women to wear *hejab*. They proposed that the Islamic dress code should not be made specific to women but that both men and women should be required to wear simple and decent clothing which covers the body in a non-arousing, modest fashion. On the Islamic Republic's policy of excluding women from the judiciary, Islamic feminists argued that 'women's emotionality is not an acceptable ground for their exclusion from passing judgement,' and said that 'Muslim women should be able to take their legal problems to female judges as much as possible, just as they take their medical problems to female doctors.'

Despite the enormous enthusiasm of these women and initial expectation that they would make a major contribution to the Islamic Republic's gender policies, Islamist feminists were marginalized by the hard-line factions of the post-revolutionary government. Ayotallah Khomeini's tendency to ignore voices of moderation, together with repressive state policies, resulted in the radicalization of the feminist strand of the Islamist women's movement. During the politically extremist years of 1981–87 the voice of Islamic feminism was thus silenced almost completely.

This took place in the context of a diversity of Islamist opinions, political power struggles, political repression, ideological control, economic stagnation, war and international isolation. These developments affected the ability of the state to establish coherent policies or ensure their effective implementation. Although the general framework of state policies on women was defined by opposition to the Pahlavi regime and 'alien Western values', actual policies of Islamization were formulated in a heterogeneous and *ad hoc* manner by a variety of agents with different and sometimes conflicting interests. The way this affected women can be seen in the pattern of their education and employment in this period. Although strongly encouraged in official rhetoric, in reality women's education and employment suffered from contradictory policies, the imposition of gender quotas and support for male dominance, combined with lack of co-ordination between the multiple centres of decision-making and lack of financial resources. Nevertheless, although the opportunities available to women were reduced, Islamization policies and mismanagement did not stop women's participation in education and employment.

The state also failed to deliver 'Islamic justice' in relation to women's position within the family. Women had been promised support for their 'natural' rights and roles. They were to receive economic and legal protection from the Islamic state and its male representatives in the home. In return, women were expected to prove their credentials as obedient wives, self-sacrificing mothers and active citizens. However, this equation failed to work in the actual political and economic circumstances of the Islamic Republic. On the contrary, measures such as the strengthening of male authority in the family not only failed to increase women's protection, but actually resulted in the reduction of women's familial rights and the deterioration of their material condition. The Islamic Republic may have given its female supporters the opportunity for popular political participation and a sense of righteousness and self-worth, but it seriously undermined women's position within the family and restricted their human rights.

All this gave greater credence to the cause of Islamist feminism. To survive during particularly repressive periods, Islamist feminists tried to be as non-controversial as possible, and in doing so they colluded extensively with state attacks on women's rights. The degree of loyalty to the state expected from Islamist feminists proved to be much higher than that expected from the pro-state feminists of the Pahlavi era. Despite this, the extremist years had a maturing effect on Islamic feminists. They realized that unless they established an autonomous existence and spoke out against state policy, women would continue to get a raw deal despite the state's claim to represent 'true Islam'. Thus, a small but vocal Islamist feminist opposition re-established itself in the late 1980s.

Since the late 1980s, Islamist feminists have been able to campaign for women's rights in a much more open and direct manner than before. They have also proved more successful in pressurizing the policy-makers to revise earlier restrictions on women's legal rights and to consider positive proposals for greater rights for women within an Islamic framework. The issues on which they have campaigned have included family, education, employment, political participation and *hejab*. On education and employment, which seem to be the most sophisticated and successful issues on which Islamic feminists have campaigned, discriminatory practices towards women have been scrutinized and proposals made for their eradication. One important achievement in this area has been the lifting of restrictions that had been placed on women's entry to technical, scientific and medical fields soon after the Revolution.

Campaigns on the family have focused on improving the balance of power between men and women in the family. The emphasis has been put on the concept of 'partnership between husband and wife' as opposed to the concept of 'male guardianship', which is the basis of the Civil Code. Islamist feminists have protested against the failure of state policy to 'facilitate the growth of women's talents and personality', 'preserve their rights in the sacred institution of family', 'protect the rights of unprotected women' and 'remove obstacles in the way of women's participation in economic, social and political activities.' The policies advocated include state remuneration for housewives and unmarried women, monogamy, automatic custody rights for mothers, protection against divorce without the wife's consent, the right of wives to half the family assets, and women's rights to undertake education, employment or travel without the consent of husbands or other male guardians.

However, despite achieving relative independence for their movement and having some success in persuading policy-makers to extend women's rights, Islamist women leaders have on the whole had limited opportunities to take on decision-making roles and have had a hard time gaining authority or influence in the Islamic polity. Only a handful have entered the Islamic parliament or the government. Eleven elections during the first decade of the Islamic Republic have produced in total only six women representatives in parliament, an even more tokenist minority than in the Pahlavi era. . . .

Conclusion

This incursion into contemporary Iranian history demonstrates that gender issues have been at the heart of Iranian politics and that they have undergone complex and sometimes paradoxical transformations. This has been nowhere more apparent than under the Islamic Republic. Indeed, the transformation of Islamist feminism from post-Revolutionary idealism to realism and pragmatism of the late 1980s has been remarkable. This being the case it is no longer inconceivable to envisage strategic alliances between Iranian strands of secular and Islamist feminisms on women's rights issues. The frames of reference of the two traditions of gender activism are, of course, very different. Iranian Islamist feminism is theoretically rooted in cultural relativism and politically rooted in anti-imperialism, while the direction taken by Iranian secular feminism in exile in the last decade has been largely universalist, anti-religious and increasingly individualistic.

However, the severity and material reality of the problems faced by Iranian women have reduced the importance of these ideological differences. To illustrate this point, it will be useful to compare the experiences of feminists campaigning to improve family laws in the Pahlavi era with those under the Islamic Republic. It took about forty years for secular feminists of the Pahlavi era to change the family law from the Civil Code of 1936 to the Family Protection Law of 1975. In 1979, it took Ayatollah Khomeini one speech to demolish the Family Protection Law in a single blast; and since then it has taken Islamist feminists over twelve years to build it again bit by bit; the task has yet to be completed.

The same family laws which had been historically presented by the Pahlavi state as part of a process of secularization and which were opposed by the clergy as contrary to Islam and therefore demolished, are now being reinstated under the Islamic Republic. The difference does not seem to be in the Islamist or secular nature of the law but in the political priorities of the era. This has created a potential for co-operation and alliance amongst ideologically diverse feminisms. Old ideological enemies may turn into new political allies when it comes to resisting the onslaughts of male supremacy. Although these alliances may be fraught and fragile, they speak of Iranian women's will to act upon their gender interests.

Erika Friedl  **NO**

Sources of Female Power in Iran

Reports of the position of women in Iran and in other Middle Eastern countries contain a seeming paradox: women are said to be subordinate to men, second-class citizens, oppressed, veiled, and confined, unequal to men legally and in access to resources. This gender inequity further is said to be validated, supported, and mystified by local gender ideologies and a superstructure formed by the teachings of the Quran and other religious scriptures, by Islamic law, and by folk notions about male–female differences. Yet, on the level of everyday life and popular culture, Iranian women, especially mature matrons, are widely perceived as 'powerful.' They are described as running the political affairs of their sons and husbands, as controlling the lives of everyone in the household—omniscient, beloved, respected, and feared matrons much like the stereotypical Jewish mother of western folk culture.

No matter how contradictory the concept of the oppressed-yet-powerful woman might seem, the contradiction is contrived. Indeed, I will even argue that subordinated people, women in this case, not only can be both oppressed and powerful simultaneously, but that they can derive power to effect changes in their own and in others' affairs from the very relations of inequality that define their position: from concrete, adversarial circumstances in their lives, from the existential conditions to which they are confined, unfavorable as they might be.

Women arrive at their position of power vis-à-vis the power elite through dynamic processes, each with its own dialectic logic. In this [selection] I will trace a few of these processes. I will focus on some examples of the power that women in Iran are said to have: on how they access it, how they use it, and where it takes them. In so doing, I will try to show the connection between women's oppression and women's power and will attempt to put the discussion of this seeming paradox into the context of an analytic-methodological frame....

Specifically, I have selected four topics that illustrate the power-potential of women. The first topic, resistance, is an abstract concept, manifested through a bundle of tactics used to counter hegemonic domination. These tactics can be used in all life situations, and create specific power dynamics. The other three topics are concrete and specific: women's work and employment, religion, and political conditions. These three pertain to everyday circumstances of life and are examined for their potential power-content through the use of several brief, illustrative examples.

Resistance as Power

Resistance can take women in three different directions.

1. Power differences between dominants and subordinates—any dominants and their subordinates—inevitably lead to resistance against demands, control, and restrictions of superiors. Dominants in turn perceive the resistance as attempts to challenge, even usurp, their power (in a Zero-Sum game) and thus label resisters as 'bad.' In our case, women do resist domination; their resistance is anticipated, and hence women are said to be by nature obstinate, shameful, foolish, sinful, or childish. As such, it is argued, they must be carefully watched and treated with commensurate firmness if need be ('need' being determined by those in authority), with yet another commensurate backlash of more resistance to be expected. Resistance therefore can, and often does, lead to more suppression: to punishment, discreditation, loss of honor, and confinement rather than freedom, choice, or autonomy.

   For example, in Iran (as elsewhere) women's compliance with the dress code is taken as a measure of both state control on the national level, and of men's control over their families on the individual level. One of the duties of male and female Revolutionary Guards is to publicly enforce the dress code (including the men's dress code, which is much less restrictive and much less focused on than the women's). If a woman's hair shows from under her headscarf the transgression not only is proclaimed a private sin but is also taken as a political statement of resistance to the nation's moral code and to women's place in the social hierarchy of the Islamic Republic, and thus may be punished. By resisting the dress code, individual women do make a statement of protest, but unless they can turn their individual resistance into a mass protest, they cannot use their gesture as a source of power to effect a desired change in the dress code or in their personal position. Their lonely protest is easily quelched.

2. Suicide is one of the most dramatic gestures of resistance. Suicide as a strategy of resistance to demands or to mistreatment by figures of authority (usually within the woman's family) is ineffective for the woman who dies, but the suicide death of one woman can give weight to the resistance efforts of another woman who can use the threat of suicide as a source of power to get her will....

3. The third extreme direction resistance can take is women's own acceptance of the dominants' view of female resistance to hegemonic authority. Women in Iran who accept this view—and there seem to be many —believe that women are inherently weak in body, intellect, and emotional resilience. In extreme but by no means isolated cases, they maintain that all women are inherently 'bad,' probably even hell-bound, and

that women's only hope for salvation lies in proper guidance which will save them from themselves, as it were. Accepting the male paradigm, women paradoxically can turn the male view into a source of power for themselves in relation to others in low positions: women can use the paradigm to control, 'guide,' and subordinate other women. For example, female Revolutionary Guards patrolling the streets to watch over the propriety of other women, mothers-in-law critically watching their daughters-in-law, or *hezbollah* (Party-of-God) women in offices and schools controlling the dress and behavior of officemates or students are enforcing conformity and quelching resistance to male authority. By taking up the cause of male/state authorities, including the expectation of resistance to domination and the perceived need to nip it in the bud, these women can achieve a substantial measure of power over other women. But this support undermines the position of women in general, including their own vis-à-vis their husbands or brothers. Not even the collaborators can easily convert this male-derived power over other subordinates into autonomy in their private lives....

In very rare cases, women manage to turn restrictive orders against the authorities themselves. For example, a woman principal of an all girl's school I know was ordered by her male supervisor not to let any man enter the school premises. When the supervisor appeared a few days later to check on administrative matters, the principal refused him entry on grounds of his own order. Tongue-in-cheek (as in this case) or seriously, women can claim the fool's freedom more easily than men. Although resistance based on the acceptance of male rule in government or in the family may lead to small personal victories for individual women, it cannot be expected to alter the skewed power balance between dominants and subordinates in general. Such resistance is a tactic for getting by and getting even, not for redress.

Resistance can take a great many forms, each with different consequences for the generation of power. I will briefly discuss four such forms which I have found to be used frequently: disobedience, subversion, refusal, and crying for help.

1. Open disobedience of male orders leads to conflict, hidden disobedience to distrust. Both conflict and distrust lead to greater oppression and tighter control, thus creating a vicious circle of tyranny and rebellion.

   For example, a young woman in a small town in southern Iran who disobeyed her husband frequently and for good reasons, as she and many others thought, was often beaten by him in the course of the resulting fights. On one such occasion she fled to her brother, who ordered her to stop arguing and to do her husband's bidding. When she now refused to obey her brother, he beat her, and her relatives and neighbors called her 'crazy' for being disobedient in such a foolishly demonstrative way. Another young woman I know had for years refused all orders by her relatives to marry one of her suitors, on pain of severe punishment at each refusal and near ostracism by her family. Although successful in her resistance, she paid a high price in comfort and reputation. Moreover, when her eventual later marriage to a man of her choosing turned out disastrous, villagers characteristically saw a direct connection between her earlier disobedience and her eventual calamity....

Disobedience as a tool of power for women works best if it is supported by dominants against other dominants: a father supporting his daughter against her husband; a son backing his mother against a half-brother. It can also be successful if one woman's disobedience is backed by other women in an act of solidarity that the men find hard to break. But because solidarity requires more organizational structure than women in Iran, especially rural women, usually have, it is relatively rare outside of the family. Within the family, solidarity is easiest to achieve between mothers and daughters and among sisters, whereas between mothers-in-law and daughters-in-law, and among sisters-in-law, relationships are potentially so fraught with tensions that solidarity seems to be hard to attain.

2. Subversion, in the form of minimal compliance with controversial rules or the outright subversion of such rules is at once a form of testing the limits of the rules and the tolerance of the rule-makers and thus is an expression of one's dissatisfaction with them. This form of resistance can very easily be interpreted as disobedience requiring respective reprisals.

   In Iran, for example, the rule for women to cover their hair in front of unrelated men is subverted when a woman drapes a big scarf loosely over her head, holding it in place not by a tight knot or a safety-pin under her chin but by slinging one end of the scarf over the opposite shoulder. The headdress which is meant to conceal has become an ornament; the intent is subverted and the woman who wears it makes a political statement by turning an object of control into one of protest....

3. A woman's refusal to obey her husband's (or father's) orders or to perform expected services challenges the man and inconveniences him. A woman who refuses a demand hopes that her husband will try to prevent the inconvenience and remedy the contested situation before precipitating a showdown. However, any kind of refusal by a woman in everyday situations, from refusing to cook or to fetch a glass of water for her son, to denying sex to her husband, is sanctioned negatively in the Islamic moral code. For a woman, refusing obedience or services to her husband (or, in varying degrees, to other men in positions of authority over her), no matter how extreme the demand, is a sin, and a very 'female' sin at that. It is a sin said to be typical of women, and this notion in turn is part of the script by which women are socialized. Women who resort to refusal as a tool of power are told they are courting punishment in the afterlife as well as in this life.

In the most extreme and most effective case of refusal, a woman leaves her husband to live with her father, brother, or grown son. Her husband then must cope with women's chores, including the care of young children, and is greatly inconvenienced. His difficulty can be compounded if his own mother and other female relatives, in tacit solidarity with his wife, refuse to help him. Sooner or later, out of necessity, he will decide to negotiate for his wife's return, presumably agreeing to measures that will redress his wife's complaints and will improve her situation. Wright reports a case from the Doshman Ziari in which two sisters even left their husbands in order to force them to make a political move the women favored. . . .

4. A cry for help, that is, informing others of wrongs one is suffering, aims to involve outsiders in one's affairs in order to embarrass one's own people into addressing the problem. This form of resistance undermines indirectly a woman's standing, the more so the more people get involved: honorable people take care of their problems themselves.

For example, a woman who has been beaten may choose to go to the public bathhouse where her bruises will tell her story without a word from her. The news will spread to her father who may then decide to have a word with her husband, usually with a little noise as possible. . . .

These examples suggest that resistance as a source of power for women is considered destructive to self and to others in Iran. Resistance supports the stereotyping of women's power as an inherently dangerous force that must be controlled. Women's resistance is taken by men and women (in what Wright calls the 'dominant model' for behavior and attitudes) as proof of women's inherent weaknesses, their unreliability, recalcitrance, childishness, and antagonism. Although all of these have to be feared as dangerous to the social and moral order, the fear is not a wholesome one, but rather leads to distrust and further curtailment of movement and options for women. Yet, despite its limited, at best short-range, benefits and high costs, resistance is the single most frequently used tactic of power, the most popular 'weapon of the weak' that women use when they feel wronged. Social developments in the Islamic Republic have neither led to equal access to resources for women and men nor to equal opportunities for self-determination and personal autonomy. Given the government's social and gender philosophy, gender equality is not even a sociopolitical agenda. Women therefore can be expected to continue to try to use traditional means to create power, such as resistance, in conducting their lives, even to intensify these power tactics when other sources of power are curtailed.

Work as Power

Women's participation in the labor market is generally taken as an indicator of the status of women, especially in developing countries, and employment of women is considered a means, even a necessity, for women's emancipation. True as this view might be in the long-range processes of women's liberation, my observations in Iran suggest that a woman's labor contribution is not in itself a reliable indicator of a woman's autonomy and power (let alone her status), at least not among the lower classes. This is especially true for manual labor, which generally is regarded as demeaning drudgery. But even clerical work has this connotation, at least among people in the lower classes. Hegland reports from a village in southwest Iran that 'employment outside the home was considered an indication of low socio-economic position and a source of shame both for the women involved and for their relatives.' Such women often find it necessary to assert that they don't *have* to work, that they are well taken care of and chose employment.

The work women do, be it in- or outside of the home, can be tapped by women as a source of power under certain conditions: (1) The work creates dependencies that the woman can exploit; (2) the work creates resources that the woman can control; (3) the work creates skills that enable the woman to access other sources of power and creates in her the self-confidence to shrewdly exploit them. I will briefly discuss [the first of] these conditions [here].

Dependencies

Within the family, it is easy for a woman to make others, for example, her children, husband, and aged parents-in-law, dependent on her services. A woman in a traditional rural household, by refusing to cook or to milk animals, for example, might force her husband to negotiate with her for better treatment. (This, however, happens at the cost of reinforcement of the negative stereotype of women as nags, or, in extreme cases, the threat of divorce.) On the other hand, as a willing, cooperative, and competent housekeeper, a woman can gain considerable manipulative power. She can gain control over most of the household resources (including even control over a co-wife). By wisely using her resources, she will build up her husband and earn the respect of relatives and others in her social circle, which in turn will empower her to have input in others' and her own affairs. In this way she will also accumulate knowledge about others, which she can incorporate into a power base that includes political as well as economic and emotional resources, and provides many angles for arranging her circumstances to the benefit of herself and her protégés. Hegland reports that the village women she observed used 'their verbal and intellectual skills in gathering information, spying, persuading, taunting, berating, threatening, shaming, discussing, interpreting, encouraging' in order to manipulate their power base. One result of such successful manipulation is the 'powerful' wife-mother figure of popular culture and folklore: the woman who knows everything, who controls children and relatives, who makes and breaks people, who keeps her sons on short emotional reins, and whom everybody loves and fears at the same time. A competent woman in this sense is using her talents, connections, and services—all her assets—to build up her husband (or sons) and herself simultaneously. The most successful will continue to give the impression of overt deferral to male authority, because it is important for the maintenance of 'face' *(aberu)* that her husband's dominance should not be challenged overtly. This pretense of submission in turn has to be accepted by the husband at face value along with his wife's manipulations which, after all, he recognizes as advantageous for himself. This is a power game which so-called successful couples seem to be playing all over the patriarchal world, and which, because of its success, makes other ways of assertion by women, including attempts at emancipation in a western sense, seem superfluous, even foolish, to many men and women in these systems.

In economically depressed post-revolutionary Iran, the household, the kin group, large families are more important than before in structuring the lives of people; the social life as well as economic assistance flow in the kind of close-knit social networks in which women operate very well. Thus, chances for wielding the kind of power that comes from cleverly creating and using dependencies have increased in importance for women. . . .

Religion as Power

Religion can empower women insofar as the religious idiom can provide the means, justifications, and rationalizations for independent actions. Religious concepts thus can be and are used as manipulative devices.

For example, during the revolution, many Iranian women participated in demonstrations against the Pahlavi regime. Hegland reports that the women (and the men who allowed them to do so) saw protest as a religious rather than a political activity: women were giving testimony to Islam by supporting Khomeini.

The paucity of occasions for women in the Islamic Republic to congregate legitimately outside their homes seems to be one of the reasons for the rapid increase in women's participation in graveyard visitation parties on Thursday afternoons. During these visits, women socialize while ostensibly fulfilling a pious obligation. Likewise, *rowzeh* gatherings and *sofrehs* (parties given in honor of a saintly personage) are used extensively for what is elsewhere called women's networking.

Likewise, pilgrimages to saints' shrines are popular among women as religiously motivated social activities. Women consider visits to a neighborhood shrine to be like informal visits to a relative, close to home and easily fit between chores. Pilgrimages to distant, important shrines, however, involve considerable expense and logistical problems, which make male approval, support, and escort necessary for women. Indeed, a woman very likely must use her manipulative powers to make her husband or son take her on a pilgrimage. Frequently a woman can keep her vow to pay a visit to a saint only after she is widowed or has found a separate source of funding for the travel.

For example, an old widow in Deh Koh, an herbalist who had been living precariously on her own for many years, wanted to make the pilgrimage to Mashhad, but was very concerned about the possible impropriety in going alone. On the bus to Mashhad she met a mullah with his eight-year-old son and contracted a temporary, non-sexual marriage with the boy. This allowed her to make the journey as a well-chaperoned married woman. Thus, she used the combination of control over her finances and two religiously sanctioned customs to gain the autonomy to venture into an otherwise inaccessible world. Temporary marriage, which can be taken to demean women, in this case became a source of power that enabled a woman to realize her wish.

Women can use expressions of piety as a manipulative strategy. Since about 1983, a code of piety has developed in Iran, a politically-piously correct way of talking, dressing, reading; a politically correct body of knowledge and phrases that one can use to one's personal advantage.

For example, a young woman (or man for that matter) seeking acceptance at a university or promotion at work will avoid the slightest hint of resistance to the dress code. In public, she will wear the plainest outer garments, correct low-heeled shoes, and a dark scarf pulled over her forehead, completely covering her hairline. She will accept a scholarship to a special Quran course in the summer, no matter how boring she might find it. She will not tell others that at home she is looking at American videos smuggled in from Kuwait. She will pray and observe the fast ostentatiously. She will not be seen with men (other than close family members) in public, and will discourage male attention. Her impeccable behavior will be noted by those who report on her morality, and this will increase her chances for advancement. The restrictive code is thus turned into a tool with which she can manipulate her career.

In the Islamic Republic many women, especially those in the middle class and the former elite, have perfected the art of dissimulation and the use of the code of piety to the extent that their private and public personae are almost totally different.

Since the war, the status of 'Mother of a Martyr' has become a potential source of power for women who have lost a son in the war. The government has given these women the moral right to demand respect and consideration from other people. These women are given preferential treatment in the allocation of subsidized appliances, and they are enlisted as watchers over the correctness of their neighbors' behavior. Some of these women, especially those with limited access to other sources of power and respect, use their position as informer to the point where conversation in a room falters when they enter. These women are seen by others as using a government-bestowed power to the detriment of other women.

In a more traditional religious domain, the prestige of a successful pilgrimage to certain shrines (expressed in the titles *haji, karbela'i, mashhadi*) and that of a descendant of the Prophet Mohammad (*sayyed*) carry respect and are thus a potential source of power for women. A *sayyed* woman often is sought out as a mediator in disputes or as a peacemaker.

For example, in Deh Koh, a man whose wife had fled to her father after a fight enlisted the help of a *sayyed* woman to persuade his father-in-law to send back his wife. Although the young woman's family had vowed they would let her go only if her husband agreed to a list of demands, they found it impossible to resist the *sayyed,* whose invocations of piety, morality, and peace were strengthened greatly by her illustrious descent. In effect, this *sayyed* used her own male-derived powers (from her ancestor, the Prophet) to undermine the protest action of another woman who, as a young wife, had very little power over her fate.

Government as Source of Power

Women in Iran have the right to vote. Yet although voting gives women a voice in political matters equal to men, not all women, especially not rural ones, consider it a source of power. A woman's vote is often regarded as her husband's or father's second vote: he will determine how she is to vote.

Similarly, women do not regard law and the courts as sources of power and rarely use them, even if in a particular instance the law would indeed be on their side. Involving the court in one's affairs is taken as a sign of failure of the informal, traditional, honorable ways of dealing with problems and thus is easily seen as shameful, especially for women. Furthermore, few women have the economic and strategic-assertive resources to go to court alone and plead their case, especially against a male relative.

For example, when in a small town a young woman's husband died, his relatives sent her back to her father without her two infant children. Although the law gave her the right to keep her children at least for a specific time, and although she missed her children badly and fell into serious depression, her father decided not to press the issue in court to avoid the embarrassment of a public fight. The woman felt completely unable to deal with the problem herself, especially over the objection of her father. For similar reasons, women who are denied their legal share of the inheritance of their brothers usually 'pardon' it rather than face a court battle with them.

As mentioned before, politically correct demeanor helps a woman with professional aspirations. In this regard, one could say the government provides a script for women who want to attain power positions, be it as a school principal, a medical professional, an elected member of a village or town council, a Revolutionary Guard, an informer in an office, or an employee of an intelligence agency. In the last three instances, 'successful' women use their government-bestowed powers against other women in the interest of the male dominants, thereby supporting women's domination. Thus, the government makes it possible for some women to advance individually without emancipation....

A final example of a government-generated source of potential power for women comes from an unexpected and controversial circumstance: the mandatory sex-segregation in schools. Although motivated by a restrictive code of sexual morality that otherwise works against women, sex segregated schools have the advantages of all-women's groups in general: they provide young women with an environment where they are not harassed, restricted, challenged, or intimidated by male teachers and male classmates. In such environments women can express themselves freely, they have more opportunity to practice leadership and intellectual skills than they would have if men were present, and they can develop confidence even in such subjects as mathematics and the sciences which in some societies are said to be the domain of men.

Summary

When legitimate sources of power for women become increasingly scarce in an androcentric, male-dominated society such as the Islamic Republic of Iran, and women's realm of action and influence becomes more restricted, women can be expected to intensify their use of the 'weapons of the weak,' that is, manipulation of resources and resistance to restrictive rules to exert control over issues important to them. Both strategies potentially lead to a reinforcement of the popular Iranian stereotype of women's negative character traits, from childishness to outright evil, and reinforce the cycle of antagonism and distrust characteristic of such power constellations. Women who use this system 'well,' that is, in such a way that men feel secure in their claim to control and superiority (regardless of how manipulated or subverted they may be) or else feel that their women's strategies and tactics are advantageous for them, can derive power to the extent that the dominant-subordinate constellation may even seem reversed. Such women are viewed not only as 'powerful' but as de facto rulers of the house. Women who control other women in the interest of dominant authority, either within the family or in public, do so to the detriment of women in general and cannot easily derive autonomy over their own lives from this position. In both cases, that of the successful wife-mother and the wielder of male-derived power, however, the existing hierarchy of domination remains not only unchallenged but is stabilized, and the gendered system of super- and subordination is cemented.

POSTSCRIPT

Has the Islamic Revolution in Iran Subjugated Women?

Since the 1970s feminist anthropologists have increasingly focused attention on the role of women in different societies. Earlier anthropologists, they have argued, had largely written women out of ethnographies, relegating women's roles to the domestic sphere while women's economic and political roles remained largely unstudied. As feminist theory developed in the West, feminist anthropologists attempted to account for and explain the subordination of women in different societies. Radical feminists developed a universal model of patriarchy—a pattern of male domination of women, their labor, their sexuality, and their reproductive capacities. Such models were invoked to explain how women continued to be oppressed in many parts of the world. Explanations of how patriarchal regimes have invoked Islamic law as justification for women being given a subordinate position in society often have emerged from this patriarchal model. Paidar's selection draws on this patriarchal model but avoids the strident, polemical stance that has characterized many feminist interpretations of Muslim society.

The most important reaction to the patriarchal model has been the view that whether these Muslim communities are patriarchal or not, women nevertheless lead rich and rewarding lives in spite of their segregation from men and their limited public role. Some ethnographers have argued that Islamic women even wield considerable informal influence and power. Some anthropologists, such as Lila Abu-Lughod in her *Veiled Sentiments: Honor and Poetry in a Bedouin Society* (University of California Press, 1986) have challenged stereotypes of Islamic women that often depict them as trapped in exploitative gender roles that have emerged from an unchanging form of Islam. Abu-Lughad has argued that we need more descriptive studies of Muslim women before we can understand whether or not these women are subjugated. Friedl suggests that even when women have little direct access to power, as in postrevolutionary Iran, women can and have been able to set agendas and define some of the parameters in which public debate over gender policy will be conducted. See *In the Eye of the Story: Women in Post-Revolutionary Iran* (Syracuse University Press, 1994), edited by M. Afkhami and Friedl, for other perspectives on women's rights and roles in Iran.

For a discussion of women's roles in pre-Taliban Afghanistan, see Nancy Tapper's *Bartered Brides: Politics, Gender, and Marriage in an Afghan Tribal Society* (Cambridge University Press, 1991). Ziba Mir-Hosseini's *Islam and Gender: The Religious Debate in Contemporary Iran* (Princeton University Press, 1999) discusses the rise of an indigenous Iranian feminism within postrevolutionary Iranian society. For a discussion of Middle Eastern feminism, see *Remaking Women: Feminism and Modernity in the Middle East* (Princeton University Press, 1998), edited by Abu-Lughod, and *Gendering the Middle East: Emerging Perspectives* (Syracuse University Press, 1996), edited by Deniz Kandiyoti.

Are Yanomami Violence and Warfare Natural Human Efforts to Maximize Reproductive Fitness?

YES: Napoleon A. Chagnon, from "Reproductive and Somatic Conflicts of Interest in the Genesis of Violence and Warfare Among Tribesmen," in Jonathan Haas, ed., *The Anthropology of War* (Cambridge University Press, 1995)

NO: R. Brian Ferguson, from "A Savage Encounter: Western Contact and the Yanomami War Complex," in R. Brian Ferguson and Neil L. Whitehead, eds., *War in the Tribal Zone: Expanding States and Indigenous Warfare* (School of American Research Press, 2000)

ISSUE SUMMARY

YES: Anthropologist and sociobiologist Napoleon A. Chagnon argues that the high incidence of violence and warfare he observed among the Yanomami in the 1960s was directly related to man's inherent drive toward reproductive fitness (i.e., the innate biological drive to have as many offspring as possible). For Chagnon, the Yanomami provide an excellent test of this sociobiological principle because the Yanomami were virtually unaffected by Western colonial expansion and exhibited intense competition for wives.

NO: Anthropologist and cultural materialist R. Brian Ferguson counters that the high incidence of warfare and violence observed by Chagnon in the 1960s was a direct result of contact with Westerners at mission and government stations. Fighting arose in an effort to gain access to steel tools that were increasingly important to the community. Ferguson asserts that fighting is a direct result of colonial circumstances rather than biological drives.

Napoleon Chagnon's work among the Yanomami Indians of the upper Orinoco River basin in Venezuela is one of the best known ethnographic studies of a tribal society. When his books and films first became available in the 1970s, they depicted a society that was intensely competitive and violent.

The Yanomami, according to Chagnon, saw themselves as "the fierce people." Chagnon views the Yanomami as a prototypic tribal society that until very recently operated independently of the forces, processes, and events that affect the rest of the world. For him they represent a pristine example of how tribal communities living in rain forest conditions may have functioned at other times and places in the world.

For many years, Chagnon has periodically revisited the Yanomami, assembling a comprehensive set of data on violence, warfare, movement of local groups, genealogies, and marriage patterns. Since the 1970s Chagnon has championed the cause of sociobiology, which is an effort to bring evolutionary biological theory into anthropology. He uses his database to test whether patterns of warfare and violence can be explained in terms of man's innate desire to reproduce as many offspring as possible, which Chagnon refers to as *reproductive fitness.*

R. Brian Ferguson also studies the Yanomami; however, he routinely uses the term *Yanomami* when discussing linguistically-related tribes studied by Chagnon. Drawing his data from the voluminous books, papers, films, and field reports of others, Ferguson has written a detailed political history of Yanomami warfare. Rather than viewing the Yanomami as innately violent, he interprets the intense violence observed in the 1960s as a direct consequence of changing Yanomami relationships with the outside world. He rejects the notion that the Yanomami of this period represent a pristine tribal society that state societies may have emerged from in the past. Although the foreign influences on the Yanomami may be seen as indirect, Ferguson believes that the Yanomami were nevertheless part of the global system of economic and political relations. Ferguson looks to the control of the material bases of life rather than to biological urges and explains the violent nature of Yanomami culture as the result of a desire to obtain Western products.

This pair of selections raises a number of questions about how anthropologists can explain the sociocultural processes that lead humans to violence. Are there biological drives and urges that lead individuals and groups to engage in violent behavior? Does a growing scarcity of key resources lead individuals to protect their access through increased violence? Is it possible to use contemporary societies as ethnographic analogies to suggest how early prehistoric societies operated? Are there any communities that are not linked to the global system of economic and political relations?

In the following selections, Chagnon develops a model to explain the incidence and character of Yanomami fighting. He asserts that human behavior can be explained in terms of the biological drive to reproduce. This innate drive leads men to maximize their access to women who can bear their children, passing as many of their genes on to the next generation as possible. Ferguson counters Chagnon's position by arguing that the Yanomami have been thoroughly influenced by the flow of steel tools into the region from the outside world. The desire for steel machetes drives Yanomami who live in settlements far from where machetes are available to fight with other Yanomami who have access to this scarce resource.

Napoleon A. Chagnon  **YES**

Reproductive and Somatic Conflicts of Interest in the Genesis of Violence and Warfare Among Tribesmen

Darwin's view of the evolution of life forms by natural selection is now a standard dimension in social and cultural anthropology, modified, of course, to apply to "cultures" or "societies." It is the modification, however, which is today a major issue, since the changes necessary to extend his original arguments by themselves distorted and changed his arguments. Specifically, problems with the "group" versus the "individual" controversy are now beginning to appear in anthropological discussions of the evolved functions of human behavior. This has long been resolved in favour of the individual or lower levels of organization in the field of biology.

Another deficiency in our use of evolutionary theory has to do with our almost exclusive focus on "survival," when, in fact, evolutionary theory is about both survival and reproduction. On the one hand, this is probably related to the difficulty of imagining cultures or societies "reproducing" like organisms. On the other, there is a general bias in materialist/evolutionary anthropology to play down or ignore the issue of the individual's role in shaping societies and cultures. Furthermore, when we deal with survival, our concerns appear to be more about the survival of systems (cultures, groups, populations, etc.) than of individuals. This makes it difficult for us to evaluate and discuss the relationship between societal rules and what individuals actually do. We thereby preclude the possibility of understanding the evolved biological correlates of conventions and institutions.

My proposed approach will treat warfare as only one of a class of conflicts which, in band and village societies, must be examined carefully to determine the extent to which they can be traced back to conflicts of interest among individuals.... [T]he focus will be primarily on individuals, who will be viewed as expending two basic kinds of efforts during their lifetimes: somatic effort (in the interests of survival) and reproductive effort (in the interest of fitness)....

Warfare as a Kind of Conflict

... Conflicts between individuals and groups of individuals break out within many band and tribal societies, but the groups contesting are not always (at the time) politically independent. Indeed, a common consequence of such conflicts is the fissioning of the groups along conflict lines, and an escalation/ continuation of the conflict. It is at this point that groups become visibly "independent" of each other and more conveniently fit into categories that enable us to define the *extended* conflicts as "warfare." However, we could not do so initially when the contestants were members of a common group. By insisting that our approach to warfare focus only on conflicts between politically independent groups, we run the risk of losing sight of the genesis of the conflict. We are also tempted to restrict our search for causes to just that inventory of things that "groups" (politically independent societies) might contest over, such as a hunting territory or water hole—resources that may be intimately identified with members of specific local groups.

This is a crucial issue. First, conflicts of interest in band and village societies often occur between individuals within the same group and are provoked by a wide variety of reasons. Second, individuals in kinship-organized societies tend to take sides with close kin and/or those whose reproductive interests overlap significantly with their own (e.g., wife's brothers). "Groups" are therefore often formed on the basis of kinship, marriage, or both, and by definition their members have overlapping reproductive interests. They usually have economic and other interests that overlap as well, but it is theoretically important to keep in mind that, from the perspective of evolution, the ultimate interests of individuals are reproductive in overall scope....

Life Effort

A basic assumption in my model is that the lifetime efforts of individuals can be partitioned into two conceptually distinct categories that incorporate all or nearly all of the activities that an individual (an organism in any species) engages in if it is to be biologically successful. These categories are *somatic effort* and *reproductive effort*. The former has principally to do with those activities, risks, costs, etc. that ensure the survival of the organism in a purely somatic sense—seeking shelter from the elements, protection from predators and conspecifics, obtaining nutrients, maintaining hygiene and health, etc. This would include most items we traditionally focus on in studies of technology, economics, settlement patterns, cultural ecology, grooming, ethnopharmacology, curing, etc.

The second category is one that is not normally considered in traditional cultural ecological/materialist approaches to intergroup conflicts, warfare, and cultural adaptation. While the category's overall content is "reproductive," it includes a number of specific variables not normally considered in traditional anthropological studies of reproduction as such (see Figure 1). Herein lies the value and power of theoretical developments in evolutionary biology that can shed new light on conflicts of interest between individuals and, ultimately, intergroup conflicts between politically independent groups such as bands and horticultural tribes.

Figure 1

Model of Individual Life Effort From a Darwinian Perspective

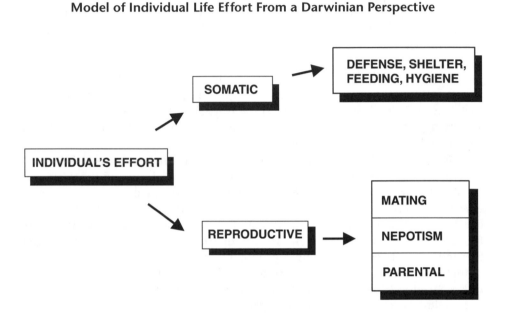

Note: Individuals expend basically two kinds of effort during their lifetimes: Somatic Effort and Reproductive Effort. The former has basically to do with the survival of the organism as such, while the latter has to do with costs, benefits, risks, etc. associated with mating, nepotism (aiding non-descendant kin), and parenting.

A review of the literature pertaining to warfare and conflict in such societies reveals that much of the conflict emanates over such factors as rape, abduction of females, failure to deliver a promised bride, niggardliness in paying bride price or executing bride service, and seduction. Whereas warfare and conflict in industrialized societies and many "ranked" or "stratified" societies can be convincingly shown to be associated with relative scarcity or protection of material resources, the proverbial "means of production," much of the conflict in most band and tribal societies is generated because of contests over the *means of reproduction.*

Let me make one thing perfectly clear at this juncture. I am *not* claiming that all conflicts of interest in band and tribal society derive from conflicts that are reproductive in overall quality, nor am I claiming that conflicts over material resources are not found in such societies. I am simply arguing that conflicts of reproductive interests occur commonly in band and tribal societies and that these often lead, as indicated above, to intergroup conflicts that we traditionally consider to be warfare. I accept (and have always accepted) explanations of specific band and village warfare patterns in which demonstrable and convincing evidence indicates that shortages of material resources are directly implicated in the genesis of the conflicts....

The category "reproductive effort" in my model is advised by and basically derived from the post-1960 theoretical developments in evolutionary biology. Reproduction entails getting copies of one's self into subsequent generations. This can occur in more than the single obvious way we normally think of reproduction: begetting and successfully raising offspring. Since related organisms share identical genes by immediate common descent, organisms can advance their reproductive interests by engaging in activities and behaviours that affect, in a positive way, the reproductive efforts and accomplishments of relatives with whom they share genes. Thus, while the original Darwinian perspective viewed success in terms of fitness measured by numbers of immediate descendants (offspring), the new Darwinian perspective views success in broader, more encompassing terms. What is significant is the number of copies of one's genes that are perpetuated in subsequent generations.

This draws attention to the enormous importance of W. D. Hamilton's now classic papers defining "inclusive fitness." Individual Egos can pass on their genes by direct acts of reproduction (having children) and by aiding genetic relatives, who, by definition, share genes with Ego in proportion to the degree of genetic relatedness between them. If the aid enhances the relatives' reproduction, Ego "benefits" in a reproductive sense by having more copies of his/her genes enter the gene pool of subsequent generations—through the reproductive accomplishments of those relatives.

The study of "reproduction" becomes, then, more than merely the collection of genealogical facts and reproductive histories of individuals. It entails the study of all social interactions that potentially affect the reproductive success of the individual and those with whom he or she is interacting. Such interactions include, for example, taking risks to protect a kinsman in a mortal duel, sharing a piece of food, tendering aid in clearing gardens, and reclassifying a covillager from the kinship category "sister" to "wife."

The study of reproduction also entails the study of both the "rules" and violations of the rules, injunctions, moral prescriptions, etc., which can and often do lead to conflicts and fighting. Thus, failure to give a piece of food might possibly reflect an immediate shortage of food and have, therefore, relevance in a purely somatic context. At the same time, it can reflect a *reproductive* strategy on the part of an individual to enhance his or her political esteem and authority—to insult a reproductive competitor, for example. It thus has relevance in a purely reproductive context as well, often in the absence of resource scarcities. Such affronts are common in meat distributions among the Yanomamö, for example, where there is a chronic struggle among men to establish individual reputations for authority, prestige, esteem, productivity, generosity, and matrimonial success. The "rule" is to give portions of large game away first to the "big men" and then to the lesser. A meat distributor can strategically conduct his distribution to indicate to the assembled that he doesn't consider a particular individual in the group to be as "important" as he himself and others might consider him to be. This can be done by deliberately giving him an unacceptably small portion, an undesirable portion, or presenting a portion after first acknowledging that others are more important than he by distributing to them first. He might even go so far as to give him no portion. This is, of course, remembered and noted by all . . . and adds to all those other factors that accumulate eventually into smouldering inter-individual hostilities and conflicts that eventually explode and are expressed in arguments, club fights and, occasionally, homicides.

Reproductive efforts, then, includes a more comprehensive set of variables than traditional anthropological concepts embrace. It can conveniently be partitioned into several broad sub-categories (Figure 1): parental effort, mating effort, and nepotistic effort. Parental effort deals primarily with those factors we are familiar with in our more traditional views of reproduction: all those costs and risks required to rear one's children successfully and, by extension, grandchildren and great-grandchildren, i.e., descendant relatives. Mating effort includes the study of all those variables that affect the success that individuals enjoy in attracting (obtaining) a mate; guarding the mate from the seductive attempts of others; and keeping the kin of that mate satisfied in terms of the expectations that they have regarding bride price, bride service, food sharing, etc. Nepotistic effort includes all those social activities entailing costs and risks that are expended in order to aid non-descendant relatives. These individuals, by virtue of receiving such beneficence, are in a position to translate it into reproductive consequences that ultimately enhance the "inclusive fitness" of the original helper, i.e., by producing additional copies of the helper's genes through their own reproductive accomplishments.

Life Effort Model

. . . By thinking of an individual's life time as a series of efforts entailing costs and risks on the one hand and benefits on the other, one can more clearly identify the factors that are likely to be significant in terms of the individual's attempts to be successful as both a member of society and as an organism constrained by societal rules. One can see how culture and cultural success is relatable to biology and biological success. The myriad factors that potentially or actually lead to conflicts of somatic and reproductive interests and, ultimately, fighting and warfare can also be appreciated.

By focusing on individual level conflicts of interests, we can more clearly see how the patterns of escalation, found widely in tribal societies, grow in such a way as to enable us to trace the sources of the conflicts back to the individual level and relate them, where possible, to reproductive versus somatic conflicts. This is particularly important for understanding warfare in band and village societies where the initial conflicts are almost always at the level of individuals. The "causes" of specific "wars" in such societies are bound up in complex, often vague, issues that transpired months or even years before the specific raid by "Group A" on "Group B" which we traditionally identify as "war" actually occurs. In contrast, by starting with the "group" as our initial level of analysis (because we usually define warfare as mortal contests between groups), we lose sight of the anterior patterns and are forced to interpret the group level phenomena as having started there.

The focus on individuals not only makes the conflict genesis clearer, it also compels us to consider the history of the conflict and how initial conflicts over one particular cause evolve into newer, more encompassing conflicts that are perpetuated by secondary causes. . . .

Striving for Esteem and Prestige

Kinship and genealogy become significant in understanding conflicts for a variety of reasons. They are as a result central variables in understanding the causes, development and escalation of violence in kinship-organized band and village societies. However, in addition to the variations in one's relative influence in his/her society as determined by the size and structure of one's kinship nexus, individuals are significantly different in their ability to achieve prestige and status through chronic or episodic acts of competition in various arenas of social life. There is marked variation from one society to another in the extent to which there is competition among individuals (viz. Benedict's classic work on patterns of culture [1934]). In some, it is so negligible that ethnographers insist that it is irrelevant or does not occur at all. . . .

This is one area in which we must do more work. Inter-individual conflicts of interest presumably exist in all societies and individuals must therefore resolve them somehow and, we would predict, in fashions that benefit *them* rather than others. In some societies, it might be very difficult to distinguish the effects that kinship power confers on individuals from those attributes of esteem and prestige that are achieved apart from or in spite of the kinship nexus. Among the Yanomamö, virtually every village I have studied is led by headmen who invariably come from the largest descent groups in the village. Yet in a large number of villages there are men from distant, essentially unrelated villages who, through their individual skills and political abilities, rise to high levels of esteem in spite of their comparatively small number of relatives. In many societies, competition for or striving for high esteem and prestige is obvious and often spectacular.

The benefits for achieving high esteem in most band and village societies normally entail polygynous marriage and/or a more desirable position in the food/labor exchange networks, which can ultimately be related to differential access to mates and differential reproductive success. Among humans, prestige leads to influence and power, and power appears to lead to high reproductive success. Betzig has convincingly demonstrated this in her analysis of a larger number of "despotic" societies, but the extent to which this is true, statistically, in a significant sample of egalitarian societies must yet be established. The correlation has been demonstrated for the Yanomamö in several of my own publications. Large numbers of ethnographic descriptions of tribal societies suggest that polygyny, one spoor of high reproductive success, is usually associated with leadership or other positions of prestige, but none of them document statistical differences in reproductive accomplishments of polygynous versus nonpolygynous males. Indeed, variations in male reproductive success have been documented in only a few instances for *any* species.

Striving for prestige entails taking risks that lead to greater or lesser amounts of success for particular individuals: there will be winners and losers. Those who lose are all the more anxious to establish or reestablish their position. As a result, conflicts and fighting arise, often over issues that appear to have no obvious direct relationship to either somatic or reproductive interests. Whether or not they ultimately do can usually be established by documenting variations in survivorship among the offspring of the successful, as well as differences in numbers of mates and numbers of offspring among the losers and winners, and the comparative reproductive success of the adult offspring of the esteemed. . . .

A Headmen's Prestige and Reaction to Insult

In about 1980, a particularly devastating war developed between the village of Bisaasi-teri, the group I described in my 1968 monograph *Yanomamö: The Fierce People,* and the village of Daiyari-teri, a smaller, neighboring group described by Lizot in *Tales of the Yanomami.*

The war was provoked by a trivial incident in 1981 that amounted to a gross insult of the Bisaasi-teri headman, but its ultimate origins go back to the mid-1950s. The Daiyari-teri are members of a larger population bloc that includes a village called Mahekodo-teri. The Bisaasi-teri had just recently fissioned from their parent group, the Patanowa-teri, and were attempting to establish themselves as an independent, viable village. To this end, they were cultivating alliances with unrelated villages to their south. Unfortunately, their erstwile allies invited them to a feast and treacherously massacred many of the men and abducted a number of their young women. The survivors fled to and took refuge among the Mahekodo-teri. The Mahekodo-teri, acting from a position of strength, took further advantage of them and appropriated a number of their young women. At the same time, they also tendered them sufficient aid to enable the Bisaasi-teri to recover and regain their independence by making new gardens further away from their enemies. The Daiyari-teri, congeners of the Mahekodo-teri, eventually located their village at a site within a day's walk of the Bisaasi-teri. For the next decade or so, relationships between the two groups varied from friendship and amity to neutrality to overt hostility verging on warfare. In 1965, for example, the Bisaasi-teri spread rumors that the Daiyari-teri were cowards. The Daiyari-teri responded by demanding to have a chest-pounding duel with the more numerous Bisaasi-teri to show them—and the world at large—that they were valiant and would not tolerate insults to their reputations. From that point until about 1980, relationships between the two groups were strained, but the Daiyari-teri were not powerful enough to threaten the Bisaasi-teri militarily. Eventually, visiting between them resumed and they became allies, albeit suspicious allies.

In 1980, the Bisaasi-teri headman decided to take his village on a camping trip up the Orinoco river, near the village of Daiyari-teri. Since they were allies, this headman decided to visit their village and ask them for plantains, a commonly expected courtesy between allies under such circumstances. When he reached the village, there were a large number of Daiyari-teri children and youths playing in the water. They began pelting the headman with mudballs and sticks, harassing him in that fashion all the way into the village—an insult of the first order. What apparently made matters serious was the fact that the Daiyari-teri adults neither scolded the youths nor prevented them from continuing their abuse. The Bisaasi-teri headman left, angry, and without plantains. He moved his people back to the village and cancelled the camping trip.

Some time later, perhaps a few weeks, a large number of Daiyari-teri men visited the Salesian Mission at the mouth of the Mavaca river, immediately across the Orinoco from the Bisaasi-teri village. The Bisaasi-teri spotted them immediately, and challenged them to a fight. They attacked them first with clubs and, ironically, pelted the Daiyari-teri men with lumps of hardened cement that had been discarded from a house-construction project on the mission side of the river. Considerable injury to the Daiyari-teri resulted, and they left for home, bleeding from their numerous wounds, threatening to get revenge. They eventually sent word to the Bisaasi-teri that they wanted to settle their dispute in a chest-pounding duel. The Bisaasi-teri enthusiastically accepted the challenge and went to their village to feast and fight. In the ensuing duel, two young men were killed. The Bisaasi-teri departed immediately, but were intercepted by Daiyari-teri archers who managed to wound one of them with an arrow. Shortly after, the Daiyari-teri raided and wounded a Bisaasi-teri man.

Some weeks later, one of the young men in Bisaasi-teri went on a fishing trip with an employee of the Venezuelan Malarialogia service. He was warned not to go on the trip because it was too close to the Diayari-teri village. He went anyway. While they were fishing from their canoe that night, a party of Daiyari-teri men discovered them and killed the young man with a volley of arrows, three of which struck him in the neck. The Bisaasi-teri recovered his body the next day and, in the ensuing weeks, mounted several unsuccessful raids against the Daiyari-teri, who had fled inland to escape retaliation. The Daiyari-teri eventually returned to their village.

The Bisaasi-teri called on their allies to join them in a raid. One of the allied groups, Iyawei-teri, attacked a day before the main group. The Bisaasi-teri raiding party reached the Daiyari-teri village a short time after the Iyawei-teri raiders had struck and fled, leaving two Daiyari-teri men dead. The Bisaasi-teri and their allies, armed with both arrows and shotguns, surrounded the village and set it ablaze, forcing the inhabitants to flee to the bank of the Orinoco river. There they took cover in a large pit they had dug into the ground in the event they were driven from their village by raiders—as they were. They were bombarded with volley after volley of Bisaasi-teri arrows, shot into the air and descending, like mortar rounds, into the open pit. Those who raised up to return the fire were shot with both arrows and shotgun blasts. A number of the adult males were killed; at least two women were deliberately shot as well, and an undetermined number of children and infants were accidentally wounded by the volleys of arrows and random shotgun pellets, some of whom later died. One of the fatalities was a woman who was a sister to the Bisaasi-teri headman and had been appropriated when the Bisaasi-teri took refuge with the Mahekodo-teri in the 1950s.

The survivors fled to an allied village when the raiders left. They solicited aid from the Mahekodo-teri and several other villages to mount revenge raids and eventually managed to ambush a young Bisaasi-teri couple who were on their way to the garden one morning, killing both of them. The Bisaasi-teri were satisfied that they had taught the Daiyari-teri a lesson and have no further interest in raiding them. However, they say they have every intention to exact revenge on the Mahekodo-teri for the two most recent killings and are presently waiting for the most opportune time to do so.

Discussion

In both of the above examples, the notion of prestige and status figure prominently and must be taken into consideration in explaining the conflicts. Moreover, the conflicts are not simply isolated incidents, provoked by a specific single act. They are continuations of smouldering antagonisms that originate in a multitude of previous acts, some involving seduction and male/male competition for women, others involving reactions to insults or testing of resolve and status, and others are purely vindictive and motivated by vengeance. Among the Yanomamö, it is relatively easy to relate all of these variables to reproductive striving, for a village that fails to respond to aggressive acts, even verbal ones, soon finds itself victimized by stronger, more assertive allies who translate their advantage into appropriating reproductively valuable females.

For the leaders, the reproductive rewards for aggressiveness are even more obvious. The above Bisaasi-teri headman, for example, has had 8 wives during his lifetime and has sired 25 children by them (not all survived). At present (1988), he has two wives, one of whom is still young and able to produce his children. Finally, the followers who take risks on behalf of and at the instigation of leaders, benefit in both somatic and reproductive terms as well. By complying with the suggestions and directions of the leaders, they contribute to the reputation of the village, as well as to their own reputations as individuals. By thus establishing the credibility of their claims for being valiant and aggressive, they also manage to prevail in a milieu of chronic aggressive threats and enjoy relatively secure and predictable somatic and reproductive opportunities compared to those who fail to make such demonstrations.

The overall aggregate of groups comprised of competitive status-seeking individuals has its social costs as well. The most obvious one is a domestic condition fraught with relatively constant stress and bickering, particularly in larger groups whose kinship composition might favor factionalism. The chronic fissioning of larger groups along lines of close kinship is a response to this internal social stress and competition whenever external threats are sufficiently low to permit them.

Summary

... Status differentials among individuals are more numerous and dramatic in so-called egalitarian societies than many contemporary theoretical arguments from anthropology assert. These are, in part, inherited in a very real sense. One's fund of kinship power is fixed largely at birth. One cannot, for example, pick his or her parents or descent group, nor alter the reproductive facts of the ascending generations, i.e., how many kin of what kinds or degrees of relatedness he or she will be surrounded by at birth and among whom he or she grows up and must interact socially with on a daily basis. An individual can, as he or she matures, modify the "luck of the kinship draw" in a number of limited ways, but all of them require the cooperation of others. One way is to produce children, but Ego must first find a mate, i.e., have elders who will find a mate for him or her. Another way is to "manipulate" kinship classifications and move people in kinship categories that are socially and reproductively more useful, an act that requires the "endorsement" of co-villagers who will go along with the manipulation by altering their own kin usage to conform to that initiated by the original manipulator. A third way is for particular men to lobby for a village fission that will divide the larger group into smaller ones permitting Ego to surround himself with a mixture of co-resident kin more congenial to his social and reproductive interests. One's ability to influence others, make demands, coerce, garner cooperation, etc. is often a direct function of the individual's kinship nexus and the kinds and numbers of kin-defined allies he or she can draw on to enforce his or her will. Conflicts of interest emerge and develop in a kinship matrix in most band and village societies, necessitating an understanding of genealogical relatedness, reproductive and marital histories, and other features of kinship and descent. In addition, high status and esteem usually confer advantage in matrimonial striving and, therefore, in reproductive success. It thus should be expected that individuals will compete over and have conflicts about relative degrees of esteem, conflicts that may, on the surface, reveal no obvious relationship to either somatic or reproductive resources. Measurements of relative status and relative degrees of reproductive success should be made to determine if there is a positive correlation between them.

A Savage Encounter

The lives of the Yanomami of the Orinoco-Mavaca river confluence of southern Venezuela have been presented in the works of Napoleon Chagnon as a kind of morality play. Embroiled in seemingly endless violence fueled by sexual competition, status rivalry, and revenge, the Yanomami are held to exemplify the Hobbesian condition of " 'Warre'—the chronic disposition to do battle, to Oppose and dispose of one's sovereign neighbors." Moreover, their lifeways are said to represent "a truly primitive cultural adaptation... before it was altered or destroyed by our culture." Their warfare is portrayed not as aberrant or unusual, but as the normal state of existence for sovereign tribal peoples, seeming atypical only because other war patterns have been suppressed by colonialism. It is "an expected form of political behavior and no more requires special explanations than do religion or economy." The conditions Chagnon describes are said to resemble those at the dawn of agriculture. The Yanomami are "our contemporary ancestors"; thus, understanding their "quality of life... can help us understand a large fraction of our own history and behavior." The same insecurities that create Warre among the Yanomami account for warfare among modern nation-states, and the same inference is to be drawn: "the best defense is a good offense."

Chagnon's portrayal is persuasive and has been widely accepted. In the Foreword to his *Yanomamö: The Fierce People,* one of the most widely read texts in the history of anthropology, the series editors write that the "sovereign tribal" politics of these Yanomami is "a product of long-term sociocultural evolution without intervention from outside alien populations and life ways." Even scholars who have been the most attentive to the violence-provoking possibilities of Western contact accept the Yanomami's relatively "pristine" character. Students of the Yanomami have been more skeptical, many pointing out that the Orinoco-Mavaca area has undergone extensive contact-related changes. None of the critics, however, has shown in any systematic way how those changes relate to observed patterns of violence.

[T]his paper was written... to explore exactly those relationships, and to challenge the idea that any ethnographic case of indigenous warfare is fully understandable apart from the historical circumstances of contact with an expanding state.... I will not dispute that [Yanomami] are less disrupted and transformed by Western contact than most of the peoples for whom we have ethnographic information. Nevertheless, I will argue that after centuries of sporadic contact with outsiders, Orinoco-Mavaca society was undergoing massive change for some two decades prior to Chagnon's arrival, and that this process of change accelerated during the time period described in Chagnon's monographs (1964–72). His statement that "it is not true, as a few of my colleagues believe, that the Yanomamo were described at a particularly 'turbulent' period of their history" is unsupportable. The "fierce people" immortalized by Chagnon represent a moment in history in which Yanomami culture was pushed into an extreme conflict mode by circumstances related to the intensifying Western presence. Their warfare and other conflicts are manifestations of this larger situation. Where Chagnon tells us that the Yanomami provide "an intimate glimpse beyond history, whither we came," I maintain that they will remain a baffling chimera until they are seen in the light of their own history....

Local History

The ancestors of the Yanomami were raided by slavers, in varying intensity, from probably the mid-seventeenth century to about 1850. The raids drove them deep into the Parima highlands, although some still came down to the rivers to trade. The rubber boom of the latter nineteenth century reached into mountain areas and was accompanied by wars and migrations for the recent ancestors of the Orinoco-Mavaca people. The collapse of rubber production left the region more isolated from Westerners from around 1920 until 1940, a brief interlude which has been misconstrued as a primeval state. For the Orinoco-Mavaca people, this was a time of peace.

Sporadic, sometimes violent, contact began in the area around 1940 and intensified over the decade. The captive woman Helena Valero was in this area, and she describes the intensifying conflicts as new tools and diseases began to filter in. In the late 1940s the Namoweiteri, the population cluster later to host Chagnon's field research, divided into hostile western and eastern (Patanowa-teri) groups. Then, in 1950, the establishment of the first mission near Mahekodo-teri on the Orinoco was followed almost immediately by the slaughter of a western Namowei-teri trading party by the more isolated Shamatari. Interior groups continued to harry the wealthier villages around the Orinoco until, in 1955, the latter demonstrated their military superiority. During the relatively peaceful half decade to follow, a second mission was established by Iyewei-teri at the mouth of the Ocamo River. The Iyewei-teri are an important contrast to other local groups: although only a few hours by launch downstream from Chagnon's field site, they had a more stable and wealthy Western power base than any upstream village, and enjoyed almost unbroken peace while the upriver villages endured several wars.

In 1958, a government malaria control station was set up at the mouth of the Mavaca River. The Bisaasi-teri, the larger of the western Namowei-teri groups, accepted an invitation to settle by the post. (The other western group, the closely allied Monou-teri, was located a short distance up the Mavaca.)

Almost immediately, the missionaries at Mahekodo-teri moved their main operation to Bisaasi-teri. The Bisaasi-teri and Monou-teri then set out to establish beneficial alliances with Shamatari groups up the Mavaca, and in one instance demonstrated their willingness to use force against potential adversaries. For the next several years, Bisaasi-teri would be the metropolitan center of the far upper Orinoco, especially in late 1964 to early 1966, when Chagnon lived there, and when another mission was attempting to establish itself directly across the Orinoco. But those years also saw the western Namowei-teri beleaguered by internal factionalism and external enemies. This was the extraordinary fighting described in *Yąnomamö: The Fierce People*. . . .

Infrastructure

Western contact brings epidemic diseases. In the Orinoco-Mavaca area, epidemics began to occur around 1940, and they continued with devastating frequency. A major outbreak of malaria in 1960 killed an estimated 10 percent of the area population, and another outbreak is indicated for 1963. Chagnon's initial census established the cause of death of 240 individuals: 130 are attributed to malaria and epidemics, and another 25 to "sorcery." A measles epidemic swept through the area in 1968. Among deaths recorded by Chagnon for 1970 to 1974, 82 (69 percent) were due to all infectious diseases (including "magic"). In a different sample gathered at Mavaca for 1969 to 1979, 53 (39.6 percent) were due to malaria.

A single influenza epidemic that hit three remote villages in 1973 shows how terrible the impact can be. One hundred six people died, 27.4 percent of the combined population. One village lost 40 percent. In this epidemic, and presumably in all of them, the young and old died in disproportionate numbers. The contagion apparently was transmitted by men coming back from a trip downstream to obtain machetes. . . .

In sum, in the Orinoco-Mavaca area, a great many families were disrupted by death during the contact period. Only about one-quarter of the children there have both parents alive and coresident by the time they reach the age of 15. For the Yanomami, family, economy, and polity are one, and this many deaths tears at the fabric of society. . . . The longer-term consequences are described by Chagnon and Melancon:

> Disruption of village life and the resulting coalescence or fusion shatters the
> social organization and creates chaos, conflict and disorder in the newly-
> constituted village(s).

. . . [Another] infrastructural consequence of contact is technological change. Of paramount importance is the introduction of steel cutting tools, which are up to ten times more efficient than stone. As with other Amazonian peoples, Yanomami have gone to great lengths to obtain these tools, relocating villages, sending trading parties on long and hazardous journeys, and raiding vulnerable possessors of steel. All known Yanomami had obtained some metal tools long before any anthropologist visited them, yet these highly valued items remained scarce until very recently. And steel tools are only the beginning. New needs develop rapidly for a range of Western manufactures, in a process that can lead to assimilation into the lowest stratum of the expanding state. In the Orinoco-Mavaca area, those with greatest access to Westerners are seen by other Yanomami as having "turned white."

Machetes, axes, and knives are unlike anything in the indigenous economy. At least at first, their utility and scarcity makes them more precious than items of native manufacture. Furthermore, they are unequally available, their sources restricted to a few points of Western presence, so procurement is the key problem. It is commonly acknowledged that Yanomami villages have moved out of the Parima highlands in order to provide closer access to sources of steel, and that in the Orinoco-Mavaca area, this is why Yanomami moved from the highlands to the insect-infested rivers. And there is more to it than movement.

> Thus there grew up two types of community—those holding manufactured goods acquired directly at source, and those (isolated ones) which were deprived of them. The entire map of economic and matrimonial circuits, along with political alliances, was transformed and flagrant imbalances appeared. Gradually, though scarcely within twenty years... the economy was disrupted, the society menaced at its roots, and dysfunctional attitudes developed....

Structure

The structural effects of contact on war are here separated into three conventional topics: economics, kinship, and political organization.

Economics

A central problem for all Yanomami economies is how to obtain Western manufactured goods. In different Yanomami areas, these have been obtained by hunting for pelts, traveling to work as farmhands, or producing manioc flour or bananas for sale or trade. In the Orinoco-Mavaca area, the way to obtain Western goods has been to work for the Westerners who come there to live or visit. Missionaries and other resident Westerners regularly give away substantial quantities of manufactures. They make large presentations on special occasions, such as visits to more remote villages, but normally give the manufactures as payment for goods (garden products, meat, firewood), for services (as guides, ground clearers, housebuilders, translators, maids, informants, etc.), and in some instances, for local manufactures with external sale potential. Very few details are available about employment and payments, but one obvious point has important consequences for understanding patterns of conflict: to work for the Westerners in most of these capacities requires that one live close to them.

... [T]he Yanomami generally make great efforts to monopolize access to the Western provider using pleas, threats, and deceptions to keep the distribution of goods within their local group. Beyond the source point, Western manufactures are passed along from village to village through networks of kinship. Often the people in one village use a tool for some time, then pass it along to the next village when they get a new one. The quantities in exchange can only be guessed, but that guess must be high. An incomplete listing of goods distributed from the Catholic mission at Iyewei-teri for 1960 to 1972 includes 3,850 machetes, 620 axes, 2,850 pots, 759,000 fishhooks, and large quantities of other items. Most of these goods were traded to more remote villages. Nevertheless, some villages separated from Western sources by two or three intervening villages are reported as receiving only poor remnants of manufactures. . . .

Most reports indicate that the exchange of Western manufactures is usually without overt contention. A request for an item is made, and that item is given, on the promise of some future compensation. On the other hand, Lizot reports that "the bargaining, however, does not procede without bitter disputes. The partners stay at the brink of rupture." Even the smooth transactions may mask tensions, and the major trading that occurs at feasts is often preceded or followed by violent confrontations. Veiled and not-so-veiled threats are made, as when a man "named the men he had killed on various raids—just before demanding a machete" from Chagnon. "In some communities, to declare, 'I will not give anything' or 'I will not give what you are asking' is to risk a clubbing." . . .

In exchange for Western manufactures, more isolated Yanomami make and trade local manufactures. Consistent with the earlier quotation from Lizot, this has led to a clear division of labor between Yanomami communities. All the villages around missions have specialized in the trade of Western items; residents of villages without such access have become specialists in producing specific local commodities which they trade to the mission villages.

But does this general pattern apply to the Bisaasi-teri? Admittedly, it would be difficult to infer its existence from reading *The Fierce People*. Cocco, however, like Lizot, describes the pattern as applying to all mission villages in the area, which would include Bisaasi-teri. In a letter written during his initial fieldwork, Chagnon reports the same pattern: "Some villages specialize in making one or another object; others who have special sources of access purvey axes or machetes and pots to the rest." The pattern is also suggested by the captions of two photographs from the same trading session: "Kaobawa trading his steel tools to Shamatari allies" and "Kaobawa . . . trading with his Shamatari allies for arrows, baskets, hammocks, and dogs," and it is implied in a passing mention of "steel tools and aluminum pots" being the trade specialization of "several contacted villages." But Chagnon follows this point immediately with a discussion that downplays the utilitarian aspect of trade in local manufactures, arguing that trade specialization is to be understood as a gambit to create political alliances. . . .

[T]he material interest in Bisaai-teri trade is apparent in regard to cotton and hammocks. Woven by men in this area, cotton hammocks are scarce and very valuable. They are traded widely, even into the Parima highlands.

> The Bisaasi-teri obtain much of their spun cotton and curare arrow points from their Shamatari allies. It takes considerable time and labor to accumulate these items. When the Shamatari are visited by the Bisaasi-teri, the latter make known their desire to have these items, and their hosts promise to produce them. When the items are accumulated, the Shamatari visit the Bisaasi-teri to inform them their cotton and arrow points are ready. A feast is arranged and the items are given over to the Bisaasi-teri after the celebration

terminates. The Shamatari then request specific items from their hosts, and the cycle continues.

The Bisaasi-teri export this cotton yarn to another ally, and it is then "brought back in the form of manufactured hammocks, the importer merely contributing labor to the process." In other words, the Bisaasi-teri come to possess a quantity of a very valuable trade item without expending any labor in its production. Curare arrowpoints, not incidentally, are listed by Cocco as the item Bisaasi-teri uses when trading at Iyewei-teri.

In sum, Yanomami with direct access to sources of Western manufactures make great efforts to monopolize them, sharp tensions surround the exchange of Western items, the quality and quantity of Western manufactures diminishes markedly at each step in the exchange network, and outpost villages acquire large quantities of various local, labor-intensive manufactures. My inference is that those groups who control sources of Western manufactures exploit more isolated peoples who depend on them for metal tools. This inference is reinforced by the more obvious exploitation by middlemen in the realm of marriage relationships, discussed in the next section. Later, we will see how all these factors generate warfare.

Kinship

The main focus of this section is marriage patterns and the much-debated "fighting over women." ...

One of the paramount concerns of a senior man is to find wives for his sons, younger brothers, and other coresident agnates. These men comprise his political supporters. But marriage makers are also vitally concerned with the question of bride service. In terms that are negotiated in advance, a groom is required to live with and labor for his wife's parents for a certain period after marriage, usually one to four years in the Orinoco-Mavaca area, before returning to the husband's village. The main duty of a son-in-law is to hunt, but other obligations are involved, including support of the father-in-law in war. The centrality of marriage arrangements is summed up by Lizot: "The highest cleverness consists in acquiring wives for one's sons by negotiating the briefest possible marital service and in seeking for one's daughters husbands who agree to settle permanently in the community."

Negotiation of marriage arrangements is made far more difficult by the circumstances of Western contact. In the Orinoco-Mavaca area, there is a well-known scarcity of marriageable females. I argue elsewhere that current evidence supports Chagnon's original observation that the intensity of female infanticide is associated with the intensity of warfare, despite his later assertion that sex ratio is skewed at birth. The local scarcity of marriageable women is aggravated by the relative predominance of polygyny. The actual incidence of polygyny is unclear. Some of Chagnon's generalizations, such as "a successful man may have had up to a dozen or more different wives, but rarely more than six wives simultaneously," appear exaggerated....

This relative scarcity of women would make finding a mate for a young man very difficult, and choosing a mate for daughters very political under the best of circumstances. The Yanomami do not live in the best of circumstances. As noted earlier, marriage arrangements are built up over years of negotiations, and they are reduced to chaos by the death waves of epidemics. Many disrupted families must be reconstituted, and arranging new marriages becomes even more difficult when the youngest generation of women dies off.

Simultaneously, the new ordering principle of access to Western goods enters in. Studies of some eastern Yanomami demonstrate a partial substitution of gifts of Western manufactures for actual bride service. The exchange is not a one-time payment. A man who has access to Western goods is expected to obtain them regularly for the wife-giver family. Although most marriages are village-endogamous, intervillage marriages are the firmest basis of alliance. Intermarriage, trade, and political support are all woven together. As noted earlier, the entire map of matrimonial, trade, and alliance networks was redrawn after the introduction of Western manufactures. The basis for this transformation is clear: women flow toward mission and other Western outpost villages. Among the eastern, Brazilian Yanomami, Peters and others describe a dramatic increase in village exogamy, with women going to the mission residents who could make bride payment with Western manufactures. In the northern reaches of their territory, Yanomami seeking Western manufactures from their well-supplied neighbors the Yekuana, gain access by a one-way ceding of women as brides or sexual partners....

The alliance between Chagnon's main field location, Bisaasi-teri and its Shamatari trade-partners to the south is perhaps the best illustration of this general pattern. In the four or five years after it moved to the government malaria station, Bisaasi-teri managed to obtain from the Shamatari "two dozen or so women... while having given or promised only a half-dozen in return." The chain of trading villages leading out from Bisaasi-teri exhibits a "cline in sex ratios": 0.8, 1.1, 1.2, 1.6. Bisaasi-teri has an unusually high rate of exogamic marriages, 53 percent, compared to 15 percent in Patanowa-teri; and the majority of exogamic marriages in at least one of Bisaasi-teri's two divisions are through alliances, while most of Patanowa-teri's are through abductions of women.

Bisaasi-teri has been equally privileged in terms of bride service.

> The men who have obtained Shamatari wives have, as well, managed to cut short their period of bride service in the Shamatari village. Conversely, Shamatari men who have been promised women of Kaobawa's group are pressed into very lengthy bride service.

The bride service of these Shamatari seems particularly difficult. Chagnon describes one young man who was "expected to do all manner of onerous tasks... [and] was subject to a considerable amount of ridicule and harsh treatment." His "father-in-law was particularly unpleasant to him. He denied Wakarabewa sexual access to the girl while at the same time he allowed the young men of the natal village to enjoy these privileges."

Viewing access to Western manufactures as the key to obtaining women from allies is a different perspective than that argued by Chagnon, who has consistently attributed success in obtaining wives to physically aggressive measures. The relevance of the Western manufactures-for-women connection is, however, indicated in a brief comment at the start of his thesis: "the disposition of desirable trade goods may affect the balance in the exchange of women between two villages." Also, in a coauthored article based on team research in another Yanomami area, Chagnon et al. note that control over steel tools gives Makiratare (Yekuana) the ability to "demand and usually obtain sexual access to Yanomama women," both in affairs and as marriage partners.

Political Organization

Having examined the unequal trade and marital relationships that develop on the basis of unequal access to steel tools and other Western items, we can now understand the nature of the antagonisms that lead to war and other political conflicts in the Orinoco-Mavaca area. Steel tools are essential means of production. In the Orinoco-Mavaca area during the period under discussion, they were available from a few source points. Compared to villages dependent on Yanomami middlemen, those with monopolistic access to Westerners received: (1) more Western items, (2) better quality Western items, (3) many local manufactures, (4) more wives, and (5) better bride service terms....

How is force applicable in this context? The most direct application of force is that aimed at obtaining Western manufactures through plunder. That has been done by Yanomami, as by many Amazonian peoples, but it is a high-risk endeavor, and unusual within the Orinoco-Mavaca area. Force is more routinely applied to affect the flow of Western items beyond their source points. This occurs in several ways. Ambush or the threat of ambush is used to discourage travel that would circumvent a middleman village, or raids and surprise attacks at feasts are used to make a village relocate. The latter course can be used by a trade controller against a village that is attempting to move closer to the source of Western goods, and by those without good access to Westerners, in an attempt to make the controlling villages abandon their monopolistic position. Finally, club fights and other violent confrontations are used within established exchange relationships in order to direct the distribution of scarce items, and (more hypothetically) to influence the implicit rates of exchange of Western goods for other valuables.

The Yanomami do not appear at all unusual in this patterning of violence. Very similar considerations shape warfare on the Pacific Northwest Coast.... Conflict over access to Western manufactures fosters intense political conflict not just because of the importance of steel, but because unequal access creates a structured, collective conflict of interest between villages or factions. One man may benefit by capturing a wife, but a whole community benefits by an enhanced flow of machetes, axes, and pots. But turning a community of interest into an action group prepared to do violence is a difficult task, requiring great leadership skills. That brings us to the topic of leaders, and how they too have changed in the circumstances of contact.

Leadership among the Yanomami falls squarely within the general pattern for all recently described Amazonian societies. The headman represents his coresident kin, either a separate settlement or a recognizable cluster of families within a larger village, in interactions with outsiders. He is more likely than other men to be polygynous, and his status relative to other headmen largely depends upon the size of his kin group. In a sense, the group makes the leader, but the leader also makes the group. By his manipulation of marriages and other movements of people, he can gain or lose followers. The headman is the capstone of coresidential group organization, and those groups often dissolve on his death.

Leadership also responds to the changes associated with contact, however. Headmen are the main recipients of Western goods, especially in the more remote villages.... The role of headmen in channeling Western manufactures in outpost villages is less clear, but there are indications that they continue to have special access. To the east, at the Catrimani mission, each mission payment to an individual had to be approved first by the headman. Furthermore, headmen often enjoy the very substantial benefit of explicit backing by resident Westerners....

Another contact-related factor affecting the status of headmen is the intensity of conflict. Increasing danger of war brings an immediate, palpable increase in the authority and jurisdiction of headmen. In a politically charged environment, a leader can be peremptory, even tyrannical, using violence against those who do not obey his orders.

During peaceful times, the need for leadership is limited, but during war and other periods of high tension, the headman has two major responsibilities. One is tending to the necessities of combat, such as organizing raiding parties or checking village perimeters for signs of raiders....

The other responsibility is managing alliances. During peaceful times, political alliances between villages are of limited development and importance. During wartime, they are essential. Allies are needed for survival and success in war, providing both warriors on raids and vital places of refuge. There are often substantial tensions between allies, which the headman must keep under control....

Given the role of the headman as the capstone of the coresidential group, and his centrality in relation to the practice of war and alliance, it is easy to understand a tactic of Yanomami warfare: targeting the headman. Headmen are frequently reported as the intended targets or actual victims of raiders. The effectiveness of this tactic is illustrated by the plight of Monou-teri in 1965, when the killing of their headman by raiders left them adrift and dependent on the leadership of self-interested neighbors....

Superstructure

[Chagnon called the Yanomami "the fierce people."] Fierceness is embodied in a commitment to take revenge, in cultivating an image that retaliation *will* follow any killing. As [one man] reportedly told potential enemies: "We are in this world to avenge ourselves; if you do it to me, I will do it to you." This image has obvious defensive value. In a climate of ongoing wars, the failure to retaliate for a hostile act creates the appearance of weakness, and this can encourage future attacks. But it is necessary to distinguish the tactical value of retaliation from the idea that wars are propelled forward by sentiments of blood revenge. In a recent publication, Chagnon places great emphasis on blood revenge as a factor itself responsible for raiding and other violence. In a commentary on that article, I argue that the vengeance motivation itself is highly malleable, manipulated to suit political needs.

   ... [I]ntensifying hostility between political groups is [also] conceptualized in terms of spirit battles, controlled by their respective shamans. An accusation of witchcraft often precedes combat, so that it may appear that these beliefs are the cause of war. But it has been a consistent finding of witchcraft studies in other parts of the world that accusations of witchcraft *express* existing hostilities rather than cause them. Here too, bad relations lead to suspicions of sorcery and villages "linked by trade and feasting ties... rarely accuse each other of practicing harmful magic."

   ... [A]ttribution of a death to sorcery is accompanied by a felt need for blood revenge. It may be that witchcraft and revenge are two sides of a coin. Witch beliefs confirm the malevolence of particular outsiders ("them"); vengeance beliefs emphasize the solidarity of the local group ("versus us"). Together, they make up an effective ideological system for the difficult task of mobilizing people for collective violence.

Conclusions

This paper has examined the multiple, interacting effects of Western contact on the war complex of Yanomami of the Orinoco-Mavaca area. Contact both generated war, primarily through conflicting interests in Western manufactures, and led to pervasive reorganization of society and culture, such that all of life became oriented toward violent conflict. Comparing these Yanomami to Yanomami elsewhere, one cannot doubt that they share a fundamental cultural identity. But the "fierce people" represent Yanomami culture in an extreme conflict mode, a mode that is clearly attributable to the exogenous factors of Western contact. These people cannot be taken as "our contemporary ancestors." They do not represent a phase in sociocultural evolution.

   No one can say if the Yanomami ancestors made war before they felt any effects of European contact. But their *known* wars are clearly products of the contact situation, and more specifically, of the infrastructural changes wrought by contact, played out through a changing structure and superstructure.

POSTSCRIPT

Are Yanomami Violence and Warfare Natural Human Efforts to Maximize Reproductive Fitness?

Although no one can dispute the fact that the Yanomami were violent in the 1960s, these selections may lead some to ask whether Yanomami violence was always as pervasive a part of Yanomami culture as Chagnon describes it. Filmmaker Timothy Asch, who helped Chagnon with some of his films, depicts a much more tender side of Yanomami life than is typical in Chagnon's films. What seems to be missing from both of these perspectives, however, is the role of basic cultural values in shaping Yanomami behavior, whether toward violence or toward tenderness. What is also absent in these two accounts is the role of regional patterns of intergroup exchange that may have been disrupted by the introduction of Western machetes.

Ferguson's argument is more fully developed in his book *Yanomami Warfare: A Political History* (School of American Research Press, 1995) in which he draws upon his own research as well as that of many other anthropologists besides Chagnon who have worked with the Yanomami. Other aspects of Ferguson's argument are developed in several papers, including "Game Wars? Ecology and Conflict in Amazonia," *Journal of Anthropological Research* (Summer 1989) and "Do Yanomami Killers Have More Kids?" *American Ethnologist* (August 1989).

Chagnon has published several ethnographic volumes about his research with the Yanomami. These include his original monograph, *Yanomami*, 5th ed. (Harcourt Brace, 1997), originally published with the subtitle "The Fierce People" in 1968, and *Studying the Yanomami* (Holt, Rinehart and Winston, 1974). His most recent monograph deals directly with aspects of cultural change and is entitled *Yanomami: The Last Days of Eden* (Harcourt, Brace, Jovanovich, 1992). He has also published a number of papers supporting his sociobiological interpretations. See "Kin Selection Theory, Kinship, Marriage and Fitness Among the Yanomomö Indians," in G. W. Barlow and J. Silverberg, eds., *Sociobiology: Beyond Natural Selection* (Westview Press, 1980) and "Sociodemographic Attributes of Nepotism in Tribal Populations," *Current Problems in Sociobiology* (Cambridge University Press, 1982).

Two of Bruce Albert's essays, "Yanomami 'Violence': Inclusive Fitness or Ethnographer's Representation," *Current Anthropology* (December 1989) and "On Yanomami Warfare: Rejoinder," *Current Anthropology* (December 1990), deal with the central question of fitness in this issue.

ISSUE 12

Is Ethnic Conflict Inevitable?

YES: Sudhir Kakar, from "Some Unconscious Aspects of Ethnic Violence in India," in Veena Das, ed., *Mirrors of Violence: Communities, Riots and Survivors in South Asia* (Oxford University Press, 1990)

NO: Anthony Oberschall, from "The Manipulation of Ethnicity: From Ethnic Cooperation to Violence and War in Yugoslavia," *Ethnic and Racial Studies* (November 2000)

ISSUE SUMMARY

YES: Indian social researcher Sudhir Kakar analyzes the origins of ethnic conflict from a psychological perspective to argue that ethnic differences are deeply held distinctions that from time to time will inevitably erupt as ethnic conflicts. He maintains that anxiety arises from preconscious fears about cultural differences. In his view, no amount of education or politically correct behavior will eradicate these fears and anxieties about people of differing ethnic backgrounds.

NO: American sociologist Anthony Oberschall considers the ethnic conflicts that have recently emerged in Bosnia and contends that primordial ethnic attachments are insufficient to explain the sudden emergence of violence among Bosnian ethnic groups. He adopts a complex explanation for this violence, identifying circumstances in which fears and anxieties were manipulated by politicians for self-serving ends. It was only in the context of these manipulations that ethnic violence could have erupted, concludes Oberschall.

Since the 1960s anthropologists and other social scientists have debated the causes, origins, and necessary conditions for ethnic differences to erupt into ethnic violence. Such discussions have built on an older debate about the origins of ethnicity. In the earlier debate, two key positions emerged. The first is the *primordialist* view, in which ethnic attachments and sentiments emerge from the fact of being members of the same cultural community. Although cultural in origin, the primordialists see kinship, language, and customary practices as the source of ethnic identity and social bonds between people of the same ethnicity. Ethnicity in this view is something one is born with, or at least born into, because it develops as one learns kinship, language, and culture. A second position, often called the *circumstantialist* perspective, was developed by the Norwegian anthropologist Fredrik Barth in his book *Ethnic Groups and Social Boundaries* (Little, Brown, 1969). For Barth, a person's ethnicity is neither fixed nor a natural condition of his or her birth. One's ethnicity could be (and often was) manipulated under different circumstances. By dressing differently, by learning a different language, and by intermarriage, people in many ethnic groups within a generation or two could become members of another ethnic group and have a different ethnic identity. Later, if it became advantageous to be members of the first ethnic group, these same people could acknowledge their past and become members of the first group.

The following selections shift the ethnicity debate to the problem of whether or not ethnic conflict is inevitable. Sudhir Kakar uses a psychological approach to develop a primordialist argument to explain the frequent and almost continual problems of ethnic violence in India. For Kakar, ethnic sentiments and attachments emerge from deep psychological concerns at the unconscious or even preconscious level. He contends that psychologically there are primordial differences between Indians of different ethnic backgrounds, and such differences lead to conflicts over access to resources, jobs, and the like.

Anthony Oberschall considers possible explanations for the sudden appearance of ethnic conflict in the former Yugoslavia. He acknowledges that the primordialist variables of kinship, religion, and language may play some role in explaining why Serbs, Croats, and Bosnian Muslims behaved as they did once ethnic conflict broke out. Traditional animosities existed for centuries in the Balkans, and they reemerged suddenly after 50 years of peace and cooperation. But such variables cannot explain why these groups started fighting with one another in the first place, says Oberschall, after nearly half a century of living together peacefully, regularly socializing, and even intermarrying with one another; such ties as kinship, language, and religion do not explain why tensions flared up or why neighbors suddenly tried to eliminate people of other ethnic backgrounds from their towns and villages. Drawing on a complex pattern of circumstantial variables, Oberschall develops a circumstantialist model, arguing that politicians were manipulating local sentiments for their own ends. In the context of great uncertainty and crisis, people of all ethnic backgrounds bought into the anxieties suggested by their different leaders.

What leads people to hate people of different ethnic backgrounds? Is it deeply held fears of cultural differences? Or does conflict emerge because individuals fear losing what they have worked hard to obtain? How could people in Yugoslavia live together harmoniously for 50 years and then suddenly participate in the "ethnic cleansing" of their neighborhoods? Could the willingness to commit such acts of violence against neighbors have been suppressed for half a century by a strong central government? What is the source of this kind of group hatred, since differences in skin color and physical features are largely not present in either the Indian or Yugoslavian cases?

Sudhir Kakar

 **YES**

Some Unconscious Aspects of Ethnic Violence in India

T he need to integrate social and psychological theory in the analysis of cultural conflicts, i.e. conflicts between ethnic and religious groups, has long been felt while its absence has been equally long deplored. Though everyone agrees on the theoretical questions involved—how do these conflicts originate, develop, and get resolved; how do they result in violent aggression—a general agreement on the answers or even on how to get these answers moves further and further away.

A large part of the problem in the study of these questions lies with the nature of and the crisis within the social sciences. The declining fortunes of logical positivism, hastened in the last twenty years by the widespread circulation and absorption of the views of such thinkers as Gadamer, Habermas, Derrida, Ricouer and Foucault, has led to a plethora of new models in the sciences of man and society. The dominant model of yesteryears—social science as social physics—is now only one among several clamouring for allegiance and adherents. It incorporates only one view among many on the nature of social reality and of social science knowledge. Anthropology, sociology, political science, psychology and even economics are all becoming more pluralistic and scattering into frameworks. In such a situation, the calls for a general theory of ethnic violence or indeed (as Clifford Geertz has remarked) of anything *social,* sound increasingly hollow, and the claims to have one science seem megalomaniacal. Thus, without taking recourse to other disciplines and even ignoring the grand theories of human aggression in psychology itself—those of animal ethology, sociology, Freudian Thanatos and so on—I would like to present some limited 'local knowledge' observations on ethnic violence in India from a psychoanalytic perspective.

In the manner of a clinician, let me begin with the concrete data on which I base my observations on the first question, namely the origins of ethnic conflict. The data for these observations, and those which follow, come from diverse sources: spirit possession in north India, dreams of psychotherapy patients, eavesdropping on group discussions at the Golden Temple complex in July 1984, and finally, personal participation in large religious assemblies.

The Other in Ethnic Conflict

Some years ago, while studying the phenomenon of possession by spirits in rural north India, I was struck by a curious fact. In a very large number of cases, 15 out of 28, the *bhuta* or malignant spirit possessing Hindu men and women turned out to be a Muslim. When, during the healing ritual, the patient went into a trance and the spirit started expressing its wishes, these wishes invariably turned out to be those which would have been horrifying to the patient's conscious self. In one case, the Muslim spirit possessing an elderly Brahmin priest vigorously insisted on eating kababs. The five women surrounding the man who had engaged the *bhuta* in conversation were distinctly disheartened that he had turned out to be a *Sayyad* and one of them lamented: 'These Mussulmans! They have ruined our *dharma* but they are so strong they can withstand our gods.' In another case, the *bhuta* inhabiting a young married woman not only expressed derogatory sentiments towards her 'lord and master' but also openly stated its intentions of bringing the mother-in-law to a violent and preferably bloody end.

Possession by a Muslim *bhuta,* then, seemed to reflect the afflicted person's desperate efforts to convince himself and others that his hunger for forbidden foods and uncontrolled rage towards those who should be loved and respected, as well as all other imagined transgressions and sins of the heart, belonged to the Muslim destroyer of taboos and were furthest away from his 'good' Hindu self. In that Muslim *bhutas* were universally considered to be the strongest, vilest, the most malignant and the most stubborn of the evil spirits, the Muslim seemed to symbolize the alien and the demonic in the unconscious part of the Hindu mind.

The division of humans into mutually exclusive group identities of tribe, nation, caste, religion and class thus seems to serve two important psychological functions. The first is to increase the feeling of well being in the narcissistic realm by locating one's own group at the centre of the universe, superior to others. The shared grandiose self, maintained by legends, myths and rituals, seems to demand a concomitant conviction that other groups are inferior.

India has not been exempt from this universal rule. Whatever idealizing tendencies we might have in viewing our past history, it is difficult to deny that every social group in its tales, ritual and other literature, has sought to portray itself nearer to a purer, divine state while denigrating and banishing others to the periphery. It is also undeniable that sharing a common ego-ideal and giving one's own group a super-individual significance can inspire valued human attributes of loyalty and heroic self-sacrifice. All this is familiar to students of culture and need not detain us further here.

For the psychoanalyst it is the second function of division into ethnic groups, namely the need to have other groups as containers for one's disavowed aspects, which is of greater significance. These disavowed aspects, or the demonic spirits, take birth during that period of our childhood when the child, made conscious of good and bad, right and wrong, begins to divide himself into two parts, one that is the judge and the other that is being judged. The unacceptable, condemned parts of the self are projected outside, the projective processes being primitive attempts to relieve pain by externalizing it. The expelled parts of the self are then attached to various beings—animals and human—as well as to whole castes, ethnic and religious communities. This early split within our nature, which gives us a future license to view and treat others as if they were no better than the worst in ourselves, is normally completed by the time the child is six to seven years old. The earliest defenses for dealing with the unacceptable aspects of the self—namely their denial, the splitting from awareness and projection onto another group—require the active participation of the members of the child's group-parents and other adults who must support such a denial and projection. They are shared group defenses. The family and extended group of a Hindu upper-caste child, for instance, not only provides him with its myths and rituals which increase his sense of group cohesion and of narcissism in belonging to such an exalted entity, but also help him in elaborating and fleshing out his demonology of other ethnic and religious groups. The *purana* of the Muslim demon, for instance, as elaborated by many Hindu groups, has nothing to do with Sufi saints, the prophet's sayings or the more profound sentiments of Islam. Instead, its stories are of rape and pillage by the legions of Ghazni and Timur as well as other more local accounts of Muslim mayhem.

The Muslim demon is, so to say, the traditional container of Hindu conflicts over aggressive impulses. It is the transgressor of deeply-held taboos, especially over the expression of physical violence. Recent events in Punjab, I am afraid, are creating yet another demon in the Hindu psyche of north India. Over the last few years, tales of [Sikh militant leader] Bhindranwale's dark malevolence and the lore of murderous terrorists has led to a number of reported dreams from patients where Sikhs have appeared as symbols of the patient's own aggressive and sadistic superego. A group of Sikhs with raised swords chasing a patient who has broken into an old woman's shop, a Nihang stabbing a man repeatedly with a spear on the street while another patient as a frightened child looks down upon the scene from an upstairs window—these are two of many such dream images. Leaving aside the role played by these images in the patients' individual dramas, the projection of the feared aggressive parts of the self on the figure of the Sikh is an unhappy portent for the future relationship between the two communities. The fantasy of being overwhelmed by the frightening aggressive strength of the Sikhs can, in periods of upheaval and danger—when widespread regression in ego takes place and the touch with reality is weakened—lead to psychotic delusions about Sikh intentions.

Sikh Militancy

Until this point I have used some psychoanalytic, especially Kleinian, concepts of splitting and projective identification to understand data that bears on the question of ethnic conflict. More specifically, I have outlined the origins of certain pre-conscious attitudes of Hindus towards Muslims and Sikhs. These attitudes reflect the psychological needs of the child, and the adult, to split off his bad impulses, especially those relating to violence, and to attach them to other communities, a process supported and reinforced by other members of the group. Let me now use another set of analytical concepts of group identity and narcissism, narcissistic hurt and rage, to understand the phenomenon of Sikh militancy. To avoid any misunderstanding let me state at the outset that I am primarily talking about the militant Sikh youth of Punjab, not of all Sikh youths, and certainly not of the Sikh community as a whole. Also, the word narcissism in psychoanalysis is not used in a pejorative sense but, together with sexuality and aggression, as the third major and fundamental motivational factor in human beings which is concerned with the maintenance of self-esteem. The data for these observations comes from being an observer of heated and anguished discussions among randomly formed groups which were being spontaneously held all over the Golden Temple complex in Amritsar, five weeks after Operation Blue Star.* said elsewhere, the aftermath of Blue Star, which heightened the awareness of their cultural identity among many Sikhs, also brought out in relief one of its less conscious aspects. I have called it the Khalsa warrior element of Sikh identity which, at least since the tenth guru and at least among the Jats, has expressed itself in images of 'lifting up the sword' against the 'oppression of a tyrannical ruler', and whose associated legends only countenance two possible outcomes—complete victory (*fateh*) or martyrdom (*shaheedi*) of those engaged in the battle. The surrounding society has of course reinforced this identity element over the years by its constant talk of Sikh martial process and valour. The Sikh youth's acceptance of these projections of heroic militancy made by the Hindu can lead to his overestimation of this aspect of his identity as he comes to feel that it is his very essence. All other qualities which may compromise heroic militancy, such as yearnings for passivity, softness and patience, will tend to be denied, split off and projected onto other, despised groups. The damage done to the Akal Takht —as much a symbol of corporate militancy as of religious piety—reinforced the two M's—militance and martyrdom—the inner counterparts of the well-known five K's which constitute the outer markers of the Khalsa warrior identity. The exaggerated value placed on martyrdom is hard to understand for Hindus since oppressors in *their* mythology—the Hindu equivalent of Sikh legendary history —tended to be destroyed by divine intervention rather than by the sacrifice of martyrs.

The army action was then a hurt to Sihk religious sentiments in a very different way from the sense in which a Hindu understands the term. It was an affront to group narcissism, to a shared grandiose self. The consequent feelings were of narcissistic hurt and rage. This was brought home to me again and again as I listened to groups of anguished men and women in front of the ruins of the Akal Takht. Most men stood in attitudes of sullen defeat, scorned and derided by the women with such sentences as 'Where is the starch in your moustache now?'

Given the collective need for the preservation of this core of the group identity, the Golden Temple action automatically completed a circle of associa-

---

* [Operation 'Blue Star' was the code name for the army action to clear the Golden Temple of Sikh militants in June 1984, in which Bhindranwale died. The operation resulted in extensive damage to the sacred site.—Ed.]

tions. The army action to clear Akal Takht from desperadoes became an attack on the Sikh nation by a tyrannical 'Delhi durbar'. It was seen as an assault designed to wipe out all its traces, its *nishan*—since this is how it was in the past. The Sikhs killed in the attack were now defenders of the faith and martyrs— since this too is a pattern from the past. The encounter was viewed as a momentous battle, an oppressive empire's defeat of the forces of the Khalsa. The relatively heavy army losses are not a consequence of its restraint but a testimony to the fighting qualities of the Khalsa warrior. Paradoxically, the terrorist losses were exaggerated to simultaneously show the overwhelming strength of the army and the Khalsa readiness to die in martyrdom when victory is not possible.

Bhindranwale, in dramatically exemplifying the two M's of militancy and martyrdom, has touched deep chords. His status with much of the Sikh youth today is very near that of an eleventh guru. Initially, Bhindranwale may have been one of many *sants,* though more militant than most, who dot the countryside in Punjab. What began the process of his elevation was his successful defiance of the government—echoes, again of Sikh history, of defiant gurus contesting state authority. In setting the date and terms of his arrest (*'Santji* gave arrest', and not 'He was arrested', is how the people at the Temple complex put it), and predicting the day of his release, Bhindranwale began to be transformed from a mortal preacher to a 'realized' saint with miraculous powers. (And the reputation of being able to work miracles is, we know, essential for those aspiring to enter the portals of gurudom in all religious traditions.) His 'martyrdom' has now cemented the transformation and made his elevation into the Sikh militant pantheon irreversible. The tortures and murders in the Temple complex or outside are no longer his responsibility, being seen as the doings of deluded associates, acts of which Santji was, of course, unaware.

It is obvious that after the army action there was a threat to the cultural identity of at least a section of the Jat Sikh youth. This led to regressive transformations in the narcissistic realm, where reality is interpreted only as a balm to narcissistic hurt and as a coolant for narcissistic rage. It needs to be asked what precisely constituted this threat. I would tend to see the threat to the Jat Sikh group identity as part of a universal modernizing process to which many groups all over the world have been and continue to be exposed. This group though has preferred to change a social-psychological issue into a political one. The cultural decay and spiritual disintegration talked of in the Anandpur resolution are then viewed as an aspect of majority-minority relations rather than as an existential condition brought on by the workings of a historical fate. A feeling of inner threat is projected outside as oppression, a conflict around tradition and modernity as a conflict around power.

Narcissistic rage, then, is the core of the militancy of Sikh youth and Sikh terrorism. As Kohut says about this rage: 'The need for revenge, for righting a wrong, for undoing a hurt by whatever means, and a deeply anchored, unrelating compulsion in the pursuit of all these aims, gives no rest to those who have suffered a narcissistic injury.' For the analyst, this becomes paramount in the understanding of youthful militancy, the foreground, while political, social and other issues recede into the background.

Let me now make a few observations on the question of ethnic conflict resulting in violent aggression, i.e on mob violence. My data for these remarks is, paradoxically, personal participation in largely peaceful and loving groups engaged in religious and spiritual endeavours. Yet many of the psychological processes are common to the two kinds of groups. Both emotionally charged religious assemblies and mobs on the rampage bring out in relief the vulnerability of human individual ego functions confronted with the power of group processes. In the face of these, the 'integrity', 'autonomy', and 'independence' of the ego seem to be wishful illusions and hypothetical constructs. Mobs, more than religious congregations, provide striking examples of the massive inducement, by group processes, of individuals towards a new identity and behaviour of the sort that would ordinarily be repudiated by a great majority of the individuals so induced. They illustrate, more clearly than in any other comparable social situation, the evanescence of rational thought, the fragility of internalized behavioural controls, values, and moral and ethnical standards.

The most immediate experience in being part of a crowd is the sensual pounding received in the press of other bodies. At first there may be a sense of unease as the body, the container of our individuality and the demarcator of our boundaries in space, is sharply wrenched away from its habitual way of experiencing others. For, as we grow up, the touch of others, once so deliberately courted and responded to with delight, increasingly becomes a problem. Coming from a loved one, touch is deliciously welcomed; with strangers, on the other hand, there is an involuntary shrinking of the body, their touch taking on the menacing air of invasion by the other.

But once the fear of touch disappears in the fierce press of other bodies and the individual lets himself become a part of the crowd's density, the original apprehension is transformed into an expansiveness that stretches to include others. Distances and differences—of class, status, age, caste hierarchy— disappear in an exhilarating feeling that individual boundaries can indeed be transcended and were perhaps illusory in the first place. Of course, touch is only one of the sensual stimuli that hammers at the gate of individual identity. Other excitations, channelled through vision, hearing and smell, are also very much involved. In addition, there are exchanges of body heat, muscle tension and body rhythms which take place in a crowd. In short, the crowd's assault on the sense of individuality, its invitation to transcend one's individual boundaries and its offer of a freedom from personal doubts and anxieties is well nigh irresistible.

The need and search for 'self-transcending' experience, to lose one's self in the group, suspend judgement and reality-testing, is, I believe, the primary motivational factor in both religious assembly and violent mob, even though the stated purpose is spiritual uplift in one and mayhem and murder in the other. Self-transcendence, rooted in the blurring of our body image, not only opens us to the influx of the divine but also heightens our receptivity to the demonic. The surge of love also washes away the defences against the emergence of archaic hates. In psychoanalytic terms, regression in the body image is simultaneous with regression in the superego system. Whether the ego reacts to this regression in a disintegrated fashion with panic that manifests itself (in a mob) in senseless rage and destructive acts—or in a release of love encompassing the group and the world outside—depends on the structure provided to the group. Without the rituals which make tradition palpable and thus extend the group in time by giving assurances of continuity to the beleaguered ego, and without the permanent visibility of leaders whose presence is marked by conspicuous external insignia and who replace the benign and loving functions of the superego, religious crowds can easily turn into marauding mobs. Transcending individuality by merging into a group can generate heroic self-sacrifice but also unimaginable brutality. To get out of one's skin in a devotional assembly is also at the same time to have less regard for saving it in a mob.

Some Implications

The implications of my remark, I know, are not too comforting. The need for communities, our own to take care of our narcissistic needs and of others to serve as recipients for our hostility and destructiveness, are perhaps built into our very ground-plan as human beings. Well meaning educative efforts in classrooms or in national integration seminars are for the most part too late and too little in that they are misdirected. They are too late since most of the evidence indicates that the communal imagination is well entrenched by the time a child enters school. They are misdirected in that they never frankly address the collective—and mostly preconscious—fears and wishes of the various communities. Demons do not much care for 'correct' interpretations of religious texts by scholars, nor are they amenable to humanist pleas of reason to change into good and loving beings. All we can do is accept their existence but reduce their potential for causing actual physical violence and destruction. The routes to this goal, the strategies for struggle with our own inner devils, are many. One strategy strives for the dissolution of small group identities into even large entities. Sikhs and Hindus in Punjab can move towards a group identity around 'Punjabiyyat', in which case the despised demon shifts outside to the *Purubia* or the *Madrasi*. One can go on to progressively larger identities of the nationalist Indian whose *bete-noire* can then be the Pakistani or the Chinese. One can envisage even larger groupings, for instance of the 'Third World', where the sense of narcissistic well being provided by this particular community needs a demonic West as the threatening aggressor.

A second strategy is, in a certain sense, to go the opposite way. By this I mean less the encouragement of various ethnic identities than in ensuring that all manifestations of ethnic group action—assemblies, demonstrations, processions—are given as much religious structure as possible in order to prevent the breakout of archaic hate. Vedic chants and Koranic prayers, *mahants, pujaris* and *mullahs* in their full regalia and conspicuous by their presence, are fully encouraged to be in the forefront of religious processions and demonstrations. Traditional religious standards, flags and other symbols are liberally used to bind the religious assemblies.

Yet another strategy (and let me note that none of these are exclusive) is to concentrate all efforts at the containment of the communal demon on the dominant community. We know that the belief of the dominant party in a relationship often becomes a self-fulfilling prophecy, involuntarily changing the very consciousness of the weaker partner. In India the Hindu image of himself and of other communities is apt to be incorporated in the self image of non-Hindu minorities. Even when consciously accepted, the denigrating part of the image is likely to be a source of intensive unconscious rage in other communities. Their rage is stored up over a period of time, till it explodes in all its violent manifestations whenever historical circumstances sanction such eruptions.

The Manipulation of Ethnicity: From Ethnic Cooperation to Violence and War in Yugoslavia

Four views on ethnicity and ethnic violence are common. In the 'primordial' view, ethnic attachments and identities are a cultural given and a natural affinity, like kinship sentiments. They have an overpowering emotional and non-rational quality. Applied to the former Yugoslavia, the primordialist believes that despite seemingly cooperative relations between nationalities in Yugoslavia, mistrust, enmity, even hatred were just below the surface, as had long been true in the Balkans. Triggered by fierce competition for political power during the breakup of Yugoslavia and driven by the uncertainties over state boundaries and minority status, these enmities and hatreds, fuelled by fear and retribution, turned neighbour against neighbour, and district against district, in an expanding spiral of aggression and reprisals. Although the primordial account sounds plausible, and it is true that politicians activated and manipulated latent nationalism and ethnic fears, some evidence contradicts it. Ethnic cleansing was more commonly militias and military against civilians than neighbour against neighbour. In seventeen assaults against villages during the ethnic cleansing of Prijedor district in Bosnia in May/June 1992, we found that the aggressors wore military and paramilitary uniforms and insignia. In fourteen assaults, the survivors did not recognize any of the aggressors, who did not bother to wear masks or disguises. These 'weekend warriors' from central Serbia openly bivouacked at the Prijedor police station. The primordial theory omits the fact that ethnic hatreds can subside as a consequence of statecraft and living together. [President Charles] de Gaulle and [Chancellor Konrad] Adenauer managed to reconcile the French and German people. Why no lasting conciliation in Yugoslavia after forty years of ethnic peace?

In the second, 'instrumentalist' view, ethnic sentiments and loyalties are manipulated by political leaders and intellectuals for political ends, such as state creation. For Yugoslavia, the instrumentalist explanation highlights Serb nationalists' goal of a Greater Serbia, and a similar Croat nationalism. Ethnic cleansing resulted from a historical longing by Serbs in Croatia at first backed moderate nationalists, for a Greater Serbia, with deep cultural roots. [Slobodan]

Milosevic and Serb nationalists tried to implement it when the opportunity arose in the late 1980s and early 1990s. Greater Serbia required ethnic cleansing of non-Serbs from areas inhabited by a majority of Serbs and the corridors linking Serb population clusters. Although there is evidence that ethnic cleansing was a state policy, orchestrated by the highest authorities in Serbia and the Bosnian Serb leadership, this explanation ignores that many Bosnian Serbs did not want secession, that many Serbs in Croatia at first backed moderate nationalists, and that many Serbs evaded the draft. The instrumentalist view assumes an ethnic consensus that initially does not exist. But if many were reluctant to wage war and to participate in ethnic cleansing, how did ethnic extremists prevail over these moderates?

The third 'constructionist' view of ethnicity and ethnic conflict was originally formulated by [Leo] Kuper. It supplements the insights of the primordial and of the instrumentalist views. Religion or ethnicity are very real social facts, but in ordinary times they are only one of several roles and identities that matter. There is a great deal of variance in a population on ethnic attachments and identities. In the words of [Juan J.] Linz and [Alfred] Stepan 'political identities are less primordial and fixed than contingent and changing. They are amenable to being constructed or eroded by political institutions and political choices'. The constructionist view offers insights but is incomplete. How are nationality and ethnicity constructed and eroded by political mobilization and mass media propaganda?

A fourth model of ethnic violence centres on state breakdown, anarchy, and the security dilemma that such conditions pose to ethnic groups who engage in defensive arming to protect their lives and property against ethnic rivals, which then stimulates arming by other ethnic groups like an arms race between states. The driving motivations are not ethnic hatreds but fear and insecurity. In the Yugoslav crisis Michael Ignatieff puts it thus:

> Once the Yugoslav communist state began to split into its constituent national particles the key question soon became: will the local Croat policeman protect me if I am a Serb? Will I keep my job in the soap factory if my new boss is a Serb or a Muslim? The answer to this question was no, because no state remained to enforce the old ethnic bargain.

There is a security dilemma in ethnic conflict, but why so much ethnic violence without state breakdown? Can insecurity and fear be spread by propaganda even when daily experience contradicts the allegations of ethnic hostility and threat? Can the powerful fear the weak?

Building on the four views and mindful of [Rogers] Brubaker and [David] Laitin's criteria for a satisfactory theory of ethnic violence, I use the idea of latent nationalism at the grass roots, and show how it was activated; I highlight ethnic manipulation by political leaders, and explain why manipulation was successful; I take into account the variance in ethnic identities and analyse why extremists prevailed over moderates; I focus on the security dilemma and ethnic fears and insecurity, and show how fears and insecurity grew from lies and propaganda. To this arsenal of concepts and models for generating the dynamics of ethnicization and collective violence, I add 'cognitive frames'. Combining all, I seek to explain how forty years of cooperative ethnic relations ended with collective violence and war.

Prijedor: A Case-Study

To get a sense of what is to be explained about ethnic conflict and violence at the grass roots, consider the Prijedor district in Northwest Bosnia where major ethnic violence took place in the spring of 1992. In the 1991 Census, Prijedor district was 42.5 per cent Serb and 44 per cent Muslim. It was surrounded by districts that had either a slight Serb majority or were close to even, as Prijedor was. Prijedor Serbs were not an isolated Serb minority island surrounded by a sea of Muslims and Croats.

There had been no Serb complaints of mistreatment, discrimination, or intimidation in Prijedor by non-Serbs, or vice versa. On the contrary, as a bewildered Muslim refugee from Prijedor stated,

> In Prijedor there were no conflicts between nationalities. We didn't make the distinctions. My colleague at work was an Orthodox Serb, we worked together. When we were children we went to the Orthodox church or the mosque together... I don't understand. Before there were never any problems between us. We lived together. My sister is married to a Serb, and a brother of my wife is married to a Croat.

According to the [United Nations] Bassiouni Report, Serbs held the leading positions in Prijedor in 1991, as they had done for decades.... In the 1991 elections, the predominantly Muslim SDA [Party of Democratic Union in Bosnia] won thirty seats; the Serb SDS [Serbian Democratic Party] twenty-eight, and thirty-two went to other parties. The Muslims refrained from taking over a number of leading posts to which their electoral victory entitled them because they believed in power-sharing. Even so, the SDS blocked the work of the Prijodor Assembly and organized a parallel governance for Serbs, in alliance with the SDS leaders in nearby Banja Luka. In Bosnia as a whole, the Serbs shared political power and controlled the most important military forces.

As in other towns and cities in Bosnia, the SDS in Prijedor organized a successful Serb plebiscite for Greater Serbia. A parallel Serb governance, called the 'Crisis Committee', secretly created an armed force of Serbs with weapons obtained from Serbia. Serb crisis committees were also formed among Serbs in some of Prijedor district's towns and villages. On the night of 29 April 1992, without any provocation or a shot being fired, 1,775 well-armed Serbs seized the city of Prijedor in a *coup d'état*. By this time the Prijedor local government had completely lost power to various Serb groups. Paramilitaries had seized the radio and television transmitters and cut off all but Serb transmissions. The Serb *coup d'état* in Prijedor is similar to what happened elsewhere in Northern Bosnia.

Non-Serb leaders were arrested and shortly afterwards disappeared, presumed executed. The Muslim police and other officials were fired from their posts. Schools closed; the newspaper ceased publication, and a Serb paper was started. Non-Serbs were harassed, intimidated, fired from their jobs. Amid incessant house searches, weapons, mostly hunting guns, belonging to non-Serbs, were rounded up. After the attempt on 30 May by the Patriotic League of Croats and Muslims—an armed formation of 150 fighters—to retake the old city, many non-Serb inhabitants were arrested and sent to the infamous Omarskca camp. At Omarska, prisoners were tortured, brutalized, starved and killed. The guards were rural Serbs from nearby villages; the interrogators were Prijedor police inspectors.... People were rounded up and some were executed: those shot were Muslim leaders whose names appeared on a list. Atrocities took place elsewhere in the district.

Several observations should be made about the events in Prijedor. Muslims and Serbs had lived in peace before the conflict erupted. The Serbs were neither a numerical minority, nor discriminated against. They not only had a share of power, but they had the biggest share, and they were well armed. Why, then, did Serbs fear their fellow citizens in Prijedor? A cartoon from this period expresses the puzzle well. It shows a bearded Serb paramilitary, armed to the teeth, with guns, hand-granades, ammunition belts, knives, waving a machine gun, looking worried, and yelling at the top of his voice, 'I am being threatened!' There was no anarchy, no state breakdown in Prijedor. The Serbs used the police and military of a functioning government to subdue the non-Serbs. Serbs may have been apprehensive about their future in an independent Bosnia, but even in Bosnia they had a big presence—numerical, military, political, economic. There was no spontaneous violence initiated by Serb civilians against non-Serbs, nor vice-versa. Instead, there was a highly organized, secretly prepared *coup d'état,* like the 1917 Bolshevik seizure of power in Russia.... As in the Russian revolution with the Soviets, the Serb parallel government was not only an instrument for seizing power from non-Serbs but of stripping the moderate Serbs of any influence and authority.

What was the reaction of ordinary Serbs to these events? Though there is no information on Prijedor itself, one can learn from what observers recorded in nearby Banja Luka. Peter Maas reports that a Serb lawyer there estimated that 30 per cent of Serbs oppose such things [ethnic cleansing], 60 per cent agree or are confused and go along with the 10 per cent who 'have the guns and control the television tower'.... An armed, organized 10 per cent who control mass communications can have its way when the majority supports it overtly or tacitly or is confused, and when the opposition is unorganized, divided, and scared. One has to explain how it was that 60 per cent were supportive of or confused on ethnic cleansing, since their support and quiescence were necessary for the success of the extremist 10 per cent.

Was Violent Conflict Inevitable?

In a multinational state such as Yugoslavia, nationality will be a salient dimension of political contention, and there will be leaders and intellectuals with a nationalist ideology and agenda. The Yugoslav constitution and its political institutions were delicately balanced and crafted to deal with nationality. A nationalist challenge would inevitably zero in on stateness, minority rights and power-sharing: if accepted boundaries of political units are renegotiated or remade, who decides which peoples and territories belong to new and old political entities? Will all peoples in the new units be equal citizens for governance, or will majority ethnonational affiliation become the admission ticket for full citizenship?

Once unleashed, nationalism in Yugoslavia set on a collision course the two largest nationalities, the Serbs and the Croats. With a quarter of Serbs living outside Serbia, a centralized Yugoslav state was a guarantor of Serb security. For Croats and their history of opposition to Hapsburg rule, a decentralized state and weak federation meant control of their own destinies, unencumbered by inefficient state agencies and enterprises staffed and controlled by Serbs. Nevertheless, nationality issues could have been sorted out with democratic institutions in a confederation, with collective rights for minorities, and with systems of political representation in elections and collective decision rules in assemblies that would protect minority voice and favour coalitions rather than majority domination. With these reforms, nationalist leaders would have found it difficult to rally the citizenry to their cause.

In a country with great differences in economic development and standards of living between the Republics, there will be disagreements over economic policies, taxation, transfer, subsidies across regions, and abandoning socialism for a market economy. All Republics had experienced dramatic economic gains since World War II. Yugoslavia was not beyond economic repair.

As in other communist states in the late 1980s, the Yugoslav communist leaders wanted to remain in power. Some reprogrammed as reform communists, and hoped to move into European-style social democracy. Others chose ethnonationalism as the issue that would carry them to power and create a new principle of legitimacy for the post-communist regime. Moderate nationalists stood for conciliation among nationalities; extremists were willing to pursue their goals with force and violence. The defeat of the moderates was not inevitable. Why did xenophobic nationalism resonate with the citizenry? How is it that when the media unleashed the war of words and symbols before the war of bullets, so many believed the exaggerations, distortions and fabrications that belied their personal experiences?

Ethnic Relations Before the Crisis

Survey research on ethnic relations in mid-1990 found that in a national sample of 4,232 Yugoslavs, only 17 per cent believed that the country would break up into separate states, and 62 per cent reported that the 'Yugoslav' affiliation was very or quite important for them. On ethnonational relations, in workplaces, 36 per cent characterized them as 'good', 28 per cent as 'satisfactory', and only 6 per cent said 'bad' and 'very bad'. For ethnonational relations in neighborhoods, 57 per cent answered 'good', 28 per cent 'satisfactory', and only 12 per cent chose 'bad' and 'very bad'. For the majority of Yuogoslavs, on the eve of the Yugoslav wars, nationalist contention in the public arena did not translate into hostile interpersonal ethnic relations....

Ignatieff is puzzled, 'What is difficult to understand about the Balkan tragedy is how ... nationalist lies ever managed to take root in the soil of shared village existence.... In order for war to occur, nationalists had to convince neighbors and friends that in reality they had been massacring each other since time immemorial.'

The Manipulation of Ethnicity

For explaining ethnic manipulation one needs the concept of a cognitive frame. A cognitive frame is a mental structure which situates and connects events, people and groups into a meaningful narrative in which the social world that one inhabits makes sense and can be communicated and shared with others. Yugoslavs experienced ethnic relations through two frames: a normal frame and a crisis frame. People possessed both frames in their minds: in peaceful times the crisis frame was dormant, and in crisis and war the normal frame was suppressed. Both frames were anchored in private and family experiences, in culture and in public life. In the normal frame, which prevailed in [Josip Broz] Tito's Yugoslavia, ethnic relations were cooperative and neighbourly. Colleagues and workers, schoolmates and teammates transacted routinely across nationality. Some did not even know or bother to know another's nationality. Intermarriage was accepted. Holidays were spent in each others' Republics. Except in Kosovo, the normal frame prevailed for most Yugoslavs throughout the 1980s.

The crisis frame was grounded in the experiences and memories of the Balkan wars, the first and second world wars—and other wars before that. In these crises, civilians were not distinguished from combatants. Old people, children, women, priests were not spared. Atrocities, massacres, torture, ethnic cleansing, a scorched-earth policy were the rule. Everyone was held collectively responsible for their nationality and religion, and became a target of revenge and reprisals....

Tito had wanted to eradicate the crisis frame, but it simmered in the memories of older people, the families of victims, intellectuals and religious leaders. Milosevic, Tudjman and other nationalists did not invent the crisis frame; they activated and amplified it....

If the normal frame prevailed in the 1980s as shown by ... survey findings, how did nationalists activate and amplify the crisis frame after decades of dormancy? The emotion that poisons ethnic relations is fear: fear of extinction as a group, fear of assimilation, fear of domination by another group, fear for one's life and property, fear of being a victim once more. After fear comes hate. The threatening others are demonized and dehumanized. The means of awakening and spreading such fears in Yugoslavia were through the newsmedia, politics, education, popular culture, literature, history and the arts.

The crisis frame in Yugoslavia was first resurrected by Serb intellectuals over the plight of the Kosovo Serbs....

Fear of extinction was spread with highly inflated figures on the ethnic killings in World War II....

In my interview with a Serb refugee one can trace how the atrocities discourse switched on the crisis frame: 'We were afraid because nationalists revived the memory of World War II atrocities ... nationalist graffiti on walls awakened fears of past memories; it was a sign that minorities [Serbs in Croatia] would not be respected and safe'.

Fears of domination, oppression and demographic shrinkage were roused by the incessant rape and genocide discourse....

Ordinary people echo the intellectuals' and the media crisis discourse.... Peter Maas asks a Serb refugee couple why they had fled their village. Their answer: Muslims planned to take over, a list of names had been drawn up, Serb women were to be assigned to Muslim harems after the men had been killed. They had heard about it on the radio; the Serb military had uncovered the plan. The journalist probes: 'Did any Muslims in the village ever harm you?' They reply, 'Oh no, our relations with the Muslims in the village were always good, they were decent people'. In the minds of the Serb couple, the crisis frame had eclipsed the normal frame. What under peaceful circumstances were totally implausible events—young women become sexual slaves in harems for breeding janissaries; a fifteenth- and sixteenth-century style Turkish/Islamic invasion of Europe—become credible narratives of ethnic annihilation and domination within the crisis frame.

Fear and the crisis frame provided opportunities for nationalists to mobilize a huge ethnic constituency, get themselves elected to office, and organize aggressive actions against moderates and other ethnics....

Populist nationalism worked. The Vojvodina and Montenegro party leaderships resigned and were replaced by Milosevic loyalists. Abolishing the autonomous provinces of Kosovo and Vojvodina precipitated a constitutional crisis.... The nationality balance in Yugoslav politics was thus disturbed. Serbia gained control of over half the votes in all federal bodies and institutions. Slovenes and Croats reacted with their own nationalism.

There was grass-roots resistance to nationalism and to activation of the crisis frame. A content analysis of news stories in *Oslobodjenje* for 1990 indicates that municipalities, youth and veterans' organizations, and trade unions repeatedly protested against ethnic polarization and hatreds.... Important as this opposition was, it was countered by the spread of populist nationalism. *Oslobodjenje* in 1990 is full of affirmations of national symbols and identities: the renaming of localities; the reburial of bones of atrocity victims from World War II; nationalist graffiti on churches, mosques, monuments and in cemeteries; fights over flags, ethnic insults, nationalist songs, ethnic vandalism. To many, these were signs that normal times were sliding into crisis, and the authorities had lost control.

Mass communications and propaganda research help to explain why ethnic manipulation worked and why the crisis frame eclipsed the normal frame. First, ... fear arousing appeals, originating in a threat, were powerful and effective in changing opinion and belief. Furthermore, the most important reaction to fear is removing the source of threat, precisely what nationalists were promising to do in Yugoslavia. Second, studies of propaganda routinely find that repetition is the single most effective technique of persuasion. It does not matter how big the lie is, so long as it keeps being repeated.

Third, much of what we know is vicarious knowledge and not based on personal experience. We accept the truths of authorities and experts whom we respect and who have socially recognized positions and titles. Who could really tell or check how many Serbs had been massacred by Ustasha? Fourth, outright falsehoods were common and intentional. According to a media analyst, 'In Serbia and Croatia, TV fabricated and shamelessly circulated war crime stories... the same victims would be identified on Zagreb screens as Croat, on Belgrade screens as Serb'....

Fifth, mass communications studies of the two-step flow of communication show that in ordinary circumstances crude propaganda from 'patriotic journalism' is discounted because people are exposed to a variety of broadcast messages and because they check media messages against the beliefs and opinions in their social milieus in interpersonal relationships and conversations. Ethnic crisis politics breaks down the two-step flow....

Nationalists Win the 1990 Elections

Second only to the mass media wars for the revival of the crisis frame were the 1990 elections. Every town and city experienced the founding of political parties, often at a huge rally in a public building or a sports stadium, during which speaker after speaker gave vent to exaggerated nationalist rhetoric and hostile pronouncements and attacks against other nationalities....

Nationalists persuaded voters not to 'split the ethnic vote' but to vote as a bloc for the nationalists because the other nationalities would bloc-vote and gain power. Bloc-voting became a self-fulfilling prophecy.... The politicians elected were more nationalist than their voters....

Repression of Minorities and Moderates

The demise of the moderates was due to a combination of electoral defeats, loss of credibility about being effective in a crisis, and intimidation and threats from extremists....

The nationalist winners purged their ethnic opponents and moderates of their own nationality from party and state positions. The targets were sent anonymous threat letters, were fired from their jobs, forced into military service, charged with treason, subversion and plotting armed rebellion, and subject to office and house searches for weapons, radio transmitters and 'subversive' literature.... In a Bosnian example reported by [Tadeusz] Mazowiecki, 'According to a witness [from Bosanska Dubica], the elected authorities who were moderates and who tried to prevent acts of violence were dismissed or replaced by Serbian extremists'.

Other methods were cruder.... Ordinary people could not escape ethnic polarization. In an interview a Serb taxi driver explained: 'No one wanted the coming war, but if I don't fight, someone from my side [Serb] will kill me, and if my Muslim friends don't fight, other Muslims will kill them'.

The overthrow of moderates by extremists or radicals is well known in the great revolutions: Girondins were overthrown by the Jacobins in the French revolution and all groups were overthrown by the Bolsheviks in the Russian revolution. The means of seizing power are similar. The radicals create parallel governance to the state and come to exercise *de facto* authority in many institutions, and militias and mutineers execute a *coup d'état*. Then the remaining moderates are purged. It happens in ethnic violence as well. It did so in the mixed ethnic districts of Croatia and Bosnia, and it happened in Prijedor.

Militias Take Over

Militias and paramilitaries roamed far and wide and perpetrated ethnic cleansing, massacres, atrocities and other war crimes, as in the Prijedor district....

Militiamen were not necessarily fanatics filled with hatred to start with. [Tim] Judah described how a Serb militiaman got recruited by his peers from the local SDS who pressured him for weeks: 'We've all got to take up arms, or we'll disappear from here'. He had Muslim and Croat friends. Would they protect him against extremists of all nationalities? Not likely, if it got violent. So he 'took out a gun'. Peer pressure, fear, not only of Muslims but of extremist Serbs who might finger him as a 'traitor', were the major reasons for joining a militia. Some of these men were unemployed and expected a job in the coming Serb government as militia or police.

Once the young man 'took out a gun' he became encapsulated in a quasi-military unit subject to peer solidarity and ethnic loyalty. He was trained in weapons and indoctrinated with the beliefs and norms of the crisis frame about other ethnics:

a. *Collective guilt:*   'They' act in unison; children grow into adults; women give birth to future warriors; even old people stab you from behind; 'they' will never change.

b. *Revenge and retaliation:*   'They' massacred 'us' in the past, and are about to do it again, in fact they have already started. A setting of scores is justified; an eye for an eye.

c. *Deterrence/first strike:*   Disable them before they strike, which is what they are about to do, despite appearances, because they are secretive and treacherous.

d. *Danger/survival:*   These are extraordinary times, one's entire nationality is threatened, and extreme measures are justified.

e. *Legitimacy:*   Ordinary people and militias are justified in taking extreme measures because the constituted authorities have not come to the defence of our people.

These are the rationalization and the justifying norms for unrestrained, collective, ethnic violence. Other motives for collective violence were economic gain, peer pressure and lack of accountability. From being an ordinary man in normal times the militiaman changed into being a killer at crisis times.

The Bassiouni report (UN Security Council 1994) counted eighty-three paramilitaries in Bosnia alone operating between June 1991 and late 1993, fifty-three for Serbs, with an estimated 20,000–40,000 members, thirteen for Croats, with 12,000–20,000, and fourteen for Bosniac, with 4,000–6,000 men. In view of 700,000 Bosnian Serb men aged fifteen to thirty-five, militiamen were 10–20 per cent of the Serb men of military age in Bosnia. Ten to 20 per cent of adult males in militias, added to the military and police, are more than enough for death and destruction against civilians on a massive scale.

Conclusion

My account is not a narrative of events but an analytic explanation for the breakup of Yugoslavia amid collective violence.... On the eve of the wars, Yugoslavs reported cooperative interpersonal ethnic relations and opposed a breakup of the state. Nationalist leaders succeeded in manipulating ethnicity by spreading fear, insecurity and hatred, which advanced their political agenda of separate national states.

To explain their success I draw on elements from the primordialist, instrumentalist and constructionist views on ethnicity and on the theory of ethnic violence originating in fear and insecurity. To these I add the concept of a cognitive frame which clarifies élite-grass-roots linkage and ethnic manipulation. Nationalism, ethnic identity and attachment alone, however intense, do not explain grass-roots ethnic actions. Yugoslavs possessed two frames on ethnic relations: a cooperative frame for normal, peaceful times, as in the decades of the fifties to the eighties. They also possessed a dormant crisis frame anchored in family history and collective memory of wars, ethnic atrocities and brutality. Threats and lies that were implausible and dismissed in the normal frame could resonate when the crisis frame was switched on: they became persuasive, were believed, and inspired fear.

In the waning days of Communism, nationalists activated the crisis frame on ethnicity by playing on fears of ethnic annihilation and oppression in the mass media, in popular culture, in social movements, and in election campaigns. Élite crisis discourse resonated at the grass roots, made for ethnic polarization, and got nationalists elected. Once in office, nationalists suppressed and purged both moderates in their own ethnic group and other ethnics. They organized militias who perpetrated acts of extreme violence against innocent civilians. They conducted war according to the crisis script. Without the tacit, overt or confused support of the majority, the nationalist leaders could not have escalated ethnic rivalry and conflict into massive collective violence.

POSTSCRIPT

Is Ethnic Conflict Inevitable?

Although Kakar's argument draws heavily on psychology, he clearly adopts a primordialist perspective that ethnic differences are inherently threatening; such differences lead to tension and will ultimately emerge as conflict. Individuals may keep their fears and anxieties in check for a time, but preconscious fears and anxiety will eventually emerge. For Kakar, no amount of education or politically correct training will eliminate these anxieties or permanently overcome them.

Oberschall's argument accepts the reality of primordialist variables such as kinship, language, and religion as more important than did Barth in his original formulation of the circumstantialist perspective. But for Oberschall, such variables must be triggered by circumstantialist factors before they can be aroused. The Balkans case is a particularly apt one, as ethnicity in Bosnia is largely based on religious differences. All three "ethnic" communities have emerged from essentially the same pool of genetic material. The language spoken by all three groups is essentially the same language, often called Serbo-Croatian by linguists, though the Serbs use a Cyrillic alphabet and the Croats use a Roman one. The main "ethnic" differences emerge from their three different religions: Eastern Orthodox, Roman Catholic, and Islam. Religious differences in Bosnia correspond to traditional political alliances, but, as in the conflict in Northern Ireland, they are not fundamentally based on significant biological or linguistic differences. In Bosnia, unlike Northern Ireland, people of all three ethnicities had lived and worked side by side; they socialized together and had even intermarried. The primordialist variables are, in Oberschall's view, insufficient to trigger the ethnic violence and brutality that erupted in Bosnia. Ethnic violence, massacres, and ethnic cleansing could only have emerged if people in the towns and villages were manipulated into fearing their neighbors, concludes Oberschall.

Anthropologists and sociologists have long recognized that racial and ethnic tensions in the United States and other countries are linked to issues about access to jobs, land, resources, and opportunities. But it is not clear whether or not such circumstantialist variables are sufficient to explain why social conflict so often allows ethnic affiliations to become so central.

For further reading on genocide and ethnic cleansing, see Alexander L. Hinton's edited volume *Annihilating Difference: The Anthropology of Genocide* (University of California Press, 2002). For another view on ethnic conflict in India, see Ashutosh Varshney's *Ethnic Conflict and Civic Life: Hindus and Muslims in India* (Yale University Press, 2002). For a recent perspective about ethnicity, see André Burguière and Raymond Grew's edited volume *The Construction of Minorities: Cases for Comparison Across Time and Around the World* (University of Michigan Press, 2001). For more circumstantialist discussions of ethnic conflict, see Jack Eller's *From Culture to Ethnicity to Conflict* (University of Michigan Press, 1999) and *The Myth of "Ethnic Conflict": Politics, Economics, and "Cultural" Violence,* edited by Beverly Crawford and Ronnie D. Lipschutz (International Area Studies, University of California at Berkeley, 1998).

ISSUE 13

Do Some Illnesses Exist Only Among Members of a Particular Culture?

YES: John E. Cawte, from *"Malgri*: A Culture-Bound Syndrome,"
in William P. Lebra, ed., *Culture-Bound Syndromes, Ethnopsychiatry,
and Alternate Therapies,* vol. 4 of *Mental Health Research in Asia and
the Pacific* (University Press of Hawaii, 1976)

NO: Robert A. Hahn, from *Sickness and Healing: An Anthropological
Perspective* (Yale University Press, 1995)

ISSUE SUMMARY

YES: Physician and medical anthropologist John E. Cawte asks
whether or not one particular illness, called *malgri* by the Lardil
Aborigines of Australia, is restricted to this one cultural group. After
documenting how this condition does not fit standard psychiatric
diagnoses, he concludes that *malgri* is indeed a "culture-bound syndrome" that can only occur among people who share Lardil cultural
values and beliefs.

NO: Medical anthropologist Robert A. Hahn counters that the very
idea of the so-called culture-bound syndrome is flawed. He contends
that culture-bound syndromes are reductionist explanations for certain complex illness conditions—that is, explanations that reduce
complex phenomena to a single variable. Hahn suggests that such
conditions are like any illness condition; they are not so much peculiar diseases but distinctive local cultural expressions of much more
common illness conditions that can be found in any culture.

For most of a century anthropologists have observed that people in many
tribal societies suffer from peculiar health complaints that seemed only to occur
among members of particular cultures. Most of these illnesses were psychiatric
in nature, including various kinds of "wild man" behaviors, such as *amok* in
Malaysia, the *witiko* (or *windigo*) psychosis of the Ojibwa, the "Arctic hysterias"
of some Eskimo and Siberian groups, startle reactions like *latah* in Indonesia
and Malaysia, and various panic reactions found among certain Australian aboriginal groups. In some Australian tribes, observers have reported that people

have died of no apparent physiological cause after learning that they were victims of sorcery performed against them by an enemy. These diverse conditions appeared quite different from mental illnesses observed in Western countries, and some seemed to have physiological symptoms that were not seen in industrial countries. Such cases raised the possibility that some illnesses might be rooted in a specific culture or even caused by aspects of the cultures themselves. Thus, the idea of the culture-bound syndrome was born.

For medical anthropologists, these culture-bound syndromes seemed to define a special niche in the medical world where anthropologists could contribute valuable insights that physicians, psychologists, and psychiatrists could not provide. Most anthropologists accepted the premise that anthropology could offer few new insights about such conditions like pneumonia, malaria, gastrointestinal diseases, and cancer. But if psychological conditions in different cultures were profoundly shaped by culture or even caused by aspects of a particular culture, then anthropology seemed to have a special role to play in medicine.

For these medical anthropologists the question that confronted them was, How different are these syndromes from Western psychiatric conditions and neuroses? How can such different symptomatologies be explained? How do the details of local cultural traditions actually influence the symptoms of a particular condition, or alternatively, how does culture actually cause such illnesses?

These are some of the questions that John E. Cawte addresses in the following selection. He focuses attention on a particular syndrome called *malgri*, which he observed among the Lardil Aborigines in Australia. Lardil people explain *malgri* as a kind of spirit intrusion, which typically afflicts visitors or intruders in another clan's territory. *Malgri* is also associated with violations of traditional taboo against mixing land and sea; for example, if a person enters the sea without washing his hands after handling land foods. Cawte observed that sufferers generally experienced severe abdominal pains, anxiety, and other psychological symptoms, but none of these symptoms appeared to fit standard Western diagnostic categories. He asks whether or not the mental disorder known as *malgri* is different from the diagnostic categories familiar to psychologists and psychiatrists in Western countries. After considering how *malgri* is associated with cultural concerns about territoriality, contact with strangers, and crowding, as well as other cultural aspects, Cawte concludes that *malgri* does not map onto customary psychological diagnoses and represents a syndrome that could only emerge among the Lardil and other related peoples.

Robert A. Hahn challenges the very notion that any specific syndrome is so closely linked to any particular culture that it would justify the label "culture-bound syndrome." All illnesses, he argues, are shaped by the local cultures in which they occur. These illnesses would include psychological and psychiatric conditions as well as those we ordinarily assume to be strictly physiological, such as infections, diabetes, chronic pain, and so on. Thus, for Hahn, *malgri, amok,* Arctic hysteria, and the *witiko* psychosis are merely distinctive local symptomatic expressions of conditions that are found in industrialized nations.

Malgri: A Culture-Bound Syndrome

Are the mental disorders of preagricultural "primitives" different from those found in modern society, or are they variants of the familiar Western diagnostic categories? This [selection] presents an account of a previously unreported but superbly interesting culture-bound syndrome, *malgri,* which sheds light upon this question and upon other questions commonly asked about such syndromes. Some of the issues involved in a study of culture-bound syndromes should be outlined (with reference in this case to *malgri*), at the outset. The reader may consider how far these issues pertain to the well-publicized culture-bound disorders or "ethnic psychoses," including *latah* (in Malaysia), *koro* (in Malaysian Chinese), *witiko* (in Indian cultures of northeast America), and *amok* (in Malaysia).

1. *Malgri* describes a pattern of symptoms and behaviors specially characteristic of the culture in which it appears.
2. The culture exerts both a causal and a shaping influence in cases of *malgri.*
3. There is no one-to-one correspondence between cases of *malgri* and Western psychiatric categories—*malgri* cases cover a range of Western diagnoses.
4. Not all cases of *malgri* are psychopathological. Some are; others represent culturally acceptable expressions of anxiety or other discomfort, not amounting to psychiatric disorder.
5. Individual differences in susceptibility to *malgri* are traceable to variations in personality and experience.
6. *Malgri* serves the functional purpose of social regulation in the culture (by contributing to the maintenance of territorial boundaries). *Malgri* is found only in the Wellesley Islands of the Gulf of Carpentaria. Focal distribution of such sicknesses is to be expected in view of the comparatively restricted diffusion between the various cultural blocs of Australia, probably associated with marked ecological differences.... The disorder might perhaps be termed culture-specific rather than merely culture-bound.

Malgri was encountered, in a typical sequence, through children's games. Two of my children, a girl of seven years and her brother, six, were visiting Mornington Island with me: they spent much of their time playing with a Lardil girl. During a ramble near "Picnic Place" a mile or more from the settlement, the Aboriginal girl found, exuding from a tree, some resin that was good to chew. After chewing a while, the European children ran toward the beach. The Aboriginal child called out to them to stop; they must wash their hands and mouth in a freshwater hole before going to the sea. Otherwise the rainbow snake would come out of the sea and make them sick or even kill them. My daughter, impressed with this warning, complied; her brother was skeptical but washed his hands and mouth just the same. He was not going to be the one who got *malgri* and died. An event of the next day showed how justified the precautions were. A Lardil man came to the Mission carrying his small son in his arms. The boy was very distressed and complained of pains in the legs and stomach. He kept moaning and asking his father to "Rub me guts." The Missionary gave him a sedative and he gradually recovered. The story came out that despite warnings about poisonous jellyfish, he had been bathing in the sea. But it was not a jellyfish that had stung him; his grandfather, Jacob, a tribal practitioner, confirmed that it was *malgri*. The boy was lucky to recover, said his grandfather, who was irritated that he had not been called on to treat it. He did, however, demonstrate how he would have treated it, using his grown son for the subject, in a posed demonstration for the camera.

It was ascertained from Jacob and from other Lardil men and women that *malgri* is a prominent disorder in the Lardil medical system at Mornington Island. It appears to be a spirit-intrusion syndrome linked with the totemic organization of the people and their territory. All seemed agreed on the phenomenology.

The central theme in *malgri* is the mutual antipathy between land and sea. A person who enters the sea without washing his hands after handling land food runs the risk of succumbing to *malgri*. Traces of land food are dangerous in the sea and must first be rubbed off with sand and water; even body paint and grease must be removed. If these precautions are neglected, the totemic spirit that is guardian of that particular littoral is believed to invade the belly "like a bullet." The *malgri* victim grows sick, tired and drowsy. His head aches, his belly distends, he writhes and groans in pain, and may vomit. The pain is described as constant rather than colicky, although the precise symptoms depend on the nature of the possessing spirit. The distended abdomen might result from diaphragmatic fixation coupled with air swallowing, as in the pattern of pseudocyesis, or false pregnancy; some uncertainty exists as to the accuracy of this description of distension. Most islanders seemed to have some anxiety about contracting the illness.

To appreciate this disorder one must know that a feature of Lardil cosmology is the division of the coastline of Mornington Island into upwards of thirty littorals, each the sea frontage for a particular subsection of the tribe or class of totemites, and each with its distinctive totem. In many cases the totems, such as the shark, stingray, coolibah tree, and rock cod, are obvious local natural species; in other instances (such as totems of the moon and sea serpent) the legendary associations of the site are represented. *Malgri* spirits can also operate in the reverse direction—from the land: for example, when a person who has been fishing in the sea uses a freshwater rockpool or lagoon without first cleansing his hands of all traces of salt-water food. With the aid of several islanders, and later, map-makers, I spent a good deal of time making a chart of Mornington Island as the people saw it. Understanding the territorial scheme is essential to an accurate appreciation of the disorder.

Malgri is a sickness of intruders. The social group occupying the estate enjoys some immunity in its home range. The Lardil elder, Gully Peters, described this feature. "Me boss belong that Sandalwood River country. Yarragarra [sea eagle] is boss of the sea around that part. I can eat swamp turtle belong to that land and I can go down to that sea and I can't *malgri*. I say: 'It's me, I'm boss of this country, don't *malgri* me, Yarragarra.' If somebody doesn't belong to my country, he will *malgri* there. If I go to South Side, Sydney Island way, I can *malgri* there—not my country. If people walkabout a long time at my place, like Fred, they're all right—the sea gets their smell and knows them. It's strangers that *malgri* all the time."

When the cry goes out that somebody has fallen victim to *malgri*, everybody runs to help. A fire is made near the prostrate victim. From the throng emerges a native practitioner or other elder with knowledge. Kneeling, he massages his axillary sweat into the victim's body. A grass or hair belt is unraveled to provide a long cord which is tied by one end to the victim's foot while the other end is run down to the water, to point the way home for the intruding spirit. The healer commences the song of exorcism, which is sung through the night, with innumerable verses, while the assembled people scan the sky for a shooting star. The star is *malgri's* eye personified, at last diving from the sky to indicate the spirit's dispossession and banishment. The string is then snapped. The victim recovers. So runs the procedure for treatment. . . .

Histories were collected of cases of *malgri* occurring around the time of my visit. Various sickness and behavioral patterns were represented.

Pattern 1

A middle-aged woman contracted *malgri* shortly after our expedition arrived on the island. She had been on a picnic with two friends and had eaten some dugong meat before washing her hands in the river. A truck had to be sent to fetch her, since she insisted she could not move because of *malgri*. On arrival at the Mission hospital she complained of prostration and severe abdominal pain. No physical abnormality was detected, and she was reassured. After a few hours she recovered and was discharged. Her hospital record showed frequent attendances for complaints of pain in the head and in the chest, probably psychogenic. Medical interviews with her revealed deep dissatisfaction with her family life. Her husband had left her to take a job on the mainland, and she had to look after her boy aged two and an adopted son of seven. Her various complaints of headache, "angina," and *malgri* had to be evaluated in this context.

Pattern 2

A party of five children was taken to nearby Denham Island in charge of an intelligent and literate Aboriginal matron. *Malgri* spoiled the picnic. She subsequently reported: "The children ate bread and tinned meat. Then they went in swimming in the channel. Two of the children got pain in the stomach in that water. It could not be a jellyfish sting, because only the stomach got sore. It was tight and bulging. I took them to Sister—she only given them aspirin, she didn't know what to do. So I took them down to the camp, and an old woman said, 'See Kitchener Steele.' he treated those children. He used body sweat and that *malgri* song." The nursing Sister reported: "Both children were rolling all over the hospital verandah, clutching their stomachs and yelling. I examined them. Maybe their stomachs were distended but they were soft to palpation. They seemed healthy apart from all the screaming, so I didn't admit them. They were better that night." Further discussion with the Aboriginal woman in charge of the picnic revealed a transactional situation of possible relevance. She was envious of the Mission nursing sister and lost few opportunities of disparaging her in an indirect way. She seemed gratified at being the central figure in an illness context that the nurse was not competent to handle. It is not suggested here that the situation was consciously engineered with this in mind, but, having once arisen, it was exploited in this way.

Pattern 3

A middle-aged man is reporting a hunting trip that was interrupted by *malgri*.

> That morning we got a sea turtle and had it for breakfast. Then we split up and D. B. went along the north side and he went into a freshwater hole. He should know better than that. He should have gone home. You can't take sea turtle into freshwater; this would *malgri*. You should eat it on the beach and then wash your hands. D. B. had to turn back and come to our camp. We helped him in; stomach was all blown up. We got hair string from a belt and put it from a toe to a spear under a tree. We sang him till five in the morning. I saw a star traveling over the sky from the east like a white cloud, very slow. It disappeared at five o'clock and that man got better. People said it was the rat spirit, Dowa—it was rat country—you see these rats at Birri and Rocky Island. We could see light all along the beach, in the water.

It was hard to discover the transactional background of this incident, and I was left speculating why the party of four had split up before the isolated member committed his error and contracted *malgri*.

The traditional illnesses of the Kaiadilt group from Bentinck Island were less closely studied than those of the Lardil because of the greater difficulty in communication. From discussions in the village it appeared that Kaiadilt intrusion syndromes were also common and involved the spirits of the soldier crab, reef octopus, and particularly, the mangrove rat called Wadn't by the Kaiadilt. There was no evidence that these syndromes achieved the complexity of *malgri,* though their generic name, *malgudj,* is similar. They illustrate the confluence between the two cultures and languages that developed in spite of the geographical separation and biological divergence.

Pattern 4

An old Kaiadilt woman was in the habit of talking excitedly to herself a good deal, and was generally morose to others. Routine physical examination revealed a number of highly cheloidal cicatrices on the front and back of her chest. She said that the scar in the fold under her right breast was made by her mother with a firestick during her childhood on Bentinck Island, presumably as a decoration. The wounds on her back were made by her father when she was sick as a child, to remove Wadn't, the sea rat, who was making *malgudj* inside her. The old woman volunteered this information separately from my *malgri* enquiry.

Analysis

The significance of the *malgri* syndrome was the subject of much discussion by the sociomedical team. In fact it sparked off a flurry of conjecture, which—even if we did not arrive at a full understanding of the condition—illustrates the fascination of applying modern interpretations to traditional patterns. Small wonder that exotic culture-bound syndromes provide a happy hunting ground for speculative interpretation. For example, *malgri* might be viewed, from a functionalist perspective, as a part of the total belief structure maintaining social institutions and organization, and ultimately, adaptation. From the psychiatric viewpoint it is necessary to scrutinize the pathogenic and conflictual elements of the pattern. In doing so, several elements attract comment: the antipathy expressed between land and sea, the handwashing ritual, the violated taboo, the possibility of a corresponding Western diagnosis, and the widespread phobia of the condition.

In classical psychoanalytic idiom, the preoccupation of the islanders with the sea-land antipathy would suggest to the analyst a displacement of a family antipathy, for example that between father and son, as emphasized in the Oedipal theorizing of Freud's *Totem and Taboo* (1946), or Roheim's *The Eternal Ones of the Dream* (1945). This would represent a case of the lesser fear displacing the greater terror, as suggested by Freud. In terms of neoanalytic interpersonal theory, the displacement might rather be from the individual's current family and social transactions. Some support for these interpretations could be found in day-to-day observations of the islanders' behavior, in which displacement was a common feature. It had been observed that displacement of hostility is part of the ethos of Mornington Island, an ethos that values the "happy" man, the peacemaker who is consistently generous and congenial, who avoids confrontation, and who constantly looks for ways to attribute village quarrels and fights to forces beyond anyone's control.

From the phenomenological viewpoint, the displacement might not represent an antipathy having reference to the family tensions, but refer rather to the essential difference, for the individual, between the land-sea elements. The conflict between the land and the sea is real and earnest to the islander of the Gulf. Sometimes the sea yields its food, sometimes the land. A hunting-gathering people is in a condition of sustained competition with nature and with its own members for survival. From the phenomenological perspective, the syndrome is more specifically "totem and trespass" than "totem and taboo." It is part of the network of ecological relationships evolved to prevent trespassing and to conserve proper distances between human groups. It exemplifies the ethological concept that "territory" of a social group is a pertinent consideration in behavior; indeed, often a mainspring of motivation and social interaction. What ethologists call reaction distance has been described in psychiatric patients as the "body buffer zone." *Malgri* is perhaps the most specific instance in medicine of an illness associated with the concept of territoriality. While it cannot be said to represent simple extrapolation of animal territoriality to human behavior, it offers a striking example of the universal fear of leaving one's own territory and of the danger inherent in breaking the rules on foreign ground.

Some details of the *malgri* syndrome, especially the handwashing and/or contaminatory themes, do not at first sight possess a clear association with the territory theme. The handwashing pattern might be interpreted psychoanalytically as a ritual cleansing of blood after killing the land animal (symbolically father), but phenomenological examination of the situation suggests another interpretation. The injunction underlying the *malgri* taboo is not directed against killing and eating land food, but reflects the need to propitiate the sea by refraining from mixing spirits from land and sea. The sea, like the mother, is the main food-giving element for the Lardil. Offending it could lead to engulfment, failure of the food supply, or attack by its contained objects. This interpretation does not deny a possible historical origin of the handwashing precaution in terms of an actual event; the sea does periodically enter these islands in the form of an exceptionally high spring tide. Where might the contaminatory theme come from? Enquiries revealed that the traditional Lardil toilet training schedule differs from the pattern in Western culture, where weaning precedes bowel control. On Mornington Island the child is taught to hide his excreta around the age of weaning, roughly when he is four years old, and he is taught by his peers rather than by his parents. This coincides with the time of the first major development crisis of the Lardil child: weaning or displacement at the breast by the newborn sibling, a time of tantrums and distress. It may be inferred that oral-dependent needs are frustrated and aggressive drives provoked at the same time that control of anal drives is developing. Under these circumstances, a man's desire to invade the sea to take fish might symbolize the repressed urge to enter and take food from mother, an urge that was controlled contemporaneously with the desire to soil, and might provoke projective fantasies of being entered, in retaliation.

We found that in the discussion of *malgri* among our expedition members, "wild" psychoanalytic interpretations were heady stuff, not always palatable to those reared in the more pedantic biological traditions. Observers of the latter type pointed out that the act of handwashing itself contains biological advantages that possibly operate outside of conscious awareness to reinforce it. The advantages of handwashing might, for example, reside in more successful fishing with clean hands, or in better health from removal of hand-borne pathogens of conditions such as dysentery. But it has to be conceded that if biological advantage underlies the ritual of handwashing, it does so at an unconscious level; the explanation is one that would occur to a biologically trained team of doctors rather than to primitive fishermen.

Functional explanations of culture-bound syndromes, of whatever doctrinal origin, are not completely satisfying. Room must be reserved to account for the finding that some individuals are susceptible to *malgri* while others are not, a difference traceable to individual variations in personality and to individual experience of interpersonal or ecological transactions. Because of these individual variations, exact correlations need not be expected between modern medical syndromes and culture-bound disorders. In my casebook, *malgri* corresponds most frequently to a gastrointestinal disturbance (often with constipation) overlaid with a psychogenic, culturally determined superstructure. In other cases it corresponds to a conversion reaction, and in yet others to a paranoid development. In most instances, the "spirit intrusion" explanation is applied *post hoc* to various entities by the Lardil. Interpretation has to be made individually in each case in the light of all the circumstances, especially considering the social interaction pattern in which the patient is enmeshed.

The implications that an awareness of ethology may have for the *malgri* syndrome call for further comment. Some readers may interpret the syndrome as an extrapolation to man of the phenomenon of territoriality that occurs throughout the animal kingdom. But territoriality is not universal throughout the animal kingdom, especially among nonhuman primates. It would be facile to relate the territorial behavior that occurs in some lower animals directly to man, as a biological justification of property rights. Klopfer points out that territoriality is in fact subject to great diversity, and represents not one but many different adaptations serving different purposes for various animals. Thus, it would be misleading to extrapolate from birds to men without attempting to account for all relevant evolutionary and ecological factors. Nevertheless, without resorting to the possible analogies with animal behavior, it is likely that *malgri* may have something to teach about the composition of the horde in hunter-gatherer society, and about the horde's territorial rights.

The aspect of the *malgri* sickness that should not be overlooked in concentrating upon its intricacies is that the Lardil's fear is directed toward the intruding spirits that ring the island, rather than toward the illness itself. The fear is thus a policing agent in Lardil society. In any definition of medicine and the law, a limited correspondence between these institutions in primitive and modern society may be pointed out. The law of real property may be cited as an example, it being assumed that primitive hunting-gathering society has no comparable concept. Yet we find the island home of the Lardil seemingly legally partitioned (by a fear of local spirits producing sickness) as distinctly as hereditary estates partition an English country.

Malgri therefore provides a source of material for social anthropology in its task of evaluating the nature of the relationship between local group organization and the geographical territory that it occupies. As described by Hearne, the current debate on this issue concerns several interrelated questions of both social organization and territory, including:

1. The composition and stability of local group membership.
2. The distinctiveness or exclusiveness of the local group's territorial boundaries.
3. The availability and variety, as well as the utilization patterns, of the food and water resources to which the local group has access rights or ownership claims.
4. The nature of the social, economic, and political ties that may bind local groups to one another.

We are reminded by Hearne that Radcliffe-Brown in the 1930s proposed that "the horde" was the residential unit in the social organization of Australian Aborigines. The horde was composed of males and unmarried females who were members by birth, and the wives of the male members. It was thus an exogamous unit, patrivirilocal in residence, owning and occupying a territorial area containing the horde's totemic sites and the food and water resources necessary for subsistence. Radcliffe-Brown's model has been subject to question. Hiatt argues that local groups failed to form autonomous, separate, and self-sustaining economic units opposed, in a structural sense, to similar units.

The apparent distinctiveness and exclusiveness of the Lardil estates may be attributable to the fact that the Lardil occupy an island, limited in resources and capable of supporting only a limited population, so that territorial rights might be jealously safeguarded. The *malgri* syndrome itself appears connected with the fact that the territory is an island; it is not encountered among mainland tribes. But there are ways in which the "ideal" territorial scheme elaborated by the Lardil might be modified or relaxed. One is that the littorals are not guarded by spirits equally dangerous in terms of *malgri,* suggesting that some littorals are better fishing sites and therefore need stronger policing. "Burned serpent" and "moon" are reputed to be particularly dangerous spirit guardians, and even today the littorals of which they are totems are prolific sources of food. Thus, ecological factors, as well as structural factors, enter into the determination of the territorial units or estates. The "ideal" scheme is relaxed in another way, by the practice of admitting outsiders to live with the local social unit. Gully Peters, boss of the sea-eagle country, had Fred, from the other side of the island, in his social unit. This was possible, according to Gully, because the sea-eagle spirit eventually come to know Fred's smell and accepted him as a resident.

It seems reasonable to infer that ecological or subsistence tensions were factors leading to the modification of the composition of island social units. The composition of the social units, after fifty years of European contact, is not known with any precision, although, with the help of the islanders, I have made an approximation to begin with. It is in any case more a task for the social anthropologist than for the psychiatric anthropologist.

Malgri illustrates problems of crowding, stranger contact, and aggressive behavior, to which attention has been directed by Hamburg. Hamburg reviewed the information available on these relationships in primates and in man. He suggests that millions of years of vertebrate and primate evolution may have left us with many legacies, one of which is a readiness to react fearfully and aggressively toward strangers, especially if we are crowded in with them, competing for valued resources. Whether or not this tendency is part of our biological inheritance, *malgri* shows how a group of preagricultural, pretechnological men appreciated it, and regulated it by means of "medical" theory and practice.

This quest for regulation of aggression has become an acknowledged aim of modern medicine. Hamburg points out that hostility between human groups represents one of the great dangers of our era, perhaps even greater than most diseases. It may well be that it was regarded as a greater danger in a preagricultural era. The quest is certainly not new, as our subjects show.

The technical question with which we began, concerning the correspondence between culture-bound syndromes and Western diagnostic categories, can be answered with respect to *malgri*. There is no simple relationship, because the social dimensions of illness are different in the two cultures. We conclude that crowding and stranger contact are connected with illness in each culture. But we would need to hold to too narrow a "medical model" of disease to expect to find a direct relationship between individual cases of *malgri* and modern Western diagnoses.

NO

Robert A. Hahn

Culture-Bound Syndromes Unbound

One of the jumpers while sitting in his chair with a knife in his hand was told to throw it, and he threw it quickly, so that it stuck in a beam opposite; at the same time he repeated the order to throw it, with cry or utterance of alarm resembling that of hysteria or epilepsy. He also threw away his pipe when filling it with tobacco when he was slapped upon the shoulder.... They [the jumpers] could not help repeating the word or sound that came from the person that ordered them any more than they could help striking, dropping, throwing, jumping, or starting; all of these phenomena were indeed but parts of the general condition known as jumping.... All of the jumpers agree that it tires them to be jumped and they dread it, but they were constantly annoyed by their companions.

— "Jumpers," Moosehead Lake, Maine, described by Beard

E. A. B. at the time of the event was 20 years old, unmarried, the third of four siblings and an Iban. At the time he ran amok *he had been uprooted from his normal surrounding, a longhouse in one of the upper reaches of the Batang Lupar river. He was working in an oil drilling camp, approximately 200 miles from home with no direct communication. One night, while living on a barge near the camp, he grabbed a knife and slashed five of his fellow workers, three Malay and two Chinese.*

— A man with *amok* in Malaysia, described [by] Schmidt

A man, about age 45, with wife and children, took a second wife. Afraid of the first wife's jealousy, he tried to keep the new relationship secret, but in time the second marriage became known. One evening, he came home tired and fatigued. He got the shivers, broke out in a cold sweat, and felt that his penis was shrinking. At his cry for help, the neighbors came running. Only men helped him. One man tightly held the patient's penis while another went for a sanro, *a native healer. The* sanro *performed one ritual and after a while the anxiety disappeared, ending the day's attack.*

— An Indonesian man with *koro*, reported [by] Chabot

Observers of seemingly strange behavior have distinguished a variety of behavioral syndromes that, because of their apparent uniqueness and fit to local cultural conditions, are described as culture-bound. The observers of such behavior have most often been from Western settings, the behavior observed principally in non-Western ones. In this [selection], I examine the logic by which the generic diagnostic label "culture-bound syndrome" is ascribed to some conditions and not to others. I claim that the idea of culture-bound syndromes is a conceptual mistake, confusing rather than clarifying our understanding of the role of culture in sickness and fostering a false dichotomy of events and the disciplines in which they are studied. All conditions of sickness are affected in many ways, and none is exhaustively determined by its cultural setting. Physiology, medicine, psychology, and anthropology are complementary rather than contrary and exclusive; all are relevant and necessary to the comprehensive understanding of human phenomena of sickness and healing. . . .

The very notion of a culture-bound syndrome indicates a form of reductionism—the explanation of a given phenomenon by a single principle or body of knowledge. Other explanatory principles are thus denied relevance. Reductionists may claim that they have fully explained a culture-bound syndrome and that, in consequence, this phenomenon falls exclusively within their domain of inquiry. This mistaken effort is apparent in versions of anthropology as well as in Western medicine, psychiatry, psychoanalysis, and psychology. I argue that such claims fragment human function and its study into falsely opposed divisions.

Although anthropologists may believe that they have established a firm position by appropriating culture-bound syndromes to their own domain of explanation, their claims are at once excessive and too modest, claiming too much for culture-bound syndromes and too little for the diseases staked out by Biomedicine. I argue that full explanation requires an opening of the inner sanctum of Biomedicine to anthropological review and a concomitant recognition of pervasive physiological constraint in the workings of culture. Humans are bound by their cultures—but not rigidly. Nor is culture the only binding principle; body, mind, society, and the broader environment also bind. An exploration of culture-bound syndromes thus reaches the variety of forms of sickness and the range of human disciplinary approaches.

To assess the notion of culture-bound syndrome, I briefly define *syndrome* and *culture* and suggest how syndromes might be *bound* by culture. I distinguish three ways in which culture-bound syndromes have been understood. . . . I propose that we discard the misleading concept of culture-bound syndrome in favor of a broader study of the role of human mind, physiology, culture, and society in pathology and its relief.

Syndromes, Cultures, and Binds

A *syndrome* (from the Latin "things that run together") is a group of conditions, generally pathological, that may be physical and/or mental, signs and/or symptoms, and that is thought to constitute a discrete entity. One syndrome,

AIDS (acquired immunodeficiency syndrome), has gained recent attention; it is defined by a complex set of signs and symptoms that has evolved with changing knowledge as well as political economic circumstances. Numerous other syndromes are named in Biomedicine, some after their discoverer, others after their symptoms. Syndromes are distinguished from other events that co-occur in that their co-occurrence is thought to be not simply coincidental; a syndrome is a part of a unifying phenomenon—for example, a recognized biological process. The constituents of a syndrome may reflect a group of similar causes. What makes AIDS a syndrome is the acquisition of a specific virus, the human immunodeficiency virus, which causes a range of outcomes constituting AIDS.

The specificity with which a syndrome is defined will substantially affect what can validly be said about it—its distribution by nation and ethnic group, and other characteristics....

A culture, in the anthropological sense, is the set of beliefs, rules of behavior, and customary behaviors maintained, practiced, and transmitted in a given society. Different cultures may be found in a society as a whole or in its segments—for example, in its ethnic groups or social classes.

A syndrome may be regarded as culture-bound if particular cultural conditions are *necessary* for the occurrence of that syndrome; thus the culture-bound syndrome is thought not to occur in the absence of these cultural conditions. Some analysts of culture-bound syndromes may regard specific cultural conditions as *sufficient* for the syndrome's occurrence; in this view, no conditions other than these cultural ones (for example, other cultural conditions or noncultural ones) are necessary to provoke the occurrence of the culture-bound syndrome.

A Hypothetical Ethnography of the Diagnosis Culture-Bound Syndrome

Some of the dilemmas inherent in the notion of culture-bound syndrome are apparent in the ethnographic sources of this diagnosis. The history of specific terms and interpretations of these conditions is most often lost in the memories and notes of colonial settlers. Winzeler provides a rare historical account of the development of notions of latah. Edwards formulates the history of another condition, koro, its multiple names, and purported cases; as in the example of koro described at the outset of this [selection], a person who experiences koro is usually under great stress or anxiety, suffers a retraction of the genitals, and may fear death.

In general, we may guess that the application of the generic label culture-bound syndrome and of terms for specific conditions, such as latah, and "wild-man behavior," occurs in a sequence approximating the following:

1. Observers, most often trained in Western medicine, psychiatry, or psychoanalysis, or in anthropology or psychology, visit a foreign setting or an ethnic setting at home. Most often, ethnic settings are those that differ in their culture from the observers' own. Most often, though not always, the observers are white Americans or Europeans.

2. The observers notice behavior that seems strange (that is, unusual by their standards of normality) and indicative of deviance and disturbance. According to their interpretive bent, the observers are likely to take the observed behavior as pathological in some way—medically, psychiatrically, psychodynamically, behaviorally, and so on. Yet they may not know how to diagnose this pathology since it does not fit the familiar criteria of Western nosology. The culture-bound syndromes were early described as "exotic," a term that may tell us more about its users than about its intended referent.

3. The people among whom the strange behavior occur may offer a solution to the diagnostic dilemma. They may distinguish and label the observed behavior, although recognition of such labels in an unfamiliar setting is problematic. A response to an observer's question (such as, "What and I observing, and what is it called?"), which perhaps is not well understood, may not truly indicate what nevertheless comes to be accepted as an indigenous label for the observed condition. Vallee, for example, suggests that the term for one such condition, *piblogtoq* (also referred to as "Arctic hysteria"), is the fabrication of early explorers rather than a usual term of Eskimo usage. . . .

4. The observers return home with their prized possession: a new syndrome that, because it seems to be found only in the cultural setting from which they have returned, is labeled culture-bound. Culture-bound syndromes are residual; they are conditions that do not fit the nosological scheme of a Western observer. Rather than questioning the completeness or validity of the Western nosology, the new syndrome is set apart as an oddity from another culture.

5. The observers now face the ambiguous challenge of showing how this culture-bound syndrome actually fits into their own explanatory paradigm. The dilemma here is that, as the phenomenon is encompassed by the observers' explanatory system, it may lose its uniqueness and become a version of the broader phenomenon. Explanatory gain may be culture-specific loss. Analysts of culture-bound syndromes have attempted to keep their syndrome while reducing it also, by showing how social, cultural, and psychological conditions—general elements of their own scheme—are so distinctively configured in the local scene as to make this particular syndrome unlikely to occur elsewhere. Their reductions combine the universal principles of their own discipline —for example, the learning theories of psychology—with the unique cultural peculiarities of the local setting—for example, the specifics of who teaches, what is taught, and how. The local fit and indigenous label appear to give these conditions an immunity from spreading elsewhere; they may *look* like the "xyz" syndrome found elsewhere, but they are really different.

6. Having established a new condition, often distinguished by an ascribed indigenous term, the "discoverer" of this syndrome (or other observers) may then find further instances of similar conditions in new settings,

applying the established term, but now crossing cultural boundaries. Amok is the most notorious condition to be exported....

Understanding Culture-Bound Syndromes

Three alternative understandings of culture-bound phenomena are plausible. One may be described as "exclusionist," the other two as "inclusionist." I refer to one inclusionist position as "nature-culture continuum," to the second as "multiple-aspect."

The exclusionist interpretation of culture-bound syndromes is suggested by the phrase "culture-bound syndrome" itself. The phrase implies or assumes that some conditions are culture-bound and others are not. Conditions that are not culture-bound may be regarded as culture-free, culture-blind; perhaps they are thought of as nature-, physiology-, or materiality-bound. In the exclusionist view, that a condition falls in one-half of this divide implies that it does not fall in the other, and vice versa. Latah and amok are culture-bound syndromes; measles and lung cancer are not. This division is held to correspond to disciplinary divisions as well, so that culture-bound syndromes are the concern of anthropological and/or psychological or psychiatric expertise and culture-free syndromes are the subject of medical or physiological examination.

Kenny provides an excellent example of the exclusionist position in his analysis of latah. In Kenny's work, some conditions are regarded as clearly culture-bound and others as clearly universal (though universal conditions may be differently interpreted in different settings).

> Measles or smallpox, for example, are clearly identifiable disease entities, but receive very different cultural interpretations. Is this also true for "latah," "amok," and other ostensibly culture-bound syndromes? In short, are latah-like startle responses better considered [quoting Simons 1980] as the "exploitation of a neurophysiological potential," *or* are they themselves more plausibly considered as the outcome of social *rather than* biological factors? (emphasis added)

Kenny's "or" and "rather than" are exclusive connections. "Disease entities" are regarded as universal phenomena, the results of biological factors; culture-bound syndromes, in contrast, are not diseaselike and result from social factors. Kenny claims that cultural patterns "fully explain" latah; it would thus seem that biological explanation has no room....

Kenny believes the "true" nature of latah to be dramaturgic, an arena he believes unrelated or exclusive of human biology.... Kenny writes: "If this is the case, then the latah performance is taken out of the province of biomedical reductionism and is seen in what I take to be its true light—as theater." Kenny here replaces biomedical reductionism with theatrical reductionism.

Psychologist John Carr's interpretation of another Southeast Asian condition, amok, represents a version of the exclusionist position distinct from Kenny's. Though Carr writes that some syndromes are culture-bound, he goes on to formulate a plausible interpretation of amok behavior based on a theory of learning from Western psychology. Carr applies universal principles to the Malay setting, asserting that amok is a learned behavior response to a highly ambiguous yet demanding culture situation. Langness claims that similar cultural conditions—"contradictory demands and discontinuities"—account for "wildman behavior" in New Guinea.

Yet although Carr relates this culture-bound syndrome to universal principles of learning, like Kenny, he explicitly dissociates it from universal processes of disease, as formulated in Biomedicine: "The notion that culture-bound syndromes share underlying common disease forms is rejected. Instead, the ethno-behavioral model postulates that culture-bound syndromes consist of culturally specific behavioral repertoires legitimated by culturally sanctioned norms and concepts, but with both behavior and norms acquired in accordance with basic principles of human learning universal to all cultures."

Using notions of disease and illness developed by Kleinman, Carr associates culture-bound syndromes with illness behavior, which, "as distinct from the disease process, is always culturally determined." He concludes that a culture-bound syndrome is "a distinct repertoire of behaviors that (1) have evolved as the result of a social learning process in which the conceptual and value systems, and the social structural forms that mediate their effects, have served to define the conditions under which such behavior is an appropriate response, and (2) have been legitimated within the indigenous system as *illness* primarily in terms of extreme deviation from the behavioral norm as defined by preeminent culturally-specific conceptual dimensions governing social behavior."

This description of culture-bound syndromes parallels Kleinman's distinction between disease and illness and corresponds to disciplines appropriate to each [as seen in Table 1].

Table 1

| | **Explanatory Principle** | |
	Culture	**Nature**
Condition	Culture-bound syndrome	Culture-free syndrome
	Illness	Disease
Discipline	Psychology	Physiology
	Anthropology	Medicine
		Psychiatry

Carr notes, however, that culture-bound syndromes "may be precipitated by any number of etiological factors, among them physical, as well as sociocultural determinants." Thus, the basic cause of amok is thought to be psychological; the particular elements that are psychologically incorporated are culturally specific, and given this established syndrome, a number of precipitants, including physical ones, may elicit this behavior. Carr regards diseases as phenomena that appear universally, in "inviolate" form, and that are the legitimate concern of medicine and psychiatry, whereas illnesses are "always culturally determined" and are thus the legitimate concern of psychology and anthropology....

The inclusionist nature-culture continuum position maintains that all human events, including the supposed culture-bound ones, have cultural *and* biological *and* cognitive *and* psychodynamic aspects, though some events are more profoundly shaped by one of these aspects than by others. Thus, although no conditions are exclusively culture-bound or culture-free, some may be largely culturally shaped and others principally determined by universal physiology. In this conception, the notion of culture-bound syndrome remains a valid one. An example of the nature-culture continuum position is the work of Leighton and Murphy:

> So far as the total process in the development of psychiatric disorder is concerned, it would seem best to assume that heredity, biological, and psychological factors are all three engaged. To claim dominance for one, or for any subarea within one, *as a matter of general theory,* is to express a linear conception of cause and effect which is out of keeping with what we know about all the processes in the world around us. More germane is an approach to the topic that aims to discover and map out the interrelated factors and the nature of their interrelationships.

The recommendation that the relative importance of heredity, biology, and psychology cannot be theoretically determined in advance but must be empirically analyzed suggests that these factors may have more or less weight for different sicknesses.

The continuum understanding would make the extent to which a condition is culture-bound a matter of degree. It might be possible, at least theoretically, to quantify the proportions in which different factors contribute to given outcome conditions. Measles might occupy the natural, physiological end of this spectrum, the culture-bound syndromes the other; it is not clear what sorts of conditions might fall between—perhaps depression and alcoholism....

Anthropological Queries and Logical Doubts...

Defining Syndromes: Category and Context

The prevailing view of culture-bound syndromes is that these behaviors are distinctive of their cultural circumstances. Taken to its extreme, this view has implications that make scientific comparison impossible. All phenomena and events are unique, each differentiable from all others by some or, more likely, by many characteristics: each screw produced in a factory, every case of depression and tuberculosis, every episode of latah. The variations of each occurrence of a phenomenon are explicable, though perhaps not by current knowledge, in terms of the context of that occurrence. Indeed, such explanation is what we mean by "context"—a phenomenon's context is its circumstance, its environment. It is the explanatory power of a phenomenon rather than its simple physical contiguity that constitutes the context of something to be explained.

Because one phenomenon is significant in the explanation of another, however, does not bind the two to the exclusion of other explanatory principles. Occurrences of latah may well be different in large and small communities, as manifested by older and younger performers, by one person and another, even by an individual person at different times or in different circumstances. Do we then talk of community-bound, age-bound, person-bound, person-time-circumstance-bound syndromes?

By contextualizing in this way, we end up with a list of occurrences-for-persons-at-times-in-circumstances, and so on, ad infinitum....

In Search of the Whole: Interpretive and Causal Explanation

The exclusionist claim that some behavioral complexes are culture-bound and that others are not, and that the latter fit into some universal scheme, suggests that the culture-bound phenomena are so distinctive that they are beyond comparison. The explanation of such phenomena, exclusionists assume, connects them with other local phenomena and patterns of meaning, rather than with phenomena and patterns elsewhere. This perspective parallels one of two radically different positions that divide anthropology as well as literary studies, historiography, and psychology: interpretive and causal. Culture-bound syndromes provide a perfect example of the interpretive school, since they are thought to be explicable only by their local context.

According to the interpretive understanding, a position also called hermeneutic and phenomenological and sometimes associated with the philosopher Ludwig Wittgenstein, social and cultural phenomena are fully explained when they are shown to fit with their local phenomena in a system that "makes sense." In this view, questions about the causes of the phenomena of interest are regarded as misconceived or tangential. Thus, Kenny objects to attempts to explain culture-bound syndromes by universal, causal principles: "These medical or pseudo-medical labels evoke the notion that there is some kind of causal process underlying *latah*. The interpreters of *latah* seek to identify factors in the life experience of the victim which make her condition inevitable." It is implied that no kind of causality underlies latah. In a more general vein, Geertz writes, "Believing, with Max Weber, that man is an animal suspended in webs or significance he himself has spun, I take culture to be those webs, and the analysis of it to be therefore not an experimental science in search of law but an interpretive one in search of meaning."

Although it is obvious that anthropology is not an experimental science, Geertz goes further to assert that a search for law, presumably causal, excludes a search for interpretation. Interpretation is deemed appropriate only in the study of the workings of culture. Thus Geertz distinguishes blinks, which may be causally analyzed by science, from winks, which are intentional acts shaped by cultural systems to be analyzed by an interpretation of meaning in society and the circumstances of the winker. Yet, at some level, human biology is the mechanism of winks and may be involved in their motivation as well, and blinks, too, may express a symbolic meaning; these two forms of eye movement are not as distinctive as Geertz claims them to be.

... [I]f comprehensive explanation rests with those who perform an action, we become ensnared in webs of meaning that lead logically to solipsism [a theory holding that the self can know nothing but its own modifications and that the self is the only existent thing]. If local phenomena and labels for them can be understood only in terms of other local phenomena and their labels, then research across localities, as in much of anthropology, becomes impossible. Anthropologists may pursue their own tales, but not those of others.

Anthropology, Sibling Disciplines, and the Spectrum of Sickness

A conceptual and theoretical solution to the troubles of the exclusionist position might be founded in four principles:

1. A cross-cultural theory of sickness should begin, though not necessarily end, with the indigenous and personal understandings of the sufferer. Forms of suffering that do not fit the Biomedical mold will not be excluded as culture-bound. Patients at home will not be rejected as superstitious or as "crocks" because they fail to fall into Biomedical diagnostics. Pathology would be defined by the experience of the patient rather than by principles that seem a priori universal because they work fairly well among some groups at home and because they can be significantly explained by physiology, also apparently universal. Although a person may be (asymptomatically) unaware of the conditions that might later affect his or her well-being, still the state of well-being itself, and thus the sources of threat to it, are defined by the thought world of the patient him- or herself.

2. Interpreting a human act or syndrome—that is, showing its fit to the understandings and to the local circumstances in which it occurs—may be necessary, but it is not sufficient for full understanding. Minimally, an explanation that some phenomenon occurs in one place because of such-and-such conditions must also show that it does not occur elsewhere, where these conditions are not met. Comparison is a necessity and requires the development of comparative categories so that we may say that this is found here but not there, and that that is found there but not here. Even interpretation itself requires comparative categories; without them, the terms of one language and culture (say, the interpreter's) could not apply to those of another; translation would be impossible; and interpretation could thus be made only in local terms and only for local consumption. Exclusionism, by insisting on the exclusive local fit of all cultural phenomena, thereby precludes comparison; indeed it precludes communication across cultural boundaries.

   The difficulties of causal explanation are notorious, though perhaps better recognized than the hazards of interpretation. Nevertheless causal explanation, however systematic and nonlinear, must be pursued. In this way a universal scheme will come to take local meaning into account.

3. The course of human events is inevitably many-leveled, so that neither our disciplines—such as anthropology, physiology, psychology—nor their central concepts—culture, biochemical exchanges, human experience—can exclusively appropriate any event. That is, human events are not simply cultural or psychological, but inevitably bear these aspects and others.

4. ... [T]here are several ways in which the organization and culture of societies affect their processes of pathogenesis and healing. Societies inform their members about how the world is divided up and put together. With regard to pathogenic and healthful processes I have recommended three forms of understanding: *disease* models, *illness* models, and *disorder* models. Societies also engage in the production of sickness because of the ways in which they organize cultural beliefs and social relations. Carr's psychosocial analysis of amok illustrates the pathogenic powers of the social environment.

Such a sociocultural framework applies not only to conditions that are obviously affected, but to the purportedly hard-core diseases as well. The Biomedical model has obscured rather than enlightened such effects. Yet the history of tuberculosis, as brilliantly portrayed by René and Jean Dubos forty years ago, illustrates sociocultural effects in this condition whose biological characteristics appear to be clearly defined. The variety and power of ideology in tuberculosis-like conditions in European society are visible in a great range of attitudes toward this former (and reemerging) "captain of the men of death," its victims sometimes believed to manifest intensified creative powers as they were "consumed." Ideologies continue to be modified. The Duboses suggest that the term *tuberculosis,* already bearing a denotation not directly indicative of contemporary etiological conceptions, could be modified to fit current knowledge. The bacterium itself was then being shown to be neither necessary nor sufficient to the symptomatic complex that we call tuberculosis. The Duboses insisted on the causative importance of the host's sociocultural and natural environment. They also noted that though psychological factors were likely to be of importance, their extent and workings were unknown. A great variety of remedial efforts have also followed beliefs about this condition and about the broader order of social life. Tubercular patients have been revered and isolated, placed in dry climates and wet ones, required to rest and to exercise exhaustively.

Culture, nature, and the human mind between play central roles in diseases commonly thought of in terms of microorganisms and toxins as well as in apparently strange behavioral complexes. Only an inclusionist framework can encompass the range of pathological (and healthy) forms.

Culture-bound syndromes constitute an important frontier between anthropology, Biomedicine, and the medical systems of other societies. Built in premises different from our own, they challenge our standard divisions of things. In striking fashion they have reminded us that our own forms of sickness and of reacting to events do not cover the spectrum of the humanly possible. A comprehensive theory of human reactions and pathology must take them into account.

I have argued that the exclusionist understanding of culture-bound syndromes, implicit in the term, yet not intended by early proponents, distorts the role of culture and of physiology in human affairs. It claims too much of culture at the margin of our nosological scheme and too little of culture at medicine's core. Medical professionals, anthropologists, and others have conspired in a false division of labor. False divisions obstruct understanding. The abandonment of the erroneous category, culture-bound syndrome, might serve to redirect our attention to the formulation of a theory of human sickness in which culture, psychology, and physiology were regarded as mutually relevant across cultural and nosological boundaries.

POSTSCRIPT

Do Some Illnesses Exist Only Among Members of a Particular Culture?

In discussing *malgri*, Cawte accepts this condition as a medical problem that he believes occurs only among the Lardil Aborigines and their neighbors. As he outlines the syndrome, he links its occurrence to cultural factors not found in industrialized societies. He also finds no correspondence between *malgri* and psychological diagnoses in the West, and this he concludes that *malgri* is a culture-bound syndrome. Hahn steps back from the details of specific conditions described as culture-bound syndromes to ask what they all have in common rather than focus simply on *malgri*. He asks, In what sense can these syndromes be seen as distinct from Western diagnostic categories? Hahn concludes that authors like Cawte have typically reduced what must be complex illness experiences to a single set of cultural factors. He concludes that there are no culture-bound syndromes; all illness conditions are rooted in the biology and psychology of individual patients but shaped by the cultures in which they live. Thus, culture plays no more important role in *malgri* than in malaria, pneumonia, cancer, or depression.

Cawte and Hahn differ on whether or not conditions like *malgri* are really so different that they cannot be explained as manifestations of more common psychological problems. Cawte argues that *malgri* is unlike anything described in the standard reference manual, *Diagnostic and Statistical Manual of Mental Disorders* (*DSM-IV*), (American Psychiatric Association, 1994). Hahn contends that the symptoms associated with conditions such as *malgri* are usually so vague and ambiguous that they only seem not to fit *DSM-IV*.

A similar issue concerns whether or not we could actually compare culture-bound syndromes if they genuinely were bound to particular cultures. Hahn argues that if they were truly culture-bound, comparisons among different kinds of hysterias, wild man behaviors, startle reactions, and the like would be impossible. Such syndromes would have no common basis for comparison since it is the distinctive cultures, not something in the bodies and psyches of patients, that are causing the conditions. Hahn suggests that comparison among different conditions, such as the comparison Cawte provides in his selection, would be impossible.

Ronald C. Simons and Charles C. Hughes edited *The Culture-Bound Syndromes: Folk Illnesses of Psychiatric and Anthropological Interest* (D. Reidel, 1985), which surveys the various syndromes and attempts to sort them into general patterns. This volume has an exhaustive bibliography of primary sources about most culture-bound syndromes. Although Simons and Hughes accept the premise of the culture-bound syndrome, they conclude that some conditions probably should not be considered culture-bound, while others, such as Arctic hysteria, *amok*, and *latah*, probably should be accepted as legitimate culture-bound syndromes. Despite the fact that this volume accepts some culture-bound syndromes as distinctive, Hughes challenges the suitability of using this terminology, since most of the conditions can be related to conditions described in the *Diagnostic and Statistical Manual*.

Cawte's selection comes from one of the first collections to document many of the culture-bound syndromes: *Culture-Bound Syndromes, Ethnopsychiatry, and Alternate Therapies*, William P. Lebra, ed. (University Press of Hawaii, 1985). The collection contains detailed discussions of *latah, amok, witiko* psychosis, Arctic hysteria, and other syndromes mentioned here. Another volume of interest to psychological anthropologists and students interested in the relationship between culture and mental health is *Cultural Conceptions of Mental Health and Therapy*, edited by Anthony J. Marsella and Geoffrey M. White (D. Reidel, 1982). For a good discussion of *latah*, see Robert L. Winzeler's *Latah in Southeast Asia: The History and Ethnography of a Culture-Bound Syndrome* (Cambridge University Press, 1995).

On the Internet ...

Hands Around the World: Yanomamo Indians

The Hands Around the World: Yanomamo Indians Web site provides links to dozens of Web sites dealing with the Yanomamo (currently called the Yanomami) Indians of Venezuela and Brazil.

`http://indian-cultures.com/Cultures/yanomamo.html`

Rigoberta Menchú

This Web site offers a biography of Rigoberta Menchú as well as a link to an interview between Menchú and the Odyssey World Trek Team. Information on Menchú's home of Guatemala is also provided.

`http://www.worldtrek.org/odyssey/latinamerica/`
`rigoberta/`

The Politics of Indigenous Identity, Ethnicity, and Tradition

The Politics of Indigenous Identity, Ethnicity, and Tradition Web page is de-signed as part of a course taught by Dr. Bronwen Douglas at the Australian National University. Explore this site for additional suggested readings on the invention of tradition in the Pacific.

`http://library.kcc.hawaii.edu/psiweb/pacific/`
`pol_of_indig_indent.html`

The Hindmarsh Island Bridge Royal Commission: Transcript of Proceedings

The Hindmarsh Island Bridge Royal Commission: Transcript of Proceedings page provides a link to the Royal Commission's report concerning the Hind-marsh Island controversy.

`http://library.adelaide.edu.au/gen/H_Islnd/`

Hindmarsh Island Bridge Legal Defense

This Web site, entitled Hindmarsh Island Bridge Legal Defense, explores and discusses the court case involving the Hindmarsh Island bridge. This site also provides links to the latest news involving the case, history and background information, as well as various articles.

`http://www.ccsa.asn.au/HIB/HIBindex.htm`

PART 3

Ethics in Cultural Anthropology

*T*he ethical treatment of other peoples has come to play an increasingly important role in contemporary anthropology. Ethical issues directly affect how cultural anthropologists should treat their human subjects. What harm, if any, can be brought to a group being studied? How important is accuracy when writing of one's experiences in the field? What are the responsibilities of the anthropologist when writing of field experiences? Similarly, we may ask what the ethical responsibilities of Western anthropologists should be when they find certain cultural practices abhorrent or unjust. Should anthropologists work to change these practices? All of these issues raise questions about how involved anthropologists should become with the people with whom they work. Should anthropologists take a passive, objective, and even scientific position or should they use what they know to support or change these native communities?

- Did Napoleon Chagnon and Other Researchers Harm the Yanomami Indians of Venezuela?

- Does It Matter if Nobel Peace Prize Winner Rigoberta Menchú's Memoir Contains Inaccuracies?

- Should Anthropologists Work to Eliminate the Practice of Female Circumcision?

- Do Anthropologists Have a Moral Responsibility to Defend the Interests of "Less Advantaged" Communities?

ISSUE 14

Did Napoleon Chagnon and Other Researchers Harm the Yanomami Indians of Venezuela?

YES: Patrick Tierney, from "The Fierce Anthropologist," *The New Yorker* (October 9, 2000)

NO: John Tooby, from "Jungle Fever," *Slate,* http://slate.msn.com/?id=91946 (October 25, 2000)

ISSUE SUMMARY

YES: Investigative journalist Patrick Tierney contends that geneticist James Neel caused a measles epidemic among the Yanomami Indians of Venezuela by inoculating them with a virulent measles vaccine. He also states that Neel's collaborator, anthropologist Napoleon Chagnon, exaggerated Yanomami aggressiveness and actually caused violence by indiscriminately giving machetes to tribesmen who helped him, sometimes even inducing them to break their own taboos.

NO: Anthropologist John Tooby counters that medical experts agree that it is impossible to produce communicable measles with the vaccine that Neel used. He also argues that Tierney systematically distorts Chagnon's views on Yanomami violence and exaggerates the amount of disruption caused by Chagnon's activities compared to that of such others as missionaries and gold miners.

In September 2000 a startling message flew around the e-mail lists of the world's anthropologists. It was a letter from Cornell University anthropologist Terry Turner and University of Hawaii anthropologist Leslie Sponsel to the president and president-elect of the American Anthropological Association (A.A.A.), with copies to a few other officers, warning them of the imminent publication of a book that they said would "affect the American Anthropological profession as a whole in the eyes of the public, and arouse intense indignation and calls for action among members of the Association." The book in question, which they had read in galley proofs, was Patrick Tierney's *Darkness in El Dorado: How*

Scientists and Journalists Devastated the Amazon (W. W. Norton, 2000). The letter summarized some of Tierney's charges that medical researcher James Neel, anthropologist Napoleon Chagnon, and others seriously harmed the Yanomami Indians of Venezuela, even causing a measles epidemic that killed hundreds.

The leaking of the letter and the subsequent publication of Tierney's article in *The New Yorker* caused great excitement at the annual meeting of the A.A.A. in San Francisco, California, in mid-November 2000. Discussion climaxed at a panel discussion. The panel included Tierney, anthropologist William Irons (representing Chagnon, who declined to attend), and experts on the history of science, epidemiology, and South American Indians. (Neel could not defend himself, as he had died earlier that year.) Numerous members of the audience also spoke. Most speakers argued that Tierney was wrong in his accusation that the measles epidemic in 1968 was caused by Neel's and Chagnon's inoculations, but opinions about whether or not Chagnon had treated the Yanomami in an ethical manner during his research were mixed. Later, the executive board of the A.A.A. established a task force to examine the allegations in Tierney's book. The 300-page *Task Force Final Report* was completed on May 18, 2001, and is posted at http://www.aaanet.org.

Why would a book about researchers' treatment of a small Amazonian tribe have caused such an uproar? The reason is that due to the enormous sales of Chagnon's book *The Yanomamö* (now in its fifth edition) and the prize-winning films he made with Timothy Asch, the Yanomami (as most scholars spell their name) are probably the world's best-known tribal people and Chagnon one of the most famous ethnographers since Margaret Mead. Chagnon's use of his Yanomami data to support his sociobiological explanation of human behavior has also had influence outside anthropology, for example, in evolutionary psychology. The idea that the most aggressive men win the most wives and have the most children, thus passing their aggressive genes on to future generations more abundantly than the peaceful genes of their nonaggressive brethren, is a cornerstone of the popular view that humans are innately violent. Thus, Tierney's attack on Chagnon's credibility sent shock waves through the scholarly community.

Is it inherently unethical for scientists to treat other people as mere subjects for investigation or experimentation? Should scientists always place the welfare of their subjects ahead of the success of their research? Do researchers have a moral obligation to compensate people for their help and information? Are researchers responsible for the sometimes harmful effects of those payments? Are there ways of doing research that are mutually beneficial? Finally, is it fair to condemn a scholar for breaking a code of ethics that was not in place at the time of the research?

Tierney charges that Neel and Chagnon deliberately exposed Yanomami to a potentially fatal disease in order to test their theory of natural selection. He also contends that Chagnon's ethnographic research harmed the Yanomami by pitting person against person and group against group, leading to the violent conflict that he attributes to their heredity. Tooby counters that Tierney's book is a hoax, a systematic attempt to distort the facts and to blame the researchers for events that were beyond their control, like the measles epidemic.

Patrick Tierney  **YES**

The Fierce Anthropologist

In November, 1964, Napoleon A. Chagnon, a twenty-six-year-old American anthropology graduate student, arrived in a small jungle village in Venezuela, to study one of the most remote tribes on earth—the Yanomami Indians. At the time, the boundaries between Venezuela and Brazil were still uncertain. The upper Orinoco, with its tumultuous rapids and impassable waterfalls, had frustrated conquistadores since the sixteenth century, making its mountain redoubts a perfect blank slate for the dream of El Dorado and other fantasies about the New World. The German naturalist Alexander von Humboldt, who visited the area at the turn of the nineteenth century, wrote, "Above the Great Cataracts of the Orinoco a mythical land begins ... the soil of fable and fairy vision." The Yanomami themselves were rumored, by other tribes and by the earlier explorers, to be "wild" and dangerous—so dangerous that, in 1920, one of the first Americans to encounter them, the geographer Hamilton Rice, opened fire with a machine gun, fearing that the Yanomami were cannibals. Four years later, Rice met the Yanomami again and wrote that they "are not the fierce and intractable people that legends ascribe them to be, but for the most part poor, undersized, inoffensive creatures who eke out a miserable existence."

The reality that Chagnon encountered was, in many ways, stranger than anything previously imagined. In "Yanomamö: The Fierce People," which was published in 1968, Chagnon gave both a harrowing account of a prehistoric tribe and a sobering assessment of what life was like for people whom he later referred to as "our contemporary ancestors." "The Fierce People" eventually became one of the most widely read ethnographical books of all time, selling almost a million copies in the United States alone. Buttressed by subsequent films about the Yanomami made by Chagnon and a documentary filmmaker, Timothy Asch, the book became a standard text in anthropology classes worldwide, and it has gone through five revised editions, the last one in 1997.

"The Fierce People" was written with the verve of an adventure story but was grounded in extensive empirical research. The book opens with this description of Chagnon and an American missionary named James Barker, stumbling into a Yanomami village:

> I ... gasped when I saw a dozen burly, naked, sweaty, hideous men staring at us down the shafts of their drawn arrows! Immense wads of green tobacco

were stuck between their lower teeth and lips making them look even more hideous, and strands of dark-green slime dripped or hung from their nostrils. We arrived at the village while the men were blowing a hallucinogenic drug up their noses.... I just stood there holding my notebook, helpless and pathetic.... What sort of a welcome was this for the person who came here to live with you and learn your way of life, to become friends with you?

By 1968, Chagnon had spent nineteen months with the Yanomami. During this time, as he writes, he "acquired some proficiency in their language and, up to a point, submerged myself in their culture and their way of life." He studied the Yanomami in a broad variety of aspects, from their travel habits to their technology, use of hallucinogens, agriculture, intellectual life, social and political structures, patterns of settlement, division of labor, marriage practices, trading, and feasting. What was most striking about them was, he wrote, "the importance of aggression in their culture." The Yanomami, he concluded, lived in a "state of chronic warfare":

> I had the opportunity to witness a good many incidents that expressed individual vindictiveness on the one hand and collective bellicosity on the other. These ranged in seriousness from the ordinary incidents of wife beating and chest pounding to dueling and organized raiding by parties that set out with the intention of ambushing and killing men from enemy villages.

Between 1968 and 1972, Chagnon made five more expeditions into Yanomami country, exploring increasingly remote villages. In a 1974 book, "Studying the Yanomamö," and in subsequent editions of his first book, he describes surviving a murder attempt by his hosts—whom he frightens off with a flashlight—and a close encounter with a jaguar, which sniffs him in his hammock. Despite repeated death threats, he pushes on into uncharted territory, where he discovers an isolated group, whose members he calls "the Fiercer People." Abandoned by a Yanomami guide, he hollows out a log canoe and returns downriver.

Since the turn of the twentieth century, anthropologists had been inspired to venture farther and farther afield in search of "pure" people, uncontaminated by the Industrial Revolution. In the nineteen-twenties, Margaret Mead went to the South Pacific and wrote her bestseller "Coming of Age in Samoa." Mead described native life in idyllic terms that spoke to the war-weary mood of the time, while overlooking some of the less pleasant aspects of Samoan life, such as the high incidence of violent rape.

"The Fierce People" was the product of a different period. Chagnon, who was born in 1938, had spent an austere childhood in small-town, rural Michigan; his father was an undertaker, and he was the second of twelve children. He earned his doctorate in anthropology at the University of Michigan, and obtained a grant from the National Institute of Mental Health to study the Yanomami. "The Fierce People" was published at the height of the Vietnam War, when violence was the subject of national debate, and it became, in effect, the ethnographic text for the sixties. In 1997, Chagnon told an interviewer for the Los Angeles *Times* that he had written about the Yanomami in reaction to the "garbage" he had learned in graduate school about "noble savages."

⌘

When Chagnon first encountered the Yanomami, they were thought to be the largest unacculturated aboriginal group on earth. They slept on bark hammocks slung around the periphery of communal roundhouses with open centers, called *shabonos*. They practiced ritual combats—a graded series of exchanges, starting with chest pounding and escalating into duels with long poles. For gardening, they relied on cutting tools that had been obtained through circuitous trade links with the outside world. Their staple food, which constituted seventy per cent of their diet, was plantains, an import to the New World. Even their genetic makeup was unusual. The Yanomami lack the so-called Diego Factor, an antigen found in other Mongoloid peoples, including Amerindians. Some scientists have hypothesized that they are descended from the first people to cross the Bering Strait, twenty thousand years ago.

The Yanomami had developed a complex belief system about their origins, their afterlife, and their vulnerability to an underworld of demons who were out to destroy souls by spreading disease. (Like many tribal societies, the Yanomami believed that their souls were also threatened by the taking of photographs.) Each village had shamans who maintained constant vigil against the forces of evil by casting spells on perceived enemies.

Today, there are an estimated twenty-seven thousand Yanomami living in hundreds of villages, spread out over about seventy thousand square miles in southern Venezuela and northern Brazil. They speak four distinct dialects, and there are enormous regional variations in trade, warfare, and degrees of contact with the outside world. At the time of Chagnon's first expedition, most of the Yanomami were mountain dwellers. They did not have much in the way of metal tools or personal possessions. They practiced slash-and-burn agriculture, and they spent much of their time on long treks of hunting and gathering. They did not use canoes—there are no navigable rivers in the mountains—and they had little use for clothes, other than a cotton waistband for women and a penis string for men. Increasingly, however, the Yanomami were leaving the mountains to settle along the main course of the Orinoco. There, during the nineteen-fifties, missionaries had established outposts, and Venezuelan government workers had set up centers for treatment of malaria, which had become endemic along the river. Some of the Yanomami in the lowlands were beginning to wear Western clothes, and they had settled into a relatively sedentary life style, which they supported by growing crops, begging, and performing services for outsiders. It was among these Yanomami that Chagnon established his headquarters, at the confluence of the Orinoco and Mavaca rivers, next door to the Mavaca mission in the village of Bisaasi-teri.

Chagnon arrived in Yanomami territory in an aluminum rowboat with an outboard motor. He was carrying axes and machetes to give to the villagers as payment for their coöperation. Although the people of Bisaasi-teri were accustomed to receiving a trickle of trade goods in return for their work in the mission, the sudden windfall created a sensation. In a letter from the field, Chagnon writes that the first recipients of his gifts, all of whom were male, immediately left the village for remote settlements, where the axes and ma-chetes could be used for trade. One of the most startling conclusions of "The Fierce People" is that Yanomami warfare was caused largely by competition among marriageable men over females, who—thanks to the widespread practice of female infanticide—were in scarce supply. In another letter from the field, Chagnon noted, "This particular war got started the day I arrived in the field (cause: woman stealing), and it is getting hotter and hotter." The Yanomami's need to wage war, he observed, encouraged the breeding of males—and this, in turn, led to more war. Among anthropologists, this conclusion contradicted the conventional wisdom that primitive warfare was the result of competition for hunting territories, cropland, or trade routes. Chagnon later said that his find-ings had come as a surprise to him, too. In 1988, he told a reporter for *U.S. News & World Report,* "I went down there looking for shortages of resources. But it turns out they are fighting like hell over women."

Over a period of thirty years, Chagnon led some twenty expeditions into Yanomami territory and collected an unparalleled body of data, which he pre-sented in two books and more than thirty articles. Perhaps Chagnon's most enduring achievement was explaining the Yanomami's seemingly savage behav-ior in a way that shed new light on natural selection. In 1988, he published an article in *Science* entitled "Life Histories, Blood Revenge, and Warfare in a Tribal Population," in which he reported that the Yanomami men who murdered had twice as many wives and three times as many offspring as non-murderers had. He concluded that, among the Yanomami, the act of killing bestowed status.

This paper had considerable impact beyond the field of anthropology. Ed-ward O. Wilson and other sociobiologists accepted it as important evidence of the genetic origins of human violence. In a preface to Chagnon's 1992 book, "Yanomamö: The Last Days of Eden," which is "The Fierce People" adapted for a general audience, Wilson lauded Chagnon's synthesis of evolutionary biology and culture as a "master work."

⋘◉⋙

Like most undergraduate anthropology students in the nineteen-seventies, I ad-mired "The Fierce People" for its vivid research and unsentimental approach. In part inspired by Chagnon's example, I set out, in 1983, to do a study of rit-ual murder in the Andes. Like Chagnon, I concluded that, among some tribes, committing ritual murder was a prestigious act. In 1989, I decided to study the Yanomami, first in Brazil, where the Amazon gold rush had brought epidemics, guns, alcohol, and prostitution, and then in Venezuela, along the Orinoco and in the mountains. Over the next ten years, I made six trips to the Amazon-Orinoco region, spending fifteen months in the field and visiting thirty of the villages that Chagnon had studied. What I found was sharply at odds with what Chagnon described.

In "The Fierce People," Chagnon wrote that the Yanomami were "one of the best nourished populations thus far described in the anthropological/ biomedical literature." Unlike Chagnon's "burly" men, the villagers I encoun-tered were—as Rice had observed in 1924—tiny and scrawny, smaller than most

African Pygmies. According to data compiled by Darna L. Dufour, a biological anthropologist at the University of Colorado, the adult males average four feet nine inches in height, and the women four feet seven inches. The children have some of the lowest weight-for-height ratios among Amazonian Indians. More-over, Chagnon's account of Yanomami warfare seemed greatly exaggerated. I visited a village on the Mucajai River, in Brazil, where Chagnon had spent some time in 1967, and where he claimed to have found a group that demonstrated the most extreme form of Yanomami "treachery." However, according to the au-thoritative sociologist John Peters, who lived there from 1958 to 1967, the group had participated in only four raids in half a century. These raids, he said, had been provoked not by competition for women, as Chagnon had written, but by the spread of new diseases, which prompted angry accusations of witchcraft.

Others, too, were bewildered by some of Chagnon's writings. The linguist Jacques Lizot, who had been encouraged by Claude Lévi-Strauss at the Collège de France, has lived for twenty-five years with the Yanomami. In 1994, Lizot crit-icized Chagnon in the *American Ethnologist* for obscuring the identity of twelve villages in his homicide study, making it difficult for other anthropologists to verify his data. The German ethnologist Irenäus Eibl-Eibesfeldt, a former head of the human-ethnology department at the Max Planck Institute, outside Mu-nich, has been conducting research among the Yanomami since 1969. In 1994, he and another Yanomami researcher at the institute wrote a letter to the Amer-ican Human Behavior and Evolution Society, which claimed that Chagnon had got important mortality-rate statistics wrong.

In the past decade, some of Chagnon's colleagues, as well as Catholic mis-sionaries in the field, have expressed concern about the impact of his research on Yanomami culture. Kenneth Good, who worked with Chagnon while re-searching his Ph.D., has lived among the Yanomami for twelve years—longer than any other American anthropologist. Good calls Chagnon "a hit-and-run anthropologist who comes into villages with armloads of machetes to purchase coöperation for his research. Unfortunately, he creates conflict and division wherever he goes." During his years among the Yanomami, Good witnessed a single war, and the only time he felt endangered was on his first, nervous night in the field, in 1975, when Chagnon and another anthropologist, both drunk, burst into his hut, tore his mosquito netting, and pushed him out of his hammock in a mock raid.

✦

In 1995, Brian Ferguson, an anthropologist at Rutgers University, published a book entitled "Yanomami Warfare: A Political History," which challenged the sociobiological theories drawn from "The Fierce People" and other studies by Chagnon. Ferguson, whose book analyzes hundreds of sources, wrote that most of the Yanomami wars on record were caused by outside disturbances, particu-larly by the introduction of steel goods and new diseases. Ferguson noted that axes and machetes became highly coveted among the Yanomami as agricultural tools and as commodities for trade. In his account, evangelical missionaries, who arrived in Yanomami territory during the fifties, inadvertently plunged the region into war when they disbursed axes and machetes to win converts. In time, some of the missions became centers of stability and sources of much needed medicine. But Chagnon, whose study of Yanomami mortality rates took him from village to village, dispensed steel goods in order to persuade the people to give him the names of their dead relatives—a violation of tribal taboos.

In a chapter entitled "The Yanomamo and the Anthropologist," Ferguson described how these methods destabilized the region—in effect, promoted the sort of warfare that Chagnon attributed to the Yanomami's ferocity. By Chagnon's own account, he shuttled between enemy villages and cultivated "informants who might be considered 'aberrant' or 'abnormal' outcasts in their own society," and who would give him tribal secrets in exchange for beads, cloth, fishhooks, and above all, steel goods. To get the data he wanted, Chagnon, by his own account, began " 'bribing' children when their elders were not around, or capitalizing on animosities between individuals." Ferguson writes that Chagnon stirred up village rivalries by behaving like a regional big man and an "un-Yanomami... wild card on the political scene."

This depiction of Chagnon was supported by many of the Yanomami with whom I spoke. In 1996, in the village of Momaribowei-teri, a man named Pablo Mejía told me that when he was twelve he had witnessed Chagnon's arrival in his village: "He had his bird feathers adorning his arms. He had red-dye paint all over his body. He wore a loincloth like the Yanomami. He sang with the chant of his shamanism and took *yopo*"—a powerful hallucinogen used by Yanomami shamans to make contact with spirits. "He took a lot of *yopo*. I was terrified of him. He always fired off his pistol when he entered the village, to prove that he was fiercer than the Yanomami. Everybody was afraid of him because nobody had seen a *nabah*"—white man—"acting as a shaman. He said to my brother Samuel who was the headman, 'What is your mother's name?' My brother answered, 'We Yanomami do not speak our names.' Shaki"—the Yanomami's name for Chagnon—"said, 'It doesn't matter. If you tell me, I'll pay you.' So, although they didn't want to, the people sold their names. Everyone cried, but they spoke them. It was very sad."

Ferguson described an incident, in 1972, when Chagnon arrived in the village of Mishimishimabowei-teri, approximately seventy miles upriver from Bisaasi-teri. In exchange for blood samples, which he was collecting for his genealogical study, Chagnon distributed machetes to a nearby rival village, whereupon the headman of Mishimishimabowei-teri, an aggressive man named Moawa, threatened, Chagnon wrote, to "bury an ax" in his head if he didn't give his last machete to a man Moawa designated. Chagnon complied, but when he was safely back at his home base, in Bisaasi-teri, he vented his feelings in a way that shows how deeply he had become enmeshed in local politics. In "Studying the Yanomamö," Chagnon writes, "I told the Bisassi-teri that I planned never to return to Moawa's village.... I was tired of having people threaten to kill me. I was alarmed at how close some of them had come. I told them that I would do 'the same' to Moawa as he did to me, should he ever venture to come to Mavaca [mission] to visit."

In a review of Ferguson's book in *American Anthropologist,* Chagnon blamed the missionaries for any destabilization, pointing out that the conflicts had broken out long before 1964, when he arrived. In the 1997 edition of "The Fierce People," he wrote that he had been something of a savior to the people of Mishimishimabowei-teri, helping to broker "neolithic peace" between them and the antagonistic people of Bisaasi-teri. He said that, in return, the Mishimishimabowei-teri had bestowed on him the name of their village—an honor usually reserved for chiefs. "I was their village," Chagnon writes. "Their village was me."

Chagnon, who retired this year as a professor of anthoropology at the University of California in Santa Barbara, still retains his eminence in the field. Irven DeVore, a professor of biological anthropology at Harvard, says, "Chag was both first and thorough. First in the sense that very, very few anthropological studies have been carried out by an anthropologist who was first on the scene. Thorough in the sense that Chag has visited at least seventy-five Yanomami villages on both sides of the Venezuela and Brazil borders. I cannot think of a comparably thorough survey among any cultural group by an anthropologist. Chag gathered very detailed and documented data on the villages—so much so that another investigator could study the same population and come to a different conclusion. Chagnon's study was 'scientific' in the best sense of the word."

In 1995, Chagnon agreed to meet with me in his office in Santa Barbara. By this time, I had become a human-rights activist on behalf of the Yanomami and other Amazon tribes. I had written a piece in the New York *Times* that was critical of one of Chagnon's Venezuelan friends and colleagues, Charles Brewer-Carías, and Chagnon was angry about it. In recent years, he had become such a controversial figure for his research among the Yanomami that the Venezuelan government had prohibited him from reëntering Yanomami country. Chagnon refused to answer any of my substantive questions about his troubles, saying that, at some later date, he planned to write about them himself. During the preparation of this article, he was again asked to answer questions about his work with the Yanomami. After first agreeing to talk in depth to *The New Yorker*, he changed his mind a few days later and declined to comment.

One of Chagnon's most important academic mentors was the celebrated geneticist Dr. James Neel, who was a member of Chagnon's Ph.D. advisory committee at the University of Michigan. Neel, who died earlier this year, first achieved fame in the field of inherited disease and then headed the Atomic Bomb Casualty Commission, which was established after the war to study survivors of the bombings of Hiroshima and Nagasaki. Between 1965 and 1972, he received more than two million dollars from the Atomic Energy Commission to compare the cellular-mutation rates of the Japanese survivors with those of the Yanomami and other "primitive tribes" that had not been exposed to radiation. The immediate goal was to determine the effects of radiation on the genetic material of cells. The ultimate goal was to help set radiation safety standards in the United States.

Chagnon became, as Neel put it, the "indispensable cultural anthropologist" in Michigan's Human Genetics Department. Between 1966 and 1971, Chagnon made six trips to Brazil and Venezuela, as a member of a multidisciplinary team led by Neel to make what Neel described as the most comprehensive study of a tribal people ever attempted.

Neel had long been interested in unadulterated societies. A self-professed eugenicist, he believed that modern democracies, with their free breeding among large populations, violated the process of natural selection and promoted genetic entropy. Tribal people, in his view, were likely to have superior genetic material because they lived according to the survival-of-the-fittest principle—that is, they were ruled by polygamous chiefs who had triumphed over their rivals. He hoped that by studying the Yanomami he might be able to isolate specific genes for male leadership—or, as he put it, an "Index of Innate Ability." This view of the Yanomami as a superior breeding stock was not generally shared by Neel's medical colleagues. Most of them believed that the Yanomami, like other Amerindian tribes, were immune-depressed.

In January, 1968, Neel's team, which included Chagnon, Asch, and a Venezuelan doctor, Marcel Roche, arrived on the upper Orinoco. Chagnon was sent ahead of the others to secure, as he later wrote, "agreements from the Yanomamo to provide endless outstretched brown arms into which many needles would be stuck for the next weeks." Asch described the process in notes for one of his films: "The villagers are studied on a production line: numbers are assigned to them; specimens of their blood, saliva, and stools are collected; impressions of their teeth are made; and they are weighed and measured by the physical anthropologists." Each person was also photographed and paid with what Neel called "a 'cash' transaction based on trade goods."

Neel had learned of an outbreak of measles that had occurred the previous fall among Brazilian Yanomami in villages more than a hundred miles from the Venezuelan missions. For what he later called "an exercise in preventive medicine," Neel's team brought a thousand doses of live measles vaccine into the upper-Orinoco region. Neel was eager to collect data on vaccine responses. At the time, geneticists wanted to study tribal people who had no measles antibodies, in order to determine how their immune responses differed from those in modern societies. In 1966, Francis Black, a geneticist at Yale, had vaccinated a Brazilian tribe, the Tiriyo, with a measles vaccine, in the hope of using the vaccine virus as "a model of natural measles." He found that the Tiriyo's postvaccination fevers were extraordinarily high; the temperature elevations were nearly three times those of other races that had been given the same vaccine.

Black had chosen the widely used Schwarz measles vaccine, rather than an older vaccine, the Edmonston B, citing "the risk of severe febrile response" with the Edmonston B vaccine. In 1962, when an immune-compromised child with leukemia died after receiving Edmonston B, one of the vaccine's inventors, John Enders, of Harvard, had cautioned that the strain was dangerous for immune-depressed people. Measles vaccines were also known to produce unusually severe reactions in people suffering from anemia, dysentery, or chronic exposure to malaria—and the Yanomami suffered from all three.

Two years after Black conducted his study, Neel took the Edmonston B vaccine, rather than the Schwarz, into Yanomami territory. None of the other members of Neel's team seem to have participated in this decision, and there is no evidence that any of them would have known the difference between the two vaccines. In January, 1968, Venezuela had begun a national vaccination project, administering the Schwarz vaccine in three diluted doses, on the recommendation of the Centers for Disease Control, in Atlanta. In the United States, where many children still received the Edmonston vaccine—it is no longer used anywhere in the world—it was given with an accompanying dose of gamma globulin, which reduces the fevers by half. Neel had his researchers administer Edmonston B without gamma globulin to forty tribespeople at a mission on the Ocamo River. According to the director of Venezuela's vaccination department, Dr. Adelfa Betancourt, they did so without the department's permission. (A science historian at the University of Pennsylvania, Susan Lindee, was recently quoted in *Time* to the effect that Venezuelan officials gave permission for the vaccinations. She has since told *The New Yorker* that her evidence for the claim was erroneous.)

Over the next three months, the worst epidemic in the Yanomami's history broke out. On the basis of three mission journals, data of the expedition itself, and interviews with Yanomami survivors and with other witnesses, I determined that the course of the epidemic closely tracked the movement of Neel's team. It broke out in the three settlements that received the vaccinations—the Ocamo mission, the Mavaca mission, and a village called Patanowa-teri. Because quarantines were not rigorously imposed, the disease spread to dozens of villages scattered across thousands of square miles. It is estimated that between fifteen and twenty per cent of the Yanomami who contracted measles died in the epidemic.

A child's unmarked grave lies next to a dirt airstrip at the Catholic Ocamo mission. Thirty years ago, a small cross was erected at this spot, but it could not withstand the tropical weather. The remains in the grave are those of a year-old boy named Roberto Baltasar, who died on February 15, 1968; he was the first clearly diagnosed case of measles among the Venezuelan Yanomami recorded in the mission journals. According to Vitalino Baltasar, the boy's father, Roberto had come down with the disease after being vaccinated by Chagnon, under the direction of Neel.

In a 1970 paper entitled "Notes on the Effect of Measles and Measles Vaccine in a Virgin-Soil Population of South American Indians," Neel and Chagnon tell a different story. In their account, a single case of measles coincidentally broke out among the Venezuelan Yanomami as soon as Chagnon and Asch arrived at the Ocamo mission. The measles, Neel and Chagnon wrote, had been brought by a fourteen-year-old Brazilian worker, who had come to Ocamo with other workers. They said that Roche had made "a tentative diagnosis of measles" in the Brazilian teen-ager, and added that Roche's diagnosis was "uncertain," because the boy's symptoms could not be distinguished from "any of a variety of 'jungle fevers.' " (And the boy showed no signs of a measles rash.) Twenty-eight years later, I talked to Roche in Venezuela, in the offices of a scientific journal of which he was the editor. He told me that he did not remember having diagnosed measles in the Brazilian boy. Indeed, according to the Mavaca-mission records, Roche and another doctor reported that the team's arrival had coincided with an ongoing epidemic of bronchopneumonia, whose symptoms match those that Neel and Chagnon described in the fourteen-year-old boy.

Chagnon and Roche began vacinnating the Ocamo Indians with Edmonston B for purely "preventive" reasons, Roche later told me. According to Neel and Chagnon, cases of "moderately severe measles" appeared among the vaccinated Yanomami six days after they were inoculated. The fevers Neel and Chagnon recorded were, on average, far higher than previous responses to the Edmonston B vaccine—so high that they could not be distinguished from the fevers of natural measles. Then Roberto Baltasar died. According to his father, vaccinated Yanomami began fleeing the Ocamo mission, and going into the hills. "They already carried the disease," he told me, twenty-eight years later. "Few of them returned, because the majority died."

It cannot be determined with any accuracy how many died after receiving the vaccination. Chagnon has said that no one who was vaccinated got measles, and, according to the medical consensus at the time, the Edmonston B vaccine virus was not, in itself, contagious. Today, scientists still do not know whether people who have been vaccinated with Edmonston B can transmit measles. What is certain is that the effects of an epidemic, in which hundreds died in a relatively short period, were especially devastating on a people who believed that some new black magic must have brought on the disease and who, at the first sign of the measles rash, panicked and fled from their homes into the forests, away from further medical attention.

A government nurse who was in the area at the time, Juan González, helped the Yanomami collect the bodies of the dead for cremation. "They hung the children in baskets from the trees," he recalls. "The cadavers were placed inside the baskets, all rolled up tightly, like a metallic foil. The women were more loosely wrapped, in leaves, and they were left hanging in hammocks out in the wild among the trees. They tied the men up on poles, higher up in the branches. What a stench there was. Nothing but dead Yanomami. The Yanomami say that they died from that vaccine. That's why even now some of them don't want to be vaccinated. I don't know how to explain it either, because we initially believed that that first vaccine had come to help us. Instead, it came to destroy us."

Asch, who died in 1994, left about twenty thousand feet of raw footage of the expedition, along with the sound tapes, to the Smithsonian Institution. The first mention of the measles outbreak on the soundtrack is heard on the eighteenth of February, three days after Roberto Baltasar's death. On that day, Asch recorded Neel giving him instructions on filming measles victims at the team's base camp, at Mavaca, where a second vaccination center had been established. "Let me tell you what we want to get—extreme severe morbilliform rash," Neel says. "Can you get this? ... Both eyes. He has the typical morbilliform rash on both cheeks.... I'm afraid you're going to [see] some severe cases of measles.... We're going to be able to document the whole gamut of measles in this group."

Later, Chagnon asks Neel to summon more doctors, from Caracas, to treat the measles, and Neel agrees. Their radio operator, whom they call Rousseau, says that he will contact people in Caracas and request antibiotics *"por los efectos de la vacuna"*—because of the effects of the vaccine—and adds that the vaccine may bring *"brotes de sarampión,"* outbreaks of measles. After listening to Rousseau, Chagnon cautions Neel, "But he's trying to interpret all of them to mean that it's a reaction to the vaccination, which I don't think is a wise thing to do." Chagnon seems bewildered by the extent of the outbreak. He says, "Now we have measles at Mavaca and Ocamo, and I don't know where else it is—I don't know when it arrived."

Later, he tells Neel that the Ocamo Yanomami could easily spread the disease to others by journeying to nearby villages to trade. (Apparently, this happened. A group of Ocamo Yanomami who had sold blood to Neel's researchers for knives, machetes, and other trade goods travelled upriver to visit a village called Shubariwa-teri, which was then devastated by measles.) Chagnon suggests that Neel take quarantine precautions at Mavaca, and he urges that doctors be flown in from Caracas to care for the Ocamo Yanomami. Neel agrees. He then orders his younger colleagues to move farther up the Orinoco, into the tribe's heartland.

◈

During the epidemic, Neel, Chagnon, and Asch made two award-winning films. One was "Yanomamö: A Multidisciplinary Study," which presents a general overview of Neel's research objectives. The other was "The Feast," which documents the celebration of a military alliance between two formerly hostile villages. "The Feast" is widely considered one of the finest ethnographic films ever made, because of how it depicts the Machiavellian underpinnings of tribal festivities. In Asch's notes, he explained the background to the film: "To conduct raids and to protect itself from attack, a Yanomamö village must ally itself with neighboring villages. The feast is a means by which these intervillage alliances are formed. To prepare for a feast, the village is first cleaned. Gallons of banana soup for the guests are cooked and stored in large troughs. The guests, waiting outside the village, send in an emissary who chants a greeting and brings back food to his people. The guests burst in, dancing and brandishing their weapons, while the hosts recline in their hammocks. Feasting, trading, and games of ritual violence then take place. Sometimes these 'games' escalate into real massacres."

Both "A Multidisciplinary Study" and "The Feast" were filmed in the village of Patanowa-teri. Twenty-eight years later, when I visited there, a tribal elder named Kayopewe told me, through a translator, that before Chagnon and Asch arrived with their equipment the village had fallen into ruins and was largely abandoned. It was reconstructed and reoccupied, he said, only after Chagnon promised that if the villagers moved back in and held a peacemaking feast with their neighbors from a hostile village called Mahekoto-teri he would give every man among them a machete. Kayopewe said that the whole affair had, in effect, been brokered by the filmmakers.

Asch partly confirmed this account in an article published in the film journal *Sightlines,* in 1972. In a description of the making of "The Feast," he said that Chagnon had sent him, three Yanomami, and a young Protestant missionary, Daniel Shaylor, on an eleven-day trek to Patanowa-teri, a "mountain hideout" far from the vaccination centers along the Orinoco. "After finding [the] Pataowa-teri we set up an aircraft radio and reached Napoleon at Mavaca. He convinced the headman to move back into an old garden near the Orinoco River where the genetics expediction could work with them and we could take film." A large shipment of metal pots duly arrived as payment for the villagers' coöperation. In 1995, according to an article in the *Visual Anthropology Review,* Chagnon said, "I did not 'stage' this—it happened naturally. They could not have cared less about our interests in filming and are the kind of people who would not do something this costly and time consuming for two whole communities simply to accommodate the filming interests of outsiders."

Other payments were required—so many that Chagnon radioed for another plane to bring in more trade goods. When Chagnon distributed the goods, he created what seems, on the soundtrack, to be pandemonium. Later, when Chagnon and Asch asked a group of Yanomami to cut some bananas in front of the camera, they suddenly burst into a frenzied dance—"screaming at the top of their lungs, waving branches of leaves in the air," as Asch later wrote in *Sightlines.* Asch filmed the scene, assuming that it was a "garden ritual." When the Yanomami finally stopped, Chagnon asked them, "What was that all about?"

"Isn't that what you just asked us to do?" the headman replied.

The filming of "The Feast" also had unforeseen consequences. When Chagnon invited the Patanowa-teri's former enemies, the Mahekoto-teri, to participate as guests, he created a new alliance. According to Chagnon, it is Yanomami custom for two villages to celebrate such a union by choosing a new enemy, and after feasting together the new allies launched a raid on a third village, killing a woman in the process. One day, when Asch tried to film a doctor who was treating a sick man from the village of Mavaca, Neel interrupted him. "I don't want any of this," he said. "You're here to document the kind of study we're trying to make. Anyone can walk into a village and treat people. This is not what we're here to do."

After Neel's researchers departed many of the Mahekoto-teri and Patanowa-teri became sick and died. It is not clear what they died of, because they may have been exposed to many different pathogens, including colds, the Edmonston B virus, and malaria. (Shaylor, the expedition's translator, had arrived in Patanowa-teri with malaria, where he became so sick that he had to be evacuated.) In 1996, when I showed the elders of both villages a video of "The Feast," many of the old men wept. Kayopewe said, "We broke out in sores and rash on our faces, and it burned really badly. One of us died at the village [where the filming took place]. We left him there and fled into the jungles. An old man would die. We would tie him up in the trees. And then a young woman would die, and we would leave her in a basket. We kept dying off and dying off." When the men heard a translation of the soundtrack of "A Multidisciplinary

Study," in which Neel claimed that the Patanowa-teri had been saved from measles, thanks to the vaccinations, there was a chorus of protest. *"Horemu! Horemu!"* ("Lies, lies.") One man told me, "Shaki stole our spirits, and we have never been the same."

⋘◆⋙

By the mid-seventies, the Yanomami had become the most intensively studied and filmed tribal group in the world. In Paris in 1978, a festival was devoted to films about them. As scientists, news teams, filmmakers, and others competed for footage and new data bout the tribe, some of the Yanomami along the Orinoco became part-time film extras and anthropological informants.

At the same time, native-rights advocates began to criticize outsiders—gold miners, journalists, missionaries, scientists—claiming that cultural disruption and epidemics invariably followed their visits into the tribal territories. The first group to defend Yanomami rights was formed in Brazil, and a split developed in anthropology between the researchers who wanted simply to observe tribal culture and those who wanted Indians to have land rights and health care. From 1976 until 1985, Chagnon was prohibited from reëntering Yanomami territory. During those years, he and his wife, Carlene, raised two children, and he became a popular lecturer at Northwestern and then at the University of California at Santa Barbara.

In 1985, Chagnon, accompanied by a University of California graduate student, Jesús Cardozo, who was Venezuelan, succeeded in reëntering Yanomami territory. He returned to Mishimishimabowei-teri, where he hoped to finish his long-term study of the relationship between Yanomami homicide and reproductive success. Cardozo, who no longer has cordial relations with Chagnon, went on to help create the Venezuelan Foundation for Anthropological Research, which promotes Yanomami education and land rights. As Cardozo later recalled of the expedition, "We hadn't even got our boat moored to the shore at Mavakita"—a Mishimishimabowei-teri village that had broken off from the main group following various epidemics in the early seventies—"when Yanomami started coming out and shouting, 'Go away! Shaki brings *xawara* [illness].' Within our first twenty-four hours there, three children died—two in the night and another in the morning." Although there was no connection between Chagnon's arrival and the deaths, the events were seen as further evidence of the anthropologist's malefic power. "On our second night, half of the village fled into the forest to get away from us."

After another day of searching for a community where he could continue his genealogical research, Chagnon found a village, Iwahikoroba-teri, that was willing to receive the expedition. "When we arrived at Iwahikoroba-teri, everybody was sick, throwing up and moaning and lying down in their hammocks," Cardozo said. "I remember a little girl, Makiritama. She was vomiting blood. She was defecating blood, too. I remember her husband—she was very young, she was to be his future wife—showed me where she was spitting up everything. And I went up to Chagnon and said, 'You know these people are really sick. Some of them could die. I think we should go and get medical help.' Chagnon told me that I would never be a scientist. He said, 'No. No. That's not our problem. We didn't come to save the Indians. We came to study them.' "

For the next several weeks, Chagnon collected homicide data, numbering each Yanomami's chest or arm with a Magic Marker, posing the Yanomami for identification photographs, and paying them with trade goods. He summarized his findings in an article in *Science,* which was published in February, 1988. The article was noted in *Scientific American* for providing a new, though grim model for human evolution: "Through violence a Yanomamö male seems to enhance his reproductive success and that of his kin: he becomes 'fitter.' "

But Yanomami specialists generally rejected the study. In a number of anthropological journals, they challenged Chagnon's findings on ethical, statistical, linguistic, and interpretive grounds. And Chagnon's presence in the media—he was mentioned in the Los Angeles *Times,* in February, 1988, as having said that when the Yanomami were not hunting, or searching for honey, they were often killing one another—became provocative. Less than a year after the *Times* article appeared, the Brazilian military chief of staff cited the Yanomami's trulculence as a reason for breaking up their lands. A past president of the Brazilian Anthropological Association, Maria Manuela Carneiro de Cunha, wrote a letter to the *Anthropology Newsletter* in which she held Chagnon accountable, in part, for the government's actions against the Yanomami. In an article entitled "The Academic Extermination of the Yanomami," which was published in the Brazilian cultural journal *Humanidades,* two anthropologists, Alcida Ramos and Bruce Albert, wrote, "Few indigenous people... have had their image as denigrated as have the Yanomami, who had the misfortune of being studied by a North American anthropologist named Napoleon Chagnon."

Chagnon responded to da Cunha in the *Anthropology Newsletter* by saying that he could not control the press's tendency to sensationalize his findings, and that he should not be held responsible for the failure of Brazilians to defend the rights of indigenous people. In his 1992 revised edition of "Yanomamö," for which he dropped the subtitle "The Fierce People," he drew a distinction between researchers who sought objective facts, like him, and other anthropologists, who were motivated by a sense of political activism and who "hold a romanitc, Rousseauian view of primitive culture."

In 1989, Chagnon proposed bringing a BBC film crew to Bisaasi-teri to commemorate the twenty-fifth anniversary of his arrival in the village. By this time, many more Yanomami had left the highlands to live near missions along the Orinoco and its tributaries, where they could attend schools, get medical care, and eat a more varied diet. The Yanomami at the missions were considerably more robust than those in the hills, and they had learned how to market their own handicrafts through a trade coöperative run by elected representatives. Along the Orinoco and Mavaca rivers, it was no longer easy for researchers to hire Yanomami porters, informants, or film extras. When the Yanomami at Bisaasi-teri learned that Chagnon was returning, they instructed their representative, a former guide of Chagnon's named César Dimanawa, to write a letter asking the anthropologist to keep away, because his films contained so much "fighting and bloodshed." Dimanawa wrote, "We do not want you to make any more films." Again, the Venezuelan government cancelled Chagnon's permit, citing the "turmoil" that his vist would provoke.

⌘

Chagnon turned for help to Brewer-Carías, his old friend. A distinguished botanist, Brewer-Carías had been criticized by environmentalists and human-rights activists for allegedly acquiring, under the pretense of doing research in rain forests, land for gold mining—charges that he emphatically denies. Through Brewer-Carías, Chagnon made another powerful ally, Cecilia Matos, the mistress of the Venezuelan President, Carlos Andrés Pérez, and the head of a foundation that had been set up to assist indigenous and peasant families. Chagnon, Brewer-Carías, and Matos devised a plan to create a Yanomami re-serve in the Siapa Highlands—an area of thousands of square miles in which the Indians would live in protected isolation. Only scientists would be allowed into the area, to study the Yanomami at a research center run by Chagnon and Brewer-Carías.

Between August, 1990, and September, 1991 Chagnon and Brewer-Carías organized a dozen expeditions by helicopter into the Siapa region for journal-ists and scientists, in order to build up national and international support for their project. Three of the villages that were visited by Chagnon, Brewer-Carías, and their entourage were badly damaged by the helicopters. In 1991, Chagnon described one of these events in an article for the magazine *Santa Barbara*, en-titled "To Save the Fierce People": "A few feet from landing, we aborted when we saw the leaves of their roofs being blown away by the chopper's downblast. We saw people fleeing in terror and men throwing sticks and stones at us as we retreated up and away."

Dr. Carlos Botto, the director of the Amazon Center for the Investiga-tion and Control of Tropical Disease, in Puerto Ayacucho, was in the village of Ashidowa-teri when Chagnon landed in his helicopter and part of the *shabono* collapsed. "When the poles of the roof fell, a number of Yanomami were in-jured, and we had to treat them," Botto recalls. "We had to rescue people who were buried under the poles and roofing of the *shabono*. The expedition left a tragic scar."

In September, 1993, Chagnon and Brewer-Carías were named to a Pres-idential commission, which was given broad powers over the Yanomami's land and political future. The attorney general's office, leaders of the Catholic Church, and native-rights groups opposed the appointments, and three hun-dred representatives from nineteen Indian tribes rallied in the streets of Puerto Ayacucho, the capital of the state of Amazonas, in an effort to have Chagnon and Brewer-Carías expelled from Yanomami territory. On September 30th, Chagnon was escorted to Caracas by an Army colonel, who confiscated his field notes and advised him to leave the country—which he did.

In the United States, Chagnon remained highly regarded. Earlier that year, he had been elected president of the prestigious Human Behavior and Evolution Society.

❦

In September of 1996, after undergoing a weeklong quarantine, I trekked for seventeen days into the Siapa Highlands with a Brazilian malaria-control worker, Marinho De Souza. We were the first outsiders to revisit the area since Chagnon's tumultuous helicopter descents, and we found the villages very different from his description. In articles and interviews, Chagnon had said that the Siapa Yanomami were healthy, well fed, and peaceful. Here, in the tribe's unspoiled heartland, steel goods were scarce, and the homicide rate among men was much lower than it was in the lowlands along the Orinoco.

What De Souza and I discovered, however, was a fearful, broken society. At Narimobowei-teri, the first village that Chagnon's helicopter had damaged, men with drawn arrows greeted us, fearing that we were enemy raiders. At night, we listened to the chanting of shamans who were trying to exorcise the demonic flying machine that had descended upon their village, dispensing both wonderful trade goods and, they believed, terrible disease. At another village, Toobatotoi-teri, which Chagnon described as "the last uncontacted group in this region," we came to a clearing where shamans were trying to induce helicopters to land by chanting and dancing. The plan, apparently, was to trick any outsiders into unloading their steel gifts and then to scare them into leaving—quickly, before they could infect the people with colds and fevers. Life in the Siapa Highlands had always been a struggle. The villagers had combatted malnutrition, intestinal parasites, and, more recently, malaria. But what they could not comprehend—and what had shaken their world—was the sudden arrival of visitors who seemed to offer an easier life and, at the same time, sowed so much confusion. For them, Chagnon had come to personify everything that both attracted and repulsed them about our culture. They wanted him, and they didn't want him, and they could not forget him.

After twelve days of trekking, we reached Ashidowa-teri, the village where a number of Yanomami had been injured when Chagnon's helicopter blew away a roof. They were living in what looked like woefully inadequate lean-tos, and they were the most sickly, dispirited Yanomami I had seen in Venezuela. As soon as we entered their clearing, a man grabbed by hand, held it to his feverish forehead, and cried, "*Hariri!*" ("Sickness.") Many of the people had painted their faces black, in mourning, and most of the children looked malnourished.

At night, in the firelight of circled hearths, the Yanomami sang about the mysterious arrival of the helicopters and their strange riders. Then the people around the campfires began mourning for their departed kin. The headman, Mirapewe, said to me, "If you could count the dead, you would see how many of us there were."

Jungle Fever

Lately I've been engrossed in—and in some sense involved in—the most sensational scandal to emerge from academia in decades. The scandal erupted last month when two anthropologists, Terry Turner and Leslie Sponsel, sent a searing letter to the president of the American Anthropological Association. The letter distilled a series of chilling "revelations" made by the journalist Patrick Tierney in his forthcoming book *Darkness in El Dorado: How Scientists and Journalists Devastated the Amazon*. According to Turner and Sponsel, the scandal unearthed by Tierney, "in its scale, ramifications, and sheer criminality and corruption," is "unparalleled in the history of Anthropology." Turner and Sponsel listed a horrifying series of crimes—"beyond the imagining of even a Josef Conrad (though not, perhaps, a Josef Mengele)"—including genocide, allegedly committed by U.S. scientists against the Yanomamö, an indigenous people living in the Venezuelan and Brazilian rain forest.

Turner and Sponsel's letter spread like a virus over the Internet, quickly driving the controversy into the mainstream press. A story in Britain's *Guardian* —"Scientist 'killed Amazon indians to test race theory'"—was followed by accounts in *Time* and the *New York Times,* on NPR's [National Public Radio's] *All Things Considered,* and so on. The accusations drew strength from two institutions that endorsed Tierney's credibility: *The New Yorker,* known for its obsessive fact-checking, published an adapted excerpt from the book;... and the fact that the book is scheduled for publication... by W.W. Norton, which is highly respected by academics.

Prepublication galleys of the book show why it inspired such trust. Tierney's argument is massively documented, based on hundreds of interviews, academic articles, and items uncovered under the Freedom of Information Act, not to mention his own visits among the Yanomamö. Through 10 years of dogged sleuthing, it would seem, Tierney dragged a conspiracy of military, medical, and anthropological wrongdoing into the light. [In October 2000], when finalists for [the] year's National Book Awards were announced, *Darkness in El Dorado* was listed in the nonfiction category.

There is only one problem: The book should have been in the fiction category. When examined against its own cited sources, the book is demonstrably, sometimes hilariously, false on scores of points that are central to its most sensational allegations. After looking into those sources, I found myself seriously wondering whether Tierney had perpetrated a hoax on the publishing world. Of course, only he knows whether he consciously set out "to trick into believing or accepting as genuine something that is false and often preposterous"—the dictionary definition of a hoax. But the book does seem systematically organized to do exactly that. And, to a frightening extent, it has succeeded.

The accusations are directed primarily against James Neel, a physician and a founder of modern medical genetics (now dead), and Napoleon Chagnon, perhaps the world's most famous living social anthropologist. Tierney describes Neel as an unapologetic "eugenicist" who believed as a "social gospel" that "democracy, with its free breeding for the masses and its sentimental supports for the weak" is a eugenic mistake.

Tierney argues that, starting in the 1960s, Neel and his researchers were funded by the Atomic Energy Commission to conduct horrifying medical "experiments" on the Yanomamö. Far and away the most serious allegation is that the researchers killed hundreds or even thousands by knowingly releasing a contagious measles virus into the previously unexposed Yanomamö population. As Turner and Sponsel put it, "Tierney's well-documented account... strongly supports the conclusion that the epidemic was in all probability deliberately caused as an experiment designed to produce scientific support for Neel's eugenic theory." Chagnon—described by Tierney as a "disciple" of Neel's —was implicated in this crime and charged with inadvertently bringing other devastating diseases as well. What's more, Chagnon was said to have been the main cause of the violence he saw among the Yanomamö and more generally to have twisted his scholarly portrayal of them to bolster his Hobbesian theories of human nature.

I was an early recipient of this ethics complaint, in that small number of Internet nanoseconds when it was still considered confidential. As president of the Human Behavior and Evolution Society, of which Chagnon was a prominent member, I was obliged to investigate the allegations, just as the American Anthropological Association would be doing. Chagnon had been my departmental colleague since I moved to the University of California, Santa Barbara, a decade ago, and I consider him a friend. But I'd never met Neel, and for all I knew, he really was a eugenics crackpot, exploiting the isolation of his field site in some warped way. And as for Chagnon—well, how much do we really know about the person in the next office?

Starting with the most serious charge—genocide—I looked up what Neel himself wrote about the measles epidemic. Tierney alleged that a measles vaccine Neel's team administered to the Yanomamö, Edmonston B, was a dangerous agent—and was known to be so at the time—and triggered the epidemic. In Neel's account (a cover-up?), what Tierney finds suspicious—that a measles outbreak started around the time Neel first administered the vaccine—has a different explanation: After Neel learned about the incipient outbreak, he started vaccinating people, trying furiously to head off an epidemic.

To my nonspecialist ears, Tierney's theory sounded possible: Many vaccines, including measles vaccines (then and now), use attenuated live virus, which, when injected, gives the recipient an infection that is supposed to stimulate the immune system. So why couldn't a live virus have spread contagiously from Yanomamö to Yanomamö, launching a deadly epidemic?

I started putting in calls to the Centers for Disease Control and Prevention [CDC] in Atlanta. Conversations with various researchers, including eventually Dr. Mark Papania, chief of the U.S. measles eradication program, rapidly discredited every essential element of the Tierney disease scenarios.

For example, it turns out that researchers who test vaccines for safety have never been able to document, in hundreds of millions of uses, a single case of a live-virus measles vaccine leading to contagious transmission from one human to another—this despite their strenuous efforts to detect such a thing. If attenuated live virus does not jump from person to person, it cannot cause an epidemic. Nor can it be *planned* to cause an epidemic, as alleged in this case, if it never has caused one before.

Experts elsewhere have confirmed this—and have confirmed the safety of the Edmonston B vaccine under the conditions in which it was used. All told, the evidence against Tierney's genocide thesis is now so overwhelming that even Turner, its once-enthusiastic supporter, has backed off. He concedes that the medical expert he finally got around to consulting took Tierney's medical claims and "refuted them point by point."

You'd think the Tierney book, 10 years in the making, might mention the relevant and easily discoverable fact that, as the Michigan medical report puts it, "live attenuated vaccine has never been shown to be transmissible from a recipient to a subsequent contact." Somehow it omits it (even though this information is featured prominently in a paper Tierney cites five times!). The *New Yorker* piece also fails to mention it and instead says, "Today, scientists still do not know whether people who have been vaccinated with Edmonston B can transmit measles." This is literally true, but only because scientists use the word *know* very carefully. Scientists also do not *know* that *The New Yorker* is not riddled with a cult of pedophilic Satan worshipers or that the Pentagon is not in the control of extraterrestrials masquerading as generals. If you ask a *good* scientist about each of these allegations, she would be forced to answer, yes, it's possible. But she will consider it relevant and worth mentioning, as *The New Yorker* does not, that the failure to substantiate a hypothesis given millions of opportunities floats the hypothesis out toward the scientific neighborhood inhabited by ESP and UFOs.

Once I had seen Tierney's most attention-getting claim crumble, I started through the galleys of his book systematically, evaluating it against available sources with the help of various colleagues. Almost anywhere we scratched the surface, a massive tangle of fun-house falsity would erupt through.

We had to accept from the outset that scores of conversations reported in the book are with people scattered through the rain forest, virtually impossible to contact (even for *The New Yorker*'s energetic fact-checkers). So Tierney's veracity would have to be judged on the basis of sources that could be reached. I had already run into one such source—Papania of the CDC, whom Tierney had interviewed for the book. Papania told me that he was troubled to find, in galleys he'd recently been sent, that Tierney had misquoted him. Tierney had him endorsing the idea that the vaccine was a plausible cause of the epidemic, which was not, in fact, his view.

It soon became evident that Tierney was no more faithful to written sources than to oral ones. To begin with, comparing Neel's autobiography with Tierney's use of it is an education in audacity. Whatever Tierney might have wished to convey by calling Neel a "conservative" and claiming that "Neel's politics were too extreme for Reagan's council on aging," Neel's book shows him to be a supporter of Al Gore ("superb," "the most hopeful recent sign"), a Reagan-Bush basher ("chilling," "myopic"), pro-nuclear-disarmament, and an enthusiastic environmentalist. Neel's conflict with the advisory council on aging, it turns out, came when he objected to the diversion of money from poor children into research on how to artificially extend the human life span—research that, Neel speculated, would wind up benefiting mainly the affluent.

And what of Tierney's claim that Neel was a "eugenicist" who believed as a "social gospel" that "democracy, with its free breeding for the masses and its sentimental supports for the weak" was a eugenic mistake? It turns out that Neel had been a fierce opponent of eugenics for 60 years, since his student days. To dramatize his opposition, he labeled his beliefs *euphenics*, emphasizing the medical and social importance of environmental interventions. As Neel put it, the "challenge of euphenics is to ensure that each individual maximizes his genetic potentialities" through the creation of environments in which each can flourish, and "to ameliorate the expression of all our varied genotypes"— ameliorate the *expression* of our genes, not the genes themselves. Neel lists, as examples of good social investments, prenatal care, medical care for children and adolescents, good and equal education for all children, and so on.

There is not a word on any of the pages Tierney cites about how "democracy... violates natural selection." Indeed, though worried about overpopulation, Neel argues that there is no scientific or moral basis for preventing anyone from being a parent, and he says that guaranteeing the equal rights to reproduce would "preserve insofar as it's possible all of [our species'] poorly understood diversity." Neel even does an extended calculation to debunk the eugenicist fear that reproduction by those with genetic defects threatens the gene pool!

Neel does analyze, in the standard way population geneticists do, how unfavorable genetic mutations were "selected out" more rapidly before the invention of agriculture and subsequent creature comforts, and before the transition from polygamy to monogamy (which slows the form of natural selection known as "sexual selection"). Here, as elsewhere in the book, Tierney works feverishly to erase the simple distinction—basic to all scientific discussion— between describing something and endorsing it. In this case, it was a difficult erasure, since Neel, far from wanting to return humanity to a lost world where natural selection is more intense, had called this "unthinkable." (Incidentally, if you're wondering why Neel might have found a measles epidemic useful as a test of his supposed eugenic theories, as Tierney claims, the answer is that Tierney never provides a coherent explanation.)

This pattern of falsification—of which I have mentioned only a small sampling—extends to Tierney's assault on Napoleon Chagnon. To begin with, Tierney—like some other Chagnon critics—carricatures Chagnon's view of human nature, as if Chagnon considered people innately violent, period. In reality, Chagnon, pondering the relative rate that "people, throughout history, have based their political relationships with other groups on predatory versus religious or altruistic strategies," concludes that "we have the evolved capacity to adopt either strategy," depending on what our culture rewards.

Still, there's no doubt that Chagnon has a more Hobbesian view of human nature than is popular in most anthropological circles. Tierney claims that Chagnon, to support this view, exaggerates Yanomamö violence. He doesn't mention the fact that the rates of violence Chagnon documents are not high compared with the rates found by anthropologists in other pre-state societies. Nor does he mention Chagnon's view that, if anything, the Yanomamö's rate of lethal violence is "much *lower* than that reported for other tribal groups."

Not only does Tierney generally ignore inconvenient data, citing only anthropologists who disagree with Chagnon. He also, time and again, has a way of magically turning anthropologists whose data support Chagnon into anthropologists who contradict him. For example, Tierney cites a study of the Jivaro by Elsa Redmond that he claims undermines one of Chagnon's Yanomamö findings: that the effective use of violence contributes to social status, the acquisition of multiple wives, and the having of many offspring.

Here is Tierney's summary of Redmond:

> Among the Jivaro, head-hunting was a ritual obligation of all males and a required male initiation for teenagers. . . . Among the Jivaro leaders, however, those who captured the most heads had the fewest wives, and those who had the most wives captured the fewest heads.

Here is what Redmond actually says:

> Yanomamo men who have killed tend to have more wives, which they have acquired either by abducting them from raiding villages, or by the usual marriage alliances in which they are considered more attractive as mates. The same is true of Jivaro war leaders, who might have four to six wives; as a matter of fact, a great war leader on the Upano River in the 1930s by the name of Tuki of José Grande had eleven wives. Distinguished warriors also have more offspring, due mainly to their greater marital success.

Similarly, Tierney cites anthropologist John Peters at various points in his argument that Chagnon exaggerates Yanomamö violence. But what Peters actually writes in his book *Life Among the Yanomamo* is far stronger than anything Chagnon has written: "Anyone who is even minimally acquainted with the Yanomami is familiar with the central role of war in this culture. Violence seems always just a breath away in all Yanomami relations."

Throughout the book, Tierney is comically self-aggrandizing, often presenting as his own discoveries things plainly described in Chagnon's publications. After complaining that Chagnon concealed the identity of villages from which some of his more controversial data were drawn, Tierney writes, "It took me quite a while to penetrate Chagnon's data, but, by combining visits to the villages in the field with GPS [Global Positioning System] locations and mortality statistics, I can identify nine of the twelve villages where all the murderers come from in his *Science* article." Or, if he didn't want to do all that walking and calculating, he could have gotten this information by consulting sources listed in his own bibliography, such as a 1990 Chagnon article and Chagnon's *Yanomamo Interactive* CD.

Although Tierney's many misrepresentations are riveting, his omissions are equally important—and harder for fact-checkers to spot, since omissions don't have footnotes. They figure centrally in two of Tierney's core accusations: that Chagnon inadvertently introduced various diseases besides measles into the region just by going there; and that Chagnon, by giving pots, machetes, and other steel tools to the Yanomamö, somehow exacerbated the rate of warfare, thus influencing the very data he gathered.

Both of these claims are logically possible. But Tierney fails to mention some relevant facts (well known to him) that call them into question.

Tierney presents the Yanomamö as if they were isolated in a petri dish, except when Chagnon visited and sneezed. In reality, the Yanomamö are tens of thousands of people, surrounded by other people with real diseases who have regular transactions with them. Moreover, this 70,000-square-mile area is penetrated by thousands of non-Yanomamö: missionaries, gold miners (over 40,000), highway workers, government officials, tin miners, loggers, ranchers, rubber tappers, drug smugglers, soldiers, moralists like Tierney, and on and on. This whole area is beset by epidemics of various kinds, as the Yanomamö tragically encounter diseases from the industrialized world. So, the probability that Chagnon or Neel or Tierney in particular is the source of any specific epidemic is, crudely speaking, one divided by these tens of thousands. Yet Tierney strangely insists that disease, like war, somehow specifically dogs Chagnon's movements.

To reliably identify the major sources of disease, one would need to collect demographic data in many villages and map it against the various forms of contact. As it happens, this is just what Chagnon did, and he gradually concluded that the Catholic missions were serious sources of disease, largely because of their regular roles as points of contact and entry. Yanomamö living at the missions benefited from the medical care, but those living close enough to catch their diseases yet too far to get the medical care suffered. When Chagnon saw the pattern, he blew the whistle. This did not endear him to the missionaries, who have ever since been the source of enough anti-Chagnon anecdotes to keep an enterprising journalist busy for years.

Similarly, Tierney says that competition over the pots and machetes and other steel tools that Chagnon gave the Yanamamö sometimes led to war. This too is logically possible. The Yanomamö certainly valued Chagnon's gifts, since cutting the jungle back for their crops was much easier with machetes. But Tierney fails to mention that Chagnon's contributions (made so that he would be allowed to collect data) were dwarfed by all the other sources of such items, such as the military, who hired Yanomamö laborers, and especially the vast mission system, which imports boatloads of machetes and other goods, and even has its own airline.

While Tierney considers Chagnon's distribution of steel tools an outrageous threat to peace, he amazingly gives a free pass to the introduction by others—including some missionaries—of hundreds of shotguns. These weapons are known to have been used by the Yanomamö in raiding from mission areas to the less well-armed villages where Chagnon worked. Chagnon blew the whistle on this, too.

In short, what Tierney leaves out of his story is that what his key sources have accused Chagnon of—causing disease and warfare—just happens to be what Chagnon had previously accused some of them of doing. Indeed, a prerequisite of Tierney's ability to do research in this restricted area was almost certainly his endorsement of one side in this feud. Tierney's translators, his guides, his selection of interviewees—all carry the strong implication that he received a guided tour drenched with these local politics. Throughout the book, Tierney goes to extraordinary lengths to explain away real causes of disease and violence that trace back to his patrons. (He has a whole appendix devoted to attacking evidence that the missionaries spread disease.) When this context is supplied, the unremitting denunciations of Chagnon start to sound different, and Tierney, *The New Yorker*'s intrepid "Reporter At Large," appears in a less flattering light.

Chagnon has made enemies in academia as well as in the rain forest. Anthropology is full of people who still subscribe to Rousseau's "noble savage" view of human nature, and their battles with Chagnon have been intense. That is why Tierney could pepper his *New Yorker* article, and his book, with anthropologists who question Chagnon's Yanomamö data—a technique of great rhetorical power unless you know about all the anthropologists Tierney doesn't mention whose data support Chagnon. Chagnon's longtime critics include Turner and Sponsel, a fact that explains their uncritical and hyperbolic embrace of the Tierney book, and a fact that isn't mentioned in their incendiary letter to the American Anthropological Association.

With experts increasingly coming forward to debunk various aspects of the Tierney book, the accusations against Neel and Chagnon "are crumbling by the hour," as it was put by Lou Marano of UPI, one of the few reporters to deeply examine the credibility of Tierney's charges. But much damage has already been done—and not just to the reputations of Neel and Chagnon. Tierney's claim that an immunization program can start an epidemic has been carried around the world in media reports. This myth could compromise the ability of health workers to administer such programs, especially in poor countries, and people could die as a result. Moreover, indigenous cultures will not benefit from the public's impression that they are endangered only by the occasional anthropologist, when in fact they are victims of far more powerful forces, ranging from well-meaning missionaries to untrammeled modernization.

The slow-motion tragedy of the world's indigenous peoples continues, and Tierney's thoroughly dishonest book is just one more exploitation of them.

POSTSCRIPT

Did Napoleon Chagnon and Other Researchers Harm the Yanomami Indians of Venezuela?

This controversy exposed a deep rift in the anthropological community. The rift has been variously defined as between those who see anthropology as a science and those who consider it a humanistic discipline, between sociobiologists and cultural determinists, and, at the basest level, between scholars who personally like or dislike Neel and Chagnon. The battle lines are sharply drawn, and few anthropologists have remained neutral. The antagonists are pulling no punches in their charges and countercharges.

The El Dorado Task Force of the A.A.A., which investigated Tierney's accusations, concluded, among other things, that Neel and his associates should be praised, not condemned, for vaccinating the Yanomami against measles, an action that "unquestionably... saved many lives" (see the *Final Report* on the A.A.A. Web site at http://www.aaanet.org). However, the task force criticized Chagnon on ethical and professional grounds for working with a group of wealthy and corrupt Venezuelans to gain access to the Yanomami in 1990, despite having been denied a research permit by the Venezuelan government. It also criticized him for misrepresenting the Yanomami as the "fierce people," a view used by others to justify violence against them, and for not correcting that image or supporting their human rights. Not surprisingly, the report has been criticized by Chagnon's supporters as too harsh and by his enemies as too lenient.

An extremely comprehensive and balanced guide to sources is the Web site of Douglas Hume, a graduate student at the University of Connecticut (http://www.anth.uconn.edu/gradstudents/dhume; click on "Darkness in El Dorado"). It includes a full list of articles published from September 2000 to the present, an extensive supplementary bibliography, and links to relevant Internet sites and documents. The paperback edition of Tierney's book contains an 11-page "afterward" responding to his critics. Other printed publications include Terry Turner's "The Yanomami and the Ethics of Anthropological Practice," Cornell University Latin American Studies Program Occasional Paper (vol. 6, November 2001) and the *Current Anthropology* forum entitled "Reflections on Darkness in El Dorado," which presents comments by six scholars (vol. 42, no. 2, 2001). A relevant earlier source is Leslie Sponsel's article "Yanomami: An Arena of Conflict and Aggression in the Amazon," *Aggressive Behavior* (vol. 24, no. 2, 1998).

ISSUE 15

Does It Matter if Nobel Peace Prize Winner Rigoberta Menchú's Memoir Contains Inaccuracies?

YES: David Stoll, from "The Battle of Rigoberta," in Arturo Arias, ed., *The Rigoberta Menchú Controversy* (University of Minnesota Press, 2001)

NO: Carol A. Smith, from "Why Write an Exposé of Rigoberta Menchú?" in Arturo Arias, ed., *The Rigoberta Menchú Controversy* (University of Minnesota Press, 2001)

ISSUE SUMMARY

YES: Anthropologist David Stoll argues that Rigoberta Menchú misleads readers of her book by implying that she experienced events to which she could never have been a witness. Contrary to what Menchú implies, he asserts that the guerrillas used violence to force otherwise complacent Mayan peasants to join their fight.

NO: Anthropologist Carol A. Smith contends that Menchú's misrepresentations are inconsequential. She states that what is more important is that Menchú's book was instrumental in drawing national attention to the plight of the Guatemalan Maya, who, Smith maintains, were ripe for revolution and eager to fight with the guerrilla army.

In 1983 Rigoberta Menchú Tum, a Guatemalan Maya peasant woman, published her autobiography, *I, Rigoberta Menchú* (Verso, 1984). This book graphically detailed the plight of indigenous Guatemalan Maya people, who faced oppression and racism at the hands of Guatemala's Ladino (non-Indian) minority. Civil war had been raging in Guatemala for 23 years (and would continue for another 13). Menchú had ties to groups like the Guerrilla Army for the Poor (EGP) and Guatemalan National Revolutionary Unity (URNG), who were fighting a guerrilla war against the Guatemalan National Army. The atrocities committed by the Guatemalan army are now well known, and Menchú's book further illustrates the brutal violence carried out by soldiers. Over 200,000

Guatemalans perished in the war, most of them Maya. *I, Rigoberta Menchú* speaks of the abject poverty, hunger, and racism Menchú encountered while growing up, the violent deaths of many in her own family (including her father, brother, and mother) at the hands of the army, and her own transformation into one of Guatemala's leading revolutionary figures. The book was instrumental in bringing international attention and aid to the Maya and in eventually bringing an end to the war. In 1992, Menchú was awarded the Nobel Peace Prize.

In 1998, David Stoll published his book *Rigoberta Menchú and the Story of All Poor Guatemalans* (Westview, 1999), which caused an angry response from many scholars. Stoll challenged the veracity of many events described in *I, Rigoberta Menchú*. For example, Menchú wrote that she had watched her younger brother Nicolás die of malnutrition while her family worked to feed themselves on a coffee plantation in southern Guatemala. But Stoll discovered that Nicolás is still alive, and in any event Menchú could not possibly have worked on such a plantation since at the time she was in boarding school. Menchú also described her father Vincente's struggle against wealthy Ladino landlords to gain title over the land he farmed. A land dispute had occurred, but Stoll learned that it was between Vincente and his in-laws and did not involve wealthy Ladinos whose gunmen threatened Vincente's family. In one of the most gruesome and memorable scenes in her book, Rigoberta wrote of the death of her brother at the hands of the army. She described how her brother and other revolutionaries were marched into the town square "bloated like bladders" from days of torture. They were doused with gasoline and burned alive. In reality, Menchú's brother was killed by the army, but he was never burned alive publicly in the manner Menchú describes.

In the following selection, Stoll argues that Menchú's untruths undermine her work and misrepresent the reality of most Maya. He contends that by representing herself as a sort of "composite Maya" with a "wider range of experiences than a single person could have," she wrongly suggests that all Maya were revolutionaries eager to fight with the rebels. Instead, Stoll contends that the Maya felt "trapped between two armies." If they did not support the guerrillas, they would die; if they did not support the National army, they would also die. He concludes that Menchú exaggerated and fabricated events to suit her own political needs and the needs of the guerrilla army, rather than offering an honest account of the lives of most Maya.

In a paper published soon the after release of Stoll's book, Carol A. Smith criticizes what she sees as Stoll's attempt to blacken Rigoberta Menchú's name. She argues that whatever the details of Menchú's actual life and that of her family, her book represents a greater historical truth: the plight of the Guatemalan Maya people. Whatever minor untruths Menchú may have fabricated, argues Smith, her book brought international attention to conditions in Guatemala. She also notes that *I, Rigoberta Menchú* is written as a *testimonio*, a genre of Latin American literature in which it is standard and appropriate for the experience of an entire group of people to be represented as if it happened to one individual.

The Battle of Rigoberta

... the critics have mixed their scholarly calling with their political beliefs, in the process converting oral literature—the most supple of genres and the most subject to personal invention—into an almost religious canon, bordering on the absolute. By delegitimizing every attempt at critical skepticism, they have obtained a contrary result: the status of the texts, specifically in this case that of Rigoberta Menchú, has actually become fragile, vulnerable to any misstep.

— Elisabeth Burgos (1999, 86)

For many of the contributors to [*The Rigoberta Menchú Controversy*], my decision to publish the problems with a beloved story is hard to fathom. The dismay is not surprising in view of how and why the Nobel laureate told her story and why I decided to challenge it. Rigoberta Menchú was not the first to tell us that the Guatemalan dictatorship of the early 1980s was slaughtering peasants. The story that she told and Elisabeth Burgos turned into a book was instead an answer to the question: Why should we care? About another far-off conflict in which people we don't know are being killed for reasons we don't understand.

The first-person nature of the story provided an immediacy and credibility that no other narrative style would have achieved. That is why the book has been so effective in spreading interest in Guatemala to wider circles, especially in colleges and churches. That is why it could not have been as effective as anything but eyewitness testimony—the kind of account that I demonstrate it was not. How can you question the eyewitness nature of Rigoberta's story without suggesting that she is guilty of a hoax, fraud, or lie? None of these labels is appropriate for a person telling how she lost three members of her family, but that is the implication. Once my book was translated into the column inches of journalism, the issue was the veracity of a Nobel laureate.

Ordinarily, cultural anthropologists such as myself are more interested in perspective than accuracy. That includes autobiographical accounts where partisanship is only to be expected. But in the case of *I, Rigoberta Menchú,* the story has been so appealing to foreigners that it has overshadowed other Mayan perspectives on the violence. I felt obliged to point out gaps between Rigoberta's story and that of neighbors because of the enormous authority that so many readers have attributed to it. If you take the book at face value, as an eyewitness account, you will probably conclude that guerrilla warfare in Guatemala grew out of peasants' need to defend themselves from intolerable conditions.

Because of the different story I heard from many peasants, this is what became the most important issue for me: Was the Guerrilla Army of the Poor (EGP) that Rigoberta joined, and whose version of events she gave us in 1982, an inevitable response by the poor to oppression? Should the conflict be understood primarily in social terms, as the inevitable outcome of centuries of oppression suffered by Guatemala's indigenous population? Or is it better explained on the political level, as the result of particular decisions made by particular groups including the U.S. government, the Guatemalan oligarchy, the Guatemalan army, and the opposition groups that decided to fight back with guerrilla warfare?

The Ixil Mayas whom I interviewed in the late 1980s had been a bastion of the largest of the three guerrilla groups, the EGP. Nearly everyone, including myself, assumed that the guerrillas had been a deeply rooted popular movement. If not, why would the army kill so many people? In the wake of repression, the EGP's support might seem impossible to gauge because survivors would be afraid to discuss it. This has become the most common rejoinder to my argument: that peasants were too repressed to say much about their experiences. Yet many Ixils were willing to acknowledge that they had supported the guerrillas. Some were also rather candid about the atrocities committed by the army, even in the late 1980s and early 1990s when they were still under army occupation.

Typically, Ixils said that the army had done most of the killing but blamed the guerrillas for being the first to show up in uniform with guns. If the EGP was to be believed, the Ixils were so oppressed that they had no choice but to join the insurgency. It is true that they were living under a dictatorship. Most were poor; many had suffered discrimination. When the EGP sent cadres into the area, some Ixils were eager to join. Many more were interested in the revolutionary message, of a Guatemala where they would enjoy the same privileges as wealthy ladinos. But the pre-EGP Ixils were not facing intense repression. Despite patronal backlashes, they were regaining control of local governments from ladinos. Although the region was policed by a dictatorship, it was not militarized, because the army had no reason to be there.

Once the EGP began to assert control, a succession of Ixils told me, they were on the horns of a dilemma. If they cooperated with the guerrillas, the army would kill them in droves. If they cooperated with the army, the guerrillas would kill them more selectively. They were "entre dos fuegos" (between two fires), the peasant expression I turned into the title of my much-excoriated *Between Two Armies in the Ixil Towns of Guatemala*. Once the army began to lash back at the guerrillas by punishing nearby civilians, in 1979–82, waves of Ixils joined the less homicidal EGP for protection. You can call this a popular movement if you want, but the connection with prewar political organizing was often weak.

My skepticism about why Ixils supported the guerrillas, and the anger of some of my colleagues that I expressed it, reflect the divide between *indígenas* and ladinos in Guatemalan life. On the national level, the guerrilla movement was a seemingly inevitable response to the 1954 CIA intervention and the right's destruction of democracy. But the leadership of the insurgency was urban and nonindigenous, with little participation by the country's Mayan population. Only in the late 1970s did the guerrillas recruit large numbers of Mayas. The most widely read account of that relationship is *I, Rigoberta Menchú*. So what do my interviews in Rigoberta's hometown tell us about the EGP's popular base there? Did her village join the guerrillas to defend itself from ladino landlords? Did many of her neighbors see the insurgency growing out of their own needs?

As I have often pointed out, oral testimony from a repressed town such as Uspantán could be affected by fear of the army or distrust of myself. That is why I checked what Uspantanos told me against land records and human rights reports. Judging from both kinds of information, the epic struggle against plantation owners in *I, Rigoberta Menchú* was actually an internecine conflict between K'iche' Maya in-laws. The first local political murders were committed by the EGP. These are mere details in terms of who bears responsibility for most of the subsequent killing—the army. But the import of Rigoberta's story is not just a detail, because it turned her family and village into model revolutionaries of the kind desired by the EGP.

Judging from her story, five hundred years of indigenous resistance to colonialism had finally joined the larger revolutionary struggle. She gave foreign readers a firm sense of which side they should be on, even though the divided feelings expressed by Victor Montejo in his less-read testimonio *Death of a Guatemalan Village* were probably more widespread. Certainly there was Mayan support for the EGP—lots in the Ixil area and some in Rigoberta's *municipio*. But most of it was rather brief, for a year or two, and Rigoberta was telling her story at its apogee. When Rigoberta's story acquired the permanence of a book—not the original purpose of the tape recordings, which were for a magazine interview—it became a rationale for guerrilla warfare that acquired more weight than the many forms of Mayan alienation from this strategy. Over the next decade, as foreign readers fell under the book's spell, it consecrated a brief period of support for the guerrillas at the height of peasant consciousness, the golden age of militancy.

Still, the result was not just an EGP script or fabrication. Even if you object to Rigoberta's approach, her story became a parable about the social context of the violence that is easy to defend as truthful. By claiming to have suffered in ways that she never had herself, Rigoberta turned herself into a symbol for an entire people. By blaming all the violence on the army, she targeted the side that did 93 percent of the killing, according to the UN truth commission.

The main problem with Rigoberta's story is not that she chose to communicate the problems facing Guatemalan Indians by turning herself into a composite Maya, with a wider range of experiences than a single person could have. It is not important if her relatives died a bit differently than she says they did. Even if readers should know that *I, Rigoberta Menchú* is not a literal account of her life, it is not hard to defend her narrative strategy because her most important claim is true—the Guatemalan army was indeed slaughtering defenseless villagers. In a crisis situation, Rigoberta was dramatizing herself the way a Hollywood scriptwriter might, to stir an audience and move it to care about far-off victims. What mattered most in 1982 was orchestrating international pressure against the Guatemalan army to stop the killing.

That said, there is a problem with Rigoberta's story. Arguably it was not a major problem in the early 1980s, when the killing was at its peak and what mattered most was drawing attention to a human rights emergency. But now that truth commissions are delivering reports, what may have been a secondary issue is no longer so. I refer to the social background of the killing, including how it spread to previously quiet areas. If you interpret Rigoberta's story as the eyewitness account that it claims to be, you will conclude that the rebel movement grew out of the basic needs of her people, which is not what many of them have to say about it.

My books are controversial because they take the intense localism that many anthropologists have found in rural Guatemala, then use it to challenge the assumption that the insurgency of the late 1970s and early 1980s was an inevitable Mayan reaction to oppression. That Mayas had very mixed feelings about the guerrillas is not a discovery made by myself. Although the EGP was stronger in Rigoberta's region of the Sierra Cuchumatanes than in most others, a string of ethnographers ([e.g.,] Davis, Watanabe, Kobrak, Montejo) have had doubts about the depth of its support, as have Yvon Le Bot and Carol Smith. Because Smith misconstrues my argument, let me quote some of her previous writings on the subject:

1. Did support for the insurgency spring from the steady immiseration of the poor? "Obviously, then," she concluded from her surveys of the prewar peasant economy, "it is incorrect to describe as general a pattern of increasing impoverishment of peasant communities in this period [to 1978], though one could point to increasing penetration of market relations into the fiber of indigenous society.... Both individuals and communities generally reported a much lower dependence on plantation income than was formerly the case ... there was no general trend toward increasing dependence on plantation wages, no general impoverishment, relatively little internal class polarization, and much less destruction of indigenous community organization than would be expected from the usual accounts of the period." No one denies that most Mayas were poor, that some welcomed the guerrillas, and that more joined the insurgency to protect themselves from repression. However, the tapestry of conditions that Mayas faced was not compatible with the ideological justification for the high cost of armed struggle, that the Mayas were being impoverished en masse.

2. Was the insurgency a last resort for peasants who had no other way to defend themselves? The last-resort paradigm fits some local situations, but more broadly it is not compatible with what we know about the origins of the Maya movement, which is led by people who are taking advantage of expanding opportunities. Nor is the last-resort paradigm

compatible with the Maya movement's critique of the guerrillas as well as the army: that both sides imposed the war on Mayas. If the insurgency was an inevitable response to oppression, then ladino-led guerrilla organizations would not be guilty of imposing it. Here is what Smith had to say just as I was finishing *Between Two Armies:* "The guerrilla insurgency of the 1980s, in which many Maya participated, was not the kind of resistance described above—limited in goals, leaderless, localized. There was a clear strata of leaders, most of them middle- or even upper-class Ladinos, who had little experience with Maya culture or people.... From interviews with guerrilla leaders, as well as their own accounts, it seems fairly clear that they chose to recruit in the Maya area; Mayas did not seek out Ladino leaders for their own insurgency."

3. Should blame for starting the violence be laid exclusively at the door of the Guatemalan army? Here I must repeat what so many peasants told me: although the army did most of the killing, it was often the guerrillas who were the first to visit their villages, as part of their announced strategy of spreading the war to new areas. Returning to Smith: "Both [Mario] Payeras [of the EGP] and Gaspar Ilóm of the Revolutionary Organization of the People in Arms (ORPA) have discussed how difficult it was to enlist Maya, but how recruitment snowballed after army repression began. It is now widely recognized that many Maya joined the insurgency *after* they were attacked by the army for merely living in places the guerrillas visited. For these people, following the guerrillas into the montaña was little more than an act of self-preservation. We do not yet know what revolution meant to those who joined the insurgency as voluntary participants, since Maya accounts of the 1980s are mainly those of victims rather than rebels."

Contrary to Smith, our colleague Paul Kobrak was not the first to point out that "we're caught in the crossfire" rhetoric was a protective response to army repression. "Because so much coercion and concealment is involved in this kind of warfare," I noted in *Between Two Armies,* "how can we be sure that statements of neutrality or alignment with the army are anything but tactical, James Scott's 'public transcript' as opposed to a 'hidden transcript' of support for the guerrillas? ... At the most public level, that is, face to face with the army, Ixils mimic its rhetoric, as when civil patrollers volunteer that 'we're protecting our communities from the subversives.' Almost as public, that is, offered to just about anyone except perhaps an army officer, are protective statements of neutrality such as 'we're between two fires.' This is the safest possible presentation of self, the least compromising in many situations where one's interlocutor is not clearly marked politically. Needless to say, sharper feelings operate below the surface ... it was not hard to elicit frank descriptions of how the army imposed itself in the early 1980s, and few or none could be said to share the army's point of view. Even ex-army sergeants, civil patrol leaders, and military commissioners recounted their experiences from the in-between position of the beleaguered civilian."

Like Victor Montejo, Duncan Earle, and Mario Roberto Morales, Kay Warren appreciates the importance of debating the painful issues I raise. Was the "just war" of the disenfranchised Guatemalan left also a just war for the Mayan population that paid so much of the price? Does an anthropologist have a duty to report the kind of information that I discovered? I'm flattered by Warren's suggestion that *Rigoberta Menchú and the Story of All Poor Guatemalans* is an experimental ethnography. She is right that I adopted some of the conventions of the exposé genre, and her juxtaposition of it with the testimonial approach is interesting. However, she minimizes the defensive attitude about Rigoberta that more than a few Guatemala scholars have shown. If the essays from our colleagues Smith, George Lovell, and Christopher Lutz are not sufficient evidence, compare some of Warren's interpretations of what I wrote with what I actually wrote. Any reader of my two books about northern Quiché can verify that (1) I do not accuse Rigoberta of fraud; (2) I do not neglect the scholarly literature on Mayan communities; (3) I am not trying to discredit popular opposition to state violence; and (4) I have no objection to reading testimonial literature as a mediation between individual and collective veracities.

Far from seeking to discredit *I, Rigoberta Menchú* or testimonial literature, my book insists on interpreting it on the multiple levels that its significance requires....

[T]he laureate received the Nobel Peace Prize for her work as an indigenous human rights activist, not as an author. She and her editor Elisabeth Burgos-Debray were trying to persuade readers to stop massacres, not to create world literature. That they managed to do both is a huge accomplishment, but not one that can protect Rigoberta from obvious questions. The right to compare narratives about the violence cannot be confined to scholars with advanced training in literary theory. Human rights activists cannot hold the Guatemalan army to a factual standard while making excuses for the most widely read book about the conflict.

I would like to thank Arturo Arias for putting together [a] collection, as well as the contributors for taking the time to respond to my work. It is an honor to be the subject of a book, and I am sorry that the occasion requires me to point out its limitations. One is that few of the editorialists reprinted [in the collection] had read *Rigoberta Menchú and the Story of All Poor Guatemalans* before they damned or praised it. In particular, I should respond to an accusation that cannot be answered simply by referring readers to my book. It is that I "entered war zones in the friendly embrace of the army, interrogating—excuse me, 'interviewing' informants in the presence of armed soldiers." The author of this statement was the editor of [the] collection (Arias)....

It is not hard to see how some of the recrimination could have been avoided. In the realm of might-have-been, there could have been a less injured response to my first presentations to small academic gatherings a decade ago. Some of the contributors to [the collection] do not grasp that much of the scandal is over their own phobic reactions. The result was to discourage communication, convince me to undertake a major research effort, and encourage Rigoberta to think that she would never have to face certain facts about her life. It is much easier to defend the story that Rigoberta told in 1982 than some of the arguments in [the] collection. Like a Bill Clinton scandal, the denials and cover-ups are more consequential than the original transgression. Why didn't someone persuade her to preempt my findings with a well-timed statement? She was already preparing a new book about herself with the help of Dante Liano. Supposedly it was going to set the record straight. That is why I sent her a complete draft of my book in June 1997, to spell out what she would have to deal with. The only response was a delivery receipt from the post office.

When the scandal broke, Rigoberta countered that challenges to her story were an attempt to discredit all victims of the violence. Except for a few admissions in press conferences, this was her main response, and it was a popular one with many of her supporters, who decided that questioning her 1982 story was tantamount to defending the Guatemalan army. In the national press the bulk of the editorializing was against me, not her, with the implication that there was no need for Guatemalans to read my work. To make sure that they will not have the chance, some of Rigoberta's supporters pressured the Mayan publishing house Editorial Cholsamaj into killing its Spanish edition of my Ixil book.

Many have asked why I published the Rigoberta book just before the report of the truth commission—was I trying to discredit it? My book appeared when it did because it took two years and more than thirty queries to find a publisher, even in the North American academic presses. Finding a publisher for the Spanish translation has been impossible. For some of the contributors..., there never has been a good time to compare Rigoberta's story with that of her neighbors, and there probably never will be. Had I agreed to talk to the *New York Times* in October 1990, I would be responsible for adding to the backlash against political correctness. Two years later, had I not declined comment to Tim Golden of the *Times,* I would have been guilty of discrediting the Nobel award. Had I published my findings prior to the signing of the peace agreement, I would have deflected international pressure on the Guatemalan army. Now that the reports of the two truth commissions are being digested, I am sabotaging them. If I waited longer, I would be distracting attention from the latest human rights trial or wrecking Rigoberta's bid to become president of Guatemala.

Fortunately, the controversy over my book did not divert attention from army atrocities or shatter the human rights consensus. The *New York Times* soon devoted more column inches to the truth report and a massacre exhumation than it did to Rigoberta's veracity. The indictment against the army does not depend on a story that was told eighteen years ago. Exhumation teams are digging up more evidence every month. In May 1999 the U.S. government released documents in which the army listed how it disposed of 183 kidnapping victims. Soon Rigoberta persuaded a Spanish court to indict General Efraín Ríos Montt and two other former Guatemalan dictators for genocide, terrorism, and torture.

Of the possible costs of my book, the one I take most seriously is that of depriving Mayas and other Guatemalans of a national hero. Until the press reaction to my book, I could not be sure that there would be much wounded feeling because Rigoberta had become so unpopular with her allies in the Maya movement and on the left. By the late 1990s it took some effort to hear anything but complaints about her, usually for being peremptory and unreliable. Perhaps because she receives such an uncritical reception abroad, she still spends much of her time there and is often criticized for failing to recommit herself to Guatemala. Significantly, however, the criticism focuses on Rigoberta as a person, not as a symbol for victims of the violence. The reaction against my unread book helped her overcome some of the enmities she faces, but the relief is probably only temporary. As Diane Nelson has pointed out, jokes about the laureate condense the ambivalence of Guatemalans over their ethnic, gender, and national identities. Feelings about her have become barometric.

There is no need to apologize for Rigoberta's stature. Nobel Peace prizes are not a reward for personal virtue. You get one because it serves a larger purpose in the opinion of the Norwegian social democrats on the Nobel committee. Once that is understood, it was clearly a good idea to give Rigoberta the 1992 prize, regardless of what you think about the guerrilla movement. Internationally, the prize increased pressure on the Guatemalan power structure to make concessions to a rather weak opposition. Even now, the upper class has to face the fact that the Guatemalan with the most name recognition in the world is a Mayan woman from a peasant village. At least in human rights symbolism, the first is last, and the last is first. The award told the upper class that it could not regain international respect without acknowledging the rights of the poorest Guatemalans. . . .

Using *I, Rigoberta Menchú* to canonize the revolutionary political claims of the early 1980s does not leave enough room for how many victims of the violence feel about it. If the story told in Paris remains sacrosanct, it will perpetuate a colonialism of images in which one person is held to be the indispensable intermediary between Mayas and the international community. Within Guatemala, Mayan intellectuals know that they do not have to fall into line behind a single leader; why do they still think they must on the international level? Perhaps this is what Rigoberta's foreign admirers have unwittingly communicated.

The most constructive suggestion in the controversy over my book has been made by the anthropologist Gary Gossen. In the Mexican state of Chiapas, according to Gossen, Mayas are reading *I, Rigoberta Menchú* as a charter text, one that speaks to their identity as a people even though, strictly speaking, it is not about them. This is also how many Mayas in Guatemala hear the laureate's story. Because of the almost biblical power of the narrative, about a village girl who loses her parents to the army, flees abroad, tells the world what happened, and returns home in triumph, one woman's story becomes the story of a people.

Maybe it is time to liberate *I, Rigoberta Menchú* from the category of testimonio, which by its very name will continue to arouse expectations of eyewitness truth that this particular example cannot withstand. Let us instead think about Gossen's suggestion to teach Rigoberta's story as an epic. And not just for Mayas, as no small number of ladinos also identify with it. According to Gossen, epic narrative is about a time of tribulation; has a basis in historical fact; is told from a very partisan point of view; yet becomes a charter for a broader identity. An epic is, by the nature of its appeal, more or less beyond refutation for those who find it meaningful. But that does not mean that we should avoid historical exegesis of it. If *I, Rigoberta Menchú* is becoming national scripture for Mayas and other Guatemalans, that is all the more reason for scholars to be producing the historical criticism for which they will be asking us.

NO

Carol A. Smith

Why Write an Exposé of Rigoberta Menchú?

In the preface and first chapter of his book, David Stoll notes the following about Rigoberta Menchú's book. "There is no doubt about [her] most important points: that a dictatorship massacred thousands of indigenous peasants, that the victims included half of Rigoberta's immediate family, that she fled to Mexico to save her life, and that she joined a revolutionary movement to liberate her country." She is only misleading or wrong about the "situation of her family and village life before the war," as well as about her presence at some of the situations she describes. He adds, "most of the pressure that forced the army and the government to negotiate [with the guerrilla, leading to a peace accord at the end of 1996] came from abroad, and it was generated by human rights imagery" in which Rigoberta's book played an extremely important role. After these concessions, Stoll asks, "if Rigoberta is fundamentally right about what the army did, if her story expresses a larger truth about the violence, why dissect a personal account that is inevitably selective?" He answers his question with the following four points.

First, the catastrophes that befell Rigoberta's family, her village, and other indigenous villages in western Guatemala were brought on by the revolutionary guerrilla as much as by the army. In the particular case of Rigoberta's village, Rigoberta's father, Vicente, appears to have invited the guerrilla there—or at least to have received them warmly. Hence the targeting of him and his family by the army was quite natural. In the case of Vicente Menchú's death through conflagration at the Spanish embassy, it may be that the victims (who were protesting army murders of their relatives) immolated themselves. More generally, guerrillas pursue "a high-risk strategy that usually ends in defeat and disillusion, after sacrificing peasants to romantic images of resistance." Despite Stoll's previous efforts to make this general point about guerrilla warfare in his first book on Guatemala, few seem to have paid much attention—because of the influence of Rigoberta's book, according to Stoll.

Second, Rigoberta's testimony suggests that there was powerful support among indigenous people for the guerrilla, when in fact support was very weak. In this way Rigoberta played a major role in mythologizing the popular roots of

From Carol A. Smith, "Why Write an Exposé of Rigoberta Menchú?" in Arturo Arias, ed., *The Rigoberta Menchú Controversy* (University of Minnesota Press, 2001). Originally published in *Latin American Perspectives* (November 1999). Copyright © 1999 by Latin American Perspectives, Inc. Reprinted by permission of Sage Publications, Inc. and the author. Notes and references omitted.

Guatemala's revolutionary movement. Although dissecting the legacy of guerrilla warfare may require "beating a dead horse"—since even leftists no longer support a guerrilla strategy—Stoll feels it must still be done because Che Guevara and the third-world guerrilla continue to provide a romantic legacy to Western solidarity types and to the middle-class urbanites of the third world—giving them the illusion that they could wield real political power in an unjust world. More important, Rigoberta has displaced authentic indigenous perspectives about the violence—most of which equate the guerrilla with the army. "Rigoberta's version [of events] was so attractive to so many foreigners that Mayas who repudiated the guerrillas were often ignored or discounted."

Third, Rigoberta's story depicts "noble Indians [being dispossessed by] evil [Ladino] landlords ... [which has] encouraged the Guatemalan Left and its foreign supporters to continue viewing the countryside as a contest among social classes, ethnic blocs, and structural forces." But the real problems of peasant villages are not these. Most contestation over land is not between Indians and large Ladino landholders but *among* Indian smallholders. The poverty of those peasant villages is brought on by the indigenous livelihood practices, which involve

> a degenerative process of population growth, slash-and-burn agriculture, and migration [to frontier areas] that is complicated, but not altered in any fundamental sense, by the Ladino-indígena conflict and inequitable land tenure to which Rigoberta gives so much attention. Romanticizing peasants is a hoary tradition that has the virtue of dramatizing their right to their land.

Fourth, in the world of human rights activism, journalism, and scholarship, a "new standard of truth" is forcing Westerners to cede authority to the non-Western subaltern and to local witnesses—that is, to people such as Rigoberta—and thus to support those who are invariably apologists for one side or another in situations that cannot be reduced to two sides. Created under the influence of multiculturalism, postmodernism, and postcolonialism, this new criterion for veracity has discredited "objective" portrayals of complex situations. "The underlying problem [with Rigoberta's book] is not how Rigoberta told her story, but how well-intentioned foreigners have chosen to interpret it." She is taken as the only authentic voice on "all poor Guatemalans" because as an Indian, a woman, and a poor Guatemalan, she (unlike Stoll) represents the "new standard of truth."

Given that Rigoberta and her story on the violence in Guatemala have been granted more authority in the West than David Stoll and his story, Stoll had to discredit her if he was to make his point. So I will take Stoll's arguments seriously and evaluate exactly what Stoll wants to assert in contradistinction to Rigoberta: that is, about guerrilla warfare, indigenous support for revolution in Guatemala, the extent of and reasons for indigenous poverty, and the impact of multiculturalism and the "new standards of truth" on the nature of reportage. We will also have to consider what exists in the way of evidence for the two positions. We cannot go to the same eyewitness (or hearsay) accounts Stoll used. But we can go to other accounts—not on the truthfulness of Rigoberta's testimony (which Stoll concedes "expresses a larger truth about the violence"), but on Stoll's points about the economic and political situation in Guatemala —the reasons he gives for writing his exposé of Rigoberta Menchú.

1. Did Guatemala's guerrillas recklessly target those indigenous areas least able to defend themselves? Were the guerrillas responsible for the brutal massacres carried out by the Guatemalan military governments? Can one equate the guerrilla and the army as two similar sources of violence affecting peasants? Stoll documents two guerrilla killings to nearly one thousand army killings in the *municipio* where he interviewed Rigoberta's neighbors and family members (Uspantán), which would lead most of us to wonder about the disparity. Stoll also wonders about it. After rejecting the argument of racism (which many specialists on Guatemala consider a powerful factor influencing Guatemalan violence over the years, he argues that the "fanatical anti-communism of Guatemala's government that allowed it to slaughter so many men, women, and children could not have happened without the spectre of foreign communism as provided by the revolutionary theatrics from Cuba." And because insurgents muddy the distinction between themselves and noncombatants, according to Stoll, "brutality toward civilians is the predictable result." He does not ask why civilian massacres by armies were *much* less common everywhere else in Latin America where guerrilla warfare was waged—as in El Salvador and Nicaragua....

So who is at fault for the murders and exile of more than 150,000 Mayan peasants in Guatemala? Most experts on Guatemala consider the army responsible, especially because it showed a consistent tendency to avoid encounters with the guerrilla, preferring to attack unarmed civilians. I can think of no one other than Stoll who would blame persons like Vicente Menchú, even if he were a "guerrilla collaborator." Many solidarity types blame the Cubans as much as Stoll does, but for reasons quite different from Stoll's—the Cuban failure to arm the Guatemalans. Guatemalan insurgents were not supplied with the arms they expected from the Cubans, unlike the insurgents in Nicaragua and El Salvador. The fact was enormously important to the fate of Guatemala's revolutionary movement, especially its ability to "protect" its peasant recruits. Those who know Guatemalan politics well blame the United States for replacing one of Guatemala's first democratically elected governments with a lawless military government in 1954, instilling Guatemalan elites with an enormous fear of "communism" together with the certainty that the United States would do whatever needed to support them against communism, that is, helping to arm, train, and provide intelligence to what had formerly been a poorly organized army, and advising that army about guerrilla counterinsurgency techniques— such as drying up the ocean (killing civilians) to eliminate the fish (the guerrilla). (Stoll occasionally mentions U.S. guilt in the situation, but invariably undercuts it.) There are, it would seem, a surplus of people and groups to blame. I personally see the situation as a national tragedy that had been brewing ever since a military government took power in 1954. Military dictatorships motivated various forms of leftist protest, nonviolent as well as violent, and mark the period when death squads began to eliminate political activists, union leaders, indigenous leaders, and Christian Democrats. Many such murders occurred before there was a guerrilla presence. Racism accounts for the nature of the "final solution" in the 1980s—the huge massacres of indigenous people.

2. Let us now consider how much the peasants blame the guerrilla for what happened to them. Stoll bases his entire analysis of indigenous response to the guerrilla and army on information from four *municipios*—three in the Ixil area plus neighboring Uspantán, where Rigoberta's family lived. Hence I cannot use information I have about the impact of and support for guerrilla warfare in other parts of Guatemala (mainly Quezaltenango, Chimaltenango, and San Marcos), where circumstances were quite different. Instead, I use a recent Ph.D. study undertaken by Paul Kobrak in a *municipio* neighboring the Ixil, Aguacatán, to discuss changes in support for the guerrilla there. In some respects Paul Kobrak, whom Stoll seems to admire, is no more flattering to the guerrilla operating in Aguacatán (also the EGP) than Stoll is of those in the areas he covers. But he makes two extremely important points that Stoll fails to make. First, he observes that support for the guerrilla in the remote and very poor K'iché-speaking hamlets was initially quite strong, even though the guerrilla spent relatively little time in the area. Locals told him that the entire population could have gone either way—that is, with the guerrilla or with the army in mid-1982—but after careful consideration, as a group decided that it was much more dangerous to go with the guerrilla because of the greater army brutality. Nonetheless, a large number of them joined the CPRs (civilian resistance communities) in the Ixil area.

Second, and most important, Kobrak provides a historical context for the period when he was interviewing survivors in Aguacatán (roughly the same time Stoll was working in the nearby Ixil area). As Kobrak describes it, the male civilian population had been so militarized and exposed to army propaganda under the civil patrols (groups of village men made responsible for "protecting" their communities under the direction and control of the army) that they had significantly reconstructed their local history. Like Stoll, Kobrak notes the common use by villagers of the phrase "[we were] between two armies," but he observes that this local construction was a way for peasants in the patrols to "neutralize" their own position in the war:

> In the 1990s context in which I collected these reconstructions of the violence, the army was the preeminent power in Guatemala, having decisively defeated the guerrilla movement and established their civil patrols throughout the countryside. The army had committed far more abuse against the civilian population, but the army's victory made it easy (and satisfying) to vilify the rebels. With their participation in the civil patrol system [which involved carrying out many brutalities ordered by the army] villagers had a strategic and psychic need to justify collaboration with the army. Residents of civil patrol villages [and this included virtually all villages in the five *municipios* discussed here] are most comfortable with rhetoric that equates the two sides, putting them in the middle as unwilling participants in the war, as spectators to the repression, rather than as participants.

The point here is that in the late 1980s and 1990s it was virtually impossible to obtain a clear view of how villagers in the affected regions (where village civil patrols operated twenty-four hours a day from 1982 to 1996) viewed the guerrilla or the army. Historical memory in a time of extreme violence is volatile, all the more so when the victorious side takes direct control of village life. Almost certainly the victims of army brutality, who then had to become directly *complicit* in army brutallity, are going to put a different construction on their history, on the army, and on the guerrilla—who are blamed by the army for all of their suffering....

What most differentiates Kobrak from Stoll is that Kobrak makes it clear that indigenous peasants were not the dupes of either the army or the guerrilla. Many Indians supported the guerrilla, but changed their position when they saw what hapened to guerrilla supporters and sought army protection. Others were able to flee the country under guerrilla protection. Obviously, not all succeeded in finding protection. But according to Kobrak, the peasants had a fairly clear idea of what they were doing—they were not, as Stoll would have it, "lured into confronting the state" in the absence of knowledge about the state, which they had confronted in various ways for more than two hundred years....

3. The question now becomes, How intolerable was the poverty of Guatemalan Indians in the early 1980s and what were its causes? This is something on which institutions such as the World Bank have information and comparative statistics; the World Bank is also a good source for an evaluation of Guatemala's land distribution and its significance, because it rarely makes revolutionary recommendations. The World Bank reports in a study done just before the peace accords were signed, that on virtually every indicator of poverty (income, malnutrition, infant death, life expectancy, literacy) Guatemala was close to or the most poor of all Latin American countries in both time periods. In 1995, the poverty rate of all Indians was 93 percent, whereas the poverty rate of urban Ladinos was 40 percent. Even when they controlled for all the poverty indicators—such as rural locality and education— Indians had a 15 percent higher chance of being poor than Ladinos did. More than three-quarters of the indigenous population (81 percent) lived in "extreme poverty," defined as lacking the income needed to purchase sufficient food.

My own work before the violence showed (as Stoll notes) that many fewer indigenous people in the western highlands were migrating to the south coast to work seasonally for wages on plantations than before. But that does not mean that they were prospering. My work has always emphasized the significant differences between peasants in the periphery (most of highland San Marcos, Huehuetenango, and El Quiché, which includes the area covered by Stoll and Kobrak) and peasants in the core (the area near Quezaltenango). Virtually no peasants from the core had migrated to plantations since the 1960s, only peasants from the periphery. Commercial diversification occurred in both parts of western Guatemala in the 1970s, but large numbers of people from the periphery still worked on the plantations and many in the core were becoming increasingly indebted. The statistics on poverty from the World Bank, which covers both the previolence and postviolence periods, speak for themselves—*the majority of indigenous people were not getting enough food to eat!*

What about the causes of poverty? Was it limited indigenous access to economic and political power, caused by Ladino monopolies, which is what I argued? Was it the extremely unequal distribution of land, as Rigoberta argued? Or was it uncontrolled population growth among the Maya and their destructive farming practices, as Stoll argues? My data on 124 *municipios* in western Guatemala from 1976 showed a higher correlation between indigenous poverty and Ladino monopolies than with any other municipal variable (e.g., population density, place in region, average indigenous landholding, economic specialty). But Stoll could dismiss these data with the argument that I am simply another scholar who "views the countryside as a contest among social classes, ethnic blocs, and structural forces"—thus supporting the leftist interpretation of economic reality.

The World Bank highlights land distribution—which puts it in the same "structuralist" category Rigoberta is in. . . .

The World Bank's three main recommendations for dealing with poverty and inequality include providing greater access to land for the poor and supporting an increase in tax revenue to improve education (human capital) and infrastructure in the rural areas. There is no mention of introducing new ("less destructive") farming practices or population control measures, policy issues with which the World Bank is quite familiar.

If land distribution is as important as the World Bank (and Rigoberta) think, why do peasants fight each other over small amounts of it rather than fight the few major landowners in the country (only 2.5 percent of the farm owners own more than 65 percent of the land)? This is Stoll's question. By implication, the countless squabbles over small amounts of land waste time, energy, and resources that could be better spent in a more "rational" attack on the big landlords. Stoll apparently does not know what happens to peasants who attack major landlords in Latin America. Almost everywhere they end up in jail—if they are lucky; as often they end up dead. . . . Most of us who work with peasants do not assume, as Stoll believes we do, that peasants are noble. But we have discovered that they are relatively rational. I find it very odd that Stoll asks the questions he does about struggles between smallholders. Does he believe that his (weakly supported) argument that these struggles are more common than struggles against major landlords will prove that land inequality is not a major problem in Guatemala?

Stoll's claim that the real development issues in Guatemala are uncontrolled population growth and ecologically destructive farming practices is much more serious. He is quite right that Guatemala's (especially its rural, indigenous) population has a high rate of population growth. But what he appears not to appreciate is the difference between cause and effect. Most population experts believe that the underlying *cause* of high population growth is poverty and a primitive economy—where most income is made through expenditures of raw, unskilled labor. It is now well known that in economies where the rates of infant mortality, income inequality, *and land inequality* are low, where most children are sent to secondary school (true of a very small minority in Guatemala), and where most women work outside of the home (again, Guatemala's rate is very low), birthrates fell dramatically. In other words, transforming a country with a high population growth rate calls for a "revolutionary" economic reform that Guatemala may well never see—for the only political sector that has supported such an economic policy has been the left. Such a radical economic reform in Central America has been most fully achieved in Costa Rica (through land reform, high taxation, and high educational achievement), where the birthrate has significantly fallen. High birthrates are not a church or cultural problem, as Stoll implies. Catholic Italy currently has the lowest birthrate in the world, well below national reproduction.

A similar relationship exists, with some differences, between wealth and ecologically sound farming practices. Farmers have to be rich enough to be able to afford ecologically sound farming. Or they have to have been pushed out of full-time farming. The farmers of San Miguel Totonicapán, where no one has had enough land to be a full-time farmer for more than fifty years, are the only Guatemalan farmers I know who have the time to terrace, rotate trees over their fields, and use organic fertilizer. Those who are clearing new land in frontier areas (the situation of Vicente Menchú and others in areas that Stoll knows) are probably in the worst possible situation in this regard. They have insufficient labor, very little infrastructural support, and a pressing need to produce enough to keep their families alive each year. Under such circumstances, clear-cutting is typical—whether undertaken by a small-holding peasant or by a larger plantation. Regardless of whether peasants or plantations are the worst offenders in this situation, it seems rather bizarre to blame Guatemalan peasants for their poverty by noting their "destructive" farming practices (not to mention uncontrolled population growth). Stoll gives no review of the literature on either issue, and I very much doubt that his analysis of Guatemala's poverty would be accepted as it stands for an M. A. or Ph. D. by any social-science department emphasizing development issues. Blaming the victims for their poverty in the case of Guatemala also seems utterly gratuitous.

4. Objective reportage, according to Stoll, is no longer appreciated in the social sciences, heavily influenced by literary theory, postmodernity, and a general postcolonial or multicultural uncertainty about the trustworthiness of white first-world men. Witnesses who represent the subaltern—people like Rigoberta, who are from oppressed classes in third-world countries—are better sources on the oppressed and on the meaning of their lives than are outside reporters. This has given Rigoberta an "unfair" advantage over Stoll—the objective reporter, just trying to get at the truth. Perhaps the best response to this charge would be a brief synopsis of the discussion and debate around "situated knowledges" in feminist theory. This literature pointed out that men could not be trusted to represent women, that white women could not be trusted to represent black women, that anthropologists from the imperial centers could not be trusted to represent the "natives"—not because they were less "objective," but because everyone is positioned and situated in the world with bias so that they cannot fully see the reality of another world. The subaltern herself sees the world through a distinct positionality or bias and thus needs to be in dialogue with people and scholars who represent other positions and positionalities. Hence the encouragement by most contemporary scholars to bring

new and different voices into the canon that have not previously been represented—not just Marx, Weber, and Durkheim on oppression and exploitation, for example, but Marx, Weber, Durkheim, and Rigoberta.

Most scholars consider the argument about new voices, new ways of representing the world, new ways of seeing such things as truth and responsiblity to be a very progressive move. There may have been excesses. And it is not always a sure bet that the representative from the third world will have a more useful take on its problems than a representative from the first world. But David Stoll's very positionality in the debate he has set up between himself and Rigoberta Menchú makes it seem all the more important that Rigoberta exists as one (not the only) voice for "all poor Guatemalans," and that Stoll exists to represent the illusory truth of "objective" reportage.

I have used Rigoberta's book for many years in my classes and have always emphasized the phrase she uses on her first page: "[T]his is my testimony... [but] I'd like to stress that it's not only *my* life, it's also the testimony of my people.... My story is the story of all poor Guatemalans. My personal experience is the reality of a whole people." I tell my students to read the book as if it is a general rather than particular depiction of life in Guatemala, noting that in *testimonios* it is typical for a person to present the experience of a whole people as if it happened to a single individual—because that may be the only way outsiders can understand and emphathize with another way of life. Even though I do not teach—and I doubt many students go away with—the literalist reading that Stoll feels compelled to refute, my students learn a great deal about a life of poverty, politicization, and struggle in Guatemala by reading Rigoberta's book.

... [I]n most courses where various new subaltern or postcolonial voices are introduced, they are almost always introduced in dialogue with very different perspectives. In the future I will probably even introduce chapters from Stoll's exposé. The "postmodern and/or postcolonial" move to add new voices to our experience is not an attempt to *restrict* the repertoire of perspectives, it is an attempt to expand it to include voices never before represented. Only reactionaries in the academy object to this move.

One reason we now emphasize the complexity of truth and the need to hear many voices rather than a single "objective" source is that facts do not speak for themselves, they always have to be interpreted. Let me illustrate this point with one simple example from Stoll's book. Stoll asserts that Guatemala's conservatives immediately recognized the falsehoods in Rigoberta's testimony, and it is almost certainly "factually true" that most did reject her depiction of indigenous life in Guatemala from the beginning. But on what basis did they recognize falsehoods? What do Guatemala's conservatives know about Rigoberta's or Guatemalan peasant life? I was always shocked at how very little they knew. What makes Stoll think that their rejection of Rigoberta's testimony was anything other than a statement of their political convictions? To present conservative knowledge as some kind of bolstering "factual" evidence for his own position without any interpretation of who the characters are and why they believe what they do is quite ludicrous. It seems to be little more than a rhetorical device—of which there are a great many in Stoll's book. It nonetheless rests on an absurd kind of "truth."

For this reason, then, I have to conclude that if forced to take out one of the perspectives listed above from a course on Central America, it is more likely to be Stoll than any of the others. The reason is that he is the least clearly positioned of all the authors. He *is* positioned—having at least an antileft, antipostmodern, antistructuralist, and antisolidarity position—but he claims not to be positioned and then tries to bolster weak scholarship on the larger issues (Guatemala's guerrillas, historical memory, poverty and its causes, and multiculturalism) with spurious claims of objectivity on unrelated phenomena (who Rigoberta's father battled over land). Stoll basically produces a polemic about Rigoberta and his four issues, which comes less from scholarly conviction and more from personal frustration about losing a monopoly on authority. This, I think, explains why Stoll wrote an exposé of Rigoberta Menchú. One wonders if he will try to topple all the alternative voices on Guatemala with exposés.

Does It Matter if Nobel Peace Prize Winner Rigoberta Menchú's Memoir Contains Inaccuracies?

Despite the controversy provoked by Stoll's book, Rigoberta Menchú remains a national hero for many Guatemalans. The Nobel Peace Prize committee has come forward to state that there is no possibility of Menchú's prize being rescinded. It would seem that Menchú's status as a popular Maya leader as well as an internationally recognized human rights advocate remains untarnished, despite the doubtful veracity of some of the claims she makes in her book.

Menchú went on to produce a second book, *Crossing Borders* (Verso, 1998), which details her life after winning the Nobel Peace Prize. The decision to award the prize to Menchú was a significant event in the struggle for indigenous rights. In addition to drawing international attention to the human rights abuses in Guatemala, the prize forced the Guatemalan government to recognize Menchú and the peasants she represented as a viable political voice. Many upper-class Ladinos were incredulous that a poor Mayan woman could achieve such notoriety.

The debate surrounding Menchú's book has produced vibrant and heated anthropological criticism. The first academic forum on the debate appeared in the November 1999 issue of *Latin American Perspectives*. It included the essay by Smith, from which this selection has been taken, as well as articles by Stoll and Elisabeth Burgos-Debray (who compiled *I, Rigoberta Menchú* from tapes of her 1982 interviews with Menchú). Much of the work written on the Menchú controversy has centered upon the "primacy of larger truths" versus literal veracity of specific details. It has also been about whether or not the Guatemalan peasants were ripe for revolution (as Smith contends) or merely caught between two armies and forced into fighting (as Stoll suggests). Anthropologist Duncan Earle made several important points in an article published in a volume edited by Arturo Arias entitled *The Rigoberta Menchú Controversy* (University of Minnesota Press, 2001). This volume is the most comprehensive collection yet published about the Menchú controversy. Earle's essay sides with Stoll on two important points. He agrees that many facts in Menchú's book are fabricated and agrees that most Guatemalan peasants felt forced to join the conflict. But Earle takes issue with what he views as Stoll's obsession with the misrepresented facts in Menchú's life. Like Smith and many other Menchú supporters, he argues that the international attention that Menchú brought to the atrocities in Guatemala is far more important than "who died where."

Anthropologist John Watanabe, who has also worked in Guatemala, has written an important review article, "Silence and Solidarity Across a Watershed of War: The Heritage of U.S. Complicity in Guatemala," *American Anthropologist* (March 2002), which helps contextualize the debate in terms of United States, and especially CIA, involvement in the Guatemalan civil war.

Students may also be interested in *When the Mountains Tremble*, a 1984 documentary film from Skylight Productions loosely centered on Menchú's life, which appeared soon after the publication of her memoir.

ISSUE 16

Should Anthropologists Work to Eliminate the Practice of Female Circumcision?

YES: Merrilee H. Salmon, from "Ethical Considerations in Anthropology and Archaeology, or Relativism and Justice for All," *Journal of Anthropological Research* (Spring 1997)

NO: Elliott P. Skinner, from "Female Circumcision in Africa: The Dialectics of Equality," in Richard R. Randolph, David M. Schneider, and May N. Diaz, eds., *Dialectics and Gender: Anthropological Approaches* (Westview Press, 1988)

ISSUE SUMMARY

YES: Professor of the history and philosophy of science Merrilee H. Salmon argues that clitoridectomy (female genital mutilation) violates the rights of the women on whom it is performed. She asserts that this operation is a way for men to control women and keep them unequal.

NO: Professor of anthropology Elliott P. Skinner accuses feminists who want to abolish clitoridectomy of being ethnocentric. He states that African women themselves want to participate in the practice, which functions like male initiation, transforming girls into adult women.

For more than a century anthropologists have seen cultural relativism as an essential antidote to ethnocentrism, a perspective that evaluates and judges the practices of other peoples according to the standards and sensitivities of one's own culture. This issue raises questions about the boundaries and limits of the anthropologist's cultural relativism. By evaluating cultural practices in a culture's own terms, anthropologists have long defended cultural diversity and the general principle that dominant cultures should not force members of weaker cultures to abandon traditional customs and practices, simply because practices appear peculiar, bizarre, or wrong to those in power. But today the world is increasingly integrated, and a number of international organizations have emerged whose purpose is to defend a single universal vision of human rights. Few anthropologists would object in principle to the notion that human rights should be defended for all people, but universal moral codes also challenge the rights of cultural groups to be different.

In this issue two scholars debate whether or not anthropologists should interfere with the cultural practice, found in many parts of Africa and the Middle East, of clitoridectomy and infibulation, variously called female circumcision or female genital mutilation. The practice is typically part of female initiation ceremonies and takes different forms in different ethnic groups, varying from relatively minor surgery to the clitoris (clitoridectomy) to the complete surgical removal of the clitoris and much of the woman's external sexual organs, after which the vagina is sewn up, leaving only a small opening (infibulation).

Merrilee H. Salmon refers to this practice as female genital mutilation and argues that it is fundamentally wrong, a violation of a woman's human rights. She contends that the practice is part of a male-centered power structure, which allows men to control women. Although Salmon acknowledges that women often control the ritual and even the surgery, the practice of female circumcision nevertheless supports male dominance within the community. In her view this cultural practice is an immoral one, and anthropological calls for moral relativism in this case are fundamentally ill-founded.

Elliott P. Skinner counters that female circumcision is only found in African societies where male circumcision is also practiced. Both practices involve mutilation of the genitals and are the means of transforming male and female children into adult men and women, respectively. Skinner maintains that not only are the female rituals entirely in the hands of other women, but that the practices empower women within a society where men might otherwise dominate them. Feminists who argue that this practice is an example of male power over women, in his view, have got it wrong. Calls for the abolition of female circumcision began with Western missionaries who found the practice repugnant. He states that Africans supported female circumcision as a form of resistance to white domination, and in Skinner's view current calls from Western people for the abolition of this practice is another example of Western domination of African societies.

At issue here are several key questions: Is female circumcision morally repugnant? Should anthropologists defend it or work to stop it? How should anthropologists deal with such practices when they see them occurring in their village communities where they work?

Although this issue seems very narrowly focused on a particular traditional custom in only one part of the world, it has important general implications for cultural relativism and universal human rights. Should anthropologists defend cultural practices simply because they are traditional? Do anthropologists have a responsibility to help end practices that they find morally abhorrent? If so, whose moral notions should be followed? Is moral relativism fundamentally flawed, as Salmon asserts?

Merrilee H. Salmon

 **YES**

Ethical Considerations in Anthropology and Archaeology, or Relativism and Justice for All

Cultural Relativism and Ethical Relativism

Respect for the beliefs, practices, and values of other cultures, no matter how different from one's own, is a hallmark of anthropological wisdom. Franz Boas, the father of American academic anthropology, rejected invidious comparisons between European "high culture" and indigenous American languages, myths, art forms, and religions. Boas, dismissing absolute scales of cultural development such as those proposed by Condorcet and L. H. Morgan, insisted on studying the culture of each group in the context of its own historical development. Boas's work forms the historical basis for the anthropological doctrine known as *cultural relativism.*

Many anthropologists regard *ethical relativism* as an easy corollary of cultural relativism. I show that this view is incorrect. Cultural relativism does not entail ethical relativism; an anthropologist can consistently embrace cultural relativism while rejecting ethical relativism. As most anthropologists understand it, ethical relativism identifies the concepts of good and evil, or right and wrong, with what a particular culture approves or disapproves. Because ethical standards arise within particular cultures and vary from culture to culture, ethical relativists deny any extracultural standard of moral judgments. According to them, moral judgments of good or bad are possible only within a given culture, because such judgments refer only to compliance or noncompliance with that culture's norms.

The fact that a belief arises within a cultural context, however, does not imply that it can have no other basis. Although moral beliefs, like all other beliefs, arise within a given cultural setting, some of those beliefs may transcend the cultures in which they arise. Condemnation of murder and recognition of obligations to help others who are in extreme need, for example, are common to many cultures. Moreover, societies that differ in derivative moral judgments about marriage between close relatives frequently agree about more fundamental moral judgments, such as the immorality of incest. This modicum of moral consensus has encouraged some critics to try to refute ethical relativism by identifying a set of universally acceptable moral principles.

Whether universal agreement exists on any specific basic moral judgment is partly an empirical matter and partly dependent on how such terms as "murder," "cruelty," and "incest" are defined. Colin Turnbull's (1962) admittedly controversial studies suggest that the Ik do not embrace the most likely candidates for fundamental moral principles, on any reasonable definition of such principles. In Turnbull's account, the Ik provide a striking counterexample to general views that cruelty to children, for example, is universally condemned. Even if Turnbull's account is rejected, the search for moral principles that are both reasonably specific and universally acceptable is problematic.

The lack of agreement about principles, however, is not sufficient to demonstrate the truth of ethical relativism. What a culture regards as right or wrong conduct depends to some degree on both the members' factual beliefs about the state of the world and their beliefs about the likely consequences of their conduct. The absence of any universally accepted standards would support ethical relativism only if cultures that shared all the same factual beliefs and agreed about the consequences of particular behavior nevertheless disagreed in their ethical judgments. This situation has not been demonstrated. In fact, many apparent differences in ethical matters are resolved by bringing forth pertinent facts about the conditions under which moral choices are made. Even Turnbull (1962) goes to considerable trouble to show that severe hardship and deprivation of material resources in Ik society have altered their perceptions of reality. Whereas lack of universally accepted moral principles does not prove ethical relativism, however, neither would the universal acceptance of some specific moral principles disprove ethical relativism. The agreement could be accidental instead of arising from some feature of the human condition. Berlin and Kay's (1969) refutation of the relativism of color classification was convincing only because they were able to demonstrate the physiological—and thus cross-cultural—basis for color classification.

Ethical relativism apparently accords with anthropologists' determination to reject ethnocentrism and maintain a nonjudgmental stance towards alien cultural practices. Nevertheless, both anthropologists and philosophers have noted a serious problem with relativistic ethics: it seems to rule out condemning even such obviously immoral acts as genocide so long as they do not conflict with prevailing cultural norms. Ethical theories about what constitutes right and wrong behavior are severely tested when they go against our deepest moral intuition in this manner; in such cases one naturally questions the theory rather than giving up the intuition. H. Russell Bernard (1988:117), for example, says that

> cultural and ethical relativism is an excellent antidote for overdeveloped ethnocentrism. But cultural relativism is a poor philosophy to live by, or on which to make judgments about whether to participate in particular research projects. Can you imagine any anthropologist today defending the human rights violations of Nazi Germany as just another expression of the richness of culture?

Bernard's use of "is" in the first sentence shows that he does not distinguish cultural from ethical relativism. If he had done so, his point would be less confusing. *Cultural* relativism, in Boas's sense of trying to understand and evaluate the practices of other cultures in their own historical context, is a good antidote for ethnocentrism. Identifying the practices of any culture as the ultimate moral standard for that culture, however, is a different matter and rightly raises problems for a reflective anthropologist. Bernard in mentioning Nazi Germany has offered the standard counterexample to the claim that morality recognizes no extracultural authority.

Despite its fatal flaw, however, ethical relativism still enjoys wide acceptance among practicing anthropologists. Ethical relativism, for example, played a role in testimony by a French ethnologist in the trial of Bintou Fofana Diarra for complicity in the genital mutilation of her infant daughter. As reported in the *New York Times* (Weil-Curiel 1993), the unnamed ethnologist testified that "Africans should not be punished [for genital mutilation of infant girls] because they act under social pressure." The principle implicit in this statement—that one should not be punished for acts done under social pressure—is uncomfortably similar to the defense offered by Nazi war criminals.

A second problem with making cultural standards the final arbiter of morality is that this practice presumes a uniformity in cultures that current research denies, even for small, isolated, and tightly knit societies, or it gives a privileged moral position to powerful subgroups within the society. In the latter case, for example, the power to set cultural norms may belong to a minority whose control of valuable resources enables it to force others to follow its standards. Conversely, the power to set norms may accrue to those who are members of the majority, while significant minorities have no voice. In either case, one can only refer to the norms of "the culture" by ignoring ethical disagreement within the culture.

Some anthropologists believe that relativism is the only ethical stance that is compatible with a scientific investigation of other cultures. A scientific anthropologist presumably formulates "neutral" descriptions of the culture, reporting such quantifiable information as the frequency of occurrence of behaviors and perhaps the observed attitudes (approval, disapproval) of members of the society, while refraining from judging the culture or interfering with it in any way. Whether such detachment is required to maintain scientific integrity and whether such detachment is even possible are points raised by D'Andrade (1995) and Scheper-Hughes (1995). D'Andrade (1995:399) points to the alleged subjectivity of ethical judgments and contrasts these with the objectivity of scientific judgments. Scheper-Hughes (1995), however, objects to a scientific detachment that would prevent anthropologists from taking an active role in alleviating suffering among their research subjects. This debate is somewhat at cross-purposes because D'Andrade's main concern seems to be with an epistemic relativism that claims that such notions as knowledge and truth have no extracultural basis.... Scheper-Hughes, in contrast, is worried about the behavioral implications of a relativist ethics that takes the existing social arrangements in a culture as the ultimate moral authority.

The strict separation of science and values, a cherished principle of logical positivism, is increasingly difficult to defend in the face of ethical problems raised by scientific advances in many fields. In particular, current biomedical techniques for genetic engineering and research on human embryos raise important problems that tend to blur lines between scientific and value judgments. Bernard (1988) notes that when resources are limited, the very choice of anthropological research topics is value laden. The possibility of an ethically neutral or completely value-free science of human behavior now seems to many scientists both unattainable and undesirable, but recognition of the interrelationships between science and values need not prevent the limited type of objectivity that D'Andrade argues is possible for anthropological research.

Anthropologists may continue to avow ethical relativism despite its difficulties because they have not articulated an alternative ethical theory that is consistent with their distaste for ethnocentrism and their respect for cultural diversity. Nevertheless, maintaining a consistent form of ethical relativism is highly problematic in the present research climate. Facing the loss of valuable anthropological and archaeological resources, anthropologists have re-examined traditional relationships with their subjects, their colleagues, and the general public. To resolve problems and achieve clarity, they are currently debating and revising professional ethical standards. Despite the traditional commitment of anthropologists to relativism, the ethical principles that underlie their professional codes are not relativistic. The codes refer to their duties and responsibilities, and—by implication at least—to the corresponding rights of their research subjects, colleagues, and the general public. The conflict, often unacknowledged, between the avowed relativism of anthropologists and their sincere concern with justice and rights can lead to confusion and ineffectiveness in achieving the important goals of preserving anthropological resources and protecting cultural minorities. . . .

An Anthropological Example—Female Genital Mutilation

The arguments of feminist anthropologists for altering discriminatory practices of other cultures similarly compromise a commitment to ethical relativism. In some cultures, all females are subjected to genital mutilation. In its severe form, this involves cutting away most or all of the external sex organs (euphemistically called "circumcision") and sewing or sealing (infibulating) the vagina so as to leave only a pinhole opening for urination and menstruation. The practice affects an estimated ninety-five million or more women in at least twenty-five countries, mostly, but not all, in Africa (Lightfoot-Klein 1989). Within the cultures that practice genital mutilation, little disagreement exists about its value, though different groups offer various justifications for the practice. Most, but not all, of the countries that engage in the practice are predominantly Muslim, but it is absent in many other Muslim countries. The operation typically is performed on girls from six to nine years old but also on younger girls and infants. Sometimes when a bride is an "outsider," she is infibulated just before she marries into a group that follows the custom.

Anthropologists have attempted to document, understand, and explain this practice, which, aside from its harshness, strikes most Westerners as extremely bizarre. Why do they do it? What possible benefit do they see from it? How could it be so widespread? In contrast to most accounts in the contemporary press which dismiss the practice simply as a way of oppressing women, anthropologists' explanations are appropriately complex. They refer to the cult of virginity, the cultural association between female purity and the society's honor, and the antiquity of the tradition—Herodotus, writing in the fifth century B.C., obliquely refers to its practice in Egypt, and some mummies show evidence of infibulation. Anthropologists also cite the symbolic role female circumcision plays in distinguishing the Arab-Muslim African societies that practice it from their culturally distinct neighbors.

In places such as the Sudan, where the practice is nearly universal, anthropologists discuss genital mutilation in the context of social practices that involve other forms of mutilation practiced upon both males and females, such as tribal scarring of the face and piercing of body parts. Anthropologists also emphasize the cultural value of enduring pain without complaint. Economic explanations are also proposed. Midwives who perform the operations are sustained by the fees not only from the original circumcision and infibulation but also from treatment of the inevitable medical problems that result. Other explanations are psychological, such as those that refer to the attitudes of older women who say that they have gone through the experience and therefore do not see why the younger ones should be spared.

Besides offering their own historical and cultural explanations, anthropologists report the explanations of the people who engage in the practice. These include such claims as we have always done it, our religion requires it, no one will marry an uncircumcised woman, it makes us clean, it makes us more beautiful, it improves health, it limits the sex drive, it is good for fertility, and— referring to reinfibulation after childbirth—it deters a husband from seeking additional wives.

Some—relatively few—women and men in such societies do question the practice or its supposed benefits, particularly if they have been exposed to modern Western culture. But when asked why they nevertheless have their daughters circumcised, they refer to tradition, or say that their female relatives insisted, or insist that no one would marry the girl unless she were circumcised. Most explanations of female genital mutilation come from women, since few men can be persuaded to discuss the issue, claiming for the most part that it is women's business. Jomo Kenyatta, the revered former leader of Kenya and member of the Kikuyu tribe, who earned a Ph.D. in anthropology under [Bronislaw] Malinowski, however, said, "No proper Kikuyu would dream of marrying a girl who has not been circumcised" (Kenyatta 1938, quoted in Lightfoot-Klein 1989:71).

Women in cultures that practice genital mutilation claim that it is done for the benefit of the men, but women alone are responsible for arranging and performing the operations. Even the question of the acceptability of bridal candidates is largely under control of the women since arranged marriages are the rule, with the groom's mother having a prominent voice. (Recently a young woman from Togo sought and was granted asylum in the United States to avoid genital mutilation. The woman became endangered, however, only after her father had died. Her guardianship then passed to her aunt, who attempted to commit the woman to an arranged marriage.) Thus the practice is unusual inasmuch as it is intended to control women, it affects them almost universally, and they suffer the greatest harm from it; but they manage and control it almost exclusively.

The presence in European cities of sizable African communities that maintain the practice—despite local laws that prohibit it—has brought female genital mutilation to the attention both of the courts and of feminists who see it as "butchery intended to control women" (Weil-Curiel 1993). Anthropologists who claim to be relativists face the ethical dilemma of whether their responsibility ends with describing the practice and placing it in a cultural context, whether they are obligated to protect the practice from outside interference, or whether they should help to end the practice. Relativism might suggest that they have a further responsibility to protect, or at least not interfere with, this culturally sanctioned practice. At the same time, as relativists, they must also consider their responsibility to cooperate with members of their own culture who are trying to end the practice on the grounds that human rights are being violated.

Although relativistic anthropologists are reluctant to try to alter the values of other cultures, many think it appropriate to try to correct mistaken factual beliefs when this would benefit the welfare of members of the culture. Value judgments that are based on mistaken factual beliefs may be revised without undermining the values themselves. Clearly some beliefs of cultures that practice genital mutilation are factually mistaken. Contrary to those who say the practice is beneficial to sanitation or health, mutilation causes severe medical damage in many cases. The operation can cause immediate infection, excessive bleeding, and even death. Delayed common effects of the operation are infections of the urinary tract, menstrual problems, painful intercourse, reduction in fertility, and complications in childbirth. Nor does the Muslim religion command infibulation, as some believe. The practice does not guarantee virginity, since reinfibulation, which simulates the virginal state, is widely practiced. Because sex drive is more a matter of endocrinology than external organs, the claim that infibulation limits sex drive is likewise questionable.

Insofar as genital mutilation is motivated by sanitary or medical considerations, therefore, knowledge of the facts would tend to undermine the practice without reducing the cultural commitment to the values of purity, fertility, or health. Insofar as genital mutilation is motivated by other factors, such as maintenance of cultural distinctiveness and increasing the ability to endure pain, its medical harm could be alleviated by practicing less severe forms of circumcision without infibulation and by performing the operation only in a sterile clinical setting.

Such a medical solution, while it would save lives and preserve health, does not address the ethical question, raised by feminists, of the right to control one's body and whether or to what extent this right is inalienable. Since genital mutilation is usually performed on children, an important issue is whether parents have the right to harm the child in this way. Parents and guardians cannot violate *inalienable* rights of their children even for some supposed benefit.

Parents may, however, subject children to some kinds of discipline, as well as to dangerous and sometimes painful medical treatment, when it is for the good of the child. Erroneous views about the supposed benefits of genital mutilation, of course, cannot justify harming the child.

Unlike mistaken claims about the medical benefits of mutilation, other claims are apparently correct. Marriage within the culture *as things now stand* may not be an option for an uncircumcised woman. Moreover, for females in that culture, marriage is a prerequisite for obtaining any other rights. So being able to marry is a clear benefit and may outweigh the harm of circumcision from the point of view of the girl. (According to principles of justice, the benefit that justifies a harm must accrue to the individual who undergoes the harm, not merely to her extended family. Thus, loss of a bride price for the family would not, without further argument, justify the harm to the child.) Feminist anthropologists, as well as others who are concerned with human rights, want to take both educational and legal means to end the practice of genital mutilation. Their attitude, however, is not consistent with a commitment to ethical relativism....

Individual Rights and the Common Good

... In looking at the question of genital mutilation, the following pertinent questions arise. How fundamental is the right not to have one's body altered? At what age does the girl have the right to decide for herself whether to undergo a mutilation? Young girls in the Sudan who are not circumcised by their eighth year usually ask to have it done. Should we disregard these requests because the children are mere dupes of the culture? If they are, can they ever reach an age of consent? Many Western cultures practice ear piercing on infant girls, and many others accede to the wishes of six or eight year olds to have their ears pierced. Circumcision of male infants is common. Bodily mutilations are as much a part of cultural identity for some cultures as distinctive styles of clothing. Some mutilations we regard as attractive, some as beneficial to health, some as harmless, some as aesthetically offensive, others as brutal. Severe genital mutilation surely falls into the brutal category. Moreover, its rationale is empirically flawed, and because its harms disproportionately affect females, it raises serious questions about violating rights. In cases such as this, anthropological understanding of the practice can legitimately be used to aid attempts to eradicate or modify it for the benefit of the members of the culture where it is practiced. Those who disagree should at least argue for the practice on stronger grounds than the value of cultural diversity....

Anthropologists who work in cultures that withhold fundamental human rights from women, children, or any other subgroup face difficult choices about taking any *action* to restore rights. Some anthropologists would say that their decision to work in such cultures obligates them to alleviate the problem. Others hold that their role as anthropologists is to observe cultural phenomena and record and analyze them as accurately as possible, but not to try to alter conditions. In either case, the anthropologist has a minimal obligation to report the observed and analyzed state of affairs in normal anthropological outlets for publication. Anthropologists do not betray secrets or violate confidences when they describe a custom that is almost universally practiced in the culture. By calling attention to an unjust practice, however, anthropologists at least implicitly invite groups devoted to the protection of rights to take action. By presenting the offensive practice in its full cultural context, which may involve revealing its latent functions in addition to its manifest or stated functions, anthropologists also provide valuable information about how to control or prevent the practice.

After the anthropologist acts to present information in an appropriate way to a suitable audience, his or her responsibility to try to alleviate the injustice seems to me neither greater nor less than that of any person who is in a position to help the victims of an unjust practice. Even if no further action is taken, I think that the anthropologist who refuses to recognize that the value of cultural diversity is morally subordinate to that of protecting rights is on shaky moral ground. The anthropologist who retreats into ethical relativism in such situations, as did the ethnologist at the trial of Bintou Fofana Diana, does not demonstrate tolerance by appealing to social pressures in another culture but instead risks being committed to the same morally untenable position as the "Nazi defense."

Conclusion

I have reiterated some criticisms of ethical relativism, a position which once seemed to offer anthropologists a way to profess tolerance and avoid criticizing the morality of some practices of other cultures. My arguments try to show not so much that ethical relativism is "false" but that its consequences conflict with our deepest held moral intuitions and that it cannot be held consistently while embracing those intuitions. I have tried to show also that anthropologists need not forego tolerance if they abandon relativism in favor of a morality based on principles of justice and fairness. The concern with justice that guides anthropologists' codes of professional conduct can provide the starting point for a more sophisticated analysis of rights, which can be used to analyze cultural practices. (The philosophical literature on rights is vast, but a useful entry for anthropologists is available in Baker 1994.) Ethical judgments of another culture's practices, especially when based on deep understanding of their life, customs, and tradition, are indicative neither of ethnocentrism nor of intolerance. Instead, they show respect for the basic anthroplogical belief in "the psychic unity of humans" and a commitment to justice and fairness for all.

References

Baker, J., ed., 1994, Group Rights, Toronto: University of Toronto Press.

Berlin, B., and P. Kay, 1969, Basic Color Terms: Their Universality and Evolution. Berkeley and Los Angeles: University of California Press.

Bernard, H. R., 1998, Research Methods in Cultural Anthropology. Newbury Park, N.J.: Sage Publications.

D'Andrade, R., 1995, Moral Models in Anthropology. Current Anthropology 36(3):399–408.

Kenyatta, J., 1938, Facing Mount Kenya. London: Secker and Warburg.

Lightfoot-Klein, H., 1989, Prisoners of Ritual: An Odyssey into Female Genital Circumcision in Africa. Binghampton, N.Y.: Haworth Press.

Scheper-Hughes, N., 1995, The Primacy of the Ethical. Current Anthropology 36(3):409–20.

Turnbull, C., 1962, The Forest People. New York: Simon and Schuster.

Weil-Curiel, L., 1993, Mutilation of Girls' Genitals: Ethnic Gulf in French Court. New York Times, November 23.

Female Circumcision in Africa: The Dialectics of Equality

Culture and society must, of course, always take account of human biology, but they do so in complex ways. The distinctive characteristics of culture is that it transcends nature; but this does not mean that it has left it behind—rather, it has turned it upside down.

— Robert F. Murphy (1977)

Female circumcision or clitoridectomy, called by the Mossi, the *Bongo*, is [a] not too subtle mechanism of Mossi women to challenge the superiority of men. This was the thought that flashed through my mind, as I watched with amazement, the quiet pride of the women and girls performing the rituals of the graduation ceremonies of their own Bongo. Here were women doing things that they usually never did, and more importantly, should not have been doing. They had procured the drums from men and, much to my surprise and their amusement, were beating them. Where had they learned? Oh yes! They must have practiced these rhythms while pounding millet and sorghum in their mortars. Inexplicable was the source of their knowledge of the songs and dances of the Bongo which were allegedly the sole province of males, but which they performed equally well. True, I had learned both the dances and songs of the Bongo during my numerous visits to the circumcision lodge, but these female graduates did them better than I ever did. Surely some Delilah had tricked a Samson who had then revealed the secrets of arrogant men. During the Bongo ceremony, Mossi women were showing to the men publicly, that they knew male secrets, and moreover, these were not important after all. . . .

The subject of male circumcision and female clitoridectomy and infibulation in African societies has been the source of great speculation and controversy, primarily because it involves the "fundamental ontological differences between the sexes—conditions of simple *being*—based in the first instance on anatomical distinctions" and what flows from these. Questions raised have been: 1. Are these operations cruel? 2. Do they have anything to do with sex? 3. Do they reveal anything about the relative merits of various cultures' sexual sensibilities? and 4. Do male and female versions of the operations differ with regard to the answers to questions 1 and 2? Some anthropologists and some non-anthropologists have already strong views on these questions.

Fran P. Hosken discussing "Genital Mutilation in Africa," severely criticized those "Anthropologists (mostly men) who have studied African traditions have done no service to women by utterly disregarding women's health while they attribute 'cultural values' to such damaging traditions as excision and infibulation." Considering these practices "deleterious to health and indeed dangerous," Hosken lamented that many African groups "subject their female children to genital mutilation for a multitude of 'reasons,' many of which conflict and all of which are based on total ignorance concerning reproduction." She wondered aloud whether it was really in the interest of such populations "that such damaging myths are perpetuated under the cloak of silence and are praised as 'culture' in the literature? I think not. The time has come to face the facts." (Hoskin 1976:6) Hosken is tired of, and angry about those "explanations" of men and of what she calls "brain-washed women" who attribute clitoridectomy "to the fear of female sexuality," and the need to "prevent adultery." (*Ibid.*)

Simon D. Messing, an applied anthropologist, feels that he and his colleagues "cannot evade the issue of such a serious and widespread problem as genital mutilation of females, if they are concerned with public health... they should not leave the burden of this task entirely on the shoulders of radical feminists—and the latter in turn should welcome our cooperation." (Messing 1980:296)

Neither the radical feminists nor the anthropologists have considered the possibility that in the frequent dialectics that we find in social life, female circumcision might well be one of the numerous ways in which women challenge the vaunted superiority of men....

Given the contemporary controversy surrounding "female" circumcision (really an interesting misnomer), it is generally ignored that circumcision is predominantly a "male" ritual. Many well-known ancient peoples, such as the Hebrews (who probably adopted this ritual in ancient Egypt as they borrowed other interesting aspects of that culture) limited circumcision to males. The same thing is true for many African populations. As far as I can ascertain, there is not a single African society in which female circumcision exists without its male counterpart. The reasons for this are as intriguing as they are germane to this article....

Initiation ceremonies preparatory to marriage, sexual relations, and the creation of families, are widespread in African societies, but are not necessarily linked to either circumcision or clitoridectomy.... Characteristic of this *rite de passage* is the customary withdrawal of the initiates from the world of people; their education into the knowledge and lore of their societies; and their subjection to a great deal of physical pain and other hardships....

The Mossi initiated and subjected their pre-pubescent youth to both circumcision and clitoridectomy. In the Manga-Nobere districts of Burkina Faso (formerly Upper Volta) in southern Mossi country, every three or four years, during December, the coldest part of the year, and depending upon the food supply, the Mossi opened the "Bongo" or the initiation ceremony for boys, in a secluded area in the woods. Here were gathered about twenty to thirty boys, age seven or eight to twelve years old, from the surrounding villages and their helpers. Known as Bankousse, these youths built a camp called the *Keogo,* placing barriers on the paths leading to it so as to warn off uncircumcised children and women. The mothers of the boys brought food daily to the barrier, but did not cross it.

The Mossi considered circumcision to be a simple surgical act which was only incidental to the Bongo—a veritable initiation to life involving a great many hardships. Almost immediately after arriving at the Keogo the boys were circumcised by the head of the camp, known as the *Nane* who used a sharp razor for the operation. As in other parts of Africa, the initiates were not expected to cry, and their wounds were cared for by the Nane. Then came the important post operation period called *komtogo* or "bitter water" by the Bankousse because of the pain involved. Despite the cold nights, they had use of only a small fire and were not permitted to use any covers. Every morning they were forced to bathe in a cold pool, and when they returned, they had lessons to learn involving history, nature study, and life.

The Bongo had its own mystery language whose words turned out on analysis to be synonyms for ordinary More (the language of the Mossi) with the prefix "na." The camp had its own rules on which rank was based, not on those on the outside, but on the order in which the youths were circumcised. What the Nane attempted to do was to forge a link between the boys in opposition to himself, who acted like a veritable ogre. Walking about the camp with a long stick, he whipped the youngsters into line, threw sand in the food brought by the women, and made the Bankousse dance and sing until they were exhausted.

Graduation ceremonies of the Bongo involved going into the woods, cutting grass for the horses of the chiefs, and wood for their fires. Then on the appointed day, the mothers brought new clothes for their sons, hoping that none of them had died during the ordeal of the Bongo. Then on the appointed day the graduates dressed in their new clothing marched through the market place, and visited the chief. Then they engaged in dancing and singing at a public place just outside the market place.

As usual in almost all parts of Africa, the Mossi women were in complete charge of their Bongo from which they excluded all men. Their *Keogo* was not in the woods, but was in the compound of a woman who lived by herself. But as usual for males, I could find out nothing about the nature of the excision that took place. I did hear the drumming and singing that took place there all night until the wee hours of the morning, and did observe the young girls going backward and forward to their homes. Invariably they carried a tufted staff, said to have been given to them by their prospective husbands. The women would say nothing about the symbolism involved, considering the information specific to women alone. The most that they would say about what went on in the female Bongo was that the males have their secrets and so did the women.

Like the graduation exercises of the male Bankousse, the female ritual was a village-wide affair, but strictly within the province of the women. Market days before, the relatives and prospective husbands of the graduates, shopped for the clothes and headties, and makeup for them. Then on the day of the exercise, the young girls went to the home of the female Nane and accompanied by their mothers and sisters who were beating drums and singing, went to the village square where the Bankousse danced and sang the traditional airs of the Bongo. From time to time, male relatives and husbands would detach themselves from the line of spectators and approach the dancers, giving them presents of money. To all intents and purposes, the female Bongo was structurally and functionally quite similar to that of the males. This ceremony demonstrated to all that the Mossi women were just as capable as the men in performing an initiation ceremony whose function was to transform girls into women, as the male version transformed boys into men. Moreover, they had more effectively kept men from knowing their secrets than did the males, whose secrets they had obviously shared. . . .

What is important about the puberty rituals in African societies, whether they involved painful initiation, and whether they involved genital mutilation with recognizable pain, are the emic and etic features involved. The Africans do have their own views of their rituals even though others have ignored these views and insist upon their own interpretations. This is perhaps par for human beings involving as it does relative power. There is no doubt that had they the requisite power, Africans would insist that the world accept their interpretation of their own rituals, as well as their views of the rituals of others. Anthropologists would do well to keep this in mind.

The Mossi are not much given to speculating on the imponderables of social life, or the world in general, judging such ratiocinations quixotic. To them the Bongo for men and for women have the same meaning and serve the same function for both men and women: preparation for marriage and rearing families. Indicative of this equality is that the two genders control their own initiation rituals, even though women have to borrow drums from the males. When badgered about the sexual features involved in genital mutilation, an admittedly chauvinist Mossi male might suggest that since females are inferior to males they are not permitted to touch the male organ during sexual congress, and that clitoridectomy makes sexual congress easier. This may be as good a rationalization as any other, but flies in the face of the anxiety of Mossi men over the conduct of their wives, and their stated axiom: "Women are so important that if a man receives as a wife, either a blind woman or a leper, he should close his eyes, close his mouth, and close his ears, and keep her."

The equally male chauvinist Dogon explicitly associate both circumcision and clitoridectomy with elaborate myths concerning creation and cosmology. Both operations are said to have been instituted as punishments and are indicative of the incomplete state of human beings resulting from the primordial crime of a godling. There is the removal of the opposite sex complement with which all human beings were originally intended to be equipped. Thus for the Dogon there is complementarity in the operation. Mary Daly criticizes the Dogon for what she considered an emic patriarchal obfuscation of the true purposes of the operation, namely the intimidation and humiliation of women. What she conveniently ignores is the fact that the Dogon forbid men to have intercourse with their wives against their will and that the sexual responses of wives are in large part conditioned by the treatment they generally receive from their husbands (Daly 1978).

Somewhat like the Dogon, both the Egyptians and the Northern Sudanese stress the complementarity of circumcision and clitoridectomy. Referring specifically to the Sudanese, [Janice] Boddy asserted that

> Through their own operation, performed at roughly the same age as when girls are circumcised (sic) (between five and ten years), boys become less like women: while the female reproductive organs are covered, that of the male is uncovered, or, as one Sudanese author states, of a child's sex... by removing physical characteristics deemed appropriate to his or her opposite: the clitoris and other external genitalia, in the case of females, the prepuce of the penis, in the case of males. This last is emphasized by a custom now lapsed in Hofriyat wherein one of the newly circumcised boys' grandmothers would wear his foreskin as a ring on the day of the operation (Boddy 1982:687–8).

Paying special attention to the widespread African emic notion of complementarity in the rituals of circumcision and clitoridectomy, Boddy insists that

> By removing their external genitalia, women are not so much preventing their own sexual pleasure (though obviously this is an effect) as enhancing their femininity. Circumcision as a symbolic act brings sharply into focus the fertility potential of women by dramatically de-emphasizing their inherent sexuality. By insisting on circumcision for their daughters, women assert their social indispensibility, an importance that is not as the sexual partners of their husbands, nor in this highly segregated, male-authoritative society, as their servants, sexual or otherwise, but as the mothers of men. *The ultimate social goal of a woman is to become, with her husband, the cofounder of a lineage section. As a respected haboba she is "listened to," she may be sent on the* hadj *(pilgrimage to Mecca) by her husbands or her sons, and her name is remembered in village genealogies for several generations* (italics supplied) (*Ibid.:*687).

Although Boddy had her own etic views of female genital mutilation among the Sudanese, her ethnographic data support the etic argument of this paper, namely that in this instance of the dialectics of social life, clitoridectomy rather than a ritual performed by women, to demean their already low status in many African societies, is a declaration of equality. What is interesting is that there are few, if any, cases in the ethnographic record where African women (as contrasted to the normally sexist African men) see this ritual as reducing their status. Feminists may consider the African women who defend this practice as "brain-washed," but should be aware that many African women, as well as men, take the same jaundiced view of many rituals of Western Christendom. True, some contemporary African women object to clitoridectomy, but few had dared to confront their mothers and grandmothers over the issue for fear of being taken for "black" white women. The implication here is that these women have failed to assert that cultural equality for which Africans have fought long and hard.

What is important about the controversy about clitoridectomy in Africa is that African women were never part of it. The issue grew out of a Judeo-Christian concern over human sexuality, involved Christian missionaries in Africa, and was used by African men in their struggle for cultural autonomy from Europeans, and ultimately for political independence. . . .

Missionary opposition to clitoridectomy among the Kikuyu was very much linked to their opposition to all aspects of African culture that could frustrate their attempts to impose Western Christendom. We are told that

> The missionaries recognized the significance of the initiatory rites, of which circumcision was the outward physical symbol, and they were appalled at what they saw in them. The physical operation they considered brutal and unhygenic and in the case of girls a barbaric mutilation with permanent ill-effects. *But the atmosphere in which the ceremonies were carried out seemed to them even more evil, with what they took to be the sexual innuendo of the dances and songs, the licentiousness of the old men and women and the gloating cruelty of the operators and their attendants. They taught against the practices and prayed that the people might forego them altogether* (Italics added) (Murray–Brown 1972:50–51).

. . . What had started out as an issue over clitoridectomy, and a practice which many African Christians were prepared to change, became a cause célèbre over the issue of African cultural and political freedom. Much to the alarm of the colonial government, it became known locally in October 1919 that "John [Jomo] Kenyatta" who had gone to Britain to protest settler colonialism, had been to Moscow and was "in close touch with Communists and Communist Organizations." Songs praising Kenyatta and ridiculing the governor were outlawed as seditious, creating anger among anti-mission Kikuyu. . . .

The problem now was that clitoridectomy had become inextricably linked to the Kikuyu desire for equality in their homeland. The missionaries were insisting that Kenyatta "should tell his people to obey government officers, Kikuyu chiefs, and missions in control of schools. . . ."

Kenyatta's subsequent defense of clitoridectomy as an operation in which the operator had "the dexterity of a Harley Street surgeon . . . with a stroke she cuts off the tip of the clitoris . . . the girl hardly feels any pain" (Jomo Kenyatta 1962) is only understandable in light of the role that clitoridectomy had played in the drive of the Kikuyu to achieve equality for their institutions in the face of Europe's arrogance. Like Bob Murphy, Kenyatta was very aware of the dialectics of social life. For him colonial tutelage was oppressive and alien. He wrote:

> In our opinion, the African can only advance to a 'higher level' if he is free to express himself, to organize economically, politically, socially, and to take part in the government of his own country. In this way he will be able to develop his creative mind, initiative, and personality, which hitherto have been hindered by the multiplicity of incomprehensible laws and ordinances (*Ibid.*:192).

What the conflict over clitoridectomy did was to bring to "an abrupt close the paternalistic phase of missionary activity; henceforth the emphasis would be on the growth of native churches. The high noon of imperialism... [and the attempt] to extend white dominion over all of East Africa, was over." (*Ibid.*:151)

Kenyatta has been pilloried by many female scholars and feminists, for defending a practice (which he was prepared to see abolished), in the greater interest of political equality for Africans. Few noted, as did Harriet Lyons, that Kenyatta had suggested, perhaps as an after thought, that clitoridectomy may have been practiced to prevent masturbation, a practice condemned in both Kikuyu boys and girls, and that his major emphasis was "largely on social structure." (1981:510) Moreover, he was fully prepared to use education to abolish it. A more intemperate view of Kenyatta's action is that of Fran Hosken who declared that

> An international feminist observer cannot help but wonder why the male African leadership does not speak out about the mutilation of women, a custom that was reinforced by Kenyatta in Kenya and is also supported by the independence movement under his leadership.... It clearly affects the status of women in political affairs (Hosken 1976:6).

Understandably, there are some African feminists who agree with Hosken. Nevertheless, it should be noted that "the resistance of African feminists to anti-clitoridectomy agitation—evident at the United Nations World Conference on women held in Copenhagen in 1980" accords fully with the demand of Kenyatta for African cultural autonomy. Like him, these women realize that African practices must be brought into line with those characteristics of the emerging global civilization. What they insist upon is respect, and the end of European arrogance.

The problem with blaming Kenyatta and other African men for clitoridectomy misses the important point that African women have always been in control of this ritual (until now when male doctors may perform it in modern hospitals), and probably used it, to declare their equality with men. Faced with discrimination for not possessing those characteristics with which dominant social strata have linked their dominance, African women, like other women, and subordinate groups, have striven to acquire the traits viewed as valuable. These practices vary cross-culturally in time and space, and can be as different as Japanese females surgically operating on their eyes to approximate those of American males during the occupation of their country; to certain American females bobbing their noses; other Americans bleaching or darkening their skins; and still others dressing like males, and creating female counterparts of such organizations as Masonic lodges, veteran groups, and institutions of higher learning. In many of these cases, the males or dominant groups whose characteristics were being imitated, were not aware of the attempts to achieve equality with them, or to win their favor. That they were responsible for the behavior in the first place may well have been true, but a dialectician like Robert Murphy, whose eyes were probably opened by his wife, Yolanda, would smile at the irony of it all.

References

Boddy, Janice, 1982. "Womb as oasis: the symbolic context of Pharaonic circumcision in rural Northern Sudan," *American Ethnology,* 9: 682–698.

Daly, Mary, 1978. *Gyn/Ecology: The Metaethics of Radical Feminism,* Boston: Beacon Press.

Hosken, Fran P., 1976. "Genital Mutilation of Women in Africa." *Munger Africana Library Notes,* #36, October, p. 6.

Kenyatta, Jomo, 1962. *Facing Mount Kenya,* New York, Vintage Brooks.

Lyons, Harriet, 1981. "Anthropologists, moralities, and relativities: the problem of genital mutilations." *Canadian Review of Sociology and Anthropology,* 18: 499–518.

Messing, Simon D., 1980. "The Problem of 'Operations Based on Custom' in Applied Anthropology: The Challenge of the Hosken Report on Genital and Sexual Mutilations of Females." *Human Organizations,* Vol. 39, No. 3, p. 296.

Murphy, Robert F., 1977. "Man's Culture and Woman's Nature," *Annals of the New York Academy of Sciences.* Vol. 293, 15–24.

Murray-Brown, Jeremy, 1980. *Kenyatta.* London, George Allen & Unwin Ltd.

POSTSCRIPT

Should Anthropologists Work to Eliminate the Practice of Female Circumcision?

The issue of female circumcision raises important questions about whether or not there are limits to cultural relativism. Critics of cultural relativism have often pointed to the Nazi atrocities during the Second World War as examples of immoral practices that can be understood in culturally relative terms but should not be condoned. Cultural relativists in such cases counter that unlike male or female circumcision in Africa, genocide was never morally acceptable in German society.

At issue here is whether or not an unhealthy practice should be suppressed because it is unhealthy. If anthropologists work to abolish female circumcision, should they also work to prohibit use of alcohol, tobacco, and recreational drugs in our own society because such products are unhealthy? Are there limits beyond which cultural relativism has no power? If anthropologists and international organizations are right to stop female circumcision, would they also be justified in working to abolish male circumcision in Jewish and Muslim communities on the same grounds?

Without dealing directly with issues of cultural and moral relativism, Skinner argues that anthropologists should take seriously the concerns of both African men and women, the majority of whom want to continue to practice clitoridectomy and resent Western attempts to suppress the practice. For another view from a similar perspective, see Eric Winkel's essay "A Muslim Perspective on Female Circumcision," *Women & Health* (vol. 23, 1995).

There are many essays by authors who wish to abolish female circumcision, and nearly all of them refer to the practice as female genital mutilation. A lengthy bibliography can be found at http://www.fgmnetwork.org/reference/biblio.html. Typical examples would include Harriet Lyons's "Anthropologists, Moralities, and Relativities: The Problem of Genital Mutilations," *Canadian Review of Sociology and Anthropology* (vol. 18, 1981) and Anke van der Kwaak's "Female Circumcision and Gender Identity: A Questionable Alliance?" *Social Science and Medicine* (vol. 35, 1992).

For a balanced anthropological view of female circumcision and cultural relativism, see Carole Nagengast's "Women, Minorities, and Indigenous Peoples: Universalism and Cultural Relativity," *Journal of Anthropological Research* (vol. 53, 1997).

For a discussion of issues dealing with cultural relativism and anthropological ethics, see *Ethics and the Profession of Anthropology,* Carolyn Fluehr-Lobban, ed. (University of Pennsylvania Press, 1991).

ISSUE 17

Do Anthropologists Have a Moral Responsibility to Defend the Interests of "Less Advantaged" Communities?

YES: James F. Weiner, from "Anthropologists, Historians, and the Secret of Social Knowledge," *Anthropology Today* (October 1995)

NO: Ron Brunton, from "The Hindmarsh Island Bridge and the Credibility of Australian Anthropology," *Anthropology Today* (August 1996)

ISSUE SUMMARY

YES: Anthropology professor James F. Weiner asserts that anthropologists have a moral obligation to defend the interests of the native communities with whom they work, even if it means halting development projects. In his view, anthropologists have a responsibility to defend traditional native cultures, particularly if secret cultural knowledge is involved.

NO: Applied anthropologist Ron Brunton argues that even when hired as consultants, anthropologists have a moral and professional responsibility to the truth. This responsibility applies even when such evidence does not support the interests of a native community.

Over the past 30 years anthropologists have increasingly been asked to serve as consultants on various mining and development projects. Anthropologists sometimes work for a government department or developer, but more often work for the native communities whose land will be developed or resources exploited. In such instances, anthropologists are asked to provide expert testimony about traditional native cultures. This testimony can cause government bodies or developers to reshape a project's design or, if matters of serious cultural heritage are involved, may even halt a project. Anthropologists are trained to respect the cultures and traditions of people very different from themselves. However, in legal proceedings involving the development of native lands, they must generally take a stand defending either the native communities or the developers.

The controversy concerning the Hindmarsh Island Bridge in South Australia raises a number of questions about the responsibilities of anthropologists toward the native communities with which they work. Like the United States, Australia has laws intended to protect the sacred sites of native Aboriginal tribes from desecration by developers. Some Aboriginal women of the Ngarrindjeri tribe tried to stop construction of a bridge connecting Hindmarsh Island to the mainland, stating that Hindmarsh Island is a sacred site where women conduct secret ceremonies. The proposed bridge, they asserted, would desecrate this site and threaten the tribe's future prosperity. Until recently, secret women's rites have received little attention from anthropologists studying Aboriginal societies, but some anthropologists have demonstrated that "women's business," as these secret ceremonies are publicly called, are an important part of traditional life. When a female anthropologist working on this case reported that the proposed bridge would indeed desecrate a site sacred to women, the project was halted. Developers raised charges of misrepresentation and the state government established a Royal Commission to investigate whether there had been falsification of anthropological data.

Anthropologists have typically supported the rights of less advantaged communities against exploitation by more powerful individuals and groups. Initially, the Hindmarsh Island Bridge case seemed straightforward—an anthropologist was defending the rights of an Aboriginal group to protect sacred land from desecration. But this case raises a number of other concerns because the knowledge used to support the native community's concerns was secret knowledge that only women should know. The case was further complicated because the Ngarrindjeri are one of the most acculturated tribes in South Australia, and none of its members have lived a traditional lifestyle for more than a century. At issue before the Royal Commission was whether the information that the Ngarrindjeri women gave the anthropologist was based on traditional knowledge of cultural practices or fabrication.

In the following selections, James F. Weiner argues that cultural knowledge is relative and contingent, and that only a few senior Ngarrindjerri women could be expected to know female secrets relevant to "women's business" at Hindmarsh Island. Weiner contends that we should expect all traditions to change, including those of native communities, and it is the anthropologist's responsibility to explain traditional cultures to mainstream society and to defend the rights of less advantaged groups. Recognizing that cultures do change, Ron Brunton asserts that anthropologists have a professional responsibility to find out what traditional beliefs, customs, and practices really are, even if such facts work against the interests of native groups. Brunton maintains that it is simply bad anthropology to accept the statements of any informants without a thorough analysis of all available data.

James F. Weiner  **YES**

Anthropologists, Historians, and the Secret of Social Knowledge

In the state of South Australia, we are currently witnessing two remarkable things. First, the validity and authenticity of Australian Aboriginal culture and belief are being openly challenged by the State government and the media. Second, the status of anthropological expertise and the procedures used by anthropologists in explicating that culture and belief to Anglo-Australian society are being disparaged, and unfavourably compared with other disciplinary expertise, specifically, that of the historian.

Briefly, the background to these events is as follows. A group of Aboriginal women of the Ngarrindjeri tribe, the traditional indigenous inhabitants of the Lower Murray region in South Australia, claim that there is what they call 'women's business' on Hindmarsh Island, a small island in the mouth of the Murray River. 'Business' is a pan-Aboriginal English word used throughout Australia nowadays to refer to any religious, sacred or ritual knowledge or activities or procedures that pertain to a specific site or landmark.

Hindmarsh Island is the site of a marina development project and the developers, in partnership with the local government councils and the State Government, planned to build a bridge from the mainland to the island. The Ngarrindjeri women who wished to see the plans for the bridge abandoned, claim that the island had to remain separate from the mainland, and that any attempt to compromise the discreteness of the two bodies of land would have an adverse effect on Ngarrindjeri women's ability to reproduce. On the strength of their assertion of this ritual significance, and acting on advice from a professor of law and an anthropologist (both women) who were charged with assessing the nature and extent of this women's business, the Federal Minister for Aboriginal Affairs intervened and placed a 25 year ban on the bridge's construction in May 1994. The ban was subsequently overturned by an Australian Federal Court decision in February 1995.

In May 1995, the Adelaide television station Channel 10 broadcast allegations that the women's secret knowledge which was the justification of the original Federal ban was 'fabricated' by some Aboriginal men and the Anglo-Australian lawyer employed by the South Australian Aboriginal Legal Rights

From James F. Weiner, "Anthropologists, Historians and the Secret of Social Knowledge," *Anthropology Today*, vol. 11, no. 5 (October 1995). Copyright © 1995 by The Royal Anthropological Institute. Reprinted by permission of Blackwell Publishing Ltd.

Movement, who was acting on behalf of the women. Importantly, a group of so-called 'dissident' Ngarrindjeri women also publicly proclaimed shortly afterwards that they had no knowledge of women's business on Hindmarsh Island. This contestation of the existence of women's business by other Ngarrindjeri women encouraged other commentators who sought to discredit the original claim, and ultimately emboldened the State government. In June, a State Royal Commission was appointed to inquire:

> 1. Whether the 'women's business', or any aspect of the 'women's business', was a fabrication and, if so:
> (a) the circumstances relating to such a fabrication:
> (b) the extent of such a fabrication: and
> (c) the purpose of such a fabrication...[1]

It is at this point in the growing controversy, now having achieved national scrutiny, that this criticism of anthropology by a historian took place. In the June issue of the *Adelaide Review,* University of Adelaide emeritus professor of history Austin Gough published an article entitled 'Hindmarsh Island and the Politics of the Future'. He first commented mordantly on the 'remarkable contrast between the scant evidence for "women's business" coming from Aboriginal sources and the positive cornucopia of interpretation, evaluation and embroidery coming from anthropologists and lawyers, always on hand to explain what is culturally appropriate to Ngarrindjeri women'.[2] Gough went on to say:

> Anthropologists have been better placed to find career-building subjects since the spread throughout the social sciences of postmodern relativism, according to which there is no such thing as empirically verified truth, and all belief-systems are of equal plausibility. There is an overwhelming temptation to leave behind the Western bourgeois ideal of the impartial observer, and to adopt the paradigm of the anthropologist as a culture-traveller totally immersed in the beliefs of his subjects, sharing their interests and willing to go to bat for them against the materialist Western world. The principle accepted by the American Anthropological Association and followed by many Australian practitioners is that 'the anthropologist's first responsibility is to those whose lives and customs they study. Should conflicts of interest arise, the interests of these people take precedence over other considerations'.[3]

After this diatribe against the hopelessly non-objective and witlessly committed anthropologist, the author goes on to express his unqualified belief in the documented knowledge of two earlier representatives of the Ngarrindjeri people:

> It is worth noting that Albert Korloan and Pinkie Mack, the greatly respected sources for Ngarrindjeri culture interviewed in the nineteen-forties by Ronald and Catherine Berndt and reported in their magisterial study *A World That Was,* expressed pleasure that their knowledge would now be available for all Australians.[4]

The author did not see fit to comment on the vast difference in relations between Aborigines and Whites in the 1940s—when, apart from people like the Berndts, most Australians lent neither credence, value nor authenticity to any Aboriginal beliefs, secret or otherwise, and when no Aboriginal practice or belief, however important, could have made the slightest difference to the government, graziers, miners, land developers and atomic weapon testers—and the 1990s, when such beliefs are part and parcel of a newly acquired political autonomy and cultural identity and hence of much more urgency and value. This itself is a curious act of disregard by an historian. Finally, the author comments that:

> [the anthropologist] briefed by the [Aboriginal] Legal Rights Movement as a 'facilitator' of evidence... should have aroused scepticism when in 1994 she could find... women's secrets unknown to Pinkie Mack, who was born in the eighteen-fifties and was revered by all Ngarrindjeri women as the custodian of their culture...[5]

Issues pertaining to the nature of social science research are raised by Gough's questioning of the discipline and practice of anthropology. They concern the role and function of secret knowledge in a social formation, the different perspectives that the anthropologist and the (oral) historian must necessarily bring to this phenomenon, and how each is likely to evaluate what we might call the social and epistemological status of such secret knowledge, given the very different notions each has as to what constitutes social life. In addressing more broadly the theoretical and methodological issues that underpin the controversy, I wish to clarify what I take to be the role of the anthropologist (in particular as against that of the oral historian), the role of secrecy in a non-western culture, and the nature of knowledge of sociality in non-western societies.

Although what I have to say applies very widely to non-western societies throughout the world, let me begin with the Ngarrindjeri. The book that Gough referred to in his article, published by Ronald and Catherine Berndt (two of the most renowned anthropologists of Aboriginal society in Australia this century) and entitled *A World That Was*,[6] is not an ethnography strictly speaking: it is a work of oral history. It was an attempt to *reconstruct* a culture from the memories of several surviving members of a tradition that no longer existed in that traditional form. Despite Ronald Berndt's understanding of the fractional nature of his informants' 'data', the assumption behind *A World That Was* is that such a thing as a whole culture exists. It is important to understand that when I say it no longer existed in traditional form. I am not making any claims as to what pieces of secret knowledge have or have not been forgotten by surviving Ngarrindjeri, or how much was still remembered when the Berndts compiled their interviews: I mean that such knowledge was not generated within an intact social system in which it functioned to label and describe people's places and interpersonal relationships in such a system. We must understand at the outset that there is no precise number of secrets or secret knowledge that defines or compiles a culture or society; rather, from the anthropological point of view it is the other way around: the necessity and function of secret or re-stricted knowledge is generated by the particular strategy or mode of social differentiation of a given community, as I will explain shortly.

But an oral history of the kind approved of by Gough would have to take the content of particular remembered secrets at face value. It must necessarily concede that whatever version of culture one elicits through its methodology, it is confined to the discourse of personal memory, and that such a portrait of culture itself would be exhausted by the sum total of subjective memories of each of its constituent members. As Robert Tonkinson himself remarked in the foreword to the Berndts' book: 'One of the problems with this type of re-constructive research, as the Berndts note . . . , is the intermingling of normative statements about what ideally ought to have been the correct behaviour, with accounts of what actually happened . . .' (p. xix). The Berndts would have had to pretend, along with their informants, that culture was in this instance equiv-alent to a narratable story or text, and that included in such texts in this case were the particular items of knowledge themselves.

The task of the oral historian is then to transcribe these narrated memo-ries. The resulting texts become the material record of the culture of its narra-tors, and can be appealed to as documentary evidence.

It may not be surprising that in our current post-structuralist period, where textuality is exalted as a general model of social life, the notion that a culture resides largely in the narrated memories of its members would find a high degree of credibility. Because texts can readily be compared across lan-guages and cultures, and across times and places, such a procedure absolves the oral historian of the difficult and laborious task of accounting for the differences between cultures, social systems and epochs themselves. Gough, though tacitly arguing for the superior empirical grounding of history over anthropology, finds his empirical facts solely in written documents, and thus oddly enough demonstrates his own peculiar adherence to a version of post-modernism in his steadfast belief in the sanctity of the text and its particular form of representation. But many anthropologists would still maintain that this is a narrow view of culture, and could even be pernicious, especially as applied to Aboriginal and other non-western societies, such as those in Papua New Guinea. What are the dangers of such a view, from the anthropologist's perspective?

First, if we see something that we can call 'cultural knowledge' as always unevenly and restrictedly distributed amongst members of a community, then an oral history will always be only a partial account and could never stand as a document of the total repertoire of a culture. Secondly, human social life is not reducible to its narratable form. It is not exhausted by a story one tells about it, or any number of stories, any more than we would say that the history of the Third Reich was accurately or comprehensively given to us in the memoirs of either Albert Speer or Karl Löwith or both together. Social life as I understand it lies in the contrast between the stories we tell in order to represent it to our-selves, and the actual, observable behaviour of those same story-tellers which is often at odds with or contradicts such accounts. It is in the contrast between what we do and what we say we do that some essentially human aspect of life, Aboriginal, Papua New Guinean, Western or otherwise, is revealed to us.

Thus, unlike the oral historian, who interviews the person divorced from any actual social life they are enmeshed in, the ethnographer is obliged to participate in and observe people in such social settings, in order to gauge the contrast between what language avers and what behaviour reveals. The oral historian cannot convey the social situatedness of a narrator's speech and action, because the extent to which we are influenced and constrained in such a way is very often concealed from us. This is the job of the anthropologist, in much the same way as it is the job of the psychoanalyst, to reveal the influences affecting people's behaviour and speech of which they may be unaware.

When it is suggested that 'historians alone have as their preoccupation and responsibility the reconstruction of the past by questioning all the surviving evidence',[7] I would urge that we understand the difference between *historiality* or *historiography,* a western fetishizing of the document and documentary evidence, and *historicity.* The latter refers both to (1) the manner in which the local construction, reconstruction and invocation of the past and the future play a constitutive role in people's discourse and social life, and (2) the phenomenon by which such construction is dialectically related to all those forces and influences which escape our constructionist efforts but which nevertheless impinge upon our perception and motivation. It is this dialectical relation, concerning broadly what we call the role of ideology in culture and human action, which is the anthropologist's subject matter, and apparently not that of Gough, though it is the concern of many responsible and intelligent historians. It is the identification of living history, if I may call it that, which makes the anthropological description of a community's social and cultural life 'historical' through and through, just as it is a concern for the social siting of the historical that makes the discipline of history so necessary to anthropology. From this point of view, those who suffer history often have a very different view of it from those who write it, authorize it and legitimate it.[8]

It is the anthropologist's understanding that many non-western societies were and continue to be very differently ordered than our own. Let us consider a social world where the point of social life, its rationale, was *not* to reveal, assemble and collate knowledge and information, as is the case in our own, but to prevent its spread, to restrict its transmission and to fashion a system of social statuses out of this variable distribution and restriction of knowledge. In both Aboriginal Australia and Papua New Guinea, there are many occasions in which ethnographers witness people's attempts to both *minimize* and *delay* the amount of information they publicly reveal about things, especially matters pertaining to land ownership, secret names and certain kinds of myth. Papua New Guinea people such as the Avatip and Foi characteristically seek to *not* reveal names and other information in public. The reasons are much the same as those that Aboriginal people give in the same context: if people know what you know, 'proof of ownership could become the opportunity for raids and thefts which could be used against people'.[9] Discursive strategies then become to force others to reveal these names or other items of restricted knowledge. Such an approach to talk and to the act of 'saying' does not then support any simple constructivist approach to knowledge. It also appears that it is precisely this non-constructionist approach to saying and knowing that is the hardest thing to convey to westerners who are not familiar with non-western modes of social and perceptual engagement. *Such an approach would see dispute, contestation and disparity of viewpoint as constitutive of social life, rather than an adventitious and unwelcome by-product of it.*

What we must consider is a social world founded not on consensus, uniformity, solidarity, cohesiveness, collective argument, or law in our sense. We must consider a social world founded on the opposite: relations are made between people by creating and stipulating the gaps and discontinuities between them. By assuming an uneven distribution of sacred knowledge, people create functional relationships of ritual specialization. People with specialized and secret knowledge must be called in to perform ceremonies necessary for other persons who lack such knowledge. Obligations are created between people based on their differences, rather than their similarities.

Under such conditions, knowledge is selectively, differentially and unevenly distributed within a society. It could now be argued that no piece of knowledge, no single datum of cultural information by itself could then 'stand for' the entirety of a culture. What one man or woman knows about the sacred character of a particular locale or piece of territory, and which is not known by other people who are identifiably members of the same community, does not therefore constitute in any direct way the culture or tradition.

But it is my point that *this argument rests on a divorcing of knowledge from its pragmatic, communicative, relational origin.* Let us consider the idea of a dreaming track, one that perhaps stretches the entire length of Australia, from the South Australian coast to the Top End. This track can be considered a single thing, the sum total of the marks and traces left on the landscape during the single journeys of a creator being or beings. We might even concede right at the outset that the track is a culture in and of itself. It certainly seems to be a coherent story of a cultural moment, circumscribed by the beginning and end of a journey of a being or beings. It links what we would at first identify as distinct linguistic and cultural groups: if the creator being passed through the territory of any particular group, then that group is linked to all others through whose territory the being also passed.

Now it is reasonable to assume, as is the case, that even if they were aware of the trans-local nature of a dreaming sequence or track, each local group might only intimately know the parts of the landscape that pertain to the journey of the creator being through their territory. They might not know, or be unable to know in any detail or in their experience, what happened to that being when it left the territory. The local territorial groups are linked by the route of the journey, yet the sum total of the linkages does not make a whole thing. The whole thing is assembled by the anthropologists who have collected the parts of the story from each group along the track and fitted the parts into a whole story with a beginning, middle and end. One would not dispute the wholeness of this story nor its facticity, yet prior to the assemblage by the anthropologist, *it never existed as a whole, complete thing.*[10]

Thus an important point has to be made. If dreamings, or mythical journeys, did not constitute a whole thing between different territorial groups, why should we assume that they performed such a unifying function *within* the group? Could it be that among the different clans and lineages that constituted the local territorial group, knowledge of mythical journeys and linked dreaming sites was similarly discontinuous, fragmented and selectively distributed? The point of social communication would then be to release the evidence of knowledge in a controlled and allusive way, to show the proof that it exists rather than the knowledge itself: *that is, to demonstrate the social implications of the revealed disparities between sites and possessors of knowledge.*

We could say then that Aboriginal and Papua New Guinea cultures seek always to make visible such points of rupture, that this is the supremely creative act for them. We would then find the clearest evidence for the intactness of Aboriginal society, whether it be in South Australia or northeast Arnhem Land, in the surfacing of disputes over possession of secret knowledge and restricted access to territorial and cosmological mythopoeia.[11]

We can now return to the point with which I began. Oral historians believe an account of a culture to be complete when they feel that all the data have been documented. Anthropologists, insofar as they would concede that something as open-ended and ongoing as 'social life' is ever complete, or ever comes to an end, only admit that it does so in the form of the system or theory one devises to describe or model it.

·◀❀▶·

We have now cleared the way for consideration of what most of us will see as the more important issue in this case, that of the 'fabrication' of secret, sacred knowledge for political purposes by indigenous people. The questions I wish to ask now pertain not to whether some Ngarrindjeri women truly believe in the existence of sacred, secret women's business, but to the social conditions of its elicitation: how and when they acquired those beliefs, under what social and political influences and conditions. From a strictly historical perspective, all beliefs are 'recent' at one stage. The enduring and stable in what we call culture and religion is always negotiated and made visible through the contingent and mutable conventions of the present; to the extent that there is never any perfect instauration of law or convention, then every conventional act or belief is, as Roy Wagner maintains,[12] innovative or 'new' or 'fabricated'.

Thus the perception of antiquity of a belief or custom, in a strict phenomenological sense, can only be negotiated in a present moment. How can we distinguish between the recent acquisition of old knowledge from the recent creation of knowledge per se? The day after the creation of Magna Carta it was already a vital part of the British legal tradition—but we know this only with hindsight, as it might have been retracted on the third day of its life and never heard of again. Now we have had the Magna Carta for centuries. The fact that I may have found out about it at school only two days ago may make my knowledge recent in terms of acquisition, but the knowledge itself is of long duration. The question, again, is thus not one of recentness or antiquity of a belief as a measure of its 'authenticity' or 'truth content', but of the political conditions and motivations for its evocation. A false belief nevertheless can serve a positive social function and be 'true' in the ordinary sense in which we as anthropologists construe such social function.

Peter Sutton, an Australian anthropologist with long experience with a number of Aboriginal communities, remarked to me that he has seen sacred sites 'discovered' by Aboriginal people in the bush where there was absolutely no threat to the site or the land tenure. The site content, from its inception, and the method of 'finding' it, was, according to him, perfectly true to Aboriginal cultural conventions in these cases. To repeat what I suggested earlier, the manifestation of supernatural presence, in particular features of the landscape, is not just a catalogue of religious events; it is a conceptual and a perceptual mechanism with which Aboriginal people make hypotheses about affairs and events in their current life. 'Discovering' sacred sites, including those that have not previously been recorded by anthropologists or anyone else, is a common and inevitable product of such a perceptual and conceptual strategy.

Finally, these strategies of elicitatory fabrication, must be formally situated within a larger system that is now based on a hierarchy of western legal rational authority and Aboriginal traditional knowledge. Within any such hierarchical system, different forms of knowledge preempt and obviate others. The *internal* pre-empting and cancellation of knowledge at work within Aboriginal society is now embedded within a system that encompasses two incommensurable sub-systems (White and Aboriginal) to which it also appears at the same time *external*. There is a new 'inside' (i.e. secret or restricted) and 'outside' (i.e. public) to Aboriginal knowledge now, based on the realization that all knowledge is subtended by western legal canons of verification. This means that the question of whether the Ngarrindjeri women 'made up' the knowledge as a ploy to stop the bridge, or whether they knew of it beforehand, might not be as important as tracing the demands made upon Aboriginal knowledge within this larger 'system'. Performatively, knowledge creation and asseveration now serve the function of combating racism and cultural ignorance, and is no less knowledge put to pragmatic situated social use than it had been in its traditional religious context.

Anthropologists, because they go and live in a community, are both participants in it and yet always an outsider, have the opportunity to see connections which the members of that community do not see, or which are institutionally or otherwise concealed from them. I maintain that such an approach, essential to anthropology, is what is missing in oral history, which inevitably equates a living culture with the set of documents one can reduce it to. For myself, I prefer this more difficult task of reconciling the inevitable slippages between language, assertion, contestation and avowed knowledge through long-term observation and interview. And I would hope that anyone contemplating what must result from such a long-term involvement in people's lives realizes that this implies more than recording people's stories: it means being entailed in and by their lives and bearing the inevitable consequences of having the effects of those lives impinge upon one's own.

The whole rationale of anthropology stems from the constructive dilemma of managing descriptive veracity in the midst of profound engagement in a community's life. It appears as if it is exactly the theoretical and ethical implications of this engagement which are either avoided or denied by Gough, though I hardly think he is representative of many historians these days. But if one admits confronting this dilemma as a sound strategy for understanding people and their social life, then being obliged to them, as our anthropological code of conduct insists we must be, means something much more than the debased and politically self-interested advocacy that some ill-informed opponents of anthropology construe as our true motivation. It means that we are professionally bound to ask awkward questions on behalf of the less advantaged, and to challenge the complacency of the status quo and the so-called rationality of a system which would set indigenous beliefs and culture in amber and deny indigenous communities the possibility of life, transformation and political autonomy that rests on the ongoing invention that is social life.

Notes

1. Terms of Reference, Hindmarsh Island Bridge Royal Commission, 16 June 1995.
2. A. Gough, 'Hindmarsh Island and the Politics of the Future', *Adelaide Review,* June 1995, pp. 8–9.
3. ib. p. 8.
4. ib. p. 9.
5. ib.
6. Milbourne U.P., 1993.
7. Professor Wilfred Prest, in a letter to *The Australian,* 1 June 1995.
8. See *The Past is a Foreign Country,* ed. Tim Ingold, Group for Debates in Anthropological Theory No. 5, 1993. Department of Social Anthropology, University of Manchester.
9. Rose, D. (1994) 'Whose Confidentiality? Whose Intellectual Property?' in *Claims to Knowledge, Claims to Country: Native Title, Native Title Claims and the Role of the Anthropologist.* Canberra: The Native Title Research Unit, AITSIS: p. 6.
10. The Berndts say the following: 'As a rule, no local descent group, clan, or dialect unit owns a complete myth. Even though at first it may appear to do so, what it has is usually only a section, dealing with some actions of a certain being. The men over in the next stretch of country may own another section and can perform the rites associated with that—and so on, all over the country. Members of several local groups come together from time to time to perform their separate, but linked sections. But the myth is never acted out *in toto* because all its owners could not meet, and in fact would probably not even know one another' (*The World of the First Australians,* Adelaide: Rigby Publishers, 1985, pp. 243–44).
11. See Ian Keen's *Knowledge and Secrecy in an Aboriginal Religion,* Oxford U.P., 1994.
12. *The Invention of Culture,* U. of Chicago P., 1981.

NO

Ron Brunton

The Hindmarsh Island Bridge and the Credibility of Australian Anthropology

The Hindmarsh Island Bridge affair has become a turning point for Aboriginal heritage claims in Australia. For the first time, Aboriginal objections to a proposed development were denounced as a 'hoax' by another group of Aborigines with no discernible interest in the development itself. As a result of these denunciations by the so-called 'dissident Ngarrindjeri women', the South Australian state government established a Royal Commission to investigate, and in December 1995 the commission found that the original claims had been fabricated to prevent the construction of the bridge. Because of the role that anthropological arguments played in supporting the anti-bridge Ngarrindjeri, the profession has undergone an unprecedented degree of critical scrutiny, and now faces widespread doubts about its credibility.

Unfortunately however, people whose only knowledge of this bizarre case comes from James Weiner's ANTHROPOLOGY TODAY article will have a poor understanding of the matters at stake.[1] Even allowing that Weiner wrote without the benefit of the Royal Commission's findings, his article omits a great deal of vital information. He displays a surprising indifference to the ethnographic particularities of the Ngarrindjeri, and his approach to questions arising out of anthropological involvement in public policy is evasive and naïve.

Hindmarsh Island is one of a number of islands near the mouth of the Murray River, 70 km south-east of Adelaide. At present, travel to the island is by ferry, and the bridge was necessary for the increased traffic that would result from major extensions to a marina on the island. A state government instrumentality was to build the bridge, and the marina developers would reimburse the costs later. The bridge first received widespread publicity in local and Adelaide newspapers in 1989, and the following year archaeological and anthropological surveys revealed that the Ngarrindjeri were concerned about possible damage to middens and burial sites on the island and the mainland opposite. But these concerns could be met without preventing the bridge's construction, and there were no Ngarrindjeri objections when preliminary work was undertaken in May 1990. This preliminary work continued over a couple of years.[2]

By late 1992 however, a number of property owners began to complain that the bridge would affect their visual amenity, and that the increased traffic would cause environmental deterioration. Ngarrindjeri opposition first emerged in October 1993—apparently after the anti-bridge group decided that Aboriginal involvement would strengthen their hand. But formal applications in December 1993 to state and federal governments for the prohibition of the bridge were based on the existence of archaeological sites, and nothing else.

In late March 1994 a couple of prominent Ngarrindjeri were visited by an anthropologist, Lindy Warrell, on another matter. When Hindmarsh Island was mentioned, Warrell said she had been working on 'women's business' in the state's north and it would be nice if the Ngarrindjeri had something similar. About two weeks later the first public indications of 'women's business' emerged, perhaps coincidentally, but shortly after it had become clear that the archaeological sites did not provide sufficient basis for the then federal Minister of Aboriginal Affairs, Robert Tickner, to override the state government and prohibit the bridge.

In April the developer and his solicitor were told by the regional chairman of a major Aboriginal organization something to the effect that 'Hindmarsh Island is significant because it is shaped like a woman and there are woman's issues to do with the island associated with birth'. These claims had supposedly been 'researched' by Doreen Kartinyeri, a Ngarrindjeri employee of the South Australian Museum who was well-known for her work on Aboriginal family histories, and who had been involved in other heritage disputes.

On May 9 about 15 Ngarrindjeri women travelled to Hindmarsh Island. There, according to Dorothy Wilson, who was present, and who became a key 'dissident' after she started making her own inquiries into the claims, Doreen Kartinyeri told them about 'women's business'. Kartinyeri also said that neighbouring Mundoo Island was sacred to men as a place where bodies were prepared for burial. Apart from Kartinyeri herself, none of the women claimed to have known about 'women's business' before, but all agreed to send a fax to Tickner demanding that he prohibit the bridge. A few days later Kartinyeri also sent a letter to the Minister, which was composed with the help of Steve Hemming, a historian-anthropologist at the Museum.

In response, the Minister commissioned Cheryl Saunders, a University of Melbourne law professor, to inquire into the significance of the region as the relevant legislation required. On June 17, the Aboriginal Legal Rights Movement (ARLM) appointed Deane Fergie, an anthropologist in Weiner's department at the University of Adelaide, to 'facilitate' a meeting between Saunders and the Ngarrindjeri women 'proponents'. Fergie knew Kartinyeri, but she had no particular knowledge of Ngarrindjeri culture. At the time of her appointment she had not even read the major text on the traditional culture, Ronald and Catherine Berndt's *A World That Was*. Little more than a week later however, the ARLM told Fergie that the brief had changed, and that she should write a report within five days.

Fergie's report. which contained two confidential appendices to be read only by women, clearly had a major impact on Saunders' own discussion, and Saunders referred to it many times.[3] Both reports went to the Federal Minister, and on July 10 Tickner announced a declaration which effectively imposed a 25 year ban on the bridge. This decision was widely reported in the Australian media the following day. As a consequence of the ban, the developers' company went into liquidation, and the developers, Tom and Wendy Chapman, are now on the dole.

⚜

Fergie and Saunders both stressed that the bridge would desecrate Ngarrindjeri traditions. In Fergie's words, it would 'form a permanent link between two parts of the landscape whose cosmological efficacy is contingent on separation'. The region around Hindmarsh Island, was 'crucial for the reproduction of the Ngarrindjeri people.' Fergie stated that she had been told that there were 'very strict laws' relating to people's movement on Hindmarsh and Mundoo Islands, and that some Ngarrindjeri women who had made a bus tour of Hindmarsh Island in June 1994 had refused to leave the bus at many places for fear of breaking these laws.

Fergie gave the clear impression that the beliefs were not a recent invention. She claimed that the supposed Ngarrindjeri custodians, two of whom are in their seventies, have had the relevant knowledge 'since their puberty', which was around the time that the Berndts were conducting their field research in the early 1940s. She also stated that the case 'demonstrates the specificity and persistence of womens [sic] tradition in Aboriginal society'.[4] The 'proponent women' themselves claim that it is ancient—40,000 years old'.

Fergie and Saunders both referred to the Berndts' book. Fergie in particular cited it in an apparent attempt to suggest a ready familiarity with the key text, and to point to supposed continuities in nomenclature, mythology, treatment of the dead, and symbolic motifs—although in the last case she actually misrepresented the data.[5] But both Fergie and Saunders chose to omit one crucial piece of information from their respective reports. The Berndts had specifically noted that there was no evidence that the Ngarrindjeri had any gender-based secret-sacred domain. In his summary foreword to *A World That Was,* Robert Tonkinson also noted that Catherine Bernt had previously written that 'gender-based differences, in the sense of inclusion-exclusion, in religious and other affairs, were minimal', and that she had suggested 'this as one of the remarkable features of [Ngarrindjeri] society'. The book even has an index entry, 'secret-sacred issues, absence of'.[6]

During the Royal Commission Fergie said that her findings about the women's secret traditions represented a 'significant anthropological discovery'.[7] But even the loosest canons of research require that a 'significant discovery' should be identified as such, and this was not done in Fergie's report. In his article, Weiner also ignored the Berndts' statements about the absence of gender-based secret traditions. Indeed, Weiner's overgeneralized and ultimately irrelevant discussion of secret knowledge in Aboriginal Australia and

Papua New Guinea gives no indication that there was anything unusual about the Ngarrindjeri. And he invokes Austin Gough's remarks in a manner that implies that Fergie had merely discovered traditions relating to a specific site, rather than a totally unexpected domain of Ngarrindjeri culture.[8]

⋅◉⋅

The professional imperative for Fergie—and Saunders[9]—to note a seemingly fundamental conflict between their findings and those of two of Australia's most experienced and distinguished ethnographers is quite separate from the question of whether the Berndts' assessment of the Ngarrindjeri was justified. Of course, the Berndts could have been wrong. Nevertheless, the evidence indicating that the secret women's traditions are a very recent invention is highly compelling.

It is necessary to make the obvious distinction between knowing the content of secrets, as against knowing that secrets exist. By their very nature, and in the light of the restrictions the proponents are demanding, the women's traditions would have had highly significant and visible consequences for the behaviour of all Ngarrindjeri. The possibility that these could have completely escaped the notice of all researchers and other observers until April 1994 is beyond belief, as the region is one of the most intensively studied in Australia, and the records go back over 150 years. When the Berndts carried out their fieldwork, Catherine was fully aware of the possibility of Aboriginal women's secret religious traditions, both from her own work at Ooldea, and from Phyllis Kaberry's work in the Kimberley.[10] The Berndts' major informant, Albert Karloan, was passionately committed to telling them all he could about the traditional culture, seeing his task as a 'sacred trust'. And he and other Ngarrindjeri had no hesitation about telling them specific things that once had been highly restricted.[11]

Even more significantly, when the Berndts were working with the Ngarrindjeri, barrages designed to control the salinity of the Lower Murray were just being completed. The Goolwa barrage joins Hindmarsh Island to the mainland in the south, and a series of barrages—which can carry a single lane of vehicular traffic—form a similar connection to the east. The construction of these barrages between 1935 and 1940 involved major engineering work, some of which, such as the driving of pylons into the river bed, would have been desecrating in itself according to the present claims. Ngarrindjeri workmen participated in the construction, but Betty Tatt, one of the 'dissident' women who was living in the area at the time, told the Royal Commission that there were no suggestions from anybody that the barrages posed any danger of desecration or threat to women's reproductive abilities.[12]

The existence of the barrages was too obvious a problem for Saunders and Fergie to ignore. They attempted to explain it with two different kinds of arguments, neither of which can be sustained. The first involved subtle, but completely uninformed, distinctions between barrages and bridges in terms of permanence, solidity, function and effect on the flow of water.[13] In fact, for some of the supposed distinctions the barrages are far more 'desecrating' than the bridge would ever be.[14] In addition, the subtleties of the distinctions that are now being made would have been extremely difficult to sustain around the time when the barrages were being completed, as the cosmologically damaging effects would not yet necessarily have manifested themselves. At the very least it would have been a period of intense anxiety and widespread speculation, and it is extremely unlikely that any concerns would have been kept from the Berndts or from other anthropologists who were working with the Ngarrindjeri at the time, such as Norman Tindale—who was assisted by his wife Dorothy—and Alison Harvey. Yet as the Royal Commission noted, 'None of the ethnographers and historians working in the area during the period of construction of the barrages and afterwards recorded any indication of desecration.'[15] And had the Berndts heard any concerns about the barrages, it is impossible to see how they would have produced the interpretation of traditional Ngarrindjeri culture that they did.

The second kind of argument advanced by Fergie and Saunders was that when the barrages were built the Ngarrindjeri had no prospect of preventing them. While not specifically addressing the problem of the barrages, Weiner makes a similar point, noting that in the 1940s, 'no Aboriginal practice or belief, however important, could have made the slightest difference to the government,' etc.[16] Certainly any Ngarrindjeri complaints would have been ignored or ridiculed by the authorities. But Ngarrindjeri men and women had no hesitation in conveying their anger and concerns about other matters such as land clearing and archaeological research—which they had equally little hope of preventing— to the Berndts and to Norman Tindale. The Berndts note that older people 'were outspoken about those who excavated burial mounds and camp sites', activities which were seen as desecration of the land.[17] Such protests also show the inappropriateness of Weiner's attempt to dismiss the relevance of the Berndts' work to the present case by suggesting that it is only an 'oral history', based on interviews with 'people divorced from any actual social life they are enmeshed in'.[18] The 'cultural knowledge' of the older Ngarrindjeri generated certain kinds of responses to circumstances that the ethnographers were able to observe and record, and which contributed to their understanding of Ngarrindjeri culture.

Another obvious problem for those who suggest that it was the Berndts who got it wrong is that it took four years for any Aboriginal opposition to emerge. Fergie and the 'women's business' proponents have attempted to explain this in a number of ways. Some of these are mutually contradictory, and none of them stand up to any examination. For instance, in her report Fergie suggested that the women who knew of the secret traditions were living in different parts of South Australia, and were unaware of the bridge proposal. Elsewhere she stated that Doreen Kartinyeri had not heard about the bridge until January 1994.[19] But important information flows readily throughout the Ngarrindjeri community as there is a lot of long distance visiting and attendance at ceremonies, as well as telephone contact.[20] Important information flows readily throughout the Ngarrindjeri community. In any case, in 1990 one of the supposed custodians, Edith Rigney, was a member and attended meetings of the Lower Murray Aboriginal Heritage Committee with a number of other Ngarrindjeri who had been involved in consultations over the bridge.[21] The real implications from Fergie's suggestions are that the custodians of 'women's business' were cavalier about their obligations and did not bother to keep themselves informed of potentially threatening developments.

In her May 1994 letter to Tickner, Doreen Kartinyeri made a different claim, stating 'I have always known about the stories associated with... Women's Business, but until recently I didn't know the exact place that they referred to'. However, two of the three women she named as having passed on the information to her had died many years previously, and the other woman denied knowing anything about women's business'. And in a magazine interview she claimed to have known that the stories referred to Hindmarsh Island in 1954.[22]

The Royal Commission identified many other major inconsistencies and defects in the research and arguments of Fergie and the other supporters of women's business. The transcripts also show that Fergie, her counsel, and other 'proponent' anthropologists seriously misrepresented the texts in attempts to suggest that the existing literature does contain hints of secret-sacred Ngarrindjeri traditions.[23] Certainly, Fergie was given very little time in which to complete her original report. But one of the best ways of compensating for this problem would have been to seek advice from Philip Clarke, a former colleague of hers at the South Australian Museum. Clarke had been studying Ngarrindjeri culture for over a decade, he had just submitted his Ph.D. thesis on the Aboriginal cultural geography of the Lower Murray, and he was married to a Ngarrindjeri. Fergie told the Royal Commission that she had intended to contact Clarke, but that his telephone was not answering.[24] Clarke's office is a couple of minutes walk from Fergie's own office at the University, the Museum has receptionists who take messages, and at the time Fergie was sufficiently friendly with Clarke to ring him at home.

Nevertheless, a few days after the Royal Commission's report was released, Weiner defended Fergie in comments to the press, stating that he 'maintained absolutely', that she 'did the best job she could under the circumstances'. He added that 'in many ways' the Royal Commission's attacks on her were 'gratuitous and unwarranted'.[25]

❧

But if Fergie was being defended—at least publicly—by a leading anthropologist, the same did not occur for those who helped to expose the fabrication. When the 'dissidents' denounced 'women's business' in May 1995, they were widely attacked as stooges of conservative politicians, and ridiculed by sections of the media. Privately, a great many anthropologists were scathing about the 'women's business' claims, but they kept a public silence. Angered by this silence and the treatment the 'dissident women' were receiving, Philip Jones, then head of the Anthropology Division at the South Australian Museum, told the media that there was 'not a shred of evidence to suggest that secret sacred women's business existed on Hindmarsh Island'.[26]

He was later joined by Philip Clarke, and the two provided the bulk of the anthropological support for the 'dissident women's' position during the Royal

Commission. The only other anthropologist to assist the commission was Bob Tonkinson, who acted as a consultant. Despite its efforts, the commission was unable to obtain the services of any female anthropologist from Australia, and had to engage Jane Goodale from the United States.[27]

Like Weiner, other prominent anthropologists such as Diane Austin-Broos, Julie Marcus and Peter Sutton, criticized the scholars who were publicly complaining about the unconscionable behaviour of the profession in regards to Hindmarsh Island.[28] When, in an attempt to recover some credibility for the profession, Clarke told the Royal Commission that anthropologists were 'appalled by what they believed to be in Deane Fergie's report' and that the report was 'bad anthropology', he too was condemned.[29] Gillian Cowlishaw from Sydney University was introduced on television as stating that Clarke had done an 'immense disservice to his profession'. Cowlishaw also suggested that his comments were at variance with a statement released by the Australian Anthropological Society (AAS), and even implied that Clarke's right to call himself an anthropologist might be questioned, as he was not a member of the AAS. (A line of attack that was also pursued by Fergie and her counsel at the Royal Commission, who attempted to make much of the fact that Clarke's Ph.D. was jointly in geography and anthropology.)[30]

The AAS statement was largely drafted by Cowlishaw, though with her original reference to 'genocidal threat' omitted in an apparent concession to wider Australian sensitivities. While carefully worded, it is a clear attack on those with a 'crudely empiricist understanding of culture' who were arguing that 'women's business' had been fabricated to prevent the bridge. The statement wrongly pretended that the controversy had cast anthropology as having to 'judge the truth or falsity of Aboriginal beliefs'—the frequent refrain of Tickner and the 'proponent women'. This ignores the role that matters of truth or falsity necessarily play in any assessment of the sincerity, contexts and explanations of those beliefs, and indeed—current fashions notwithstanding—in all anthropological work. There are many assertions in the Fergie report, for instance, which are clearly intended to be taken as true, although quite a number of them have turned out to be false. A failure to acknowledge this situation ultimately casts the anthropologist as merely an amanuensis for informants.

Yet at the same time the AAS statement did acknowledge the possibility that deliberate fabrication had taken place, though without offering any plausible means of finding out whether this had occurred—hardly surprising given the expressed attitudes towards 'truth or falsity'—or even accepting that it mattered very much.[31] A similar kind of indifference is apparent in Weiner's article and in his remarks about those who would 'set indigenous beliefs and culture in amber'. From a theoretical viewpoint, the more important questions may well relate to the 'demands made upon Aboriginal knowledge' within the contemporary Australian system.[32] (In fact, the most interesting and important theoretical questions are very dependent on whether the beliefs were recently invented. For if the 'proponent's' claims really are of some antiquity, the implications for our understanding of knowledge transmission, the maintenance of what are, in effect, secret conspiracies, and the veracity of anthropological data are very great indeed.)

But anthropologists who accept professional consultancies on heritage matters are being asked for practical assessments, because heritage claims can have enormous impacts on the interests of other people. Are anthropologists really saying that if a group of Aborigines wishes to stop any development, anywhere in Australia, at any time, they should be at liberty to do so, for all that matters is what people currently say they believe? That is certainly how it appears to many observers, and it is an inference not far removed from what the AAS, Weiner, and some other prominent Australian anthropologists have actually stated.[33]

The Hindmarsh Island case also suggests that despite all the moral posturing—the professional obligation 'to ask awkward questions on behalf of the less advantaged' as Weiner puts it[34]—many anthropologists are only comfortable with those of the 'less advantaged' who take an adversarial position in relation to the wider Australian society. The 'dissident women' showed great courage and honesty. They wanted to tell the truth about their history and culture, and to counter what they saw as degrading representations of their past. They were ostracised and subjected to death threats, and a sorceress from Central Australia was brought down to Adelaide—apparently on public money—in order to intimidate them.[35] Yet, when I travelled to South Australia to meet them early this year, I discovered that, apart from Jones and Clarke, I was the only anthropologist who had attempted to contact them and hear their stories.

The Hindmarsh Island saga is far from over. The developers have already initiated damages claims against Tickner and Saunders, and further claims against others involved—including anthropologists—are likely. Two days before the Royal Commission released its report, a group of Ngarrindjeri women and men made a fresh application to Tickner to stop the bridge, using similar claims to those that had been considered by the commission. Instead of dismissing the application as vexatious, Tickner established another enquiry, this time under a judge, Jane Mathews. Soon afterwards, the Labor Government lost power—and Tickner lost his seat in a massive swing against him, at least partly attributable to Hindmarsh Island. However, the new Government appears legally obliged to continue with the enquiry (although Mathews' appointment is currently subject to a High Court challenge). Unlike the Royal Commission, this enquiry is not open to the public, and participants have to sign an undertaking that they will not disseminate any submissions that they receive—conditions that mean its findings, should they differ from those of the Commission, will be widely disbelieved. And also unlike the Royal Commission, the enquiry has encountered no shortage of anthropologists willing to assist Judge Mathews. For this is a 'good' enquiry, established by a man who had made his support for the proponents of 'women's business' abundantly clear, and whose politics are more congenial to most anthropologists than those of the conservative South Australian state government.

Nevertheless, there are some welcome signs. Two anthropologists—Grayson Gerrard and Ken Maddock, renowned for his work on Aboriginal law and religion—have prepared submissions to the Mathews enquiry for the developers' solicitors. And another internationally renowned anthropologist, Les Hiatt, who was outside Australia during the Royal Commission hearings, has offered to make a submission to the enquiry for the 'dissident women's' solicitors, and has indicated his support for Clarke and Jones. It is to be hoped that their actions will encourage more Australian anthropologists to recognize their responsibilities to the wider public and thus help to restore the profession's credibility.

Notes

1. James F. Weiner, Anthropologists, historians and the secret of social knowledge. ANTHROPOLOGY TODAY, October 1995.

2. Except where indicated, information in this section is taken from Iris E. Stevens, *Report of the Hindmarsh Island Bridge Royal Commission.* State Print. Adelaide. 1995: 54–143.

3. Cheryl Saunders, *Report to the Minister for Aboriginal and Torres Strait Islander Affairs on the Significant Aboriginal Area in the Vicinity of Goolwa and Hindmarsh (Kumarangk) Island,* July 1994, e.g. pages 23–24, 27–29, 31–32, 35, 37–39.

4. Dean Fergie, *To All the Mothers That Were, To All the Mothers That Are, To All the Mothers That Will Be: An Anthropological Assessment of the Threat of Injury and Desecration to Aboriginal Tradition by the Proposed Hindmarsh Island Bridge Construction.* July 1994, pages 19, 15, 10, 16, 12.

5. *Ibid.,* pages 13, 15, 6:cf. Stevens, *op. cit.,* page 278; Ronald M. Berndt & Catherine H. Berndt, with John Stanton, *A World That Was.* Melbourne University Press. 1993, 154–155.

6. C. Berndt, Retrospect and prospect, in Peggy Brock, ed. *Women, Rites & Sites,* Allen & Unwin. Sydney, 1989, page 11; *A World That Was, op. cit.,* pages xxix, 621; see also pages 24, 163, 210. One element of the male initiation ritual was supposedly secret-sacred, but the ritual as a whole was not.

7. Transcripts of the Royal Commission into the Hindmarsh Island Bridge, page 5330.

8. Weiner, *op. cit.,* pages 5, 4.

9. Saunders said she had consulted the Berndts' book (*op. cit.,* page 9), and it requires no particular anthropological skills to recognise that the Berndts' and Tonkinson's remarks were very relevant to her report.

10. C. Berndt, *op. cit.,* pages 2–6: P. M. Kaberry, *Aboriginal Women, Sacred and Profane.* Routledge, London, 1939.

11. *A World That Was, op. cit.,* pages 282, 148, 176.

12. Stevens, *op. cit.,* pages 245–246, 261: cf. Fergie, *op. cit.,* page 18.

13. Saunders, *op. cit.,* pages 38–39; Fergie, *op. cit.,* pages 19–20.

14. Stevens, *op. cit.,* pages 245–250.

15. *Ibid.* page 246.

16. Saunders, *op. cit.,* page 38; Fergie, *op. cit.,* page 22; Weiner, *op. cit.,* page 4.

17. Norman Tindale, Prupe and Koromarange: a legend of the Tanganekeld, Coorong, South Australia. *Transactions of the Royal Society of South Australia,* volume 62, number 1, 1938, page 20; R. M. Berndt. Some aspects of Jaralde culture, South Australia. *Oceania,* volume 11, 1940, page 166; *A World That Was, op. cit.,* page 16.

18. Weiner, *op. cit.,* pages 4–5.

19. Fergie, *op. cit.,* page 16; Pamela Lyon, Hindmarsh Island bridge: taking care of women's business. *The Adelaidean,* 1 August 1994, page 6.

20. Foreword, *A World That Was, op. cit.,* page xvii.

21. Stevens, *op. cit.,* page 254.

22. *Ibid.*, pages 134–137; Craig Henderson, Troubled waters. *Who Weekly,* 17 July 1995, page 274. In a telephone conversation, Henderson told me that the words of the interview were checked back with Kartinyeri before publication.

23. Stevens, *op. cit.*, pages 156–162; Chapter 6: Ron Brunton, The False Culture Syndrome. *IPA Backgrounder,* volume 8, number 2, March 1996, pages 6–7.

24. Transcripts *op. cit.*, page 5326.

25. John Kerin, Call for sacred-site index to avert repeat of bridge debacle. *The Australian,* 27 December 1995.

26. Transcripts *op. cit.*, pages 4427, 4431. Although Jones would not have known, Ken Maddock wrote an article for the Melbourne *Herald-Sun* in March 1995 stating his belief that the traditions were a recent invention.

27. *Ibid.*, pages 6667–6668.

28. Dianne Austin-Broos, Evidence that is contemporary. *The Australian,* 16 November 1995; Julie Marcus, Ill-founded in fact and logic. *The Australian,* 22 November 1995; Peter Sutton. Forensic anthropology, expert evidence and legal culture in Australia, paper presented at AAS Conference. Adelaide, 29 September 1995.

29. Transcripts, *op. cit.*, page 3573. Although few anthropologists had seen Fergie's report, its broad thrust could be inferred. When he wrote his article Weiner probably had not seen it, as in February 1996 he asked if I could send him a copy, because legal considerations prevented Fergie from giving one to him. However, by the time of the AAS Conference in September 1996, well before Clarke made his statement, many anthropologists had at least been informed of the crucial omission of the report.

30. ABC TV (Adelaide) *7:30 Report,* 18 October 1995; Gillian Cowlishaw, What really appalled anthropologists, *The Australian,* 18 October 1995; Transcripts, *op. cit.*, pages 3563–3571, 5933–5935.

31. Hindmarsh and anthropology. *Australian Anthropology Society Newsletter* 62, December 1995, page 24.

32. Weiner, *op. cit.*, pages 6–7. Perhaps I should note that I have attempted to deal with these issues, though in a broad-brush way, in *Blocking Business: An Anthropological Assessment of the Hindmarsh Island Dispute,* Tasman Institute Occasional Paper B31, August 1995, pages 22–32, which was based on a submission I made to the Royal Commission. But such discussions are often unwelcome to many Aboriginal organizations, because they raise embarrassing questions.

33. See e.g. Ian Keen, Undermining credibility: advocacy and objectivity in the Coronation Hill debate, A. T. 8.2, April 1992, page 8; Aboriginal beliefs vs. mining at Coronation Hill: the containing force of traditionalism. *Human Organization,* volume 52, 1993, page 344.

34. *Op. cit.*, page 7.

35. Chris Kenny, Witchcraft, *The Adelaide Review,* May 1996.

POSTSCRIPT

Do Anthropologists Have a Moral Responsibility to Defend the Interests of "Less Advantaged" Communities?

Native communities in the United States, Canada, Australia, and New Zealand are increasingly hiring anthropologists to assist them in a variety of public policy concerns. Cases like the Hindmarsh Island Bridge affair show that there are grey areas at the boundaries of established cultural tradition and that anthropologists may not always be able to defend the political and legal positions advocated by native communities.

The Hindmarsh Island Bridge affair has been one of the most divisive controversies in Australian anthropology in recent years. It has been debated in the Australian courts, by a Royal Commission, in newspapers, on television, in several books written for popular audiences, and in anthropological journals. At times the debate has been rancorous and personal both in public discourse and among anthropologists.

Robert Tonkinson's discussion in "Anthropology and Aboriginal Tradition: The Hindmarsh Island Bridge Affair and the Politics of Interpretation," *Oceania* (September 1997) raises a number of questions for academic anthropologists, including: How can secret knowledge that is essential to a society's survival exist yet remain hidden from a general public awareness? How should anthropologists deal with knowledge that is not generally shared within the community, as is the case with most secret knowledge? Building on these concerns, Weiner's essay, "Culture in a Sealed Envelope: The Concealment of Australian Aboriginal Heritage and Tradition in the Hindmarsh Island Bridge Affair," *Journal of the Royal Anthopological Institute* (June 1999), argues that both the state and the anthropologists who were involved with the case have failed to consider the relational nature of social knowledge and culture. An essay that suggests that the Hindmarsh Island Bridge affair has feminist implications is M. Langton's "The Hindmarsh Island Bridge Affair: How Aboriginal Women's Religion Became an Administerable Affair," *Australian Feminist Studies* (October 1996).

In 2001 the developers of the proposed bridge sued the Ngarrindjeri tribe for damages caused by stopping bridge construction. When the Royal Commission met, none of the Ngarrindjeri women had been willing to appear for testimony about secret women's business. But a number of them did testify in court when their tribe was being sued for damages. The court found in favor of the tribe, contending that there was secret women's business on Hindmarsh Island that justified halting the bridge project.

Contributors to This Volume

EDITORS

ROBERT L. WELSCH is a visiting professor of anthropology at Dartmouth College and adjunct curator of anthropology at The Field Museum in Chicago. He received a B.A. in anthropology from Northwestern University in 1972, an M.A. in anthropology from the University of Washington in 1976, and a Ph.D. from the same department in 1982. He has conducted field research among the Ningerum people of Papua New Guinea, the Mandar people of South Sulawesi, Indonesia, and the diverse peoples of the Sepik Coast of Papua New Guinea. He is the author of *An American Anthropologist in Melanesia* (University of Hawaii Press, 1998) and coeditor, with Michael O'Hanlon, of *Hunting the Gatherers: Ethnographic Collectors, Agents, and Agency in Melanesia* (Berghahn Publishers, 2000).

KIRK M. ENDICOTT is a professor and the chairman of the Department of Anthropology at Dartmouth College. He received a B.A. in anthropology from Reed College in 1965, a Ph.D. in anthropology from Harvard University in 1974, and a D.Phil. in social anthropology from the University of Oxford in 1976. He has repeatedly conducted field research among the Batek people of Malaysia. He is the author of *An Analysis of Malay Magic* (Clarendon Press, 1970) and *Batek Negrito Religion: The World-view and Rituals of a Hunting and Gathering People of Peninsular Malaysia* (Clarendon Press, 1979), and is coauthor, with Robert K. Dentan, Alberto G. Gomez, and M. Barry Hooker, of *Malaysia and the "Original People": A Case Study of the Impact of Development on Indigenous Peoples* (Allyn and Bacon, 1997).

STAFF

Theodore Knight   List Manager
David Brackley   Senior Developmental Editor
Juliana Gribbins   Developmental Editor
Rose Gleich   Administrative Assistant
Brenda S. Filley   Director of Production/Design
Juliana Arbo   Typesetting Supervisor
Diane Barker   Proofreader
Richard Tietjen   Publishing Systems Manager
Larry Killian   Copier Coordinator

AUTHORS

SERGE BAHUCHET is Chargé de Recherche at the Laboratoire de Langues et Civilisation à Tradition Orale at the Centre National de la Recherche Scientifique in Paris. He has conducted research among pygmies in the Congo.

RON BRUNTON is a senior fellow of the Institute of Public Affairs at Queensland, Australia. An anthropologist by training, he has conducted research on environmental policies in Australia and Melanesia.

JOHN E. CAWTE is an emeritus professor of psychiatry and community medicine at the University of New South Wales. He is the author of many books and articles dealing with Aboriginal conceptions of health and illness, including *Healers of Arnhem Land* (New South Wales University Press, 1996).

NAPOLEON A. CHAGNON is a professor emeritus of anthropology at the University of California at Santa Barbara. He is best known for his extended work over many years among the Yanomami Indians of Venezuela, about whom he has written many books, including *Yanomamö,* 5th ed. (Harcourt Brace, 1997).

JAMES CLIFFORD is a professor of the history of consciousness at the University of California at Santa Cruz. He has written many books and articles about postmodern anthropology, including *Routes: Travel and Translation in the Late Twentieth Century* (Harvard University Press, 1997).

IGOR de GARINE is at the Centre National de la Recherche Scientifique in Gan, France. He writes about topics in human ecology, including a volume coedited with G. A. Harrison, *Coping With Uncertainty in Food Supply* (Oxford University Press, 1988).

JAMES R. DENBOW is an associate professor of anthropology at the University of Texas at Austin. He has conducted field research in southern Africa and was curator of archaeology at the National Museum of Botswana.

DENIS DUTTON is associate professor of art theory in the School of Fine Arts at the University of Canterbury at Christchurch, New Zealand. He is a specialist on aesthetics and tribal art and is the author of *The Forger's Art: Forgery and the Philosophy of Art* (University of California Press, 1983).

R. BRIAN FERGUSON is a professor of anthropology at Rutgers University. He has conducted field research in Puerto Rico and among the Yanomami in South America.

DEREK FREEMAN (1916–2001) was an emeritus professor of anthropology in the Research School of Pacific and Asian Studies at the Australian National University. He conducted field research among the Iban of Borneo and the Samoans of Western Samoa.

ERIKA FRIEDL is a professor of anthropology at Western Michigan University. She is a specialist on the lives of women and children in Iran. She is the author of many books and articles, including *Children of Deh Koh: Young Life in an Iranian Village* (Syracuse University Press, 1997).

CLIFFORD GEERTZ is a professor at the Insitute for Advanced Study in Princeton, New Jersey. He has conducted field research in Indonesia and Morocco. He is the author of *Works and Lives: The Anthropologist as Author* (Stanford University Press, 1988).

STEVEN GOLDBERG is chairman of the Sociology Department at City University of New York. He has written many articles and books, including *Seduced by Science: How American Religion Has Lost Its Way* (New York University Press, 1999).

JOHN J. GUMPERZ is an emeritus professor of anthropology at the University of California at Berkeley. His research interests have concentrated on sociolinguistics and issues of language and culture. He is the author of numerous books and articles, including *Discourse Strategies* (Cambridge University Press, 1982).

ROBERT A. HAHN is an epidemiologist with the Centers for Disease Control and Prevention and an adjunct professor of anthropology at Emory University. He has published many articles and books on various topics in medical anthropology, including *Anthropology in Public Health: Bridging Differences in Culture and Society* (Oxford University Press, 1999).

MARVIN HARRIS was a professor of anthropology at Columbia University until 1980, when he was appointed graduate research professor of anthropology at the University of Florida. He is the author of many books on anthropology and anthropological theory, including *Cultural Materialism: The Struggle for a Science of Culture* (Random House, 1979).

THOMAS N. HEADLAND is international anthropology consultant at the Summer Institute of Linguistics and an adjunct professor of anthropology at the University of Texas at Arlington.

ELLEN RHOADS HOLMES has conducted field research in Samoa. She is coauthor, with her husband Lowell D. Holmes, of *Samoan Village: Then and Now* (Harcourt Brace, 1992) and *Other Cultures, Elder Years: An Introduction to Cultural Gerontology* (Sage, 1995).

LOWELL D. HOLMES is an emeritus professor of anthropology at Wichita State University. He has conducted field research in Samoa and in contemporary America. He is the author of *Quest for the Real Samoa* (Bergin & Garvey, 1986).

SUDHIR KAKAR is widely known as the father of Indian psychoanalysis and has practiced for many years in New Delhi. He has been a visiting professor of psychology at the University of Chicago and is currently a senior fellow at the Center for the Study of World Religions at Harvard University. His books include *The Colors of Violence: Cultural Identities, Religion, and Conflict* (University of Chicago Press, 1996).

ROGER M. KEESING (1935–1993) was a professor of anthropology at McGill University. He is best known for his research among the Kwaio people of Malaita in the Solomon Islands and published four books and many articles about them, including *Custom and Confrontation: The Kwaio Struggle for Cultural Autonomy* (University of Chicago Press, 1992).

RICHARD B. LEE is a professor of anthropology and chair of the African Studies Programme at the University of Toronto. He is best known for his research among the San peoples of the Kalahari Desert. He is the author of *The Dobe Ju/'hoansi*, 2d ed. (Harcourt Brace, 1984).

MARIA LEPOWSKI is a professor of anthropology at the University of Wisconsin. She has conducted field research in Papua New Guinea and is the author of *Fruit of the Motherland: Gender in an Egalitarian Society* (Columbia University Press, 1993).

STEPHEN C. LEVINSON is director of the Language and Cognition Group at the Max Plank Institute for Psycholinguistics at Nijmegen in the Netherlands. His research has focused on linguistic anthropology and cognitive anthropology. He is the author of numerous books and articles, including *Presumptive Meanings* (MIT Press, 2000).

BETTY JEAN LIFTON is a therapist, freelance writer, and adoption rights advocate who has published widely on adoption in the United States. Her books include *Twice Born: Memoirs of an Adopted Daughter* (St. Martin's Press, 1998).

DOYLE McKEY is a biologist at l'Université Montpellier II, Montpellier, France, and specializes in the relationship between insects and plants in the tropical rain forest.

JUDITH MODELL is a professor of anthropology, history, and art at Carnegie Mellon University in Pittsburgh, Pennsylvania. Best known for her research on adoption, she has written many articles and books, including *A Sealed and Secret Kinship: Policies and Practices in American Adoption* (Berghahn Books, 2001).

ANTHONY OBERSCHALL is a professor of sociology at the University of North Carolina at Chapel Hill. He has written many books and articles dealing with social conflict, including *Social Movements: Ideologies, Interests, and Identities* (Transaction Books, 1993).

PARVIN PAIDAR works in international development and is currently with UNIFEM in Afghanistan. Her research has focused on gender and social development in developing countries, especially on feminism and Islam in Iran. She is the author of *Women and the Political Process in Twentieth-Century Iran* (Cambridge University Press, 1997).

STEVEN PINKER is a professor of brain and cognitive sciences at the Massachusetts Institute of Technology. His research has focused on the relationship between language and cognitive function. He has written numerous books, including *Words and Rules: The Ingredients of Language* (Basic Books, 1999).

MERRILEE H. SALMON is a professor of the history and philosophy of science at the University of Pittsburgh. Her recent research concerns the philosophy of anthropology.

ELLIOTT P. SKINNER is an emeritus professor of anthropology at Columbia University. He has conducted fieldwork in Burkina Faso (Upper Volta) where he formerly served as United States ambassador. He is the author of *The Mossi of Burkina Faso* (Waveland, 1990).

CAROL A. SMITH is a professor of anthropology at the University of California at Davis. She has conducted more than five years of field research in Guatemala since 1969. She has written many articles and books, the best known of which is her edited volume *Guatemalan Indians and the State, 1540 to 1988* (University of Texas Press, 1990).

DAVID STOLL is an assistant professor of anthropology at Middlebury College. He has published several books based on his fieldwork in Guatemala, including *Between Two Armies in the Ixil Towns of Guatemala* (Columbia University Press, 1993).

JOHN TERRELL is curator of oceanic archaeology and ethnology at the Field Museum in Chicago. He has conducted extensive field research in Papua New Guinea as well as in New Zealand, Tonga, Samoa, and Fiji. He has written numerous articles and books, including *Darwin and Archaeology: A Handbook of Key Concepts* (Bergin and Garvey, 2002).

PATRICK TIERNEY is a freelance journalist and center associate/visiting scholar with the Center for Latin American Studies at the University of Pittsburgh and has spent much of the past decade conducting research for his critique of Napoleon Chagnon's fieldwork with the Yanomami Indians of Venezuela and Brazil. He is the author of *Darkness in El Dorado: How Scientists and Journalists Devastated the Amazon* (W. W. Norton, 2000).

JOHN TOOBY is a professor of anthropology at the University of California at Santa Barbara and codirector of UCSB's Center for Evolutionary Psychology. He is a specialist on the evolution of hominid behavior and cognition. He is coeditor of *The Adapted Mind: Evolutionary Psychology and the Generation of Culture* (Oxford University Press, 1992).

HAUNANI-KAY TRASK is a professor of Hawaiian studies at the University of Hawai'i at Manoa. She is a well-known Native Hawaiian activist with Ka Lahui Hawai'i, one of several organizations advocating Native Hawaiian sovereignty. She is the author of *From a Native Daughter: Colonialism and Sovereignty in Hawai'i*, rev. ed. (University of Hawai'i Press, 1999).

JAMES F. WEINER is currently a research associate at the Australian National University. He has written many books and articles about the Foi people of Papua New Guinea, including *The Empty Place* (University of Indiana Press, 1991).

EDWIN N. WILMSEN is a research fellow at the University of Texas at Austin. He has conducted research in Botswana and is the author of *Land Filled With Flies: A Political Economy of the Kalahari* (University of Chicago Press, 1989).

Index